TEENAGERS
with ADD and ADHD

TEENAGERS
with ADD and ADHD

A Guide for Parents and Professionals

Chris A. Zeigler Dendy, M.S.

WOODBINE HOUSE   2006

All rights reserved. Published in the United States of America by Woodbine House, Inc., 6510 Bells Mill Rd., Bethesda, MD 20817. 800-843-7323. www.woodbinehouse.com

Cover photograph: Alex Zeigler and Chris Dendy.
Illustration on p. 25 is by Derek Engram.
Illustration on p. 13 is reprinted courtesy of Alex Zeigler.
The photograph on p. 26 is reprinted by permission of *The New England Journal of Medicine*, Alan J. Zametkin, M.D., Volume 323, p. 1365, Figure 4. Copyright 1990. *Massachusetts Medical Society*. All rights reserved.
The photograph on p. 59 originally appeared in the December 2004 issue of *ATTENTION!* and is reproduced with permission of the editors.

Library of Congress Cataloging-in-Publication Data

Zeigler Dendy, Chris A.
  Teenagers with ADD and ADHD : a parents' guide / Chris A. Zeigler Dendy. -- 2nd ed.
     p. cm.
  Includes bibliographical references and index.
  ISBN-13: 978-1-890627-31-7
  ISBN-10: 1-890627-31-3
 1. Attention-deficit disorder in adolescence--Popular works. I. Zeigler Dendy, Chris A. Teenagers with ADD. II. Title. III. Title: Teenagers with attention deficit disorders and attention deficit hyperactivity disorders.
  RJ506.H9Z45 2006
  618.92'8589--dc22

     2006022615

*This book is dedicated
to all the teenagers and their families around the world
who struggle daily with the challenges
of ADD and ADHD.*

Table of Contents

Acknowledgements ix

Introduction xi

Chapter 1: What Is Attention Deficit Disorder?..1

Chapter 2: Causes: Understanding ADD/ADHD and the Brain............................23

Chapter 3: Diagnosis of ADD or ADHD 31

Chapter 4: Moving Beyond Guilt, Anger, and Fear to Optimism! 53

Chapter 5: Treatment of ADD and ADHD in Adolescents..................................75

Chapter 6: The Medication Dilemma: Should Your Teen Take Medicine? 99

Chapter 7: Attention Disorders and Coexisting Conditions 127

Chapter 8: Raising a Healthy, Well-Adjusted Teenager 143

Chapter 9: Common Behaviors of Teenagers with ADD or ADHD 171

Chapter 10: When Teenagers Continue to Struggle…..203

Chapter 11: The Parent's Role in Eliminating Academic Agony 233

Chapter 12: Working on the Home Front...249

Chapter 13: Success, Not Just Survival, in School...267

Chapter 14: Legal Leverage for Pursuing Academic Success 293

Chapter 15: After High School…What Next? 325

Chapter 16: Parents Have Permission to Take Charge 353

Chapter 17: Words of Wisdom from the Kids 369

Appendix 1: Medication Rating Scale 384
Appendix 2: Sample Contract 385
Appendix 3: The ABCs of ADD/ADHD: Impact on School Performance 387
Appendix 4: Sample Medical Report 390
Appendix 5: Developing and Implementing Effective IEPs 391
Appendix 6: OHI School Eligibility Report 394

Resource Guide 395

Bibliography 399

Index 403

Acknowledgements

Special thanks are due to former teens Alex, Lewis, Shawn, Chad, Robert, Damian, and Steven, who were my inspiration and extraordinary teachers for the original book.

Over 100 people from all walks of life contributed to the original version of *Teenagers with ADD* (TWA). The diverse contributions of these parents, teachers, and treatment professionals laid an incredibly strong foundation for the first edition. This new edition builds upon the earlier work but adds the most up-to-date science-based information available.

Three stalwart experts have been among my major resources for all three of my books and the rewrite of TWA: William Buzogany, M.D., a psychiatrist and former Commissioner of Mental Health in Wisconsin; Ted Mandelkorn, M.D., a Washington pediatrician specializing in treatment of ADHD; and Claudia Dickerson, Ph.D., a licensed school psychologist in Georgia. Other generous colleagues have been available to answer specific questions as needed: Peter Jensen, M.D., Tim Wilens, M.D, Tom Brown, Ph.D., Steve Evans, Ph.D., Ed Gotlieb, M.D., Mary Durheim, B.S., Joan Helbing, Joan Teach, Ph.D., David Kinsley, Pharm.D., Harvey Parker, Ph.D., Art Robins, Ph.D., Karen White, Ph.D., Kathy Hubbard Weeks, M.S., Bob Reid, Ph.D., Jonathan Jones, M.S., Linda Katz, Ph.D., Mathew Cohen, J.D., Jeff Prince, M.D., Edna Copeland, Ph.D., Russell Barkley, Ph.D., Edward Hallowell, M.D., Pam Esser, M.S., and Dixie Jordan.

Key parent/professional contributors include Jill Murphy, Gale Gordon, M.D., Pamper Garner Crangle, Evelyn Green, Janice Bond, Cindy Evans, Mary Robertson, Andrea Bilbow, Lisa Fairman, Nancy Sayers, Sue Hammond, Penny Mundt, Elaine Carroll, Sandra Dendy, and Audrey Dendy Grabowski. Two parents, Don and Penny Dieckman, have lived a parallel journey as their son Jeremy grew up and have continued their wise input to all three of my books.

I was very, very lucky ten years ago, when Woodbine House decided to take a chance on an unknown author who was writing about teenagers with attention deficits. From the beginning, my partnership with my editor, Susan Stokes, has been extraordinary. Not only is she a superb editor, but she is an expert on ADHD in her own right. The other members of the team, Fran Marinaccio, Beth Binns, and Brenda Ruby, have also been exceptional.

Over the last ten years, several amazing teenagers have been invaluable in educating me more fully about ADD and ADHD. They have agreed to interviews, given advice, participated on teen panel discussions, and allowed their pictures to be included in my books. I owe them a very special debt of gratitude.

Alex	Allie	Alyssa
Andrew	Ari	Ashley
Bart	Billy	Chad
Chris	Dan	Emily
Eric	Erik	Hunter
Jake	Jay	Jerry
Katie	Kati	Khris

Kyle	Lewis	Marina
Marlie	Max	Nathan
Nick	Paul	Perry
Robert	Samantha	Shawn
Spencer	Steven	Tate
Travis	Tyler	Will

Finally, since the publication of the first edition of TWA, sadly my parents have both passed away. This acknowledgement is given in memory of two special people who helped shape my life and gave me so many opportunities:

Lillian J. Abney
1918-2003

Judge W.L. Abney, Jr.
1916-1997

Introduction

Although it's hard to believe, it has been over ten years ago since the first edition of *Teenagers with ADD and ADHD* (TWA) was published as a result of our family's difficult personal struggles coping with attention deficit disorders. During the past decade, I've been honored and humbled that parents and professionals have made it one of the best selling books on adolescents with attention deficit disorder. Books sales of TWA have reached nearly 100,000. It makes my husband and me so happy that we have achieved our goal of *helping other families avoid the painful teenage years we experienced with our children.*

First, a Little History...

When our son, Alex, was a teenager, there were no books or resources on adolescents to help us understand his attention deficit. Basically, I had to research attention deficit disorders, find my own material, and rely on my experience as a teacher and mental health professional to cope with his challenging teenage years. So the books that I have written and videos we published were produced because they were the very resources we needed when we were parenting our teens. A parent once lamented to me that she wished she had had this book five years ago and I immediately laughed and commented in return, "You're not the only one. I wish I had it five years ago when my son was fourteen."

My Goals for This Book...

My goals in writing the first edition of this book were very basic:

1. Create a comprehensive, one-stop source of information for parents on teenagers with ADD and ADHD.
2. Reassure parents that they are not alone in struggling with this sometimes baffling condition.
3. Educate parents about attention deficit disorders so they will have realistic expectations and can once again love their child.
4. Answer all the questions that I had about my own teenaged son's challenges; for example, his impulsive, daring behavior, academic struggles, sleep problems, disorganization, tardiness, and forgetfulness.
5. Give parents a sense of hope by throwing them a lifeline that will help them successfully survive their son's or daughter's attention deficit.

I am happy to report that over the last ten years I have received hundreds of heartfelt letters, emails, and phone calls from parents and professionals telling me that the first edition of this book did, indeed, accomplish all of these goals. I will be immensely gratified and proud if this new edition continues to achieve these goals for a new generation of parents.

The Book Content...

Most books describe ADD and ADHD and its impact on the family in academically sterile terms. Yet, coping with ADD and ADHD can be an intensely emotional experience for both teenagers and their families. If we as parents are aware of the typical behaviors of teens with attention deficit disorders, we are less likely to be shocked by our children's misbehavior, overreact emotionally, and jump to frightening conclusions about their future. Simply put, the more we parents learn about ADD and ADHD, the easier our parenting job becomes.

In an effort to provide you the most current information, this second edition contains significantly rewritten material plus the most up-to-date research and information that we hope will help you be even better parents for your child. As you can see from reading the Table of Contents, many critical topics are addressed in *Teenagers with ADD and ADHD*:

- The basics: inattention, impulsivity, and hyperactivity
- Common behaviors: arguing and talking back, sleep issues, tardiness
- More serious concerns: speeding tickets, substance use, sexuality, suicide risk
- Common learning problems and challenges at school
- Medication
- ADD and ADHD from a teen's perspective

My Perspective...

My unique perspective on ADD and ADHD comes from experiences as a former teacher, school psychologist, and mental health counselor and administrator. However, my most valuable education came from the humbling experience of being the mother of Alex and second-mother for Steven, both of whom have attention deficits. I have great admiration for my sons, who have struggled to cope with this disorder. They are delightful adults now and are doing well. Both are college graduates. Steven is general manager of a manufacturing plant and a wonderful husband and father, and Alex is an author, graphic artist, and research and development director for a specialty ammunition company. You can read more about both of them in Chapter 17. I believe that having both lived with and extensively studied attention deficits has enriched my writings.

Other parents and professionals who have also lived with ADD or ADHD give added wisdom to this book through their personal experiences. Their powerful stories are shared throughout the book. I am deeply grateful to my friends and colleagues who have been so generous with their time. Their personal insights and advice will help families cope in a healthy and loving way with this stressful disorder.

Parents Need Help and Hope

Raising a teenager with an attention deficit disorder can be an extremely painful and lonely job for a parent. Because ADD and ADHD are "invisible disabilities," most parents of these teenagers feel isolated and receive little support and understanding from others. The teenager looks "normal," but may perform erratically at school and seldom does as parents ask. Some family members and friends may be quick to give advice, saying that strict discipline will solve all the teenager's problems. However, when your life is personally touched by an attention deficit, your attitude changes dramatically, as my husband explains:

As a graduate of the U.S. Naval Academy, I thought stern discipline would solve all Steven's problems. Now that I understand ADHD, I find myself frustrated that most adults have the same attitude I had toward my son. They feel that these children are lazy and don't care. There are a lot of children in our society who need our understanding. They need to be protected against that type of negative attitude. If all adults had to raise a child with ADD or ADHD and if they could see the dramatic difference medication can make, we could improve the lives of so many children and families."

When their teenager struggles, parents experience a great deal of anxiety and self-doubt. Sometimes they wonder if they have been "bad" parents or if they have a "bad" child. If, however, they are informed about typical behaviors that teenagers with attention deficits exhibit, as well as potential interventions, parents are able to anticipate and weather the challenges of raising their child.

It may help to know that—with appropriate supports and treatment—most of these teens make it through this difficult period successfully. During the ages from seventeen to twenty-one, many of these teenagers seem to mature and establish a clearer direction for their lives. In fact, researchers tell us that their maturation continues into their early thirties. As they achieve more successes, their self-esteem is bolstered. They appear to settle down and be happier. In addition, many children mature and exhibit milder symptoms as they reach adolescence and adulthood. With proper diagnosis and treatment, most teenagers with ADD or ADHD will grow up to be well-adjusted adults.

Parents Must Advocate for Their Teenager

Since parents know their teenager better than any professionals involved with the family and are committed to their child's success, they make excellent advocates. They know their offspring's strengths and weaknesses, and often know which medications and interventions work best. This knowledge makes parents indispensable as respected partners in the treatment process. It is critical for parents to learn everything they can about ADD and ADHD. The more parents learn about these conditions, the more effective they become at advocating on behalf of their teenager.

Education of teachers, treatment professionals, and other adults who work with these teenagers is also essential if these young people are to succeed in school and grow up to be happy, productive adults. This is because a teenager's ability to cope successfully with ADD or ADHD depends a great deal on how the teenager and others perceive the condition. Having people who believe in the teenager is essential for successful adjustment.

Many professionals are well informed about attention deficit disorders and do an excellent job monitoring the teenager's response to medications and adjustment at home and school. However, other professionals do not. Until all key professionals become better informed about ADD and ADHD, *parents may have to take charge of helping educate the professionals and ensuring coordination among them.* This book offers concrete information and suggestions that will enable parents to feel confident enough to take charge of helping their teenager cope successfully with his or her attention deficit.

Now Let's Start at the Beginning

The most elating experience of my life occurred the day my son, Alex, was born. He was delivered at 1:11 a.m. after a brief three hours of labor. Natural childbirth procedures allowed me to be awake and alert during his birth. When the doctor pronounced the delivery of a healthy baby boy with an APGAR score of 10, I heaved a sigh of relief. Ten fingers and ten toes, they were all there. He was beautiful! No problems.

I promptly rejected the doctor's suggestion that I skip Alex's 6:00 a.m. feeding. I wasn't tired. I was exhilarated! At thirty years of age, I had been waiting for this day for a long time. I lay awake waiting for the nurse to bring him for his scheduled feeding. He arrived. I held the world's most beautiful child while he nursed, savoring the joy he had brought into my life.

The joy of watching my precocious, happy child crawling undaunted into the ocean as an infant, diving at age two, and water-skiing at age four was rudely interrupted when he entered first grade. For some reason, he could not keep up with his classmates, in spite of his high intelligence and good intentions. My sensitive, loving six-year-old child was reduced to tears because he could not quickly finish his class work, and, as a result, his teacher thought he was "bad." Our high expectations for him in school were dashed as he struggled to cope with overwhelming academic demands. I knew he was a good child who wanted to do well at school, but I was at a loss to understand the contradictions between his ability and poor academic performance. This battle with an undiagnosed adversary—ADD—created a cruel learning environment for the next six years. The major thing my son learned was to hate school. Alex was twelve before we discovered that ADD was the culprit behind his devastating struggles at school.

Our Hopes and Dreams for Our Children

Our hopes and dreams for our children are so grand when they are born. We dream of school successes, athletic or artistic talents, solid values, leadership skills, and a spiritual strength to sustain them in difficult times. As the years roll by, we watch our child's life unfold. Some teenagers' lives seem to unfold easily in a very logical and orderly fashion. Other teenagers' lives, including many of those who have attention deficit disorders, are much more difficult and stressful. Nothing seems to come easily.

Upon learning that their child has ADD or ADHD, some parents are devastated at first. But given time to absorb this information and its positive potential for enabling their child to live a happier and more productive life, most parents are relieved and grateful. At last, you know the reason for your child's puzzling behavior. Now, you can begin to tap into the growing body of knowledge about attention deficit disorders and use it to help your child succeed. *Teenagers with ADD and ADHD,* based as it is upon the research of professionals and the collective wisdom and experience of contributors, should help you begin to understand and appreciate your child's world. It is my fondest hope that what we—the author and contributors—have learned from living with this disorder will make a meaningful difference in your life as you and your family learn to cope with this challenging disorder.

Sincere best wishes to you and your family,

Chris Abney Zeigler Dendy

P.S. To find out more about me and my family, visit our website at **www.chrisdendy.com***. As always, I welcome your comments or suggestions for improving our book. I look forward to hearing from you at* **chris@chrisdendy.com***.*

What Is Attention Deficit Disorder?

"When you have an attention deficit disorder, you don't know what 'normal' attention and concentration are. You just assume that everyone concentrates the same way you do. It's like having a vision problem. You don't realize what the real world looks like or that you have a vision problem until you are tested and get glasses. The same thing is true with ADD. You don't know you have ADD and problems with attention and concentration until you take Adderall and find out what it's like to be able to concentrate." —Alex, age 16

The ABC's of ADD and ADHD

Attention deficit disorders are neurobiological disorders. That is, researchers believe that the symptoms of attention deficits are caused by chemicals in the brain that are not working properly. In addition, there are differences in actual brain structure. As a result, many children and teenagers with these disorders have problems with attention and learning that may cause significant difficulty both at home and school. The most common characteristic observed in these teenagers is *inattention*. *Impulsivity* is also a classic symptom of teens who have attention deficit disorder—perhaps more so for those with hyperactivity (ADHD) than for those who have the primarily inattentive form of the disorder (ADD). Although *all* children may be inattentive and impulsive at times, youngsters with ADD or ADHD behave this way more frequently.

Another hallmark of many teenagers with the disorder is *underachievement in school*. That is, these students don't perform as well academically as would be expected, given their level of intelligence. Additionally, for some, but not all, *hyperactivity* during childhood is also a classic indicator. By adolescence, this hyperactivity has usually subsided, to be replaced by restlessness or sometimes rebelliousness. Beyond these core characteristics, there is great vari-

A Note on Terminology

Sometimes the terminology used to distinguish between the various types of attention disorders is confusing, since doctors and teachers use different names for the same conditions. The terms teachers use—ADD and ADHD—were established by federal education law. The terms doctors and other treatment professionals use are more complex and can be somewhat confusing. For example, they use the term AD/HD for all three conditions, even when the teen isn't hyperactive. These official diagnostic terms are explained later in this chapter.

In this book, I will use these abbreviations:

- **ADHD**, unless otherwise noted, refers to both the hyperactive and combined types.
- **ADD** refers to the inattentive non-hyperactive type.

ability in behavior among young people with this disorder. Seldom will two teenagers with an attention deficit disorder behave exactly the same way.

Teenage students may have one of two distinctly different types of attention deficit disorders, plus they may have a combination of the two:

1. teens who were hyperactive and impulsive as children, and
2. teens who are inattentive but were never hyperactive.

Teens with the hyperactive type look very different from those with the inattentive type. In fact, teens with the hyperactive or combined forms often have high energy levels, while teens with the inattentive form are almost the exact opposite. The low energy and day dreaming associated with ADD inattentive often confuse parents and professionals, leading them to believe the child does not have an attention deficit.

"My son wasn't hyperactive so I thought he couldn't possibly have ADHD."

ADD and ADHD: Practically Speaking

Before reviewing the official criteria for diagnosing attention deficit disorders, it is important to discuss the practical implications of living with a teenager who has an attention deficit. Clearly the technical diagnostic criteria alone don't tell the whole story about the challenges of having ADD or ADHD. So this next section gives an overview of the challenges of living with these teens day-in and day-out. More detailed descriptions of everyday behaviors these teenagers exhibit at home are provided in Chapters 9 and 10. The actual diagnosis of ADD or ADHD is discussed in detail in Chapter 2. In addition, school issues are addressed in Chapters 11 through 15. You will also find a great deal of helpful information in the companion guide to this book, *Teaching Teens with ADD and ADHD,* since it is devoted singularly to coping with challenging issues at school. Plus, my son Alex and I, with input from twelve teens, have coauthored a survival guide for the teens themselves, *A Bird's-Eye View of Life with ADD and ADHD.*

All this information should make it easier for parents and teachers to identify teenagers with the disorder, plus understand more about the disorder from the teen's perspective. *A Bird's-Eye View* may also give you the easy-to-understand words and drawings you need to discuss these complex issues with your teenager. But first let's talk briefly about why these children are so difficult to raise.

Why Is Parenting a Teen with an Attention Disorder So Hard?

Parenting a teenager with ADD or ADHD may be compared to riding a roller coaster: there are many highs and lows, laughs and tears, and breathtaking and terrifying experiences. Although parents crave calm, uneventful weeks, unsettling highs and lows are more likely the norm with these teens.

A wise child psychiatrist once observed:
"I'm so glad I had the opportunity to raise 'an easy child' in addition to my child with ADHD. Otherwise I would have always doubted my parenting skills."

Another expert on attention deficits, psychiatrist Peter Jensen, M.D., concurs that many of these children are much more difficult to parent and that parents will, in effect, need a "black belt" in parenting. So let's clarify this key point from the very beginning—the leading experts agree, "bad parenting" does not cause ADD or ADHD. At times, these children baffle even the experts. We all—the teen, parents, and professionals—struggle with the best way to treat this condition.

Although this chapter reviews many reasons that ADD or ADHD may cause parents to question their parenting skills, that is not to say that raising a teen with an attention deficit disorder is unrewarding. In fact, people with attention deficit disorders are often very personable and have many special talents. Often a parent's major contribution is helping the teen tap those talents to find her special niche in the work world. Tips on finding your teen's positive qualities are discussed in Chapter 4.

Immaturity and Developmental Delays

Since 1995, when the first edition of this book was published, researchers have made us aware of two heretofore unrecognized factors that have a profound impact on the behavior and academic performance of teenagers with attention deficits:

1. *deficits in executive function*, in other words, the management functions of the brain that control self-regulation and the individual tasks that are critical for success at school. See box below.
2. A *30 percent developmental delay* in executive function skills. For teens, that translates into as much as a four- to six-year delay.

What Is Executive Function?

During the early 1990s, several researchers including Russell Barkley, Ph.D., and Martha Denckla, M.D., a pediatric neurologist at John's Hopkins University, recognized the importance of a group of key cognitive skills known as *Executive Function.* These skills are believed to be controlled by the prefrontal cortex of the brain and are what enable us to consciously manage our learning and behavior to prioritize and meet our goals. Denckla also describes "executive dysfunction as the zone of overlap between ADHD and learning disabilities." Although deficits in executive skills are common among those with attention deficits, they also may occur in people who do not have attention deficits.

Thomas E. Brown, Ph.D., a well-known authority on ADHD at Yale, gives us a helpful visual image by comparing executive skills to the conductor's role in an orchestra. The conductor organizes various instruments to begin playing singularly or in combination, integrates the music by bringing in and fading certain actions, and controls the pace and intensity of the music. In a similar manner, the brain's executive functions control several individual skills that are required to complete complex tasks. For example, here is a simplified explanation of the skills that must be coordinated when a student writes an essay. The student must hold information and ideas in mind, select, organize, and sequence key facts, retrieve grammar and spelling rules, and put this information in writing.

Although researchers do not all agree on the components of the executive function process, typically most lists include many of these skills:

1. **Working memory and recall** (holding facts in mind while manipulating information; accessing facts stored in long-term memory; and then using this information to guide actions). This skill is essential for imagining the past, anticipating what will happen next, avoiding repetition of the same mistakes, planning for the future, comprehending what is read, writing essays, working complex math problems, and having a sense of the passage of time.
2. **Activation, arousal, and effort** (getting started; paying attention; staying awake in class; finishing work).
3. **Controlling emotions** (ability to tolerate frustration; thinking before acting or speaking). Being able to internalize or keep private one's own emotions is essential for development of internal or intrinsic motivation.
4. **Internalizing language** (using "self-talk" to control one's behavior, guiding one's daily activities, and directing future actions).
5. **Reconstitution** (taking an issue apart, analyzing the pieces, reconstituting and organizing it into new ideas). This skill is critical for creative, analytical problem solving, speaking and writing fluently, and sequencing ideas for writing and problem solving.

Executive function has a profound impact on a teenager's school performance, plus her ability to cope with the challenges of everyday living. Executive function deficits cause major problems in areas such as organization, time management, and self-control. The ability to plan for the future is also a critical element of executive function.

Here is the good and bad news about executive function: your teen's executive skills, although delayed, will continue to develop and improve over the years—until her early thirties, according to Dr. Barkley, or even her forties, according to Dr. Denckla's research. Although people with attention deficits will never quite catch up with their non-ADHD peers, most learn compensatory strategies and are capable of functioning quite well in the adult work world.

Problem behaviors resulting from executive function deficits are discussed in detail in Chapters 8 through 13 of this book.

These two topics will be described briefly here, but are discussed in more detail throughout this book and in Section 3 of *Teaching Teens with ADD and ADHD*. These topics are also addressed in *A Bird's-Eye View* in words and examples teens can easily understand.

Dr. Russell Barkley, one of the leading international researchers on attention deficit disorders, has validated what parents have known for many years—our children are less mature than their peers. Dr. Barkley was the first to document that many of these children experience a 30 percent developmental delay in executive skills such as self-management, organization, awareness of time, the ability to plan ahead, and control of emotions. For example, your 16-year-old may act more like a 10- or 12-year-old with regard to these behaviors. But let's be clear: the term "developmental delay" does not imply mental retardation; in fact, teens with attention deficits can be very bright. Unfortunately, these teenagers are often unintentionally put in environments, such as unsupportive school settings, that they are unprepared to handle and then blamed when they fail.

On the surface, the teenager's immaturity and executive function deficits make it appear as though he or she is simply making a conscious choice to be lazy and unmotivated. But in reality, the majority of our teens are victims of a very complex disorder. Unfortunately, the invisible nature of attention deficits—our teens look perfectly healthy—makes it more difficult for many adults to fully understand and accept the magnitude of the disability. [In recognition of the significant impact ADD and ADHD have on both teenage boys and girls, the pronouns "he" and "she" will be used in alternating chapters throughout the book.]

For these teens to succeed in high school or college, parents must be more involved than usual.

Unfortunately, you may be criticized for being too involved, when in reality you are simply providing *developmentally appropriate supervision* for your eighteen-year-old, who, for all practical purposes, acts as though she is twelve. However, it is also important to continually assess your level of support, allowing your teen to do as much for herself as possible, and gradually reducing your level of involvement over time. The concept of developmentally appropriate supervision is discussed in more detail in Chapter 12.

A Conflict in Roles. Because of the developmental delays and executive function deficits, during adolescence, the *"job descriptions" for parents and teens are often in conflict.* The parents' primary job is to gradually *decrease* their control, "letting go" of their teenager with grace and skill. In contrast, the teenager's main job is to begin the process of separating from her parents and becoming an independent, responsible adult. For better or worse, part of the teen's job is to experiment with making her own decisions, testing limits, and exercising her judgment. When teens with attention deficits start this process, parents may feel they are "losing control." Ironically, the natural tendency is to exert *even more* control. After all, giving freedom and responsibility to teenagers with an attention disorder is enough to unnerve even the most stouthearted parent.

Challenging Behavior

In addition to developmental immaturity, teens with ADD or ADHD usually have other characteristics that adults find difficult to deal with. They include:

Inattention and Noncompliance. A primary complaint from parents and teachers is that these teenagers have *difficulty following rules and instructions.* Specifically, two core characteristics of ADD or ADHD, inattention and impulsivity, are involved. *Inattention* is most obvious when teenagers need to sustain attention to boring, repetitive tasks such as schoolwork, homework, or chores. In order to pay attention, these teenagers actually need high-interest activities that offer a more stimulating, immediate reward. Specific comments from parents and teachers that pinpoint inattention frequently include: doesn't listen, doesn't pay attention, can't concentrate, loses things, can't work alone, doesn't finish tasks, and shifts from one task to another. Parents frequently complain that their teenager doesn't complete her chores.

Impulsivity. *Impulsivity* is the second primary characteristic of attention deficit disorders that concerns adults. Parents and teachers describe impulsivity as it relates to school issues as follows: responds quickly without waiting for instructions, makes careless errors, doesn't consider consequences, takes risks, carelessly damages possessions, has difficulty delaying gratification, and takes shortcuts in work. Sometimes these youngsters, especially those who were hyperactive as children, talk a lot, are bossy, say things without thinking, offend people without realizing it, don't pick up on subtle social cues, and interrupt conversations. Consequently, they may have more *difficulty making and keeping friends. Talking back and arguing* with adults may also be a problem. However, these issues tend to be less problematic for teens with ADD inattentive as opposed to ADHD. Teens with either ADD or ADHD also may inherit a gene that makes them more likely to be somewhat impulsive risk-takers.

Conflict with Adults. Because teenagers with attention deficits often have difficulty following rules and are impulsive, they are likely to have *conflicts with their parents, teachers, and other authority figures.* Conflicts most often arise when they don't do their class work, homework, or chores. Power struggles between teenagers and parents are common. As many as 60 to 65 percent of these youngsters have problems with *stubbornness, defiance, refusal to obey, temper tantrums, and verbal hostility.* Many chafe for independence from their parents, typically before they are ready for this independence. Parents have long observed that youngsters with attention deficits are more difficult to parent and discipline. They simply *do not respond to rewards and punishments* like other youngsters do. This behavior may help explain why they receive more criticism, rejection, and punishment than other children their age.

Easily Frustrated. *Low frustration tolerance* is also common. Teenagers with attention deficits seem to respond more emotionally to stressful situations than other teenagers do. For example, breaking up with a girlfriend or boyfriend is often a more emotionally devastating experience than for those without ADHD. They may become angry easily, have a "short fuse," and "blow up" over trivial things. Some may be defiant and argumentative with their parents and other authority figures. *Anxiety and depression* are also common, but their importance and impact on the teenager's behavior may be overlooked.

Sleep Disturbances. Sleep issues—getting up and going to bed on time—are also a major source of conflict within families, yet may not be addressed by treatment professionals. Several researchers found that more than half of all teenagers with ADHD reported sleep problems. To be specific, 56 percent of these teens had difficulty falling asleep compared to only 23 percent of their non-ADHD peers. They may also have difficulty waking up each morning. Thirty-nine percent report problems waking up frequently during the night. In addition, they may wake up each morning feeling tired (55 percent vs. 27 percent). Although sleep issues in children with ADD haven't been studied, parents report similar problems. Three critical issues for families seem to be:

1. the teen's difficulty falling asleep once she gets in bed
2. fewer hours of sleep
3. major battles each morning over the teen's difficulty waking up and getting to school on time.

(These sleep disturbances are a separate problem from those caused by taking stimulant medication such as Ritalin or Adderall too late in the day.) Sleep issues are discussed in more detail in Chapter 7.

Special Challenges of Attention Disorders during Adolescence. Although elementary school children with attention deficit disorders also have problems with inattention and impulsivity, the challenges facing teenagers are more complex. Problems common in younger children—talking excessively, blurting out answers in class, not sitting in their seat, and doing sloppy work—are not the major issues facing middle and high school students. During the teenage years, the risks of school failure, school suspension or expulsion, dropping out of school, substance abuse, pregnancy, speeding tickets, car wrecks, and suicide are greater for these youngsters. Because of their academic struggles, many teenagers develop an aversion to school. Yet school success is critical for developing a healthy self-esteem. These troubling issues are discussed in more detail in Chapters 9 through 12.

Brushes with the Law. Unfortunately, a few of the more impulsive and aggressive teenagers may have problems with law enforcement agencies. These "brushes with the law" are usually minor and not the result of any malicious or criminal intent. Instead, they result from poor impulse control, risk-taking behavior, and/or failure to anticipate the consequences of their actions. For example, teenagers with attention deficits have been known to receive speeding tickets, talk back to police officers, shoplift inexpensive items, sneak out of the house after city curfew, drink under age, and experiment with drugs. Parents are understandably frightened by these impulsive behaviors and may fear that this kind of acting-out behavior may become more serious. Fortunately, parents can often prevent more serious problems by learning to intervene when their child misbehaves, imposing appropriate yet reasonable consequences, and continuing to believe in and support their child. See Chapters 8 through 10 for these parenting strategies.

When our son was twelve and before ADD inattentive was diagnosed, he sneaked out of the house one night. The police called at three A.M. telling us that he had been picked up inside the mall about a mile from our home. He had not done any damage or stolen anything. I know my son. I don't believe he was up to any malicious mischief. Primarily, I think he enjoyed the adventure of sneaking out of the house. Plus, because of his sleep problems, he sometimes would still be awake, and bored, after I fell asleep. He and a friend had found an unlocked door and were walking through the mall. They got scared and ran when a security guard shouted at them. He had to do community service and we put him on restrictions. Although his actions worried us sick at the time, he is nineteen now, a freshman in college and doing well. Just because a teenager has a brush with the law does not mean he will be a delinquent.

These teenagers are not "bad, lazy, or unmotivated," as sometimes suggested by parents or teachers, but are struggling to cope with ADD or ADHD.

Most of us have known children or teenagers like this, whether they are our own, a relative's, or a friend's child. Some readers may even recognize themselves in the descriptions of teenagers presented in this book. Consequences for these types of misbehavior are discussed in more detail in Chapters 8-10. Obviously, if problems are serious and potentially life threatening, parents should seek professional help.

Academic Agony Unique to ADD and ADHD

Many students with attention deficits have *major problems at school*. Roughly 90 percent struggle terribly at one time or other. As you can guess, parents often identify this as the major source of conflict within their homes.

Unfortunately, our educational system is highly structured, and demands strong executive functions such as organizational skills, a good memory, good listening skills, and the ability to stay on task, follow up, and complete work rapidly. In other words, many teens with attention disorders spend much of their day in an unfriendly, hostile environment, attempting tasks that require skills that they do not have.

This system requires students to delay gratification for their "rewards." For example, they must work today for a grade (reward) that they will receive nine weeks, a semester, or a year later. High school and college present the most structured and demanding environments these teenagers will face in their lifetime. Consequently, these students are under incredible pressure during their school years. Teens with attention deficits face unique academic challenges, as described briefly below and in depth in Chapters 11-13.

Underachievement. Parents and teachers may be puzzled because teenagers with attention deficits may be bright but often *underachieving academically*. Frequently, teachers comment that these teenagers are not doing well in school mainly because they don't pay attention, don't complete class work and homework, forget to do make-up work, make a lot of zeros on daily work, and sometimes, sleep in class. Even when they do their homework, they may forget to turn it in. Students with attention deficits often have tremendous difficulty getting started on schoolwork and frequently may turn in assignments late. At times, teenagers with attention deficits must be baffled by their own behavior.

I have always been curious why it is that so many kids feast at the table of knowledge, when all I get is indigestion.

—Nick, an intellectually gifted eight-year-old upon learning that he had ADHD

Uneven Academic Performance. Some days these students can do the work; other days they can't. This unevenness in performance is extremely confusing to both parents and teachers. On the surface, it looks as if they can do the work but choose not to. Unevenness of schoolwork is one of the primary problems of youngsters with ADD and ADHD.

It is not unusual to hear a teacher say, 'Your son could do the work, if he would just try. He has a high IQ.' Parents and teachers often assume, incorrectly, that intelligence is the only prerequisite for good grades.

—Steven Evans, Ph.D., Director, ADHD Clinic, James Mason University

Learning Disabilities. Unidentified learning problems often contribute to academic difficulties and underachievement. Sometimes the source of the problem is an undiagnosed specific learning disability; other times, the symptoms of the attention deficit cause problems. After all, if students can't pay attention, they can't learn.

Older research studies reported that 25 percent have specific learning disabilities (SLD)—a special education category in federal law that is used to describe learning problems that are not due to low intelligence. However, a 2002 Center for Disease Control (CDC) study reported that roughly 50 percent of students with an attention deficit have learning disabilities.

Common learning disabilities in these students occur in these areas:

- written expression,
- working memory,
- math computation,
- listening comprehension,
- reading comprehension.

Some teenagers have serious learning problems and deficits in executive functions that do not meet the criteria for specific learning disabilities and that may not be brought to parents' attention by school personnel. Nonetheless, these learning problems may seriously interfere with school performance.

The characteristics of attention deficit—*inattention, disorganization, poor memory, and fine motor problems (especially poor handwriting)*—can also cause significant problems in school. These learning problems may result in poor and sloppy handwriting, slow, decreased production of written schoolwork, and failure to memorize information such as multiplication tables. Obviously, avoidance of written work often becomes a problem. Common learning problems and classroom accommodations are listed in Table 13-2 in Chapter 13.

Executive Function Deficits. Although difficulties with executive skills have a profound impact on a student's school work, their significance went unrecognized by educators and parents until relatively recently. Unfortunately, these deficits are often viewed as simple laziness or lack of motivation. The bottom line is that the student often has the brain power to do the work, but her ability to organize and implement a plan to actually do homework, school projects, or chores is greatly impaired.

Deficits in executive skills may contribute to:

- disorganization,
- difficulty getting started and finishing work,

- forgetting assignments,
- "procrastination" on long-term projects,
- forgetting to turn in assignments,
- difficulty memorizing and later quickly recalling facts, especially multiplication tables,
- trouble writing essays or reports,
- difficulties controlling emotions,
- problems socializing with friends, and
- planning for the future.

These are all common complaints from parents and teachers. Because of these behaviors, these teenagers may appear to be irresponsible, immature, and rude. Not surprisingly, they experience more criticism, punishment, and rejection from parents and teachers than their peers do.

As a result, many children with ADD or ADHD may have lower self-esteem as early as first and second grade. Yet on the surface, some children with attention deficits seem to have an over-inflated sense of self-esteem. At times, they don't seem to know how badly they are doing and may be clueless to rejection by their peers. A more detailed explanation of executive function is provided in Chapters 3 and 13.

"For me, discovering the concept of executive function deficits was like finding the missing piece of the puzzle. I was always baffled as to why my intellectually gifted child always teetered on the brink of school failure in high school. Now I understand."

—a school psychologist

Transition to Middle and High School. Transitions to both middle and high school can be extremely difficult for these students. Academically and emotionally, many children with attention deficits are able to cope adequately with the demands of elementary school. And some teenagers with attention deficits are able to succeed with minimal problems even in middle and high school. For most youngsters with attention deficits, however, frustration begins building in fourth and fifth grades. It increases still more in middle school, when demands increase significantly for academics, organization, and independent completion of school work. Strong executive skills such as organization, analysis, problem solving, and planning ahead are essential for middle and high school. If students' frustrations are not recognized and if adjustments are not made at home and school, parents may be faced with a very hostile, angry teenager who is miserable at school.

Transitions to Technical School or College.
Postsecondary education may be extremely challenging for our children. Options such as technical school, college, Job Corps, and the military are discussed in more detail in Chapter 15. Keep in mind that our teens need additional supports and accommodations if they are to be successful.

Section 504 of the Rehabilitation Act ensures that eligible students will receive additional help in these settings. Unfortunately, researchers tell us that only a small percentage of students with attention deficit disorders graduate from college. However, we have good reason to be optimistic that more of our students will graduate, if appropriate supports are put in place.

The Official Diagnostic Criteria for Attention Deficit Disorders

Often parents, teachers, pediatricians, or others strongly suspect that a teenager or child has an attention deficit disorder because of behaviors like those described earlier. The diagnosis of attention deficit disorder is not "official," however, unless the child meets certain criteria developed by the American Psychiatric Association (APA) and published in their *Diagnostic and Statistical Manual of Mental Disorders (DSM)*. The most current edition of the manual is the fourth edition, text revision, so the book is referred to as DSM-IV-TR. (See the box on the next page about expected changes in the next DSM.)

In determining whether a child has an attention deficit disorder, a licensed counselor, psychologist, or physician will compare the teenager's behavior (or the parents' reports of his behavior) with the characteristics listed under each of the types of attention deficits included in the DSM-IV-R. If the teen has a sufficient number of the characteristics to a degree that is "maladaptive and inconsistent with developmental level," he or she will be diagnosed with an attention deficit. Typically, this means the symptoms of the condition are serious enough to interfere with the teenager's

ability to function successfully at home and school. See Chapter 3 for a more detailed explanation of what comprises a good evaluation for ADD and ADHD.

As useful as the DSM criteria can be in reaching a diagnosis, many educational and medical professionals think there are a few shortcomings:

- DSM diagnostic criteria are based upon the behavior of boys, not girls, so accurate diagnosis of girls is more difficult. Girls who are diagnosed based upon these criteria tend to have worse cases of the disorder. In addition, girls are less likely to be hyperactive and aggressive, so they may be overlooked until later.

- DSM criteria for the hyperactive impulsive type are most accurate for children ages 6-14. Older teens and young adults may have ADHD yet not have six of the nine characteristics.

- Many leading researchers, including Dr. Russell Barkley and Dr. Joseph Biederman, do not agree with using age seven as a cutoff for diagnosing the disorder. For example, very bright children can compensate sufficiently until middle school when they may be overwhelmed by increased organizational demands. These doctors suggest this criteria instead: "childhood onset, but prior to puberty."

- Another aspect of the DSM-IV-TR may be problematic: the "H" for hyperactivity is included in the term AD/HD, Predominately Inattentive Type, for diagnosing children who are *not hyperactive*. Consequently, this diagnostic title of AD/HD does not accurately describe children with ADD inattentive who are *not hyperactive*. Most likely, this incongruity will continue to cause confusion among parents, educators, and treatment professionals. Parents and professionals will ask, "How can a teenager have attention-deficit/hyperactivity disorder and not be hyperactive?" The myth that a youngster has to be hyperactive to have an attention deficit disorder may be perpetuated, and problems diagnosing ADD inattentive will probably continue. Hopefully, these problems will be corrected when the new DSM-V is published.

Table 1-1 DSM-IV-TR Diagnostic Criteria for Attention Deficit Disorders

[Comments in brackets are the author's and are not part of the DSM-IV-TR]

POSSIBLE DIAGNOSES:

- 314.00 **Attention-Deficit/Hyperactivity Disorder, Predominately Inattentive Type:** if criterion A(1) is met but criterion A(2) is not met for the past six months.

    [Inattention is the predominate feature of this disorder. Formerly called Undifferentiated ADD or ADD without hyperactivity. The predominately inattentive type is much more than just a simple case of ADHD without hyperactivity.]

- 314.01 **Attention-Deficit/Hyperactivity Disorder, Predominately Hyperactive-impulsive Type:** if criterion A(2) is met but criterion A(1) is not met for the past six months.

- 314.01 **Attention-Deficit/Hyperactivity Disorder, Combined Type:** if both criteria A(1) and A(2) are met for the past six months.

- 314.9 **Attention-Deficit/Hyperactivity Disorder Not Otherwise Specified:** This category is for disorders with prominent symptoms of inattention or hyperactivity-impulsivity that do not meet criteria for Attention-Deficit/Hyperactivity Disorder.

    [Licensed treatment professionals use these 314. numbers as shorthand for diagnosis and billing procedures.]

OFFICIAL CRITERIA:

Attention-Deficit/Hyperactivity Disorder

A. Either (1) or (2)

(1) six (or more) of the following symptoms of **inattention** have persisted for at least 6 months to a degree that is maladaptive and inconsistent with developmental level:

Inattention
(a) often fails to give close attention to details or makes careless mistakes in schoolwork, work, or other activities
(b) often has difficult sustaining attention in tasks or play activities
(c) often does not seem to listen when spoken to directly
(d) often does not follow through on instructions and fails to finish schoolwork, chores, or duties in the work place (not due to oppositional behavior or failure to understand directions)
(e) often has difficulty organizing tasks and activities
(f) often avoids, dislikes, or is reluctant to engage in tasks that require sustained mental effort (such as schoolwork, or homework)
(g) often loses things necessary for tasks or activities at school, home, or the work place, (e.g., toys, school assignments, pencils, books, or tools)
(h) is often easily distracted by extraneous stimuli
(i) is often forgetful in daily activities

(2) six (or more) of the following symptoms of hyperactivity-impulsivity have persisted for at least six months to a degree that is maladaptive and inconsistent with developmental level:

Hyperactivity
(a) often fidgets with hands or feet or squirms in seat
(b) often leaves seat in classroom or in other situations in which remaining seated is expected
(c) often runs about or climbs excessively in situations where it is inappropriate (in adolescents or adults, may be limited to subjective feelings of restlessness)
(d) often has difficulty playing or engaging in leisure activities quietly
(e) is often "on the go" or often acts as if "driven by motor"
(f) often talks excessively

Impulsivity
(g) often blurts out answers before questions have been completed
(h) often has difficulty awaiting turn
(i) often interrupts or intrudes on others (e.g., butts into conversations or games)

[Most of the symptoms in A(2) above describe the behaviors of younger children. So, parents may find it helpful to compare their teenager's behavior as a young child with these criteria.]

B. Some hyperactive-impulsive or inattentive symptoms that caused impairment were present before age 7 years.
C. Some impairment from the symptoms is present in two or more situations (e.g., at school [or work] and at home).
D. There must be clear evidence of clinically significant impairment in social, academic, or occupational functioning.
E. The symptoms do not occur exclusively during the course of a Pervasive Developmental Disorder, Schizophrenia, or other Psychotic Disorder and are not better accounted for by another mental disorder (e.g., Mood Disorder, Anxiety Disorder, Dissociative Disorder, or a Personality disorder).

Changing Criteria; Changing Terminology

The labels for attention deficit disorders have changed several times during the last 50 years. In earlier years, it was called Hyperkinetic Syndrome. In 1980, the condition was first included in the DSM and was called Attention Deficit Disorder. The next revision of this manual (DSM III-R), which was in effect from 1987 to 1993, contained *two* diagnoses of attention deficits in youngsters: *Attention-deficit Hyperactivity Disorder (ADHD) and Undifferentiated Attention-deficit Disorder (ADD)*. The DSM IV was released in May of 1994. This edition established the four categories of attention deficit disorders described above, and a new name for the condition as a whole: Attention-Deficit/Hyperactivity Disorder (AD/HD). The latest revision, DSM-IV-TR™, was released in 2000 but did not change the criteria or labels for attention deficits.

New diagnostic criteria for the fifth edition of the DSM are slated to be developed in 2009. The new criteria may include some major changes. Several leading researchers have expressed concerns about the names currently given this disorder. So, don't be surprised if the committee that rewrites the DSM criteria changes the names again. As will be discussed subsequently, there is a possibility that ADD inattentive will be re-named and classified as a separate disorder rather than a subtype of AD/HD. Currently, AD/HD is classified under the DSM category of "disruptive behavior disorders." Obviously, the inattentive type does not typically have major behavior problems and does not fit well in that category. In addition, criteria for girls may be modified somewhat.

How Frequently Do Attention Deficit Disorders Occur?

The number of people thought to have attention deficit disorders has varied widely from one research study to another, from as low as 1 percent to as high as 20 percent of children under 18. A more accurate estimate, based on several recent, well conducted studies, is more likely between 5 and 12 percent. Another way of describing the *prevalence rate* is to say that approximately one to three students in every classroom of thirty students has the disorder.

International Rates. This diagnosis is not just limited to the United States. Researchers have reported comparable rates of attention deficits in developed countries worldwide: Japan—7.7 percent; Germany—9.6 percent; Canada—3.8 to 9.4 percent; Spain—8 percent; China 6 to 9 percent; Puerto Rico—9.5 percent; and India—5 to 29 percent. Other countries may use different diagnostic criteria, known as the ICD-9-CM, and in some countries like England, parents often have difficulty finding doctors who are knowledgeable about diagnosis of attention deficits.

Minorities. Attention deficits occur at about the same rate in all races. For example, researchers have found comparable rates of ADHD in African-American and Hispanic youth, yet they are much less likely to receive treatment. One North Carolina study reported these percentages of children diagnosed with ADHD who were also receiving medication: Caucasian, 8 percent, African-American 5 percent, and Hispanic, 2 percent.

Boys vs. Girls. Based upon the old DSM-III-R that did not include the criteria for ADD inattentive, attention deficit disorders were diagnosed three times more frequently in boys than girls. In addition, boys were six to nine times more likely to be seen at treatment clinics than girls. However, the male-female ratio has *not* been carefully studied under the current DSM criteria. Two leading authorities on attention deficits in women and girls, Patricia Quinn, M.D., a developmental pediatrician, and Kathleen Nadeau, Ph.D., a psychologist, believe that attention disorders may occur almost as frequently in girls as they do in boys. Refer to "Unique Challenges for Girls," below.

Family Members. The likelihood that a brother or sister will also have an attention deficit is 25 to 35 percent. Researchers also tell us that roughly 45 to 50 percent of children with an attention deficit will have at least one parent who has the condition.

Adoption. Children who are adopted are more than twice as likely to have ADHD as other children. The assumption is that the attention deficit may be inherited from young parents who impulsively have unprotected sex. In addition, use of alcohol or cigarette smoking during pregnancy increases the risk of having a child with an attention deficit.

Children vs. Adolescents vs. Adults. Depending upon which diagnostic criteria are used and who is asked, estimates of persistence of attention deficits into adolescence and adulthood vary. Researchers have reported that 70 to 80 percent of individuals diagnosed with ADD or ADHD in childhood still exhibit symptoms when they reach adolescence. Among young adults, 46 percent still meet the full eligibility criteria for an attention deficit. In addition, many adults still exhibit some symptoms that interfere with daily functioning, according to parents. Few adults will meet these child-based diagnostic criteria: can't remain in seat, difficulty playing or engaging in leisure activities quietly, blurts out answers, difficulty awaiting a turn, and runs about or climbs excessively. Roughly 50 to 65 percent of adults still struggle to varying degrees with symptoms of the condition. Clearly, attention deficits are a lifespan disorder—children do not outgrow it.

ADD vs. ADHD. Researchers now believe that ADD inattentive is more common than originally thought. According to information from a study conducted by Dr. Mark Wolraich, of the 11.6 percent of students with attention deficit disorder,

- 47 percent had ADD inattentive
- 21 percent had ADHD/H predominately hyperactive-impulsive only
- 32 percent had ADHD combined type

Interestingly, Dr. Wolraich also found that 4 percent of the students who had an attention deficit were not adversely affected by their condition at that particular time. Researchers also gleaned other interesting facts: students with ADHD tend to have behavioral problems, while students with ADD inattentive are more likely to have academic problems. As expected, those with ADHD combined type had both academic and behavioral problems.

It is important to note here that far more is known about *ADHD* than about *ADD,* and that more is known about ADHD in *children* than in *teenagers and young adults.* This is because most research conducted to date has been on boys with ADHD. Consequently, the implications of these research studies for adolescents with ADD inattentive are not always clear. [When studies are referenced, this book uses the terms ADHD or ADD inattentive to specify the target population for the study.]

Why Does It Seem Like Everyone Is Being Diagnosed with ADD or ADHD?

The media sometimes feature stories about the alarming rise in prescriptions for AD/HD medications in the United States, which could give you the impression that the incidence of attention deficit disorders is exploding. It is true that more people are being treated for ADD and ADHD, but there are legitimate reasons for this increase. Although over-diagnosis is often portrayed as a major problem, in reality, *underdiagnosis* and under-treatment are of greater concern. Let's look at the facts and some possible reasons why more people are being treated for ADD and ADHD.

- **ADD and ADHD have been under-diagnosed for years.** Some researchers speculate that we "are finally playing catch-up." Many researchers believe this is the primary reason for increases in the number of children and teenagers being diagnosed. In 1987, less than 1 percent were receiving medication. Public education and awareness of ADD and ADHD have increased, making diagnosis more likely. More teenagers and girls are being treated than ever before. Finally, treatment professionals now realize that teens don't outgrow attention deficits.

- **ADD and ADHD may be increasing because of environmental trauma.** Although ADD and ADHD are often inherited, trauma or toxins in the environment may also cause attention deficits. For example, exposure to lead, or having a mother who drinks or smokes during pregnancy, may cause children to exhibit symptoms of this condition. In February 2003, the Environmental Protection Agency (EPA) issued a report which identified attention disorders as an emerging issue of concern. Specifically, the report identified PCBs and lead in the environment as possibly causing these symptoms. Children living below the poverty level had the highest rate of ADHD—14 percent—which is well above the national average.

- **The criteria for the inattentive type of ADD were not included in the DSM until 1994.** This means that some teenagers with the inattentive type of ADD who would have been overlooked previously are now being diagnosed, albeit at a later age in middle and high school or even college.

- **Children and teenagers with borderline ADD or ADHD may be receiving treatment now.** Perhaps children and teenagers who have a borderline attention deficit (with 5 but not 6 characteristics of the DSM IV criteria) are being identified and referred for treatment by parents who are desperate to find help for their struggling child. This is especially true for girls with ADD or ADHD, who typically don't have major problems with hyperactivity or aggression and may only meet five instead of six of the criteria. In fact, some researchers argue that the number of criteria should be reduced for girls.

- **More adults are being diagnosed with attention deficits and are being treated with medication.** Although there has been a significant increase in the amount of stimulant medications prescribed over the last few years, that doesn't mean that they are all being given to children.

Obviously, there may be some cases of both over-diagnosis and under-diagnosis. However, neither extreme should occur. Providing a thorough assessment should help ensure an accurate diagnosis, avoiding both under- and over-diagnosis.

The ADD/ADHD Iceberg: Understanding the Complexities of ADD and ADHD

ADD and ADHD are often incredibly complex conditions. Understanding this fact is critically important for helping teens succeed at school and for implementing an effective treatment plan. One way to help parents, teachers, and treatment professionals understand this more fully is through use of this metaphor: The characteristics of ADD and ADHD may be compared to an *iceberg*: *often the most challenging aspects of this disorder are hidden beneath the surface.* (See figure on next page.)

Typically, parents and professionals see the tip of the iceberg—the more obvious problem behaviors such as hyperactivity, talking back, and failure to complete homework. However, they may not recognize the significance of issues such as disorganization, sleep problems, impaired sense of time, inability to plan ahead, or the presence of coexisting conditions such as depression and anxiety.

For more information: Chapter 7 provides a discussion of the most common coexisting conditions found in teenagers with attention deficits; Chapter 13 describes common learning problems.

Unique Challenges for Girls

Recently, Patricia Quinn, M.D., and Kathleen Nadeau, Ph.D., have pressed for more research and a better understanding of the unique impact of attention disorders on girls and women. In 2001, these pioneers founded the National Center for Gender Issues and ADHD to study females with this condition (www. ncgiadd.org). Many leaders in the field believe that the current DSM diagnostic criteria, which were based upon the behavior of boys only, do not adequately identify females with the condition.

Drs. Quinn and Nadeau remind us that girls are often eager to please, so tend to suffer in silence and perhaps hide their struggles from parents and teachers. Since girls typically are not aggressive or a behavior problem, it is more difficult for them to meet diagnostic criteria, even when they have all the other symptoms of impairment that boys do. This factor has led some experts to argue that girls should be diagnosed with attention deficits with five of nine symptoms instead of the required six. Much is still unknown about ADD or ADHD in females. Of the thousands of studies on ADHD, Quinn and Nadeau point out that only 36 studies have been done on females and many of those are flawed. Quinn and Nadeau also believe that attention disorders continue to be under-diagnosed in females and that, in fact, the condition occurs in girls as often as it does in boys.

Girls' symptoms also tend to worsen after puberty; fluctuating levels of estrogen have a major influence on the levels of the neurotransmitters dopamine and serotonin. In turn, female hormones have a tremendous impact on girls' attention, memory, moods, and cognitive functioning. Joan Helbing, M.S., an ADHD consultant from Appleton, WI, is also the mother of two daughters with attention deficits. She offers these helpful insights. Additional information regarding the emotionality often observed in girls in provided in Chapter 9.

"One unique characteristic of girls that I have observed and other parents have confirmed is the high level of emotionality. Emotions can become a real challenge, especially when girls reach adolescence. It can put them over the edge a lot. They can be unpleasant to be around. Daughters with ADHD are pretty emotional anyway, but when you add hormonal and PMS problems, the situation can be very difficult."

Boys and girls with attention deficits may struggle with different issues, as explained by this mother of both a son and daughter. Some of these differences, however, may be explained by their having different kinds of attention deficits.

"My son and daughter both have attention deficits, but they are very different. My son has ADD inattentive and my daughter, ADHD. The things I notice most about her are her impulsivity, talking a lot,

THE ADD/ADHD ICEBERG
Only 1/8 of an iceberg is visible!!
Most of it is hidden beneath the surface!!

THE TIP OF THE ICEBERG:
The Obvious ADD/ADHD Behaviors

IMPULSIVITY
Lacks self-control   Difficulty awaiting turn
Blurts out   Interrupts
Tells untruths   Intrudes
Talks back   Loses temper

HYPERACTIVITY
Restless   Talks a lot
Fidgets   Can't sit still
Runs or climbs a lot   Always on the go

INATTENTION
Disorganized   Doesn't follow through
Doesn't pay attention   Is forgetful
Doesn't seem to listen   Distractible
Makes careless mistakes   Loses things
Doesn't do school work

HIDDEN BENEATH THE SURFACE:
The Not So Obvious Behaviors!!

NEUROTRANSMITTER DEFICITS
IMPACT BEHAVIOR
Inefficient levels of neurotransmitters,
dopamine, norepinephrine, & serotonin,
result in reduced brain activity
on thinking tasks.

WEAK EXECUTIVE FUNCTIONING
Working Memory and Recall
Activation, Alertness, and Effort
Internalizing language
Controlling emotions
Complex Problem Solving

IMPAIRED SENSE OF TIME
Doesn't judge passage of time accurately
Loses track of time
Often late
Doesn't have skills to plan ahead
Forgets long-term projects or is late
Difficulty estimating time required for tasks
Difficulty planning for future
Impatient
Hates waiting
Time creeps
Homework takes forever
Avoids doing homework

SLEEP DISTURBANCE (56%)
Doesn't get restful sleep
Can't fall asleep
Can't wake up
Late for school
Sleeps in class
Sleep deprived
Irritable
Morning battles with parents

30 PERCENT
DEVELOPMENTAL DELAY
Less mature
Less responsible
18 yr. old acts like 12

NOT LEARNING EASILY FROM
REWARDS AND PUNISHMENT
Repeats misbehavior
May be difficult to discipline
Less likely to follow rules
Difficulty managing his own behavior
Doesn't study past behavior
Doesn't learn from past behavior
Acts without sense of hindsight
Must have immediate rewards
Long-term rewards don't work
Doesn't examine his own behavior
Difficulty changing his behavior

COEXISTING CONDITIONS
2/3 have at least one other condition
Anxiety (34%)   Depression (29%)
Bipolar (12%)   Substance Abuse (5-40%)
Tourette Disorder (11%)
Obsessive Compulsive Disorder (4%)
Oppositional Defiant Disorder (54-67%)
Conduct Disorder (22-43%)

SERIOUS LEARNING PROBLEMS (90%)
Specific Learning Disability (25-50%)
Poor working memory   Can't memorize easily
Forgets teacher and parent requests
Slow math calculation (26%)
Spelling Problems (24%)
Poor written expression (65%)
Difficulty writing essays
Slow retrieval of information
Poor listening and reading comprehension
Difficulty describing the world in words
Difficulty rapidly putting words together
Disorganization
Slow cognitive processing speed
Poor fine motor coordination
Poor handwriting
Inattention   Impulsive learning style

LOW FRUSTRATION TOLERANCE
Difficulty Controlling Emotions
Short fuse   Emotionally reactive
Loses temper easily
May give up more easily
Doesn't stick with things
Speaks or acts before thinking
Concerned with own feelings
Difficulty seeing others perspective
May be self-centered
May be selfish

****
ADD/ADHD is often more complex than most people realize!
Like icebergs, many problems related to ADD/ADHD are not visible. ADD/ADHD may be mild, moderate, or severe,
is likely to coexist with other conditions, and may be a disability for some students.

the need to be active constantly, and, at times, her anger. In contrast, my son has major issues with executive function skills like organization and forgetfulness.

"*If you asked me which one was harder to parent, I'd have to say my daughter. Each responds differently when they are angry. She becomes very emotional and will get in your face. For example, she can be irritable, argumentative, and defiant. Sometimes it can be scary when she gets so angry. My daughter is extremely open with me. She likes to think out loud, so she has to discuss everything when she is trying to solve a problem. Sometimes she tells me things I wish I didn't know. I sense that she is frustrated with herself because life is such as struggle.*

"*On the other hand, when my son becomes irritable, he has learned to walk away. When he is upset, he keeps all his emotions inside and has a tendency to simply shut down under stress.*"

Childhood Characteristics of ADD and ADHD

If your teenager was only recently diagnosed with an attention deficit, you may find it helpful to look back on her early childhood and see which of the typical behaviors she had. If you are not yet sure that your teenager has ADD or ADHD, comparing her behavior as a child to the behavior described here may help you decide whether to pursue a diagnosis. In either case, the information below should help you understand some of the differences between attention deficit disorder in younger children and in teenagers and young adults.

Classic ADHD with Hyperactivity

Frequently, when people think of ADHD, they picture Dennis the Menace—a child who is constantly moving and getting into mischief. Most parents of children with ADHD, however, say that their children were active but *not* overly active. These children may run and climb, but they can sit still long enough to watch TV, play Game Boy or Nintendo, or play with their favorite toys.

"*In reality, very few ADHD children are hyperactive in the true sense. I see maybe one or two a year, referred in by kindergarten or first grade teachers. Most ADHD children and teenagers are fidgety, playing with something in their hand, standing by their desk, but not overtly hyperactive or antisocial.* "

—Theodore Mandlekorn, M.D. pediatrician

Approximately one-third of all children with ADHD may be sufficiently hyperactive to be diagnosed during early childhood. The average age for diagnosis of ADHD is three or four. Because of their hyperactivity, many children with ADHD are diagnosed before entering school or soon after they enter kindergarten. They may be extremely independent from an early age.

"*Our son always had this 'No, I'll do it myself' attitude from the time he was about one year old. When he went to nursery school, the teacher said she had never met a more independent four-year-old.*"

Extreme Hyperactivity. A few children with more severe or complex cases of ADHD are extremely hyperactive at an early age. Their parents often tell professionals that their child with ADHD has been different from their siblings or other children since birth. Some are more active in the womb. These children may stand or walk at an early age. They may learn as young toddlers to "escape" from their cribs, strollers, and playpens. They may be very talkative and may seem to be in constant motion.

"*Cassie walked at seven months and it seemed like all hell broke loose. At seven months she weighed eleven pounds. She was tiny and very agile. Nothing was safe! We couldn't have any knickknacks in our house. Nothing could be in her reach. By nine months she had kicked two slats out of her crib. At ten months, our pediatrician recommended putting a mesh roping over the top of her crib because she climbed out every time we put her in. It was quite a sight to see a tiny nine-month-old swing from the top bar of the crib and drop to the floor. We were afraid that she was going to hurt herself.*"

Some extremely hyperactive children may have trouble sitting still and are in constant motion—running, jumping, and climbing the unclimbable. These toddlers and nursery school children race from one activity to another. They may become upset and kick things or hit or bite other children if they don't get what they want, when they want it.

Early School Adjustment. When these children enter preschool or elementary school, some have a difficult time adjusting and following rules. They may have difficulty remaining in their seats. A few may be overly aggressive, fighting with other children, biting, or taking their toys away. In extreme cases, day care or school officials may call and ask parents to take their child home because her behavior is out of control or even ask them to withdraw the child from day care or kindergarten.

ADD Inattentive

A different picture emerges for children with ADD inattentive. They are sometimes described as underactive or even lethargic. Typically, these children are not as impulsive, not as emotional, not behavior problems, and have more friends than their peers with ADHD. They may also have lower energy levels, be more passive and possibly shy. Some studies indicate higher levels of anxiety for these children and others don't.

Since the symptoms of ADD and milder ADHD are not as obvious, diagnosis is often more difficult and may not be made until after a child enters school. However, *all children with ADD or ADHD share one characteristic in common—inattention,* which may negatively affect their school performance. Although school adjustment may not be as traumatic initially for these children as for those with classic ADHD with hyperactivity, school may cease to bring joy or a sense of success in the early elementary school years.

The ADD Inattentive Controversy

Recently, several researchers, including Dr. Richard Milich, a professor of Psychology at the University of Kentucky, have presented persuasive arguments that *ADD inattentive is a totally unrelated and separate disorder and is not really a subtype of ADHD.* These discussions were printed in the February 2001 and 2002 editions of *ADHD Reports.* Dr. Milich and his colleagues even suggest establishing a new name for this condition that does not have any association with ADHD. Viewing ADD inattentive as a separate disorder could help in several ways by:

- Focusing research on the unique aspects of ADD rather than doing research on young people with ADHD and applying those findings to ADD.
- Developing a theory that may explain the dynamics of this condition, thus improving treatment strategies.
- Providing a more accurate classification of the disorder by removing it from its current location as a "disruptive disorder" in the DSM.

Dr. Barkley believes that *ADHD* involves problems with output of messages from the brain, and *ADD inattentive* involves sluggish cognitive processing or "*sluggish cognitive tempo,*" a problem with the brain receiving and processing information quickly and accurately. These issues are discussed in more detail in Chapter 3.

Secondary Childhood Characteristics

Health Problems. Studies offer conflicting results regarding whether or not children with attention deficits are slower to walk and achieve other developmental milestones. However, researchers have found that many children with ADHD have more *health problems* than children without an attention deficit. Allergies, colds, ear infections, asthma, and upper respiratory infections (39-44% vs. 8-25%) occur more frequently. As infants, they may have colic, have irregular eating and sleeping patterns, be more fitful and restless, cry easily, and have trouble adjusting to change in routine. A few infants with attention deficits may be undemonstrative and noncuddlers. Some may have delays in talking or speech problems.

"From the time our son was born, he had a mind of his own. He resisted being held or cuddled by arching his back to get away from us. If he initiated cuddling, that was okay, but it very rarely happened. Mostly he would squirm down out of our reach and do what he wanted to do."

Accidents. Children with ADHD who are hyperactive tend to have more than their share of *accidents* and visit emergency rooms more often than other children. Researchers found that up to 57 percent of these youngsters may be considered accident-prone, and that 15 percent have had serious accidents such as broken bones, cuts, head injuries, lost teeth, or accidental poisonings. They may get into everything, climb the unclimbable, get into childproof cabinets and containers, have accidental burns and electrical shocks, or rush into the street or other dangerous situations. Toys and household items may be damaged or broken if parents take their eyes off the child for one moment. In adolescence, teens with attention deficits are at greater risk for traffic accidents and speeding tickets than their non-ADHD peers. Not surprisingly, medical costs for children with ADHD were significantly higher than for non-ADHD children, according to a 2001 study conducted by the Mayo Clinic.

Bladder Control. Some researchers have reported that children with ADHD have more trouble with *bladder control and bed wetting.* However, research is contradictory with no clear evidence that this problem occurs more often in youngsters with ADHD. Perhaps these children are "too busy" to go to the bathroom and as a result may have "accidents."

Motor Coordination. Slightly more than half of children with ADHD (52 percent) have poor *motor coordination,* compared with only 35 percent of non-ADHDers. Children with ADHD also have more problems with fine motor coordination, which is often manifested in their poor handwriting.

Friends. Children with ADHD may have *problems making friends and keeping them.* They may be bossy, demand their own way, or may not follow rules of fair play. Some youngsters must be the center of attention. They may monopolize conversations, talk too loudly, and show off. Researchers have found that they may be rejected by their playmates within only twenty or thirty minutes. As many as 70 percent of children with ADHD may have no close friends by the fourth grade. Their playmates may react with aversion, criticism, rejection, counterattack, or withdrawal from their aggression, unpredictability, and disruptiveness. According to Dr. Barkley, the inability to control anger is typically the best predictor of rejection by their peers. Anecdotally, parents report that their children with ADD inattentive don't experience these problems with friendships.

Sleep Problems. These children may also experience sleep problems such as resisting going to bed, having more "curtain calls" for one last goodnight, and getting fewer total hours sleep than their non-ADHD peers. In extreme cases, children with ADHD may sleep only two or three hours a night, driving their parents to exhaustion. When problems like this are so severe, it may be worthwhile to review the characteristics of other coexisting conditions such as bipolar disorder in Chapter 7 and discuss the possibilities of this diagnosis with your physician.

"*She would sleep all night once we got her to sleep. The problem was getting her to fall asleep. At first, we would spank her every time she got out of her bed. Our pediatrician recommended that we pick her up, say, 'Bedtime is for sleeping,' and then put her back in her bed. For four or five months, we had to sit outside her door and keep putting her back in bed.*"

Exceptions. Some youngsters with an attention deficit don't exhibit any of these secondary characteristics or may exhibit only a few. Perhaps it is because they have ADD inattentive or a milder case of hyperactivity.

Eliminating the Myths

Several common myths have sometimes prevented diagnosis and treatment of ADD and ADHD. It is extremely important to eliminate these myths so that parents, teachers, and treatment professionals recognize and treat this condition earlier. These myths will be discussed in Chapters 2 and 4.

Myth I: All children and teenagers with attention disorders are hyperactive.

Myth II: Hyperactive children and teenagers with ADHD can't sit still for ten minutes.

Myth III: ADD and ADHD will always be diagnosed in childhood.

Myth IV: ADD and ADHD disappear in adolescence and adulthood.

Myth VI: ADD and ADHD are over-diagnosed.

Myth VII: ADHD is not a real disorder.

Myth V: Stimulant medications such as Ritalin no longer work when the child reaches adolescence.

Myth VIII: Use of medications like Ritalin will lead to drug abuse and addiction.

"*My son who has ADD inattentive really didn't have very many of the textbook symptoms. He was never hyperactive, his developmental norms were normal, and he never had colic. However, he was inattentive, very adventuresome, and moderately active. He never seemed to need as much sleep as other children. Getting him to bed at night or to take a nap was frequently a battle.*"

The overview in this section is not intended to give in-depth information. For the interested reader, several excellent books are available regarding younger children who are hyperactive. See the Bibliography for a list of reading materials on younger children with ADD or ADHD.

Understanding Teens with ADD OR ADHD

Each Teenager with ADD or ADHD Is Unique!

Just to say that a student has ADD or ADHD really doesn't tell you very much at all about an individual teenager. There are many reasons why each teen with an attention disorder is unique.

1. Teenagers with attention deficits do not all act alike or have the same strengths or problems.
2. Symptoms of inattention, impulsivity, and hyperactivity, if present, may vary from mild to severe.
3. Learning problems (up to 50 percent) may also occur in one or more academic areas and may vary from mild to severe.
4. Other coexisting problems (69 percent) such as anxiety, depression, and aggression may be present, further contributing to the unique make-up of the teenager.
5. Teenagers with ADHD and hyperactivity often face different challenges from those who have ADD with inattention.

Furthermore, many factors, including basic personality, temperament, intelligence, severity of the ADD or ADHD, response to medication, learning disabilities, and family and school support all affect a teenager's behavior and his or her ability to adapt successfully. So, too, do outside stresses such as divorce, sexual or physical abuse, family moves, ill health, a death in the family, lack of supervision, lack of family supports, single parenting, remarriage (step-parenting), out-of-home placement, and poverty. Keep in mind that your teenager's attention deficit is really only one aspect of who he or she is!

To get an idea of the uniqueness of each teenager with an attention deficit, review the sample profile included as Table 1-2 on pages 18-19. This profile for a teen with ADHD can help you become more aware of the many factors that influence your teenager's development and to identify areas which you can change. If your teen has ADD inattentive, his or her behavioral profile probably will be very different from the teen with ADHD.

Develop a Profile of Your Teenager

To better understand your teenager with ADD or ADHD, you may want to develop a profile by completing the blank form (Understanding the Teenager) in Chapter 16. This form identifies a broad spectrum of factors, both positive and negative, which may affect your teenager. Many rating scales focus only on problems, and thus fail to identify strengths (which may inadvertently discourage parents and teenagers.) By filling out this form, you can clearly see your teenag-

er's strengths and difficulties, and important areas in which you can make changes. This information can be helpful to both parents and teachers in targeting specific behaviors for improvement.

Build on Strengths. Remember that the behaviors associated with attention deficits are not the only ones that influence your teenager's ability to cope successfully with the disorder. Parents and teachers are urged to identify the teenager's positive qualities as noted in

Table 4-1 in Chapter 4 and build upon those strengths. Parents are also encouraged to cherish their teenager's strengths and zest for living. The more "positive factors" in a teenager's life and the fewer stresses and hostile interactions, the more likely she will successfully adjust at home and school. Several chapters explain how parents can forge partnerships with professionals to help capitalize on their teenagers' strengths: issues regarding treatment professionals are discussed in Chapter 5; working with school personnel, in Chapters 11, 12, and 13 and in *Teaching Teens with ADD and ADHD.*

What Does the Future Hold?

Scenes from Ron Howard's movie *Parenthood* humorously capture the hopes and fears many parents have for their children. In the movie, the father (Steve Martin) daydreams about the future of his 10-year-old son. Will he be a success or a failure? In the first scene, he proudly envisions his grown-up son as the valedictorian of his class delivering the commencement address. In the next scene, his crazed son has barricaded himself atop a tower and is shooting innocent people.

The pain within the child as he struggles to understand himself and find understanding from others is poignantly portrayed in the movie. "Dad, what's wrong with me? Why am I going to see a psychiatrist?" Teenagers with ADD or ADHD must experience a similarly intense emotional struggle as they try to figure out "What's wrong?" or "Why am I having so much trouble in school?"

Table 1-2   Understanding the Teenager with Attention Deficit Disorder

Name: Student with ADHD   **Age:** _____   **Date:** _____

By completing this form, parents should gain a better understanding of their teenager's unique characteristics, personality, strengths, difficulties, and how he or she is different from other teenagers with an attention deficit. In addition to the list of symptoms, all the factors listed below also influence the teenager's behavior, self-esteem, and ability to cope successfully with ADD or ADHD. The severity of the behavior will also vary. Please circle words that best described your teenager.

DIAGNOSIS: Symptoms of ADD or ADHD may range from mild to severe.

	mild	moderate	severe
ADHD	mild	(moderate)	severe
ADD Inattentive	mild	moderate	severe

Coexisting Diagnoses: ADD and ADHD frequently coexist with other disorders

	mild	moderate	severe
Anxiety	mild	moderate	severe
Depression	mild	moderate	severe
Learning Disability	mild	moderate	severe
Learning Problems	(mild)	moderate	severe
Sleep Disturbance	mild	(moderate)	severe
Oppositional defiant	(mild)	moderate	severe
Conduct Disorder	mild	moderate	severe
Substance Abuse	mild	moderate	severe

FACTORS INFLUENCING ADD OR ADHD: Other factors influence a teenager's personality and ability to cope successfully with attention deficit disorder. These factors may also vary in intensity: mild/moderate/severe. Teenagers with ADHD and ADD Inattentive may be almost exact opposites in some behaviors. Circle the words that describe your teenager's behavior most of the time.

TEMPERAMENT	GENERAL ISSUES	FAMILY STRESS FACTORS
calm / (fidgets)	Self-esteem: (fair) / good	Family understand ADD/ADHD: (yes) / no
easy going / (aggressive)	Response to meds: fair / (good)	
low energy / (High energy)	Intelligence: average / (high)	Reasonable discipline: (yes) / no (not too harsh or lenient)
depressed / (happy)	Inattentive: (yes) / no	
irritable / (pleasant)	Impulsive: (yes) / no	Open communication: (yes) / no
sullen / (charming)	Disorganized: (yes) / no	Few hostile interactions between teen and parents: (yes) / no
shy / (class clown)	Loses things: (yes) / no	
anxious / (relaxed)	Forgets things: (yes) / no	Relatives understand ADD/ADHD (supportive): yes / (no)
(cautious) / daring	Complies with requests: (yes) / noo	
gives up / (tenacious)	Will do chores: (yes) / no	Family stresses (money, illness, divorce (remarriage): (yes) / no
(compliant) / (defiant) sometimes	Truthful: (yes) / no	
copes well / (frustrated)	Difficulty falling asleep: (yes) / no	Moved to new community: yes / (no)
calm / (angry outbursts)	Difficulty waking up: (yes) / no	Attending new school: (yes) / no
quiet / (talks a lot)	Restless: (yes) / no	Two parent family: (yes) / no
	Self-centered: (yes) / no	Step parents: (yes) / no
	Accident prone: (yes) / (no)	
	Interrupts: (yes) / no	
	Few friends: (yes) / no	

AREAS OF SUCCESS	POTENTIAL PROBLEM AREAS	MORE SERIOUS PROBLEMS
sports: (yes) / no	Argues: (yes) / no	Lies or cons others: yes / (no)
computers: (yes) / no	Loses temper: (yes) / no	Starts fights: yes / (no)
Game Boy: (yes) / no	Blames others: yes / (no)	Bullies or threatens others: yes / (no)
music/art: yes / (no)	Annoys others: (yes) / no	Physically cruel to others: yes / (no)
religious activities: (yes) / no	Easily annoyed: (yes) / no	Physically cruel to animals: yes / (no)
hunting/fishing: (yes) / no	Spiteful/vindictive: yes / (no)	Steals without confronting: yes / (no)
theater: yes / (no)	Defies/disobeys: yes / (no)	(shoplifting, credit card fraud)
add others:	Skips school: yes / (no)	Robs someone: yes / (no)
	School suspension: yes / (no)	Breaks into houses, cars: yes / (no)
	School expulsion: yes / (no)	Destroys other's property: yes / (no)
	Drops out of school: yes / (no)	Sets fires: yes / (no)
	Speeding tickets: (yes) / no	Uses weapons to harm: yes / (no)
	Substance abuse: yes / (no)	Forces others to have sex: yes / (no)
	Sexually active: (yes) / no	Substance abuse: yes / (no)
	Access to weapons: (yes) / no	Runs away from home: yes / (no)
		Pregnancy: yes / (no)
		Suicide risk: (yes) / no
		Car accidents: yes / (no)
		Before age 13:
		Stays out all night: yes / (no)
		Truant from school: yes / (no)

SCHOOL PERFORMANCE	LEARNING PROBLEMS	SPECIFIC LEARNING DISABILITY
Good handwriting: yes / (no)	Poor concentration: (yes) / no	Verbal expression: yes / (no)
Good reading skills: (yes) / no	Poor organizational skills: (yes) / no	Listening comprehension: yes / (no)
Good writing skills: yes / (no)	Poor memory: (yes) / no	Written expression: (yes) / no
Good vocabulary: (yes) / no	Lacks attention to detail: (yes) / no	Reading comprehension: yes / (no)
Good spelling skills: (yes) / no	Slow reading: (yes) / no	Mathematics calculation: (yes) / no
Good math skills: yes / (no)	Poor reading comprehension: yes / (no)	Mathematical reasoning: yes / (no)
Good organization: yes / (no)	Slow writing: (yes) / no	Basic reading skills: yes / (no)
Knows times tables: yes / (no)	Slow math calculation: (yes) / no	
Good at history: (yes) / no	Poor handwriting: (yes) / no	
Good at foreign languages: yes / (no)		
Dislikes school: yes / (no)	**SCHOOL ENVIRONMENT**	
Forgets assignments: (yes) / no		
Forgets make-up work: (yes) / no	School personnel:	
Forgets special projects: (yes) / no	Positive: (yes) / no	
Forgets instructions: (yes) / no	Flexible: yes / (no)	
Difficulty getting started: (yes) / no	accommodations: yes / (no)	
Test anxiety: yes / (no)	reasonable discipline: (yes) / no	
Failed a class: yes / (no)	Services, section 504: yes / (no)	
Failed a grade: yes / (no)	Services, special ed.: yes / (no)	

Many teenagers with attention deficit disorders experience an overwhelming sense of despair—especially if they are not receiving optimal treatment for their AD/HD. Some become so depressed about failures in school and conflicts with parents and teachers that they see no way to succeed in school or life. They may comment that they feel dumb, crazy, and overwhelmed, and sometimes they come to believe that they are "bad." As a result, their ambitions or expectations may plummet. They may give up on pursuing positive goals for their future. Much to their parents' dismay, they may select friends who are experiencing similar or even more serious difficulties.

If you have a teenager with ADD or ADHD, you may be extremely concerned about her future. Perhaps you worry about whether she will become a productive, well-adjusted adult. You may even secretly fear that she may become a juvenile delinquent. Since these teenagers seem to take longer to reach their potential and establish themselves as adults, parents have a number of years to "worry and worry some more."

> **"P**arents of teenagers without ADHD worry. The concerns of parents of teenagers with ADHD are greatly magnified!"*

The Good News

For some parents and teenagers, simply having the diagnosis of ADD or ADHD is good news.

> **"I**thought a good title for this book would be Good News: Your Teenager Has ADHD! It was a relief for me to find out why Steven had so much difficulty in school and to learn that his problem could be treated."*

Although ADD and ADHD are considered *"life-span" conditions* (children don't outgrow their attention deficit), the characteristics of the disorder change over time. In addition, there are some things they can do to cope more successfully. Plus, as they enter adolescence, many teens begin maturing and learning new skills and coping mechanisms. Their symptoms of impulsivity and over activity decrease, and their ability to sustain attention improves. Fortunately, the maturation process continues into young adulthood. For example, according to Dr. Barkley's research, executive functions don't reach full maturity until the early thirties.

Keys to a Good Outcome

Take Charge: Change the Things You Can Change

Many factors determine how successfully a teenager is able to cope with having ADD or ADHD. These will be discussed in Chapter 5. Some factors are beyond anybody's control. Fortunately, however, some important factors may be within your control by ensuring proper treatment, ensuring school success, or if needed, getting treatment for yourself.

Be Aware of Resilience Factors

Researchers have always found it interesting that two sets of teenagers can have a challenging condition like ADD or ADHD, yet one is successful and the other is not. So they have tried to figure out what makes the difference. One key factor seems to be resilience—or having the "capacity to cope and feel competent." Three leaders in the field of attention disorders have written about the importance of resilience—Drs. Robert Brooks, Sam Goldstein, and Mark Katz. (See the Bibliography.)

Resilience seems to be linked to several factors such as supportive adults, reframing ADD and ADHD, persistence, self-awareness, and redefining oneself in positive terms. As a parent, you need to be aware of these factors and try to ensure that they are incorporated into your teen's life. In other words, ***you must change the things in your teen's life that you can change!*** Tips for building resilience will be discussed in more detail in Chapters 4 and 5.

Be Supportive of Your Teenager

Clearly, parents play a critical role in helping their teenager cope with ADD or ADHD. This fact is supported by further observations from Dr. Gabrielle Weiss, a leading researcher on attention deficit disorders:

> **"W**hen the adults who had been hyperactive were asked what had helped them most to overcome

their childhood difficulties, their most common reply was that someone (parents were listed first, teachers second) had believed in them. . . ."

Unfortunately, giving your teenager the support she needs is sometimes easier said than done. *First,* you may not have much quality time to spend with your teenager if both you and your spouse work or if you are a single parent. The little time that is available may be spent on negative interactions—nagging or criticizing her for misbehavior and things not done.

Second, thanks to our hectic lifestyles and the technology boom, teens spend a lot of time in their rooms alone with their video games, music, and videos or TV.

Third, it may be difficult to support your teenager: sometimes when she misbehaves, she is not very lovable. Teenagers with ADD and ADHD tend to be inattentive, impulsive, and less likely to follow instructions. In response, their parents tend to be more commanding, negative, critical, and angry, and to use punishment more often. The teenager's misbehavior and attitudes actually affect her parents' actions and attitudes, and vice versa. Most people recognize that what parents say and do affects their children, but they forget that *children's behavior also has a major impact on their parents' actions.*

In fact, as Dr. Barkley explains somewhat tongue-in-cheek, an interesting side effect of a child's taking a stimulant medication is that *"parents and teachers get better."* When youngsters with attention disorders take medication, parents and teachers are less critical, rejecting, and punitive. Since the teenager's behavior improves when she is on medication, it is easier for parents to create the loving, positive, nurturing environment their child needs.

Finding the Road to a Successful Life

With proper diagnosis and treatment, most teenagers with ADD or ADHD will grow up to be well-adjusted adults. Unfortunately, finding and implementing the "proper" treatment for your child can be a long and complicated process. Because each teenager with ADD or ADHD is unique, treatment must be tailored to his or her individual symptoms, strengths, and needs. There is no "one-size-fits-all" plan for treating attention deficits.

Ideally, treatment plans should be aimed at helping these teenagers get along better in all aspects of their life—home, school, and community activities.

Treatment is defined broadly to include any activities that build self-esteem and help a teenager succeed in life. Keep in mind that many activities—not just taking medication and counseling—can be extremely therapeutic for your teenager. These activities include succeeding in school; mastering sports, debate, art, modeling, or other skills; and building positive relationships between parents and teenagers.

Chapter 5 covers treatment for ADD and ADHD in detail. Briefly, however, components of your teenager's individualized treatment program will probably include:

- medication
- ADD/ADHD education
- treatment of coexisting problems
- identification of learning problems, including executive function deficits
- accommodations at school
- extra support and supervision at home and school (coaching)
- activities that build self-esteem
- counseling for yourself and/or your teenager
- parent training and parent support groups
- reframing ADD and ADHD to look for positive elements of your teen's personality, believe in your teenager, and build on his or her strengths
- promoting your teen's resilience

The teenager must be involved as a respected partner in the treatment process! Your teenager is probably just as mystified and frustrated by her disorder as you are. Treatment is more likely to be successful if she is working with you rather than against you and sabotaging everything you attempt to do.

Because your teenager's attention deficit disorder can lead to so many problems within the family, getting proper treatment for her symptoms should be a family priority. See Chapter 5 for in-depth information on treatment approaches; Chapter 8 for information on positive parenting practices.

Speaking Personally from the Benefit of Ten Years of Hindsight

Looking back over the ten years since the first edition of *Teenagers with ADD* was published, I have learned some very important lessons. Many of the lessons will be shared throughout this most recent version of this book. Perhaps most important of all, I should let you know that our family has successfully survived both our sons' ADD/ADHD teenage years. In fact, we have two wonderful sons and a daughter who are all college graduates, and that, as you know, is a major accomplishment. But it has not been an easy journey. In fact, it has been the most challenging experience of my adult life. It will be important for you to remember that you are not alone; others have survived this struggle, and with careful work and planning, you should be able to do this too.

Conclusion

As you already know, to parent your teenager with an attention disorder, you will need to invest more time, energy, and patience than other parents. In fact, parenting your teen may well be one of the toughest and most humbling challenges of your life. You will need to do more hands-on behavior management, provide more supervision, and be more involved in ensuring that your teenager completes schoolwork and chores. Parenting your teenager is not, however, an impossible job or insurmountable challenge. Nor do you have to do it all alone. As later chapters explain, a wide range of professionals and other parents have expertise that can be of tremendous help to you.

After treatment is begun, you may see immediate rewards when your teenager comes home all smiles with passing grades, thanks to identification of learning problems, executive function deficits, accommodations in the classroom, and medication. Other rewards may come later when he or she reaches the late teenage years and looks at you and says, as our youngest son did, "Thanks for believing in me. I couldn't have done it without you." I can personally attest to how sweet the tears of joy are when you hear these long-awaited compliments.

Research into causes and treatment of attention deficit disorders continues and is producing exciting new information for families. As a result, the professionals who treat ADD and ADHD are becoming better informed about the disorder. Just as importantly, we may be on the threshold of major discoveries and breakthroughs about this challenging condition. In short, the future for teenagers with ADD and ADHD and their families has never been more hopeful.

2

Causes:
Understanding ADD/ADHD and the Brain

Until relatively recently, parents were sometimes singled out as the cause of their child's attention and behavior problems. They were accused of "bad parenting" and often criticized for failing to discipline their child properly. Although researchers and medical experts have not yet reached unanimous agreement about the causes of attention deficits, they agree that the vast majority of the symptoms of ADD and ADHD are beyond the teen's—and his parents'—control. Parents do *not* cause their children's attention deficit disorder. Research has shown that people with ADD and ADHD have demonstrable differences in their brains that may well be responsible for their symptoms.

The Role of Brain Chemicals in ADD and ADHD

Much research into the causes of attention deficit disorders is presently focused on differences in brain chemicals, or neurotransmitters, in the central nervous system (CNS). The CNS is comprised of the brain and nerves in the spinal cord. It acts as the main control system of the body, directing and coordinating actions. Within the CNS are billions of nerve cells or neurons that carry messages throughout the body (see Figure 2-1). These messages might direct a teenager to listen, pay attention when parents or teachers are talking, remember the assigned task, and stick with the task until it is finished.

Courtesy of Leonard Kong and Green Lake Crew—2006

Technically speaking, the nerve cells, or neurons, carry electrical impulses (nerve signals) from one end of the cell to the other—from the dendrite to the axon. Once the impulse travels down the neuron, it triggers a chemical reaction at the receptor genes on the next neuron, so that it is ready to receive the message. There is a space between neurons—known as the synapse or synaptic cleft. Since the axon and dendrites of the next neuron do not touch, messages must jump across the synapse. Neurotransmitters—the chemical messengers of the brain—are released at the synapse to help the message move across to the next neuron. Once the message has passed, the neurotransmitter is taken back up into the neuron to await the next message. This process is known as *reuptake* or more simply stated, recycling.

When an attention deficit is present, it is believed that messages move down the neuron, but stop and don't always cross the synapse to the second neuron. This disruption in the reuptake process is most likely caused by a chemical deficiency in neurotransmitters, which interrupts the normal flow of messages throughout the body.

The two primary neurotransmitters thought to be involved in attention deficits are *dopamine and norepinephrine.* Another neurotransmitter, *serotonin,* which is essential for restful sleep and feelings of well-being, is also thought to be involved, especially in some of the coexisting conditions such as depression. When availability of these neurotransmitters is inefficient, inattention, distractibility, aggression, depression, and irritability may result.

Researchers have documented *decreased levels of brain dopamine,* in the cerebral spinal fluid in children with ADHD. Not surprisingly, stimulant medications such as Concerta and Adderall, which are known to increase availability of the neurotransmitter dopamine in the central nervous system, *reduce symptoms of attention deficits.*

People with attention deficit disorders also have a higher percentage of dopamine transporter genes, DAT1—70% more than usual. Since transporter genes remove dopamine, this means that too much dopamine is removed too quickly from the synapse during the *reuptake or recycling process.* This prevents the passage of messages across each synapse. When neurotransmitters do not work properly, youngsters have difficulty paying attention, controlling impulses, suppressing inappropriate responses, and regulating motor activity.

This complex process is explained more simply and in more detail in "What Do I Need to Know about My Brain?" in our book, *A Bird's-Eye View.* Neurotransmitters, their role in attention deficits, their impact on behavior, and use of medication to improve their functioning are also discussed in Chapter 6.

Stimulant medications, such as Adderall, Concerta, and Ritalin can often improve symptoms of ADD and ADHD. Stimulant medications are so called because they stimulate the central nervous system. They are known to increase the amount of dopamine and sometimes norepinephrine that is available in the synapse—the very neurotransmitters that appear to be deficient in children with attention deficits. A new non-stimulant medication for treating attention deficits, Strattera, was released in 2002. More information on neurotransmitters and medications that enhance their functioning is in Chapter 6.

According to ADHD researcher and author Dr. Paul Wender, the production of neurotransmitters in-

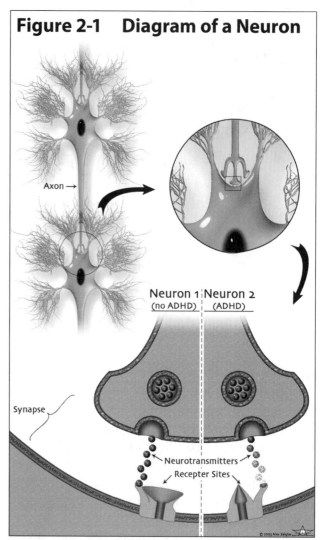

Figure 2-1   Diagram of a Neuron

Axon →

Neuron 1 | Neuron 2
(no ADHD) | (ADHD)

Synapse

Neurotransmitters
Recepter Sites

© 2003 Alex Ziegler

Our son Alex Ziegler created this drawing of a neuron for our book, *A Bird's-Eye View.*

creases with age, which may explain why many youngsters with attention deficits seem to have milder symptoms as they get older. In addition, executive functions continue maturing. In *Gender Issues and ADHD,* however, Drs. Patricia Quinn and Kathleen Nadeau remind us of a factor unique to girls—that estrogen has a major impact on both the dopamine and serotonin levels. This means that attention deficits may actually appear to worsen somewhat in girls after puberty.

Other Brain Differences in Attention Disorders

Several important studies over the last several decades have shed new light on the nature and causes of attention disorders. Although still not conclusive, much of this research points to neurological, biochemical, and genetic involvement in these conditions. However,

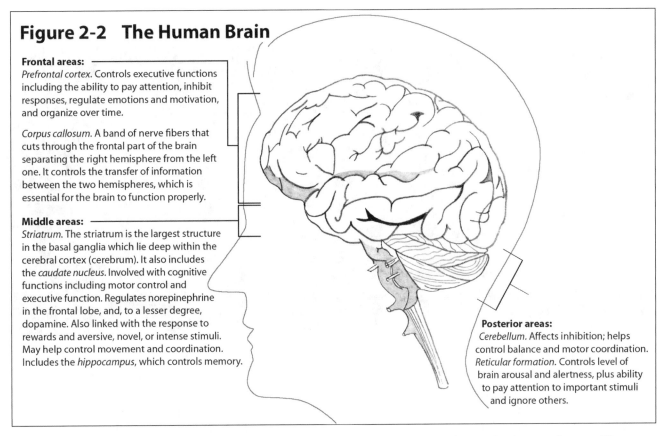

Figure 2-2 The Human Brain

Frontal areas:
Prefrontal cortex. Controls executive functions including the ability to pay attention, inhibit responses, regulate emotions and motivation, and organize over time.

Corpus callosum. A band of nerve fibers that cuts through the frontal part of the brain separating the right hemisphere from the left one. It controls the transfer of information between the two hemispheres, which is essential for the brain to function properly.

Middle areas:
Striatrum. The striatrum is the largest structure in the basal ganglia which lie deep within the cerebral cortex (cerebrum). It also includes the *caudate nucleus.* Involved with cognitive functions including motor control and executive function. Regulates norepinephrine in the frontal lobe, and, to a lesser degree, dopamine. Also linked with the response to rewards and aversive, novel, or intense stimuli. May help control movement and coordination. Includes the *hippocampus,* which controls memory.

Posterior areas:
Cerebellum. Affects inhibition; helps control balance and motor coordination.
Reticular formation. Controls level of brain arousal and alertness, plus ability to pay attention to important stimuli and ignore others.

please note that to date, research regarding the brain's involvement in this disorder has been limited to ADHD only. Most likely, the same areas of the brain are also involved in ADD inattentive. Studies on ADHD pinpoint three areas of the brain that are believed to be the major sites with neurotransmitter problems:

1. the prefrontal cortex,
2. the striatum, which is part of the basal ganglia, and
3. the cerebellum

The major sections of the brain thought to be involved in attention deficits and the probable actions each controls are noted in Figure 2-2.

Some important research findings about physical differences in the brains of people with ADHD include:

- According to the results of quantitative electroencephalographs (QEEG), there is "*slow wave, or theta, activity, particularly in the frontal lobe and excess beta activity.*" This indicates that children with ADHD are *under-responsive to stimulation.* In other words, they will have problems paying attention. This problem, however, can be corrected by stimulant medication.

- Studies have also shown *reduced cerebral blood flow* and thus less activity in the prefrontal region of the brain and the striatum during thinking tasks, specifically in the caudate region. These areas of the brain control several functions:
  - attention,
  - impulsivity—the ability to "stop and think" before acting,
  - insensitivity to rewards/punishment,
  - emotions, and
  - memory.

- *Diminished glucose metabolism* has been reported by Dr. Alan Zametkin, M.D., a psychiatrist and researcher at the National Institute of Mental Health (NIMH) in Bethesda, Maryland. Dr. Zametkin conducted Positron Emission Tomography (PET) studies of the brains of adults with ADHD. A PET scan is a procedure that is similar to taking a color x-ray of a cross section of the brain to depict its activity levels. These studies showed that the rate at which the brain absorbs glucose, its main energy source, is lower in adults with ADHD than in adults without this condition. This indicates *under-activity or under-arousal* in the brain. The largest reductions in glucose absorption are in the prefrontal regions of the brain.

Figure 2-3

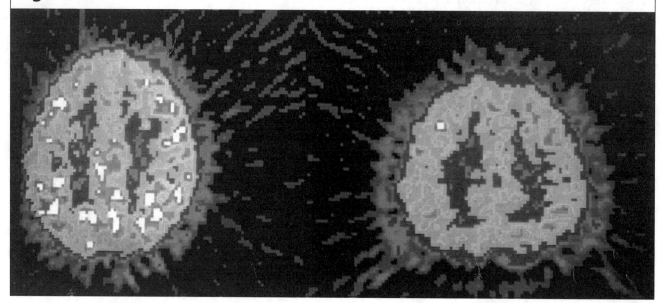

The frontal lobe of the brain controls complex mental processes such as memory, speech, and thought. These areas of the brain are where dopamine and norepinephrine are most involved in transmitting messages. Figure 2-3 shows the difference in brain activity between adults with and without ADHD. In the brain on the left (non-ADHD), there are a number of white areas indicating a great deal of brain activity, while there is only one area of white in the brain on the right (ADHD).

This NIMH research was conducted initially on adults with ADHD. Later, when Dr. Zametkin conducted the same study with male and female adolescents, the results were mixed. Girls showed the same underactivity as adults, but boys did not. Researchers are uncertain as to why this difference occurred, but the small number of youngsters in the study may have influenced the results.

- Researchers have **identified genes** that are involved in ADHD. Of the thirteen or so genes that have been identified that are linked to attention deficits, four are of primary interest to researchers: two *dopamine receptor genes—DRD2 and DRD4—plus a dopamine transporter gene—DAT1.* Dr. Barkley's group has also discovered another gene, DBH, that breaks dopamine down into norepinephrine.

    Scientists speculate that a cluster of these genes may be overrepresented in individuals who exhibit certain symptoms of ADHD. The gene receptors and transporters *control the level of dopamine* in the

synapse between neurons. DRD4 is found in the regions of the brain that are linked to executive function and attention. Dr. Jim Swanson, a developmental psychologist at the University of California/Irvine, reports that this same DRD4 gene is associated with high novelty-seeking or risk-taking behavior. This gene has also been associated with nicotine addiction and some forms of depression.

As explained earlier, a Harvard researcher has found that people with attention deficits have *70 percent* higher levels of dopamine transporters in the synaptic space. Because these receptors and transporters are not working properly, the right levels of dopamine are not available in the neurons. Researchers have shown that inefficient levels of dopamine interfere with attention, learning, and proper behavior.

- Some *sections of the brain are smaller,* according to magnetic resonance imaging (MRI) studies: the right *prefrontal lobe,* the right *cerebellum,* the left region of *the caudate nucleus,* and *the corpus callosum.* No brain damage has been found in these sections; they are simply smaller. The reduced volume is primarily attributed to smaller areas of white matter, which contain the connections between the nerve cell bodies located in the brain's gray matter. Researchers report that these sections of the brain carry messages between the neurons and ultimately affect:

1. alertness,
2. executive function,
3. the ability to control shifts from one task to another, and
4. the ability to assist with the transfer of information between neurons and between the two hemispheres of the brain.

"There is no problem with the brain cells; instead the problems lie in the 'transport system' in between the brain cells."

—Theodore Mandlekorn, M.D., pediatrician

All these research studies offer increased reassurance that the difficulties that youngsters with attention deficit disorders face are the result of physiological problems, not "bad parenting." Parents cannot cause their teenager's ADD/ADHD behavior because of the way they raise him. However, as discussed in later chapters, they can help him make a better adjustment at home and school.

Having an underlying biochemical problem doesn't mean the teenager is totally at the mercy of chemicals in his brain and is powerless to control his life or impulses. It does mean, however, that he will have to work much harder to pay attention, obey his parents, and complete chores and schoolwork. Obviously, seeking appropriate treatment, learning the facts about attention deficits, and learning to compensate for having this disorder is critical for teenagers.

Inherited vs. Noninherited Causes of Brain Differences

How do these brain differences in teens with attention deficits come about? Usually, the differences are inherited from a parent, before birth, but they can also be acquired through various types of trauma.

Inherited Causes

About four times out of five, the brain differences in attention disorders are inherited. As explained earlier, parents often seem to pass ADD or ADHD on to their children. Family histories frequently show that a parent (usually the father), or an uncle or grandfather acted the same way the child with the attention deficit

acts. Attention deficit disorders are the most often inherited childhood disorder identified in the DSM.

Researchers have shown that if one parent has ADHD, there is a 57 percent chance the couple will have a child with ADHD. Brothers and sisters of a children with ADHD have a 32 percent chance of also having the condition. If one twin is diagnosed, then 81 percent of identical twins will also have ADHD and 29 percent of fraternal twins will. Presumably, the parents have passed on to their children one or more of the genes thought to cause this condition.

"I suspect that my father, sister, and son all have ADD or ADHD. My father recently retired after 43 years of elected public service. He was honored this summer at a retirement ceremony after serving 35 years as probate judge. Although Dad was not a good student in school, he graduated from law school when he was in his early thirties. Subsequently, he was elected to the Georgia House of Representatives and later county probate judge. My sister finished her doctorate when she was in her mid-thirties.

"Some of my favorite stories about my Dad reflect his creativity and high energy level. In 1949, when Dad was elected to the Georgia House of Representatives, he gave new meaning to the term campaigning by airplane. Dad and his brother rigged up a public address system in an open cockpit airplane and flew low over houses asking people to vote for him. People were impressed!! He was elected with the highest vote of any of the eight candidates."

Noninherited Causes

According to Dr. Russell Barkley, one in five children may have an acquired case of ADHD. He explains that 10 to 15 percent of ADHD may occur as a result of prenatal injuries—trauma at birth or to the fetus during pregnancy and 3 to 5 percent may be caused by postnatal injuries—trauma or head injury in childhood or adulthood. Four common sources of prenatal injuries include

1. prenatal complications,
2. premature birth with minor brain hemorrhaging,
3. maternal cigarette smoking, and
4. maternal alcohol use during pregnancy.

ADHD is also common in children with disabilities such as *spina bifida, cerebral palsy, Tourette syndrome, and fragile X syndrome.*

Postnatal injuries may result from:

1. a serious head injury, or in rare cases,
2. streptococcal infections, or
3. chemotherapy or radiation of the brain.

In the rare situation involving strep, the child's autoimmune response attacks key parts of the brain that can predispose the child to ADHD. A teen being treated for cancer could also experience some ADHD symptoms.

ADHD, alcohol and cigarettes. Consequently, children with *fetal alcohol syndrome* (FAS) or *fetal alcohol effects* (FAE) often have symptoms of an attention deficit. So, too, do some children whose mothers abused drugs during their pregnancy. Mothers who smoke during pregnancy increase the risk that their child will have attention deficit disorder.

ADHD and TV viewing. In 2004, research was published implying that there is a link between inattention and too much television viewing among young children. However, Dr. Barkley explains that the research did not prove that TV viewing caused ADHD. Instead, he believes that the ADHD behavior is present first and these children simply prefer watching TV.

ADHD and thyroid problems. A few years ago, the media reported a link between children with thyroid disease and ADHD. However, most researchers do not think adequate research is available to confirm the thyroid/ADHD link. Thyroid problems are so rare in children with ADHD (1 in 2,500), that thyroid dysfunction is a highly unlikely cause of the these symptoms.

Thyroid screenings should be done on youngsters who have a depressed rate of growth or swelling of the thyroid gland. The effects of hormone treatment for an underactive thyroid have been contradictory: in some children, ADHD behaviors improve; in others, they worsen. If parents have concerns about potential thyroid problems, they should discuss them with their physician.

ADHD and sugar. Some have suggested that too much sugar in the diet can cause ADHD. Research clearly indicates, however, that neither sugar nor artificial sweeteners produces hyperactivity.

Other Factors Influencing ADD and ADHD Behaviors

Although current research supports the hypothesis that attention disorders have a genetic/biological basis, other factors may also influence the teenager's behavior. Dr. Bill Buzogany, a psychiatrist, and Dr. Steven Evans, a psychologist, remind us that many problems parents and teenagers face are the result of an *interaction between biochemical, psychological, and social factors.* For example, a student who is impulsive as a result of ADD or ADHD (biological cause) may act worse if his parents provide no rules or structure, or are hostile, physically abusive, or inconsistent in their discipline (psychological factors). The influence of his friends (social factors) will also have a major impact on his behavior.

Biological, psychological, and social factors, or in other words, *biopsychosocial factors,* must therefore be considered in your teenager's treatment. Medications alone are usually not sufficient to solve every problem related to ADD or ADHD. Many experts believe that a multi-faceted approach—also known as *multimodal treatment*—including medication, ADD/ADHD education, academic consultation, classroom accommodations, behavioral programming, and counseling—is best for these children and their families. Treatment methods, medications, and parenting skills are discussed in detail in Chapters 5, 6, and 7.

Unfortunately, a few teachers and counselors still believe solely in a *psychological basis* for attention disorders—in other words, they assume incorrectly that "bad parents" raise "bad children." Thus, some believe that these children can control their behavior without medication, especially if they just try harder. So these professionals urge parents to use behavior-modification techniques, family counseling, training in social skills, and educational remediation instead of medication. As explained in Chapter 5, however, studies have shown that *behavioral interventions alone are not nearly as effective as medication!* In fact, researchers tell us that stimulant medication is effective in reducing the symptoms of attention deficits for all but approximately 5 to 10 percent of children. See Chapter 6 for a more detailed discussion of medication issues.

How Research Refines Our Understanding of Attention Disorders

Interestingly, some research challenges a few of our previous assumptions about characteristics of ADD and ADHD. For example, some studies have shown that youngsters with ADD and ADHD *can pay attention* and in fact are *not distractible* in the true sense of the word.

Inattention

Parents often say, "See, he can pay attention when he wants to. Just watch him when he plays with his Game Boy." It's true; children with ADD and ADHD *can* pay attention…under certain circumstances. Sometimes they can *hyperfocus* to the point where they lose all track of time and may spend hours on the computer or playing with Game Boys or Nintendo. Parents and teachers are often baffled by this. What they fail to understand is that these electronic gadgets are *interactive and self-reinforcing*—in other words, these devices create the ideal teaching tool. The teen is active in a hands-on activity, plus gets immediate feedback. Unfortunately, few activities at school or chores at home provide the ideal learning situation—in other words, interesting, fun activities with a high level of interactive stimulation and immediate feedback.

Let me explain why it is so difficult for these teens to pay attention for less interactive and non-reinforcing tasks like school work. When tasks are boring or rote, these students have difficulty with *lack of persistence of effort.* An example of persistence of effort should clarify what is meant by this term: when most people listen to a speaker, they pay attention for a few seconds, look away, shift in their seats, and then redirect their attention to the speaker. Teenagers with ADD and ADHD cannot do this easily. They must struggle to constantly redirect their attention to the original task—to persist with the activity.

Unfortunately, they quickly grow tired of listening and begin looking for something more stimulating. From a biochemical perspective, their brains *require* that activities must be stimulating in order for them to maintain their alertness, attention, and effort. Consequently, as explained earlier, these students have problems with *uneven academic performance.* One day they can do their school work and the next day they can't.

Distractibility

Dr. Sydney Zentall, professor of Special Education at Purdue University, has not found children with ADHD to be particularly distractible, although they appear to be so to the casual observer. Instead, she explains that these children actually lose interest in their work very quickly and then actively begin seeking more interesting stimulation. In fact, when distractions were introduced into research studies, youngsters with ADHD actually did *better* on tests. That may be why placing a child in an isolated study carrel may not be particularly effective. Dr. Zentall found that these students actually work better when learning is active and in a classroom with more stimulation, for example, with Christmas lights and fish in an aquarium.

Dr. Barkley provides further clarification regarding distractibility: he explains that distractions only interfere with these children on tasks that require executive function skills—which obviously include most school assignments. This may explain why they can play video games for hours, but can't focus as easily on homework. These children seem to have great difficulty resisting distractions, persisting in paying attention, and returning to a task if they do become distracted.

New Theories about ADHD

Although we are a long way from understanding everything about the nature and causes of ADHD, we are fortunate that many talented experts continue to propose new theories and research them. For example, Dr. Russell Barkley has recently proposed a theory that ADHD is not really an attention deficit disorder, but a behavioral inhibition disorder. He believes that current research supports his theory. Of course, not everyone agrees with him, but his theories will certainly gener-

ate heated discussions, more study of this issue, and additional theories. Hopefully, one day researchers will also focus on ADD inattentive. Until then, we must rely on speculation that there are many physiological similarities between the two disorders.

Dr. Barkley believes that problems with the ability to inhibit behavior—waiting, stopping what you are doing, resisting distractions, changing behavior when it is a mistake, and resisting the urge to act—are the primary problems that define this disorder, not the attention deficit. In turn, inhibition is the foundation upon which the brain's executive function system is built, thus allowing humans, self-control, self-regulation, and the ability to plan for the future. (Dr. Barkley is also quick to point out that the ADD inattentive type *does have* a true attention disorder plus problems processing information.)

If you are interested in more detailed scientific information on his theory, you may want to read *AD/HD and the Nature of Self-Control.* I have also found Dr. Barkley's 600+ page volume, *Attention Deficit Hyperactivity Disorder,* extremely helpful with its more advanced commentary on research, diagnosis, and treatment of attention deficits.

If you would like to keep up with research into attention deficit disorders, several helpful resources are available: CHADD's *Attention* magazine, the CHADD website (www.chadd.org), www.help4ADHD.org, *ADDitude* magazine, and Dr. Barkley's more scientifically detailed quarterly publication, *ADHD Reports.*

Learning from Research

Perhaps you wonder why it is important to know about new research or studies that may challenge traditional assumptions about the nature of ADD and ADHD. The reason is that treatment for attention disorders is based on the perceived causes of the symptoms. As the quantity and quality of research on attention disorders increases, our knowledge base is expanding significantly. If the underlying causes of the symptoms are different than we originally assumed, then intervention strategies must change, too. For example, if teenagers with ADD or ADHD have problems with working memory and slow processing speed, then teaching strategies must be revised to include a more visual, concrete, hands-on approach to learning rather than simply isolating the child in a study carrel from so called "distractions." In addition, assignments must be shortened or extended time must be given.

3

Diagnosis of ADD
or ADHD

"The school psychologist and doctor who diagnosed ADHD were both a godsend! Finally, we had found someone who understood, who had a name for the elusive problem we were confronting. The emotional relief that followed was bittersweet. We had some answers now, but why had it taken so long to find them? My son and I had been living for twelve years with a disorder for which there had been no name and little sympathy and understanding from family, friends, and school personnel."

Many children with attention deficit disorders, especially with hyperactivity, are diagnosed in early childhood or elementary school. By adolescence, they have usually been receiving treatment for several years. However, *it is not unusual for teenagers to reach adolescence or even adulthood without having the disorder diagnosed.* Teenagers who are extremely bright, girls, minorities, or teens who have ADD inattentive are more likely to reach adolescence without a diagnosis.

The information in this chapter will help parents determine whether or not their teenager should be referred for a formal evaluation. It may also help parents identify other children in the family who may have a milder form or a different type of attention deficit. Some parents may even diagnose themselves with the disorder. However, even if ADD or ADHD has already been diagnosed, the information in this chapter will help parents ensure that a proper evaluation is conducted. Chapter 7 will provide information to identify coexisting problems such as depression or learning problems.

"Because of his hyperactivity, I had known for some time that my nine-year-old son had ADHD. However, after reading this book, I was shocked to realize that my sixteen-year-old daughter exhibits all the symptoms of ADD inattentive. I feel guilty about all the time we wasted when we could have been treating it. Now I understand why she has struggled in school all these years.

"She has an IQ of 132, but she is failing her sophomore year in high school. As a special education teacher, I feel guilty for all the times I sat her down with a stack of papers and made her practice math facts. She said them, sang them, but just couldn't memorize them."

Why ADD or ADHD Can Go Undiagnosed until Adolescence

Perhaps you think it is unlikely that your teenager has ADD or ADHD because you believe she would have been diagnosed with the disorder by now if she had it. After all, wouldn't one of her teachers have referred her for an evaluation if she showed signs of having an attention deficit? Or perhaps your child actually *was* evaluated for ADD or ADHD at one time, but you were told that she didn't fit the criteria. Could it be that your child really is just lazy and disobedient? Or has his or her attention deficit simply been overlooked? There are, in fact, many reasons why attention deficits may go undiagnosed for years. Just because no one has sought you out with the diagnosis does not mean that you should not have your teenager evaluated (or reevaluated). In truth, teachers are often instructed *not* to tell you that your child might have an attention deficit.

Common Myths

Several common myths have sometimes prevented diagnosis and treatment of ADD and ADHD. It is extremely important to eliminate these myths so that parents, teachers, and treatment professionals recognize and treat this condition earlier.

Myth I: All children and teenagers with attention disorders are hyperactive.

Some professionals and parents still mistakenly believe that a child or teenager with an attention deficit must be hyperactive. They may be unaware that by the teenage years, hyperactivity is usually no longer present and has been replaced by restlessness. In addition, few children with ADHD are excessively hyperactive. In contrast, students who have ADD inattentive often have low energy. Consequently, *teenagers* who have ADHD and are restless or have ADD inattentive may be overlooked.

Myth II: Hyperactive students with attention deficits can't sit still for ten minutes.

Hyperactive youngsters with attention deficits do better in one-to-one and novel situations. They can sit still and maintain a conversation with a doctor or other treatment professional during an office visit.

> *"It has been my experience that even the most hyperactive child with ADHD can be relatively quiet during a ten-minute evaluation, especially when they are bright. Some physicians and clinicians are still using this unreliable criteria to say if they can sit still in my office for that period of time they must not have ADHD."*
>
> —a school psychologist

Myth III: ADD and ADHD will always be diagnosed in childhood.

Unfortunately, attention deficit disorders are overlooked in a number of teenagers and adults. Most parents and high school personnel presume incorrectly that an attention deficit, if present, would have been diagnosed in elementary school. They may not even consider ADD or ADHD as a potential culprit underlying student underachievement. The age of diagnosis may vary depending on the severity and type of attention deficit. Although children who are extremely hyperactive are usually diagnosed early, other children may be overlooked until they are older.

Myth IV: ADD and ADHD disappear in adolescence and adulthood.

One of the reasons that parents, teachers, and physicians believe that youngsters outgrow their attention deficit disorder is because their hyperactivity decreases as they reach adolescence. The attention problems often persist, however. The hyperactivity appears to be replaced with restlessness, inattentiveness, or sleeping in class. The teenager with ADHD who feels "hyper" knows it isn't acceptable to get up and walk around in class, so instead she may tune out mentally or sleep.

Myth V: ADD and ADHD are over-diagnosed.

Although the number of children diagnosed with attention deficits has significantly increased over the last twenty years, research does not show that ADHD is being over diagnosed or that stimulant medications are being over prescribed. For example, data gathered from a study conducted by Dr. Julie M. Zito show reasonable rates of prescriptions for these medications. After reviewing ten years of data from two Medicaid and one HMO site, they found that roughly 7 percent of 5- to 14-year-olds were receiving medication for ADHD and only 1.2 percent of 15- to 19-year-olds were.

Taken out of context, however, some of the data in that study seemed to indicate over prescription of medication. Although the percentage increase in medication use sounds terrible—600 percent—it went from less than one percent (.36) in 1987 to roughly 2.54 percent in 1996, still well below the expected rate of 5 to 12 percent. Unfortunately, then the media gets this information and scares parents and other professionals to death about the "600 percent increase." This is a good reminder that information published in newspapers or magazines can be misleading.

Several other studies have confirmed that over prescription of medication is not a problem. For example, a study reported in *Pediatrics* and *USA Today* in 2003 showed an average of 4.3 percent of children were on stimulant medication. Another report, published in the *Journal of the American Medical Association* in 1999, stated that although some children are being diagnosed without good evaluations, "there is little evidence of widespread over diagnosis or misdiagnosis of ADHD or over prescription" of stimulant medications by physicians. A 1997 study in Baltimore County, Maryland found that 5.6 percent of middle schoolers and 1.6 percent of high schoolers were on medication.

In fact, *under-diagnosis and treatment* appear to be a greater problem. Dr. Peter Jensen conducted a survey in 1999 in which he found that only one-eighth of those diagnosed with ADHD were taking medication. *So it always pays to find out the facts!* The facts tell us that only 2 percent of teenagers with attention deficits are being treated, far below the expected 5 to 12 percent who have the condition.

Myth VI: ADD and ADHD are not a real disorder.

During the 1990s there were several frivolous lawsuits generated by a group that charged falsely that ADD and ADHD were not real disorders, but rather were invented as part of a conspiracy between the pharmaceutical companies, doctors, and CHADD (Children and Adults with Attention Deficit Disorder). All these lawsuits were eventually dismissed, and in one state the group was ordered by the judge to pay legal expenses.

Since then, several highly respected scientific experts and national organizations have publicly rec-ognized the profound impact attention deficits have on individuals and families, confirming that, indeed, ADD and ADHD are very real disorders.

1997: *U.S. Department of Education*: ADD and ADHD were added to the list of eligible disabilities under IDEA.

1998: *NIMH/NIH*: A Consensus Conference on ADHD was sponsored.

1999: *CDC*: The Centers for Disease Control and Prevention sponsored a conference, *ADHD: A Public Health Perspective.*

1999: *U.S. Surgeon General*: The Surgeon General's Report on Mental Health identified ADHD as a significant mental health issue.

1999: *NIMH*: The National Institute of Mental Health reported on their landmark MTA study on ADHD.

Other Factors

Several additional reasons why attention deficits are frequently overlooked are discussed below.

1. All Teenagers with ADD or ADHD Are Not Alike

Because two teenagers with attention deficits seldom behave the same way, parents may become confused when trying to determine if their teenager has the disorder. Their teenager may not act like other teenagers who have an attention deficit. One of the major reasons teens with attention deficits are not alike is that symptoms may be mild, moderate, or severe, and two-thirds have at least one other coexisting condition such as learning disability, depression, anxiety, or sleep disturbance. The teenager's basic temperament, academic achievement, successes in non-school activities, the level of family support, and the presence of coexisting conditions, all contribute to making each teenager with ADD or ADHD unique. See Chapter 1, Table 1-2, as well as the Iceberg drawing in Figure 1-1.

"Educators who fail to understand the widely varying skill levels and behaviors among students with ADHD may sometimes say, 'John has ADHD and he can do this skill....Why can't you?'"

2. Students May Be Able to "Get By" Until Middle School or High School

"*Students with undiagnosed attention deficit disorder seem to fall apart in middle school with so much to keep up with. Gaps in their fund of knowledge from five years of having tuned out in school finally catch up with them. . . .*"

—Ed Gotlieb, M.D., The Pediatric Center, Stone Mountain, GA

Frequently, academic problems do not become obvious until the middle and high school years, when demands for academic performance and executive skills increase dramatically. Children with *milder* forms of ADD or ADHD often are able to keep up with schoolwork when they are in elementary school. Extremely bright teenagers may compensate for their attention deficit and elude diagnosis until middle school, high school, or even college.

In middle school or high school, students are expected to accept greater responsibility for completing their schoolwork. Although teenagers with attention deficits frequently have the intellectual ability to do the work, they lag behind their friends in their organizational skills, the ability to accept responsibility and other measures of maturity. Because of their *four to six year developmental delay*, many students with attention deficits are unable to accept full responsibility for their schoolwork. Teens with attention deficits frequently need *more* supervision and structure than their peers.

3. ADD or ADHD May Be Overlooked during Evaluations

When teachers and parents realize that a teenager is struggling in school, he may be referred for a psychological evaluation. Unfortunately, referral and evaluation provide no guarantee that an attention deficit disorder will be diagnosed. Several groups are more likely to be overlooked during these evaluations: 1) intellectually gifted students, 2) girls, 3) minorities, 4) students who have ADD inattentive, and 5) students who are already in special education with another diagnosis. Sometimes multiple psychological evaluations may be conducted, yet ADD or ADHD is never detected.

"*Our son was not diagnosed until his third psychological evaluation. His first evaluation in kindergarten was to determine eligibility for a program for intellectually gifted children. He missed the* cut-off score by two points because he couldn't sit still long enough to finish the test. The second evaluation was conducted in the fourth grade because he was underachieving. His high IQ score made him eligible for programs for gifted students.*

"*His ADD inattentive was finally diagnosed by accident when he was in the seventh grade. When we moved that year, he had to be retested for the gifted program. We were fortunate that the school psychologist picked up on his attention deficit and referred us to a physician who specialized in this area.*"

Diagnosis of ADD or ADHD is *not* an easy, clear-cut process. Teenagers with attention deficits do not have identical test profiles. In addition, interpreting information obtained during an evaluation is not an exact science and requires good clinical judgment that is developed through experience working with these teens. In one research study, even skilled clinicians missed the diagnosis at least 10 percent of the time.

"*Our son Bill who has ADD inattentive is 19 now and a sophomore in college. We had him checked for an attention deficit when he was younger. But the results were inconclusive. He was so bright that he scored in the 97ᵗʰ percentile on achievement tests. I thought, how can he possibly have ADHD when he was able to do so well on the tests? It took the doctors a long time to figure out what was going on with him. First the neurologist diagnosed an anxiety disorder when he was 13, next came a diagnosis of a mood disorder, and finally ADHD when he was 15.*"

If you feel strongly that your teenager has an attention deficit, yet a professional says that neither ADD nor ADHD is present, seek a second opinion. By familiarizing yourself with diagnostic criteria and procedures discussed in this chapter, you can ensure that proper evaluation procedures are used so that all major learning and attentional problems are identified.

4. Girls with Attention Deficits Are Often Overlooked

Girls may go undetected until middle or high school because typically they are less likely than boys to have behavior problems. According to Yale researchers Bennett A. Shaywitz, M.D., and Sally Shaywitz, M.D., girls with attention deficits exhibit *less physical aggression and loss of control.* Moreover, Harvard researcher Joseph Biederman, M.D., has found that girls

STR:2133 REG:006 TRN:3706 CSHR:Brad B

EDUCATOR

Dear God, I need to talk
9781591172774
(1 @ 16.95) Educator 20% (3.39)   13.56

QUIZFEST
0071896461725   N
(1 @ 3.99)   3.99

Teenagers with ADD and A
9781890627317
(1 @ 24.95) Educator 20% (4.99)
(1 @ 19.96)   19.96

Subtotal   37.51
Sales Tax (8.750%)   2.93
TOTAL   40.44
CASH   40.50
CASH CHANGE.   0.06-

V101.17   06/29/2009   5PM

will be issued for (i) purchases made by check less than 7 days prior to the date of return, (ii) when a gift receipt is presented within 60 days of purchase, (iii) textbooks returned with a receipt within 14 days of purchase, or (iv) original purchase was made through Barnes & Noble.com via PayPal. Opened music/DVDs/audio may not be returned, but can be exchanged only for the same title if defective.

<u>After 14 days or without a sales receipt</u>, returns or exchanges will not be permitted.

Magazines, newspapers, and used books are not returnable. *Product not carried by Barnes & Noble or Barnes & Noble.com will not be accepted for return.*

Policy on receipt may appear in two sections.

Return Policy

<u>With a sales receipt</u>, a full refund in the original form of payment will be issued from any Barnes & Noble store for returns of new and unread books (except textbooks) and unopened music/DVDs/audio made within (i) 14 days of purchase from a Barnes & Noble retail store (except for purchases made by check less than 7 days prior to the date of return) or (ii) 14 days of delivery date for Barnes & Noble.com purchases (except for purchases made via PayPal). A store credit for the purchase price will be issued for (i) purchases made by check less than 7 days prior to the date of return, (ii) when a gift receipt is presented within 60 days of purchase, (iii) textbooks returned with a receipt within 14 days of purchase, or (iv) original purchase was made through Barnes & Noble.com via PayPal. Opened music/DVDs/audio may not be returned, but can be exchanged only for the same title if defective.

<u>After 14 days or without a sales receipt</u>, returns or exchanges will not be permitted.

Magazines, newspapers, and used books are not returnable. *Product not carried by Barnes & Noble or Barnes & Noble.com will not be accepted for return*

receipt may appear in two sections.

with ADHD have half the rate of oppositional defiant and conduct disorders as boys do, 33 and 10 percent respectively. These gender differences complicate diagnosis for girls.

Because the symptoms of attention disorders are often less obvious for girls, the initial referral for treatment may actually be for depression resulting from the untreated attention deficit.

"I have had Emily, my fifteen-year-old daughter, in therapy for three weeks now. She is angry, not doing school work, and impossible to do anything with. Her therapist says she is depressed. I said, "Of course she is depressed; she is not succeeding at anything!" He is leaning toward a diagnosis of depression without the ADD. What can I do or say to help him understand that there is more to it? Where does the ADD with depression differ significantly from just depression? He's only known her a few weeks, but we have a lifetime of monitoring that makes my husband and me certain that she has ADD."

Lack of Research on Girls. Two pioneers in research on females with attention disorders, Patricia Quinn, M.D., and Kathleen Nadeau, Ph.D., question the current research on females. Quinn and Nadeau remind us that the diagnostic criteria for ADD and ADHD were developed based upon the behavior of boys. So for girls to meet the current diagnostic criteria, they must exhibit more severe behavior with regard to hyperactivity and aggression. Yet clearly, most girls with attention disorders are not as aggressive or hyperactive as boys.

The *under-diagnosis* of girls with ADD or ADHD is a serious problem. Because attention deficits are more prevalent in boys, most parents and teachers don't think to look for it in girls. Some researchers argue that current criteria should be revised and new ones developed specifically for girls. Quinn and Nadeau also report that the symptoms for girls worsen during adolescence, primarily as a result of hormonal changes. So girls may actually show fewer symptoms until middle and high school, when these hormonal changes take place. Then they may become even more reactive and emotional. Obviously, many girls do not meet the criteria of exhibiting symptoms by the age of 7. A discussion of the arbitrary nature of this age cut-off is provided below.

"It was a nightmare getting diagnosed. The school just thought I wasn't trying hard enough. Finally I was diagnosed with ADD the middle of my freshman year. It took forever (my sophomore year) before the

school finally accepted my diagnosis and did something to help me. Although I already knew I had it, I was relieved that I was finally going to get the help and hopefully the understanding I needed."

—Emily, age 16

School Performance. According to Drs. Quinn and Nadeau, academic problems may not be as apparent in girls since they work harder to hide them. Parents often report that girls who are anxious may work harder to compensate for their disorganization, for example, studying longer hours or compulsively making lists. Since girls seem more eager to please their teachers and are more likely to conform to teacher expectations, teachers are less likely to refer them for evaluation.

"In high school, I had to work extra hard to make As and Bs. My homework often took at least four or five hours to finish each day. My senior year, the only way I passed algebra is that I went for tutoring after school with my algebra teacher three days a week. She was amazing."

—Amelia, age 18

5. Underdiagnosed in Minorities

African-American and Hispanic children are also more likely to be overlooked. For example, they are two and a half times *less* likely to be receiving treatment than white children. Gail Mattox, M.D., a professor and chair of the psychiatry department at Morehouse School of Medicine, identified two factors that are possible barriers to treatment: 1. African-American parents may be less informed about ADHD, and 2. they are more likely to believe that ADHD symptoms are caused by other things like "sugar intake."

Polls have identified several barriers to diagnosis and treatment:

1. stigma—most parents were concerned that their child will be "labeled,"
2. racial identification—one-third felt that their child was identified because of his race or ethnic background,
3. belief that ADHD is a condition that occurs mainly in white children,
4. lack of adequate information on ADHD,
5. fear of drug addiction,
6. not knowing where to go for treatment,
7. poor access to care,
8. language barriers, and
9. cost of services.

José Bauermeister, Ph.D., a researcher at the University of Puerto Rico, has found similar challenges for Hispanic families that are underserved to an even greater degree than African-American youth. Puerto Rican cultural norms do not necessarily view improvement in self-control as a desirable change for teens. Adolescents may refuse medication since they may prefer to continue to horse around, joke, and entertain their friends at school.

6. Diagnostic Criteria Were Developed for Children, Not Teenagers

The diagnostic criteria for ADHD (difficulty staying in seat, difficulty awaiting turn in games, difficulty playing quietly, and blurting out answers) describe the behavior of younger children ages 6 to 14. Fortunately, the revised DSM IV criteria in Table 2-1 *do* provide an accurate description of ADD inattentive in teenagers. The inattentive aspect of attention deficits is a greater problem for teens than the hyperactivity.

7. The School Might Not Have Recommended an Evaluation

ADD and ADHD were not even listed as eligible "handicapping conditions" under federal education law until 1997 when they were added under *Other Health Impairment.* That is, attention deficits were not mentioned in these laws as a disability that might qualify a student for special educational help at public expense. As would be expected, some schools identified attention deficits anyway and others did not. Many schools were reluctant to diagnose attention deficits and did not direct school psychologists to screen students for this condition. If you believe your child has been overlooked, you may still request an evaluation for an attention deficit even though your teenager is in high school.

Do not assume that the school will suggest an evaluation for ADD or ADHD. In some school districts, teachers are specifically told not to discuss these disorders with parents. Plus, some teachers still don't recognize the symptoms of attention deficits, especially the inattentive type.

8. ADD or ADHD May Slip through the Cracks

Students with attention deficits can easily get lost in large, unresponsive school systems. Unless educators make a special effort, school personnel may not know students or their parents, especially in urban areas where students move frequently. In high schools with 1,000 to 3,000-plus students, the teenager is more likely to become a number with no name. In these large schools, teachers may not feel responsible for monitoring their students' progress or calling parents if a student is struggling academically.

"The high school environment is less structured and teenagers are expected to take full responsibility for completing their schoolwork. Since students change classes every period and have at least six teachers, typically, their teachers do not get to know them as well or understand their disability. Frequently, they don't notify parents in advance if their teen is in danger of failing."

Currently, too many teenagers with ADD or ADHD are slipping through cracks in the system! It is important that teachers develop a personal interest in their students, regardless of the size of their school. Parents must ask teachers to let them know when their teen is struggling. Parents also need to stay involved and ask teachers how they may help.

9. Parents Are Reluctant to Believe It Is an Attention Deficit

When children first enter school and begin struggling, parents are often hopeful that this is just a temporary problem that will be resolved with age and maturity. Many parents are fearful about the diagnosis of an attention deficit and possible use of medications because of the negative but inaccurate press coverage that has been so prevalent in the last few years. Frequently parents must go through a process that includes denial, acceptance, and finally grieving, as they accept the reality that their child has an attention deficit. Sometimes parents are unable to accept the diagnosis until middle and high school, when they are absolutely desperate and their teenager is in danger of failing school.

The First Step toward a Diagnosis

Parents often wonder whether to seek an evaluation for an attention deficit. Since the *DSM-IV-TR* diagnostic criteria are the best indicator of whether or not a child has ADD or ADHD, a quick review of these symptoms in Chapter 1 should be helpful. Each of the two major types of attention deficits have nine symptoms listed—a total of eighteen symptoms. So if the child has six of the nine under either ADD or ADHD, that is a pretty good indicator that parents should proceed with an evaluation.

The diagnostic criteria also state that the symptoms should be causing *clinically significant impairment*—in other words, the evaluator will make a subjective judgment about whether or not the child is having significant difficulties in at least *two settings*, for example, at home and school. Another criterion states that symptoms should have appeared before *age seven*. However, leading researchers in the field explain that the selection of this age cutoff is arbitrary and that there is no research to back up this cutoff age. In reality, some children may not show any significant symptoms of ADD or ADHD until much later. For example, some bright teens, especially girls, compensate and are not diagnosed until middle or high school. On the other hand, when parents take the time to look back on their teenager's performance in elementary school, the symptoms are often present. Unfortunately, the problems may not have been recognized for what they were—an attention deficit.

The same DSM-IV diagnostic criteria are used for adults, teenagers, and children. For adults, a childhood history of symptoms of ADD or ADHD, with continuing problems into adulthood, are the primary indicators of the disorder. Additional helpful information on evaluation of learning issues is available in Chapter 13.

Seeking an Evaluation by the School System

There are two ways the evaluation process may be set in motion if your teenager is struggling in school or if there is a suspicion that your teenager has ADD or ADHD. *First,* a teacher or other school staff member may recommend that your child be evaluated. Typically they will not say they are evaluating for an attention deficit, but rather they are trying to determine why your child is struggling in school. In this case, the school will schedule the evaluation, select the individuals who will conduct the evaluation, and pay all expenses. (They must first obtain your permission, however.)

*"*M*y son was not diagnosed with ADHD until he was eight. I had always assumed that if he had it, the teacher would say something to me about it. Since she never mentioned it, I assumed that my son could not have the disorder."*

Second, you, as a parent, may decide that you would like your child to be evaluated. You may then either re-

quest an evaluation from your child's school, or find a professional in private practice to conduct the evaluation. If you want the school to do the evaluation, here is a word of caution. Don't ask that your teenager be "evaluated for an attention deficit"; the school may reply that they do not evaluate for ADD or ADHD. Instead, simply ask for an evaluation "because my teen is struggling."

Usually, a reasonable first step is for you to talk with the teacher or call the guidance counselor at your local school and *request an evaluation to identify your child's learning problems.* Fortunately, the data that the school collects may also confirm that an attention deficit is present. This data should be shared with your physician. Schools have the right to determine what constitutes an adequate evaluation. If they do not believe the student has an attention deficit, they may not do a comprehensive evaluation.

State laws affect this decision process. In some states, a physician has the final say in diagnosing ADD and ADHD. In these states, the school must have a statement and signature from a doctor confirming diagnosis of the attention deficit. Chapter 14 explains how a student with learning difficulties in addition to an attention deficit can qualify for special educational services from the school.

Seeking a Private Evaluation

If the school doesn't do a thorough evaluation, parents may decide to seek a private evaluation. If the private evaluation confirms a diagnosis of ADD or ADHD that "*adversely affects their child's ability to learn,*" parents may ask the school system to reimburse them for the evaluation. On rare occasions, the school system may pay for this private evaluation. However, reimbursement will be more likely if the parent asks the school in advance for this evaluation.

The specific wording you should use is that you are requesting "an independent evaluation at public expense." You should be prepared to give a reason. If possible, find out what reasons might be accepted by your school district as justification for independent testing—for example, a six-month waiting list for evaluation, your seventeen-year old-child is intellectually gifted but is failing four of six classes, or your school system is a small one that does not have access to licensed school psychologists. However, there are no guarantees of reimbursement. If they have the financial means, parents may also prefer to seek a private evaluation especially if lengthy waiting lists prohibit prompt evaluation by the school.

If you decide to pursue a private evaluation, there are a variety of routes you can take. You might ask members of local parent support groups—CHADD, ADDA-SR, LDA, or Federation of Families—to recommend competent treatment professionals who have extensive experience working with ADD or ADHD. Occasionally, school systems have a list of approved private evaluators. A variety of licensed treatment professionals are capable of conducting a proper evaluation. The competence of the individual professional is more important than the field in which he or she is trained. Ultimately, however, if ADD or ADHD is diagnosed and medications are required, your teenager must be referred to a physician.

You should use some caution if the evaluation is done privately rather than by school personnel:

1. The evaluator must be experienced in diagnosing ADD or ADHD, or the evaluation may not be helpful.
2. The evaluator should not only identify problem areas, but also give constructive advice about coping with the teenager's problems.
3. Schools may require classroom observations plus interviews from the student's teacher before they will recognize a diagnosis of ADD or ADHD. Some private evaluators do not take the time to conduct this critical part of the evaluation.
4. Private evaluators must be familiar with the tests and eligibility criteria required by the state and the local school system for purposes of documenting ADD, ADHD, or learning disabilities.

A psychological evaluation conducted by a private treatment professional may cost between $500 to $3,000 and may take up to two full days to complete. Additional time will be required to write up the formal evaluation, although they may give you an overview of their impressions after the evaluation. Private evaluators may also have waiting lists, further delaying this process. Insurance policies vary, so you will need to check your coverage. Generally, insurance companies are more likely to pay for evaluations conducted by physicians, state-licensed psychologists with a Ph.D., or, sometimes, licensed social workers or counselors with a master's degree.

Components of a Comprehensive Diagnostic Evaluation

Guidelines for a comprehensive diagnostic evaluation for attention deficits have been issued by both pediatricians and psychiatrists. It is important for parents to familiarize themselves with these guidelines so that they will know whether their teen's evaluation covers all the bases.

AAP Diagnostic Guidelines. Many skilled professionals have a pretty good idea of whether or not a teenager has an attention deficit after the first interview. Although a diagnosis of ADD or ADHD may be given after one interview, the American Academy of Pediatrics (AAP) recommends a more in-depth evaluation. In May of 2000, the AAP released clinical guidelines for *assessment* of ADHD. AAP *treatment* guidelines were released a year later. Key elements of the AAP guidelines include use of DSM-IV-TR criteria, interviews with parents and teachers, and assessment of coexisting conditions. A copy of both sets of guidelines is available on their website, www.aap.org.

If you are paying for a private evaluation, you would do well to ask the evaluator whether he or she follows the AAP guidelines. Typical elements of a diagnostic evaluation are listed in Table 3-1. If there are tests or procedures discussed here that you think would be helpful in evaluating your child, don't hesitate to discuss them with your doctor. If the assessment is conducted through a physician's office, it may be at least partially reimbursable by insurance companies. The Bibliography contains a list of books that provide more detailed clinical information about evaluations for ADD and ADHD.

Table 3-1   Diagnosing ADD or ADHD

ADD or ADHD cannot be diagnosed on the basis of a single test.

Underachievement in school should be a red flag signaling parents to evaluate for attention deficits or other learning problems.

The best indicators of ADD or ADHD are the diagnostic criteria contained in the DSM-IV-TR in Table 1-2.

The assessment may include:
1. Completion of a **behavior checklist** based upon the DSM-IV-TR diagnostic criteria
2. **Family interviews**, including a medical history
   - an interview with the teen;
   - the childhood history from the parents
     - a developmental and social history
     - birth and developmental milestones
     - a family medical history
     - teen medical history
   - a description of the teen's behavior as she is today
   - a description of the behaviors or issues of greatest concern to the family.
3. A thorough **physical examination** to rule out other disorders.
4. An **academic assessment** to identify specific learning problems
   - a description of school performance by parents and the teenager
   - review of school report cards, e.g., grades and teacher comments
   - review of official school records, e.g., standardized academic achievement tests such as the IOWA Test of Basic Skills; Individualized Education Programs (IEP); school psychological evaluations
   - a curriculum-based assessment, e.g., review of current class and homework assignments, samples of a student's handwriting or essays
   - classroom observations
   - interviews with teachers and other key school personnel
5. **Formal testing:**
   - behavior rating scales, like the Conners, Brown Scales, or BERS
   - academic and intellectual testing, such as the WISC, to help identify academic strengths, learning problems, and executive function deficits.
6. **Diagnosis and treatment of common coexisting problems** such as learning problems, sleep disturbances, anxiety, depression, defiance, and aggression. Typically, treatment of ADD or ADHD in isolation is not sufficient to ensure that a teenager will be successful in school and life. Coexisting conditions must also be treated and are discussed in detail in Chapter 7.

Additional Comments on Key Evaluation Components

Most of the components of the evaluation listed in Table 3-1 are self-explanatory, but a few deserve more attention. Although a good evaluation will establish the presence of ADD or ADHD, more importantly it should also identify hidden learning problems, including deficits in executive skills. Often this is the more challenging part of the evaluation.

1. Academic Assessment

The academic assessment of students with attention deficits may be the most important part of the evaluation. Hidden learning problems including executive function deficits are often at the root of the teenager's struggles at school.

Usually, a profile emerges of a teenager who has been an *underachiever in school.* He or she may be bright but just getting by or failing classes in middle and high school. In addition, approximately a third of the youngsters evaluated at the Pediatric Center in Stone Mountain, GA, have developed some *school avoidance symptoms.* They may refuse to go to school, skip school, have physical symptoms such as stomachaches and headaches, or fight with their parents about getting up for school each morning.

REVIEW OF PERMANENT SCHOOL RECORDS

Reviewing the students "cumulative" school records is often very instructive. Teacher comments about these children on old report cards are often very similar: "needs to use time wisely," "needs to follow directions," "needs to listen," "needs to complete assignments," "talks too much," and "not working up to potential."

STANDARDIZED TEST SCORES

Many teenagers with attention deficits are bright, yet their performance on standardized tests in school may be erratic. Occasionally students with ADD or ADHD make high scores in spite of poor academic performance in school. The discrepancy between high standardized test scores and low grades is confusing to both parents and teachers. They may think that the teenager's biggest problem is that she is just not applying herself or that she is lazy.

"My son's scores on standardized academic achievement tests in elementary school were usually in the 90th percentile and above with the exception of math computation. The discrepancy between his academic performance and high achievement on these tests was extremely puzzling to teachers and reinforced their thinking that he was not trying and could easily do much better class work. My son was learning in the classroom in spite of not completing written assignments."

ACADEMIC ACHIEVEMENT TESTS

Academic achievement tests are helpful because they give you an estimate of the student's current grade level performance in key academic areas such as math and reading. Tests such as the *Woodcock-Johnson Psychoeducational Battery (WJ III), Kaufman Test of Educational Achievement,* or the *Wechsler Individual Achievement Test (WIAT-II)* may give important information about the teenager's academic strengths, an estimate of intellectual ability, plus identify potential learning disabilities. Subtests of the WIAT include Basic Reading, Mathematics Reasoning, Spelling, Reading Comprehension, Numerical Calculations, Listening Comprehension, Oral Expression, and Written Expression. One benefit of using the WIAT is that it can easily be compared with the Wechsler intelligence test scores (WISC) for discrepancies between ability and achievement.

Often, the evaluator may find lower scores on sections of these tests which measure *math computation* skills, as many teenagers with attention deficits tend to have problems with memorization, slow processing speed, and observing symbol changes in computation. Some of these teens have never mastered rapid recall of basic math facts, such as simple addition, subtrac-

tion, and multiplication. Sometimes they don't notice when the signs on the math problems change from addition to subtraction or from multiplication to division. They may add all the problems, failing to see the change in symbols.

While reading, some teens may be visually distracted and see a lot of other words at the same time. They may also skip words, lose their place, or overlook errors when proofreading their work. Sometimes it helps to slide a ruler down the page as they read each line. Frequently, scores that measure skills in punctuation, capitalization, or spelling are also low.

"Sometimes after I have finished administering the Woodcock-Johnson, I will have the youngster read questions aloud in the proofing section even though they are asked to read silently. Teenagers with ADD or ADHD tend to correct the errors in the sentences as they read them silently. For example, the sentence reads 'Jeff is look for his wallet,' but the teenager reads it silently as 'Jeff is looking for his wallet.' Then he responds incorrectly by saying there was no error in the sentence."

—a psychologist

2. Intelligence Tests

Intelligence tests are intended to measure a student's innate cognitive ability or IQ and not information learned at school like achievement tests do. However, in reality an IQ test will measure both to some degree. Although there is no single test available that confirms the diagnosis of ADD or ADHD, intelligence tests can be helpful in several ways. They can:

1. determine the general level of a teenager's intellectual ability,
2. identify learning problems,
3. indicate problems with attention, and
4. identify problems with slow processing speed and working memory.

The WISC is the most commonly administered intelligence test, but the Stanford Binet may also be used. One key advantage of the WISC is that is provides subtest scale scores that give the evaluator greater information about possible learning problems.

THE WISC

The WISC, officially known as the Wechsler Intelligence Scale for Children, underwent major revisions in 2003. In earlier versions of the WISC, Full Scale, Verbal, and Performance IQ scores were reported. However, now the focus has shifted and the indices

Identification of Learning Problems

At the same time the evaluator is determining whether or not your teen has an attention deficit, she will also be identifying any learning problems. Researchers estimate that approximately 25 to 50 percent of teenagers with attention deficits have learning problems that are serious enough to be categorized as a specific learning disability (SLD). Keep in mind, however, that these students may have serious learning problems yet not meet the school's criteria for SLD. Specific types of learning disabilities are discussed in greater detail in Chapter 13.

One of the most challenging learning problems for many students with attention deficits appears to be in *written expression,* where, according to one study, 65 percent experience difficulty. Consequently, a test such as the TOWL, *Test of Written Language,* offers helpful information regarding the extent of the learning problems in written expression. The WIAT also has a section that is helpful for identifying problems with written expression.

Several learning problems are commonly associated with symptoms of ADD or ADHD:

1. Inattention,
2. poor working memory,
3. poor reading comprehension,
4. slow processing speed which may result in slow reading and writing,
5. poor concentration in class and during homework,
6. poor fine motor coordination, and
7. poor organizational skills.

Even if the attention deficit is being treated, there is no guarantee that the teen's learning problems are being adequately addressed. Some teachers are not aware of common learning problems associated with ADD or ADHD. If after reading Chapter 13 in this book and Chapter 2 in **Teaching Teens,** parents feel their teen has unidentified learning problems, they should discuss them with school officials. It is important to discuss the teenager's potential learning problems, accommodations currently being made at school, and additional ones that may be needed. It may also help to describe the accommodations that previous teachers have found to be effective.

are more important. Both the old and new versions of the WISC will be discussed briefly, since parents may be faced with trying to compare results of WISC scores reported in two different formats.

The WISC IV, the most recent edition of the test, displays a full scale score plus four indices. The full scale score provides a broad-based, combined IQ score that reflects both verbal and nonverbal visual perceptual skills. In contrast, the indices are designed to show more specifically where an individual's cognitive strengths and weakness lie. As shown in one student's test profile in Table 3-2 on the next page, these indices are composite scores comprised of from two to four subtests:

1. Verbal Comprehension Index (VCI),
2. Perceptual Reasoning Index (PRI),
3. Working Memory Index (WMI), and
4. Processing Speed Index (PSI). Indices—comprised of several scale scores—that fall above or below a range of scores from 90 to 109 are identified as areas of relative strengths or weaknesses.

The WISC IV has ten core subtests that must always be administered and five supplemental or optional subtests. Three new subtests were added and three old ones deleted from the third edition of the WISC. The actual scores for each subtest (the number of points earned) are converted to a scale score, which is adjusted for age and allows comparison with other students' scores. These scores are helpful for identifying potential learning problems. Scale scores range from 1 to 19, with a score of 10 falling at the fiftieth percentile or median. If a teenager obtained scale scores of 10 on all her subtests, her Full Scale score would be 100, or exactly average for her age. The average range for subtest scale scores is between 7 and 13. Two-thirds of all scores fall in this range. Approximately half of youngsters with ADD or ADHD, however, have widely varying scores.

FACTOR ANALYSIS OF THE WISC BY INDICES AND SUBTESTS

Indices. Although analysis of indices or subtest scale scores is helpful, it does not provide conclusive proof of ADD, ADHD, or specific learning problems. With regard to indices, evaluators look for a 15 point difference between the student's *Verbal Comprehension (VCI)* Index or *Perceptual Reasoning* Index Scores (PRI) (whichever was higher), compared to his Working Memory *(FDI)* or *Processing Speed (PSI)* Index (whichever was lower). Any wide variation in subtests scores could also be indicative of a learning disability. In Table

Table 3-2   WISC-IV Scores for a Student with ADHD

Optional subtests are noted by an asterisk (*)

12-year-old male, ADHD   Full Scale Score: 113

Verbal Comprehension Index—110 (percentile rank 75)
(VCI measures verbal abilities utilizing reasoning, comprehension, conceptualization, stored knowledge access, and oral expression.)
> Similarities 12
> Vocabulary 13
> Comprehension 11
> *Information N/A
> *Word reasoning N/A

Perceptual Reasoning Index—121 (percentile rank 92)
(PRI measures visual perception, nonverbal reasoning, and organization.)
> Block Design 14
> Picture Concepts 11
> Matrix Reasoning 15
> * Picture Completion N/A

Working Memory Index—99 (percentile rank 47)
(WMI measures attention, concentration, and working memory for orally presented sequences; this index was formerly labeled Freedom from Distractibility.)
> Digit Span 9
> Letter-number sequence 11
> * Arithmetic N/A

Processing Speed Index—91 (percentile rank 27)
(PSI measures the speed of mental processing and graphomotor (writing) skills that are required for copying symbols. Executive control of attention and sustained effort are required.)
> Coding 8
> Symbol Search 9
> * Cancellation NA

3-2, the student's PRI was 121 and the PSI was 91, a difference of 30 points.

Subtests. The evaluator looks for discrepancies of 5 points or more between the individual subtest scale scores. The student profiled above had a high of 15 (in Matrix Reasoning) and a low of 8 (in Coding), or a 7-point discrepancy. Information from the WISC may be helpful in selecting classroom accommodations or a teaching approach.

Not all teenagers with an attention deficit will show a wide range between highest and lowest scores on the WISC subtests. All of their subtest scores could fall within a five-point range of each other. In a one-to-one testing situation with the examiner, some teens are able to stay on task, so they score well on an IQ test. The novelty of the testing session may also help the teenager stay on task, thus masking attentional problems.

"One teenager I tested recently scored pretty well on the WISC with low scores on only one of the three 'attentional' subtests. Yet, he had all the classic symptoms of ADHD as reported by him, his parents, and teachers. His performance on the sentence completion, a test unrelated to the WISC, was revealing. The teenager's handwriting was terrible and he worked very slowly, taking 15 minutes to do 10 sentence completions. Based upon this I would assume that he has slow processing speed and would have difficulty completing schoolwork in a timely manner."

—Pediatric Center Staff

The ACID Test. When the WISC III was in use, the ACID Test had some relevance as an indicator of an attention deficit. ACID Test referred to the grouping of scale scores on the **A**rithmetic, **C**oding, **I**nformation, and **D**igit Span subtests. Although not conclusive, low scores on these subtests were a red flag for an attention deficit or learning problems.

"My son's scale scores ranged from 7 on the Coding subtest to 19 on the Vocabulary subtest. His lowest scores were all on the ACID subtests. His full scale IQ was 141, yet he could not learn his multiplication tables. What a puzzle! Later I learned he had ADD inattentive plus executive function deficits."

SUBTESTS OF THE WISC

A brief description of the individual subtests of the WISC by index may be helpful. Academic implications are also provided for two key indices that may be indicative of an attention deficit.

Verbal Comprehension Index (VCI). This group of tests measures an individual's ability to express ideas in words in response to oral questions from the examiner; no reading is required. The questions require common sense reasoning, vocabulary knowledge, and the ability to describe the relationship between words.

Similarities, Vocabulary, and Comprehension subtests. Students with ADD or ADHD may do fairly well on these subtests, which measure verbal reasoning, word knowledge, concept formation, and use of common sense and practical information.

Word Reasoning. In this optional subtest, the student is asked to identify the common concept being described in a series of clues.

Information. Low scores on *Information,* an optional subtest which asks questions about basic facts often learned in school, may indicate that the teenager has difficulty quickly *retrieving information stored in long-term memory, or has gaps in knowledge* due to his inattention or learning problems. These gaps in knowledge may occur as a result of the teenager's inability to pay attention, memorize, or complete work. Practically speaking, the student may know information but may be slow or reluctant to respond to questions in class.

Perceptual Reasoning Index (PRI). These subtests measure a student's visual perception, organization, and reasoning to solve problems that are not taught in school. Testing involves visually presented, nonverbal tasks.

Block Design. Students are shown a design with blocks that they must copy. They may be able to arrange the blocks correctly but obtain lower scores because they tend to work so slowly. Low scores on Block Design may indicate *poor organizational and analytical skills* or *slow information processing speed.*

Picture Concepts. Two or three rows of pictures are presented and the student must select one picture from each row to form a group with a common characteristic. It measures *abstract, categorical reasoning ability.*

Matrix Reasoning. The student looks at an incomplete matrix or image and then selects the missing portion from five options.

Picture Completion. The student must observe important details to discern what is missing from a picture in the Picture Completion (PC) subtest. Low scores may indicate problems with *inattention to details* or *retrieving learned information.* Obviously, attention to detail is critical for doing math operations, following sign changes, and noting punctuation, capitalization, or spelling errors.

Working Memory Index (WMI). These test items require the student to hold in mind and manipulate orally presented information, arrange the information in proper sequence, and then repeat it to the examiner.

Digit Span. In the Digit Span subtest the teenager must remember and repeat an increasing sequence of numbers presented to him orally. The teenager is also asked to repeat numbers in order backwards. Again, the inability to concentrate, poor working memory, and poor listening comprehension may result in lower scores. Repeating the numbers backward is an especially good indicator of a student's working memory skills. This subtest assesses *short-term and working memory*—whether a teenager can remember and manipulate numbers for a few seconds.

Letter-Number Sequence. The student is read a list of numbers and letters that are mixed together and must remember what she heard, mentally separate the numbers from the letters, reorder them in her head, and repeat back the numbers in ascending order and the letters in alphabetical order. Like Digit Span, this is also an indicator of *working memory.*

Arithmetic. Arithmetic, an optional subtest, measures increasingly difficult basic math skills. The teenager is asked to respond to arithmetic word problems that are read aloud. To solve the problems, the student must use her working memory, holding and manipulating information about the problem in her head, and quickly retrieving the correct math rule from long-term memory. This subtest is a better measure of *working memory, attention, and concentration* than of mathematical skills. Impulsivity and poor listening comprehension may also interfere with the teenager's ability to do well on this subtest.

Implications of Low WMI Scores. In the classroom, the teenager's poor memory skills may impair her ability to memorize information such as basic math facts, especially multiplication tables, history facts, spelling words, or foreign languages. The implications of low Arithmetic scores on math problems are obvious. The student will probably work math problems slowly, will not be able to recall math facts quickly, and will need more time to complete her work. Students with low scores on the WMI may also have problems with written expression since they must hold information in mind, manipulate and sequence ideas, remember ideas long enough to write them down, and quickly retrieve grammar rules from long-term memory.

A student could make a decent score on this index and still have memory problems. For example, one student obtained a scale score of 12 on Digit Span, yet she could not memorize her multiplication tables. Obviously, this subtest does not measure all the memory skills typically used in a real world classroom. In a classroom, the student must memorize facts one day and recall them the next day, week, or month. She must remember homework assignments for several hours.

Processing Speed Index (PSI). This index measures visual perception and organization by requiring the student to copy the visually presented symbols as quickly as possible. These subtests are timed; so if a student processes or writes slowly, scores may be lower.

Coding. The Coding subtest requires the teenager to copy a series of symbols that are paired with simple geometric shapes or numbers. Youngsters with an attention deficit, especially the inattentive type, may make low scale scores on the Coding subtest. In addition, teenagers who are distractible or who have processing speed problems such as *writing or processing materials slowly* also make low scores.

Symbol Search. For this subtest, the student scans to see if the target symbol matches any symbols in the search group. Like the Coding subtest, this is also an indicator of *processing speed.*

Implications of Low PSI Scores. From a practical standpoint, the teenager with an attention deficit who has processing and/or fine motor problems will probably *read and write slowly, produce less written work, and have trouble completing work on time.* Written work is so time consuming, the teenager may give up and not even try to finish class work or homework. In addition, she is unlikely to have the time to double-check answers after finishing an assignment or test. As one would expect, students with low scores on the Coding subtest and/or Processing Speed Index often need extended time on school work and tests. Clearly,

the teenager has a learning problem that will significantly affect her classroom performance, even though it may not meet special education criteria for a Specific Learning Disability (SLD). The student, however, may meet criteria for special education eligibility under Other Health Impairment (OHI). (See Chapter 14.)

UNDERESTIMATES OF INTELLIGENCE

Because of their attention problems and gaps in knowledge, it may be difficult to obtain accurate estimates of intelligence for teenagers with attention deficits. The IQ test results may reflect an underestimate of the teenager's intelligence, possibly because of related learning problems, deficits in executive skills, or difficulty staying focused on the test. Students with ADD inattentive who write or process slowly may not do well on timed portions of tests.

Sometimes these teenagers are conversationally very bright, yet give short, concrete answers, resulting in lower test scores. Since teenagers with attention deficits may have problems with slow processing speed or verbal expression, they may give brief answers. Other teenagers who are hyperactive may want to get the test over with as quickly as possible and impulsively give the first answer that pops into their head. Consequently, although an attention deficit doesn't affect intelligence, teenagers with ADD or ADHD may show an "unevenness" of intellectual development, as reflected by high scores on some subtests and low scores on others.

3. Assessment of Executive Function Deficits

Executive functions, which have been likened to the CEO of your brain, have a profound impact on a student's school performance. For example, experts report that a majority of students with attention deficits have problems in these areas: difficulty getting organized, getting started and finishing work, remembering homework assignments, memorizing and later recalling facts, writing essays or reports, working math problems, being on time, controlling emotions, completing long-term projects, and planning for the future. So it is absolutely critical to assess whether or not the student with an attention deficit also has deficits in her executive skills! Of course, a student may have these deficits, yet not have an attention deficit.

Unfortunately, recognition of the link between executive skills and ADHD and ADD occurred so recently that there is no standard evaluation procedure. In fact, scientists have not even agreed upon a uniform definition of executive functions. At present, clinicians are struggling to adequately evaluate this deficit. A good clinical assessment is critical.

Warren Walter, Ph.D., a neuropsychologist in Atlanta, uses several tools to identify deficits in specific executive skills. Dr. Walter advises that a key part of this evaluation is conducted through interviews that take a careful family history. He believes that important questions to address during interviews include:

1. *Describe the manner in which the student organizes his or her school work.* How does the student organize her academic life? Evidence of disorganization becomes obvious especially during the difficult transitions from elementary to middle school and then middle to high school. The increased organizational demands and increasingly complex academic materials make each passing school year more and more difficult.

2. *Describe the student's study skills.* Can the student get started on her own, prioritize, organize, and complete work independently?

3. *Describe the student's management of his or her academic materials.* Does the student come home with the correct books and assignments, take them back to school, and actually turn in homework to the teacher?

4. *Describe the student's bedroom, closet, dresser, book bag, desk, or locker.*

5. *Give examples of forgetfulness or property that the student has lost.*

6. *Determine the level of external and internal disorganization.* The preceding examples are observable examples of *external* disorganization; that is parents can easily see these problems. However, examples of *internal* disorganization are more difficult to see and may include difficulty organizing and retrieving ideas to write an essay or retrieving rules or formulas to work math problems.

FORMAL TESTS

Because assessment of executive skills is still relatively new, no really good formal tests have been developed. However, Dr. Gerard A. Gioia, a pediatric neuropsychologist, has developed a promising rating scale: *Behavior Rating Inventory of Executive Function, the BRIEF.* The scale, which has both a parent and teacher form, takes roughly 15 minutes to administer and 20 minutes to score. The *BRIEF* includes 86 questions that tap 8 critical executive skills:

1. inhibiting thoughts and actions,
2. shifting,
3. controlling emotions,
4. initiating,
5. working memory,
6. planning and organizing,
7. organizing materials, and
8. monitoring.

USE OF EXISTING TESTS

Some subtests of existing tests also measure at least three key elements of executive function:

1. working memory,
2. retrieval of information stored in long-term memory, and
3. analysis, reconstitution, and organization (complex problem solving).

For example on the WISC IV, the Working Memory Index (WMI) and its subtests—*Letter Number Sequence, Digit Span (backward), and Arithmetic*—measure working memory. In addition, working memory is required for the *Matrix Reasoning* and *Picture Concepts* subtests. The *Information* and *Vocabulary* subtests also measure some working memory skills, plus recall and retrieval of information from long-term memory. The *Coding* and *Symbol Search* subtests of the WISC identify problems with slow processing speed and fine motor coordination. In addition, the *TOWL* gives a good look at a student's written expression skills that require strong analytical, sequencing, and organizational skills.

4. Behavioral Assessment

Behavioral rating scales contain a list of behaviors a child or teenager might exhibit that are characteristic of attention deficits and other conditions. Parents and teachers are asked to rate these behaviors in terms of severity. Behavioral rating scales fall into two general categories:

1. *ADHD-specific scales,* which are more helpful for the actual diagnosis of an attention deficit, and
2. *broadband scales,* which screen for other coexisting conditions.

One of the most commonly used ADHD-specific scales is the *Conners' Behavior Rating Scale* (1997), which has short and longer versions for parents, teachers, and adolescents to fill out. The *Brown Attention-Deficit Disorder Scales* (2000) are also available and are based upon the behavior of adolescents and adults. Sometimes the behaviors listed in the DSM IV diagnostic criteria are also used as a checklist.

Among broadband scales, The *Achenbach Child Behavior Checklist* (CBCL), which takes longer to administer, identifies emotional problems such as depression, anxiety, and aggression, as well as attention deficits. Another frequently used scale is the BASC or *Behavioral Assessment System for Children.*

Results of behavioral rating scales are not infallible. Keep in mind that a mother or father who is depressed may be less tolerant and may rate the child's defiance or aggression more negatively. So, it is important for both parents to complete the scales. Additionally teachers who don't believe in ADD or ADHD may be less likely to give accurate ratings on these scales. Having ratings from more than one teacher may avoid this problem. These scores are potential indicators of problem areas only; in isolation, they cannot diagnose attention deficits.

STRENGTH-BASED ASSESSMENT

Unfortunately, most behavioral rating scales are deficit based—in other words they only look for problems rather than strengths. However, Michael Epstein, Ph.D., of the University of Nebraska has developed the *Behavioral and Emotional Rating Scale: A Strength-Based Approach to Assessment [BERS].* By identifying the child's strengths, the evaluator may encourage parents to also look for and build on the teen's strengths. Five areas evaluated by the BERS include:

1. *Interpersonal Strengths*—the student's ability to control his or her emotions or behavior;

More about the Brown Scales

Dr. Tom Brown's scales are especially helpful because they detail the breadth and complexity of attention deficit disorder and the profound impact it has on day-to-day living. So many scales, including the DSM-IV, give a rather narrow perspective of attention deficits. Brown identifies some of the more subtle inattentive characteristics of ADHD plus elements of executive function. These Scales include both a 50-sentence self-report and a parent-report checklist. A brief summary of the six core clusters of symptoms is listed in Table 3-3. Dr. Brown asks the teenager to give a score of from 0 to 3 for each question. A score of 50 or more is considered indicative of ADD or ADHD combined type. More information is available from www.brownaddscales.com.

The list of behaviors included in the Brown Scale should remind adults of the profound academic challenges some teenagers with attention deficits face in their efforts to master schoolwork. It is sobering to realize that seemingly simple tasks, such as reading, finding the main point, and processing information rapidly may be extremely difficult for these teenagers. Moreover, just getting started on a task or knowing how and where to begin can be a monumental job. Sometimes parents and teachers overlook just how courageous these teenagers are as they continue to struggle with academics when the task can be so difficult and overwhelming.

2. *Family involvement*—the student's relationship with his or her family;
3. *Interpersonal Strengths*—the student's feelings of competence and accomplishment;
4. *School Functioning*—the student's competence in school;
5. *Affective Strengths*—the student's ability to accept affection and express feelings.

Questions are also asked about the student's favorite hobbies, activities, or sports; best school subjects, best friend, favorite teacher, job responsibilities, and closest adult relationship. The scale may be completed in ten minutes by teachers, parents, a counselor, or others who are knowledgeable about the student. Then a school psychologist or other trained professional may score and interpret the results. More information is available from the publisher at www.proedinc.com or 800-897-3203.

Table 3-3 The Brown Attention-Deficit Disorder Scales

Scores show how much a feeling or behavior has been a problem within the past month.

0 not at all a problem; never occurs
1 just a little problem; occurs rarely
2 pretty much a problem; occurs a few times in a week
3 very much a problem; occurs almost every day

Organizing, Prioritizing and Activating to Work: Difficulty getting organized, starting work tasks, and setting priorities; procrastination, misunderstanding directions; difficulty waking up; exhibiting counterproductive perfectionist tendencies that interfere with prompt work completion.

Focusing, Sustaining and Shifting Attention to Tasks: Problems related to excessive daydreaming or distractibility when listening or doing required reading; must reread frequently; loses the main point in reading.

Regulating Alertness, Sustaining Effort, and Processing Speed: Difficulty keeping up consistent energy and effort for work tasks; daytime drowsiness; slow processing of information, needs extra time on assignments, doesn't finish work; inconsistent work quality, not working up to potential, sloppy writing; work effort fades quickly; academic underachievement; receives criticism for being lazy.

Managing Frustration and Modulating Emotions: Struggles to regulate moods and emotional reactions; impatient; sensitive to criticism, easily discouraged; easily frustrated, short fuse; depressed; appears to lack motivation.

Utilizing Working Memory and Accessing Recall: Problems with short-term and working memory, excessive forgetfulness; loses things; difficulty recalling intentions or learned information, retrieving words or other facts, and following through.

Monitoring and Self-Regulating Action: Difficulty regulating behavior; grabbing things or starting actions without waiting for permission; doing things too fast, not slowing down to write school work carefully.

5. Other Assessment Tools

OPEN-ENDED SENTENCE COMPLETION

The teenager may also be asked to answer some open-ended sentence completion items, such as "my mother gets angry when I_____," "I am happy when I_____." This activity provides a sample of handwriting, provides insights about the teenager's feelings and concerns, and shows how rapidly she writes.

CONTINUOUS PERFORMANCE TESTS

One of the newest tests that has been developed to identify attention deficit disorders is called a *continuous performance test or CPT*. However, reviews are mixed regarding its ability to accurately identify attention deficits. The test formats vary but typically a child is required to press a button when she sees a certain sequence of numbers, letters, or sounds on a computer screen. The score reflects the number of correct answers, the number missed, plus the number of wrong responses. Several different tests are available: *Conners' CPT, Gordon Diagnostic System (GDS), and the Test of Variables of Attention (TOVA).*

Currently, the American Academy of Pediatrics (AAP) does *not* recommend a CPT as part of an evaluation since these tests do not consistently differentiate between children with and without an attention deficit. In fact, according to Dr. Barkley, 35 to 50 percent of children with ADHD can pass the test. Researchers have found CPTs to be even *less* accurate for identifying ADHD among teens than among children. Video savvy teens may score well on the test but still have an attention deficit.

PET SCANS, SPECT SCANS, AND MRIS

Although Position Emission (PET) Scans, Single Photon Emission-computer Tomography (SPECT), and Magnetic Reasoning Images (MRIs) have been used in research to identify areas in the brain that are involved in attention deficit disorders, their use for diagnosis of attention deficits in the general population is impractical. First, the tests are very expensive and may not be covered by insurance. In addition, most researchers don't want to take the risk of injecting children with radioactive materials. Currently, most leading researchers do not believe these tests are appropriate for diagnosis of ADD or ADHD.

6. *Physical Examination*

A good physical should help identify any medical or mental health conditions that coexist with or mimic ADD or ADHD. Several disorders have symptoms similar to attention deficits, including: lead poisoning, fetal alcohol syndrome, bipolar disorder, and thyroid problems. And some common health problems, such as anemia and mononucleosis, have symptoms of low energy which may be mistaken for symptoms of ADD inattentive. An attention deficit disorder cannot be diagnosed as the sole cause of a teenager's behaviors until other conditions are ruled out. See Chapter 7 for a discussion of common conditions that frequently coexist with ADD and ADHD.

7. *Common Sense Timing of Evaluations*

During a crisis, parents and teenagers may need immediate help with the most pressing problems. Parents should not be afraid to ask professionals for what they need—for example, help with a crisis now, and a comprehensive evaluation only after the crisis is resolved. Families in crisis often prefer development of a behavioral action plan that targets the current problems such as failing a class in school, rather than conducting a lengthy evaluation.

"Once when my teenager was failing four of six classes, a psychologist wanted to do a two-day evaluation. After thinking it over, I said no. I wanted a plan to help him immediately. If needed, we could do more lengthy evaluation later. So a plan was developed to help him pass as many classes as possible. Teacher conferences were held and make-up assignments were identified. Some teachers agreed to assign projects for extra credit. A friend, a 'study buddy,' was invited over to study for final exams. My son earned passing grades in five of the six classes."

Getting the Evaluation Results: Does Your Teen Have an Attention Deficit?

Once the interview, tests, and physical examination are completed, the evaluator will meet with the family to give them the results of the assessment and recommendations for treatment. You may *take notes or ask for permission to tape record the session*. This may be a period of high anxiety, and it is difficult to remember everything that is said in these meetings. Initially a verbal report may be given and then later a written report will be finalized and given to the parents. If parents request, a copy of the report will be sent to the school. In addition if you request it, the doctor will write a letter to the school confirming the presence of an attention deficit. Schools often require such a letter be on file to confirm eligibility for special education services under the category of "*Other Health Impaired.*"

No matter where your child receives her diagnostic evaluation, you, too, should be given the results of her evaluation. You may want to *request a written copy* of the evaluation for future reference so that you will have the opportunity to study the results more thoroughly. You should feel free to *ask questions* about anything you don't understand. Sometimes reports include a lot of jargon. If so, *ask what the practical implications of the test results* mean for your teenager's schoolwork. The results of each test battery will probably be written up in the report. If not, ask which tests were used and request certain scores such as the subtest scores for the WISC. Then you can compare the subtest scores with the information in this chapter.

If a diagnosis of ADD or ADHD is confirmed, the test results should also help the school determine whether your teenager is eligible for special education services under IDEA. If she is eligible, an individualized education program (IEP), including recommendations for specific academic interventions, will be developed jointly by your family and the school system. Development of an IEP is discussed in Chapter 14.

What Does Your Teenager's Diagnosis Mean?

As discussed in Chapter 1, there are three major categories of attention deficit disorders listed in the *Diagnostic and Statistical Manual of Mental Disorders* (DSM-IV-TR). The DSM contains the *official criteria* used by licensed treatment professionals in diagnosing ADD and ADHD. So, if your teenager is found to have an attention deficit, the evaluator should tell you which of these types he or she has. This section describes what each of these diagnoses may mean to you and your teenager on a day-to-day basis.

1. *AD/HD, Hyperactive-Impulsive Type (ADHD)*

Since the DSM-IV criteria for ADHD describe behavior exhibited in elementary school, most teenagers with ADHD probably won't meet six of the nine diagnostic criteria. So parents and evaluators may want to ask this question: "Did this teenager exhibit six of these characteristics when she was in elementary school?" As teenagers, children may still have the hallmark characteristics of inattention and impulsivity, but the hyperactivity is usually replaced by restlessness. As a result, parents and treatment professionals must rely on a past history of hyperactivity in childhood to help make a diagnosis. Characteristics of younger children with attention deficits are described in Chapter 1.

In addition, most teenagers with ADHD don't seem to listen, don't obey rules, don't finish tasks, can't concentrate, don't work well independently, and shift from one task to another. They may also have difficulty delaying gratification, difficulty getting along with peers, and exhibit disruptive behavior in the classroom. Although teens with ADHD may talk more than their peers, when asked to respond to specific questions with concise answers, they often talk less. Sometimes they learn to be the class clown or become adept at "charming" the teacher as a survival skill to compensate for their academic difficulties. These teenagers are more likely to be aggressive, oppositional, and defiant than teenagers with ADD inattentive. Some students who are more aggressive may receive an additional diagnosis of Oppositional Defiant Disorder (ODD) or Conduct Disorder (CD). ODD and CD are discussed in more detail in Chapter 7.

2. AD/HD, Inattentive Type (ADD)

To be diagnosed with ADD inattentive, teenagers must exhibit six of the nine DSM-IV diagnostic criteria established in the DSM in 1994. In the early 1980s, this diagnosis was known as ADD without hyperactivity. Teens with ADD tend to be daydreamers who are not hyper, are more laid back, and are not aggressive. They are less likely to act out, and cause few, if any, behavior problems during the early school years. In elementary school, their teachers may describe them as well behaved. As teenagers, they tend to have *low energy levels,* rather than hyperactivity, and some may even appear lethargic at times. Teenagers with ADD inattentive are not as talkative as those with hyperactivity. Often inattentive teenagers with ADD are overlooked until they reach middle or high school, when they seem to fall apart academically due to their deficits in executive skills.

Possibly a Separate Condition from ADHD. Three leading researchers on attention deficits—Russell Barkley, Ph.D., Tom Brown, Ph.D., and Richard Milich,

Ph.D.—have observed that the behaviors of teenagers with major inattention problems are different from those who are hyperactive. As explained in Chapter 1, Dr. Barkley believes that *ADD inattentive involves problems with focused or selective attention and processing speed, rather than problems with sustained attention and impulse control observed in ADHD.*

In fact, some researchers now believe that ADD inattentive is a totally separate disorder rather than a subtype of ADHD. Although researchers who wrote the DSM-IV characterized people with ADD inattentive as having "sluggish cognitive tempo (SCT)" —drowsiness, lethargy, and underactivity—they did not include these characteristics in their diagnostic manual. Don't be surprised if sometime in the coming years, the name for ADD inattentive is changed.

Distinguishing Features. Teenagers with ADD inattentive have several distinguishing behaviors, with the common thread often being *slow processing speed,* even though the teenager may be bright. Slow processing speed combined with *expressive language* problems may contribute to difficulties at school and home—for example, slow reading and writing; slow response to requests; poor memory recall; slow completion of work; and eventually avoidance of homework.

These teenagers may also *appear unmotivated, low in energy, and at times even apathetic. Getting started and sustaining effort* on tasks such as schoolwork is also extremely difficult for them. When teenagers can no longer sustain attention to school tasks, they may sit quietly in their seats, tapping their pencils or foot, playing with their hair or paper, staring into space, daydreaming, or sleeping in class rather than exhibiting physically hyperactive behavior. School issues are discussed in Chapters 11 to 13.

"Shawn's problems didn't begin to show up until third grade. At first, it seemed to be the result of an unstructured second grade class combined with two moves. At that time the problem was minor. In fourth grade, his disorganization began to show up: not getting assignments home, wrong book, etc. By fifth grade, his grades really began dropping. By sixth grade, it seemed that he couldn't pass tests. Although he needed and received tutoring in test taking skills, his grades continued to drop. By ninth grade he was failing. He was diagnosed with ADD inattentive when he was fifteen."

In contrast to teenagers who have ADHD, teenagers with ADD inattentive don't seem to have as many problems related to impulsivity and intrusiveness. They are less likely to be socially aggressive, oppositional, or defiant. They may get along better with their peers and don't seem to have problems with social rejection that some teenagers with ADHD have.

Depression and anxiety may be more common in teenagers with this type of attention deficit. In addition, family members tend to have a history of learning disabilities and anxiety disorders more often than in families with ADHD.

Parents should be aware that one reason ADD may be overlooked is because of the misleading labeling of this condition. The technically correct DSM-IV diagnostic term—attention-deficit/hyperactivity disorder—may discourage parents and professionals from considering the diagnosis of ADD inattentive. A reasonable person would expect a teenager diagnosed with AD**H**D to be *hyperactive*.

"I always thought a child had to be hyperactive to be diagnosed as having ADHD. Consequently, since my son sat quietly at his desk, I assumed incorrectly that he could not have an attention deficit."

3. AD/HD, Combined Type, Hyperactive, Impulsive, and Inattentive (ADHD)

To be diagnosed with ADHD combined type, the teen must have a least six characteristics under both ADD/inattentive and ADHD/hyperactive-impulsive, for a total of twelve or more symptoms. So, the diagnostic label for this disorder is self-explanatory. The teenager is or was hyperactive and also has significant problems with inattention. He or she exhibits a combination of the characteristics described in the two preceding sections.

4. AD/HD, Not Otherwise Specified (ADHD/NOS)

Rarely, parents might hear that their teenager has Attention-Deficit/Hyperactivity Disorder Not Otherwise Specified. This diagnosis is given when the teenager has prominent symptoms of inattention or hyperactivity, but does not meet the full criteria for AD/HD. For example, the teenager may have fewer than the required six DSM IV symptoms to be diagnosed with an attention deficit disorder. Typically, if the doctor reports your teen's diagnosis to the school at your request, she will probably refer to the diagnosis simply as ADHD, rather than specifying ADHD/NOS. Obviously, the child is struggling at school and at home, even if the diagnosis is ADHD/NOS.

A Summary of Similarities and Differences Between ADD and ADHD

There are some similarities in behaviors between teenagers with ADD and ADHD, and also several differences, as shown in Table 3-4. Because each teenager with an attention deficit is unique, however, remember that not everyone with ADD or ADHD will have all the behaviors listed here.

Parents as Partners

Three sets of experts must be involved in diagnosis and treatment of attention deficits:

1. the *treatment professionals* (pediatricians, clinical psychologists, psychiatrists, family physicians),
2. *school officials* (teachers, school psychologists, administrators, social workers, and/or guidance counselors), and
3. the *family* (parents and the teenager). Each group has a unique contribution to make to the diagnostic and treatment process.

Your Partnership with Professionals

As a parent, you know your teenager best, having lived with him or her and the attention deficit for many years. It is important to trust your instincts regarding the best interests of your child. Believe in yourself and your teen. As you prepare to read Chapter 5 on treatment, here

Table 3-4 Comparison of ADD and ADHD

Similarities: Students with ADD and ADHD share these characteristics:

- inattentive
- impulsive
- trouble getting started on homework/chores
- poor sustained attention (persistence on tasks)
- problems with written expression and math
- poor handwriting (fine motor skills)
- positive response to medications
- short term memory problems
- working memory problems

Differences: Students with ADD and ADHD also have very distinct differences. However, students with combined ADHD will have symptoms from both columns.

ADHD/Hyperactive or ADHD combined

- hyperactive
- out of seat
- talkative
- blurts out answers
- talks and acts before thinking
- class clown
- difficulty making and keeping friends
- misses social cues

ADD /Inattentive

- low energy/ not hyperactive
- sits in seat, daydreaming
- quiet, less talkative
- math computation difficulties
- slow to respond in class
- slow processing speed (seems confused at times)
- slow retrieval of information stored in long-term memory
- slow perceptual-motor speed
- slow writing
- quiet, socially distant
- gets along better with peers

Less Common Characteristics: The following behaviors are not present in all teenagers with attention deficits but when present, they are more likely to be associated with the type of ADD or ADHD noted.

ADHD (hyperactive-impulsive type)

- aggressive
- oppositional defiant behavior
- conduct disorder

ADD (Inattentive type)

- anxious
- less impulsivity
- less oppositional
- less defiant

Shared School-related Problems:

- disorganization (forgetting or losing books or homework assignments, not returning work to school, forgetting due dates);
- math computation problems (difficulty memorizing math facts, especially multiplication tables);
- listening comprehension problems (difficulty following instructions, confusion with verbal directions, difficulty taking notes, difficulty identifying main points);
- spoken language problems (slow verbal responses, difficulty giving clear concise answers, avoidance of responding in class);
- written language problems (slow writing, less written work produced, difficulty getting ideas down on paper, difficulty writing essays, difficulty taking written tests, slow reading, and poor reading comprehension).

is some general advice for a better working relationship with school officials and your treatment professional:

- *You and your teenager should be treated with respect* by any professional who is working with you.
- Professionals should *not make you feel guilty* or that you are to blame for your child's behavior.
- In addition, they should *ask for your input* as the treatment strategy is developed.
- They should be *open about answering questions* you ask about the evaluation, treatment approaches, or medications.
- Ideally, the treatment professional will *identify your teenager's strengths* and tap those as part of the treatment plan.
- If you or your teen do not like and respect a professional, consider finding someone else. If your teenager is willing to go to counseling, it is important to *select someone she likes and respects.*
- It is also important for you to *treat professionals with respect.*
- You will need to *work closely with school officials* to help your teenager succeed at school. A positive parent/teacher partnership is critical.
- *Avoid conflicts* with school officials. Sometimes parents are so frustrated and angry, they may inadvertently alienate school officials by misdirecting their frustration and fear about the attention deficit toward them. Usually, you will be more successful at having your teenager's needs met by working collaboratively *with* school personnel.
- Typically, students with ADD or ADHD need more support from teachers at a time when the system expects more independence and offers less support. Many of our teenagers are four to six years behind developmentally. So teachers will need to spend more time and energy than usual with your teen if her educational program is to succeed. Parents and teachers must provide "*developmentally appropriate levels of support and supervision.*"
- Occasionally, "being nice" doesn't work and you may have to *be more assertive* to get the help you need. Legal rights under federal laws are discussed in Chapter 14.

ADD and ADHD: the Past, Present, and Future

Although the symptoms that comprise the diagnosis of ADD and ADHD have been observed since at least the early 1900s, researchers did not make much headway in understanding the disorder until the last few decades. In fact, only a generation ago children with attention deficits were sometimes diagnosed inappropriately as having minimal brain damage. It was not until 1972 that Dr. Virginia Douglas at McGill University in Montreal first identified the problems with sustained attention and poor impulse control associated with this condition. She noted that hyperactivity was just one of several symptoms of the disorder. And it was not until the publication of DSM III in 1980 that the condition was first labeled attention deficit disorder. Two categories of attention deficits were included: ADD with and without hyperactivity. Prior to that time, attention deficits were called Hyperactivity or Hyperkinetic Syndrome.

Although we have made great progress, proper diagnosis and effective treatment strategies for ADD and ADHD are still evolving, especially for teenagers. Through additional research, the subtle characteristics and problems related to diagnosis and treatment of attention deficits should become clearer during the coming years. However, as with diagnosis and treatment of any fairly new disorder, you should *not* assume that all the symptoms related to your teenager's ADD or ADHD have been identified and are being properly treated. As I explain in Chapter 7, if your teen continues to struggle, there is a good possibility that a key coexisting condition has been overlooked or the correct medication and dosage has not yet been found. So you must continue to be vigilant in the years after your child is diagnosed to ensure that his or her needs are being properly met and that all coexisting conditions have been identified and treated!

4

Moving Beyond Guilt, Anger, and Fear to Optimism!

Parenting a teenager with ADD or ADHD can be compared with riding a roller coaster: there are many highs and lows, laughs and tears, and breathtaking and sometimes terrifying experiences. Most parents of teens with attention deficits would give anything for a week that was relatively calm and free of turmoil. However, unsettling highs and lows are likely to be the norm for many of these families.

When parents encounter difficulties raising their teenager with an attention deficit, they often have deep feelings of self-doubt, fear, and guilt. Some parents worry that they have been "bad" parents and have caused their teen to act the way he does. Other parents believe that they have a "bad" child. Because of their teenager's behavior, parents may experience a wide variety of emotions ranging from embarrassment and depression to anger. All of these feelings are perfectly normal and understandable, under the circumstances. Learning to handle these stressful feelings in a constructive way should make it easier for parents to raise these teenagers.

Despite your teenager's difficult behavior and the stressful demands of parenting, you undoubtedly still love him and want the best in life for him. You may be desperately seeking special guidance to help him succeed, since traditional child rearing techniques don't seem to work as effectively. This chapter in particular will help put you in a more positive frame of mind so you can follow the guidance in the rest of the book. Its goal is to help you understand your teen's behavior, plus your own negative feelings that may have built up over

the years, and then to cope with those feelings constructively. By first dealing with your feelings, you can begin to deal more realistically and optimistically with the attention deficit disorder. In addition, the chapter offers a review of specific therapeutic steps that parents can implement to help teens cope successfully.

The Emotional Impact of Attention Deficit Disorder

Raising a teenager with ADD or ADHD can exact a tremendous toll on the family, especially when the attention deficit is more serious and is not being properly treated. Family arguments and fights over homework, skipping school, school failure, and medication refusal can thrust the family into an emotional pressure cooker. It is not unusual for parents to feel inadequate and overwhelmed. Researchers have found that *parents of youngsters with ADHD experience more feelings of depression and doubt about their parenting skills.* According to Dr. Russell Barkley, parents whose children's ADHD is more severe are three times as likely to separate or divorce as parents who do not have children with an attention deficit.

"In the midst of a major crisis when her son had been suspended from school again, one mother cried, saying, 'I don't want to give up my whole life for this child.' Yet by the next day, after this brief angry outburst, she was back at the job of helping her son cope with the blow-up at school."

As parents, your whole world may revolve around your teenager with an attention deficit. You may expend tremendous amounts of time and energy worrying, providing supervision and support, and, occasionally, "rescuing" him. At times, you may become exhausted and depressed. Conflicts with your teen, your family, or your spouse can contribute to exhaustion, depression, or feelings of being overwhelmed. So, too, can coping with your own conflicting emotions. The typical conflicts facing families with an attention deficit are discussed below.

Conflicts with Your Teenager
Noncompliance

One of the most common sources of conflict between parents and teenagers is their failure to do as parents ask. *Their inattention, forgetfulness, and, sometimes, defiance play a major role in their noncompliance with parental requests.* Many teens with ADD or ADHD are not doing well at school and are disobedient at home. As a result, parents spend a lot of time monitoring school work, nagging about homework and chores, dealing with teachers, and setting limits for their teenager. They grow weary of constantly having to handle these problem behaviors. This is particularly true if the behaviors have not improved with treatment or if the teen has coexisting problems such as depression or a learning disability.

Although parents know intellectually that their teenager's misbehavior is often related to his attention deficit disorder, this does not make it any easier to cope emotionally with these problems. Even when ADD or ADHD is a contributing factor, behaviors such as defiance, stubbornness, talking back, and disobedience can infuriate, frustrate, and embarrass most parents.

"It is so embarrassing when my son talks back to me or disobeys me in front of others. I know other people must think I am a terrible parent. At times, I feel like such a failure."

Emotionality

Teens with ADD and ADHD often have *low tolerance for frustrating situations* and then respond with *intense emotional reactions.* They have great difficulty handling their anger, stress, and disappointment, and therefore approach situations more emotionally than other teenagers do. This is especially true for girls, who are more emotionally reactive, especially during their menstrual cycle. The changes in hormones seem to wreak havoc on their emotions. Emotional problems also are compounded for both boys and girls because of their four- to six-year developmental delay. Like younger children, they show their emotions more overtly. If they feel something, they may say it or take action impulsively.

"Breaking up with a girlfriend often triggered emotional blowups for our son. We learned the hard way that we should put preventive strategies in place. When he was a junior in high school, his girlfriend left him for someone else. He ran into the boy in the hall and they got into a fight. Both boys were suspended. Later we set up a system whereby he could go to the guidance counselor's office, no questions asked, if he felt like he was about to blow up."

In turn, the teen's increased emotionality may trigger a strong emotional response from parents, setting in motion a vicious cycle of yelling fights. Typically, if parents respond in a loud, angry manner, the teenager gets even angrier. He then becomes increasingly aggressive and less likely to do as he is asked.

In an emotionally tense situation, the best response for parents and teachers is to *lower their voice, stay calm, and give the teenager some time and space to cool off.* This is easier said than done, however, when the teen yells, talks back, curses, or cries. Most parents wisely pick and choose their battles, ignoring less serious problems. The good news is that this emotionality does improve with medication; age and maturity also help.

Sometimes because parents dread the emotional blow-up, they may avoid confronting their child about his behavior or misbehavior (poor grades, missed curfew, drinking). Since parents know these issues *must* be dealt with eventually, anxiety about the inevitable confrontation builds up and is very stressful.

Crisis Situations

Crises occur far too frequently and often contribute to family friction. Some parents dread receiving "bad news" phone calls about their teenager. If their teen is out with friends at night, they start worrying when the phone rings. "Mom, I got a speeding ticket tonight." "I had a wreck." "Dad, I'm at the police station—can you come get me?" Other "bad news phone calls" come from school: "Your son is failing chemistry." "Your son was in a fight at school today. Please come take him home." Parents long for the time when they receive no more bad news phone calls.

"There were times when my daughter was in high school when I thought, 'I just can't go through another day or another moment.' I would be so tired of having the phone ring and having it be the police department or school saying she wasn't at school today."

Some parents have had to face police bringing their teenager home for violating curfew, or judges when accompanying their teen to juvenile court. These trips to court are typically over less-serious issues—speeding tickets, violating curfews, or sneaking out of the house at night.

Any crisis, major or minor, may throw the whole family into emotional turmoil. *Tremendous emotional energy is required to parent these teenagers when they are in crisis.* It is perfectly normal for parents to be angry and depressed about the stress their teen causes. No doubt, the teenager is also angry with himself, and, sometimes, with the whole world.

"I live with a constant underlying feeling of anxiety when my teenage son is out at night during the weekend. I wonder what's going to happen next."

Daily Friction

Crises aren't the only thing that cause conflicts between parents and their teenager. *The teen with ADD or ADHD often has difficulty meeting the seemingly simple demands of daily living.* He doesn't do chores. He seems lazy and appears eager to avoid helping around the house. His room is a disaster zone. The yard is never mowed on time. The teenager is argumentative and talks back to parents. He stays out late or parents don't know where he is. He may be moody, irritable, and explosive at times. If parents had to deal with just a few of these behaviors on an occasional basis, it wouldn't be terribly stressful. Dealing with one behavior on top of another, however, quickly wears down even the most patient parent. Yelling battles may be common.

"Knowing the value of the child and experiencing the love of the child do not keep parents from feeling weary unto tears."

"By his early teens, all of my son's anger and frustration were directed toward me. We ended in verbal conflicts even over the weather, date, time . . . everything. I would go to work early so we wouldn't have conflicts before school to start both our days on the wrong foot."

Communication Problems

A host of communication problems may strain relationships between parents and teenagers with attention deficits. According to Dr. Barkley's research, many parents and teens with ADHD say mostly negative things to each other. Sometimes parents can't find anything positive to talk about with their teen. Because of the child's disobedience and defiance, experts tell us that *parents tend to issue more commands and putdowns, plus make more negative comments.* Parents must work very hard to avoid falling into this counterproductive trap.

Before parents are educated about attention deficits, they may assume incorrectly that their teenager is acting maliciously. Initially, many view their teen as "lazy, stupid, unconcerned, irresponsible, unmotivated, a liar, or selfish." And that may be exactly what they tell their teenager. Not surprisingly, arguments can be very heated and intense. Parents may say things in the heat of anger that they later regret. It is so difficult for parents to maintain their composure when they are angry and frustrated. Parents and teens may begin distancing themselves from each other emotionally if these negative exchanges persist.

"We used to put our son down like this. Fortunately, he seemed to have an insight telling him we were wrong. The major point I would like to convey to other fathers is, don't say degrading things to your child. Don't call your child stupid or a lazy bum.

Don't tell him you wish you never had children or that you wish he were never born. I've said some of those things and I'll regret those put-downs until the day I die."

To add to communication problems, the teenager's perception of family interactions is not always accurate. Often, he sees his parents' rules as unfair and too restrictive. This leads to even more arguments.

As a result of these frequent conflicts, experts tell us that the primary caregiver, usually the mother, may feel more depression, self-blame, and social isolation. Frequently, depression contributes to a vicious cycle of problems. Parents who are depressed are more critical, disapproving, and punishing with their children. Depressed parents are less tolerant, and may consequently see their child's behavior more negatively than it actually is. In addition, depressed parents often use inconsistent child management techniques, which undermines their effectiveness. For their part, children of depressed parents are more likely to be aggressive toward their parents.

A mother's depression is not a minor issue. According to findings from the NIMH/MTA study, the second most important factor in determining how well a child coped with ADHD was having a mother who was not depressed. Mothers who are depressed must seek treatment for themselves!

There *is* some good news about communication between parents and teenagers. As discussed earlier, *communication becomes more positive when the teen is taking medication.* Families with children with an attention deficit always have more conflict than other families, however, regardless of the child's age.

To help improve communication skills, Gale Gordon, MD, a California pediatrician, recommends *How to Talk So Kids Will Listen and Listen So Kids Will Talk.* This book offers parents the words to use when talking with their teen.

Conflicts within Your Family

Attention deficit disorder has a tremendous impact on the whole family. *Brothers and sisters in particular often feel strong, conflicting emotions.* On the one hand, they feel terribly *sorry* for the struggles their sibling must go through. But on the other hand, they are equally as *angry and resentful* that he messes things up, gets into trouble, embarrasses himself and his family, harasses their friends, and makes his parents angry and depressed. To a large degree, it must seem to them that family life unfairly revolves around their sibling's needs. They may resent their sibling for "hogging" the lion's share of their parents' time and energy and feel as if they are shortchanged as a result.

Some siblings believe that their parents have a *double standard* for behavior. They often think that the teenager with the attention deficit gets away with more misbehavior than they do. They may second guess and be angry with their parents because the teen with ADD or ADHD "isn't punished often enough."

In comparison with a teenager with ADHD, the brother or sister may *seem angelic* to parents. In some families, siblings may feel they have to be the "model child" to make up for the teen with an attention deficit.

"My daughter felt guilty that her brother had a disability instead of her. She wished she could have the ADHD to relieve her brother's pain for a while. She was always a good student. She was trying to make up for her brother's problems. If I had it to do over again, I would be more honest and explain the disorder better. I would give her something to read about ADHD. I didn't give her credit for being able to understand what was going on."

For their part, teenagers with attention deficits are *not particularly sensitive to how their behavior affects others.* They *borrow* things without permission and sometimes *lose or break* them. This may lead to frequent arguments that escalate into screaming or shoving matches or occasionally fights.

"My older sister, who has ADHD, makes me so angry because she borrows things from me without asking and never returns them. She doesn't respect my property. My irritation level with her on a scale of 1-10 is 12. I've tried everything to get her to stop taking my things. Yelling doesn't work. Asking doesn't work. I threatened to beat her up. I am starting to dislike her. I hate to admit it, but I can't trust her. She's very selfish. She doesn't care about anyone's feelings but her own. She eggs me on and tries to get me mad. She plays with my mind. My parents are tougher on me because of things my sister has done."

Often, teenagers with attention deficits don't handle their anger very well. Consequently, they may *take their frustration and anger out on younger siblings.* If the teen comes home angry because of frustrations at school, he may yell at younger brothers or sisters, boss them around, threaten them, or hit them. The teen's sense of powerlessness or impotence often is translated into anger directed at others. Obviously, younger siblings get upset and come crying to parents. Then another battle is set in motion between the parents and the angry teenager. Younger siblings with attention deficits may pester their older siblings.

If more than one family member has an attention deficit, problems may be even more complicated. According to researchers, 54 percent of all children with ADHD have at least one parent with the disorder. In addition, 35 percent of siblings, most likely a brother, also have the condition. Obviously, if several family members are inattentive, impulsive, disorganized, and have difficulty handling anger and stress, family life may frequently be in an uproar.

Conflicts with Your Spouse

There is great potential for conflict between parents who are raising a teenager with an attention deficit. *Many mothers and fathers often have difficulty agreeing on the best method for disciplining their teen.* In addition, some parents blame each other for their child's difficulties. Often, one parent is the disciplinarian in the family. Frequently, the "disciplinarian" believes that if the other parent were less permissive, their teen would not have so many problems. Agreeing on appropriate discipline is especially ticklish if one parent does not understand attention deficit and wants to impose punishment that is too rigid and harsh.

Parents may argue or fight over the teenager's behavior. Sometimes, if one parent is too tough on the teen, the other parent compensates and is too easy. The "easy" parent may "protect" the teen from the disciplinarian by covering up his misbehavior. Communication between spouses becomes strained. They talk less, withhold information about misbehavior from each other, or actually lie to cover up for the child. Obviously, parents in these situations don't act as a united team in disciplining their teenager. Although this problem is relatively common, it can be emotionally damaging for both the parents and the teen. Parents may benefit from talking with a licensed treatment professional such as a psychologist or family counselor who can mediate and help them agree on parenting strategies.

Different Parenting Styles

Differences in parenting styles may also cause conflict. Generally speaking, mothers talk more, reason more, and are more affectionate with their children. Fathers talk less and take action by using punishment or consequences more quickly. Obviously, these roles can sometimes be reversed. Parents need to *understand and respect each other's parenting style*, as well as their teenager's unique response to each and *avoid being judgmental* of each other. You can also take heart from the knowledge that research on ADHD has shown that the mother/child relationship improves with age and involves fewer negative interactions.

Although research on families with teenagers with ADD or ADHD is lacking, it is clear that the parenting approach used with younger children must be modified to be effective with teens. Parents must learn more sophisticated strategies, such as those discussed in Chapters 8, 9, and 10.

Fathers and Mothers: Differing Perspectives

Sometimes parents' perceptions of their child with ADD or ADHD is influenced by traditional parental roles. For example, a mother's self-esteem may be closely related to the house, its appearance, and her children's accomplishments and behavior. As a result, she may be more upset than the father about a dirty room, chores that are not completed, or poor grades. Conversely, many fathers' personal satisfaction is wrapped up in their professional accomplishments at work, so they are bothered less by some things that upset mothers. Of course, these generalizations do not apply in every family.

Misunderstandings between spouses also can arise if the teenager behaves better with one parent than the other. As researchers have found, this is often the case among *children* with ADHD. Researchers have yet to study whether the same holds true for teens. Dr. Russell Barkley and Dr. Sydney Zentall have each speculated why *children behave better for their fathers.* Dr. Barkley explains that these children respond better to immediate consequences, which fathers are more likely to use. And Dr. Zentall points out that children with ADHD do better in novel situations. Typically, children spend more time with their mothers (familiar) and less time with their fathers (novel). In addition, fathers are usually stronger and physically more intimidating. On the other hand, children may feel safer expressing their feelings, including anger, with their mothers.

According to Dr. Barkley, a father sometimes mistakenly assumes that the mother is not an effective parent because their child behaves better with him. As a result, he may believe that the child's problems are not as serious as described by the mother. Some men believe that if only the mother was less permissive and used more discipline, the teenager would behave better. A few fathers may even believe that it is the mother, not the child, who needs help. Or the father may think that the mother is overly sensitive to behavior that he sees as being normal in an "all American" boy.

"My husband didn't really say it, but I know he really felt the problems were my fault too. I felt guilty and a failure as a mother. But with me working, there just were not enough hours in the day."

"When my wife and our son's teachers began talking about his problems at school and mentioned ADHD, I was very skeptical. There was nothing wrong with my son. He acts just like I did when I was in school. Later it became clear to me that I also have ADHD."

Researchers emphasize that *the child's response to his mother is usually not a negative reflection on her parenting skills*. Dr. Barkley noted that, "It is time for fathers and male professionals to realize that children, especially ADHD children, do show differences in the actual manner in which they respond to their mothers compared to their fathers. This does not necessarily implicate flaws in the mother's caretaking abilities or an excessive sensitivity to normal child behavior." Dr. Barkley also suggests that if fathers and mothers switched daily responsibilities, fathers would most likely experience many of the same problems mothers do. Obviously, the parent who places the most demands on the teenager to complete work will be involved in more conflicts.

Maintaining Relationships

Parents may need to *compromise on their parenting strategies—talk less and take action—*when misbehavior occurs. Or as Sam Goldstein, Ph.D., author of several books on attention deficit disorders, is often quoted as saying, "*Act. Don't Yak*." If it is necessary to punish your teenager, *talk and reason later* after a consequence has been imposed. Keep in mind, however, that harsh punishments are not particularly effective and should be avoided.

Other problems may arise within a marriage if parents are afraid to go out and leave their teenager at home for fear of the impulsive misbehavior he may get into. Although the teen doesn't really need a "baby-sitter," his parents may feel that he needs some kind of adult supervision. Unfortunately, if a husband and wife spend little or no time together, they will have trouble nurturing their own relationship. Their limited time together may be spent fighting about their teenager. They begin to think of themselves only in the role of parents, and may lose sight of the common interests and values that originally drew them to one another. Resentment and depression at having no life outside of their family can follow.

Your Own Conflicting Emotions
Confusion, Self-Doubt, and Embarrassment

You may be *bewildered and frustrated,* and at times, *embarrassed* by your teenager's behavior, both before and after the diagnosis of an attention deficit. Your teen doesn't mind at home and may not be doing well in school. He is angry and defiant. If you have raised other children "successfully," it is especially hard to understand why this teenager is different and more difficult to raise. Discipline worked for the other children. Why doesn't it work for this child?

"I'm so glad I had an 'easy child' in addition to my child with ADHD or I would have always doubted my parenting skills."

—a child psychiatrist

Your teenager himself is likely at a loss to explain his own behavior. He is probably confused and bewildered also because he wants to do well in school and at home but can't seem to follow through on his good intentions. As a teen or young adult, he may struggle to find his niche in life.

"I remember a touching conversation at bedtime one evening when Alex was in elementary school. He described his eagerness to turn over a new leaf when the new school year started and made a sincere commitment to make all A's. His ADD hadn't been diagnosed at that time. Without medication, he could not sustain this commitment. He genuinely wanted to do better in school but could not."

"I truly believe that my daughter Elizabeth really wanted to succeed. I also believe there is a 'fear of trying'—that is, 'if I don't try and I fail, then it is because I didn't try, not because I'm not smart enough.' I believe they have great fear of failure."

A teenager's bewildering misbehavior may lead parents to doubt their own feelings about their child's worth. Intuitively, many parents know their teen is basically a "good child" who wants to do well at home and in school. In the midst of a crisis, however, it is difficult for even the most devoted and loving parent to maintain faith in their teenager's goodness. This is true even if they know that the attention deficit is responsible for a lot of their teen's struggles.

To add to your self-doubts, other well-meaning adults voice opinions that "a good spanking will straighten the child out" or "he just needs to be disciplined." Because they may see no other logical explanation prior to diagnosis of the attention deficit, some parents come to believe their teenager is lazy, "doesn't care," and "doesn't try" to complete work or chores. Some classroom teachers make similar comments, reinforcing this idea.

"The school suggested that my son Steven be evaluated by a psychologist. I felt that would be a terrible waste of money. I thought if he would just apply himself, he would do fine in school. His biggest problem appeared to be that he made way too many zeros in class. I was convinced he was just lazy and was not willing to give up any of his play time to devote to his studies.

"Since Steven has been diagnosed as having ADHD, I realize he has much more difficulty concentrating on school work than I had. As a graduate of the U.S. Naval Academy, I thought anyone who tried could discipline himself to accomplish what I had in school. I have learned so much and have come to understand how difficult school is for teenagers with ADHD."

"A lot of parents think their child is lazy. As a psychologist, I believe there is no such thing as a truly lazy child. They may act lazy outwardly because everyone expects them to act that way. Usually, they get into that because something is wrong. The problem just hasn't been diagnosed."

"After we held Scott back in the eighth grade and his maturity level was more appropriate to his grade level, things got better, but there was always the 'laziness' issue. No one could explain his behaviors any other way, but I always knew in I my heart he was not lazy."

Unfortunately, *some teenagers come to believe what adults have said about them*—that "they are lazy" and that's why they don't do well in school. Parents are trapped with their offspring in a complicated web of self-doubt, misinformation, and subtle blame. Hopefully, the research on the neurobiological basis of ADHD that has been produced during the last decade by the National Institute of Mental Health (NIMH) and other researchers gives parents some reassurance that they have not been "bad" parents, nor are their teens "bad" children. (See Chapter 5.)

Avoiding moral judgments about your teen's behavior is one of the toughest challenges parents and teachers face. If teens are told to correct their misbehavior and they still don't do as asked, it is only natural for adults to assume "this teen made a conscious choice to defy and disobey me. It has to be willful disobedience. It looks, smells and tastes like intentional defiance—so it must be." But …it's not! Furthermore, Dr. Barkley reminds us that this is not a knowledge deficit—our teens know what to do most of the time—it's a performance disorder. They don't have the maturity, self-discipline, and forethought to use the right skill at the time it is needed.

Parents are often so overwhelmed, they may feel confused and uncertain about where to turn for help. You may feel embarrassed about having to seek help.

"I will never forget the first time I was sitting in a psychiatrist's waiting room. I felt like the whole world was coming down on me. I was so stressed, I wondered if our life was ever going to be happy. I was so frightened, sitting there not knowing what would happen to me and my child. I felt so sorry for myself. I was so panicky I had literally made myself ill. Even though I am an educated parent, I didn't know what these diagnoses meant. I doubted my parenting skills and found myself asking, what kind of parent have I been? Are people looking at me, wondering what I have done wrong?

"Parents must remember to think of this as a medical problem. Stigma is still such a huge issue for a lot of families, they delay getting treatment. Looking back, I

wasted a lot of energy on fear and worry. My son's psychiatrist is really fantastic and we have a great working relationship!! Now I urge other parents to get help from a psychiatrist. It's not the end of world. It's the beginning of a much improved life."

Resentment and Anger

Strong emotional feelings may surface over common ADD/ADHD problems such as talking back, messy rooms, unfinished chores, and incomplete homework. What's more, in moments of anger or crisis, some parents may even wish their teen had never been born. If their child is involved in one serious problem after another—speeding tickets, car wrecks, drinking, and school suspensions—parents may have fantasies of "running away from home" or trading their teen in for a "newer model" with fewer problems.

When parents are angry, they may have trouble finding any lovable characteristics about their teenager. They may be so stressed out and depressed that they focus only on his negative behavior. Then they must struggle with overpowering feelings of guilt and inadequacy as a parent.

"I wished we didn't have teenagers. I only wanted babies. I really loved the early years. I felt really good about the way the babies were developing. I wish I could say that now. I feel like such a failure as a parent."

Guilt

When ADD or ADHD is diagnosed, especially if the diagnosis is delayed until adolescence, some parents experience overpowering feelings of guilt. They second guess themselves and question why they didn't figure out their teenager's problem earlier. Parents "beat themselves up" and ask themselves a thousand questions.

"Why didn't I find this out sooner? Why did I push so hard? Why did I degrade my child so much? I should have known he was basically a good child. A better parent wouldn't have done the things I've done. I'll regret some of my putdowns until the day I die."

"Every parent must work through the guilt, particularly those of us who are teachers and counselors and should have recognized the ADHD!"

Make peace with yourself and your teenager. You did the best you could with the knowledge and skills you had. Any past negative interactions between you and your teen were not intentional, nor were they done in a malicious manner. You were simply dealing, as best you could, with your teenager's behavior. Parents need to forgive themselves.

"We have made peace with our son. After all, for most parents, it is on-the-job training . . . . No course prepares us for ADHD parenthood. Our own self-esteem as parents also needs to be worked on. We always did the best we could at the time."

Sometimes parents get upset with their teenager even after they learn of the implications of the attention deficit. They yell or overreact, and then feel very guilty. These feelings are normal. It would take a saint to always maintain a calm, reasonable exterior when dealing with these teens. Some parents may benefit from training to cope with typical behaviors related to attention deficits. Parent training and support are discussed at the end of this chapter, in Chapter 8, and in *Teaching Teens with ADD and ADHD*, Chapter 2.

Inadequacy: "I Don't Have the Answers"

Parenting a teenager with ADD or ADHD can be a very humbling experience. Typically, parents are aware early in their child's development that this child is different. In their more positive moments, parents see the teen as a unique and special person. During a crisis, however, parents may view their teenager as a "pain in the neck" and an unwanted burden. Often, they feel inadequate and overwhelmed. Parents are acutely aware that they don't have all the right answers for raising their teen. Furthermore, many of the experts they consult don't have all the answers either. Several parents with professional training in this field echo the difficulties inherent in raising a teenager with an attention deficit:

"As the parent of a child with ADD, I have had the humbling experience of living with, loving, and 'sweating bullets' raising a child whose world inside his head was not like the world I knew growing up. I have struggled to understand my son's thoughts and actions, and provide loving but firm support and direction in a world, particularly a structured academic one, which in large measure did not understand him, his disability, or value the very special person he is."

"When we who are 'professionals' in this field have trouble, it is a double blow. We feel we should have the

answers. If we have difficulty, surely parents without formal training would have even more so."

"Despite all my 'expert skills and knowledge of children,' I have experienced strong feelings of inadequacy as a parent and definitely have not felt like an 'expert' raising my own child. Too many times I have not had the answers; too many times the professionals to whom I have turned for advice have not had the answers. Too many times I have questioned my own judgment in 'disciplining' my son. Too many times I have felt the disapproval of my son's teachers, principals, and some family members, regarding how I chose to discipline and raise my son."

"I fall back on, 'I live with her, know her best, and do the very best I can with the help I receive.'"

Emotional Pain

Although it can be hard to remember during a crisis, parents aren't the only ones who live with the daily stress of an attention deficit. Having ADD or ADHD is no picnic for the teenager either. If the teen had a choice, no doubt he would not choose to have the disorder. It's true that many teenagers with ADD or ADHD eventually cope successfully with the disorder. Others, however, struggle to find a place in school and in the work world where they can succeed and feel good about themselves. Teens with attention deficits frequently have difficulty verbalizing the pain they feel, but the perceptive parent knows it's there.

*"M*om, am I going to feel this way all my life? Sometimes, I feel like I am going to die of a heart attack or anxiety."

*"D*ear God, please don't let me have ADD."

*"W*hy are these books about ADD so cheerful? ADD SUCKS!!!"

When teenagers hurt, their parents hurt too. *No pain can be any greater than the pain a parent feels for their teen in distress.* Parents and teenagers *both* hurt because this world does not understand attention deficit disorder and has not been particularly kind to them.

*"T*here is nothing worse than not being able to help my child, and there is nothing better than seeing her succeed. As parents, we hurt when we see our child suffering and we can't fix it. It's very frustrating and de-

pressing. That's why it is so important for us to latch on to the successes and to reinforce those every time we see them

"I've found myself, at times lately, struggling to find the positive behaviors. While I know they exist, the negative ones that involve peer relationships in particular rip my heart out. I have trouble sometimes sorting out what is normal (whatever that is) teenager separation struggles and the impulsive, naive behavior that comes from the need for immediate gratification. The scary part is she thinks she's making sound judgments. I love the highs but the lows are the pits."

Worry and Concern for the Future

As discussed in Chapter 1, parents worry a lot about the future. "Will our teenager graduate from high school? Will he find a good job and support himself as an adult?" Because parents worry so much, they may focus most of their energies on their teenager's negative behavior. Some days parents feel tired and overwhelmed just thinking about everything they'll have to go through until their teen becomes a responsible adult. Since most teenagers eventually cope successfully with their attention deficit, parents probably waste a lot of time worrying unnecessarily.

Perhaps you worry that if your teenager is having trouble succeeding in high school, how can he possibly manage technical school, college, or a job? Keep in mind that although he is not ready to attend college *today*, that's all right. He doesn't have to cope with those demands right now. When your teen reaches eighteen or nineteen, he will be older and more mature. In addition, you can help him obtain needed supports and accommodations to succeed in high school, technical school, or college. Issues related to succeeding in school and career options are discussed in Chapter 15 and in *Teaching Teens with ADD and ADHD*.

*"O*nce accommodations were made in college, my son did better there than he did in high school."

Sometimes your good intentions (worrying) about helping your teenager succeed in life may backfire. When parents nag, regardless of their good intentions, conflicts with their teen get worse. Your teenager's high school performance won't improve if you nag at him about making good grades for college and preparing for his future job. There will, however, be more animosity between you.

When parents worry too much about tomorrow and the future, they may forget to enjoy their relationship with

their teenager today. Learning to live one day at a time is a difficult lesson for most adults to master. Trying not to worry about problems that may arise next month or next year is easier said than done. You and your teenager should try to maintain a belief in your ability to cope successfully with each problem—when it arises.

Isolation and Loneliness

As if it weren't bad enough to have so many conflicts within the family, *parents often have no place to turn for support or help outside the family*. Parents feel a tremendous sense of isolation because they assume that no other parent could possibly have gone through the same struggles they face on a daily basis. They have trouble confiding their pain and concerns to other adults who do not have teenagers with ADD or ADHD. In truth, other parents can't fully understand how difficult these teens can be to raise. Sometimes other adults come across judgmentally, sending the message: "Your child wouldn't do these things if only you would discipline him properly." Even grandparents and other relatives don't always understand attention deficits, are critical of the teenager's behavior, and judgmental of your parenting skills.

> *"When my father told my new husband that my son just needed discipline, I was devastated. My feelings were so hurt because my own father thought I was not doing a good job as a parent."*

> *"Sometimes at midnight on a Friday, I would be hoping that my husband and daughter would both be coming in soon. I would be exhausted from work and would be waiting for my husband to get home from the airport. When a crisis arose, I would be crying and thinking, I don't want this and I don't need this. I bet all of my sisters and brothers-in-law have never had kids who have done all these 'terrible' things."*

Over the years, parents often have difficulty taking a break from the stresses of raising these children. Frequently, when the children were younger, babysitters were hard to find. After experiencing a hyperactive youngster, the babysitter often was not willing to come back. Even grandparents or other family members were reluctant to keep these youngsters overnight, for a weekend, or a week in the summer. When these problems arose, parents had to seek creative solutions, such as hiring two or more babysitters.

Sometimes even professionals fail to give parents the support they need. Parents can't always find

the services their teenager needs, or don't know where to request help. It is very difficult to find someone who understands the full implications of having an attention deficit and can work effectively with the disorder. When other adults don't understand the disorder or provide support, parenting a teen with ADD or ADHD can be an extremely lonely job.

Special Parenting Issues
Unique Issues for Single Parents

Divorce is a fact of life in the world today and may have a negative impact on many teenagers with attention deficits. The exploding divorce rate (approximately 50 percent) has resulted in roughly 40-50 percent of all teenagers living with a single parent, typically their mother. Adolescence alone is a difficult adjustment period for many young people. If the teen has an attention deficit, plus parents who are divorcing, it is an even more stressful time in his life.

Researchers tell us that divorce is harder on youngsters with attention deficits than it is on their peers. *So single parents face a special challenge raising these teens*. Although experts aren't certain why, children with attention deficits who live with a single parent are more aggressive than those living in a two-parent family. Having the sole responsibility of raising a teenager with this disorder is an exhausting job, especially if no family members live nearby to provide support and help. This doesn't mean single parents cannot be good parents. However, the job of raising these teenagers is usually easier when two parents work together and give each other some relief from the stress. Two-parent families who move a lot and have no relatives nearby also miss the extra support an extended family can provide.

Exhaustion and lack of support are often huge problems for single parents, especially when their teen has undiagnosed coexisting problems:

The turning point for me as single parent came when I was trying to hold down a job and keep my son in school. Those two things together were about the death of me. I was exhausted physically and emotionally but I never got a break from the stress of raising him. At times, I just needed to be away from him, to get my emotions under control—so that I didn't do any harm to him or myself.

"Once I was feeling so overwhelmed, I locked myself in my room and found myself praying, 'Am I the right parent for this child?' I couldn't open the door until I got an answer to that question. I finally realized that I was the only hope for this child. No one else could do it for me. I had to do whatever it took to help him, in a world that just didn't understand him. I prayed to God to give me strength because I was absolutely at the end of my rope.

"Here's my advice for other single parents: Never doubt that you have what it takes to stay the course. In fact you may be the only person who can or will.

"Looking back on this incident now, I can laugh about it. I so badly needed just a little time alone, that's why I put myself in 'timeout' by locking myself in my room. But even then I couldn't get any peace. He was banging on the door and screaming at the top of his lungs, 'Mama, let me in.' It's hard to believe he was only five years old. Much later I came to understand why he was so challenging; he had both ADHD and bipolar."

The isolation and rejection by others are incredibly painful for these families.

When Jeremy was small, I was so isolated. Nobody wanted my child to be around their child. We were both excluded. He was not invited to parties or invited over to play. He was not picked for teams. No one seemed to understand. These were just little things, but it was so hurtful for me as a parent to watch that happen and to feel helpless to do anything about it. Feelings of helplessness and hopelessness will eat you alive. I struggled on a daily basis with feelings of being excluded and nobody wanting us. That was such a lonely and terrible place to be. Occasionally, I even felt like I was on the verge of a mental breakdown.

"There was no place I could go and be accepted except at CHADD meetings. That was the only place I felt I could just be myself and not be judged. They had been there too; they understood."

Single parenting is 'doable' when you have a support system of family, friends, and professionals. But when access to resources is denied because of finances, location, or availability, isolation and depression can become your worst enemy. This was one of my biggest struggles."

PARENT-CHILD RELATIONSHIPS

The mother-son or father-daughter relationship may be extremely intense and difficult during this period for several reasons. First, the teenage male with ADD or ADHD is becoming a man and that means behaving like husbands and fathers do. He may want to be the male head of the household in his father's absence. Consequently, he may feel threatened by men dating his mother. He may be possessive for fear the man may take his mother away from him. After all, he has already "lost" one parent. Competition with the "other man" for his mother's attention is likely to occur. Similar problems may occur if the daughter has an attention deficit and her father is dating or decides to remarry.

In addition, the teenager with ADD or ADHD may act like his father did, or even look like him, and some of the problems the divorced parents had may be played out between the mother and the son. If the divorce is recent, then the teen may struggle with depression and anger as well as with the attention deficit.

PARENT RELATIONSHIP WITH AN EX-SPOUSE

After a divorce, the relationship between parents can be strained and at times outright hostile. It takes a special effort from both parents to make it work positively in the best interests of the child. There are numerous potential areas for conflict: disagreements over diagnosis, medication use, the level of structure, and discipline.

It was always a huge adjustment for Jeremy when he came back home from his Dad's. His dad had a very loose environment and there was absolutely no structure. Jeremy could do anything he wanted to do there. Then he would come back home where we had schedules and routines that he desperately needed. His dad was always 'fun'; I wasn't. I felt like I was always the 'bad guy.' My ex-husband didn't believe anything was wrong with Jeremy, because they acted just alike."

DATING

Single parents who begin dating again after divorce or the death of their spouse face a difficult situation. Frequently, the people they date do not understand the teenager or attention deficit disorder. Consequently, they think that increased discipline will solve all problems. These "significant others" face major conflicts and disappointments if they are rigid or expect the teen to respond to traditional discipline and instantaneously obey their requests.

"People I dated during my ten years as a single parent would try to tell me what to do to 'straighten Lewis out.' They just believed his behavior problems were my fault because I was a single parent."

Conflicts between the parent and "significant other" about child-rearing practices and discipline are almost certain to arise. If a long-term relationship develops, educating the friend about symptoms and treatment of attention deficit disorder is important. Here are some ideas that may help:

- Provide some easy reading materials about teenagers with ADD and ADHD. Start out with something brief and easy to read. Relevant sections of this book may be helpful. Excellent CHADD Fact sheets are available from www.chadd.org.
- In addition, *A Bird's-Eye View* provides an easy, but scientifically accurate "Cliff Notes" read for adults and teens.
- Attending CHADD or other support group meetings together should be extremely helpful.
- Try making a special effort to include the teen in some activities with the two adults.
- Scheduling special alone time with just the parent and teenager is also helpful.
- Avoid saying anything negative about the absent parent. To maintain strong self-esteem and cope successfully with his parents' divorce, the teen needs a strong relationship with both parents.

These steps should make the teenager less anxious and more accepting of the new person in his parent's life. Remember, it often takes a very special and understanding person to cope with a teenager with an attention deficit, especially when the teen is not his own.

The Complexities of Second Marriages

Second marriages present complex issues for all families. When a child has ADD or ADHD, the pressures on stepfamilies are compounded. You should be aware of the factors that make step-parenting difficult for all families, as well as the unique ways an attention deficit can affect stepfamilies.

First, being a member of two families can become very *complicated*. The teenager may have as many as four "parents," plus extra grandparents with whom he must interact. Parents may or may not agree on child management strategies. Each family's ability to maintain consistent family rules and consequences for misbehavior varies. This could be a nightmare for the teen with an attention deficit who needs structure, routine, and consistency. Remembering which rules apply in which family will be extremely difficult.

Second, making decisions about *living arrangements* may be difficult. Since most children of divorce live with their mothers, the typical stepfamily consists of the teenager, his mother, a stepfather, and sometimes other siblings or stepchildren. Frequently, the teen spends alternating weekends with the absent parent, most often, the natural father. Usually, the "weekend parent" spends less time with the teenager, has fewer conflicts, and may be tempted to just have fun with the teen. He or she doesn't want to be the "bad guy" and may ignore the need for routine, structure, and consequences. However, if parents have joint custody, the teenager may live alternating weeks with each parent. In this situation, it is very difficult for the teen to make transitions such as moving back and forth between families.

On a more practical level, can you imagine what havoc a teenager's attention deficit related to disorganization and forgetfulness can cause when living arrangements are divided? Now he has two homes where he can lose or leave things. If he needs the math book, homework, or computer, it is probably going to be at the wrong house.

Third, the teenager's natural *loyalty* to biological parents may result in strong conflicting feelings. The teen may think subconsciously, "If I like and have fun with my stepfather (stepmother) that means I am not loyal to my real father (mother)." The teenager may fear that the stepparent is trying to replace his natural parent. Stepparents have to carve out their own special relationship with the teen and make it clear that they are not trying to take the absent parent's place.

Fourth, the teenager and the parent with whom he lives are sometimes extremely close and develop a very special relationship. When a stepparent enters the relationship, their time must now be shared among three people, not just two. Initially, feelings of *displacement* are common among teens. Sometimes, the son (daughter) who has been the man (woman) of the house is resentful, jealous, or frightened that he or she is being replaced by the new spouse. These feelings increase the potential for family conflict.

Fifth, the stepparent's *role in parenting* is seldom clearly defined. Teenagers are unlikely to accept parenting or discipline from a stepparent until trust and a relationship have been established. According to research, being a stepmother is the more difficult role—perhaps, in part, because of our society's negative attitude toward "the wicked stepmother." Often the teen feels the stepparent hasn't earned the right to intervene or discipline until their relationship is solidified. The teenager may say, "You're not my father (mother). You can't tell me what to do." As a result, the biological parent may make decisions about most of the disciplinary actions. Unfortunately, developing trust between stepparent and teen takes time, perhaps years. You can't force or rush it. The biological parent must make a special effort to involve the new stepparent in decision making and to present a united front to the teenager. To be honest, however, sometimes parents have a spoken or unspoken agreement: you discipline your child and I'll discipline mine. That strategy works well in some families. For the best results in these situations, discuss differences in parenting strategies privately and in a calm manner.

Sixth, stepparents may consciously or subconsciously attribute a teenager's misbehavior to poor parenting. This spoken or unspoken *criticism or blame* results in the biological parent feeling hurt and defensive. The biological parent then finds herself (himself) frequently trapped between the stepparent and the child. This creates tremendous stress. Most natural parents want to build a cohesive parenting team with the new stepparent. However, this is difficult, especially if the stepparent does not fully understand attention deficits.

Seventh, most biological parents are *naturally protective* of their teenager, particularly with their new spouse or people they are dating. Feeling guilty about the divorce and their child's "loss" of a parent contributes to this protectiveness. Plus, parents are even more protective when a child has a disability. Because the potential exists for so many negative interactions, a wise natural parent often works very hard to increase positive interactions with her teen. So at times mothers may avoid conflict by ignoring less important issues. Although these parents do set limits, they may ignore more misbehavior than the average parent. Other adults may not understand this.

Eighth, *natural parents are often extremely embarrassed by their teenager's misbehavior.* Even though they know better, they may sometimes feel as if their teen's misbehavior is a negative reflection on their parenting skills. They may reluctantly withhold information from the stepparent simply to avoid conflict.

"Although I know I shouldn't withhold things from my husband about my son, I have done it before. It is so embarrassing to tell him some things that my son has done. Occasionally, when I don't tell my husband something, I feel very guilty. But if I told him everything, a huge fight would erupt between us. Sometimes, I deal with the problem myself and impose a consequence when necessary."

Finally, many of the typical problems associated with stepparenting are magnified because of the teenager's symptoms of ADD or ADHD. The "invisible" nature of attention deficit disorders makes it difficult for most stepparents to understand its profound impact on the teen's day-to-day behavior. Some stepparents perceive the teenager as lazy and his misbehavior as malicious and intentional, further adding to family conflict.

STEPPARENTS MAY BE UNPREPARED

New stepparents usually feel overwhelmed when they inherit a son or daughter with ADD or ADHD. Some stepfathers or stepmothers who are disciplinarians believe incorrectly that their strong influence and discipline will solve the teenager's problems. This attitude is more likely if the new parent has other children who don't have an attention deficit and are easier to raise, or if they have no children at all. Yet, unless the teen is receiving proper treatment and the stepparent is educated about attention deficits, problems are likely to become worse, not better.

"As a young treatment professional I gave other parents 'great advice.' I had all the right answers until I had a child with ADD inattentive. Then when I became a stepmother, I also had to learn how to deal with the unique characteristics of a stepson with ADHD."

Occasionally, both parents bring children with attention deficits to a marriage. These parents may be more understanding of the behavior associated with ADD and ADHD. However, parenting a second child—a stepchild with an attention deficit—is still very difficult.

"I know I was more tolerant of my own child's ADD inattentive behaviors than I was of my stepson's ADHD. I made a special effort to treat them equally, but it was terribly difficult. I feel guilty about it, but

unfortunately, I think it's a pretty common parental reaction. The age difference was also a factor. His son was older and I felt he should have been more responsible. Later, when my son reached the same age and did the same things, I realized I should have been more understanding of my stepson."

MARITAL BLISS? MAYBE NOT!

Conflicts over the teenager's behavior may put a serious strain on the marriage. Ideally, the couple should not wait until the relationship deteriorates, but seek counseling early from a treatment professional who specializes in working with families with attention deficit disorder.

Just looking at data about all remarriages is scary. About 50 percent of remarriages end in divorce. The primary reason these marriages fail is due to conflict over children. Stepfamilies coping with ADD or ADHD are clearly in double jeopardy, since conflict over these children is inevitable. The remarriages that have the greatest risk of failing are those in which the father has children and marries someone who does not have children. However, the family unit is strengthened and more closely bonded when the new parents have another child. The arrival of a baby strengthens the relationship between the siblings.

The simple passage of time plays a major role in cementing relationships in stepfamilies. Some research has shown that "blended families," as second marriages involving children are sometimes called, take approximately five years to bond and feel like true family members.

"We have been married eight years now. The early years in our marriage were very difficult. Our teenage sons, both of whom have ADHD, are now young adults. My husband and I have fewer conflicts with them and are closer not only to our own sons but stepsons too."

Do You Have ADD or ADHD? Should You Seek Help?

As Chapter 1 discusses, many parents of children with attention deficits have the condition themselves. Parents with this disorder may be disorganized and have difficulty being consistent in their approach to child management. If you suspect you may have an attention deficit, pursuing a diagnosis can be helpful. *Medication helps most parents be more organized and consistent, handle their frustration better, and cope*

more effectively with their teenager and his crises. See Chapters 5 and 6 for further discussion on medication.

In some respects, there are actually some advantages to being a parent with ADD or ADHD. Parents who have successfully coped with the disorder may view attention deficits more positively. "My son acts just like I did—I did okay and so will he." They can also empathize with the challenges their child faces. Sharing their personal experiences may be beneficial to their teenager. The teen may be more inclined to listen to what his parent says, because he knows his parent has dealt with similar problems. These parents also understand their teenager's pain, as one parent explains:

"I've been through so much pain in my life and I can see how so much of it is directly attributable to my ADHD. This is a mixed blessing—on one hand, I see how handicapping ADHD is. But on the other hand, I realize that those of us who are touched with this extra dimension to our souls are the dreamers and poets and gentle spirits—way down deep. If we didn't have the ability to tune out and to forget and to try again, I truly believe we would lose our minds.

"Since my ADHD was diagnosed and I began taking Ritalin, my life has been so much better. After I got home from buying groceries one night at 10:30, I started to clean up my kitchen so I could put the groceries away. I was so thrilled that I could stay organized to start and finish this process. I even washed the kitchen trashcan. I was standing there KNOWING how to clean the can. I began to cry. I wonder if anyone could possibly understand that my life is so unproductive and so disorganized that in all the fifteen years I've been a wife, I have never washed my kitchen trashcan? I have bought new ones when the old one was too gross to use. In the past, washing out the can was never even a THOUGHT."

"We can punish ourselves better than anyone else could ever dream of. The guilt, self-doubt, recrimination . . . the perfection we hold up as our role model. It's no wonder we don't try sometimes."

On the other hand, some parents with ADHD may be impulsively impatient, and criticize and punish their child for the very same things they did as children. Obviously parent training can help you deal more effectively with your child. Strategies in the next section should give you additional ideas of things you can do to help your child be successful.

Take Charge: Change the Things You Can

The remainder of this chapter offers guidance on the specific steps that parents can take to help their teenager be successful. Although these steps may simply seem like good common sense, in reality they are a key part of the treatment plan that *parents can take charge of and implement*! These steps represent non-traditional therapeutic strategies—a critical part of the treatment plan. First let's take a second look at our views about ADD and ADHD.

Is the Glass Half Empty, or Half Full?

"*It has been my experience as a parent, school teacher, school psychologist, and counselor that most teenagers are good, and our job as parents and teachers is to 'catch them being good' and praise them for what they do correctly. I prefer to view the glass as being half full, rather than half empty. I praise my teenage son for remembering to mow the yard even though he ran over a portion of my flower bed.*"

A risk inherent in writing a book about attention deficit disorders is that the teenager's negative characteristics are discussed in such detail that they inadvertently overshadow his strengths. The main reasons problem behaviors are discussed in detail is to help parents and professionals recognize the symptoms of ADD, ADHD, and coexisting problems, to begin treatment as early as possible, and to help parents cope with their own feelings of doubt and anger. So, it is important for parents to learn to view the glass as half full and not allow themselves to hyperfocus only on the negative things about their teen.

Another key strategy that is discussed in Chapter 5 is to educate yourself and your teen about ADD and ADHD. This makes it easier for parents to recognize "ADHD behaviors," have realistic expectations for their child, and a sense of self-confidence that they can cope with this disorder as a family. "ADHD education" also will help the teen understand himself better and why certain aspects of life are more difficult.

Promoting Resilience

One of the new strategies championed by Robert Brooks, Ph.D., Sam Goldstein, Ph.D., and Mark Katz, Ph.D., is to teach parents how to *promote resilience in their children*. The authors believe that resilient children are more likely to cope successfully with the challenges of having a condition like an attention deficit. Dr. Brooks and Dr. Goldstein explain this concept more fully and give specific intervention strategies in their book, *Raising Resilient Children*.

Simply put, resilience means that a child has the "capacity to cope and feel competent." Drs. Brooks and Goldstein explain that being resilient also means that the child has the ability to "deal more effectively with stress and pressure, to cope with everyday challenges, to bounce back from disappointments, adversity, and trauma, to develop clear and realistic goals, to solve problems, to relate comfortably with others, and to treat oneself and others with respect." The authors' description of the mindset of parents who help foster resilience should be helpful. Here is a brief summary of the major concepts. In addition, it will be well worth your while to read more about resilience.

1. *Be empathic*; put yourself in your teenager's shoes and try to see the world through his eyes.
2. *Communicate effectively*; listen actively and avoid power struggles.
3. *Change negative scripts*; if you wish to improve communication with your child, you must take the lead and first *change your words—choose positive phrases*.
4. *Love your children in ways that help them feel special and appreciated*; love them unconditionally. One person who believes in the child ultimately may be the deciding factor in how well the teen copes.
5. *Accept your teenager for who he is, including his strengths and challenges*; help him set realistic expectations and goals.

6. *Help your adolescent experience success*; build on his skills and talent, or "islands of competence."

7. *Help the teen recognize that mistakes are experiences that help us learn;* promote a positive attitude about mistakes—mistakes are not bad; try to learn from them.

8. *Develop a sense of responsibility, compassion, and a social conscience;* offer opportunities to contribute or help others.

9. *Teach your adolescent to solve problems and make decisions;* don't always tell him what to do, rather discuss possible solutions he may choose.

10. *Discipline in a way that promotes self-discipline and self-worth;* don't just punish the teen, use this as an opportunity to teach new skills.

"I like Bob Brooks's focus on finding each child's islands of competence. If parents aren't careful, negative thinking can be the focal point for your child with ADHD. I believe we have to be coaches, cheerleaders, talent scouts, and encouragers. We must remember to stay focused on their positive traits. We must appreciate them for who they are and help them understand more about themselves than just the negative things they hear. We should acknowledge that school is really tough—but it's just one place. Encourage them to find another place where they can be successful."

Dr. Mark Katz also provides helpful information on resilience in his excellent book *On Playing a Poor Hand Well*. His books shares several research studies, but one stands out as giving parents hope for the future: Emmy Werner's Kauai Longitudinal Study. Children who had faced serious adversity, including learning disabilities, had fared poorly in school, had not done well as young adults, but somehow managed to turn their lives around in their early thirties. Based upon their behavior at age 18, parents and other concerned adults would not have had reason to believe they would cope successfully. So the message for parents is, "Do not give up hope and remember to keep a lifespan perspective."

Dr. Katz also shares research on protective influences—characteristics that increase the likelihood of a positive outcome—identified in several studies. The young people in Werner's study who were successful later on in life shared these characteristics:

- had a pleasant disposition and related well to parents and teachers,
- set realistic educational and job goals,
- had responsibility for something that was helpful to others,
- had faith in themselves that they could cope,
- had an important adult who believed in them,
- had a second chance opportunity such as military, community college, a religious experience, marriage, or birth of a child.

Other researchers have noted these additional traits in resilient children:

- had a desire to succeed,
- wanted control over their lives,
- accepted and reframed their disability,
- were persistent,
- had a good fit between their skills and job,
- had learned creative ways to solve problems.

So, the bottom line for parents is to find ways to promote these skills and attitudes in your child. In the remainder of this section, advice will be given on ways to promote resilience, starting with taking a second look at your teenager and finding his strengths. One of the keys to coping emotionally with ADD and ADHD, however, is not to focus solely on all your teen's irritating and demanding behaviors. Instead, *you must look beyond the negative behaviors and latch onto his strengths.* You must ask one critical question: "Are we going to dwell on our teenager's deficits, or build on his strengths?" Below are a few specific steps that I have found helpful in coping successfully and in building a teen's resilience.

Discover Your Teenager's Strengths

Teenagers with ADD and ADHD have many strengths. Often, they are delightfully entertaining and charming. Most teens with hyperactivity have boundless energy. Some of these teenagers also seem to be especially creative. These teens often have a unique way of analyzing problems and coming up with creative solutions. Many have an amazing zest for living and unflinchingly tackle new and exciting adventures. When properly channeled, a teen's daring and risk-taking behavior can be a real asset. Someone must be willing to tackle daring careers such as fighter pilot, firefighter, or astronaut.

"Even though our son did not do well in school, his skills with electronics are amazing at times. He wired his car so each car door pops open when he mashes a button on his key ring. His car is modified so that there

are no external door handles. It is somewhat comical when he takes his car in to have the oil changed. The mechanics can't figure out how to open his car door."

Lucky us, parenting a teenager with an attention deficit is *never, ever boring!* Something exciting is always going on with these teens, whether it is some new project they have undertaken or a problem they have experienced. Frequently, they will be the first to volunteer to try new things. As teens and young adults they have ventured off to Europe alone and climbed the Himalayas.

The teenagers with ADD and ADHD I know have diverse interests, have excelled in academic and nonacademic areas, and include two state championship wrestlers, an excellent bow hunter, a competitive swimmer, a college football player, a college wrestler, a stand-up comedian, a professional musician, a debate team member, an artist, a horse woman, a computer and electronics whiz, a scuba diver, life guards, a skateboarder, car mechanics, and perhaps a budding poet....

There's this thing called ADD.
That's not a drug or something growing in a tree,
But an attention deficit that's been affecting me.

Before I couldn't sit and learn
Because my thoughts were all in a churn.

Even if the teacher screamed right in my ear,
My ADD wouldn't let me hear.

My grades are up and my spirits are high
'Cause I gave Ritalin just one single try.

Now I've found a part of life I'd never seen,
So I've started all over and wiped my slate clean.

—Written by Lee, age 16, a state champion wrestler

Successful adults with attention deficits who survived their difficult childhood are found in all walks of life. Some of these adults did well in school, but others were either mediocre or very poor students.

One thing that may help you view your teenager in a more positive light is to identify his strengths and help him develop them as fully as possible. Generally, parents who help their teen build on his strengths *experience more joy parenting their child*. The strengths of one teenager with ADD have been identified and are listed in Table 4-1 on the next page. Please take the time to fill out the blank form that is provided in

Chapter 16 to help you identify your teen's strengths. As you complete this form, refer to the list of challenging ADD/ADHD behaviors that have been reframed positively in the next section.

Reframe Your Perceptions of ADD and ADHD

Dr. Sydney Zentall has a refreshingly creative way of looking at youngsters with attention deficit disorder. She suggests that we *reframe* the way we look at their characteristics. For example, she explains that bossiness may be viewed as "leadership." Qualities that are not endearing in school settings may well be highly valued in the adult business world. Members of the Gwinnett County, Georgia CHADD chapter added to Dr. Zentall's list of positive aspects of the teenager with attention deficits:

- bossiness—"leadership" (albeit carried too far)
- hyperactivity—"energetic," "unlimited energy," able to conduct ten projects at the same time, work long hours.
- strong-willed—"tenacious"
- stubborn—"persistent"
- poor handwriting—"maybe they'll be a doctor one day"
- day dreamers—"creative, innovative, imaginative"
- question authority—"independent, free thinker, make own decisions"
- daring—"risk-taker, willing to try new things"
- argumentative—"persuasive, maybe attorney material"
- laziness—"laid back; Type B personalities live longer"
- instigator—"initiator/innovative"
- manipulative—"delegates; gets others to do the job"
- failure to follow directions verbatim—"creative thinking"

Some parents and teachers have learned to see "ADHD behaviors" in a more positive light and are able to be more positive with these teens.

"I often use the following personal story in my training sessions to show how teachers have different perceptions of the same characteristics. While one teacher may describe Katie as talking too much, too loud, or

Table 4-1　Identify the Teenager's Strengths

Individualized Treatment Planning: "Do Whatever It Takes"

Name: Shawn _____ **Age:** 17 ___ **Grade:** 12 _____

STRENGTHS ....

Home/Community

- Intelligent
- Creative
- Caring/kind hearted/helps others
- Fast swimmer/lifeguard
- Daring/will try most anything once
- Easy going nature
- Good with electronics/wiring stereos
- Complies with requests
- Pursues interesting hobbies: scuba diving, flying an airplane, photography
- Sensitive
- Willing to take medication
- Trying to understand ADD and himself better
- Tall and handsome
- Good caring for young children

School

- Intelligent
- Creative
- Good with computers
- Good with hands; did well in shop class
- Complies with most rules/not a discipline problem
- Allows parent to monitor and prompt when assignments are due
- Writes great creative stories
- Kept class snake during summer/helpful
- Great vocabulary
- Has ability to get algebra problems correct even when he doesn't do the problem right

too fast, most other teachers say positive things. One teacher wrote on a report card, 'Katie is a pleasure to have in my class. She is always willing to participate in class discussions.' Another teacher wrote that she loved her enthusiasm and creativity.

"Katie's symptoms of ADHD presented much later than her older sister's did. My husband and I thought we were out of the woods with her and that she didn't have ADHD. She had good reports back from daycare. Her teachers used positive words like curious, bright, very good language skills, kind to others, independent, and willing to try new things to describe her.

"I remember vividly her kindergarten year; we were all so excited about it. During the first grading period we had heard nothing negative from the teacher, not one phone call or note. We assumed everything was fine and showed up for our first parent-teacher conference, full of optimism. The teacher met us halfway to the door and her first words to us were, 'We have got to find a way to shut Katie up.' Then the teacher spent the next 20 minutes talking about how to 'shut her up.' My husband was so stunned he couldn't say anything. I too was shocked but managed to ask several questions; for example, what was Katie talking about? It turns out that Katie was on task; she was so excited about being at school that she wanted to

contribute to the discussion. The teacher's focus certainly got more positive after talking with my husband and me."

Some teenagers have clearly defined strengths that do not need to be reframed.

"*Teenagers, especially those with ADD inattentive, tend to be sensitive. They are sensitive to the needs of others, show personal warmth and affection, are kindhearted, and show remorse when they have done something wrong. However, being sensitive can also be a double-edged sword. When someone is unkind or critical, the sensitive teen also feels the pain very intensely.*"

Another issue to keep in mind is that the *desirability of certain behaviors changes over time.* Behaviors parents and teachers worry about now may not present problems in adulthood. For example, hyperactivity (high energy) and failure to follow teacher instructions verbatim (creative thinking) are not particularly valued at school, but may be highly valued in the work force. Daring behavior is required for some careers. Compliance is valued in students, but adults who are too compliant may be completely dominated by a spouse, coworkers, or supervisor.

"I heard Dr. Zentall make a wonderful presentation at a national CHADD conference. During her talk, she told us that she has ADHD. I loved her comments: 'I like my ADD friends best! They're more fun. They talk about more interesting things and go more interesting places. I have four offices and ten projects going at one time.' Talk about reframing ADHD. I came away feeling a little jealous that I didn't have it."

Believe in Your Teenager and Yourself

Short of purchasing a bulletproof vest, parents must develop certain armaments for coping with their teenager during crises. *Believing that you and your teen will cope with whatever crisis arises is probably the most important armament you will need.* Parents must believe in the "goodness" of their teenager. More importantly, parents and professionals should work together to help the teen believe in himself again. Conveying positive messages to your teenager about his worth as your son or daughter and as a human being is extremely important! Often your teen's self-esteem is battered because of repeated failures in school and frequent negative interactions with parents and teachers.

As you convey your expectations to your teenager, it is important to be aware of a concept known as a *"self-fulfilling prophesy."* That is, if you convey by word and action that you expect your teen to be responsible, he will usually rise to your expectations. A positive self-fulfilling prophesy is a powerful influence: if parents believe their teenager is "good" and will succeed in life, then he probably will. Unfortunately, the opposite is also true. If a parent thinks his teen is "bad" and treats him as though he is "bad," he will probably have more trouble succeeding.

Somehow, it is easier to believe in the "goodness" of your child or teenager if you know he exhibits inappropriate behavior because of a medical problem—ADD or ADHD. Your teen may feel better about himself too when he realizes that he has an attention deficit and isn't just being "lazy or bad." Of course, he must also learn that he still has to work hard to compensate for problems caused by this condition.

Do you need an attitude adjustment? One of the toughest challenges that parents face is recognizing and dealing with their own negative thoughts about their teenager. We often say all the right words but our body language, our raised eyebrows, sighs, and subtle putdowns give away our true feelings. Sometimes our teen's self-esteem is battered by messages we parents have unknowingly and unintentionally sent—for example,

embarrassment or anger. Praise and your belief in the goodness of the teen must be genuine, or the teen will intuitively know that you are not speaking the truth.

If you have an honest heart-to-heart talk with yourself and you know you are angry and still terribly frightened regarding your teen's future, then you need to spend some time talking with a professional to deal with your angry feelings, embarrassment, disappointment, and fear. By talking these issues through with your doctor or a therapist and getting them off your chest, you should be more effective as a parent. In truth, you may also be depressed from the daily ups and downs of parenting one of these teens. As explained earlier and in Chapters 5 and 7, treatment of depression is critical.

Acknowledge That Attention Disorders Are Tough to Handle

As mentioned earlier, having an attention deficit is no picnic for the teenagers who have the condition. It amazes me that we fail to acknowledge this fact to our teens. In doing so, we inadvertently deny the pain and challenges they face living with this disorder.

Dr. Katz explains that children have a choice of how they view adversity or challenging conditions such as an attention deficit. Katz goes on to explain that children can learn to stop blaming themselves for stressful events that are beyond their control and come up with new ways of solving problems.

Write a Healing Story. Two family therapists, Michael White and David Epson, have developed a strategy that may help your teen feel less self-blame. They suggest helping people learn to *"tell their personal stories in ways that heal."* This retelling of their personal story should be done with words that "legitimize, validate, and empower" the teenager. These words should also highlight the teen's courage and free him from immobilizing feelings of self-blame. These new words give a teen a better perspective on the challenges of having ADD or ADHD—he can step back and perhaps look at it more objectively from a distance. These healing stories may be told verbally or in writing.

An advantage of giving your teenager something in writing is that if he can find it, he can reread it at later times when he may be feeling down about his attention deficit. So think seriously about *writing your son or daughter one of these healing stories* and giving it to him sometime soon! It could have a profound impact. The next few paragraphs may give you some ideas about what to write.

As an example of this strategy, Dr. Katz wrote a touching response to a sixteen- year-old who was struggling in school—to this student the school day "lasts 20 hours." The teen was also dreading what graduation will bring. A copy of Dr. Katz's full response is available in his book, but I'd like to quote two paragraphs here:

"*While you may not realize it, you represent a group of individuals who possess a type of resilience that has become the focus of many professional people around the country. These people feel that individuals like yourself have many lessons to teach. Bear in mind that your friends have no real idea what school has felt like for you. You've been tested in ways that your friends haven't. You've stood strong, despite what likely have been some very stressful times. Individuals like yourself often become stronger as a result of this. It's like you develop "psychological antibodies." Future stresses down the road somehow don't seem so big. This isn't always the case for kids who sailed through school smoothly. Some of these kids have escaped having to contend with significant obstacles in their path. These obstacles will likely appear someday, in one form or another. They too will be tested, like you were. I hope they can stand up as well…*

"*In closing, let me just say, Kurt, that I'm typing this letter a few hours after returning from the movies, where I just saw a movie that was directed by Steven Spielberg. The story told to me about Spielberg was that he didn't do so great in school. His family, however, encouraged his creative and expressive talents. Reportedly at a relatively early age he was already experimenting with a home movie camera. Talent meeting opportunity. Keep in mind that Spielberg's talents, and those of many other well-known artists, are talents that usually aren't highlighted and nourished in most schools, as we've designed them. Nonetheless, they are extraordinarily talented individuals. In the future, Kurt, when our society becomes more aware of the diversity of human talents, and the need to nourish all of them, there'll be more options for students like yourself. For now, you're going to have to be a bit of a trailblazer. Keep in mind that you're in some great company.*"

Keep Grades in Perspective

According to Robert Brooks, Ph.D., author of *The Self-Esteem Teacher*, research has shown that *good grades are not a predictor of success in life*. Many people, some famous and some not, did not do well in school. Thomas Edison was constantly in trouble as a child

and was removed from school. Winston Churchill was hyperactive. Albert Einstein was kicked out of school because he failed some classes.

Cher and Bruce Jenner have learning disabilities and did not do well in school. Sylvester Stallone was a very poor student. His father and teachers called him dumb. His father's favorite remark to Stallone was that his "brain was dormant." Although Stallone's creative abilities were not appreciated, he went on to write and star in *Rambo* and *Rocky*. Although some may question the artistic content of his movies, their financial success cannot be denied. A former Florida governor tells of being asked to leave two kindergartens because of his active, aggressive behavior.

For most parents, *the ultimate goal is for their teenager to become a happy adult and a contributing member of society*. Successes help build a teen's self-esteem and his ability to cope with life. For many teenagers with attention deficits, school is difficult and successes are few and far between. Areas outside of school may offer greater opportunities for success. Early on, the families of teens with attention deficits should concentrate on helping their youngster succeed in nonacademic activities to compensate for any negative experiences at school.

One of the toughest challenges for parents, especially those for whom college graduation is an expected family accomplishment, is letting go of your own goals for your teen, such as getting into Harvard or becoming a lawyer. Often these teens listen to their own distinctive drummer and may select nontraditional careers that do not require a highly scheduled 9 to 5 job or a college degree. Ultimately, the parent's job is to learn to value their teenager's decisions and help him feel good about his career choice.

Maintain a Strong Sense of Humor

A good sense of humor is critical for parents of teenagers with ADD or ADHD. Crises will happen and parents must learn to roll with the punches. Remember, humor is healing! Parents must learn to laugh at themselves and their teen's crises. Typically, parents can allow their sense of humor to surface once the crisis is safely over. Remember, however, to laugh *with* your teenager, rather than *at* him. There is a difference, and your teen will sense if you are laughing at him.

"How is your son doing? Well, he hasn't gotten any speeding tickets this week."

"My son is on the six-year plan for college."

"One night I was called to come pick up my daughter at the police station because she and a friend had attempted to 'borrow' a 200-pound concrete deer and put it in the back of their Honda. They were going to put it in another friend's yard as a joke. The policeman could hardly keep from laughing when he turned them over to me. We had to go to court. We can laugh about some of these things now, but they certainly weren't funny at the time."

Weather Each Crisis As It Comes

Teenagers with ADD or ADHD often do well for a while and then exhibit problem behaviors at home or at school. Crises may erupt daily, weekly, or monthly, or, if parents are lucky, only once every six months or so. One important lesson for parents to learn is *not to overreact when their child experiences one of the typical bumps associated with being a teenager who has an attention deficit.* In moments of crisis, the teenager's problems may appear exaggerated and overblown. Behaviors such as sneaking out of the house at night, speeding, or having a party while parents are out of town are definitely inappropriate, but they do not mean the teenager will be a delinquent. Address the problem, teach a new skill, impose a consequence if appropriate, and nudge the teenager back on the "straight and narrow path." Then be prepared for the next "mini-crisis." *Learning to live one day at a time is critical!*

Be Grateful for Small Favors

Although most parents of teenagers with an attention deficit may never be able to brag about their child's Merit Scholarship or straight A's, there are other things to brag about. As explained earlier, teenagers with ADD or ADHD often excel in many areas. Regardless of their strengths, *you should take great pride in each of your teenager's accomplishments.* You can show your pride in a variety of ways: framing pictures of athletic teams, dance recitals, or debate competition and prominently displaying them; submitting photos to the local hometown newspaper; enlarging a photograph of him in some activity to poster size; sending pictures to grandparents; bragging to friends in front of the teenager; displaying ribbons and awards or things the teenager made; or videotaping his activities. With each accomplishment, your child takes another step toward overcoming a disability and becoming a successful adult.

"The thing I have seen in my daughter from age 18 to 24 was that she assumed more and more responsibility for her own actions. While she has gone to India, Thailand, Nepal, and the Himalayas all by herself, she has really had to search her own soul to be independent. Although we have paid her college tuition and room and board, she has been financially responsible for her other expenses since she was 18."

Frequently, parents of teenagers with attention deficits learn to be thankful for small favors: their teenager didn't fail any classes this grading period, didn't receive a speeding ticket this week, or even though he received a speeding ticket, it was not a ticket for Driving Under the Influence of alcohol or drugs (DUI).

Keep Attention Deficit Disorder in Perspective

Sometimes parents have to put things in perspective by stepping back and asking themselves, "What is the worst thing that could happen to my teenager?" The ultimate answer is death. Your teenager could die in a car wreck, accident, or suicide attempt. The next worst thing might include involvement in violent criminal acts such as murder, armed robbery, or rape. If your teenager truly is in danger of one of these calamities, you should, of course, take immediate action. (See Chapters 5 and 8.) But if the current crisis is something along the lines of failing to complete homework, talking back, or staying out too late, you may need to reevaluate your reaction. By identifying truly "bad behaviors or horrible events," you may be able to place minor crises in perspective. *Remember also, a teenager's life includes a much larger picture than just twelve years in school.*

"A twelve-year-old student at my son's school hanged himself because he received a mid-term warning about his bad grades at school. Apparently, he was really upset, especially because his mother was a teacher."

Many youngsters with attention deficits have rough teenage years. Parents have to develop a tough hide and learn not to be surprised by anything. They have to respond by thinking, "Oh well, my teenager is having a crisis, but in the long run, he is going to grow up to be okay." The major issue here is to deal with each problem as it arises and continue to love and support your teenager. You must believe that you and your teenager will handle each crisis as it comes up, and that ultimately, there will be a happy ending.

"The belief that we will handle whatever crisis arises is what gets me through and keeps me going."

Two additional books may help parents keep things in perspective by putting behaviors into categories ranging from minor to more serious: Dr. Thomas Phelan's *Surviving Your Adolescents* and Dr. Ross Green's *The Explosive Child*. Their strategies are discussed in more detail in Chapter 8. Depending upon the severity of misbehavior, the parent may respond by doing nothing, consulting, negotiating, or taking charge.

Beginning to See the Rewards

Some parents with whom I've spoken recently have teenagers who are now in their early twenties. Life during their twenties and early thirties continues to get even better for our teens due to maturation of their executive skills, development of compensatory skills, and schools or jobs that are more "ADD friendly" than high school could ever be. Comments from parents are extremely encouraging.

"Steven's first year in college was extremely difficult. He dropped out, worked for a year, and then went back to school. His ADHD was diagnosed when he was twenty and he started taking Ritalin when he went back to college. He made two A's, a B, and a C his last semester in college. He even qualified for the 'good student' discount for our car insurance. He graduated last year and has a wonderful job. He has so much energy he sometimes works twelve-hour days. We are so proud of him."

"Teenagers with ADHD can and usually do grow up and do okay. My daughters, who are in their early twenties, have made me feel like it was all worthwhile by saying things like, 'How did you do it, Mom?' and 'Thanks for hanging in there, Mom,' or 'For my next adventure, I think I'll try Australia.'"

Conclusion: Finding the Joy

The road to successfully raising your teenager with ADD or ADHD will probably be bumpy! You should expect crises on a fairly regular basis. In truth, you may shed buckets of tears during the teenage years. So I reiterate: *this may be the toughest job you have ever had!* Try not to become discouraged, however; cope with each crisis, one day at a time, as it arises. The next chapter will tell you specific things you can do to increase the likelihood that your teenager will cope successfully with his attention deficit.

Remember also that you don't have to do it all alone. Other parents and professionals experienced in working with teenagers with attention deficits can offer you invaluable support and advice. Although coping may be difficult at first, eventually you will become an expert "crisis counselor" through on-the-job training.

It does, indeed, take a village to raise a child, especially one with an attention deficit disorder. So, one thing I would like to encourage all parents to do is to nurture not only your child but also other teenagers with attention deficit. Consider embracing the *"pay it forward"* philosophy portrayed in a recent movie. As you learn about ADHD, share that information with others. Our teenagers get so little positive feedback from adults that it is critical for us to help each other, especially if you have the emotional energy to do so. Our children desperately need the praise and acceptance of important adults in their lives. Celebrate your teen's successes with each other. Send a card or write a note when other teenagers become an Eagle Scout, graduate from high school or college, or make the soccer team or school play. We need to work as a family to ensure that all OUR children succeed!

5

Treatment of ADD and ADHD in Adolescents

Some people think that treatment for ADD and ADHD includes only medication and maybe some counseling. This view, however, is much too narrow. Treatment should actually be defined more broadly to include any activity that has a positive therapeutic effect on the child or teenager! Typically, treatment may involve several strategies, including parent training, a parent support group, behavior management, medication, counseling for the family, and perhaps most important of all, "ADHD education." This broad-based approach is known as *multimodal treatment*.

Keep in mind that *many other activities can also be therapeutic,* even though they aren't traditionally considered "treatment." These activities involve doing well at school, succeeding at a sport or hobby, doing fun things with parents or family, maintaining positive relationships with friends, or having a girlfriend or boyfriend who is a positive influence. After all, sometimes help may come from unexpected places:

"My son's girlfriend was the most therapeutic thing in his life during his senior year in high school. She was a tremendous positive influence on him regarding schoolwork, going to church, staying out of trouble, and treating me with respect. She had a greater impact on his life than any counseling session."

In addition, as explained earlier, Dr. Sam Goldstein, a leading expert on ADHD, suggests that treatment should also include interventions aimed at

building resilience in youngsters with this condition. Children who are resilient are more likely to cope successfully with adversity. Suggestions for building resilience in your teenager are available in Chapter 4.

Taking all these issues into consideration, this chapter offers suggestions for *building a comprehensive individualized treatment plan*. The ideal treatment plan for all teenagers with attention deficits should be tailored to their individual needs and be comprehensive—designed to help them succeed at home, at school, and in the community. These suggestions for treatment are based upon the best available research, plus my own professional and personal experiences and that of several of my colleagues.

This chapter also provides a summary of exciting new research findings and their implications for treatment. Sometimes research speaks to controversial issues; for example, "Should your child take stimulant medication?" or "Is ADHD medication over-prescribed?" So I will give you the scientific evidence on these important issues. Then you can read the facts for yourself, talk things over with your doctor or counselor, and make the best decision for your family that is consistent with your family values.

Unique Challenges of Treating Teenagers with Attention Disorders

Treatment of teenagers with attention deficits is not easy, yet very little has been written to guide parents and professionals through this difficult time. If treatment procedures for teenagers were clear-cut, there would be as many books on the subject as there are about treatment of children.

Sorry to say, teenagers with attention deficits are also going through the typical transition from childhood to adulthood—a factor that complicates treatment. Roles are changing for both the teenager and the parents. The *parents' job* is to teach the teenager how to make responsible decisions, help her move toward independence, and begin "letting go of the reins" controlling the teenager's life. The *teenager's* job is to begin the process of separating from his or her parents and become an independent, responsible adult. For better or worse, part of the teen's job is to experiment with making her own decisions, testing limits, and exercising her judgment.

Unfortunately, the teenager's developmental delay in maturity and executive functions and problems with inattention and impulsivity lengthen and complicate this transition. As a parent, you must learn to alternate between sometimes giving encouragement, asking how you can help, and teaching new skills, and at other times, applying pressure or imposing consequences.

Girls with ADD or ADHD present another treatment challenge. Thanks to groundbreaking information and research by Drs. Patricia Quinn and Kathleen Nadeau, we are becoming more aware of issues that are unique to girls. Limited access to treatment by some minorities is also an important issue, as discussed in Chapter 2. Gail Mattox, M.D., chairman of the Psychiatry Department

of the Morehouse School of Medicine, suggests developing a "parents educating parents" model to reach more African American families. Mattox bemoans the lack of "culturally competent providers" and identifies it as a major barrier to treatment. Dr. Jose Bauermeister, a researcher at the University of Puerto Rico, expressed similar concerns about the number of Hispanic families that are not being served. Hopefully, more research about serving minorities effectively will be forthcoming.

Empowering Families: Parents as Partners

Traditionally, parents and teenagers have been expected to take somewhat passive roles in treatment and to do as the professionals tell them. In contrast, this book is intended to *empower families* to use their unique strengths in helping their teenager cope with his or her attention deficit. Most parents have a fierce commitment to helping their own flesh and blood that professionals can never match. The parent's insights, commitment, and love are often the greatest treatment asset a teenager has working in her favor. After all, as a parent, you know your teenager best. Often, you know which parenting and teaching strategies work best and which ones are ineffective.

This book encourages you to take an active role, as best you can, in coordinating your teenager's treatment needs by working with professionals to develop an *individualized treatment plan*. This treatment plan should:

1. be built on your teenager's strengths,
2. identify problem areas and needs at home, school, and in the community, and
3. include interventions tailor-made for your teen and family. Guidelines to help you develop an effective multimodal treatment plan are provided throughout this chapter and in Chapter 15. If you also have ADD or ADHD, it may be a very difficult task for you. So you may wish to have the non-ADHD parent take the lead in this planning and monitoring process or hire a coach or therapist to assist you.

Regrettably, some doctors are not up on best treatment practices for ADD or ADHD. According to one survey, some physicians are actually misinformed. Thirty-three percent of physicians surveyed believed the preferred way of treating attention deficits is to provide counseling first. Historically, many professionals believed you should start counseling first, and then and only then, consider medication to treat the remaining problem behaviors unresolved by counseling.

As you will read later, research is clear: *medication is the single most effective treatment for attention deficit disorders*. In fact, medication is significantly more effective than counseling or behavioral interventions. The evidence suggests that at a minimum, when a child is really struggling, medication should begin simultaneously with counseling and behavioral strategies. So, in some instances, parents must help educate doctors and professionals about the most effective treatment for ADD and ADHD. According to Peter Jensen, M.D., *parents are the most effective resource for changing the way doctors treat these conditions!* So Dr. Jensen offers this sage advice:

Don't settle for anything less than the very best treatment for your teen !!!

Parents must read all they can about medications and other treatments and then, as an informed consumer, explain to their physician what they need. For example, you might say something like this, "My son is forgetting to take his mid-day medication dose, plus he is embarrassed to go to the office. I understand that medications such as Concerta and Adderall last 10 to 12 hours. Could we try one of those medications for my son?"

Key Principles Guiding Treatment

Several philosophical themes underlie the treatment suggestions woven throughout this book. Briefly, these themes and parenting strategies include the importance of:

1. reframing attention deficit disorders in a positive light,
2. building on your teenager's strengths,
3. treating your teenager as a respected partner in the treatment process,
4. using effective behavioral and parenting strategies,
5. providing "ADD/ADHD education",
6. fine-tuning medication for peak effectiveness,
7. ensuring success at school,
8. identifying special talents and enhancing them,
9. believing in your teenager and yourself, and
10. joining parent groups.

Obviously, the treatment approach must take into consideration the current theories about the neurobiological basis of attention deficit disorders. Medication may be necessary to help neurotransmitters function properly, making it easier for your teenager to pay attention and comply with requests. In addition, common characteristics of attention deficits, such as impulsivity, inattention, difficulty following rules, decreased sensitivity to punishment and rewards, and rapid loss of interest in rewards and consequences, also will play a major role in the treatment strategies chosen. Finding effective rewards and consequences is often difficult.

"Parenting techniques that work today may not work tomorrow. Parents must develop a large repertoire of disciplinary techniques. If one fails, go to the next one, and then the next one. When that stops working, start through the list again."

—Kathleen Allen, MS, Pediatric Center

"I have found that interventions are effective for about three weeks. Parents and teachers may anticipate the need to change strategies at the time."

—Claudia Dickerson, Ph.D., school psychologist

The Teenager: A Respected Member of the Treatment Team

Including your teenager as a respected member of the treatment team and involving her in all major decisions affecting her life is critical. It may be easier to treat your teenager with respect if you are aware of your own feelings and subtle attitudes about attention deficit disorders.

Frequently, many of your teen's problems are due to *skills deficits, not malicious intentions*. So it is important to view them that way rather than as a sign of a character defect, laziness, or a lack of motivation. If you think that your teenager is maliciously misbehaving and intentionally failing to do schoolwork, then a logical response is to believe that she will get better *only* if you force her to do things or punish her. On the other hand, if you believe that she wants to do well but is struggling to cope with ADD or ADHD, then you'll convey a different attitude. You will be positive, provide support and guidance, and if needed, suggest she consider taking medication. Even when you are teaching her new skills, it is still important to treat her with respect. Of course, when appropriate, you will impose consequences for misbehavior. You may also enlist her help in solving her own problems. For example, you might say something like this:

"Ibelieve you are doing your best, but your ADHD is making school difficult for you. I truly believe you want to follow rules and do well in school. Students with attention deficits often have problems getting their homework done and remembering their homework assignments. I know that's a problem for you sometimes. How can we work together to solve this problem?" If she has no suggestions, then you may suggest something like, "Let's develop a plan to make certain that you bring home the right books and know your homework assignments every night. If you can't remember to write it down in your new Palm Pilot, maybe you could ask John or Maria to write it down for you."

"Ihave come to believe that teenagers with ADD or ADHD will do well if they can— in other words, if they have the knowledge and skills to do well. At one time I believed that the only way my son would do what he should do was if I forced him to do it. I thought punishment was the answer."

You must help teach your child needed skills rather than just punish him or her for lack of skills such as disorganization, slow reading and writing, poor time management, or impulsive comments and actions. Many of us parents are worn out from the daily struggles of parenting these teens. We often slip into angry, blaming behavior. At times we think they are simply lazy, unmotivated &*#@!! So think about what we have discussed so far in this section. Then ask yourself this question, *"Do I need an attitude adjustment about my teenager's attention deficit?"*

Obviously your teen's attention deficit cannot be used as an *excuse* for misbehavior or school failure. Rather, it is a mitigating factor that helps explain why she often has trouble doing as adults ask and completing schoolwork. Clearly, she must still accept the consequences of her actions and learn to cope with and compensate for the symptoms of her attention deficit.

The NIMH/MTA Study: Research Implications for Treatment

Parents should also pay attention to the results of research studies, since that information will often help them develop the most effective treatment plan. For example, the National Institutes of Mental Health (NIMH) Multimodal Treatment Study (MTA) is an extremely important study that has profound implications for treatment of our children.

This 1993 landmark study, the largest ever done by NIMH on any topic, was spearheaded by Peter Jensen, M.D., currently the Director of the Center for the Advancement of Child and Adolescent Mental Health at Columbia University. Researchers collected data on nearly 600 students with attention deficits ranging in age from 7 to 10 at six sites around the country.

Researchers implemented a carefully constructed study with four components. The study hoped to answer some important basic questions. For example:

1. Which interventions work best?
2. Do behavioral interventions and counseling work better than medication?
3. Does a combination of medication and behavioral/counseling work better than either of these options alone?

To answer these questions, four study groups were set up:

1. The first group received *medication only*.
2. The second group received *behavioral interventions only*.
3. The third group received *combined medication and behavioral interventions*, and
4. The last group was maintained on whatever *existing treatment* they were already receiving in the community.

Sometimes this type of research is referred to as a "Cadillac study"—two of the four groups in the study received intensive interventions that otherwise are not available in most communities. For example, participating families received:

1. 27 sessions of parent training over 14 months;
2. individual therapy;
3. day-long summer treatment camp (9 hours intensive behavioral interventions);
4. classroom aides (drawn from camp staff) during the school year;
5. teacher consultation;
6. teacher training; and
7. social skills training, self-control training, and daily school report cards. Data collection in the study will continue until 2007.

The MTA findings are significant in that they will help shape how attention deficits are treated for years to come. A summary of key findings and their implications for treatment is provided in the box on the next page.

Important Findings from the Landmark MTA Study

The MTA study on ADHD combined type produced several important findings. (According to parent reports, many of these findings are also applicable to ADD inattentive.) Here are a few facts we have learned already, plus some thoughts on their implications for treatment:

- *Over two-thirds of children with ADHD have at least one other coexisting condition* such as depression, anxiety, or learning disabilities. [Unfortunately, many coexisting conditions are not treated, so teens continue to struggle unnecessarily. Parents and treatment professionals must be vigilant to ensure that all coexisting conditions are diagnosed and treated.]
- *"Medication alone" was significantly more effective than "behavioral intervention alone."* [ADD and ADHD are neurobiological conditions, and medication is often needed to help the brain chemistry work properly.]
- *Combined treatment is preferred.* Combined treatment includes medication plus behavioral intervention strategies, education, and parent training. [If ADD or ADHD is carefully and accurately diagnosed, then medications may be started simultaneously with behavioral interventions.]
- *Two intervention strategies were almost equal in getting the best results:* surprisingly "medication alone" was as effective as the "combined treatment" for treating the symptoms of ADHD. There were some situations, however, where the "combined treatment" intervention was preferable to "medication alone."
  - "Combined treatment" was superior in treating:
    1. *ADHD with anxiety*
    2. *ADHD and conduct disorder;* and
    3. *ADHD and learning disabilities.* [Children learned skills that reduced their anxiety, impulsive aggression, and enhanced academic skills.]
  - Students receiving "combined treatment" were treated successfully on *lower doses of medication.* [It's just good common sense to keep medication doses as low as possible yet still achieve optimum results.]
  - *Parents expressed greater satisfaction* with the "combined treatment" strategies rather than "medication alone." [Perhaps parents gain a greater sense of self-confidence and control of their children as a result of participating in the parent training.]
- Many students may be receiving *stimulant medication doses that are too low for maximum improvement in school work and behavior.* [The MTA study found that students being treated by their local physician were on doses of medicine that were too low to be maximally effective. If medication doesn't bring about the expected changes as listed in Table 5-1 in Chapter 5, talk with your doctor about adjusting the dosage.]
- When students took the right dose of medication, ultimately *they took fewer total medications.* [In other words, in the past when a student's stimulant medication didn't reach the dose for peak effectiveness, doctors may have prescribed additional medications to address the remaining problem behaviors. Obviously, fine-tuning medication so that peak effectiveness is achieved is critical.]
- After the treatment interventions, there was a *significant reduction in the number of children* who were diagnosed as having ADHD and Conduct Disorder. [Parents should take hope from this; with treatment, even children with severe problems can get better.]
- Researchers looked at which factors seemed to have the *most positive impact on a child's life.* For example, 75 percent of these children had an "excellent response" to the MTA treatment if three "protective factors" were present. Having an excellent response means that you couldn't tell the difference between the behavior of these children and their peers who did not have ADHD. These three factors are listed in order of significance:
  1. taking medication,
  2. having parents who were not depressed (mom is not depressed or dad not abusing substances), and
  3. having a less severe or milder case of ADHD.

On the other hand, there is a cumulative negative impact if the child is *not* protected by these positive factors. If the child is not taking medication, the mother is depressed, ADHD is more severe, and the child has a lower IQ, he or she is less likely to cope successfully with the attention deficit. So it is critically important to implement a treatment plan to address as many negative factors as possible.

Formal Treatment Strategies
Comprehensive Individualized Treatment Planning

My colleagues and I in the children's mental health field often refer to individualized planning and provision of treatment based upon the child's needs as *Wraparound*. Wraparound, a philosophy developed by Karl Dennis and Dr. John VanDenBerg, is one form of multimodal treatment.

When I make presentations about individualized treatment and Wraparound to parents and professionals, I frequently use a metaphor, describing a treasured quilt my grandmother hand made for me. Symbolically, a quilt conveys feelings of warmth and tender loving care. A quilt may also be wrapped around someone to provide real comfort and warmth. Sewn together into one square, the whole quilt becomes much stronger than its individual pieces. These same principles apply to an individualized treatment plan. A comprehensive treatment plan covering all the important aspects of a teenager's life—home, school, community, recreational—is more effective than a plan that touches only one or two parts such as medication and counseling.

Although quilting is a dying art, I am continuing a family tradition by making a quilt for my son. As shown in Table 5-1 on the next page, I have used the design for my son's quilt to help parents visualize the important concepts of individualized treatment and Wraparound.

Specific Strategies for Individualized Treatment

As explained earlier, intervention strategies for attention deficits may include parent training, support groups, behavioral interventions, medication, accommodations at school, skills training, "ADHD education," and possibly some counseling for the parents or teenager. You may elect to use some or all of these strategies, depending on the severity of your teenager's problems and his or her specific needs.

Identifying your teenager's treatment needs may be compared to peeling layers from an onion. . . . you should continue to examine layer after layer, until all the core problems are uncovered and the services necessary for your teen's success at home and school are provided. Each teenager's treatment needs will be different. For some, medication and behavior management may be all that are needed to help improve behavior and school performance.

The first step in the treatment process is to *review the results* of your teenager's evaluation and decide their implications for treatment. Information in Chapter 3 may help you better understand your teenager's evaluation. You can also discuss the evaluation results with a knowledgeable professional: your physician, licensed clinician psychologist, a school psychologist, school social worker, or guidance counselor. Ask their opinions about the best intervention strategies for your teen. Remember, however, that you have the right to accept or reject any proposed treatment. If you disagree with the recommendations, discuss alternatives with your treatment professional. If you cannot agree on a treatment approach, look for another professional who shares your treatment philosophy and in whom you have more confidence.

Strategies for Teens and Parents

The following suggestions are divided into two categories:
1. suggestions of ways you can help your teenager cope successfully with this disorder, and
2. suggestions of things you can do to help yourself be a more effective parent.

Suggestions for Teenagers

1. PROVIDE "ADHD EDUCATION"

Peter Jensen, M.D., explains that one of the most important things that parents can do is to educate their child or teenager about his or her attention deficit. In other words, teenagers must *become experts on their own ADD or ADHD!* Some professionals may suggest providing "psychoeducational training," but that is just a fancy way of saying provide "ADHD education" for your teen. One of the first things parents should consider, even if problems are mild, is to have someone, perhaps the physician, teacher, counselor, or the parents themselves, educate the teenager about this condition. In one or two sessions, the physician or counselor should be able to help the teenager:
1. grasp the basics of ADD or ADHD and how it affects her behavior
2. understand the lesser known characteristics that often accompany attention deficits: disorganization, memory problems, sleep disturbances, and the impaired sense of time

Table 5-1   Individualized Treatment Plan

Utilizing a quilt pattern, an individualized treatment plan for a seventeen-year-old teenager is displayed below. Although the procedure for developing a treatment plan is explained throughout the book, Chapter 16 contains more details about specific development. To help in development of the treatment plan, parents are encouraged to gather information about their teenager and complete the forms in Chapter 16:

MEDICAL

M1 Physician evaluation.

M2 *Diagnosis:* ADD; sleep and learning problems; some anxiety and depression; deficits in executive skills.

M3 *Medication:* Adderall XR (dose 40 mg); Dexedrine (5 mg as needed early morning or evening); Tofranil (50 mg per night); *Fine Tune Meds:* adjust timing/dose if not working; put medication in daily pill container; if needed, use beeper/cell phone to remind.

M4 *Psychiatric Consultation:* problems are more complex (i.e., medications are difficult to fine tune, sleep and learning problems, depression).

M5 *Fine Tune Plan:* If school work and behavior don't improve, reassess medication and revise treatment plan.

FAMILY

F1 *Counseling/Parents:* learn parenting tips; ADHD Ed; get support; develop treatment plan; consider counseling for a teenager.

F2 *ADD/ADHD Education:* join local CHADD; nat'l conferences; tapes and books on ADHD.

F3 *Fun Family Activities:* water ski, boating, hunt (father); visit supportive grandparents; holiday celebrations; family reunions.

F4 *Parenting Strategies:* be positive; avoid harsh punishment; give choices; provide structure and supervision; treat as partner; build self-esteem. Chapter 8.

F5 *Target Problem Behavior:* Chapters 9-13, *misbehavior:* keep busy in positive ways; *speeding tickets:* meds when driving; *homework strategy:* supervision; monitor subjects if failing; extra algebra book at home; phone # of friend in class.

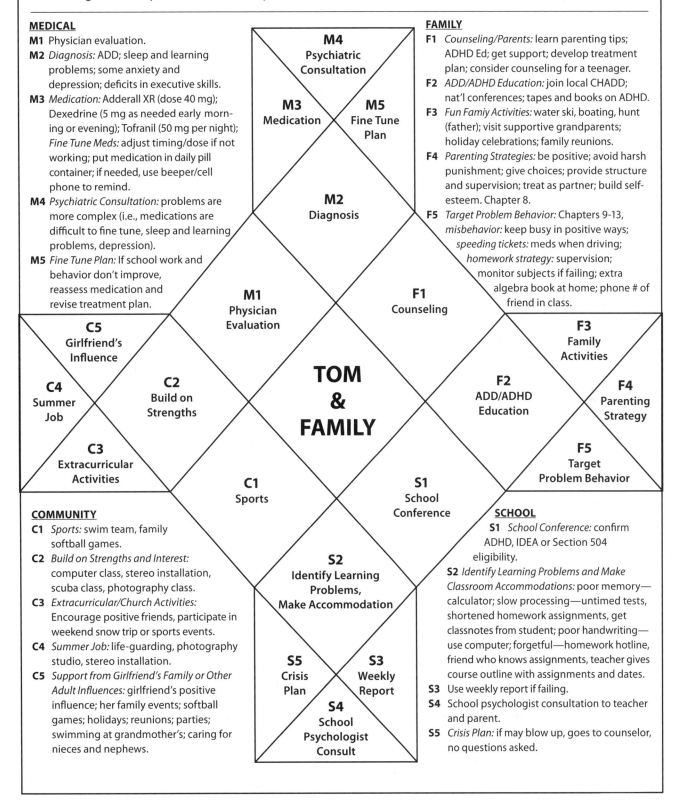

COMMUNITY

C1 *Sports:* swim team, family softball games.

C2 *Build on Strengths and Interest:* computer class, stereo installation, scuba class, photography class.

C3 *Extracurricular/Church Activities:* Encourage positive friends, participate in weekend snow trip or sports events.

C4 *Summer Job:* life-guarding, photography studio, stereo installation.

C5 *Support from Girlfriend's Family or Other Adult Influences:* girlfriend's positive influence; her family events; softball games; holidays; reunions; parties; swimming at grandmother's; caring for nieces and nephews.

SCHOOL

S1 *School Conference:* confirm ADHD, IDEA or Section 504 eligibility.

S2 *Identify Learning Problems and Make Classroom Accommodations:* poor memory—calculator; slow processing—untimed tests, shortened homework assignments, get classnotes from student; poor handwriting—use computer; forgetful—homework hotline, friend who knows assignments, teacher gives course outline with assignments and dates.

S3 Use weekly report if failing.

S4 School psychologist consultation to teacher and parent.

S5 *Crisis Plan:* if may blow up, goes to counselor, no questions asked.

3. reframe the positive aspects of her personality
4. learn about neurotransmitters in the brain and how medication helps them work properly
5. recognize that many adults are aware that it is extremely difficult to live with this condition
6. learn to cope with and compensate for her attention deficit
7. realize that many successful people have coped with this condition.

There is a tremendous need for educational materials written specifically for teenagers; yet little is available. A few available resources are listed here.

- *A survival guide for teens*: In response to the need for educational materials, my son, Alex, and I collaborated on a guide for teenagers and young adults, *A Bird's-Eye View of Life with ADD and ADHD: Advice from Young Survivors!* This humorous, easy-to-read guide is packed with cartoons, scientific facts, and advice from twelve teenagers from across the country. Dr. Barkley reports that it is "terrific…the best he has seen" and Dr. Ned Hallowell describes it as "superb."

- *A video for teens: Teen to Teen: the ADD Experience,* also available in Spanish, is a wonderful educational tool that we produced for helping teens understand themselves and others with this condition. Positive role models who are coping successfully with the challenges of ADD and ADHD are featured. Additionally, the video provides a realistic balance between the joys and challenges of living with this condition day in and day out. A video of a teen panel, *Advice on ADHD from the Real Experts*, that I facilitated at the 2004 national CHADD Conference is also available from www.chadd.org.

- *Other helpful materials*: The Girl's Guide to AD/HD (Beth Walker), *Adolescents and ADD: Gaining the Advantage* (Patricia Quinn); *I Would If I Could: A Teenager's Guide to ADHD/Hyperactivity* (Michael Gordon); *ADHD: A Teenager's Guide* (James Crist).

2. OFFER SELF-MANAGEMENT AND SKILLS TRAINING

In addition to helping them become an expert on their attention deficit, we need to give teens the skills to manage this disorder. Since teenagers with ADD and ADHD often have trouble with organizational, study, and time management skills, it seems logical that training in these executive skills should help.

Teaching your teen compensatory skills is also critical. Teens must *learn to compensate* for their symptoms by developing lists or using a beeper or Palm Pilot, by finding someone such as a friend, parent, or coach to remind them of assignments or due dates. As adults, hopefully these teens may have secretaries or administrative assistants to "coach" them.

Research to date has shown that some skills training, especially for social skills, isn't particularly effective, at least for *children* with ADHD. However, other researchers have found that social skills training *could* be helpful for those with ADD inattentive especially if they are shy, anxious, or withdrawn. Interestingly, one researcher found that providing a student tutoring that improved school performance was more effective in improving social skills than formal "social skills training."

Generally speaking, here is the main reason why skills training may not work. Frequently, these children and teens do not have a knowledge deficit; rather, they fail to use the skills they know at the proper time. Unfortunately, students are much less likely to use these skills when they are angry or are in a crisis. Regardless, this training surely won't hurt your teenager and you can make certain that she at least knows the basic skills. Perhaps she can also learn a few new strategies to help her get along better with friends.

At the same time, don't expect miraculous changes in your teen's behavior. You must recognize that even if she knows the skills, she won't always have the ability to think ahead and use them at the proper time. As children with attention deficits reach late adolescence and abstract thinking improves, their ability to learn from skills training classes *may improve and* carry over into real-life situations.

You may find a class or group that focuses on developing a skill where your teenager is especially weak; for example:

1. communication,
2. organization,
3. peer relationships,
4. anger management,
5. study habits,
6. time management,
7. test-taking,

8. problem-solving, and

9. social skills. Check with the school guidance counselor, mental health center, your doctor, CHADD, or ADDA-SR to see what teen groups may be offered. Strategies for improving specific skills such as anger management, problem solving, and self-management are available in Summary 65, *Teaching Teens*. Social skills tips are also provided in a *Bird's Eye View* and the *CHADD Educators' Manual*.

3. OFFER COUNSELING TO YOUR TEEN

At some point, your teen may benefit from some counseling. However, counseling is not a magic bullet—it will not "cure" your child. Depending on the training of the therapist, the counseling may include "ADHD education," behavioral counseling, skills training, or "talk or insight therapy."

Typically, "talk-therapy" refers to talking over your problems with an adult in an attempt to gain greater insight into your feelings, thoughts, and actions. Theoretically, when talk therapy works, the teenagers should change their problem ADD/ADHD behaviors... yet most of the time they do not. Dr. Barkley reports that traditional counseling is effective only 30 percent of the time with teens and their families. According to Dr. Barkley, treatment for children and teens should not be office based. To be effective, support and guidance must be delivered in the real world, at the point of performance. For talk therapy to be effective, the teen must be capable of self-talk and self-instruction. Neither of these skills is developed in the majority of teens with attention deficits. As teens get older and their brain and executive function systems mature, counseling may work more effectively. I have to chuckle when Dr. Barkley says, "Too many therapists take credit for maturation."

For now, "ADHD education" is probably more helpful for teens than counseling. Remember Dr. Barkley's quote: ADD/ADHD is not a *knowledge deficit*; it's a *performance deficit*—teens can't seem to access the knowledge they have at the moment when it is needed.

Initially, your teenager may rebel at the suggestion of being sent to a counselor, psychologist, doctor, or psychiatrist. If her problems are less severe and she is adamant about not going to counseling, it may be best not to force the issue. In reality, parents are often the only counselor that a teenager may ever have. So parents have a serious responsibility to educate themselves about this condition and learn more effective intervention strategies.

"I know that some teens have found counseling helpful. Personally speaking, most of the time I hated having to go. I remember I went to one counselor with my mom. The counselor was negative and kind of on my case. Neither one of us liked her so we never went back. I think it's hard for most counselors to relate to teens. To me it's hard to talk to someone I hardly know and to accept advice from them. It takes a long time to learn to trust someone. I guess that's why I liked having my mom for my counselor.

"Maybe one reason that counseling wasn't too much help is because I also had good common sense. I could figure things out. It wasn't too often that I ever had a psychiatrist tell me something that I didn't already know. Of course, that's exactly what some experts say, 'People with ADHD know what to do, but don't always do what they know.' Taking medication helped me do what I knew I should do."

—Alex Zeigler, coauthor,
A Bird's-Eye View of Life with ADD and ADHD

Some teenagers may resist counseling in the beginning, but eventually may come to perceive their counseling sessions as very positive. Hopefully, even if your teenager is resistant, you can talk her into meeting with the doctor or a counselor—at least once. For now, you may have to settle for educational programs that are less formal and may not be as threatening.

Although counseling may not prove effective for the symptoms of ADD or ADHD, it may help teens who are struggling with anxiety, depression, or learning disabilities.

"The summer before her senior year, Cassie wasn't sure of anything in her life: what she wanted to do, her boyfriend, nothing. She would get angry with us as we tried to talk with her about what she wanted to do. We suggested that she needed an objective third person to talk to—so she could process who she was, what she wanted to do, and how she wanted to get there.

"She went through the whole thing where she said, 'I don't want to go see a shrink; I don't want anyone to know; I'm not sick.' We said, 'Those things are all true, but you're obviously in distress about what you want to do and you don't want to talk to us about it.' It only took two visits for Cassie to decide that this was a good thing.

"The psychologist was very good about saying, 'Lots of people have learning disabilities or ADHD and they have gone on to lead successful lives. You just have to figure out what you want to do and how you want to do it. You don't have to have all the answers when you are eighteen.'"

"For a year, Cassie went to see the psychologist once every week or every other week. That was some of the best money we ever spent. It helped her work through independence versus dependence issues."

"One good thing Lewis knows is that it is okay to get help when you need it. He saw his Dad get help from AA and a psychologist and me getting some positive results from therapy."

In some situations, counseling is essential. For example, if problems are serious—aggression, suicidal risk, depression, substance abuse—you must talk with a professional as soon as possible and develop a plan for your teenager to be seen for counseling or a psychiatric evaluation.

You may need to shop around to find a person who is well matched for your teenager. The counselor must be someone your teenager likes and trusts. If the first one doesn't work out, try another professional. Again, other parents are an excellent referral source for finding effective treatment professionals.

If your teen participates in *group therapy*, make certain it is a "prosocial group"—in other words, with participants who will be a positive influence on your child. Dr. Barkley believes that putting children who tend to be antisocial into groups—especially if they are

extremely aggressive or break laws—ultimately may become a "deviancy training program." Participants may learn worse behaviors from others teen in the group.

When more serious problems are present.... For those who have more serious emotional problems, more than the traditional one hour of therapy a week will be required. Other treatment options such as intensive in-home services, self-contained special education classes at school, day treatment, intensive summer programs, or, as a last resort, placement in a residential treatment program may be necessary and are discussed later in this chapter.

4. CONSIDER HIRING A COACH.

In their book *Driven to Distraction,* Dr. Edward M. Hallowell and Dr. John Ratey refer to the person who provides extra support as a *coach.* According to Drs. Hallowell and Ratey, who are both psychiatrists who also have ADHD, a coach may also be needed at home to help deal with the routines of daily living such as remembering to do chores, doing homework, or remembering family events. If adults need coaches, teenagers need them even more. Our teens have a significant development delay and parents should not feel guilty about providing *developmentally appropriate support and supervision.*

5. ADVOCATE FOR ACCOMMODATIONS FOR LEARNING PROBLEMS

The identification of learning disabilities and deficits in executive skills is critical and cannot be emphasized enough! If a teenager has untreated learning problems, a vicious cycle of school failure, conflicts with adults, and lower self-esteem may occur.

Classroom accommodations should be provided to address any learning problems or executive skill deficits identified during an evaluation. Federal law mandates that eligible students who are struggling academically receive accommodations—special supports or adjustments in the classroom. For example, a teenager with memory problems who cannot memorize multiplication tables may be allowed to use a chart or a calculator. A student who has slow processing speed (slow reading and writing) may be given shortened homework assignments or extended time for tests. Likewise, students with executive skill deficits will also require accommodations to address their disorganization and forgetfulness. Accommodations might also include changing parts of the school environment. For instance, it might help to schedule difficult academic classes earlier in the day or to switch to a classroom teacher who is more understanding of students with attention deficits.

Chapter 12 discusses identification of learning problems and implementation of appropriate classroom accommodations in detail. The federal laws requiring schools to make accommodations for students are discussed in Chapter 13. Accommodations are also discussed in detail in *Teaching Teens,* Chapters 2 and 3.

6. CONSIDER MEDICATION; FINE-TUNE MEDS

Research from the 1999 NIMH/MTA study has clearly shown that *stimulant medication is the most effective intervention strategy for attention deficits.* In fact, medication is sometimes referred to as the cornerstone of a treatment program. Behavior, academic performance, emotional control, and the ability to relate to friends improves significantly in the vast majority of youngsters with ADD or ADHD when they are given appropriate medication. Most treatment professionals agree, however, that medication alone is not a panacea. It should be one part of a comprehensive treatment plan.

Deciding whether to give your teenager medication for an attention deficit is often very difficult. Most parents would prefer that their teen not take any medication at all. I certainly remember feeling that way. Ultimately, I realized that there were potentially serious negative side effects of *not* taking medication—for example, school failure, dropping out, substance abuse, and brushes with the law.

The next chapter is devoted to educating you about medications that may be prescribed for teenagers who have attention deficits.

7. ENGAGE YOUR TEEN IN TREATMENT PLANNING

Beth Kaplaneck, RN, Past President of CHADD, has identified a key question that parents ask over and over again: *"How can we engage our teenager or young adult in the treatment process?"* Rightly so, parents want their children to begin taking charge of their attention deficit. Most parents are tired of being "the memory and organizer for two people" and hope that this job will soon be over.

Unfortunately, having an independent teen is not going to happen as quickly as you would hope. You have to accept your teenager at her present skill level, which may be zero, expect her to take longer to mature, and in the interim teach her the skills she needs or help her compensate for any skill deficits. Hopefully, the material in this section will help you understand why engaging teens in treatment is difficult, plus give you some specific strategies that may help get them actively involved.

The seeds you sow in childhood set the stage for your relationship with your child when she becomes an adolescent. So you should begin using these principles during early childhood. Several key words come to mind—respect, partner, education, communication, and skills. Clearly, this journey is not for the impatient or faint of heart; it will take many years. You will need excellent communication skills to engage your teen in treatment planning. Ultimately, the more teens feel a sense of control, the more capable they will feel to solve their problems and take charge of their lives. Remember, the goal is to make your teen an expert on his or her attention deficit.

Suggestions for Parents

THINGS THAT DON'T WORK

Let's talk for a minute about what we know *doesn't* work. For years, parents have been nagging, yelling, confronting, and constantly reminding teenagers to do chores, take medication, and do homework. Yet, we know that doesn't work. Nagging and punishment can't make the teen's brain neurotransmitters work more effectively, nor can they make the attention deficit disappear. So here are a few suggestions that parents may find helpful.

1. SEEK PARENT TRAINING

While you are seeking treatment for your teenager, you may also want to seek guidance and support for yourself. After all, attention disorders are a family problem, and the whole family must learn to cope with them. Plus, as you have probably already observed, *traditional approaches to discipline don't seem to make lasting changes in the behavior of youngsters with ADD or ADHD.* In fact, these teenagers are much more difficult to parent than other children. So much so that Dr. Jensen sometimes jokes that parents of these children need a *"black belt"* in parenting. Learning additional and more creative ways to channel your teenager's energy and cope with misbehavior can be a lifesaver. Furthermore, it is unrealistic to assume that an outside treatment professional will be able to solve all of your teenager's problems for the family. So, learn all you can about attention disorders and parenting strategies.

Parent training classes may be especially helpful in introducing you to behavior management and other effective parenting techniques. Short classes, lasting perhaps eight weeks, are offered by many groups: schools, mental health centers, religious groups, and groups listed under "National Parenting Groups." An in-depth training program for parents, known as *Parent to Parent: Family Training on ADHD,* has been developed

Strategies for Engaging Teens in Treatment

Many suggestions discussed throughout this book are aimed at gradually helping teenagers take charge of their own lives. They are summarized here with references for more information to (TWA) for this book, (TT) for *Teaching Teens*, and (BEV) for *Bird's-Eye View*.

A. Adopt Realistic Expectations. Remember, your teenager will not mature as quickly as his or her classmates. So, expect her to achieve some developmental milestones such as self-control, organizational skills, and time management more slowly. Parents will need to support and teach their teenager skills for a longer period of time than parents of other teens.

B. Treat Your Teen as a Partner. In essence, you will become your teen's coach or mentor who must show her how to cope with this challenging condition. For example, when you help her solve a problem or write an essay, you are teaching by modeling or showing her how to master a new skill. You are solving these problems *with* her, not simply sending her somewhere for someone to "fix."

C. Use Positive, Respectful Communication *(Chapter 8 - TWA).*
   1. Be positive. Give help without belittling, nagging, condescending, or blaming so that he or she will always be willing to come to you when help is needed.
   2. Depersonalize situations. The use of "depersonalization" strategies replace our typical criticisms and put-downs with neutral statements of fact and offer guidance that a teenager is more likely to hear. For instance, you might say, "A lot of teens with ADD have sleep problems just like yours. The brain chemicals that control sleep aren't working right and that makes it really hard for you to fall asleep at night and wake up each morning."
   3. Really listen when teens talk. Treat any concerns they raise as important issues.
   4. Give teens choices, in most situations, rather than dictating what must be done and when. Researchers tell us that students who have choices are more compliant and produce more school work.
   5. Ask for their input or opinions.

D. Provide "ADHD education," *as discussed above.*

E. Teach Skills *(See earlier section.)* Analyze the skill you want your teen to learn, subdivide the skill into action steps that can be mastered, and then teach those skills. This process is known as "shaping behavior." Obviously, you can't teach all the skills at once, but you've got to begin somewhere. For strategies to address time management, self-management, and anger management, read Summaries 33-35, 64, and 69 (TT) and (BEV). Realistically, however, there may be some developmental skills that the teen may never master.
   1. Shape behavior. Break each skill into four or five smaller segments. Begin with the first step and build from there. See Summary 61 (TT).
   2. Model skills. One effective way to teach skills is by modeling them or doing them together. Learning skills such as writing an essay or cleaning up a room takes a lot of time and frequent repetitions. For example, see Summary 15 (TT) for tips on writing essays. Tips for organizing your teen's closet are provided in "Chaos & Clutter" (BEV).
   3. Put routines in place and practice them with the teenager until the action becomes second nature.
   4. Teach compensatory skills. Encourage the teen to use devices such as a watch, beeper, or pocket PC as a reminder of important events or to take medicine. Or teach her to involve those around her to give reminders of important events. See Summaries13-E and 65 (TT) and "I'm Late for Everything" (BEV).
   5. Teach and practice problem-solving strategies on a regular basis. Listening and not jumping in with solutions too quickly is very important. Remember to let her do things her way, when you can. As long as she can get the job done, it shouldn't matter to you *how* she does it. Specific strategies are discussed in Summary 66 *(TT)*.
   6. Build in time for maintenance. It takes a lot of time to monitor progress, so you will need to build in time to meet with your teen regularly. You'll need to informally assess her progress, identify the next small incremental step, and then teach it.

F. Expose to Expertise of Other Teens with ADD or ADHD who may also serve as successful role models. Although it may be difficult to find groups of teens, these role models can be helpful. A list of books and videos are listed earlier under "Provide ADHD Education."

    1. Attend a program for teens. Local CHADD or ADDA-SR groups have offered programs that teach about attention deficits or new skills, such as getting organized to do homework or compensating for problems with time awareness.

    2. Attend a teen panel on ADD/ADHD at CHADD or ADDA-SR to learn more about how others cope with this condition. One teen who previously refused medication began taking it after hearing one of these panel discussions.

    3. Watch an educational video. If your teen is somewhat resistant to watching the video, try this approach: simply run the video when your teen is in the house but don't make any comments about it. Maybe it will pique her interest. Teens may be more receptive to watching a video if it is presented by someone else, for example at school or a teen group meeting.

    4. Read a good book on ADD/ADHD. You may be successful by reading brief book sections on timely topics with your teen from *A Bird's-Eye View* or one of the books mentioned earlier.

G. Seek Successes Outside the Classroom. These activities will help build self-confidence, self-esteem, and resilience.

    1. Build competencies. Give your teen opportunities to participate in favorite activities: sports, debate, music, art, or dirt bike riding. Or as Drs. Brooks and Goldstein sometimes say, "Help them find or build their *islands of competence.*"

    2. Avoid withholding these activities as punishment. Avoid depriving teenagers of these special activities as punishment for their misbehavior. If punishment is appropriate, find another consequence. It is tempting to take away the things the teen loves most because they are very powerful tools. These activities, however, may be the only positive things in the teen's life, since school provides very little positive feedback. In fact, these skills may be the only positive force that is keeping your child in school or preventing her from turning to less desirable friends or illegal activities such as drug use.

    3. Build a sense of self-worth and a sense of making a valuable contribution to society. Give the teenager opportunities to help others. Try to ensure that these experiences are fun and rewarding for your teen. One young teen was "turned off" by the strong smell of urine during a nursing home visit.

    4. Become an expert. Seek opportunities for her to be the "expert" on her attention deficit. Perhaps she can participate on a question and answer teen panel at CHADD, ADDA-SR, or other group situation. Or maybe she can talk with a younger teen about how she has coped with a specific issue.

    Afterward, you may be tempted to say to yourself, "Well, she talks a good game! She says all the right things, but she doesn't do them when she should." Just remember, this is the first baby step in a lengthy, multi-step process. She has to say the right things before she can move on to believing and then actually doing them more consistently.

---

by CHADD. Plus, federally funded "parent training and information centers" for children with disabilities are available in every state. (See Resources for contact information for these and other organizations.)

Improve Communication Skills. Parents must master skills that will enable them to diffuse stressful or angry situations. The words that parents choose can make the situation better or worse. Words like "You're lazy. You're not trying. You're not going to amount to anything when you grow up" tend to make situations worse. Other words like, "I know this is difficult for you. Let's work on this together" are more likely to make things better.

You may benefit from learning some new words and ways of saying things. For example, instead of saying "You're so rude! You *always* interrupt me when I am on the telephone!", talk about your feelings and then suggest a solution. "I feel so frustrated when I am talking with my friends and I can't finish my conversation. Instead will you come to the phone, and point to yourself when you need to talk? If I can stop, I will. If not, I'll come talk to you as soon as I get off the phone."

So often the same old words or yelling haven't worked in the past, so it makes sense to try some new ones. As suggested earlier, the best selling book, *How to Talk So Kids Will Listen and Listen So Kids Will Talk* by

Adele Faber and Elaine Mazlish, may help parents not only improve communication with their teens, but also reduce conflict. A summary of a few strategies from this book is provided in Chapter 8.

2. ATTEND PARENT SUPPORT GROUPS

One coping method that many parents swear by is to join a group of other parents of children with ADD or ADHD. At first, parents may seek this companionship to reassure themselves that they are not alone in their struggles. They are able to trade war stories and share their emotions, and get the support and advice that parents of "typical" teenagers could never give them. Only another parent of an ADHDer will not be shocked by anything these teens may do.

Attending a local support group will help educate you more fully about attention deficits, expose you to treatment experts in the community, plus provide support from parents who have faced similar challenges. Many of these groups have monthly programs and offer educational materials such as handouts and newsletters. This information may also help educate other family members or school personnel about ADD and ADHD.

Sometimes parents who also have been diagnosed with an attention deficit decide to meet together as a separate group. For many parents, their diagnosis is still relatively new. They are eager to learn about

the disorder and better understand its impact on their lives. Parents with ADD or ADHD may have powerful feelings to deal with regarding their own personal struggles, and discussing them with other adults with this same condition may be helpful.

Join National Parent Groups. In addition to local groups, there are two types of national parent groups you may wish to investigate:

1. educational and support groups concerned with attention deficit disorders; and
2. support groups concerned with some of the disorders that can co-exist with ADD and ADHD. Contact information for these and other helpful organizations is listed in the Resources.

ADD/ADHD Support Groups. Parent groups related to ADD/ADHD often provide several services: support to parents and adults, fact sheets, training materials, magazines, conferences, and education of state and national policy makers about the challenges of having an attention deficit. In the U.S., CHADD and ADDA are the two national educational groups that are making a difference by educating families and professionals regarding best practice information about treatment of attention deficits. Joining one or more of these organizations can be very helpful to parents in obtaining the most up-to-date information about ADD and ADHD.

CHADD (Children and Adults with Attention Deficit Disorders), established in 1987, is the largest national ADD/ADHD educational and support group. CHADD has local chapters all across the country and publishes an excellent newsletter, *Attention* magazine, and sponsors a highly informative annual conference. CHADD also offers an outstanding website, www.chadd.org, where helpful fact sheets and lists of local chapters are available. Through local CHADD support groups, parents receive support and the opportunity to talk with other parents of children with attention deficits.

CHADD and other advocacy groups were instrumental in U.S. Department of Education issuing *a major policy memo (9/91)* regarding the special needs and supports required by youngsters with attention deficits at school.

CDC National Clearinghouse and Resource Center on ADHD. The Centers for Disease Control and Prevention (CDC) selected CHADD as the clearinghouse for information on attention deficits. Parents who contact this group can talk with staff about issues of concern regarding both children and adults with attention deficits and receive information on key topics. Visit www.help4adhd.com.

ADDA. Another important national educational and support organization is the Attention Deficit Disorders Association (ADDA), www.adda.org. ADDA's primary focus is on providing support for adults with this condition. ADDA's leadership worked actively with CHADD to obtain important educational policy changes. ADDA also has an excellent annual conference and a newsletter, *Focus,* which may be of interest to parents who also have an attention deficit.

ADDA-SR. The Attention Deficit Disorder Association-Southern Region (**ADDA-SR**) is a strong regional parent educational support group that was established in 1987. Based in Houston Texas, this group is active in the mid-southern region, specifically Texas and surrounding states. They also have strong local chapters, an excellent annual conference, plus helpful information on their website, www.adda-sr.org.

Support Groups for Coexisting Conditions. As discussed earlier, some teenagers with attention deficits have coexisting conditions that can lead to serious emotional problems. Their parents may be unable to find all the help they need from local parent support groups. The advocacy groups described below are active on behalf of children and teenagers with a broader range of emotional problems. If your teenager's problems are more serious, you should find out which of these organizations are active in your community and what support they provide. In addition, information on educational support groups for specific conditions such as bipolar disorder, Tourette syndrome, and depression is available in the Resources.

The Federation of Families for Children's Mental Health is a parent-run organization focused on the needs of children and adolescents with emotional, behavioral, or mental disorders and their families. The Federation has local chapters in many states. Contact information for each state chapter is available on their website, www.ffcmh.org.

The National Mental Health Association (NMHA), along with the Federation and NAMI, was involved in an initiative in 1992 which has resulted in a significant expansion of funding to develop services for children with serious emotional problems. Visit their website at www.nmha.org for more tips on promoting your child's mental health.

The National Alliance for the Mentally Ill (NAMI) offers information about a variety of mental disorders such as bipolar disorder and depression that can co-exist with attention deficits (www.nami.org).

You may want to become involved with one or more of these organizations if your teen has more serious emotional problems, or if you are interested in local and state level advocacy for policy changes that affect our children. In some communities, you may find chapters of these organizations, but not of CHADD or ADDA-SR.

3. SEEK "ADD/ADHD EDUCATION"

In a presentation to the 2002 CHADD conference, Dr. Barkley explained that the most effective intervention for helping parents is *education* about attention deficit disorders. *"ADHD education" is even more effective than counseling!* The better parents understand the disorder, the more effectively they can cope with it. They must develop more realistic expectations of their teen and understand that many of the irritating things their teen does are not malicious but rather a result of her ADD or ADHD. This knowledge changes how the parent interacts with the teenager. Please read the earlier section about "ADD/ADHD education" for teens for a list of important information you should learn.

4. REFRAME ADD AND ADHD MORE POSITIVELY

Look for positive elements of your teen's personality, believe in her, love her unconditionally, and build on her strengths. To reframe ADHD, fill out the blank chart in Table16-1 in Chapter 16. Activities to build self-esteem are discussed in Chapter 8. The strategies to promote resilience discussed in Chapter 4 will also be helpful.

5. TRY BEHAVIORAL INTERVENTIONS

The first intervention most parents try with children is behavior management, or *behavior modification,* as it is also known. Behavior management programs use several techniques, including:
1. positive reinforcement;
2. "shaping" or teaching desired behavior;
3. withholding rewards or privileges; and
4. punishment to change a child's behavior.
   Behavior management is a helpful tool for

parents, but it has some limitations with teenagers. Effective use of these techniques, their limitations, plus suggestions for how to use punishment wisely are discussed in Chapter 8.

Remember also that researchers tell us that behavioral interventions alone are not nearly as effective as medication. A few years ago, most treatment professionals, myself included, recommended that behavioral intervention be tried first with a child with an attention deficit and then later treat the remaining symptoms with medication. However, based upon the results of the NIMH/MTA study, many leaders in this field are now suggesting that medication and behavioral interventions be started simultaneously. Of course, this assumes that a thorough evaluation and correct diagnosis have been provided.

6. SHOULD YOU SEEK COUNSELING?

Once your teenager has been evaluated and a diagnosis has been made, you may want to seek counseling for yourself. You may need someone to listen while you let off steam, discuss your fears or feelings of guilt, and seek guidance about ways to deal with your anger toward this teenager who may be making your life so miserable.

If you also have an attention deficit, more than likely you will need to talk with someone about your own personal challenges. You may have tremendous difficulty just keeping your own life organized. Frequently, having an attention deficit makes it even more difficult to be a parent. Your teen may be taxing your limited organizational and coping skills.

Eventually, your teenager may talk with a counselor or doctor, but the least intrusive method should be tried first. I often suggest that the parent attend counseling to learn new parenting skills. If parents become more effective in dealing with their teenager, then it may not be necessary for the teen to seek counseling.

The ideal counselor for your family is a treatment professional who believes in a "wellness model" and builds on the strengths of your family. This is in contrast to an "illness model," which focuses only on identifying problems, diagnosing an "illness," and placing blame on the teenager and parents. Your teenager should not be viewed as "bad or lazy," nor should her attentional difficulties or behavior problems be viewed as the result of inadequate parenting. Local parent organizations may be excellent resources for finding professionals who specialize in treating ADD and ADHD.

> *I knew our pediatrician was exceptional when I learned that he employed a counselor in his office specifically to help parents and their teenagers learn new coping skills and to handle the stress caused by ADHD. His staff have participated in specialized training regarding treatment of attention deficits. They*

Reasons for Delayed Independence

Let me remind you why achieving independence is so incredibly difficult for our teens. In addition, let me offer a few suggestions of ways to help your teen mature, accept more responsibility, and become more involved in treatment. Remember, however, there is no magic bullet that will fix everything for our teens. We simply do the best we can to love, support, and teach them.

- First, the big picture: the characteristics of their attention deficits are a major culprit here. Their *inattention, impulsivity, and executive skill deficits* impede their developing maturity at every turn.

- These teenagers are *developmentally behind* so your 16-year-old may act more like a 10- or 11-year-old, especially with regard to her executive functions and social skills.

- Many of these teenagers have *difficulty getting started* or initiating activities due to their attention deficit. [We want them to take the initiative to do what they are supposed to do on their own; many can't do this easily.]

- They *live in the here and now*. [We'd like for them to be thinking and planning for the future, but they can't anticipate or plan ahead very well.]

- Their *impaired memory* is a huge problem. [We want them to remember to take their medication, do their chores and homework; but many can't.]

- Some teens are *depressed* because simply coping with the challenges of their attention deficit is sometimes overwhelming. [Teens who are depressed don't have the energy to become actively involved in their treatment plan.]

- Teens *don't always accept* the fact that they have an attention deficit. [They may go through the normal stages of grieving, initially denying that they have any problems. They may refuse medication.]

The good news is that they will continue to mature until their early thirties, but unfortunately at a slower rate than their friends. In addition, they can learn to compensate for skills they may never master.

were so helpful in educating me about ADD inattentive and treating my son.

"For my family, the environment that best matched the 'wellness' philosophy was having our pediatrician treat our sons. One of the major advantages has been that our sons are 'treated' at a doctor's office rather than in a psychologist's or psychiatrist's office. That has been a more acceptable (less stigmatizing) option to our boys. It is not unusual for teenagers to have an annual physical plus have their medication monitored and academic progress reviewed at the same time.

"Our doctor was extremely sympathetic and supportive. Dr. Ed, as he is affectionately known to his patients, has always been there for us when we needed him. When my son balked at talking with a 'shrink,' Dr. Ed spent an hour talking with us about the best way to handle our crisis. He has held our hands and loved us through a crisis on more than one occasion."

Try to get a general understanding of your counselor's treatment philosophy. You must find a counselor who understands the neurobiological aspects of attention disorders. Some counselors who provide traditional "psychotherapy" often look for hidden psychological reasons for behavior that may blind them to the true nature of "ADHD behaviors." From this perspective, a person who is always late for therapy or forgets sessions may be viewed as being "resistant" to therapy. The counselor may fail to see that problems with brain chemistry cause the problems with forgetfulness and tardiness. If they view "ADHD behaviors" as intentional or at best a willful subconscious act, their therapeutic interventions are unlikely to be successful.

Counseling is just one strategy that may be used in conjunction with other interventions as part of a comprehensive treatment plan. For the best results, the problem may require the involvement of the whole family—parents, the teenager with the attention deficit, and other siblings. Educated parents and teenagers are critical for effective treatment.

7. STAY ON TOP OF YOUR TEEN'S TREATMENT PROGRESS

Your teenager's treatment plan should include periodic assessment of her functioning. Is she complying with your requests more often? Is she making passing grades? Does she seem happy most of the time? If you don't know the answer to these questions, then you should seek more information. Success in school is also the key to a successful treatment plan, so monitoring school progress is critical.

8. ENSURE SCHOOL SUCCESS

When teenagers continue to struggle even after treatment has begun, you need to reassess and revise their treatment plan and probably the IEP or Section 504 Educational Plan. These terms are explained in Chapter 14. If school performance doesn't improve so that the teen is passing all her subjects, then you and the professionals should change your current strategy. Reassessing and fine-tuning both medication and the treatment plan are critical. For our son, there were three main reasons that he continued to struggle so terribly in high school. You may experience these same challenges with your child.

1. The most appropriate medication(s) and dosage were not found early enough in our son's school career. As a result, his inattention and failure to complete school work improved very little. For example, his medication was always too low for maximum effectiveness in high school and most of college.

Action Steps: Reassess the effectiveness of your teen's present medication regimen. For example, ask teachers to complete the *Medication Rating Scale* in Appendix 1 to determine if she is on the best possible medication dose. A change in the present medication dosage may be warranted or you may need to try another medication. Work with your doctor to resolve this issue. See Chapters 5, 7, and 8 for more details on possible coexisting conditions and other problem areas, plus suggestions for problem solving.

2. Coexisting conditions were present yet unidentified and untreated. When more serious problems such as aggression, agitation, explosiveness, or depression continue despite treatment, counseling or different medications may be helpful. For our son, his coexisting conditions, depression, and problems falling asleep and waking up were never adequately treated while he was in high school.

Action Steps: A licensed treatment professional should be able to diagnose coexisting conditions and make appropriate treatment suggestions. Medications effective in treating aggression or depression are discussed in Chapters 5 and 6.

3. Our son had serious learning problems related to his executive skill deficits that were overlooked in the preliminary evaluation. Up to 50 percent of these children have learning disabilities and many also struggle with deficits in executive skills.

Action Steps: Request that the school conduct a functional behavior assessment (FBA) to determine which problems are contributing to school failure. FBA is discussed in Chapters 13 and 14 and in *Teaching Teens,* Summary 63.

- Identify any learning or executive function problems; see Chapter 13 plus *Teaching Teens,* Summaries 28-38, for more details;

- In partnership with school personnel, develop a plan to implement accommodations to meet the teen's academic and executive skill deficits such as disorganization and memory problems. Extra support and supervision will also be required at home and school.

9. HELP FIND A GOOD CAREER MATCH

Career selection is critically important! Parents and professionals must help these young people match their personalities and skills with an appropriate career. Teenagers with ADD or ADHD must find careers in which the characteristics of their attention disorder are an asset rather than a handicap. Some teenagers who struggled through school may blossom once they graduate. But be prepared. Most teenagers will take longer to find themselves and their successful niche in life. Tips for finding a career after high school are discussed in Chapter 15.

Additional Treatment Options

Sometimes when a teen's problems are more serious, parents are at a loss of knowing what to do. More intensive interventions may be needed. Remember from our earlier discussions, intensive nonresidential services are available in some parts of the country. Other treatment options include:

- coaches or mentors,
- academic tutors,
- behavioral specialists or aides,
- respite care,
- intensive in-home services,
- day treatment,
- after school programs,
- summer camps and treatment programs,
- traditional and therapeutic boarding schools,
- 24-hour residential treatment.

Unfortunately, many of these services are either hard to find or extremely expensive. They can, however,

be a lifesaver for families in crisis or for a teenager who has more serious emotional problems. The majority of these treatment options can be provided in conjunction with other basic services while the teenager is still living at home. Parents can find out about the availability of these services through their local mental health center, school psychological services office, university ADD/ADHD program, parent support group, or a psychiatric hospital. If services are not available, you may be able to create some of them yourself. For example, find and train a coach to help your teenager stay organized. Additional critical interventions such as techniques for behavior management and building self-esteem and resilience are discussed in subsequent chapters.

Some people incorrectly assume that intensive services are synonymous with 24-hour residential care. If, however, intensive individualized services are "wrapped around" a teenager and her family, residential treatment can usually be avoided, even when emotional problems are serious. The services described in this chapter constitute a range of comprehensive services for children with serious emotional problems.

Note: Any reference to specific programs is not considered an endorsement. Parents should check out references for any program to which they entrust their child.

Coaches or Mentors. Teenagers with attention deficits may be bright and not really need an academic tutor, but, rather, need someone who can help them be more organized, remember homework assignments and books, memorize material more easily, and manage their time better. In other words, they need someone to help them with their deficits in executive skills.

One of the newer strategies to help people cope with such deficits is known as *coaching.* Coaches are formally trained and are paid for their services, which may include teaching organizational skills, meeting regularly with the teen, monitoring progress, or communicating regularly by email. In truth, parents have been serving as coaches for years. So, in many ways this is not anything new but the service has been given a name and has been legitimized. You may be interested in reading the six-page description of how to utilize coaching for students in *Teaching Teens, Summary 65.* Two groups, the American Coaching Association and the International Coach Federation, train coaches and provide a state-by-state listing of trained coaches: www.americoach.com; www.coachfederation.org. As with the selection of any professional who works with your family, take care to screen them carefully.

In reality, parents provide most of the coaching to teenagers. There are several reasons why this responsibility typically falls on parents:

1. teens need *daily* supervision,
2. the cost of providing the required level of supervision would be prohibitive, and
3. it is very difficult to find qualified people to provide the service to teens.

Some parents may be ambivalent and feel guilty about "being too involved" monitoring their teenager's school work. This may be true if parents are under pressure from school officials who say they should let the teen fail and then maybe she'll learn her lesson. However, considering your teen's developmental lag plus her executive skill deficits, ultimately, you *must be involved* if she is to succeed in school. Throughout this book, parents are encouraged not be embarrassed or reluctant to help their teenager when needed. It is important to *give yourself permission to be involved*. After all, you are simply providing "developmentally appropriate supervision."

Academic Tutors. Your teenager may need tutoring on writing essays, working certain complex math problems, or memorizing information more easily. Someone at your school may help you find a suitable tutor. Most schools have a list of "homebound" teachers who tutor students who cannot attend class. You may be able to hire one of these teachers to provide tutoring to your teen. Interestingly, Dr. George DuPaul, Lehigh University, found that when students who were acting out were provided tutoring, their behavior also improved without any other interventions.

Behavioral Specialists or Aides. Sometimes behavioral specialists or aides are available to help parents at home or teachers in the classroom. They have been specifically trained in effective use of behavioral strategies. These specialists have become more readily available in public schools since passage of the 1997 revisions to IDEA, when functional behavior assessments (FBA) and behavior intervention plans (BIP) were mandated. Occasionally, a doctor, university, or your local community mental health center may also have trained behavioral aides on staff who can come into your home or school and help you implement a behavioral program.

Respite Care. When raising a teenager with an attention deficit gets too emotionally demanding, parents need time away to recharge their energies. Getting

a babysitter, or perhaps two babysitters, for a night out is one form of respite. Sending the teenager on a supervised trip with friends or relatives also provides respite for parents. Sometimes parents have trouble getting babysitters or chaperones because other adults don't know how to cope with these youngsters.

Parents in this predicament may benefit from formal respite care. Respite care may be offered by mental health centers for their clients whose children have serious emotional problems. These centers may have trained paid staff who can stay with the teenager while parents go out. The teenager may stay at home or may go somewhere else for the respite care. Respite care is often one of the greatest needs parents have, but is seldom available. You might also ask your local CHADD chapter or other local ADD/ADHD or LD organization to offer training for babysitters or chaperones of youngsters with attention deficits.

Summer Camp and Treatment Programs. A few highly specialized summer programs offer success-oriented, high adventure programs. For example, the SOAR program features skill development in areas such as scuba diving, hiking, and horse-packing in exotic locations such as Florida, Wyoming, California, Belize, Peru, and Costa Rica. This structured therapeutic program teaches teens to work cooperatively with others, communicate more effectively, organize information and materials, and meet deadlines and manage time more wisely while also having the time of their lives. The program focuses on building strengths and confidence. One advantage of this type of program is that it is therapeutic but the teenagers don't recognize it as such, so it doesn't have the stigma attached with participating in a traditional treatment program. Contact information for SOAR is in the Resources.

Some organizations that specialize in treating youngsters with ADD and ADHD have developed intensive summer programs. For example, William Pelham, Ph.D., developed a model program that he now operates at SUNY, Buffalo, NY. Children are taught new social and academic skills and competencies through recreational activities, academic interventions, behavioral training, and counseling. Typically, this service is expensive, but some insurance polices may cover it.

After-School Programs. A few organizations around the country have begun offering specialized after school services for children or teenagers with ADD or ADHD. The services are similar to those offered in day treatment programs, except that they are conducted for only two or three hours each day after school. The Challenging Horizons Program at James Madison University in Virginia is one such program for middle schoolers with ADHD. It provides mentors/coaches who work with the students on social skills, recreational activities, homework, and academic skills.

Intensive In-home Services. "Intensive in-home" services are appropriate to use when a family is in crisis and the teenager's problems are considered serious enough to warrant residential treatment. Counselors from this program will come into the home and work with family members up to 20 hours a week during a crisis. Counselors are also accessible to the family by beeper or phone. This in-home crisis service is extremely effective in diffusing family emergencies, thus preventing a residential placement. Unfortunately, few intensive in-home services are accessible to the average family. Your local mental health center or Federation of Families chapter will know if this service is available in your community.

Multisystemic Therapy or MST is an intensive family- and community-based treatment program that was developed by Scott Henggeler, Ph.D., at the Medical University of South Carolina. Research has consistently shown that this intensive intervention program is effective in helping children cope successfully with their problems and keep them out of the juvenile justice system.

Day Treatment or Partial Hospitalization. In some communities, day treatment or partial hospitalization programs are available for teenagers with ADD and ADHD who are experiencing serious emotional problems. Many of these programs offer services that include academic instruction; individual, group, and family counseling; behavior management; medication evaluation/monitoring; and psychiatric evaluation and follow-up. Program staff may also identify learning problems and provide special academic tutoring or accommodations.

Frequently, the teenager lives at home while attending school at the day treatment program. Programs may be jointly operated by a local school and mental health center and located at either site. Often programs with greater medical involvement may be offered through a psychiatric hospital and housed in the hospital. Sometimes insurance coverage is available for partial hospitalization.

Boarding Schools. Some parents may consider sending their teen to a *traditional boarding school,* or, for more behaviorally challenging and out-of-control teens, to schools known as *therapeutic boarding schools.* Some therapeutic schools, such as Mount Bachelor Academy in Oregon, teach communication and academic skills that enable teens to regain control of their lives. Many of these programs are highly respected, but a few have made national headlines for abusive behavior toward students. Some boarding school use a controversial service, known as *transport or escort services*, in which teens who are described as out of control are awakened in the middle of the night and taken away to the school. Preferably, your teen will agree to attend the program without resorting to this approach. Any decision to remove your child from your home should be made very carefully. Always check out the reputation of any school you are considering, possibly interviewing parents whose children have previously attended the program. The school should provide references. Tips from the Alliance for the Safe, Therapeutic, and Appropriate Use of Residential Treatment (ASTART) should help parents make a better informed decision about the need for residential placement: http://cfs.fmhi.usf.edu/projects/astart.htm.

Residential Treatment. As a last resort, teenagers with attention deficits and more serious problems are sometimes placed in 24-hour residential care. According to Dr. Barkley, roughly 8 percent of children with ADHD will require residential treatment or psychiatric hospitalization. Typically, treatment is not for their attention deficit disorder, but rather for a coexisting condition such as depression, conduct disorder, substance abuse, or bipolar disorder. Residential care may be offered through several types of programs: group homes, specialized foster care homes (a foster home with trained parents plus mental health support), residential treatment facilities, or psychiatric inpatient hospitals. Costs vary, but inpatient psychiatric hospitalization is usually the most expensive residential service, ranging from $500 to $2,000 a day.

The decision to place must be made very carefully in conjunction with the teenager's doctor and/or counselor. Residential treatment is considered primarily when teenagers present a danger to themselves or others. Residential care may also be provided when the teenager is engaging in self-defeating behaviors such as substance abuse. Parents usually only turn to residential care when they are desperate and if other interventions have not worked.

Inpatient Hospital Programs. These programs are usually brief, lasting only a few days, and are aimed at helping find the right medication regimen to stabilize the teen's moods and reduce aggression, explosiveness, or depression. Services usually include individual, group, and family counseling; psychiatric evaluation; and medication monitoring. The inpatient program may also continue the teenager's education through day treatment. The length of stay may vary from a few days to several months. Often these programs have locked units; in other words, the teenager cannot come and go when she pleases. Keep in mind, however, that these programs tend to offer brief, intensive interventions aimed at stabilizing the teen's medications and behavior. Don't expect them to magically change your teen in such a short period of time.

Consequences of Inappropriate Placements. Decisions to place a teenager in residential care must be made with great care and caution. Inappropriate placements take a huge toll on families, both emotionally and financially. Teenagers with ADD or ADHD may be exposed to others who have more serious emotional problems and may learn new inappropriate behaviors or develop close relationships with other teenagers who aren't coping very well. Worst of all, the teenager's self-esteem may be unnecessarily damaged, leaving her to believe that she is emotionally "sick" or crazy. In addition, parents shoulder an unnecessary financial burden *without any guarantee it will help their teenager.*

"One teenager with ADD was placed in a residential 'rehab' treatment program when he was fifteen. He met a girl there who became his girlfriend. Within six months, she was pregnant and they got married. At age sixteen, he dropped out of school and went to work to support his family. They were divorced within a year."

If your teenager is placed in a residential treatment facility, you should monitor the length of stay in the hospital and work with your local doctor and counselor toward an early return home.

Sometimes the only services available to a family during a crisis are at either extreme of a continuum—either one hour of counseling or placement in a residential facility. Obviously, during a crisis, one hour of counseling will not be sufficient to help a family resolve their problems, but a residential placement may not really be needed. If you are ever in such a situation, remember, the key to deciding whether residential placement is appropriate is whether your teenager poses a danger to herself or others. Otherwise, work closely with your doctor to seek or develop services that will support you and your teenager at home during the crisis. Hopefully, this broad overview of treatment options will help you and your teenager determine which options seem to fit your family's needs.

Unproven Treatments. Over the years, many controversial or unproven treatments for ADD/ADHD have been proposed. Even though there may be some benefit, there are no scientifically rigorous controlled studies to validate that the following treatments work: play therapy, biofeedback, cognitive self-control training, elimination diets (sugar doesn't cause ADHD), megavitamins, antioxidants, minerals, sensory integration training, and skull manipulation by chiropractors. If you come across another treatment that you are unsure about, visit one of the major websites like www.CHADD.org or www.help4ADHD.com and check their fact sheets. CHADD's fact sheet, "Assessing Complementary and/or Controversial Interventions," may be helpful.

Outcomes: What Do We Know about the Future?

The potentially serious problems that teens with ADD or ADHD are at risk for are discussed in Chapters 1 and 10. Unfortunately, these problems often, but not always, persist into adulthood. Recently, however, re-

search has offered us some mildly encouraging news. Russell Barkley, Ph.D., and Lilley Hechtman, Ph.D., conducted longitudinal studies and found that roughly 10 to 20 percent of adults with ADHD combined type lead normal lives and are indistinguishable from other adults. Two-thirds still have symptoms that may interfere with their family relationships or job performance. But severe problems such as psychiatric disorders or antisocial behavior (law breaking) persist in roughly only 10 to 20 percent of adults. (A comparable study has yet to be done on adults with ADD inattentive.)

With early identification and treatment, however, children and adults can be successful. Studies show that children who receive adequate treatment for attention deficit disorders have fewer problems with school, peers, and substance abuse, and function better overall, compared to those who do not receive treatment.

The results of the NIMH/MTA study offer us additional encouraging news. When these children have ADHD plus coexisting conditions like ODD or conduct disorder, effective interventions truly can turn their lives around. The other piece of good news from the MTA study is that children who received the earliest interventions tended to fare better than those who received no interventions or treatment at a later time. So, the message is clear: intervene early and don't settle for anything less than the best possible treatment.

Additionally, all we have to do is look no further than several prominent researchers and physicians for proof that people with milder forms of attention deficit disorders can be successful: prominent experts on ADD/ADHD Sydney Zentall, Ph.D., Ben Lahey, Ph.D., Theodore Mandelkorn, M.D., Edward Hallowell, M.D., and John Ratey, M.D. also have the disorder. Patricia

Quinn, M.D., author and pioneer in women's issues, writes from her personal experiences with attention deficit. Children and teenagers with attention deficits do grow up to be successful, productive adults. ADD and ADHD can be treated effectively! Granted, not every child with an attention deficit will grow up to become a doctor, but if we match their talents to the right career, there is a greater likelihood they will be happy, productive adults.

Which Treatment Programs Work Best?

Unfortunately, research is extremely limited on which treatment strategies are most effective for teenagers with ADD or ADHD. Interventions at home with parents and the teen and at school with teachers and provision of accommodations are the most effective strategies. Remember, according to scientifically rigorous research, by far and away, *medication is the most* effective treatment for ADHD—90-plus percent show improvement. Combined medication and behavioral interventions may be the most helpful approach. According to research, other treatment programs that work include:

- Parent education about ADD and ADHD (and by extrapolation, probably teen education too)
- Parent training in child management regarding teens (25-30 percent show change)
- Family therapy with teens: problem-solving training (30 percent show change)
- Teacher education about ADD and ADHD
- Teacher training in classroom behavior management
- Special education services
- Regular physical exercise
- Parent support groups like CHADD

Remember also that most research on effective treatment for attention deficits has been done on *children*, not teenagers. To date, not nearly enough research has been done to understand the many complex issues that contribute to the success or failure of treatment in teenagers.

In addition, each teenager with an attention deficit is a unique individual with his or her own complex treatment needs. What works for one teenager is not necessarily going to work for another. Clearly, every

Table 5-2   Keys to a Good Outcome

One way to pursue a good outcome is to develop a *comprehensive individualized treatment plan* for your teenager. Common sense tells us that a treatment plan should help the teenager succeed in all aspects of his or her life—home, school, and community activities. Involving your teenager as a respected partner in the treatment process is critical. Obviously, the teen is more likely to follow a treatment plan that she helped develop. Here are several suggestions that were helpful to our family and that perhaps you too may find beneficial. Remember: take charge of your teen's and your own future by changing the things you can.

In summary, key elements of an individualized treatment plan include:

Medical/Treatment Issues: *Chapters 6 & 7*
1. *Consider taking stimulant medication* to enhance the functioning of neurotransmitters believed to be linked to symptoms of ADD and ADHD.
2. *Find the right medical doctor* (treatment professional) who understands attention deficit disorders.
3. *Treat coexisting problems* such as anxiety, depression, conduct disorder, sleep disturbances, or learning problems.
4. *Fine-tune medication;* ask teachers to complete a rating scale to assess effectiveness; ensure that the teen's medicine reaches peak effectiveness during the school day

Academic Issues: *Chapters 11-14*
1. *Identify learning problems and executive skill deficits.*
2. *Implement specialized instruction or classroom accommodations through development of an IEP or Section 504 Plan* to fit the unique learning needs and strengths of your teenager.
3. *Ensure completion of homework* through a regular homework routine, plus parental monitoring.
4. *Consider a "coach"* to help the teenager organize academics.
5. *Request classroom consultation* from school psychologists or private treatment professionals, if needed.

Community Issues: *Chapter 4*
1. Participate in community activities to *build self-esteem and confidence*; sports, religious events, art, music, modeling, or acting.
2. Promote *development of at least one friendship*; host activities and invite his or her friends.

Family Issues: *Chapters 4, 5 & 8*
Tips for helping teens
1. *Participate in "ADHD education"* program to help him or her better understand himself, ADD or ADHD, and his or her behavior, and to learn ways to cope with the disorder.
2. *Take part in skills training; self-advocacy and management, time and anger management; learn compensatory skills.*
3. *Consider counseling if needed.*
4. *Consider hiring a coach.*
5. *Advocate for accommodations for learning problems.*
6. *Consider medication.*
7. *Engage your teen as a partner* in treatment planning.

Strategies for parents
1. *Attend parent training classes* to learn about common problems of teenagers with attention deficits, new parenting skills for coping with ADD or ADHD, how to oversee the teenager's treatment, and how to promote resilience.
2. *Attend a local parent support groups* to receive support from other parents who have teenagers with the same problems; and/or *join national parent groups.*
3. Seek *"ADHD education."*
4. *Reframe ADD or ADHD* in a positive light and build on your teenager's strengths.
5. *Try behavioral interventions.*
6. *Consider counseling for yourself* to receive one-to-one guidance from a treatment professional and deal with any feelings of anger and self-doubt;
7. *Stay on top of your teen's treatment progress.*
8. *Ensure academic success.*
   - get medication right
   - treat coexisting conditions
   - identify learning problems and executive skill deficits
9. *Find a good career match.*

In Closing

Take charge and advocate for your teenager—***"Do whatever it takes to help your teen succeed!"***

treatment strategy described in this chapter is not appropriate for all teenagers with ADD or ADHD.

Factors Influencing Successful Treatment

As a parent, you should keep in mind the factors that are *predictors of a positive outcome* for attention deficit disorders. Many factors are beyond your control, but you should attempt to change any negative factors that are under your influence. Factors related to positive outcomes include:

1. a nurturing, supportive home,
2. emotionally healthy parents,
3. positive parenting practices (infrequent hostile parent/teen interactions),
4. positive friends,
5. emotional stability with less aggression, and
6. fewer emotional blow-ups.

Remember too that *resilience* plays a key role in how teens cope with this challenging condition.

Parents have greater control over these issues that are listed above. However, other factors are beyond their control:

1. higher intelligence,
2. less severe hyperactivity, and
3. middle to upper socioeconomic status.

Conclusion

So when does your involvement ever stop? Most likely, you will need to monitor and fine-tune your teenager's treatment plan on an ongoing basis through high school and probably into college or technical school training. With a little luck, someone else, perhaps a girlfriend or boyfriend, will become your child's "coach," and you may be relegated to assistant coach status. The big picture lifetime goals you hope your teenager achieves may include success in school, happiness at home, responsible behavior, good friends, honesty and integrity, and a zest for living. If he or she is doing well in these areas, then your treatment plan must be working. As teenagers mature and gain confidence in their ability to manage their own lives, your involvement and supervision gradually decline, although some parents may be involved at some level until their teen reaches 25 to 30 years of age. Regardless of when your teen matures, many treatment and support resources are now available so you won't have to tackle this job uninformed and alone.

6

The Medication Dilemma:
Should Your Teen Take Medicine?

Ideally, parents wish treatment for ADD and ADHD was simple and could be handled with a little counseling and behavior management. In fact, most parents would prefer never having to give *any* medication to their teenager; most try several strategies first before turning to medicine. Medication is often tried as a last resort. Typically, parents are desperate; their teen's self-esteem is in tatters and he may be on the verge of failing school. A few teens with a mild attention deficit may be able to cope without medicine. But the vast majority of teenagers need to take medicine to help them concentrate, pay attention, and do well in school.

Once out of school, many young people look for active, interesting jobs. If they find a good job match, some will not need to take any medicine at all or may only take it on days they need to focus—for example, to complete an adult form of "schoolwork" such as submitting sales reports or billings. Others may need to continue taking medication regularly in order to succeed on the job.

Research has clearly shown that stimulant medications are the single most effective treatment for attention deficits. These medications, which are so called because they *stimulate activity* in the *central nervous system (CNS)*, help students concentrate better, remember more information, complete schoolwork, and comply with requests from parents and

teachers. Stimulant medications are especially helpful as students advance to middle and high school and the number and difficulty of assignments increase. Plus, during these years, expectations from teachers change and students are expected to work much more independently. If a teenager continues to struggle at home and school, the benefits of medication usually outweigh any initial parental concerns about taking medicine. The decision to use medications, however, has to be a personal decision made by the teenager and family involved. This chapter is designed to give you the information you need to make an informed decision about what is best for your teenager.[1]

---

[1] *Caution:* I am not a physician, so please remember that the information about medications provided here is not intended to replace the expert advice of your medical doctor. The information is intended to educate you so you can be a better informed advocate for your teenager. No changes should be made in your teenager's prescribed level of medication without a doctor's approval. For instance, don't increase the dose or try sprinkling medication capsules on applesauce without first talking with your doctor.

Table 6-1   Behavior Changes from Stimulant Medication

Increased:	Decreased:
■ Attention and concentration ■ Compliance ■ Effort on tasks ■ Amount and accuracy of school work produced	■ Activity levels ■ Impulsivity ■ Negative behaviors in social interactions ■ Physical and verbal hostility

How Will Medicine Help My Teenager?

One of the major improvements parents and teachers should see is that the student will *do much better in school.* For instance, Bill Pelham, Ph.D., and Steve Evans, Ph.D., found that stimulant medication helped most teenagers improve their performance on quizzes and tests, improved attention, and decreased disruptive behavior. Quiz and test scores rose from an average of D minus to B or B minus. In addition, teacher ratings improved.

James Swanson, Ph.D., and his colleagues at the University of California (Irvine) conducted a "review of the review" of the research literature that included thousands of articles on attention deficit disorders. These studies provide convincing evidence that the student's school work and behavior improve significantly when stimulant medication is taken. When stimulant medications are working properly, parents and teachers should see several of the specific changes in behavior listed in Table 6-1. If you don't see these changes, the medication is not working properly. Chances are that you have not found the *right* stimulant medication for your teenager or the *dose may be too low or too high.*

"Right after Emily began taking medicine, she actually did her homework on Sunday. All I had to do was lock the door to the computer room and remind her a few times. This is a huge improvement. I promised to reopen the computer room if she did her homework and cleaned her room. Even that was a pretty minor battle. Her room was pretty messy, so instead of getting mad, I said, 'Oh Miss Emily Distracted… need help getting started?' We worked together and it went fast. We are very, very hopeful. She is already a different person. I think she is hopeful too."

Dr. Barkley has also found that medication helps improve certain executive function skills, including working memory, internalized language (self-talk),

verbal fluency, emotional control, and the ability to organize one's thinking. In addition, he reports improvements in handwriting, motor coordination, self-esteem, acceptance and interactions with peers, awareness of the game in sports, and decreased punishment from others.

However, even when medication is working properly, behaviors related to deficits in executive skills may still be problematic at times, despite some improvement. For example, issues such as disorganization, forgetfulness, and impaired sense of time must still be addressed with accommodations. Remember too, many of these behaviors immediately become problems again when the medication wears off. These medications last only ten to twelve hours at best, leaving the teen with an additional six to seven waking hours outside of school un-medicated.

So parents and teachers may still see continued problems with the following issues:
1. losing books and papers,
2. forgetting homework assignments, long-term projects, weekly reports, or after school conferences or detention,
3. planning ahead, and,
4. knowing how to budget time to complete long-term projects.

Keep in mind that these skill deficits are related to the attention deficit and *the teenager must be taught new skills or compensatory strategies and given accommodations at school!* Numerous suggestions for helping with these challenging academic and executive function issues in Chapter 12 and in *Teaching Teens,* Summaries 28-38.

Why Are ADD and ADHD Treated with Medication?

As discussed earlier, numerous studies have established a neurobiological link to attention deficit disorder, most likely a *deficiency in neurotransmit-*

ters, the chemical messengers of the brain. When these neurotransmitters don't work properly, students cannot pay attention easily and do their school work. Because of this deficiency, medication is frequently prescribed to increase the neurotransmitters in the synapse.

A second reason for prescribing medication is that researchers have shown that medication is clearly the most effective treatment for ADHD. Dr. Barkley goes as far as saying, "In a head to head comparison among all available treatments, medication produces the greatest change, bar none." In Barkley's Milwaukee study, they found that medication worked for 92 percent of children.

The medications most commonly prescribed for ADD and ADHD all affect the production or absorption of neurotransmitters. The three neurotransmitters most commonly associated with attention deficits are *norepinephrine, dopamine,* and, to a lesser degree, *serotonin*. Although the information presented in Table 6-2 is simplified, it gives a general understanding of how neurotransmitters influence the behavior of youngsters with ADD or ADHD.

Based upon a teenager's behavior, some doctors may speculate which neurotransmitters may be causing major problems and from that make educated guesses about which medications may work best. However, doctors still have to use trial and error methods to find the best medications for their patients. As you can see in Table 6-2, when norepinephrine is low, a student is indifferent, has low energy, and can't pay attention very well. According to Patricia Quinn, M.D., a medication such as Adderall or Strattera that increases norepinephrine could be helpful in treating someone who has ADD inattentive and the associated low energy levels and lack of alertness. If someone is extremely aggressive and hypervigilant, their norepinephrine may be quite high, so a stimulant like Concerta plus Clonidine might be an effective choice. Non-stimulants such as Strattera affect norepineprhrine. Antidepressants like the SSRI's and trycyclics can be useful in improving symptoms of irritability and impulsivity by decreasing norepinephrine and increasing serotonin. Specific medications are discussed in the following sections.

How Does Medicine Work? As you may recall from Chapter 2, the symptoms of ADD and ADHD are thought to be related to a deficiency in dopamine and norepinephrine in the neuron's synapse, thus preventing the brain from working properly. Since people with attention deficits have nearly twice as many dopamine transporters as the average person, these transporters carry the dopamine away too quickly before messages can

Table 6-2 How Neurotransmitters Affect Behavior

	High Level	Low Level
Dopamine	Undistracted Works intensely on tasks	Inattentive Distractible, moves from one thing to another Difficulty completing job Difficulty thinking ahead Difficulty delaying response Cognitive impulsivity
Norepinephrine	Thrill seeker Seeks new activities Impulsive aggression	Indifferent Low energy; apathy Depressed Planned aggression
Serotonin	Satisfaction Sense of well being Focus on one thing Helps with sleep	Dissatisfaction Irritability Aggression to self/others Impulsivity Obsessive compulsive Suicide risk Fire setting

cross the synapse. Consequently stimulant medications are prescribed in hopes of increasing the availability of dopamine, and, to a lesser degree, norepinephrine.

These medications trigger a chemical reaction at the receptor site of the next neuron (sometimes referred to as "binding" at the site), enabling the message to cross the synapse. After messages cross the synapse to the receiving neuron, the dopamine is taken back up into the sending neuron by dopamine transporters and recycled. This recycling process is known as *reuptake*. For additional information on medication and neurotransmitters you may enjoy reading "What Do I Need to Know about My Medicine?" and "What Do I Need to Know about My Brain?" in our *Bird's-Eye View* book.

Chemical Actions of Concerta Versus Adderall. Different stimulant medications increase dopamine in different ways. Methylphenidates (such as Concerta and Ritalin) block the reuptake of neurotransmitters, thereby allowing them to stay in the synapse longer so they can work properly. This blockage provides the higher levels of dopamine that are required for normal neuron-to-neuron communication. Specifically, methylphenidates increase mainly dopamine by slowing down the dopamine transporters, leaving more dopamine in the synapse. Dextroamphetamines (Adderall and Dexedrine) also increase dopamine but by a different mechanism—by increasing the amount of dopamine that is released into the synapse. They also affect norepinephrine, but to a lesser degree. Because methylphenidates and dextroamphetamines work via different mechanisms, scientists are wondering if there may be additional benefits from using them in combination, but in lower doses of each medication.

How Is Taking Stimulant Medication Different from Taking Illegal Drugs? While drugs of abuse share some of the same chemical mechanisms, the manner in which they are taken is totally different. Illegal drugs are often taken in high doses, not orally (sniffing or injecting), resulting in ultrahigh blood levels of the drugs. The result is euphoria, addiction, and a general overload of the system that can lead to nerve cell damage. See Chapters 7 and 10 for a fuller discussion of substance abuse issues.

How Does a Teenager Become Addicted to Illegal Drugs? According to Nora Volkow, M.D., at the National Institute on Drug Abuse, illegal "drugs of addiction also increased dopamine activity in the human brain's limbic system." The difference between stimulants and addictive drugs like cocaine is related to how long the dopamine stays in the synapse. Normally, when a stimulant is taken, the dopamine stays in the synapse only a short time—less than 50 microseconds—before it is recycled by the dopamine transporter. Drugs of addiction "block the dopamine transporter in the brain's reward circuits, allowing the neurotransmitter to remain in the synapse for a comparative eternity."

Researchers still do not fully understand why people become addicted, but research has shown that those who are vulnerable to addiction experience changes in the brain over time. For instance, there is a long-lasting reduction in dopamine type-2 receptors (D2). In fact, those prone to addiction appear to have started out life with lower numbers of dopamine 2 receptors. Others may take these same addictive drugs, "Yet the majority do not become addicted." A predisposition or vulnerability to addiction seems to be the key factor.

How Does *Not* Taking Medication Affect Teenagers?

It is also important to consider the flip side of the medication issue by asking this question: What are the "side effects" of *not* taking medication? Unless the ADD or ADHD is very mild, students with attention deficits who do not receive treatment are at high risk of having some serious problems, for example:

1. **School Failure and Family Turmoil.**
   According to Jerry M. Weiner, M.D., a former President, American Academy of Child and Adolescent Psychiatry, the risks of not treating attention deficits include "school failure, rejection by peers, and family turmoil, all of which can lead to developmental delays and psychiatric complications stemming from low self-esteem and frustration."

2. **Gaps in Knowledge.** Although some children with ADD or ADHD may appear to cope successfully in elementary school, there is a risk that without medication they may be just "getting by" and may be developing significant gaps in academic knowledge.

3. **Increased Risk for Behavior Problems.**
   Students with ADD or ADHD are at greater risk for speaking or acting impulsively, being suspended or dropping out of school. Since students who are being treated with medication have improved

school performance and compliance with adult requests, they are more likely to do well in school and thus less likely to have behavior problems.

4. **Increased Risk of Drug Use.** Students with ADHD who do *not* take medication are at greater risk for drug abuse.

A Medical Analogy. To explain the need to prescribe medication for treatment, some researchers compare attention deficits with a visual disability or diabetes. Just as people who cannot see well need glasses to help correct their vision or people with diabetes need insulin to regulate their body chemistry, students with ADD or ADHD may need medication to help their neurotransmitters work properly. Accommodations at school are comparable to providing the "glasses and insulin" that are needed to level the playing field and help them compensate for their learning problems.

Concerns about Medication

At least two myths have caused many parents to have serious reservations about giving medication to their teenager. Other reasons for parental concern include:

1. unsubstantiated, sensationalized negative publicity about Ritalin;
2. difficulty believing their teenager's problem is a biochemical one, treatable by medication;
3. Fear of immediate or long-term side effects of the medication; and
4. Guilt that they are "taking the easy way out."

Myths

Myth I: Stimulant medications such as Ritalin no longer work when the child reaches adolescence.

Research has shown that stimulant medications are effective in both children and teenagers with ADD or ADHD, and even in adults, in decreasing hyperactivity, impulsivity, negative behaviors, and verbal hostility, while improving attention, concentration, compliance, and completion of schoolwork.

Myth II: Use of medications like Ritalin will lead to drug abuse and addiction.

Some news reports have parents worried that their teenager will become a drug addict if he takes

Ritalin or other medication for his attention disorder. That means parents often unnecessarily delay starting treatment until they reach a point of desperation. But according to two major studies, students with an attention disorder who take medication are *not* more likely to abuse drugs. In fact, Tim Wilens, M.D., and Russell Barkley, Ph.D., both report that students with ADHD who take medication are actually less likely to abuse drugs than their peers who have ADHD but don't take medication

Abuse in Schools? Some news media have also implied that there is widespread abuse of Ritalin in schools. Consequently, the General Accounting Office (GAO), a federal watchdog agency, did a study to address this issue. In 2001, the GAO released its report stating that there are few incidents of medication abuse.

- Of nearly 800 middle and high school principals surveyed, only 8 percent reported knowing of attention disorder medications being diverted or abused at their school. Most principals who did report abuse reported only one incident.
- Approximately 90 percent of principals indicated that these medications were much less of a problem than the use of illegal drugs.
- Only 2 percent of students were administered attention disorder medications on a typical day, significantly less than the anticipated prevalence rate of from 5 to 12 percent.

"One educated parent who struggled with this decision finally said, 'I've decided I'm not copping out by using medication. My teenager needs to take medicine so the neurotransmitters in his brain will work right.'"

Negative Publicity about Stimulant Medication

Unfortunately, the media has unwittingly promoted misinformation about medications used to treat attention deficits. As a result, some parents are afraid to try medication. One powerful, ultra conservative organization has initiated a nationwide campaign regarding the "dangers" of medications for treatment of attention deficits. Actually, their primary mission is "to expose and eradicate violations of human rights by the field of psychiatry." So any disorder that is treated by psychiatrists may become a target for this group. Of course, the media has picked up on this campaign and has distributed information that is not based upon current science and research.

The organization alleges that the medications used to treat attention deficits may lead to "suicide, permanent severe emotional disturbance, murder, and substance abuse." Yet there are no scientifically valid research studies backing up their statements. Unfortunately, not every parent knows that this group has been behind the negative nonscience-based information that has appeared in newspapers and on television during the past decade.

In a series of lawsuits, this organization charged that three groups—the psychiatrists (APA), pharmaceutical companies, and CHADD—colluded to create a "nonexistent condition" known as attention deficit disorder. Thankfully, these lawsuits were either dismissed for lack of evidence or the group actually lost their case. This harassment has caused unnecessary stress and expense to the three targeted organizations, and, worse yet, has instilled a sense of unfounded fear among parents. As a result, it is not unusual to hear parents talk at length about the terrible struggles their child is having in school and, in their last breath, add, "but I'm not going to give him Ritalin." However, after receiving science-based information, parents often are willing to try medication. When they see the improvements, they sometimes "beat themselves up" because they waited so long to try medication.

"At first, my husband was pretty freaked out about our son taking medication. After all, our son was smart. He took the ACT in the 6th grade and got a composite score of 19, which would have gotten him into any state college. How could he possibly have ADHD? I feel badly now. The doctor said, 'You'll know right away if the medicine will work.' We were afraid to let him try it. We just didn't grasp the possibility that he really could have ADHD and that medication could make such an incredible difference."

Potential Diversion, Abuse, and Misuse of Medication

When stimulant medications are taken as prescribed, students are not likely to abuse these medicines. Obviously, the potential for abuse exists if the medicine is taken at extremely high doses, crushed and snorted, or injected. In a recent report, the Drug Enforcement Administration (DEA) indicated that they view diversion, abuse, and misuse of stimulant medications as a significant, growing problem. So it is impor-

tant for parents to be aware of the potential for diversion and abuse and act to prevent problems in these areas. Teens should always swallow their medication whole and never chew or crush it.

Diversion of medication from its originally intended purpose may happen in several ways:

1. children or teenagers may give or sell their medicine to their siblings, friends, or classmates;
2. teenagers may sell their sibling's medication;
3. teenagers may get the medicine from others;
4. medicines being held at school may be stolen;
5. some parents may take it themselves or sell it; or
6. rarely a teenager with ADD/ADHD may abuse his own medicine.

Researchers are encouraging parents to do a better job of educating their children and teenagers about the importance of taking medication as directed and not sharing the medicine with other students. Understandably, teenagers with attention deficits are pretty astute at spotting other teens who also have the condition. Obviously, they want to help their friends. If your teen may be inclined to help a friend who may have undiagnosed attention deficit by giving him some medicine, encourage him, instead, to get his friend to go in for treatment as soon as possible. Although intentions may be good, there can be serious legal consequences from sharing medicine with others.

What Is the Best Medical Treatment for My Teenager?

All of us—teenagers, parents, and professionals—would like the medical information about attention deficits to be crystal clear. We would like to know the exact cause of ADD and ADHD, the best medications, proper medication levels, and treatment outcomes. Unfortunately, medical treatment is not that simple. Response to medication varies with each child and teenager. Attention deficits must be treated by conducting an ongoing assessment of the teenager's response to medication and making appropriate adjustments to the medication and other aspects of the treatment plan. *Behavioral checklists* can be very helpful in determining when medicine is effective. Parents will find a sample medication checklist in Appendix 1.

The key to selecting the best medication is to work closely with your own doctor. This section will focus on stimulant medications such as Adderall and

Table 6-3 Stimulant Medications for Treating ADD/ADHD Symptoms

Traditional Stimulant Medications

Methylphenidates
- Concerta
- Focalin
- Focalin XR
- Metadate ER
- Metadate CD
- Methylin
- Ritalin
- Ritalin SR
- Ritalin LA
- Daytrana (a methylphenidate patch)

Dextroamphetamines
- Adderall
- Adderall XR
- Dexedrine
- Dexedrine SR
- Dextrostat

Concerta, plus the non-stimulant Strattera, and discuss other medications such as antidepressants in less detail. Although many of our teens do have coexisting conditions and may require a second medication, it is best to leave the details of those medications to your own physician or read the excellent book, *Straight Talk about Psychiatric Medications for Kids* by psychiatrist Tim Wilens, M.D. You may also ask your pharmacist for a package insert describing the medication, precautions, adverse reactions, and dosage. To stay abreast of the latest medical information, you might also want to read articles on medication in various CHADD publications: *ATTENTION* (magazine) or *CHADD Fact Sheets* (see the Resource Guide).

Stimulant and Non-stimulant Medications

Stimulants have long been considered the *medication of first choice* for improving a teenager's attention, and thus for treating attention deficits. These central nervous system (CNS) stimulants affect neurotransmitters, principally dopamine, enabling teens with ADD or ADHD to stay on task, concentrate, produce more schoolwork, behave less aggressively, be less disruptive, and have more stable moods. In addition, a newer medication—an effective non-stimulant called Strattera—was released in 2003. Now both stimulants and non-stimulants are available for treating attention deficits. All these medications also affect executive skills to some degree.

Most stimulant medications are made of one of two key ingredients: either *methylphenidate* or *dextroamphetamine*. All of the stimulant medications are classified as Schedule II controlled substances. Many experts

think this rating system, created over 50 years ago, unnecessarily implies these medications are dangerous. Practically speaking, this means that the government is monitoring these medicines more closely. Doctors must write a new prescription each month and cannot call it in to the pharmacy. When this book was first published in 1995, there were only two or three stimulant medications commonly prescribed by doctors. Now, as you can see in Table 6-3, there are many more choices. At one time, Cylert was also prescribed for ADHD. However, the FDA withdrew it from the market in 2005, because of its potential to cause liver damage.

Effectiveness

The majority of children with attention deficits respond well to one of the commonly used stimulant medications. Currently Adderall (amphetamine) and Concerta (methylphenidate) are the two most frequently prescribed stimulant medications. Stimulant medications last a limited number of hours and are then gone from the body.

Methylphenidates such as Ritalin have been around longer and have been the most frequently researched stimulant medication. According to several studies, medication effectiveness rates are in the 70 to 95 percent range. If only a single medication like methylphenidate (Ritalin) is considered, rates drop to 65-80 percent. If a teenager has only a marginally positive response or has negative side effects with a methylphenidate-based medication, the physician may try Adderall or Dexedrine, which are amphetamine-based medicines. When children who do not respond to Concerta or Ritalin are given another medication such as Adderall or Strattera, the odds of finding a medication that will work effectively jump to roughly 90 to 95 percent.

Which One Will Work Best for my Teenager?

According to researchers:

- Roughly 70% respond well to either methylphenidate or dextroamphetamine;
- 26% respond best to methylphenidate;
- 36% respond best to dextroamphetamine.

So, if your teen does not do well on a methylphenidate type medication like Concerta, you may try Adderall, another stimulant, or Strattera. As you can see, you should not assume that newer medications will always be best for your child. A physician and leader in the field of ADHD has several family members diagnosed with the condition. One is on a short-acting methylphenidate four times a day, another is on Dexedrine SR twice a day, and one is on Concerta.

Generic Stimulant Medications

According to many physicians, generic forms of stimulant medications such as methylphenidates and dextroamphetamines do not work as well as brand names (Adderall or Concerta). Other physicians, however, report that generic brands work effectively. Remember, medication response varies according to the individual, so some teenagers may respond better than others to generic medications.

PARENTS' COMMENTS ON EFFECTIVENESS

Memory improved . . .

"*Shawn's memory has improved so much since he has been on medication, it really blows my mind. He remembers to do his chores and to bring his laundry down to be washed. He never could do this before. It's like the difference between night and day.*"

Can study longer . . .

"*The most amazing observation to me was the day I saw Steven sit down at a desk and study for over three hours. That was shortly after he was put on Concerta as a sophomore in college. Before, it was rare for him to spend even fifteen minutes studying.*"

Less daydreaming . . .

"*I called one family to ask how the medication was working at school. The child said, 'I tried and tried to daydream and I couldn't.'*" —Pediatric Center Staff

Homework is no longer a battle . . .

"*When my teenage son is having academic difficulties, I tend to monitor his schoolwork very closely including completion of homework. Until he started taking Focalin in the evening, I never had the opportunity to work with him when he didn't have difficulty concentrating and completing his homework. The evening study periods seem much more productive and pleasant now that he is on the medication.*"

Grades improve . . .

"*Lewis's grades are much improved since starting on Dexedrine. No F's this semester. He even had his second A this year. Quite an achievement!*"

Improved driving, perhaps . . .

"*Will was complaining about taking Ritalin. 'When I drive, I don't think about anything else but driving.'*"

Sometimes, teenagers know themselves better than adults . . .

"*My son always told me it didn't do him any good to study for tests because he couldn't remember what he studied. I was somewhat skeptical of his comments until I talked with a psychologist who specializes in working with clients with attention deficits. The doctor told me of a twenty-year-old diagnosed as having ADHD and placed on Adderall. The young man commented that, thanks to the medicine, for the first time in his life he could remember what he studied for tests.*"

Dosages of Stimulant Medications

Researchers emphasize that the ideal dosage of stimulant medication depends on the teenager's individual response. Although different physicians prefer different medications, the key issue is the teenager's response to the medication and a careful assessment of its effectiveness.

Please keep in mind a few general points:

1. **Under-medication is common.** The NIMH/MTA study found that many children are on doses of medicine that are too low to achieve peak academic and behavioral performance. So if your teen is still struggling in school, ask teachers to complete the medication rating form (Appendix 1) and discuss the results with your physician. The doctor may consider a medication increase or change to a different drug.

2. **When stimulant medications are too low, additional medicines often are prescribed.** Another key finding of the NIMH/MTA study is that when the child takes a stimulant medication yet still has some problems, doctors tend to prescribe a second medication. However, when the stimulant medications are given at the right dose, children have fewer problem behaviors. Consequently, doctors are less likely to prescribe additional medications when doses of the stimulant are effective.

3. **Dosages of different stimulant medications may have different strengths.** According to Dr. William Pelham, most dextroamphetamine-based medications are almost twice as strong as methylphenidates. So, comparable dosages (mgs) for medications like Adderall or Dexedrine tend to be lower than for those of Ritalin or Concerta. For instance, 10 mgs of Ritalin is comparable in strength to 5 mgs of Dexedrine. Typical dosages for specific medications are discussed in subsequent sections.

Length of Effectiveness

Generally speaking, stimulant medications may be grouped into three time-release groups: *short, intermediate, and long-acting*. These options give parents and their doctors welcome choices to meet the individual teenager's needs. For example, some teens rebel at the thought of having to go to the school clinic at lunch to get their medication. The newer, long-acting medications solve this problem; they eliminate the need for remembering a midday dose. Each of these three time-release groups, however, may have a role to play in treatment, as will be explained in subsequent paragraphs. Refer to Table 6-4 for more information. Since most teenagers are more likely to be using the intermediate and long-acting medications, these longer acting medications are discussed first.

LONGER-ACTING TIME-RELEASE STIMULANT MEDICATIONS

These longer-acting medicines are known by several different terms: *sustained-release (SR), long-acting* (LA), or *extended-release* (ER, XR) tablets or capsules. Longer-acting medications act somewhat differently than short-acting tablets. They are absorbed more slowly, typically reach peak effect within about one hour, and last longer—five to twelve hours. Simplistically stated, some medicines release approximately half of the stimulant medication immediately and the remaining half two to five hours later. The newer medicines vary as to the time of release. For example, some release the medications slowly throughout the course of the day. Others release the greatest amount of medicine in the morning, and yet another group may peak in the afternoon.

Maximum Recommended Medication Dose. An explanation of the maximum recommended doses for medications is provided in at least two places: on the package insert for the medication and in a document known as the PDR—the *Physician's Desk Reference*. Typically, the pharmaceutical company gives a conservative statement of the maximum dose for each stimulant medication. Theodore Mandelkorn, M.D., a Washington pediatrician, points out that the initial PDR information on dosing methylphenidate was written in the 1950s. So, don't be too surprised if some psychiatrists or veteran physicians who specialize in treating

Table 6-4 Stimulant Medications: Length of Effectiveness

Type Medication	Time effective	Examples
Short-acting	4 hours	Dexedrine, Ritalin, Focalin
Intermediate	5-7 hours	Adderall, Metadate ER, Dexedrine SR, Ritalin SR
Long-acting	8-12 hours	Adderall XR, Concerta, Metadate CD, Ritalin LA

attention deficits actually prescribe a higher dose than is listed in the PDR. For example, some highly respected psychiatrists prescribe as high as 100 mg of Concerta for older, larger teenagers and adults, even though the recommended maximum dose in the PDR is 60 mg.

Medication Tolerance. According to researchers, some youngsters develop a tolerance to long-acting time-release medicines, so they may not be as effective after a few months. Dr. Mandelkorn reports that youngsters also may develop a tolerance to short-acting medications. Additionally, some researchers have found that a tolerance to long-acting medicines can build up during a twenty-four hour period. Accordingly, these researchers recommend that a higher dose of medication be given during the afternoon to achieve the same level of effectiveness achieved each morning. Other researchers, however, do not agree. Parents must observe the behavior of their own child and advise their doctor if tolerance becomes a problem.

Medication Build-up. Most stimulants are absorbed and cleared from the body within 24 hours. But that is not true for some of the longest-acting time-release dextroamphetamines that are in capsules. They may not leave the body totally within a 24-hour period, so may build up in the body over time. This may result in irritability after the medication has been taken for a few weeks. See the subsequent discussion on Adderall XR for information on addressing this issue.

Combining Short- and Long-acting Medicines. Occasionally doctors suggest combining a short-acting tablet with the longer-acting medicines to give more uniform dosing throughout the day and to prevent "rebound" or irritability when the medicine wears off. Benefits of using this strategy include:

1. **Easier Mornings**—*Waking Up.* If mornings are a nightmare, a teen on Concerta or Metadate ER might also be given a short-acting 5 mg Ritalin tablet to take each morning half an hour before he is scheduled to get up. (Both medicines are composed of the same core medication—methylphenidate, so they may be used in combinations.) This may help the disorganized, dawdling teen be more organized so that he can get ready and leave for school on time. The same thing can be done with Adderall in conjunction with regular 5 mg Dexedrine tablet since their core medica-

tion base (dextroamphetamine) is also the same. Dr. Patricia Quinn explains that some physicians will also combine a methylphenidate and an amphetamine; for example, Adderall XR and Focalin.

2. **Easier Homework.** Doctors sometimes prescribe a long-acting and short-acting medication together to cover the evening hours. The teen may need a 5-10 mg Ritalin or 2.5 mg Focalin or 5 mg Dexedrine in the late afternoon to tide him over so that he can concentrate on his homework. This use of short-acting medicine may help families avoid terrible homework battles.

3. **Extended Effectiveness.** The few remaining doctors who prescribe Ritalin SR usually have a special reason for this choice and do it in conjunction with regular Ritalin. Given in combination, the positive effect of Ritalin may be prolonged to five or six hours. Combining regular and SR Ritalin tends to smooth out the peaks and valleys as the medication levels swing up and down due to an uneven delivery system.

4. **Weekends.** One other time that these short-acting or intermediate time release medications may be helpful is on the weekend. Many teenagers sleep really late on Saturday mornings and taking the long-acting medications too late in the day will interfere with their ability to fall asleep that night. So instead, they can safely take a shorter-acting medication.

LONG-ACTING TIME-RELEASE MEDICATIONS (8-12 HOURS)

Long-acting medications such as Adderall XR and Concerta represent the newest group of stimulant medications to be released. Teenagers and parents especially like that the medicine lasts roughly 10-12 hours, which enables the teen to have a "normal day" for that period of time. Table 6-5 on page 110 includes more detailed information on these medications.

"When I started taking Adderall XR, it was amazing because I could concentrate all day. When I took Ritalin or regular Adderall, I could never remember to take the second dose. Or when I did remember to take it, it wasn't always timed exactly right so I didn't have a smooth release of medicine all day long. It seems like I can get a lot more done."

Medication Form, Dose, and Frequency. Although these medications give pretty good coverage throughout the day, Concerta and Adderall XR both reach a peak in the afternoon. Remember also that it typically takes an hour before the student will feel the effects of the medicine. You should take this delayed effect into consideration when determining when your teen should take medication prior to class. You may refer to Table 6-6 on page 121 to schedule the timing of medication appropriately.

When longer coverage is needed, your doctor may suggest twice a day dosing with the same long-acting stimulant. This would give sixteen to twenty hours a day coverage and does not interfere with sleep for some teens. For example, the teenager may take Adderall XR at 6:00 a.m. and then may take another one around 3:00 p.m.

Adderall XR. Adderall XR is very effective in treating attention deficits, and many teenagers like the fact that they can enjoy a fairly "normal" day for at least 10 hours. Although the beads in the capsule release a pretty strong dose of medicine in the morning, Adderall XR actually reaches its peak levels in the afternoon. In other words, Adderall XR may be slightly more effective in the afternoon. Usually, these subtle differences in when medication levels peak may not really matter. But if your teen is struggling in the afternoon, a long-acting medication such as Adderall XR may be more effective.

According to Jeff Prince, M.D., of Harvard Medical School and Massachusetts General Hospital, after taking Adderall XR for a while, it can build up in your system, resulting in increased irritability. To address this problem, Dr. Prince came up with a creative solution. He has his patients take Adderall XR capsules and Adderall tablets on alternating days.

A couple more interesting facts about Adderall: A heavy breakfast composed of eggs and bacon or acidic substances like orange juice slows the absorption of Adderall. It still reaches the same medication peak, but more slowly so the effectiveness is delayed. So avoid taking Adderall at the same time you eat a big breakfast. It may be best to take the medication before or after breakfast, but not at the exact same time.

For more information on Adderall, please read the next section on intermediate time-release medications. For teens who have trouble swallowing capsules, Adderall XR can be sprinkled on applesauce.

Daytrana. A new methylphenidate patch has been approved by the FDA and should be released in 2006. The medication release is continuous as long as the patch remains in place. This clear patch may be worn on the hip, small of the back, or forearm. Although the recommended time is nine hours, it can be worn longer and the medication effects will continue. The patch cannot be reused.

Concerta. The release mechanism for this medication is unique. The tablet is composed of three chambers. Two have different strengths of methylphenidate and one has a substance that expands when it absorbs liquid from your stomach. Methylphenidate is released initially, then the remaining medicine is pushed out as the remainder of the tablet dissolves. The highest peak of medicine is reached in the afternoon, with roughly 22 percent of the medicine released in the morning. Consequently, some researchers suggest that a booster of short-acting Ritalin be given in conjunction with Concerta to ensure effective medication coverage for the morning.

INTERMEDIATE TIME-RELEASE MEDICATIONS (4-8 HOURS)

When an intermediate time-release medication is needed, doctors may choose from several different name brand medications. A summary of the names, forms, dosages, and effectiveness of intermediate time-release stimulant medications is displayed in Table 6-5 on the next page.

Medication Form, Dose, and Frequency. Most of these medications come in several different strengths, making it easier for doctors to fine-tune the medication correctly. Although most of these medications give pretty good coverage throughout the day, some peak in the morning, others in the afternoon, and some give a steady release throughout the school day. Since levels of some of these medications may rise and fall throughout the day, the medication delivery system may not be as smooth as the "big three" long-acting medications: Adderall XR, Concerta, and Strattera. If Daytrana lives up to its pre-release publicity, it will join this group of long-acting medicines.

The time of day when peak medication is reached can be significant in treatment. If the teen is on medication but still struggling, talk with teachers and play detective. Do problems occur in all classes? Only in the morning? Only in the afternoon? Perhaps the challenge is simply a difficult subject or a challenging teacher, or the dose is too low or the peak medication is not reached during that particular class time. Parents

Table 6-5   Stimulant Medications

Long-acting Time-release Stimulant Medications (10-12 hours)

Dosage	Effective	Maximum Dose
Methylphenidates		
Concerta: 18, 27, 36, 54 mg (tablets)	Lasts 10-12 hours Begins working in 1 hour	54 mg maximum daily dose
Daytrana Patch: clear patch; dosage tied to size of patch; Larger patch; higher dose	Wear for 9 hours, effects continue for 3 hours.	One patch per day;
Adderall XR: 5, 10, 15, 20, 25, 30 mg (capsules)	Lasts 8-10 hours Begins working in 1 hour	30 mg maximum daily dose

Intermediate Time-release Stimulant Medications (4-8 hours)

Dosage	Effective	Maximum Dose
Methylphenidates		
Metadate ER: 10, 20 mg (tablets)	Lasts 6-8 hours Begins working in 1 hour	60 mg maximum daily dose
Metadate CD: 20 mg (capsules)	Lasts 8 hours Begins working in 1 hour	60 mg maximum daily dose
Methylin ER: 10, 20 mg (tablets)	Lasts 8 hours Begins working in 1 hour	60 mg maximum daily dose
Ritalin LA: 20, 30, 40 mg (capsules)	Lasts 8 hours Begins working in 1 hour	60 mg maximum daily dose
Ritalin SR: 20 mg (tablets) (only 5-10 mg Ritalin SR actually released)	Lasts 4-6 hours Begins working in 1 hour	60 mg maximum daily dose
Focalin XR 5, 10, 20 mg (capsules)	Lasts 6-8 hours Begins working in 1 hour	20 mg maximum daily dose
Dextroamphetamines (more potent than methylphenidates; comparable doses may be smaller)		
Adderall: 5, 7.5, 10, 12.5, 15, 20, 30 mg (tablets)	Lasts 6-8 hours Begins working in 1 hour	40 mg maximum daily dose
Dexedrine SR: 5, 10, 15 mg SR (capsules)	Lasts 6-8 hours Begins working in 1 hour	40 mg maximum daily dose

Short-acting Stimulant Medications (3-4 hours)

Dosage	Effective	Maximum Dose
Methylphenidates		
Ritalin: 5, 10, 20 mg (tablets)	Lasts 4 hours Begins working in 15-20 minutes	60 mg maximum daily dose
Focalin: 2.5, 5, 10 mg (tablets)	Lasts 4-6 hours Begins working in 15-20 minutes	20 mg maximum daily dose
Methylin: 5, 10, 20 mg (tablets)	Lasts 4 hours Begins working in 15-20 minutes	60 mg maximum daily dose
Dextroamphetamines (more potent than methylphenidates; comparable doses may be smaller)		
Dexedrine: 5 mg (tablets)	Lasts 4 hours Begins working in 20-30 minutes	40 mg maximum daily dose
DextroStat: 5, 10 mg (tablets)	Lasts 4 hours Begins working in 20-30 minutes	40 mg maximum daily dose

should also remember that these medications may take up to one hour to be effective. So a student who takes his medicine at 8:00 a.m. and is sitting in class by 8:30 may not be able to pay attention.

Adderall. During 2004, Adderall was the most frequently prescribed medication for treating attention deficit disorders. This medication has been carefully studied by two respected researchers: Dr. James Swanson, UC Irvine, and Dr. William Pelham, SUNY. Both Dr. Swanson's and Dr. Pelham's studies confirmed that Adderall is equally as effective as Ritalin in treating ADHD. Furthermore, in Dr. Pelham's study, many clinical staff actually favored Adderall three to one over Ritalin for the child's continued treatment. Perhaps, this choice is the result of doctor preference, a good delivery system, or good advertising. According to Dr. Swanson's research, Adderall lasts on average 6.40 hours. Adderall contains a combination of four salts of dextroamphetamine and amphetamine.

Dexedrine SR. Dexedrine SR (capsules) may be prescribed for teenagers who have not done well on Ritalin or Adderall. Although Dexedrine is considered as effective as Ritalin, it is not as widely used—perhaps because it is older. Dexedrine SR is an often forgotten, but still very effective medication.

Focalin XR. The company that makes Ritalin also makes Focalin. Basically, they have refined the Ritalin formula and produced a methylphenidate-based medication that is just as potent as Ritalin, but at a lower dose and with fewer side effects. The new XR capsules last up to eight hours. Half of the medication reaches a peak level within one hour or so and the remaining half roughly four hours later. The capsule may be opened and sprinkled on applesauce.

Metadate ER. Like other medications in this category, it may help to take Metadate extended-release tablets twice a day or augment it with a short-acting medicine. For example, a student may take the medicine at 6:00 am and then again at noon. The makers also suggest that it be taken 30-45 minutes before meals.

Metadate CD. Metadate CD capsules last roughly eight hours, in comparison to only six for the Metadate EF tablet. The Metadate CD capsule has many tiny beads, 30 percent of which are released immediately, and the remainder throughout the day. Metadate achieves its peak medication levels during the morn-ing. Metadate CD can also be opened and sprinkled on applesauce. It's important to drink water after taking medication in this manner.

Ritalin LA. Ritalin LA maintains a pretty even dose throughout the school day. Half of the beads in the capsule are released immediately, and the other half are released four hours later. Dr. Mandelkorn explains that this is like taking two doses of Ritalin four hours apart. Like Adderall XR, Ritalin LA can be sprinkled on applesauce for teens who may have trouble swallowing capsules.

Ritalin SR. Ritalin SR (sustained-release) tablets appear to provide only 5-10 milligrams (mg) of medication, instead of the anticipated 20 mg. So a higher dosage may be required to get the desired effect. In addition, Ritalin SR lasts only 4-5 hours, and some complain that it may release too slowly or unevenly so that there are peaks and valleys of effectiveness. As the first time-release medication, however, Ritalin SR was considered a godsend in the early years. Although doctors don't use it as frequently now, occasionally a child who hasn't done well on other medications responds well to the Ritalin SR. In recognition of the problems with Ritalin SR, its makers have produced the newer long-acting medication, Ritalin LA, which offers a more viable medication option.

SHORT-ACTING STIMULANT MEDICATIONS (3-4 HOURS)

Since long-acting stimulant medications came on the market, doctors don't prescribe the short-acting medications for teenagers very often. When these medications are prescribed, it is typically to augment the longer-acting medicines. For example, as discussed earlier, this practice can help teens complete their homework in the evenings and get up and get ready for school more easily.

Ritalin and Dexedrine are the best known short-acting medications. Focalin is also being used more frequently now. These short-acting medications work in a very predictable manner for most teenagers. Typically, the effect of the medication is observed in approximately 15-30 minutes. Dr. James Swanson's research showed that on average, methylphenidate lasts 3.98 hours. In actuality, drug effectiveness may be a little longer or shorter, since individual responses to medications vary. Table 6-5 gives key information about short-acting medicines.

Medication Form, Dosage, and Frequency. A summary of the names, forms, dosages, and effectiveness of short-acting stimulant medications is displayed in Table 6-5.

Ritalin. Ritalin (methylphenidate) is by far the most often researched stimulant medication. Until the last few years and the advent of long-acting medicines, Ritalin was the most widely prescribed stimulant medication. Some physicians prescribe Ritalin as the stimulant medication of first choice, especially for younger children. If the response is not positive and the doctor is limited to short-acting medicines, Dexedrine may be tried then. If the teen's primary medication is the short-acting Ritalin (10 mg), he may need to take it three to four times a day for maximum effectiveness: for example, at 7:00 a.m., 10:30 a.m., and 2:00 p.m. If a dose is needed later in the day, a smaller one (5 mg) may be taken around 5:00 p.m. or so.

Previously, physicians prescribed the dosage for stimulants based upon the child's weight—for example, milligrams of Ritalin per kilogram of weight. Researchers have noted, however, that there is no scientific data to support this practice. Sometimes younger children are on higher dosages of Ritalin than teenagers.

"When Steven was a senior in college he took Ritalin (5 mg), once a day, only when he went to chemistry class. This was pretty amazing since he stood 6 feet tall and weighed 220 pounds."

Dexedrine. Dexedrine is used in much the same way as short-acting Ritalin. Even though Dexedrine is as effective as Ritalin, some doctors have been reluctant to prescribe it, perhaps due to negative publicity generated in earlier years when it was seen primarily as an overused and sometimes abused diet pill.

Focalin. Short acting Focalin, a methylphenidate, reportedly lasts a little longer than short-acting Ritalin—4 to 6 hours, and has fewer side effects. It is more potent than Ritalin, so the maximum recommended daily dose is 20 mg.

Drawbacks for Short-acting Medications. One of the major drawbacks for teens who take only regular Ritalin or Dexedrine is that for the medication to achieve peak effectiveness, they must remember to take it three times a day. Unfortunately, by middle and high school, these youngsters often are too embarrassed to go to the office to take their medicine. Consequently, short-acting medicines are used less often for teens than the long-acting medications. When taken as directed, medications are extremely effective. However, they do have a higher potential for abuse than other medications such as Strattera, Concerta, and Adderall

XR. Interestingly, the teen receiving the prescription is not the one who usually abuses the medicine.

Side Effects of Stimulant Medications

Stimulant medications such as Adderall, Concerta, and Ritalin have unfairly received some bad press over the years. Because of lack of accurate information, parents are understandably fearful of side effects. The truth is, Ritalin has been studied carefully for over 30 years and has few side effects. Although the other medications have not been studied as often, researchers believe they are just as safe as Ritalin. The two most commonly mentioned side effects for all stimulant medications are loss of appetite and sleep problems. Irritability and weight loss are the next most often reported symptoms. Rarely, there have been more serious consequences of taking stimulants as discussed in "Safety Issues" below.

Approximately half of the children in one study who took Ritalin for their attention deficit exhibited mild side effects including loss of appetite, insomnia, anxiousness, nervousness, irritability, and/or proneness to crying. One-third reported mild headaches and stomachaches. Many of these side effects decline within one to two weeks after starting on medication.

Appetite Loss. Initially, weight loss may occur. Typically, the loss is less than five pounds and is not ongoing. Some physicians recommend that medication be taken at mealtime or sometime afterwards so that it will not suppress appetite.

Sleep Problems. Some teenagers have serious sleep problems that may interfere with their ability to function at school. For example, they may have trouble falling asleep and/or waking up, and thus may be tired the next day at school. Some of the sleep problems may be caused by taking medication too late in the day. For other teenagers, the sleep disturbance may actually be related to their attention deficit rather than a result of taking the medication. These teenagers most likely had sleep problems before they ever began taking stimulant medications. To avoid sleep difficulties related to medication and possible rebound effect, some physicians prescribe a lower dose of Ritalin in the late afternoon but suggest taking it no later than 4 or 5 p.m. Doctors may prescribe other medications such as Clonidine for sleep problems.

Paradoxically, some teens can actually fall asleep more easily when they take stimulant medicine. Apparently, it helps them slow down their minds so their brain doesn't jump from one idea to another. Then they can focus on getting ready for bed and sleep. Suggestions for dealing with sleep disturbances are provided in Chapters 7 and 9

Rebound Effect. Approximately one-third of youngsters on medication experience something referred to as "rebound" as their medication is wearing off. For half an hour or so, as the level of stimulant medication falls, the teenager may be irritable or aggressive and his activity level and restlessness may increase. He may have mood changes, and actually have more ADD/ADHD symptoms than usual. This problem is usually observed late in the afternoon or early evening. According to Dr. Gale Gordon, a pediatrician in California, rebound is much less common with the longer-acting medications. This may be another good reason for switching to a long-acting medicine.

For youngsters who experience rebound, the severity of the problem may vary from day to day. However, the problem is rarely severe enough to have to stop medication. To reduce rebound, some physicians suggest adding a smaller dose of a short-acting medication around 4:00 or 5:00 p.m. to alleviate the peaks and valleys of stimulant medications.

Growth Delay. In 2004, researchers with the NIMH/MTA Study reported mild growth suppression in the original group of children who were seven to nine when the study first started. Continuing follow-up of this group will be necessary to determine if the slowed growth is permanent. The critical question is whether these children will catch up in height when they reach the growth spurt that occurs during the teen years. In another study, Dr. Stephen Hinshaw, California-Berkeley, reported that children on stimulant medication grew more slowly by one-half inch and gained eight pounds less during a two-year period.

Previous research has found that stimulants may delay a youngster's *growth rate,* but did not permanently stunt growth. According to earlier research, when growth is delayed, it is only a temporary problem. These studies have shown that youngsters on stimulants, whose growth initially appeared slowed, gained height normally over a three- or four-year period.

Dr. Tim Wilens explains that growth is slowed for students with attention deficits in general, regardless of whether or not they are taking medicine. Our children tend to mature later and grow more during adolescence. If, however, you are concerned that your child is experiencing growth problems, perhaps unrelated to stimulant medications, you should talk with your doctor to see if referral to a specialist is warranted.

Other Side Effects. Mild increases in blood pressure and heart rate may also occur. Obviously, your teen's blood pressure, height, and weight should be monitored on a regular basis. Youngsters with ADD or ADHD may seem to lose their spontaneity if the dosage is too high. In one study, researchers found that adolescents had fewer negative side effects than children.

Safety Issues. Having been researched more than any other childhood medications including cough medicines, stimulant medications are considered very safe. However, as with any medication there are always risks. Parents must balance the minimal risks of taking medication with the risks of not treating the condition.

In 2005, the media reported 17 deaths among young people who took stimulant medications. However, there was no scientific proof showing that these medications caused the deaths. Five of the children who died had preexisting heart defects. The other causes were not as clear and involved a variety of factors: a family history of tachycardia (rapid heart beat), fatty liver, diabetes, very rigorous exercise, and heat exhaustion.

Furthermore, the media did not clarify that at that time 31,000,000 million prescriptions had been written during *one year,* while the 17 deaths occurred over a *7-year period.* Of course, these deaths are a terrible, terrible tragedy, and clearly there is a need for a thorough physical examination before children begin taking these medicines. Unfortunately, even medications that parents have long assumed were safe may have risks that most of us never hear about. For instance, during one recent year roughly 400 children died from taking penicillin because of an unexpected allergic reaction.

Fortunately, the FDA provides science-based facts and not sensationalism. According to one of their press releases, "the risk of death is no higher among children taking stimulant medicines than deaths among those who don't." According to Dr. Kate Gelperin, FDA's medical officer for drug safety, their research has shown "no conclusive link between the medications and the reported incidents in children and adults." Robert Temple, Director, FDA Medical Policy, testified, "We didn't find the sudden death data very persuasive. We don't want to "overscare" people who might benefit from taking important drugs."

However, to be on the safe side, the FDA did require a labeling change on prescriptions for Adderall advising that patients with an underlying heart defect may be at increased risk for sudden death. Obviously, when parents decide to use one of these medications, they should work closely with their physician and monitor their child's use. A physical examination to rule out any heart problems is critical. If you have had a good evaluation and trust your doctor, it may be worth considering a small dose of one of the tried and true medicines to determine your child's response. If improvements aren't significant as the dosage is raised, then you can stop the medicine.

Impact on Tourette Syndrome. Stimulant medications may cause an increase in tics if your teenager has a tic disorder and an attention deficit. Sometimes when a child begins taking stimulant medications, his tics get worse. When the medication is discontinued, the tics usually disappear. Most physicians urge a cautious approach to prescribing stimulants for combined tics and attention deficits. Sometimes Clonidine or tricyclic antidepressants may be prescribed instead. As explained in Chapter 7, some doctors have found that coexisting ADHD and Tourette syndrome can be safely treated with stimulants.

Impact on Bipolar Disorder. Teens with undiagnosed bipolar disorder (BPD) and ADD or ADHD may have an adverse reaction to stimulant medications in certain situations. If stimulant medications alone are administered to these teens, the symptoms initially may seem to get better but then may get worse. The teen may become angrier, more impulsive, more hyperactive, and more difficult to manage. Other teens with BPD have an immediate adverse reaction to stimulants. Rarely, children under 10 with undiagnosed BPD may also experience hallucinations.

Most doctors stabilize the teen's mood problems first before adding stimulants. Later, once the bipolar symptoms are under control, a stimulant may be prescribed safely. The need for careful, regular assessment of the medication's effectiveness is obvious. Diagnostic criteria for bipolar disorder are provided in Chapter 7.

Unique Aspects of Stimulant Medications

There are a few unusual facts about stimulants you should know:

- *Don't chew or snort medicines.* Chewing or crushing and snorting a tablet of stimulant medication instead of swallowing it may result in an unpredictably high blood level of the medication and toxic side effects.

- *Avoid taking aspirin and acidic foods (citrus fruit or orange juice) with stimulants* since it may interfere with the absorption of the medication. For example, your teen should avoid drinking orange juice with the medicine.

- *Avoid taking some medications with breakfast.* Some medications seem to work best when taken on an empty stomach at least 30-45 minutes before a meal. For example, research has shown that the effectiveness of Adderall XR capsules is reduced if it is taken with breakfast, especially if it contains high fat foods like eggs and bacon.

- *Monitor antihistamines and decongestants.* Antihistamines like Benadryl may *reduce* the effectiveness of stimulants. Decongestants such as Actifed may *increase* the effect of the stimulant.

- *Antidepressants may affect medication effectiveness.* According to Dr. Wilens, stimulants may change the metabolism of the antidepressant. As a result, a lower dose of the antidepressant may be equally effective when he is taking both medications.

"Medication Holidays"

In the past, some doctors recommended taking a break from stimulant medicines on the weekends or perhaps all summer long. The thinking was that attention deficits were only a school-related problem. Medication holidays are not recommended as frequently now as they were ten years ago. We now recognize that attention deficits are chronic 24-hour conditions like hypothyroidism and diabetes and should be treated 365 days of the year.

Many physicians adamantly *oppose* these "holidays," especially for teens. There are marked disadvantages to discontinuing medication during the summer. For example, a teenager's inattention and impulsivity can sometimes lead him into dangerous situations if he is driving or going out with friends, plus teens may be tempted to use other substances to compensate for not being on medicine. Parents and physicians may also decide to continue medication year round if problems are occurring at home, at school, or in relationships with friends. As a parent, you must weigh the pros and cons in making this important decision.

"Our son did not take medication in the evenings, weekends, or summers. Our initial approach to medication use was extremely conservative because of our fears about giving medication. In retrospect, it appears we made a huge mistake.

"Being the conservative parent I am and wanting to minimize the amount of medication he took, I did not give him medicine in the afternoon or evening. What I now realize is that the effects of Adderall had totally worn off by the time he started his homework in the evening. It is no wonder we continued to have so many battles over homework. Our son's behavior at home and performance at school improved significantly when we increased his medication levels and began giving him medication in the late afternoon before he did his homework. He seemed to concentrate better and remember more of his studies. We had fewer fights over homework."

A few doctors may recommend a "holiday" just to be safe, thus avoiding any unusual long-term side effects unique to a specific child. Dr. Gale Gordon suggests that "holidays" may make sense for students with milder attention deficits who don't have any major behavior problems, hyperactivity or problems relating to friends.

One reason *not* to give your teenager a "medication holiday" is for fear that he will become addicted to stimulant medications. Researchers have not found problems with addiction or drug dependence to stimulant medications in later life. In reality, as reported earlier, students with attention deficits on medicine are less likely to abuse drugs than those with attention deficits who do not take medicine.

Non-stimulant Medications for Treating ADD and ADHD

Currently, only one non-stimulant is approved in the U.S. for treatment of ADD/ADHD: Strattera. Several others are under investigation, however, and are occasionally prescribed as an adjunct to treatment for attention deficits.

Strattera (Atomoxetine)

In November of 2002, a new non-stimulant medication was released in the United States and received a lot of positive attention. It is one of the first new classes of medications for treatment of attention deficits that has been released in thirty years. Strattera has some unique advantages among medications for attention deficit. First, the medicine lasts all day, which improves behavior and social skills for a longer period of time. Second, it is not a controlled Schedule II stimulant. This means doctors can give you medication samples and can call in prescriptions to the pharmacy, so prescriptions do not need to be picked up or mailed every month.

Scientists believe Strattera acts on norepinephrine, blocking its reuptake. Some doctors speculate that this medication might be more effective with teens with ADD inattentive, although this usage has not yet been researched. Like the other two long-acting medications, it has little likelihood of abuse.

Effectiveness. According to research conducted by Tom Spencer, M.D., Strattera is effective for children. Spencer's group at Harvard also found that all of but 1 of 30 children responded favorably. Although results were seen within a week or so, research shows that significant improvements continued for up to 10 to 12 weeks. As with any new medication, there is little research about Strattera. With time, more information about both short- and long-term side effects will become available.

Word-of-mouth reviews on Strattera's effectiveness have been mixed. Some physicians consider Strattera a medication of first choice for treatment of ADHD. Other doctors have indicated that Strattera has not been that effective for their patients. Dr. Mandelkorn reports that he has been more successful starting new patients on Strattera rather than switching patients who have been on stimulants. Unlike with stimulants, patients can't feel the Strattera "kick in," so it may feel like it's not working very well. Some patients have difficulty adjusting to this difference.

Dr. Lyndon Waugh, an Atlanta psychiatrist and author of *Tired of Yelling*, reports that roughly 30 percent of his patients do well on Strattera alone. Another 30 percent or so need a stimulant in addition to the Strattera for maximum effectiveness. Finally, 30 percent prefer to remain on stimulants. So, if your teen is successful on his present stimulant medication, there may be no real reason for you to consider switching.

Medication Form, Dosage, and Frequency. Strattera is available in 10, 18, 25, 40, and 60 mg capsule strengths. The dose for this medication is based upon your weight. For example, if you weigh 125 pounds, you might start with four capsules of 18 mg for 4 days, then 25 mg for 4 days, then take 40 mg for 4 days, and thereafter take 50 to 60 mgs a day and higher if appropriate. The maximum daily dose usually does not go above 100 mg. To avoid side effects, some doctors recommend starting with even lower doses and increasing them more slowly than the package guidelines suggest.

Since this medication is new, researchers have a lot to learn about it. Some doctors prescribe Strattera in addition to a lower dose of the stimulant medication that the teenager is already taking. Researchers have studied Strattera and methylphenidate in combination and found they worked well together. Apparently, these two medications affect different neurotransmitters and different parts of the brain. So, taken in combination, the teen may get an even greater improvement in his symptoms. However, one teen I know who took both Strattera and Adderall XR at higher doses experienced severe migraine headaches. Later he was able to continue taking both medications but at lower doses.

Side Effects. The most common side effects are headache, upset stomach, and decreased appetite. Taking Strattera with food may avoid problems with gastric irritation. Tiredness, dizziness, dry mouth, and other side effects can be avoided by raising the dose slowly. Currently, the Strattera brochure mentions that allergic reactions such as swelling or hives may sometimes occur. Obviously, this could be serious so you should stop the medication and see your doctor.

An FDA Warning. The FDA issued a statement in late December of 2004, warning of possible liver damage. This warning means that Strattera must include a label that identifies liver damage as a potential side effect. "The labeling warns that severe liver injury may progress to liver failure resulting in death or the need for a liver transplant in a small percentage of patients," the Food and Drug Administration said. Most people have taken the medication with no major problems. Among more than 2,000,000 people who have taken Strattera, two people experienced liver problems. The adult and teenager received treatment and recovered

fully. None of the 6,000 people in the trial study showed any signs of liver damage. Signs of possible liver problems include jaundice, dark urine, unexplained flu-like symptoms, upper right-side abdominal tenderness, and a form of itchy skin known as pruritus. Talk with your doctor if you have concerns or questions.

The FDA also has required warning of an "increased risk of suicidal thoughts" for people taking Strattera. Although increases in suicidal thoughts were reported in several studies, there was only one attempted suicide and no deaths.

Other Medications Under Consideration

Researchers are currently looking at some new and old medications for treating symptoms of attention deficits.

Nicotinic Acetylcholine. One new drug known as ABT089 may tap the beneficial effects of nicotine. Nicotine has long been known to improve attention, alertness, and memory, which probably explains why roughly 50 percent of teens with attention deficits smoke cigarettes. This seems to be another example of teens self-medicating. Of concern, though, is a recent study that listed nicotine, not just the tars in cigarettes, as a possible cancer-causing agent.

Provigil (modafinal). A study was released in 2003 indicating that Provigil, a medication prescribed for narcolepsy (a disorder that causes extreme difficulties staying awake), also improves some symptoms of attention deficit disorder. Children in the study could pay attention better, think before acting, and were less impulsive and hyperactive. However, it is not as effective as stimulant medications like Adderall or Concerta. Headaches were listed as the primary side effect.

Aricept. In 2002, researchers at Massachusetts General Hospital found that students with attention deficits who took Aricept (donepezil), a medicine used to treat Alzheimer's patients, showed a 25 percent improvement in both attention and executive skills. The starting daily dose was 2.5 mg with a maximum daily dose of 10 mg. There were no adverse side effects. This was one of the first studies of Aricept that was conducted specifically to determine its effect on attention deficits and executive function. *Reminyl* and *Exelon* are two similar medications.

In summary, none of these new medications are considered first-line treatment choices, with the exception of the Daytrana skin patch, but might be considered if other traditional medications are not effective.

Medications for Conditions That Occur with ADD and ADHD

Sometimes a teenager with an attention deficit is prescribed stimulant medications but continues to struggle at home or at school due to aggressiveness, moodiness, or impulsivity. These symptoms may be caused by another *coexisting condition* such as anxiety, depression, or bipolar disorder.

As discussed earlier, a second medication in addition to a stimulant may then be prescribed. Sometimes this is referred to as *poly-pharmacy*. As expected, many family physicians or pediatricians are cautious about trying medication combinations, as little, if any, research is available about the long-term effects of these combinations. Most physicians won't recommend medication combinations unless they are critical for treating complex problems.

If your teenager continues to struggle and a combination of medications seems warranted, you may want to consult a psychiatrist. Psychiatrists prescribe antidepressants such as Zoloft and other medications such as Clonidine and Depakote more frequently than other physicians do, and may be more familiar with their action and effectiveness in treating attention deficits. A psychiatrist may be able to help you determine the proper medication regimen and to obtain the most up-to-date information on effective medication combinations for treating ADD or ADHD.

Several other medications may be prescribed for treating coexisting conditions. A brief overview of these medications is provided in this section. As mentioned earlier, *Straight Talk about Psychiatric Medications for Kids* by Tim Wilens, M.D. provides more detailed information on these medications.

Antidepressant Medications

As the name implies, antidepressant medications are primarily used to combat depression in adults. These medications affect the activity of the neurotransmitters, especially serotonin. Apparently, they increase levels of serotonin, which are often low in people who are depressed.

Antidepressants may be prescribed for teenagers with attention deficits in combination with stimulants, specifically for coexisting conditions. Antidepressants can help reduce inattention and hyperactivity, if they are related to a mood disorder such as depression, but they will not treat symptoms of attention deficit disorders at all. Since most teens with attention deficits have coexisting conditions, it comes as no surprise that approximately 70 to 80 percent of these youngsters respond favorably to these medications. However, antidepressants are considered a medication of second choice.

If a teen has an attention deficit and a mood disorder, both will need to be treated. If the moodiness is secondary to the attention deficit disorder, the use of a stimulant may actually relieve the mood problem. Antidepressants may be helpful for teenagers who are anxious, obsessive-compulsive, aggressive, are experiencing emotional highs and lows, or have tics. As Barbara Sayes, retired FSU professor of social work, often explains, "Aggression may mask depression." Consequently by treating depression, aggression and impulsivity are often reduced. These medications are also an effective treatment for bedwetting problems in younger children. A few antidepressants also help treat sleep problems.

For some teenagers, antidepressants may be equally as important as stimulant medications. According to Dr. Tom Brown, some teenagers and adults who have ADD inattentive, as opposed to ADHD, respond better when treated with a combination of antidepressants and stimulants.

One advantage of antidepressants is that they have a longer-lasting effect than stimulants. Teenagers can take medicine at night and benefit from the medication 24 hours a day. Two major types of antidepressants are used to treat attention deficits: selective serotonin reuptake inhibitors (SSRIs) and the older tricyclic antidepressants.

SSRIs

Selective serotonin reuptake inhibitors (SSRIs) are so called because they increase levels of the neurotransmitter serotonin in the synapse. Some of the better known SSRIs include Zoloft, Prozac, Paxil, Celexa, and Lexapro.

Doctors often prescribe SSRIs as the first choice for treating obsessive-compulsive disorder in children. In addition, they are the most frequently prescribed antidepressants for students when doctors are also treating their attention deficit. Less frequently, they are used to treat anxiety. Dr. Patricia Quinn suggests that prescribing an SSRI in addition to a stimulant may be especially helpful for girls who are emotionally reactive and may experience mood swings and emotionality related to their menstrual cycles. Dr. Tom Brown found that teenagers and adults with ADD inattentive responded favorably to a combination of Ritalin and Prozac.

Side Effects. The side effects of SSRIs may include headaches, anxiety, nervousness, insomnia, sexual dysfunction, nausea, and/or diarrhea. In some people, they also cause significant weight gain. Unlike the tricyclics, they are less likely to cause problems with sedation, blood pressure, and EKG changes. SSRIs can, however, trigger manic episodes in children who may have untreated bipolar disorder. That's why doctors may be cautious and try low doses of Zoloft or Paxil first, since they will clear the body systems more quickly than Prozac will. That way any bad reaction to this medicine will be short lived.

TRICYCLIC ANTIDEPRESSANTS

The tricyclic antidepressants such as Tofranil and Norpramin were developed before the SSRIs. When this book was first published in 1995, the tricyclics were the most commonly prescribed antidepressants for treating teenagers who also had attention deficits. They are seldom prescribed now because SSRIs tend to have fewer and less serious side effects. On a positive note, tricyclics also can be effective in treating *sleep problems*. Dr. William Larsen, a pediatrician in Anchorage, Alaska, has found Tofranil at a low dose (25-50 mg) to be very effective in treating sleep issues. Teenagers may be able to fall asleep more easily, wake up more easily, and be less irritable each morning. Perhaps the quality of their sleep is also improved. Tofranil has also been used effectively for years to treat *enuresis* (bed wetting). Anafranil is the only tricyclic that seems to help with obsessive compulsive disorder.

Side Effects. Side effects can include dry mouth, dizziness or lightheadedness, constipation, increases in blood pressure and rapid or irregular heart rate, appetite increases, nervousness, headache, and nausea. Weight gain may also be an issue for some teens. Physicians should check blood levels periodically to avoid potential toxicity and ensure that levels are not too high. An accidental overdose can be deadly. Parents should keep these medications in a safe place and monitor their use.

CAUTIONS

Don't Mix Drinking and Antidepressants. Educate your teen about the dangers of combined drinking and antidepressants. If your teenager is prescribed an antidepressant, you should work closely with your physician to monitor its use. Drinking alcohol while taking antidepressants could cause serious problems since the medication intensifies the depressant effects of alcohol. As a result, a teenager may get *drunk more easily* or have an *accidental overdose*. If a teenager is depressed and consumes excessive alcohol, he might be more prone to *consider or attempt suicide*.

Taper Off Antidepressants Gradually. This is especially true of the SSRIs. Otherwise, your teen may experience unsettling side effects known as *discontinuation syndrome*. In 1996, researchers reported that 12 percent of patients in one study experienced unsettling symptoms when they abruptly stopped taking SSRIs. Jeff Prince, M.D., Massachusetts General Hospital, explains that the core symptoms include anxiety, crying spells, and irritability. Other symptoms may include hyperactivity, slowed thinking, memory problems, confusion, dizziness, odd sensations such as prickling on the skin, lethargy, chills, vivid dreams, and lowered mood. These symptoms were also discussed on a national television program where one participant described them like little electrical jolts in the brain. These symptoms were worse for Paxil (20 percent) than for Zoloft (2 percent) and Prozac (0 percent). In other words, 20 percent of the 12 percent who had these unusual symptoms were taking Paxil. These symptoms also can occur if a teenager forgets to take these medications on the weekend. So, if your teen stops taking this medication, it is important to taper it off gradually; don't stop cold turkey.

An FDA Warning. In March 2004, the Food and Drug Administration (FDA) requested that a drug-label warning be added to ten antidepressant medications that may have potentially dangerous side effects. Specifically, there are concerns that these medications may contribute to an increased "risk of suicide," or, more accurately, self-destructive behavior. Although there is currently no proof that this is true (no deaths were reported in the study), some parents suspect that antidepressants caused their children to take their lives.

Remember too that untreated depression itself can lead to suicide. These medications have provided a tremendous benefit to many children and no doubt have *saved* many lives. No one can say with certainty whether a teen might have committed suicide whether he was on an antidepressant or not. The FDA is studying this issue, so talk with your doctor about the latest research and what is best for your child.

Certainly, teens who are extremely depressed are vulnerable to suicide risk. The period when they begin taking medication is a high-risk time and warrants cautious diligence by parents. Since these medications can take a few weeks to reach a therapeutic level, it stands to reason that teens may get worse during the initial treatment period as they are waiting for the medicine to work. Furthermore, some physicians speculate that perhaps as the antidepressant begins to work, teen may feel better and gather the energy to commit suicide.

Another possible explanation for these deaths is that some children with bipolar disorder have been misdiagnosed with an attention deficit and the antidepressants have sent them into a dangerous state of mania—with abnormal excitability, exaggerated feelings of well-being, or excessive activity.

If your teen is prescribed an antidepressant, watch for any worsening of depressive symptoms, or increased anxiety, impulsivity, hostility, irritability, or insomnia. Be vigilant and do not assume that your teen will improve immediately after starting antidepressants. Most of these medications take up to a month before you get maximum benefits. You may wish to read more about the risks and warning signs of suicide in Chapter 10.

The medications on the FDA list include:

- Prozac
- Zoloft
- Paxil
- Luvox
- Celexa
- Lexapro
- Wellbutrin
- Effexor
- Serzone
- Remeron

NEWER ANTIDEPRESSANTS

When better known antidepressants such as Zoloft or Prozac don't work, doctors may try newer medications like Wellbutrin or Cymbalta, sometimes called atypical antidepressants. Research regarding their effectiveness is limited. Although Wellbutrin may initially help with anxiety or depression, a few problems have been reported later. Patients of Dr. Patricia Quinn who were taking Welbutrin reported experiencing "cognitive clouding" after they have been on the medicine for nine months or longer. The Wellbutrin does *not* significantly improve the ability to pay attention. This medication may also make tics worse and increase the risk of seizures by lowering the threshold for seizures. Typically these medications may be given as an adjunct to treatment but not instead of a stimulant.

Medications for Treating Problem Behaviors

Two or three other classes of medications may help reduce more serious problem behaviors such as anger, defiance, or aggression. These medications are known as mood stabilizers, anticonvulsants, antihypertensives, or antipsychotics. Interestingly enough, doctors have found that medications used primarily for one purpose such as treating high blood pressure or seizures may play a major role in treating problem behaviors such as anger or aggression.

Mood stabilizers such as depakote help control volatile behavior, mood swings, overactivity, impulsivity, and aggression. These are the medications of first choice for treating children who may have bipolar disorder.

Antihypertensives such as Clonidine or Tenex are used to treat high blood pressure in adults. In children, however, they are prescribed to treat conditions that coexist with attention deficits such as aggression, tic disorders, and sleep problems. They may be used in combination with stimulants, mood stabilizers, or antidepressants. The beta-blocker Inderal (propanolol) is sometimes prescribed in low doses to students with ADD or ADHD who have extreme anxiety about making presentations in class or other events that require public speaking.

Newer *antipsychotics* such as Risperdal (risperdone), Zyprexa (olanzapine), and Seroquel (quetiapine) tend to be used as medicines of second and third choice for mood swings, Tourette syndrome, or disruptive or aggressive behavior. These medications are also called major tranquilizers or neuroleptics. These newer medications are being used more often for treating psychosis including hallucinations since they have fewer side effects. They are effective in treating symptoms such as withdrawal, loss of interest, ambivalence, and flattening of mood. Antipsychotics, especially the older ones like Haldol or Thorazine, have significant side effects and are usually tried only when all other medicines have failed.

Dr. Wilens urges parents to learn as much as they can about these medications and their side effects before agreeing to have them prescribed for their teenager. Of course, all these medications have to meet safety standards and cannot be manufactured without proper research and approval by the Drug Enforcement Administration (DEA). As with all medications, parents must monitor any disturbing changes in their teenager's behavior and discuss them with the physician.

Tips for Fine-Tuning Medication

Typically, the treatment goal is to have all day coverage of medication with peak coverage during school and homework hours. Reaching this goal will take careful monitoring. Determining the proper medication, dosage, frequency, and timing for each teenager is not a simple process, and trial-and-error fine-tuning is essential. Four critical issues are at the heart of effective medical treatment for children and teenagers with an attention deficit:

1. determining which medication works best;
2. determining the proper dose, frequency, and timing of medication;
3. educating the teen about medication; and
4. addressing any of the child's concerns so that medication refusal doesn't become a problem.

Which Medications Are Best?

As mentioned above, roughly two-thirds of students respond well to either methylphenidates such as Concerta or amphetamines like Adderall. In other words, one-third probably will respond best to methylphenidate and another one-third best to amphetamines. So if your teen tries a methylphenidate and it doesn't work, first work with the doctor to ensure that the dosage is high enough to be effective. If it still doesn't work, then talk with the doctor about trying an amphetamine or a non-stimulant. Remember, the key is to consult closely with the doctor as you and your teenager work to get the medications properly adjusted.

When a teenager with an attention deficit starts on medication, his parents typically call the physician after the first week or so and report on how the medication is working. You should get input from both your teenager and at least one or two of his teachers. The teenager himself may or may not be able to accurately gauge the medication's effectiveness. When parents ask if the medication helps, teenagers may say they can't tell for certain. Experts tell us that teachers are usually the most accurate judge of the effectiveness of medication at school.

Reports from the teenager, parents, and teachers about the medication's effectiveness are usually all that is needed to find the proper dosage. If your teenager's problems are more complex—he isn't responding well to the medication and is still struggling in school—a more formal assessment of medication

response should be done. This assessment can help determine which medication is most effective and assist in fine-tuning exact dosages and times for administering it. A more detailed description of objective medication assessment plus a rating scale are discussed later in this section.

What if the medication doesn't work? Dr. Hallowell and Dr. Ratey suggest that sometimes families conclude too quickly that "medication isn't working." It may take weeks or months to find the best dosing schedule, since each teenager responds differently to medication. In addition, medication needs may change as the teenager grows older and faces increased demands in school or on the job. Plus, many teenagers need a medication adjustment when they reach puberty and major hormonal changes occur. Medication tolerance may also become an issue. Interestingly, some teens may find that a medication that previously was ineffective may work a few months or years later.

"Jerry was doing just fine on his medicine until he reached middle school. Suddenly his grades went downhill and we were clueless as to why he was doing so poorly. During a discussion at our local CHADD meeting, it became apparent that the medication dose was now too low. He had reached puberty and his body chemistry had changed significantly. Once we talked to our doctor, adjusted the medication, and then later switched to Adderall, he did just fine."

Finding the Right Dose

Parents and doctors often struggle to find the right dosage. Obviously, there are legitimate concerns about either over- or under-medicating teenagers. It will take trial and error work to find the best possible dose. Researchers in the landmark NIMH/MTA study continued to increase medication doses "until there was no room for improvement" and the children functioned as well as other children in the classroom who did not have attention deficits.

Dr. Mandelkorn follows a similar procedure in his practice. He "pushes" the medication dose higher to find the best dosages. For example, if a teenager is taking 30 mg Adderall XR and doing pretty well, he might ask the teen to add a 5 mg capsule. Then he asks the question, "Are you doing better or worse on this dose of medicine?" He continues to increase the dose, within limits, of course, until the teen, with the concurrence of parents and teachers, finally says that things are worse. Then he drops back to the previous medication dosage.

This procedure is now considered best practice and is referred to as *titrating to the best therapeutic dose.*

Dr. Gale Gordon explains that many patients mistakenly worry that a higher dose of medicine means that their child's attention deficit is worse than for others. Obviously, that's not true. She explains that just as diabetics must have the "right" dose of insulin, our teens must have the "right" dose of Adderall, Concerta, or Strattera.

Remember, too, that children in the MTA group who were being treated in the community by their local doctor were on doses of medication that were too low to achieve the best results.

How Often Should My Teen Take Medication?

You, your teenager, and your physician must decide how frequently to take medication. All-day medication coverage is ideal. Some families, however, decide to use medication very sparingly, perhaps due to fear of side effects or the cost of the medication. This decision may cause problems, since medication may wear off before homework time. To avoid homework battles, parents may decide to augment a longer-acting medication like Adderall with a short-acting medication like Dexedrine (5 mg) to help with homework.

Table 6-6 Charting Effectiveness of Medication

Time	Medications (Adderall 20 mg; Focalin 10 mg)	Classes	Medication Status
7:00 A.M.	Wake up		
7:30	Take Adderall; effective within 1 hour		
8:00		Algebra	Not great
8:30	Meds are working		
9:00		Spanish	good
9:30			
10:00		Language Arts	good
10:30			
11:00		American Gov.	good
11:30			
12:00		Lunch	good
12:30			
1:00		P.E.	good
1:30			
2:00		Biology	fading
2:30	Meds gone		
3:00		Bus home	gone
3:30		Baseball practice	
4:00			
4:30			
5:00	Take Focalin; effective within 20-30 minutes		
5:30		Homework	good
6:00			
6:30			
7:00 +			

When teenagers take medicines that wear off during the later afternoon, their parents do not have the opportunity to enjoy the benefits of the teen being on medicine. They miss out on the pleasure of having positive interactions with him when his concentration, attention, and attitude are better.

"Lewis has a learning disability in addition to ADHD and I don't often see positive effects of the medication because he takes Adderall during school hours and skips evenings and weekends."

Timing of Medication Is Critical

Timing issues related to medication, especially shorter-acting ones, are very important. How long does the medication last? How long does it take to kick in? When does it reach peak effectiveness? This information is displayed in Table 6-6 on the previous page.

If your teenager has problems with misbehavior or failing a class, it is a good idea to identify when academic or behavior problems occurred. For example, if you look for patterns of misbehavior or class failure, you may find that the teenager is passing language arts at 9:00 a.m., but failing algebra, which is the last period of the school day—a time when his medication may have worn off. He may also have behavior problems in that class and on the school bus. Medication wearing off may well be a major contributing factor to both academic and behavior problems.

Assess Medication Effectiveness

One quick way to obtain objective information about your teen's response to medication is to complete the blank form in Chapter 16 (form 4) after your teenager begins to take medication. If only marginal improvement is noted, your doctor may decide to increase the medication. You should also look for and report any negative side effects such as loss of appetite, sleep problems, sedation, irritability, or headaches.

One parent's assessment of the effectiveness of her teenager's medication is displayed in Table 6-7. With a daily dosage of only 15-20 mg Adderall, this teenager's medication was not effective. Ultimately, the doctor prescribed 40 mg Adderall and 5 mg Dexedrine (4 p.m.) to help with homework.

Professional Assessments. If you are having major problems getting the medication right, here is another way to fine-tune your teenager's medication

regimen: seek a formal medication assessment from a treatment professional who specializes in ADD and ADHD. Your doctor or staff at a specialized program may also have the capacity to carefully monitor medication through formal behavior rating scales and observations. When the medication and dosage are working effectively, formal rating scales should show improvement academically. The Child Behavior Checklist (CBCL) typically should show a reduction in inappropriate behavior. CHADD, your treatment professional, the local mental health center, school psychological services, hospital, or a university operated program for attention deficits may be able to refer you to someone who can perform this type of assessment.

Tips for Problem-solving Medication Issues

Remember that it will take time to "fine-tune" the medication regimen. Even small adjustments such as changing the time of day or increasing the amount of medication may make a major difference in your teenager's behavior at home and school. Parents must often play "detective," analyzing all the facts to figure out why medication isn't working right. For example, if your teen is failing his first period class but passing other classes, check out what time he took his medication. If he took it on his way out the door and was sitting in class twenty minutes later, a long-acting medication will not have kicked in yet.

Medication woes may not be the only reason your teen is struggling academically. If problems are continuing at school, one area to explore further is identification of learning problems or executive function deficits and implementation of appropriate classroom accommodations. For additional help on identifying academic problems, refer to Chapters 11-14 and *Teaching Teens with ADD and ADHD*. Even if the teenager is doing okay academically, the current medication may have to be changed or adjusted if sleep disturbances, irritability, or aggression continue to be problems.

Educating Your Teenager about His Medical Treatment

It is important to explain to your teenager how the medication helps him. He shouldn't expect medication to be a miracle cure, but should understand both its benefits and limitations. He needs to understand that he is still going to have to make a conscious effort to improve his organizational skills and school-

Table 6-7   Assess Medication Effectiveness

Individualized Treatment Planning: "Do Whatever It Takes"

Name: **Sam**   Grade: **9**   Date & class: **M-F Chemistry**

Completed by: **Dr. Abney**   Time of day observed: **10:00 A.M.**

Medication: **Ritalin LA**   Dosage: **20 mg**

To assess the impact of medications is having on a student's school work, each parent and teacher should answer several key questions. When medication is working properly and learning problems have been identified, the student should be doing much better in school. Please circle the number that best describes the student's behavior.

Academic Performance:

	Strongly Agree	Agree	Neutral	Disagree	Strongly Disagree
When the student is in my class, s/he					
1. Pays attention	1	2	3	4	(5)
2. Completes class & homework	1	2	3	4	(5)
3. Does work correctly	1	2	3	4	(5)
4. Complies with requests	1	2	(3)	4	5
5. Makes passing grades	1	2	3	(4)	5

ADD/ADHD-Related Behaviors, including Executive Function Deficits

If the student is on medication and is not doing well in school, what else could be causing continuing problems? Are there any ADD/ADHD-related behaviors that are interfering with the student's ability to succeed in school?

ADD/ADHD-related Behaviors:

The student:

6. is organized (finds and turns in work)	1	2	3	(4)	5
7. remembers things (assignments, tests, etc.)	1	2	3	(4)	5
8. manages time well/ plans ahead	1	2	3	(4)	5
9. is on time to class	1	(2)	3	4	5
10. is on time to school	1	(2)	3	4	5
11. thinks before acting or speaking	1	2	(3)	4	5
12. is awake and alert in class	1	2	3	(4)	5
13. gets along with friends	1	(2)	3	4	5
14. gets angry easily & blows up	1	(2)	3	4	5

Are you aware of any sleep problems? The student

14. falls asleep easily	1	(2)	3	4	5
15. wakes up easily	1	2	3	4	5

Comments: <u>Sam wants to do well and has expressed concern that he can't concentrate. He is falling asleep in his afternoon classes according to Mr. Baker.</u>

work. He must learn to compensate for having an attention deficit. You may want to enlist the help of doctors, other treatment professionals, review with your teen the Appendix on "What Do I Need to Know about Medication?" in *A Bird's Eye View of Life with ADD and ADHD*, or attend a CHADD training session.

"One child with ADHD was talking about his 'smart pill.' I told him, 'It isn't a smart pill. You are your smart pill. This medicine simply allows you the opportunity to make choices that are more appropriate and allows you to be more successful. You can choose to complete your work or choose not to complete your work regardless of whether you have taken your Concerta. Concerta may make it easier for you, but in the long run, it is still your choice.'"

—Kathleen Allen, MS, Pediatric Center

Taking Medication Regularly

Many teenagers don't mind taking their medication regularly because they can tell that it improves their ability to concentrate. It feels good to be able to focus and make better grades in school.

"Our teenage son and his friends have come to feel special because they have ADHD. When one of them becomes too talkative or spaces out, they remind each other to take their medication. They even have a chant, 'Take your MEDICINE!' that they sing to each other. Since four or five of the boys take Adderall, they are not embarrassed to take medicine."

Never lose sight of the fact that one of the major problems with medication is that *teenagers with ADD or ADHD have difficulty* <u>remembering</u> *to take it everyday*, particularly if they have to take more than one daily dose! After all, forgetfulness is a major characteristic of

the disorder. In truth, most adults would have difficulty remembering to take medication every day, sometimes more than once a day, for the rest of their lives.

Devise a System. Help your teenager devise a system to remember to take his medicine. For example:

1. Place pills in a clear weekly container and put it somewhere he will be certain to see it—for instance, by the sink where he brushes his teeth. That way you can tell at a glance whether he has remembered to take it, without having to ask the dreaded question, "Have you taken your medicine?"
2. If you are away from home, *email, beep, or call him on his cell phone* as a reminder.
3. If your teen must remember to take medicine at school or while away from home, he could:
   a. set an alarm on his watch,
   b. ask to be prompted by teachers, or
   c. simply take a long-acting medication like Adderall XR, Concerta, or Strattera.

Try not to nag! Teenagers quickly tire of adults constantly asking, "Did you take your medicine?" This constant questioning, especially right after the slightest hint of forgetfulness or misbehavior, may lead to medication becoming the focal point of major battles between you and your teen.

"We put our son's medication and vitamins in a pill box that is marked for each day of the week. I fill it up each week and put it by his plate at breakfast. I can glance at his pill box and know whether or not he has taken his Strattera. This process is nice because now I don't have to nag him by asking if he took his medicine. I can see for myself. If he has taken it, I don't say anything. He doesn't even know I double checked it. If he hasn't taken the medicine, I simply hold out the open pill box and say, 'Here's your medicine.'"

Medication Refusal

Refusal to take medication may become a problem for some adolescents. Typical reasons may include:

1. Some teenagers don't like to be different from their friends and are embarrassed to take medicine.
2. Others don't like the way it makes them feel. They may feel like they are missing

out on things and that life isn't as much fun. Lowering the dosage may remedy this problem.

3. Denial may also play a role in medication refusal. "If I take medication that means I have a problem. There's nothing wrong with me. I don't have ADHD."

4. If they drink alcohol, they may decide it's safer not to mix their medication with drinking.

5. Most often, teenagers with ADD and ADHD simply forget to take their medication.

If you mistakenly assume the worst, that your teenager is refusing the medication, rather than just forgetting it, a nasty power struggle may develop.

"I started taking Concerta the summer before third grade. It helped me pay attention, but it didn't help me learn my multiplication tables. I thought I was taking medicine to help me do better in math. At first I didn't mind, but then I noticed Concerta took away the fun. When I wasn't on medication I was a chatterbox at school. I wasn't disruptive or hyperactive. I was just talkative. I was such a loner when I was on it. It was like I wasn't able to feel loose and fun and silly."

Don't Force Medication. It is probably wise not to force your teenager to take medication. Take time to find out why he is refusing medication. He may have valid reasons. If he is refusing to take medication, ask why he has reservations about taking it. Listen to his response and see if changes can be made to accommodate his concerns.

1. Ask him, "Do you feel like medication is helping you at all at school?"

2. If you can't talk him into continuing his medication, you might say, "Okay, let's try it without medication for a week and see how your grades look."

3. Check with the teacher for an update on grades.

4. Then the next week, state the facts: "Hmm, looks like your grades have really dropped in algebra. Your daily grades went from Bs to Ds."

You may reach an absolute impasse over medication issues:

1. If your family can't resolve problems regarding medication, talk with your physician or a close family friend to see if he can work through this problem with your teenager.

2. If that is unsuccessful, convey the message that you respect your teenager's judgment. You might say: "When you're ready and need medication, the doctor and I will be glad to help you."

3. If your teenager continues to struggle, periodically ask if he thinks he should try medication again. He may decide to try meds again but, being so forgetful, may never remember to ask you to get his prescription refilled.

4. When things get bad enough, a teenager with ADD or ADHD may ask for help or feel so overwhelmed that he is finally willing to accept your help.

Occasionally, not taking medicine may pose a safety risk. In these instances, you may want to insist that your teenager take it. For example, you might say, "You must take medication when you drive the car." Dr. Barkley tells us that teenagers who take medication are better, safer drivers. More detailed information on driving is contained in Chapter 10.

Taking Medication at School

With the advent of long-acting medications, taking medication at school has almost become a nonissue. However, some students still take shorter-acting medicines and must take a second dose at school.

School personnel should be told that your teenager has attention deficit disorder and is taking medication. The school nurse may need to be involved if a dose is given at school. Some students don't mind going to the school clinic to take their medicine—in fact, there may be several other students there taking their medication too. If going to the clinic embarrasses your teen, try to arrange a discreet schedule, such as dropping by the office or clinic on the way to lunch or another time when it may be less obvious to friends.

Although most schools don't allow students to carry medications on them, some students do anyway and take their medication unobserved by any teachers. With their natural tendency to be defiant and question authority, teenagers may perceive school rules that prohibit carrying medication as ridiculous. Although they may take their medication as needed, they may get into trouble with school officials if they are caught taking it on their own. As a parent, you should familiarize yourself with school rules about medication management and the consequences for breaking them. If punishment is stiff and your teenager may be suspended, find another way to get him to take medication at school. Or switch to a long-acting medication.

Remember also that forgetting medication or medication wearing off (antecedent) is a common cause of crises at school. Leaving some extra medication at school (intervention) would be wise. You can call the school and notify the school nurse so that your teenager will be discreetly given his medication, not called to the office over the intercom.

Should Parents with ADD or ADHD Seek Treatment?

Slightly more than 50 percent of teenagers with an attention deficit have a least one parent who also has symptoms of the condition. If you are one of these parents, you must consider whether your own symptoms are serious enough to consider taking medication. For example, do you have difficulty monitoring your teenager's behavior and consistently using effective parenting techniques? Do you fly off the handle easily and impulsively yell at your teen? As noted earlier, stimulant medications are highly effective with adults.

In one case study conducted by Drs. William Pelham and Steven Evans, a parent of a child with ADHD agreed to participate in treatment for her own symptoms of the disorder. The mother had trouble monitoring her child's behavior, couldn't use child management techniques consistently, had difficulty getting things accomplished at home, had difficulty staying on task in counseling sessions, and frequently fidgeted. She decided to take a stimulant medication and was able to improve her child management skills. This mother's symptoms were considered severe both as a child and as an adult.

Parents must make the judgment call about seeking treatment. If your symptoms are keeping you from functioning successfully as an adult, you may wish to talk with a physician about them. If you decide to seek treatment, your biggest problem may be finding a physician who is willing to treat you. How you approach the subject with your family physician may depend on your relationship with him. If you both agree that the symptoms of the attention deficit are interfering with your ability to work or fulfill your role as a parent or spouse, he may be willing to give you a trial on stimulant medication. It may help if you show the doctor the DSM criteria with your characteristics checked off, inform him

about your struggles on the job now (disorganization, forgetfulness, numerous job changes) or in relationships, and tell about your struggles during your school years. This less formal assessment may be enough for some physicians, but others may refer you to a psychologist or counselor for a more in-depth evaluation.

"After being treated for depression for several years, I realized that I have ADHD. I couldn't get organized enough to get my work done or keep my family's life organized. As a result I was always depressed."

For adults who pursue careers in which ADD or ADHD presents few if any problems, medication may no longer be needed. Some adults whose symptoms are causing difficulty may elect to continue medication daily or take it only on days requiring more intense concentration.

Conclusion

Many medications currently in use are highly effective at controlling the symptoms of ADD and ADHD in children, teenagers, and adults. Researchers see great hope in the future for development of even more effective medications for treating attention and executive skill deficits. Some predict that eventually specific medications will be prescribed based upon the subtypes of attention deficit disorder.

Hopefully, this chapter has answered your questions about whether medication should be part of your teenager's treatment and where to go to get needed information. If you and your teenager do decide that medication is key for treatment, work closely with your local doctor to find the most effective medication and dose.

In summary, here are several important facts to remember from this chapter:

1. Research has shown that medication is the single most effective treatment.
2. Medicine works for over 90 percent of children.
3. Students on medication show great improvement in school performance, behavior, and social skills.
4. Teenagers who have ADHD and are on medication are less likely to abuse drugs than teenagers with attention deficits who do not take medicine.

7

Attention Disorders and Coexisting Conditions

Many teens have one or more mental health conditions such as anxiety or depression in addition to their attention deficit disorder. In fact, according to the 1999 NIMH/MTA study, over two-thirds of children with ADHD have at least one other coexisting condition, and half of them have two other conditions. The impact of coexisting conditions on children and teenagers with attention deficits is often profound. Unfortunately, the more coexisting conditions that accompany the attention deficit, the more difficult it is to educate and treat these teenagers.

Regrettably, we are not certain just how frequently these conditions appear in children with the inattentive form of ADD, and, more importantly in teenagers. Since most of the research on coexisting conditions has been done on children, information on adolescents is extremely limited. However, we do know that risk of some of these conditions such as depression and anxiety actually increases during the teenage years. So the message to parents, teachers, and treatment professionals is clear:

Coexisting conditions are a major problem for over two-thirds of teenagers with ADHD! Thus, identification and treatment are absolutely essential for these teenagers to be successful in school and life.

A list of the most common problems that coexist with ADHD is provided in Table 7-1 on the next page. Where available, data is also provided for adolescents.

Interpreting Table 7-1: The figures reported in the table on page 128 come from two sources: the MTA study, and other leading researchers on ADHD. That means that the numbers in the first column are reported on all children in the study who were diagnosed with an attention deficit with hyperactivity—in other words a *community sample* of children who have adjusted fairly well. The other numbers may be somewhat inflated since they are from a variety of researchers, most of whom collected their information on children with more serious problems who were referred to a clinic for services—in other words, a *clinical sample*. Young people in a clinical sample tend to have more severe symptoms, as they were referred to treatment clinics or were in psychiatric hospitals, residential treatment facilities, juvenile detention facilities, or jails. So, rates

Table 7-1   Rates of Coexisting Conditions among Young People with ADHD

	NIMH/MTA	
	Children	Adolescents
Sleep problems	(56%)	[probably similar to children]
Oppositional Defiant Disorder (ODD)	40%	(45-84%)
Anxiety Disorders	33-39%	(27-44%)
Learning Disabilities (SLD)	(25-70%)	[probably similar to children]
Tic Disorders	11%	(12%) [among adults]
Obsessive-Compulsive Disorder (OCD)—	--	(3-5%) [among adults]
Mood Disorders	4%	--
▪ Depression	(9-32%)	(29-45%)
▪ Bipolar Disorder (BP)	(11%)	(6-12%)
Conduct Disorder (CD)	14%	(25-50%)
Substance Abuse (SA) or use	(5%)	(10-40%)*

Data in parentheses are from Barkley, Biederman, Goldstein, or Robin.
* higher rates of SA are linked to ADHD plus 1) Conduct Disorder or 2) Bipolar Disorder.

of coexisting conditions among children with ADHD in your community would be roughly half of the numbers reported in the second column.

Unfortunately, this information on coexisting conditions was based upon research on ADHD hyperactive and ADHD combined type only and thus may have limited applicability to those with ADD inattentive. Typically, those with ADD inattentive are intentionally excluded from these studies.

As you can see, different researchers found different rates of conditions in different populations. So the rates of conditions like ODD and conduct disorder are often reported within a range.

My Teen's on Medicine, But Still Struggling—What Do I Do?

If your teenager is being treated for ADD or ADHD yet is still struggling, **there is a high probability that a coexisting condition is not being treated!** The coexisting conditions listed in the table above are discussed in subsequent sections; potential learning disabilities or executive function deficits are addressed in Chapters 1, 3, and 13. To ensure treatment success, parents, teachers, and treatment professionals must address three major issues:

1. Identification and treatment of coexisting mental health conditions.
2. Identification of learning problems, including deficits in executive skills and if

needed, provision of accommodations to ensure academic success.
3. Ensuring that the medication and dose is right—that is, it provides peak effectiveness for optimum academic performance.

Here is one family's story about the difficulty diagnosing coexisting problems and their long and frightening journey to find the correct diagnoses for their son:

"Our son Jack was diagnosed with Tourette syndrome at around age 7 or 8, OCD when he was 11, and finally, ADHD, when he was hospitalized at age 13. When he began having physical tics and was struggling in school during the eighth grade, Jack became very depressed and felt like it was the end of the world. I trusted my former doctor, so when he said it wasn't ADHD I just dropped it. I was pretty overwhelmed by the Tourette and OCD anyway and I wasn't looking to add another diagnosis.

"Late one afternoon, the police knocked on the door. Jack had called them and said that he was having thoughts of hurting himself. Of course, my husband and I were frantic. We assumed that despondency over Tourette syndrome was the root of his problem. Much to our surprise, the neurologist at the hospital, said oh no, it was the untreated ADHD that was the major issue. He prescribed Concerta for the ADHD and clonidine to help with the Tourette. We are very lucky. Jack's Tourette symptoms are under control now and he is doing well."

The subtle differences in these disorders need to be identified in order to prescribe the proper medication and treatment regimen. If your teenager's symptoms of ADD or ADHD do not significantly improve with stimulant medications, this may be linked to failure to treat a second coexisting condition or may indicate a misdiagnosis of ADHD. But first, *double check to see that medication doses are appropriate.* If medication is dosed correctly, then work with a treatment professional to rule out other possible disorders. Since some of the medications discussed in this chapter have not been tested on children or adolescents, clearly, you will need to talk with your physician about all medication issues.

"*F*or our family, the proper medication regimen and dosages continued to be fine-tuned over a six-year period as first learning problems, then sleep disturbances were identified."

Detailed information to help ensure that medication levels are correct is provided in Chapter 6. If you are interested in more information on medications for coexisting conditions, you may consult the outstanding book, *Straight Talk about Psychiatric Medications for Kids* (2004), by Timothy E. Wilens, MD.

This chapter will help parents and professionals recognize coexisting mental health conditions such as anxiety or depression. Official diagnostic criteria from the DSM are provided for each condition. As is true for attention deficit disorders, the majority of these coexisting conditions are also linked to problems with neurotransmitters. Treatment issues for coexisting conditions will be addressed only very briefly. Obviously, a treatment professional should be consulted for help in understanding and treating any coexisting condition that might affect your teenage. Keep in mind also that for all these conditions, exercise and a healthy lifestyle will enhance the treatment plan.

National advocacy groups have been established for several of the following conditions. If a teen is struggling with a coexisting condition, parents may wish to contact the appropriate advocacy group for more detailed information that may be helpful for enhancing the treatment plan. When available, contact information for these groups, plus other helpful resources, is provided in the Resource Guide.

Anxiety Disorders

Nearly half of all teenagers with attention deficit disorders (44 percent) also experience excessive anxiety and worry. Although outwardly teens may act indifferent, they often experience tremendous anxiety regarding their school work. They may have **generalized anxiety** or may experience more severe anxiety disorders such as **panic disorder** or **obsessive-compulsive disorder.**

Sometimes a bright teenager who has undiagnosed ADD or ADHD and is underachieving in school may experience high levels of anxiety that are actually related to the attention deficit. Teens may be misdiagnosed with either generalized anxiety or panic disorder. The anxiety may mask symptoms of the attention deficit, so the ADD or ADHD remains undiagnosed. According to Dr. Patricia Quinn, when the ADD or ADHD is treated, the symptoms of anxiety disappear in roughly 60 percent of her patients. Of course, the true anxiety in the remaining 40 percent must be treated. Keep in mind that children with ADD inattentive may have higher levels of anxiety and depression than children with ADHD.

Generalized Anxiety Disorder is marked by three or more of the following characteristics:
- edginess,
- muscle tension,
- mind going blank,
- irritability,
- fatigue,
- sleep disturbance.

Students with attention deficit disorders may be especially anxious and fearful of being embarrassed in school. Typically, they recognize that they have problems listening. They're afraid if the teacher calls on them, they will be daydreaming and not hear the question. Even when listening, they may get so flustered they cannot answer the question correctly. If students also have slow processing speed, including slow retrieval of information stored in long-term memory, they may be so fearful of public speaking that they would rather accept a failing grade than give a presentation in class.

On the other hand, there may be a few positive aspects to having anxiety: students are less likely to act or speak impulsively, more likely to work harder to complete school work, and are more eager to please their parents and teachers.

Panic Attacks involve a period of intense fear, which starts suddenly and reaches a peak in roughly ten minutes. Panic disorders are believed to be inherited and are also the result of biochemical problems in the brain. The student may experience four or more of the following symptoms:

- pounding heart,
- shortness of breath,
- feelings of being outside oneself,
- chest discomfort,
- dizziness,
- fear of going crazy or losing control,
- trembling,
- nausea,
- tingling sensations.

Obsessive-Compulsive Disorder (OCD) is associated with both *obsessions*—recurring thoughts or impulses—and *compulsions*—repetitive behaviors or mental acts that the person feels driven to do such as checking locks, counting, double checking work, recopying work, ordering, hoarding, or rigidly following rules or rituals. Even when they try to suppress them, teens will still act on their obsessions and compulsions. This disorder has a tremendous impact on school performance. Students may not be satisfied with written work and may obsess over the content and neatness of their handwriting. They may feel pressure to recopy material. Obviously, obsessing over thoughts makes writing an essay especially challenging.

Around 4 percent of adults with ADHD also have OCD. When both ADHD and Tourette syndrome are present, the rate climbs to 12 percent, according to Dr. Tom Spencer, Harvard Medical School. Obviously, when a child has all three disorders, the issues are complex and make treatment difficult.

"My son has ADHD and obsessive-compulsive symptoms. Dealing with the two disorders is really complicated and frustrating. We are still trying to determine which is the primary disorder. We can't find a medication that will help with all his symptoms. We've been to see so many specialists, yet still haven't found the help we need.

"Rituals are a major issue. He has to go to the bathroom the last thing at night before going to bed. He may go several times. He has to wear certain clothes together, sit in certain places in the car and at the table. He has major dietary problems and will not eat many foods. When we find something he can eat, he must eat them in certain ways. Macaroni and cheese may be eaten only with potato chips. Pizza can be ordered only from Dominos. Things must be in order. He has difficulty with new experiences and transitions."

At some level, it is also important to remember that a healthy level of compulsive traits may actually help some people compensate by being more organized and aware of their responsibilities. Researcher Dr. Steven Pliszka, University of Texas, tells us that children with ADHD and anxiety are less likely to be diagnosed with conduct disorder than are children with ADHD who are not anxious. However, both these groups are equally as likely to have oppositional defiant disorder.

Treatment

Sometimes we underestimate the importance of treating anxiety effectively. One mother told me that even though her child has several other conditions, including severe bipolar disorder, treatment of the anxiety is paramount. Even when the bipolar was being treated, her son was unable to function well at school or home until the anxiety was properly treated.

Obviously, the simplest, least intrusive treatment strategies that are effective are preferable for all coexisting conditions. The NIMH/MTA study indicated that medication and behavioral interventions are especially effective treatments for anxiety disorders. Teens can be taught behavioral strategies to help them cope with their anxiety. Students who have an attention deficit and anxiety may benefit from both a stimulant and an antidepressant. Symptoms of anxiety, however, may also be made worse with stimulants. According to Dr. Quinn, a methylphenidate plus an SSRI may be better for treating teens with anxiety and an attention deficit. An amphetamine may make their anxiety worse.

In addition, an SSRI antidepressant such as Zoloft, Paxil, Prozac, Lexapro, or Celexa or anti-anxiety medications like Buspar may also be prescribed. Other medications that doctors may try include Serzone, Effexor, Anafranil, and Visteryl. Dr. Joseph Biederman and his colleagues at Massachusetts General Hospital report that tricyclic antidepressants such as Tofranil or Norpramin are also effective in treating coexisting anxiety and ADHD. Refer to Chapter 6 for cautions and an FDA warning regarding antidepressants. Although exercise is important for helping with most coexisting conditions, including anxiety, many teens will not consistently work out.

Tics and Tourette Disorder

Tourette syndrome (TS) is a genetic disorder that results in both motor (movement) and vocal tics. Motor or vocal tics may also occur in people who do not have Tourette syndrome.

Motor Tics involve involuntary muscle movements that are often repetitive and ritualistic, such as:

- rapid eye blinking,
- mouth opening,
- lip licking,
- sticking tongue out,
- grimacing,
- shoulder shrugging,
- stretching movements.

Vocal Tics may include:

- throat clearing,
- grunting,
- coughing,
- humming,
- spitting.

People with TS have at least one vocal tic in combination with one motor tic. Symptoms wax and wane, so sometimes they are more apparent, and sometimes less so. Frequently, old symptoms disappear only to be replaced by new ones. Stress, excitement, anxiety, or drinking caffeine can make the symptoms worse. Sometimes when students try to suppress their tics, an explosive build-up of tension may occur. Sheryl Pruitt, M.Ed., coauthor of *Teaching the Tiger*, refers to these blow-ups and loss of control as "Tourette Storms." After the storm subsides, the child calms down and sometimes will have no memory of the blow-up. Pruitt's book is especially helpful for families struggling with ADHD, TS, and OCD.

Tourette syndrome occurs in less than 1 percent of the population and is 6 times more common in males than in females. The average age of onset for TS is 6.5 years. However, the symptoms of an attention deficit disorder precede Tourette symptoms by an average of 2.5 years—around age 4. Researchers believe that hypersensitivity to the neurotransmitter dopamine may be the underlying cause of the disorder. According to Dr. Barkley, children with ADHD are not at increased risk for having TS. However, Dr. David Comings has reported that up to 85 percent of children with TS also have ADHD.

Treatment

In the past, doctors shied away from prescribing stimulant medications like Ritalin for TS because they were afraid that they would exacerbate the tic symptoms. However, David Comings, M.D., author of several helpful books on TS, and Roger Kurlman, M.D., have found that methylphenidate does *not* make tics worse. Dr. Kurlman found that initially some children's tics got worse, but, guess what—symptoms also worsened in the control group with the students who *did not* get any medication. Who knows, perhaps anxiety about the new medicine may have triggered the symptoms. By the end of the study, tic severity had decreased in all the children who received medications.

Dr. Russell Barkley reports that roughly 34 percent of children who take stimulants and who also have a dual diagnosis of ADHD and TS will experience mild exacerbation of their tics. If this occurs, talk with your doctor; medication doses may need to be reduced or a different medication prescribed. Medications commonly prescribed to treat TS include Catapres (clonidine), Desipramine, Norpramin, and Tenex.

Parents should be aware that some researchers have expressed concern that methylphenidate may trigger the onset of Tourette syndrome, although they don't think it actually causes the condition. However, Sam Goldstein, Ph.D., a leading researcher on ADHD from the University of Utah, explains that it is impossible to prove that this medication is never a primary cause of TS.

Sleep Disorders

Slightly more than half of children with attention deficits (56 percent) have sleep disturbances, which is double the rate in children without attention deficits. These teens may have major problems falling asleep, waking up, or both. Researchers tell us that these children have a much more difficult time falling asleep and get fewer hours sleep than other children do. Half also report that they feel tired when they wake up, but others appear to need less sleep. Some may have frequent night waking, nightmares, or restless sleep in which they move all around in the bed. In addition, some teens experience a delayed sleep cycle. If they could fall asleep at 4:00 a.m. and get up at noon, they might be just fine.

Lack of sleep often causes fatigue and impairs memory and the ability to concentrate. Family fights over going to bed or waking up are common. Many parents mistakenly assume that teenagers can simply fall asleep if they would just try. Unfortunately, this is not true. Even if they go to bed, they often toss and turn for a couple of hours before they can fall asleep. Parents often comment that family fights over sleep issues are a major source of conflict, yet these problems are not always addressed by treatment professionals.

Extreme difficulty waking up may also be a symptom of depression. Sometimes, even though a teenager may have slept eight or nine hours, he may wake up feeling groggy and may take an hour or more to really get going. If your teenager is persistently groggy, has stomachaches or headaches, or wakes up in an irritable mood, consider consulting a doctor. It may be difficult to determine whether the sleep disturbance is occurring as a result of the attention deficit disorder or a coexisting condition such as depression.

Sleep problems related to ADD or ADHD may be longer lasting than those related to depression, having been observed for several years, while depression may have begun more recently after a school failure or some other crisis. The family history should be reviewed to determine if depression may also be a problem for other family members. Although reasons for the sleep problems may be different, treatment may be the same.

Treatment

Specific treatment strategies such as establishing good sleep hygiene and a bedtime routine are discussed in detail in Chapter 9. Doctors may prescribe a small dose of clonidine to aid in sleep. Dr. William Larsen, a pediatrician in Anchorage, Alaska, prescribes a low dose of Tofranil to help his patients fall asleep and wake up more easily. Parents should also make certain that stimulant medications are not taken so late in the day that they prevent sleep. To assist with morning problems, your doctor may suggest waking your child up early, giving her a dose of short-acting medication like Ritalin, and letting her go back to sleep for 30 minutes. If those steps are ineffective, talk with your doctor about other options such as a sleep evaluation or medication. Because of the profound impact of sleep problems on a teenager's school performance and behavior, *parents and professionals absolutely must address this issue*.

Make certain that the physician is aware of the problem and aggressively pursues treatment.

Mood Disorders

Mood disorders are also linked to disruption of neurotransmitters. As the name implies, these disorders affect a person's moods, so that they may swing up or down. The three most common coexisting mood disorders in teens with attention deficits are: depression, dysthymic disorder, and bipolar disorder.

Depression

According to the National Institute of Mental Health, "Depression is a serious medical illness; it's not something that you have made up in your head. It's more than just feeling 'down in the dumps' or 'blue' for a few days. It's feeling 'down' and 'low' and 'hopeless' for weeks at a time."

Depression is fairly common among children with ADHD, with rates among teenagers ranging from 9 to as high as 45 percent. Dr. Barkley reports that roughly 75 percent will have a least one episode of depression during their lifetime. Researchers have found a link between ADHD and depression within families—that is, if a child has depression, then she or other family members are also at risk for having ADHD. For girls whose ADHD symptoms are less obvious, the initial referral for treatment may actually be for depression resulting from untreated ADHD.

Teenagers may experience depression just as adults do. However, the disorder may be overlooked because the symptoms may not always be the same for teens as for adults. In truth, the official diagnostic criteria for depression describe adult behaviors better than those of young people. For example, depression doesn't always involve sadness in teenagers. Adolescents may show signs of low motivation, lack of enthusiasm, and reduced enjoyment of life. Frequently, they mention difficulty concentrating, slowed thinking, and indecisiveness. A depressed person may complain of memory problems and appear easily distracted. Teenagers may comment that nobody loves them. Thoughts of death may also occur.

Generally speaking, young people who are depressed may experience:
- bad moods,
- lack of enjoyment in life,
- irritability,
- aggression.

Here is an important fact: *A teen's irritability or aggression may actually be masking or hiding depression.* Consequently, depression may be at the root of aggressive, antisocial acts such as those described below as characteristic of conduct disorder. If depression is a significant factor, adults may notice that the antisocial behavior occurred *after* the symptoms of depression were observed. When the depression is treated, the irritability and aggression often decrease significantly. Inattention may also be a symptom of depression. Occasionally, inattention related to depression may be mistaken for ADD or ADHD.

According to the American Academy of Child and Adolescent Psychiatry, up to one-third of all young people suffering from depression may actually be experiencing early onset bipolar disorder.

TREATMENT

Treatment for depression often includes exercise and an antidepressant medication such as Zoloft or Wellbutrin. One of the newer adjuncts to treatment is known as ADHD coaching. Although coaching was initially developed for adults, it doesn't take a genius to realize that teenagers with attention deficits also need a similar support system. Counseling or coaching may be very helpful, particularly if the depression is linked to problems with disorganization or sadness about underachievement in life. Specifically, teaching skills or providing prompts to accommodate deficits in executive skills should prove invaluable. For more information on coaching, see Chapter 5.

Dysthymic Disorder

A milder form of depression known as *dysthymia* also may be present in these teenagers. To meet diagnostic criteria for dysthymia, at least two of these symptoms must be present for the better part of a year:

- changes in eating habits,
- changes in sleeping habits,
- reduced mental energy,
- reduced physical energy,
- difficulty making decisions,
- low self-esteem,
- feelings of hopelessness.

Any major changes in a teen's routine behavior should raise a red flag for parents. Be observant. Any signs of consistent low energy, reduced activity, clouded thinking, and hopelessness may warrant a discussion with your doctor.

Bipolar Disorder

Bipolar disorder (BPD), formerly called manic depression, is a mood disorder, characterized by alternating periods of high energy (mania or manic moods) and low energy (depression). Adults with the disorder may have as few as four of these episodes of highs and lows per year, while some children and adolescents may have changes of mood several times a day. Until the last decade, most mental health professionals mistakenly believed that BPD could not be accurately diagnosed until the mid- to late twenties.

Recently, a controversy has been raging in the U.S. about whether bipolar disorder is being over- or under-diagnosed. Some doctors and researchers have reported an alarming increase in BPD being diagnosed among school children and are concerned that the condition is being over-diagnosed. On the other hand, according to the American Academy of Child and Adolescent Psychiatry, the first episode for 20 percent of adults with BPD occurred between ages 15 to 19. Clearly, careful assessment and diagnosis of all mental disorders is critical.

This disorder is very difficult to diagnose in young people, since many of the characteristics of ADHD and BPD are similar. At first the teen may be diagnosed with the attention deficit, only to finally show obvious symptoms of bipolar disorder during the teen years.

"One of the biggest challenges I faced was separating ADHD behaviors from 'something else,' like bipolar disorder. Information on bipolar is not easily available, and bipolar is rarer and more complicated to deal with. No one recognized the bipolar until my son was 17. The school system said that some of his behaviors weren't ADHD, and they just labeled them as intentional misbehavior."

SYMPTOMS

An awareness of the symptoms of BPD may help parents avoid an incorrect diagnosis. Several professionals, including Arthur Robin, Ph.D., professor and an authority on ADHD in adolescents, and Charles Popper, M.D., a psychiatrist and psychopharmacologist, have identified symptoms of bipolar disorder in teenagers that may help distinguish it from ADHD. Patricia Quinn, M.D., also provides helpful insights.

1. **Psychotic Symptoms:** Occasionally, people with bipolar disorder may have a psychotic episode with symptoms that reflect an impaired thought process where they

lose touch with reality. In other words, they may have hallucinations, delusions (belief in something that is not true), or feelings of grandiosity. For teens, irritability is much more common than grandiosity. Grandiosity looks different in teens. Dr. Robin gives this example: during a period of mania, one eleven-year-old mistakenly thought that all the children in her class were her good friends. During other periods, her low self-esteem surfaced and she felt that no one liked her.

Teenagers with attention deficits and no BPD will not exhibit psychotic symptoms, unless something unusual happens. For example, transient psychotic symptoms can be brought on by a chemical interaction between medications (Tofranil-imipramine) and some illegal drugs such as marijuana.

2. **Flight of Ideas or Racing Thoughts:** A rapid shift from one thought to another may be observed. In teens, these thoughts may be frightening to them and interfere with their ability to pay attention in class. In Dr. Quinn's experience, people who have bipolar disorder tend to have racing thoughts that may be repetitious, while those with ADHD jump from one topic to another and remain in touch with reality.

3. **Severe Temper Tantrums/Rages:** In younger children, a history of tantrums that release tremendous physical and emotional energy is often present. These tantrums may last longer than other children's tantrums—from 30 minutes up to 2 to 4 hours—even when they are alone and no audience is present. In adolescents, rages may result in abuse to parents such as cuts, bruises, or broken bones.

"If I ever told John no, he would fly into terrible rages. He threw furniture, threatened our lives, and once actually hit us. It was awful! And the teen years were the worst. Once when we were driving home from the beach, he flew into a rage and hit my husband (his stepfather), giving him a black eye. I was mortified that my son would hit this man who has taken responsibility for him and been the only father he has ever known.

"I literally did not know what to do. Should we call the police, have him arrested and then risk dragging him through the court system in another state? Would any of that really help him? We decided to handle it ourselves. We both had to sit on him until he calmed down. Finally we felt the rage dissipate. Later, when he was 16 or 17, we finally learned that John also had bipolar in addition to his ADHD. Finding the right medication combination is critical, yet it's very difficult to do."*

4. **Aggression and Destructiveness:** Teenagers with BPD may intentionally hit or hurt someone and may relish the fight or power struggle. In contrast, the misbehavior or destructiveness of teenagers with ADD or ADHD is often accidental.

5. **Pronounced Irritability:** Irritability may be a major problem, especially in the morning. In addition, these youngsters may be rejecting or hostile when they meet people. For example, during the first few seconds of an interview with a treatment professional, they may try to disrupt or get out of the interview or ask when the interview will be over.

6. **Sleep Disturbances:** Sleep problems may include difficulty sleeping through the night, or severe nightmares with explicit gore or images of bodily mutilation. As a result, children or teens may be afraid to sleep alone and may want the reassurance of an adult sleeping nearby. Dr. Quinn also explains teens with bipolar disorder may not sleep for two or three days and may not even seem to need sleep. Ultimately, this long period of sleep deprivation may lead to a psychotic break. With ADHD alone, however, the teen needs sleep but may hyperfocus and forget to sleep or have difficulty falling asleep.

7. **Pronounced Sexual Awareness and Interest, Danger-seeking, Giddiness, and Loud Giggling:** These behaviors may be observed, even in the preschool years.

DISTINGUISHING BETWEEN ADHD AND BIPOLAR DISORDER

One reason it is so difficult to tell an attention deficit disorder and bipolar disorder apart is that they share several common characteristics: impulsivity, hyperactivity, high physical energy, and behavioral and emotional ups and downs. The key difference between the disorders seems to be that ADHD symptoms such as hyperactivity are present consistently rather than occurring in cycles. For example, some parents of children with bipolar disorder report cycles of behavior throughout the day—their children begin the day in an almost coma-like state with moods swinging from anger to irritability, aggression, or giddiness. Teenagers with bipolar disorder are more likely to look like someone with ADHD primarily during the manic phase of BPD, when they are more talkative, have problems sleeping, and are distractible.

COEXISTING ADHD AND BIPOLAR DISORDER

Some teenagers may have both ADHD and bipolar disorder. Children who have both ADHD and bipolar tend to be extremely irritable, have multiple episodes, severe agitation, violent behavior, and rapid cycling. Leading researchers have reported varying rates of young people with ADHD who also have bipolar, ranging from 6 to 12 percent.

MISDIAGNOSIS OF EITHER ADHD OR BIPOLAR DISORDER

A few young people who have bipolar disorder may have been misdiagnosed as having ADHD during early childhood. If there is a family history of mood disorders such as bipolar disorder or manic depression, this is an important diagnosis to consider.

If a teenager isn't responding well to carefully managed stimulant medication prescribed for the attention deficit, some professionals will double check to see whether bipolar disorder is perhaps the correct diagnosis. However, *be careful about jumping to this conclusion too quickly*! A poor response to treatment may be due simply to:

1. a less-than-optimal medication regimen, and
2. failure to make accommodations for learning problems.

Some researchers believe that rather than having BPD, these youngsters have ADHD and are more emotionally reactive ("*severe affective deregulation.*")

Since bipolar disorder is often baffling to the experts, obviously parents and teachers aren't expected to recognize this disorder. My point in writing about the condition is to remind both parents and teachers that some teenagers with attention deficit disorders do, in fact, have bipolar disorder, but it may not be diagnosed for ten years or more. If a student is aggressive and extremely difficult to handle, perhaps there are hidden reasons for this behavior—for example, undiagnosed BPD. The bottom line is if you suspect your teen may have bipolar disorder, it is critical to discuss the issue with your doctor.

"Having a teenager with ADHD and bipolar has made me a better parent. It has made me be non-judgmental toward other parents who have challenging children to raise. I always try to be helpful to these parents rather than critical."

TREATMENT

When ADHD and bipolar disorder occur together, treatment planning is much more challenging. Medications known as mood stabilizers are critical for treatment of bipolar disorder. Doctors may prescribe Depakote, and, less frequently, Lithium, to stabilize moods and reduce impulsivity. Depakote, an anticonvulsant, is now the most frequently prescribed medication for treating bipolar disorder. Typically, antidepressants and stimulants alone are avoided since they can trigger emotional blow-ups, either manic episodes or depression. A few young people may not be able to take stimulant medications to help with their inattention. Dr. Quinn has successfully treated coexisting ADHD and bipolar by starting with a mood stabilizer first, and then following it with a stimulant medication. During manic phases, doctors may prescribe antipsychotic medications such as Risperdal, Zyprexa, Abilify, or Seroquel. Treating the child's anxiety and sleep problems are also very important. Drs. Demitri and Janice Papolos, authors of the popular book, *The Bipolar Child*, also offer helpful guidance.

Unfortunately, weight gain and slowed thinking are both major issues with many of the medications used to treat bipolar. Unwanted weight gain is a huge issue for teens and must be addressed. Otherwise, they may stop taking their medication. Doctors have found one anticonvulsant medication, Topomax, that is effective yet does not have the associated problem with weight gain.

Substance-Related Disorders

Ten to 24 percent of adolescents with ADHD may be diagnosed as having substance dependence or abuse issues involving cigarettes, alcohol, or illicit drugs. Treatment professionals typically describe subtstance use in three categories ranging from less to more severe, based upon how frequently they are used. Their symptoms include:

1. **Substance Use:** Characterized by occasional recreational use.

2. **Substance Abuse:** Characterized by one or more symptoms: inability to control substance use; use of substances to escape problems; failure to fulfill obligations at school, work, or home; related absences or school suspensions or expulsions; use of substances creating a hazardous situation (intoxicated while driving); related legal problems such as arrest, theft to support a habit, or shoplifting; or continued use despite related problems such as fights or family arguments.

3. **Addiction or Dependence:** Characterized by three or more symptoms: inability to control substance use; development of a tolerance, need for more drugs more frequently; use of substances to escape problems; impaired daily functioning at school, home or work; failure to fulfill important responsibilities; psychological dependence (can't live without it); withdrawal symptoms if stopped; blackouts; personality changes; a persistent yet unsuccessful desire to stop; and continued use despite knowledge of its damaging effects. Current thinking about causes of addiction is discussed in Chapter 6.

Parents should watch for these *signs of substance abuse* (alcohol and drugs) listed in Table 7-2. These signs may be more likely to surface when things are not going well at school.

Some parents believe that if their teenager is using drugs she will act like a monster. Usually, this is not true. Teenagers who are experimenting with substances will not have all the characteristics of substance abuse and thus can often hide their symptoms from parents. Drug use may be more difficult to detect than alcohol use. If your teenager is on marijuana or cocaine:

1. she may be more talkative, or
2. laugh excessively.

With marijuana, her eyes may be red and look a little glassy. When marijuana is being smoked, it has a distinctive smell like burnt rope. LSD may cause the pupils to dilate.

Research: ADHD and Substance Use

As discussed in Chapter 6, young people with ADHD who take medication for their attention deficit are less likely to have substance abuse problems than those who do not take medication. Most of these teens are no more likely to smoke, drink, or abuse illegal drugs than their peers without attention deficits.

The exception is teenagers who have conduct disorder or bipolar disorder in addition to ADHD. Dr. Barkley found that teenagers with both ADHD and Conduct Disorder (extremely aggressive and defiant) were much more likely to drink and smoke cigarettes and marijuana than teenagers with ADHD only. Dr.

Table 7-2   Warning Signs of Substance Abuse

- **Physical:** Fatigue, sleep problems, repeated health complaints, red and glazed eyes, and a lasting cough
- **Emotional:** Personality change, sudden mood changes, irritability, irresponsible behavior, low self-esteem, poor judgment, depression, withdrawal, and a general lack of interest
- **Family:** Starting arguments, breaking rules, or withdrawing from the family
- **School:** Decreased interest, negative attitude, drop in grades, many absences, truancy, and discipline problems

- **Social/behavioral:** Peer group involved with drugs and alcohol, problems with the law, dramatic change in dress and appearance
- Additional signs:
  - ❏ slurred speech
  - ❏ increased borrowing of money from parents or friends
  - ❏ stealing from home, school, or work
  - ❏ heightened secrecy about actions and possessions
  - ❏ frequent phone calls late at night or from strangers

Summarized from American Academy of Child and Adolescent Psychiatry (AACAP) Fact Sheet #3 (2004), www.aacap.org, and ***Teenagers with ADD*** (1995).

Rachel Gittleman-Klein, Director of Psychology, New York State Psychiatric Institute, found that teenagers with both ADHD and conduct disorder were more likely to experiment with alcohol and marijuana, plus were more likely to try hallucinogens such as LSD or PCP. On a positive note, however, Dr. Gittleman-Klein found that people with ADHD were no more likely than their peers to use drugs once they reached young adulthood. Dr. Barkley also found that teenagers in large cities were more likely to use drugs than those in rural areas.

Dr. Barkley has found that the substances that teenagers with ADHD are most likely to use are cigarettes and alcohol. Over 50 percent of these teens smoke cigarettes, which is double the rate for students without the condition. Studies of adults with ADHD reflect even higher rates of smoking, up to 75 percent. Unfortunately, nicotine helps people concentrate, improves their memory, and helps them calm down. Alcohol use is at about the 40 percent level and marijuana use at 17 percent. Thankfully, cocaine use is even lower at 4 percent. Keep in mind that these percentages may be somewhat inflated by two subgroups of ADHD. Teens whose attention deficit disorder coexists with conduct disorder or bipolar disorder are more than twice as likely to abuse drugs as those with ADHD alone.

Substance Abuse Predictors

"Predictors" are factors that increase the likelihood that a teen will use substances inappropriately. They include:

- school failure,
- low grades,
- low self-esteem
- hanging out with friends who use drugs,
- being aggressive and hyperactive,
- a family history of substance abuse or addiction.

If all these factors are combined and if the attention deficit is not properly treated, the increased risk of substance abuse is obvious.

The ages from 11 to 14 are critical since that is the time during which experimentation and substance use begins. According to Ari Russell, Director of GUIDE, a drug prevention program, parents often overlook early use and experimentation because they are looking for the more severe symptoms of abuse and addiction or dependency. This early use may provide the pleasant mood-altering experiences that lead some teens to continued and increased use, substance abuse, and

perhaps dependence. These patterns and experiences often begin in middle school and continue into high school, as the drugs of use become more illicit.

According to Dr. Wilens, the actual age of onset for substance abuse is typically around 19, after students have graduated from high school. So the post high school years are a high-risk time for actual abuse.

Treatment

Alcohol or drug abuse is incredibly difficult to treat; prevention of this condition is the best strategy. Suggestions for prevention of substance abuse and information on specific drugs are discussed in Chapter 10. Unfortunately, there are no guaranteed successful treatment programs. The limited research information that is available tells us that these strategies are somewhat effective:

1. **Provide interventions to ensure success in school.** School success, in turn, has a positive impact on drug use. This may be one of the most effective treatment strategies.

2. **Consider summer outreach programs** if they: a) build self-esteem, b) separate the teens from substances, c) separate the teen from a negative peer group, and d) give teens a new peer group. See Chapter 5 for more details.

3. **Provide outpatient or inpatient** services. Sometimes teens may need a *detoxification program* to help them sober up. These programs may be referred to as 28-day detox programs.

4. **Treat ADD/ADHD and coexisting conditions** such as bipolar disorder. Although individual members of Alcoholics Anonymous may say that someone with an addiction problem shouldn't take medication, AA officially recognizes that some people need medication for treatment of underlying disorders.

5. **Conduct random drug screens.** As part of her *total treatment program*, Dr. Patricia Quinn tells her patients up front that in addition to treatment with a stimulant medication she is going to conduct random drug screens. However, the national association for pediatricians does not recommend their routine use. See a discussion of the inappropriate use of drug screens in Chapter 9.

6. **Teach skills** such as anger management, time management, employment skills, or provide coaching to help the teenager cope with her skill deficits.

7. **Treat sleep disorders** since sleep problems affect school and employment performance. Students who can't get up to go to school or work often find themselves failing and in trouble with school officials or bosses.

8. **In an extreme situation, consider an "Intervention"** which involves inviting an intervention specialist to your home to jointly confront the teenager along with concerned family members. Interventions are used more often when a teen has serious substance abuse problems yet is in denial that they exist.

Asperger's Syndrome

Asperger's syndrome (AS) is one of five "pervasive developmental disorders" such as autism that are included in the DSM-IV-TR. Sometimes, Asperger's syndrome coexists with ADD or ADHD. However, other times a child with the characteristics of this condition may be diagnosed incorrectly with an attention deficit instead of Asperger's or vice versa. Additionally, Dr. Barkley reports that one in four children with autism also has ADHD.

Typically, young people with Asperger's have average to above intelligence and don't have any language delays. However, there may be exceptions. One mother reported that her son with AS didn't speak until he was nearly four years old. Some students may also have difficulty understanding the nuances of spoken language, especially irony or humor; *Pragmatic Language Disorder* may be present. In other words, they don't understand phrases when a potential double meaning is involved. For instance, when asked to select a picture of a traffic jam, the student may select a picture of a toy car stuck in a bottle of jam. In addition, they may not use the usual inflections in their speech.

A classic symptom of Asperger's is hyperfocusing on one or two interest areas such as dinosaurs or the makes and models of cars. Essentially, they may become a walking encyclopedia regarding their favorite topic.

"My son was diagnosed with Asperger's at age 5 and a year later was diagnosed with ADHD. As a teenager, one of his favorite topics is Monty Python; he often carries a two-inch thick paperback with the entire movie script. Once when we were riding a train, he went up to a total stranger, asked him if he liked Monty Python, and began talking about his script book. 'Do you remember the scene where John Cleese says…' and proceeded to quote the lines verbatim. Fortunately, the gentleman did like Monty Python and found the next hour and a half quite entertaining. However, my son would have talked regardless; he doesn't realize that others may not be interested in the same topic. Nor would it have occurred to him that he might be bothering someone."

These young people also have significant difficulties with social skills, may have few facial expressions other than anger or unhappiness, and be viewed as somewhat eccentric, or lost in their own world.

"During my son's seventh birthday party, all his classmates were playing ball while he wandered around the outside of the group, totally uninvolved. He was off in his own world doing his own thing and either found it too difficult or unnecessary to join in. Now that he is a teenager, his social skills have improved significantly. I am convinced that his behavior has changed because of all the wonderful help he has had."

According to Andrea Bilbow, executive director of ADDISS, an ADHD parent advocacy group based in the United Kingdom, teens with Asperger's have difficulty recognizing or responding with the correct emotion; they seem to lack empathy. If a classmate falls, the student may laugh inappropriately without realizing his error. After Princess Diana died, one teen asked his mother if this was a sad event. He recognized that others were saddened but did not experience that emotion. They may also be vulnerable because they are very gullible. Parents worry because someone could make sexual advances and their child may not recognize that the actions were inappropriate.

Bilbow related a story about an adult with AS who found the perfect job—he worked in a room by himself analyzing messages, manipulating numbers, and cracking secret codes for the government. However, their perfectionist tendencies may also result in depression. Researchers report an increased risk for developing depression, anxiety, or a psychosis as they get older.

Treatment. Obviously, treatment of these more complex coexisting conditions is difficult. Frequently doctors will prescribe medications for the ADHD plus an SSRI such as Prozac to help eliminate unwanted or inappropriate repetitive behaviors. For more information on medical treatment of autism spectrum disorders, see *Healthcare for Children on the Autism Spectrum* by Fred Volkmar and Lisa Wiesner. Dr. Tony Attwood, Director of the Asperger's Syndrome Clinic, Queensland, Australia, offers helpful information through his website and book, *Asperger's Syndrome*.

Disruptive Behavior Disorders

In addition to the mental health conditions discussed above, two other conditions warrant a section of their own because they occur fairly frequently and are such worrisome behaviors. These conditions are *oppositional defiant disorder (ODD)* and *conduct disorder (CD)*. Understandably, many parents are concerned when treatment professionals discuss a second diagnosis of ODD or CD. Like a diagnosis of ADD or ADHD, these labels are shorthand for behaviors that occur in a cluster. The diagnostic criteria given in the DSM-IV-TR for ODD and CD are listed below.

Oppositional Defiant Disorder (ODD)

Unfortunately, oppositional defiant disorder (ODD) is the most common coexisting condition among students with attention deficits—affecting approximately 55 percent, according to Joseph Biederman,

M.D. To be diagnosed with ODD, four of the following behaviors must be present for a period of six months:

- often loses temper,
- often argues with adults,
- often actively defies or refuses to comply with adults' requests or rules,
- often deliberately annoys people,
- often blames others for his or her mistakes or misbehavior,
- is often touchy or easily annoyed by others,
- is often angry and resentful,
- is often spiteful or vindictive.

Difficulty regulating emotions and inability to use self-talk to control behavior both play a key role in oppositional behavior. Deficits in executive skills also contribute to behavior problems in teens who have both attention deficits and ODD. For example, difficulty controlling emotions could lead to blowing up more easily than peers; working and long-term memory deficits make it difficult to pull past experiences from memory to avoid repeating misbehavior; and speaking or acting before they think of the consequences can lead to confrontations with adults or peers. Frustration with poor school performance may also contribute to these problem behaviors.

Poor parenting does not cause ODD but can make it worse. Dr. Barkley has identified four interacting factors that contribute to ODD:

1. The child's personality and temperament;
2. The parent's personality and temperament (If both parent and child have attention deficits, negative emotional interactions may be more frequent.);
3. Family stress (unemployment, marital, or money problems);
4. Parenting strategies (by learning more effective parenting strategies, parents can reduce oppositional behavior).

The major implications from these findings indicate that it is critical for parents to:

1. Educate themselves about attention deficits,
2. Learn more effective parenting strategies, and
3. Treat their own attention deficit, if they tend to be inconsistent in their parenting strategies or lash out at their children in an impulsive, angry manner.

Typically, a diagnosis of ODD is not as much a cause for concern as a diagnosis of conduct disorder. Thankfully, the problems with ODD may lessen with maturity and with proper treatment. Since oppositional behavior is fairly common among teenagers regardless of whether or not they have an attention deficit, a diagnosis of ODD does not carry as much stigma as conduct disorder.

Dr. Biederman and his associates have identified what they believe are two types of ODD: one type that seems to lead to conduct disorder and one that does not. The more serious ODD leading to conduct disorder is characterized by more negative, provocative, spiteful, and vindictive behavior. So, parents should not stick their heads in the sand and ignore problem behaviors. They need to work with treatment professionals to learn more effective parenting skills and develop a plan to cope with specific problems.

Conduct Disorder (CD)

Conduct Disorder is one of the most serious diagnoses among the DSM classifications. Teenagers with conduct disorder consistently violate the rights of others and refuse to comply with rules.

Researchers have found high rates of conduct disorder (20-50%) among teens with attention deficits. Anecdotally, however, some pediatricians report that it is rarer, with roughly 10 percent of their patients having these symptoms. Dr. Barkley explains that as adults, 18 to 27 percent of those who were diagnosed with CD as children are diagnosed as having antisocial personality disorder. Conduct disorder is a childhood diagnosis; antisocial personality disorder is a comparable diagnosis for adults 18 years and older. To be diagnosed as having a conduct disorder, a teenager must exhibit only three of the following during the past twelve months with at least one present in the last six months:

Aggression to people and animals
1. often bullies, threatens, or intimidates others
2. often initiates physical fights
3. has used a weapon that can cause serious physical harm to others (e.g., a bat, brick, broken bottle, knife, gun)
4. has been physically cruel to people
5. has been physically cruel to animals
6. has stolen while confronting a victim (e.g., mugging, purse snatching, extortion, armed robbery)
7. has forced someone into sexual activity

Destruction of property
8. has deliberately engaged in fire setting with the intention of causing serious damage
9. has deliberately destroyed others' property (other than by fire setting)

Deceitfulness or theft
10. has broken into someone else's house, building, or car
11. often lies to obtain goods or favors or to avoid obligations (i.e., "cons" others)
12. has stolen items of nontrivial value without confronting a victim (e.g., shoplifting, but without breaking and entering; forgery)

Serious violations of rules
13. often stays out at night despite parental prohibitions, beginning before age 13
14. has run away from home overnight at least twice while living in parental or parental surrogate home (or once without returning for a lengthy period)
15. often truant from school, beginning before age 13

The most common conduct problems reported are lying, stealing, truancy, and, to a lesser degree, physical aggression. According to Dr. Ben Lahey's research, children who have the most severe problems have high levels of hyperactivity and are diagnosed with attention deficit disorders by the age of 2 or 3, ODD symptoms by 4 or 5, and conduct disorder symptoms by the age of 8 to 11. Dr. Barkley observed an even earlier onset of CD symptoms—by the age of 6. So parents may feel some measure of relief if their child has reached adolescence without exhibiting symptoms of conduct disorder.

The more of these behaviors a teenager has and the worse their severity, the more serious the CD is considered to be. Teenagers with a combination of hyperactivity and conduct disorder seem to have the most serious problems and the poorest prognosis. Youngsters with ADHD and conduct disorder are more likely to be expelled from school, be arrested, abuse drugs, and break the law, possibly ending up in jail or a psychiatric treatment facility. The possible causes of ODD and Conduct Disorders are discussed in Chapter 10.

Treatment of ODD and CD

Parents can avoid some of these problems by taking steps such as those described in Chapters 5 and 8;

for example, keeping family life as organized as possible, providing supervision and structure, keeping the teenager busy in activities to build self-esteem and resilience, ensuring school success, giving medication, and if needed, seeking professional help.

One of the major findings from the MTA study was that stimulant medication is the most effective treatment for reducing aggressive behavior in children with ADHD. Other medications that doctors may prescribe include Depakote, Catapres, Tenex, or Lithium. Research from the MTA study also offers hope to parents. Initially, 40 percent of the children in the study met criteria for ODD or conduct disorder. After they received medication alone or medication plus intensive behavioral interventions, only 10 percent of the children still had ODD or CD. In other words, 75 percent of the children who had been diagnosed with ODD or CD no longer met criteria. ***ODD and CD are not permanent conditions!***

Three worrisome symptoms frequently identified in students with the diagnosis of ODD and conduct disorder are anger, aggression, and oppositional behavior. Preventing or reducing these three behaviors is very important. Reducing the number of angry confrontations between children and their parents is also critical. Common treatment strategies, in addition to medications, include interventions which help reduce frustration and increase compliance at home and success at school. These strategies are discussed in Chapters 5 and 8-13, plus in *Teaching Teens with ADD and ADHD.*

Other Possible Co-Existing Disorders

It is beyond the scope of this chapter to describe in detail every possible mental health condition or disability that can coexist with an attention deficit disorder. Attention deficits can accompany almost any condition you may name. Examples include:

- Fetal alcohol syndrome
- Specific learning disabilities (discussed in Chapters 11 and 14)
- Cerebral palsy
- Traumatic brain injury
- Mental retardation
- Fragile X syndrome
- Autism spectrum disorders
- Williams syndrome

The bottom line is, if you think there is something going on with your teenager in addition to the attention deficit, talk with your treatment professional about a thorough evaluation.

Emotional and Behavior Disorder (ED)

Some children with ADD or ADHD will develop serious emotional problems, possibly as high as 10 to12 percent. If your teenager is struggling academically and emotionally, the school may recommend evaluation for an Emotional and Behavior Disorder (ED). This category was previously referred to as SED or Severe Emotional Disturbance. ED is a special education category only—not an official medical or mental health diagnosis. In practice, many of the students who receive this label have ODD or conduct disorder.

ED may not be the most appropriate special education category for our children with attention deficits. Parents are encouraged to learn about Other Health Impairment (OHI) and, in most cases, seek eligibility under that category instead. Chapter 14 provides a full explanation of special education categories and eligibility.

Ending on a Note of Hope

Even if your teenager has some behaviors that are characteristic of a conduct disorder, oppositional defiant disorder, or emotional disorder, do not despair and give up. Your teenager's behavior may change and improve over time. A teenager diagnosed as having conduct disorder does not necessarily continue to exhibit these problem behaviors forever. Even when he or she acts out, hang on. You may be able to pull a teen back from the brink of law-breaking behavior. As Dr. Gabriella Weiss was quoted earlier in the book, *the key to successfully surviving ADHD is to have someone who believes in you, even during difficult times.* And as you will learn in Chapter 8, resilience also plays a major role in a child's ability to cope with adversity. There are many things you can do to build your teenager's self-confidence and resilience and help him or her cope successfully with the attention deficit.

True, when your teenager is in a crisis, it may be extremely difficult for you to be positive and to continue to believe in him or her. However, even though you may sometimes have doubts and get discouraged, it may help to *act* as if you believe in your teenager. You can discuss your fears in private with your family or with a treatment professional. Thankfully, most crises have a way of "blowing over" fairly soon without irreversible damage. Sometimes a parent's whispered words of hope and self-encouragement may be: *"This too shall pass."*

8

Raising a Healthy, Well-Adjusted Teenager

Parents of teenagers with attention deficit disorders often have questions about the "right" way to raise their son or daughter. Should we be strong disciplinarians or should we be more democratic? Are we being too strict or too lenient? If our teenager repeats misbehavior, should punishment be more severe? Does nagging help? How can we use positive reinforcement to help him avoid misbehavior? When punishment is necessary, what are some good strategies to use?

Although parents typically receive a lot of advice from other well-meaning adults, *there is no "magic formula" or "right way" to raise a teenager with an attention disorder.* As a parent, you must decide which techniques work best with your teenager. Here is some general advice:

- *Avoid either extreme of parenting*—that is, too harsh or too permissive.
- *Take a parenting class*. Learn a variety of parenting strategies such as those discussed in this chapter. Learning new strategies will make you a more effective parent plus make your life easier and more pleasant. Find the strategies that you feel most comfortable using.
- *Read about how to use positive reinforcement* effectively and diffuse anger.
- *Learn all you can about attention disorders* so you recognize "ADHD behaviors" and don't mistake them for malicious misbehavior.

The specific parenting approach you use—strict disciplinarian versus a more lenient approach—is not

the most crucial factor in determining whether or not teenagers cope successfully with their attention disorder. *Ongoing positive support for your teenager and medication when needed are often more important than the specific parenting approach you use.* But learning effective parenting strategies *will* be very helpful. As discussed earlier, Dr. Gabrielle Weiss believes a major key to coping with ADD or ADHD is having an adult who loves and believes in the teenager.

This does not mean that love alone cures all problems or that parents should let their teenager run wild. These teenagers need support, structure, lots of supervision, and encouragement. The challenge for parents is to achieve a balance between giving positive feedback for good behavior, ignoring minor misbehavior, teaching skills that are missing, and using negative consequences for more serious, inappropriate behavior. Parents must learn to impose reasonable consequences without obliterating their teenager's self-esteem.

"ADD/ADHD Behaviors" Make Parenting Tougher

First I want to restate the obvious: children and teenagers with attention deficits *really are* a lot more difficult to raise than other children. Consequently, you must develop strong parenting skills. Unfortunately, other adults don't realize how challenging these children can be and thus parents often face criticism from well-meaning friends and relatives about their parenting skills. However, even the experts know that treating teens with attention deficits is incredibly challenging. For example, in response to a question about what works with teenagers, Dr. Barkley replied somewhat tongue-in-cheek, "Not much!" Clearly, the most effective intervention strategy is medication—other interventions work only about 25 to 30 percent of the time.

"My sister and brother-in-law think they have all the answers. From their perspective, my son just needs to be disciplined. They cannot begin to understand what it is like to raise a youngster with ADHD. They think their child is an angel because of their superior parenting skills. I'd like to see them do any better with a child with ADHD than I have."

Unfortunately, feedback from judgmental adults makes most parents further question whether or not they are using the right strategies. Because teenagers with attention disorders are more difficult to discipline, parents may second guess themselves and question their own effectiveness. If parents assume they are doing something wrong, they may resort, unsuccessfully, to increasingly harsh punishment. It is very difficult to maintain a balanced, steady approach to parenting; it's very difficult not to overreact.

"For most parents, the teenage years are a time of letting go. But I couldn't do that with Jeremy. A friend said to me, 'Wow! Everyone else is letting go and you're still hanging on.' I thought to myself, you have no idea how much I want to let go. But my son is not equipped to handle being a teenager. It takes kids with ADHD longer to grow up because developmentally, they are so far behind their peer group.

"She didn't realize that when my son gets into trouble, I'm always the one who has to come in and help negotiate a resolution. Other teens learn negotiation and problem solving skills so that parents may not even find out about their problems. Kids who don't have ADHD learn a lesson once and retain it. But if my son does something right once, there is no guarantee he will do it right again."

Punishment Alone Is Ineffective

Remember that *punishment alone is not going to make "ADHD behaviors" go away.* Punishment will not produce more neurotransmitters or grow more white matter to help improve your teen's attention, compliance with requests, and ability to finish tasks. In fact, you may inadvertently create major problems if you take a punitive approach to parenting. Over a period of years, children who are exposed to frequent negative interactions with adults may develop negative, aggressive behavior.

As explained earlier, many teenagers with attention deficits don't respond to traditional punishment and rewards the same as teens without the condition. They don't seem to learn from their mistakes, be deterred by punishment, or be motivated by rewards as easily as other teenagers. These factors, combined with their impulsivity and sometimes daring behavior, often make them a handful for parents to manage. If parents place them on restrictions, they will turn around the next week and repeat the same misbehavior. Much to parents' dismay, when an effective consequence is found, it is not effective for very long, sometimes only a couple of weeks. In addition, traditional behavioral strategies that work with children no longer work as well with teenagers.

"Right before my daughter was diagnosed at age 10, I was at my wit's end and I spanked her for misbehaving, again. I was so frustrated. I said, 'I don't understand why you keep doing the things you do. Can you tell me, why won't you do what I have asked you to do—why don't you mind me? Are you forgetting what you should do?' She looked up at me with big, sad eyes, tears streaming down her face, and said 'Mommy, I just don't know why.'"

Teens Want To Do Well

Deep down inside, *most children and teenagers with attention deficit disorders want to please their parents and teachers, want to do well in school, and actually feel better when they do as adults ask.* It is highly unlikely that a teenager gets up every morning and makes a pledge to see how miserable he can make his parents' day. Sometimes after years of failure, however, teenagers may become so discouraged and depressed that they no longer care about adult approval. Ideally, parents will seek help before problems reach this crisis stage.

Just remember that your teenager's misbehavior is often related to his symptoms of the attention deficit disorder and deficits in executive skills—impulsively talking back, losing things, being late, being forgetful, breaking things, difficulty sitting still, waking up, listening, getting started on schoolwork, and planning ahead. I strongly agree with one of Dr. Ross Green's favorite quotes, "Children will do well if they can!" Dr. Green, author of *The Explosive Child*, believes it is our job to figure out which problems are interfering with the child's success at home and school and provide appropriate interventions.

Find a Parenting Style That Works with Your Teen

The expression "different strokes for different folks" is especially true when it comes to raising children and teenagers with attention disorders. Find someone you trust with whom you can talk and then brainstorm parenting strategies. The bottom line is, however, that you know your teen better than anyone else. Ultimately, you have to trust your own instincts. Intuitively, you often know what is best for him. Some teenagers are more sensitive and respond quickly to a raised voice or dirty look. Others require more intense parental intervention. Most teenagers with ADD or ADHD, however, respond better to stronger, more meaningful rewards and consequences.

If traditional "child rearing" methods are working effectively with your teenager, then you should continue your current methods of parenting. However, if your family is experiencing problems, you may want to try some of the suggestions given here. Techniques discussed in this chapter will work for most teenagers, not just teens with ADD or ADHD.

"Parents need to know that 'routine' parenting strategies do not work because these teens are not 'routine kids'. Parents have to think differently."

—Gale Gordon, MD, pediatrician and mother

The Big "D's": Democracy and Discipline

The authoritarian childrearing methods used by past generations don't work quite as well with the teenagers of today. Parenting techniques tend to be more democratic now, and teenagers are both "seen and heard." Teenagers are taught to be independent, speak out, and make their own decisions. Yet, when we as parents make a request, we expect the opposite—we want them to obey immediately and without question. Striking a reasonable balance between democratic principles and discipline in childrearing is challenging.

"How can you help your teenager grow up to be a responsible, happy, productive adult?" There is no right or wrong answer for this question. Generally, however, you will be more successful if you and your teenager can work together toward this goal. During the early years of adolescence, you will want to increasingly involve your teenager as a respected partner in the treatment process. You must try to educate him so that he understands the impact of an attention deficit on his life, recognizes his strengths and limitations, builds his self-esteem, accepts increasing levels of responsibility, gains some sense of control over his life, and feels confident that he can cope with whatever problems arise.

As your child reaches the teenage years, you must learn alternative ways of dealing with problems, since the time will come when physical punishment no longer works and behavior management loses much of its effectiveness. Spanking a 6'2", 180-pound 16-year-old isn't particularly feasible or effective. Nor will most teenagers be motivated by charts and stars.

There *are* several strategies, however, that should help make your job as a parent easier. These include behavior management, positive reinforcement, logical consequences, and medication management. Other helpful techniques such as ignoring minor misbehavior, active listening, negotiating, giving choices, and following Grandma's rule are also discussed in this chapter.

For additional practical and humorous insights into coping with teenagers, see Dr. Thomas W. Phelan's book, *Surviving Your Adolescents*. Having raised two teenagers, one of whom has ADHD, Dr. Phelan gives advice based upon experience, not just theory.

Guiding Principles for Parent/Teenager Interactions

This section discusses a dozen key principles to bear in mind when parenting and communicating with teenagers with ADD or ADHD. These principles are especially important if your teenager is struggling and his self-esteem is fragile.

1. Give Unconditional Positive Regard

One critical step in helping your teen cope successfully with an attention deficit is to give him what treatment professionals commonly refer to as *unconditional positive regard.* This simply means that you should make every effort to love your teenager, just as he is, with all his special strengths and faults. He needs to know that you believe in him and will be there when he needs you. Although this is all so much easier said than done, several suggestions are provided below.

Reframe Your Perception of ADD and ADHD. Reframing your perception of attention deficit disorders and your teenager's behavior in a more positive light can help you give him unconditional positive regard. As discussed in Chapter 4, viewing the cup as half full (looking at strengths), rather than half empty (looking at problems) is important. These teenagers aren't "bad," nor are you, their parents, "bad" parents. Try to understand that many characteristics that are bothersome in teenagers may serve adults well. High energy, persuasiveness, tenacity, risk-taking, creativity, and independence are characteristics that may help your teenager be successful in his chosen career. If you haven't already done so, review Table 8-2 on page 155 regarding identifying your teen's strengths and Table 4-1 on page 70 reframing negative ADD/ADHD behaviors in a positive manner.

Set Fair Expectations for Girls, Too. Guard against a double standard regarding expectations for boys versus girls with attention deficits. Because *societal expectations* are distinctly different for girls and boys, girls with this disorder often are not treated as well as boys who exhibit the same misbehavior. Even mothers give more praise and direction to their sons with ADHD than to their daughters who actually behave better. Dr. Nadeau reminds us that expectations for so-called feminine *traits* such as being neat and attractive, in control and passive, sensitive to others, and compliant are much higher for girls than for boys. Unfair expectations can be very damaging to a girl's self-esteem.

Keep a Disability Perspective. Sometimes it is hard to accept and remember that ADD and ADHD *are* disabilities for some youngsters with these conditions.

"Even though our family has been struggling with this disorder for eight years, sometimes I still forget that ADHD is a disability. Developmentally these teenagers are behind. If a child couldn't read because of a visual disability, parents wouldn't be angry. They would say, `Put on your glasses when you study.' Likewise, we, as parents, should avoid getting angry with a teenager because of misbehavior related to ADHD. We should have our teenager take his medicine, make accommodations at school, and work with him to succeed."

Write a "Healing Letter." One way to help your teen's self-esteem and increase his understanding of his attention deficit is to write him a "healing letter," as discussed in Chapter 4. In this letter, you may enumerate his strengths, acknowledge ADHD challenges, express appreciation for the difficulties he faces, offer encouragement, and refer to others who have managed to be successful in spite of painful school experiences.

Enjoy Your Teenager. Parents and their teenagers need to laugh together and have fun. By doing this, a solid base of positive memories is built that will stand the teenager in good stead when he faces difficult times. Can you remember the last time you had a really good sidesplitting laugh with your teenager? Try to find something humorous to share, even if it is just a good comedy movie. You might also suggest a "special event" for just the two of you, such as eating dinner out or an activity of the teenager's choice.

It is especially important to share activities that are fun and pleasant if your teenager is doing poorly in school. Active participation may be better than spectator activities. Many teenagers with attention deficits have trouble sitting for very long and may lose interest in watching a football or baseball game. Play tennis or basketball, ride bikes, shop, or jog together. Swim or water ski as a family. The whole family may enjoy putt-putt golf or going to a movie. Table games such as Trivial Pursuit, Pictionary, or simple card games like Skip Bo may be fun for families to share. Other hobbies such as art, music, and cooking may also be shared by family members. Make sure that the activity is fun for your teenager too. If Mom and Dad are the only ones having fun throwing the baseball, this is not the best activity for a positive interaction.

Don't avoid activities in which your teenager is more skilled than you are. Go ahead and play basketball with him, even though you are out-of-shape and your teenager may win. He may even get to teach you a thing or two. Hopefully, you can laugh at yourself. Your teenager's ego could probably use the boost.

Above all, remember that the purpose of the special time is to have fun and build a stronger bond of trust between the two of you. *Avoid the temptation to nag or discuss problems once you have your teenager "corralled."* Try to avoid these negative discussions unless your teen insists.

Nurture with Touch. Human touch is extremely healing and nurturing. Yet as children move into adolescence, touching occurs less frequently. Sometimes play wrestling or touch football are nice activities within the family to "legally allow" touching. Massage or back rubs can be very relaxing, nurturing activities. Don't be afraid to hug your teenager and tell him you love him.

2. Treat Your Teenager as a Partner in the Treatment Process

Involve your teenager in decision making as frequently as possible! For example, talk with him about best medication dosages and how frequently he needs to take it. "Does your 30 mg of Adderall XR seem to be working effectively? Does it help you concentrate better? Can you tell when your medication wears off? Do you need to take a little more medicine to get you through doing your homework?"

Be realistic during these questioning sessions. Ask one or two questions that you feel are critical. Too many questions may shut down your teen. Keep in mind that many of our teens have verbal expression problems and can't quickly and clearly tell you how medicine works. In addition, they may be oblivious to whether or not the medicine is working and may not, in fact, be very good reporters about medication effectiveness. So you may need to use a combination of observation and statements. You probably have a pretty good idea if he is struggling to concentrate and finish his homework in the evening. You may say something like, "Looks to me like you're running out of energy while you're doing your homework. Would you be willing to try a 5 mg Dexedrine in the late afternoons to get you through your homework?"

Likewise, involve your teenager in trying to solve school-related problems. You might begin by stating the obvious: "Sometimes you have trouble getting your homework done, and as a result you are failing algebra. I feel like you want to do well at school. How can we solve this problem together?" If he has no ideas, then offer a suggestion or two.

The level of your child's involvement and degree of autonomy will depend on his age. Obviously, an eighteen-year-old is capable of handling more freedom and making more responsible decisions than a thirteen-year-old. By treating your teenager as part of the solution rather than just the problem, you convey a message of respect and that you are partners working together to solve difficult problems.

Give Choices. Learning to make choices is an important part of growing up and becoming independent. Giving your teenager choices shows you respect him and his opinions, plus allows him to have more control over his environment. In addition, researchers have found that teenagers who have choices at school are more compliant, less aggressive, and produce more work.

Whenever possible, give your teenager choices. "What time is a good bedtime for you?" If you think he may give an outrageous reply, then suggest two reasonable options. "Which is better—11:00 or 11:30?" You can maintain some control by limiting choices to only two or three. Even when limited choices are given, teenagers feel a greater sense of control over their lives. "What time do you want to start on your homework? 7:00 or 7:30?" If he does suggest outrageous starting times, don't lecture him about it—just ignore it and repeat the choices. Or you can use humor without sarcasm—"Bedtime at 1:00 a.m.? Not!! Nice try."

Set Reasonable Expectations. Because teenagers with attention deficits act younger than their age and may also have learning problems, parents may have unrealistic expectations—they may expect more of a teenager than he is capable of. Keep in mind that most of these teenagers are as much as *30 percent behind their peers developmentally* (four to six years). They are less mature in their ability to accept responsibility, complete chores and homework, follow rules, or deal with their emotions. A sixteen-year-old may act more like a ten- to twelve-year-old.

"It is difficult knowing where to set expectations—not too high or too low. My frustration comes in trying to mold Lewis into just a 'normal teenager' and not taking into account his ADHD and learning disability."

Negotiate; Consider Compromise. When less serious problems come up, you might try to reach a satisfactory compromise with your teenager. Dr. Phelan suggests asking for a time to discuss the issue and to deal with only one problem at a time. For example, "When is a good time for us to talk about your room? or smoking? or coming in late?" Once the time is set, find a quiet place to talk, briefly discuss the problem, and ask if he has any ideas for solving the problem. After he explains his thoughts, state your concerns.

"Win-win" situations—where everyone gets something out of the deal—are best. Your teenager is more likely to follow through on a solution that he has helped develop. Solutions may include: a dirty room—close the door during the week and clean up on Fridays; being late—give 15 minutes leeway, have your teenager call if he is going to be late, have him set his watch alarm to go off 15 minutes before he is due home, or allow a later curfew on special occasions.

Depersonalize Problems. Sometimes it helps to take away the personal or blaming elements of a problem. Rather than criticize your teenager, try discussing the problem in terms of the typical behavior of teenagers with attention deficits.

For example, "Teenagers with ADHD (ADD) often have trouble being aware of time, so they come home late." "Most teenagers with ADD (ADHD) have trouble …getting started on their homework…remembering to take their medicine… saying things impulsively that they don't mean. Do you think this is true for you sometimes?" Listen to your teenager's response, then ask: "What can we do to solve this problem?" "How can I help you cope with this problem?" Try to have this discussion at a time when you can control your anger. For example, don't wait until your teenager comes home late for the third night in a row and then confront him as soon as he walks in the door: "You always come home late and I'm sick of it. Don't you know what time it is?"

Parents will find helpful strategies for their teens in our survival guide, *A Bird's-Eye View*. You can review this information with your teen and let him select a strategy he thinks might work. The book provides a neutral springboard for discussion—you are reading about *other* teens, not focusing on *your* teen's shortcomings. By reading these strategies together, your teen can "see" that other teens with ADHD experience the same problems and, hopefully, he or she will be less defensive.

Most parents slip into a pattern of nagging about misbehavior, even though it doesn't help change the teenager's behavior. If you have been nagging your teenager for years about something, maybe it's time to try a different approach like the ones suggested above.

Assume Good Intentions. As parents, it is easy to assume the worst intentions. Without even realizing it, you may think, "My son was late on purpose. He is intentionally lying about homework. He doesn't care if he fails his classes." Sometimes, however, it helps to assume that your teenager has good intentions. By avoiding a hostile confrontation, you avoid making him defensive. Your teenager may then be more willing to work with you to find solutions to problems. "I feel like you are willing to come home on time but you lose track of time." "I believe in my heart that you really want to make good grades in school. I know it's difficult for you. I'm willing to help you. Let's work together."

3. Maintain Good Communication

Maintaining open communication with your teenager is critically important. If the only parent/teenager communication is negative (about misbehavior), your teenager may begin avoiding you. Once this happens, your relationship may deteriorate further. If you are embroiled in negative exchanges, seek help to improve your communication skills. Dr. Barkley recommends a book for parents by Gerald Patterson, *Parents and Adolescents Living Together*. Below are some guidelines to help keep information flowing freely in both directions.

Listen When Your Teenager Talks. In the rare event your teenager wants to talk to you, you must be ready to listen.

"Maybe once or twice a month my son will come into a room where I am working, flop down in a chair or on the floor, and start talking. Whatever I am working on, I stop and set it aside. This talkative streak may last ten or fifteen minutes. Then this window of opportunity closes, until two or three weeks later when he is in the mood to talk again. I have learned that I need to make myself available when he is in the mood to talk."

If it really is a terrible time to talk because of a major conflict—an important meeting at work—set up a specific time to talk later. If necessary, call him from work after the meeting. If it is a crisis for your teenager, take at least five minutes to listen briefly, hug him, and tell him you're sorry he's hurting, you love him, and together you'll work it out. One solution may be to continue the conversation on your cell phone on the drive to work. Obviously, if it is a serious crisis, you should stay with your teenager and contact your treatment professional for advice.

Learning to listen without being judgmental is an important skill to master.

> *"My son has always told me everything both good and bad that he has ever done. Some of the things he tells me are a little embarrassing. In some ways I wish I didn't know when he has had a beer to drink or that he always carries a condom. Although I would prefer that he not drink or engage in a sexual relationship, I feel good that he tells me everything. Our communication is strong."*

The technique of active listening, described below, can help you learn to listen without judging who is right or wrong or taking sides.

Use Active Listening. Active listening may help you defuse your teenager's anger. When he is talking about things that interest him or potential areas of conflict between the two of you, you should listen and try to understand his viewpoint first. Then restate what he said to confirm that you have heard him correctly.

For example, your teenager may tell you that a teacher yelled at him in front of the whole class. You might respond by saying, "I'm really sorry your teacher yelled at you today." You can also make supportive comments. "I know it isn't fun to have a teacher yell at you. That can really be embarrassing. I always hated when my teacher did that." Don't take sides with anyone, just listen and reflect your teenager's feelings back to him.

If your teenager says he is angry with his teacher and she isn't fair, you might reflect: "I know you must have felt really angry. I didn't like it when my teachers weren't fair." He may say she gave him a zero because he left his homework at home. You may respond by saying, "I'm sorry she gave you a zero. Is there anything I can do to help?" Try to defuse anger rather than confront, criticize, or blame.

Avoid critical comments like, "If you were more organized this wouldn't happen. You probably deserved it." He needs someone to listen while he blows off steam in a healthy way. He is upset enough with himself and his teacher without you placing blame too. You can talk later about how to address the homework problem and avoid conflict with his teacher when he is calmer and less agitated.

Give "I" Messages. One technique that may keep communication more positive is to give what are known as "I" messages instead of "you" messages. "You" messages tend to be negative and blaming and frequently put the teenager on the defensive. "You didn't do your homework. You aren't being responsible." It is better to state how you feel about a certain problem—"I am very unhappy that your homework was not turned in on time. I get very angry and upset. I would like for you to help me solve this problem." Your teenager is more likely to work with you if he is not feeling defensive.

Smooth Ruffled Feathers. Teenagers with attention deficits have difficulty coping with stressful situations, yet frequently seem to find themselves in crises. As a result, parents and teachers may find themselves interacting with a teenager who is angry and argumentative. Sometimes adults can ignore the hostile questions or comments and calmly state the job that needs to be done. If your teenager refuses to do as requested, sometimes it is helpful to wade through the anger and hostility and address the real issue that may be underlying a particular incident. Smoothing ruffled feathers rather than meeting hostility with a hostile response may be effective, as described in the following example. Otherwise, a hostile response typically results in even more anger and fighting.

> *"My son advised me that he was not going to school today. I ignored most of his comments and avoided arguing with him. I told him his jeans were clean and were in the dryer. Mistakenly, he thought he would feel better if he could draw me into an argument with him. He changed tactics and asked, 'Why will it hurt me to miss one day of school?'*
>
> *"I sat and looked at him for a few moments trying to figure out what was going on behind the anger. Finally, I remembered he'd had a fight with his girlfriend the night before and said, 'I'm sorry you've been having such a rough time lately. Fighting with your girlfriend hurts.' I did not try to explain to him why he should go to school. I walked off. Within a few minutes, he started his shower in preparation for going to school."*

> *"Sometimes when my son erupts in a hostile manner, I say, "This really isn't like you to act this way. Is something wrong?' I learned this lesson one day when I was teaching school and was confronted by a hostile 14-year-old. I gave this same response. To my surprise, the student calmed down and apologized. He told me that the teacher in his previous class had yelled at him and embarrassed him. He was angry with his teacher but was taking it out on me."*

If you make comments aimed at smoothing ruffled feathers, you must genuinely mean them. If you say, "I'm sorry you've been having a rough time lately," in a sarcastic manner or give a hostile look, your teenager will pick up on it instantly. The whole purpose of being understanding and supportive will be defeated.

Additional suggestions for deescalating explosive situations with your teen are provided in *Teaching Teens with ADD and ADHD,* Summary 59. Although the suggestions are addressed primarily to teachers, they also work very effectively for parents.

Encourage Expression of Feelings. Many teenagers with attention deficits suppress painful emotions. They have difficulty being in touch with these feelings or expressing them. It is important to encourage your teenager to be aware of his feelings and to express them.

"My teenage son came home one Saturday night and he had drunk a few beers. Although I was concerned about his drinking, I just listened to him talk. He began to open up about his deepest feelings, pains, and fears. He cried as he told me that sometimes he felt like he was going crazy. He hated school and felt stupid at times. Sometimes he wished he were dead. My heart was breaking. I listened and hugged him close. I told him, 'Those feelings are not unusual for teenagers with ADD or ADHD. A lot of people worry about going crazy. Those feelings are a part of growing up. When I was younger, I wondered if I was going crazy. I love you and I'll always be here for you.' I didn't want to close the door on our communication by confronting him at that moment about his drinking. I dealt with the drinking issue later when things were calmer."

Don't be afraid to tell your teenager about personal things that make you happy or sad. When you are upset, he may learn from comforting you and listening to your concerns.

"I remember being really upset about a problem I was having at work. I wasn't afraid for my teenage son to see me crying. He sat down beside me, hugged me, and told me not to worry, everything was going to turn out okay. It sounded just like something I would say to him. I think it was good for him to feel like he was strong and was able to help me."

Another way to encourage expression of feelings is to ask questions when your teenager tells you about emotional experiences. For example, if he is telling about a teacher who has embarrassed him in class, ask him, "How did you feel when she did that?" Avoid pressuring him by peppering him with questions. It's okay to have periods of silence which give him time to think and formulate his response. Remember, his verbal expression problems may mean he needs more time to express his emotions. You may need to suggest possible feelings: "Were you embarrassed?" (listen) Or, "Were your feelings hurt?" (listen) "Did you feel angry?" (listen) "Those are pretty normal feelings. I'm sorry this was such a painful experience for you."

Teach by Example. Show your teenager through your actions how to respect others' feelings, handle conflict, and accept each other for who you are. For example, you can show your teenager that you always love *him* even though you may not love his *behavior* at times. When you are patient, you teach him to be patient. If you handle your anger about less serious issues by discussing them and reaching a compromise (or exercising, or counting to ten), your teen will learn to handle his anger in a healthy way. The converse is also true. If you are impatient, your teenager will learn to be impatient. If you are untrusting and hostile, you are teaching your teenager to be the same way.

Avoid Subconscious Negative Messages. Most messages parents give to their children are direct and the result of conscious decisions. For example, if parents are angry because their teen didn't complete his homework, they may tell him they are angry and put him on restrictions. But parents may also send indirect negative messages that are given subconsciously. Parents may not even be aware they are sending them. But these children and teenagers can be extremely perceptive: they know if parents and teachers approve of them, if adults trust them, or if adults think they're bad. The teenager will perceive the parent's or teacher's true feelings when the nonverbal messages don't match the verbal messages. Even though you don't *tell* your teen you think he's bad, you may convey this message through disapproving looks, frowns, negative comments, and lack of positive comments or touch. Monitor yourself to make sure you are not sending subtle negative messages that may be damaging to your teenager.

4. Understand ADD/ADHD Factors Influencing Behavior

Researchers tell us there are certain situations in which teenagers with ADD or ADHD seem to function better. Being aware of these situations should be helpful to you and his teachers in interacting with him (Table 8-1).

Table 8-1 Comparison of Behavior in Different Settings

Better:	Worse:
■ One-to-one setting	■ Groups
■ Novelty situations	■ Familiar
■ High interest activities	■ Low interest activities
■ Fun	■ Boring
■ Immediate consequences	■ Delayed consequences
■ Mornings	■ Later in the day
■ Frequent feedback	■ Infrequent feedback
■ Supervised	■ Unsupervised
■ Fathers	■ Mothers

5. Provide Structure and Supervision

Because of their developmental delay, *most teenagers with ADD or ADHD need more structure and supervision than their friends without attention disorders* and they will need it for a longer period of time. There are a variety of ways you can provide this structure, depending on your teenager's age, sense of responsibility, and independence.

Establish a Daily Routine. Having a set time to get up, go to bed, eat, and study each day adds needed structure to your child's life. Since these teenagers have major problems with organization, awareness of time, and time management, having a schedule and routine will help them cope better with responsibilities in life (schoolwork and chores). Involve your teenager in making decisions about his daily routine. Specific suggestions for establishing routines regarding homework are discussed in Chapter 12.

Develop Rules and Consequences. You and your teenager may jointly develop a few basic rules that address the issues that are most important to the family. Rules should be clearly stated. Consequences for breaking them should also be known in advance. For example, "You can't go out on Friday night until your homework is completed." "If you get a speeding ticket, you will have to pay the fine and you will not be able to drive for a week." Try to involve your teenager in selecting the consequence. If he suggests a consequence that is too easy or too harsh, suggest a more reasonable consequence.

"*Each year we renegotiate the rules for the school year with our daughter. We have a respectful discussion and then each of us gets to vote on the rule. We focus on how she has been able to deal with her current*

responsibilities rather than just assume more is better. After we vote, we write the rules down and post them somewhere. Here are some of our rules:

1. *Telephone Use: If it were possible, our daughter would have her cell phone surgically attached to her ear.*
   a. *No phone calls will be accepted between 6-8 p.m.*
   b. *No phone calls during homework. Once interrupted, it is too hard for her to transition back to her work.*
   c. *No phone calls in the morning before school, with few exceptions. She may call if it is something she really needs to know before seeing friends at school—for example to get a ride, or to tell them she's sick. Mornings are not social telephone times. She needs to take her time and not be rushed getting ready for school.*
2. *Dress Codes: Her school has the "3 Bs" dress code: no butts, no bellies, and no boobs.*
   a. *If she is sent home or I have to bring her a t-shirt because her clothes violated the 3B code, that item of her clothing will be discarded. If there is a question about some of her clothes, then the three of us vote to decide if it is acceptable to wear to school.*
3. *Curfew: She sees herself as more mature and likes to date older boys. So of course she wants later curfews.*
   a. *During week nights, she has to be home by 10:00 p.m. She needs to wind down before she goes to bed, plus get organized for the next day.*

She does all her organizational things at night; she gets her medicine, books, and clothes ready. Then when she gets up at 6:30 a.m., the only thing she has left to do is get dressed. She has to work when the mood strikes her, which is often at night. She may clean her room or do her laundry then. If she is not in the mood to keep her room clean every day, then she has to keep her door closed in between her cleaning moods.

b. On weekends, she can stay out until midnight. Our town has a curfew of 11:30 on weekends, unless the teen is with a parent or an adult. So she can stay out until midnight if we pick up her up."

—Joan Helbing, ADD Consultant

Develop a Contract. A contract can be developed in which you, your teen, and/or teachers clearly define expectations and consequences and rewards for appropriate and inappropriate behavior. A contract seems to work better if your teenager helps write it and chooses positive and negative consequences. It is important to build in more positive consequences so your teenager will want to uphold his end of the bargain. A sample contract is provided in Appendix 2. Feel free to modify or simplify this contract to meet your needs. Keep in mind that a contract alone is seldom enough to bring about major changes in behavior, but at least it does spell out expectations and consequences.

Schedule Chores. It helps to have regularly scheduled chores so that your teenager knows what is expected when, and can't say "but I already made other plans." If he needs a reminder, remind him the day before. If he didn't mow the yard Thursday, then remind him Friday afternoon when he gets home from school. When Friday evening rolls around and he still hasn't mowed the yard, you must "be cool." Don't nag him to mow the yard—wait until he comes to you and wants to go out. Remind him that he may go out when the yard has been mowed.

Sometimes this approach will work for only a short while. It may develop into a power struggle in which your teenager proves that he can out wait you. For example, he may refuse to mow the lawn and then contentedly stay home on Friday night. Sometimes you can extend the consequence for not doing a chore to the next day:

"When you mow the yard, you may play football with your friends." If you try this approach for a few weeks and it doesn't work, then try another intervention.

"Waiting and being cool is so difficult for me. Sometimes I slip and start nagging at him to mow the yard. Usually, a fight erupts and we both end up feeling terrible. When I can do it, it is so much nicer to look at my son and calmly and sympathetically say, 'I think it's a great idea for you to go to the movies. When you finish the yard, you may go.'"

Give Advance Notice and Timeframes. "Do it now because I said to do it" is not as effective with this generation of teenagers. Try to give your teenager advance notice and a timeframe for doing something. "I am leaving for work at 8:00. If you are ready, you can ride with me instead of riding the bus." "If you want to wear something on Monday, it needs to be in the laundry room by Saturday morning." Occasionally, your teenager is still going to forget what you told him. It may help him remember things if you remind him the next morning that you are leaving at 8:00, or write responsibilities on a calendar or Post-it note and put it where it is easy to see. A talking timer that calls out the time remaining before you must leave may also help.

Link Responsible Behavior to Privileges. For many teenagers, driving a car is one of their most cherished privileges. This privilege gives the parent tremendous leverage. Parents frequently link being responsible with having driving privileges in discussions with their teenager. Students who are responsible complete their homework, help around the house, don't get speeding tickets, and drive responsibly. Consequently, if your teenager brings home failing grades (because he isn't trying), doesn't do his chores, gets speeding tickets, or doesn't come home on time, he may not be allowed to drive for a while. For example, he can drive when his chores are completed or he brings home a good weekly report.

If your teenager is really trying but not earning passing grades, you should have him evaluated for learning problems and request appropriate classroom accommodations. If a student is doing his best on his schoolwork, punishment is not appropriate.

"As my son approached age sixteen and would soon obtain his driver's license, we talked more and more about the importance of being responsible. I have told him that if he is not responsible about his

schoolwork, then that makes me wonder if he can be responsible while driving a car. Being allowed to drive is a powerful incentive for him to do as we ask. Driving is probably the most important privilege my son has."

Try Creative Incentives. Creative incentives for completing a task are preferable, but most parents impose a punishment after the fact, often because that's what our parents did. For example, if your teen is of driving age but not completing his homework, you might try this option. First, of course, you would identify learning problems and make appropriate accommodations at school. Then you might say, "One way to ensure that you are doing your homework is for you to bring home a weekly report. Each week that you bring home a good weekly report that says you have done all your work, then you can earn the privilege of driving to school next week."

Set Limits; State Expectations. If an issue is serious, you can set limits and state your expectations without first consulting your teenager. For example, if you know or suspect that your son is planning to do something inappropriate, you might say, "Staying at a motel overnight for a New Year's Eve party is not acceptable to me. I expect you to be home by one o'clock." Or, "Cursing at me is not acceptable. I expect you to talk to me with respect." If your teenager is defiant, state your expectations ("I expect you to . . ."), and walk away. If you stay and argue, the situation will escalate. If your teenager disobeys you, follow through with a reasonable consequence.

Provide Supervision; Be a Coach. You will have to provide supervision to ensure completion of most jobs, including chores and homework. Supervision of social activities is also important. You need to know where your teenager is, what he is doing, and with whom. How much supervision should you provide a teenager with ADD or ADHD? The answer is pretty simple: as much supervision as he needs to succeed. Teenagers who act responsibly will be given more freedom and less supervision. The amount of supervision needed will vary. Some young people may need to receive support and some supervision from parents (with the teenager's permission) even in college. This is discussed in more detail in Chapter 15.

This need for supervision or "coaching" can be a major source of conflict between parents and teachers and between the parents themselves. Typically, teenagers follow certain developmental norms. For example, by age 16, most teenagers are responsible for completing their homework, passing their classes, and scheduling and remembering to take make-up exams. Parents will frequently hear teachers say (and it is true) that teenagers have to learn to be responsible for completing their work, remembering to get homework assignments, and remembering to bring home weekly reports. However, teachers and parents sometimes forget to take into consideration that many teenagers with an attention deficit are developmentally behind their peers, and that a fifteen-year-old may act more like a ten-year-old.

Most professionals still do not comprehend how difficult being responsible can be for teenagers with either ADD or ADHD. Parents need to teach, provide supervision, and "coach" while teenagers are learning to accept more responsibility and monitor their own schoolwork. Your teenager *will* master most of these important skills, but not as quickly as adults would like.

"I struggled with myself regarding how involved I should be with my son. As a former teacher and school psychologist, I felt I was more involved than I should be in his schoolwork. When I didn't provide supervision, he would fail a class or two. He really seemed sorry and wanted to do better at school. Even after he had to go to summer school, which was a very negative experience, he still didn't take full responsibility for doing his schoolwork. The hassles and embarrassment of school failure and summer school were too far removed in time to motivate him to complete his schoolwork. I had to stay involved and monitor his homework on a daily or weekly basis or he would fail. I didn't see any valuable lessons to be learned from continuing to let him fail classes. After I started monitoring his schoolwork closely, he began passing all his classes."

Courtesy of Walt Foreman.

If your teenager is in danger of failing any classes, you may have to monitor homework on a weekly basis. Don't wait until the end of the semester to get involved. Weekly reports can be very effective. Specific suggestions for ensuring that homework is done are given in Chapters 11 and 12, plus in *Teaching Teens,* Summaries 24-27.

Encourage Your Teenager to Do as Much as Possible for Himself. It may be easier and faster for you to do things yourself, but it is critically important to encourage your teenager to be as responsible as possible for doing his chores and schoolwork and for solving his own problems. You should continually lead him to take the next step in accepting complete responsibility for these activities. If he gets a speeding ticket, he must earn the money to pay for it. He should go to the police department or court, if needed, and handle the details of paying for the ticket. Don't be surprised, however, if you have to remind him when the ticket is due or go with him to court.

"Our pediatrician's motto was, 'Never do for Cooper what he can do for himself.'"

"As a parent, I am an advocate for my son. When I have worked myself out of a job, I will have been a successful parent and advocate. I don't want to be so involved in helping my son succeed in community activities or at school. I continue to decrease my involvement and encourage my son to increasingly accept more responsibility for his future."

6. Build Self-Esteem

Children who are doing poorly in school will show signs of reduced self-esteem as early as the second grade. According to reports from parents, many of our teens struggle with low self-esteem. A subgroup of those students with ADHD may also have an over-inflated sense of self-worth and may actually overestimate their skills. Perhaps they are oblivious to how others perceive their actual skills or they may simply be covering up their feelings of inadequacy.

Positive self-esteem is critical for a teenager to succeed in school and in life. Dr. Robert Brooks, author of *The Self-esteem Teacher,* reports that children who have strong self-esteem are more likely to succeed in school, to be highly motivated, to stick with a task, and to believe that they have control over their ability to succeed. A teenager who fails repeatedly and does not

receive positive messages from his teachers and parents will have difficulty developing strong self-esteem.

A teenager's self-esteem is built by the successes he achieves at home, at school, and in the community; the skills he builds and the level of competence he feels; and through positive interactions with, and positive feedback from, the significant people in his life. Helping your teenager find areas in which he can succeed is one of the greatest challenges facing you as a parent. One way to develop a plan to build self-esteem is displayed in Table 8-2. You can complete this same information on the blank form in Chapter 16. Parents must provide their teenager with the opportunity to master skills, experience success, and feel that he is a special person. The major environments in which a teenager lives and works are his home, school, community, and for some, a religious environment. You can help create a home environment that promotes the development of your child's self-esteem and take actions that make other environments more positive.

Build on Your Teenager's Strengths. Dr. Brooks uses the term "Islands of Competence" to describe the special strengths or skills in which each teenager takes great pride. Parents need to help teenagers identify and build on their strengths. The strengths of one teenager are listed as an example in Table 4-1 in Chapter 4. Remember to reframe some of the characteristics previously viewed as negative and list them as strengths.

Celebrate Strengths. Many teenagers with attention deficits receive so much criticism that they may actually begin to believe that they are lazy and unmotivated. If you ask them to list their strengths, their self-esteem may be so low they may not recognize their own assets. One way for parents to approach this is to say something like this: "I was reading this book about ADD (ADHD) and I came across this form that parents should complete. I'm supposed to write down all your strengths that I see at home and at school. This is the list I started. Can you think of any I've missed? (Wait for a response.) According to the book, sometimes teenagers with ADD (ADHD) don't always realize how many skills and talents they really have. The other interesting thing the book said is that talents you have, such as high energy (creativity, outgoing personality, or whatever skill is applicable to your teenager), may not be appreciated in school but are very valuable in adults. Oh yes, I just thought of another skill you have. You are really good at…."

Using the blank form (Identifying Strengths) in Chapter 16, you can list the strengths your teenager

Table 8-2 Building Self-esteem

Individualized Treatment Planning: "Do Whatever It Takes"

NAME: ___Tom_____ AGE: __17___ DATE: __9/18/05_____

IDENTIFY INTERESTS: Encourage your teenager to pursue his interests Give him the opportunity to participate in activities that make him feel special. Build on strengths listed in Table 4-1. List interests or talents such as sports, art, or music that could be developed further through special training.

swimming	outdoor activities
diving	stereo equipment
electronics	modifying his car
shooting rifle	

PARTICIPATE IN ACTIVITIES TO BUILD SELF-ESTEEM: Parents may arrange for their teenager to participate in a variety of activities: a summer computer class, art classes, scuba diving class, modeling, Boy or Girl scouts, acting in school plays, hunting, fishing, motorcycle racing, water or snow skiing, canoeing, baseball/football/wrestling teams, tennis or golf lessons, summer sports camps, gymnastics, karate, cheerleading camp. Religious activities should also be considered if appropriate: summer camps, Bible school, singing in a choir, public speaking on programs, or activity retreats (snow skiing, camping). Let the teenager select those activities he likes best. If he has no special interests, parents may sign him up for a variety of activities and see which skills emerge as strengths.

scuba diving	camping
diving or swim team	water skiing
lifeguarding job	install stereo equipment
computer class	work on car/install alarm
hunting	Huntsville, AL, Space Camp

has in several areas—home, family, school, academic classes, church, community, sports, social interactions, hobbies, personality, appearance, skills, and interest areas. You could save one or two talents to add to the list while sitting with your teen. Your teenager should be impressed with the long list you have compiled. He may want to keep a copy and read it on days when he is feeling down.

Encourage Pursuit of Interests. Encourage your teenager to pursue interests and activities that he enjoys. Seeking nontraditional activities that involve smaller groups and one-on-one or small group instruction may give your child a better chance to succeed. For example, you might arrange for lessons in music, gymnastics, or golf. If needed, you may be able to seek financial assistance from the school counselor or county social services agency, which may have flexible funds

available to pay for such services. Some YMCAs may offer scholarships if contacted by a school counselor or treatment professional.

Group activities such as Boy or Girl Scouts and recreational sports such as football or basketball may be difficult for your teenager if his mind is a thousand miles away while instructions are given. There are always exceptions to the rule, however. If your teenager expresses a strong interest in trying a particular activity, he may have the motivation to succeed.

"When Robert played Little League baseball, he sat down in the outfield once and began pulling up grass. Another time I looked up and he was trying to catch a grasshopper that was hopping through the outfield. My son is an excellent athlete but he had difficulty with Little League baseball, especially because he was not yet taking medication."

Select Sports Carefully. Roughly 50 percent of children with attention deficits have significant problems with coordination. That means that some teenagers with attention deficits will excel in almost any sport, and others will struggle. Many of these teens are more likely to succeed in sports that require large muscle coordination (swimming, soccer, gymnastics, karate, and wrestling). Sports that require greater hand-eye coordination (basketball and baseball) may be more difficult for them.

Sometimes giving a teenager medication when he participates in sports may help his concentration and performance. This option may not be for everyone, but some parents find it is a helpful solution.

"Baseball is very important to Andrew, but he couldn't concentrate during the game. We decided to give him his Ritalin just before game time. He played so well he won the game ball. He was thrilled. He didn't have any trouble going to sleep because he had so much exercise."

Physical activities that require self-discipline and repetition of a skill, such as swimming, wrestling, martial arts, or gymnastics may help increase a teenager's self-esteem, self-discipline, and frustration tolerance.

Provide Support in Religious Environments. Religious institutions tend to have structured environments similar to schools in which teenagers are expected to sit quietly in their seats, listen to instructions, absorb and understand what is said to them, and follow directions.

"Participating in a formal church service is not a good place to take an ADHD child. They get bored so easily. They may be more likely to attend contemporary services that are more active and relaxed."

In addition, Sunday school teachers and religious leaders may be even less prepared than classroom teachers to deal with problem behaviors in a positive, loving manner. As a result, a teenager's experiences in religious settings may be as negative as his school experiences. What some people fail to realize is that if a teenager is constantly criticized and forced to sit still in a religious setting, he may be learning to hate church or synagogue, religion, and God.

Clearly, any religious staff who interact with your teenager also need training regarding ADD and ADHD. Parents may invite interested staff to attend local parent training sessions on ADHD.

Match with Good Coaches or Leaders. Some teenagers with attention deficits can participate in sports or group activities without any extra supports, while others may struggle. Finding supportive, charismatic coaches, Scout leaders, or religious or activity leaders is critical. It takes an adult leader with the patience and skill to bring out the best in your teenager. Leaders who know how to use positive reinforcement to motivate students are especially effective.

If the leaders are receptive, give them tips on interacting with your teenager. Talk to the leader "off the record," and ask him or her to use this information discreetly and not do anything to embarrass your child in front of his teammates. As a parent you may volunteer to become one of the coaches for the team to help provide the support and supervision your teenager needs or to model how to act for other coaches.

Make the School Environment More Positive. You can take a variety of steps to help make the school environment a place where your teenager can succeed. Chapters 11 through 13 provide suggestions about consistent completion of homework, identification of specific learning and behavior problems, and accommodations to the school program that can be made under federal law. In addition, *Teaching Teens* contains 350 pages of detailed strategies for helping your teen succeed in school. Parents and teachers alike will find these strategies helpful.

7. Teach New Skills

Teaching your teenager new skills such as problem solving, time management, and anger control may be of some help. Keep in mind, however, that skills training may not be particularly effective, since ADD/ADHD is a *performance deficit* and not a knowledge deficit. These teens often know what to do, but don't use the needed skill at the right time. So you must be realistic in your expectations for what skills training can do. It can't hurt to teach the underlying skills needed to understand a concept, such as the basics of planning backward to schedule adequate time for completion of a project. Even though you taught the skill, however, your teen will not always use it when needed. Don't be surprised or angry when this happens—it's part of the attention deficit. Prompt him on what he should be doing, do the task with him, or show him how to compensate.

This job of skills training will take lots of time and patience! Practice, practice, practice will be the key. Watch for *teachable moments*—times when he brings up an important issue or things come up naturally in conversations with friends or on TV. If he asks your help solving a problem, discuss his options as explained in the next section. If he asks questions about sex or drugs, be prepared to answer the question then. Keep discussions brief. Learning to speak in "sound bites"—brief memorable quotes that capture the essence of an issue—is difficult but necessary.

Teach Problem Solving. Teaching a teenager how to solve his own problems is one of the best gifts a parent can give. A teenager who can handle his own affairs will have stronger self-esteem.

To teach problem solving, 1) begin by asking your teenager questions about *possible solutions,* and 2) help him identify *pros and cons* of a couple of options. You or your teenager should 3) write down his *options,* plus the advantages and disadvantages of each. Visually being able to see his choices should be helpful. Teenagers who write or process slowly will probably avoid writing the pros and cons themselves. In this case, you may write the information for your teen.

Keep this process as brief as possible, since it will be difficult to keep your child's attention for more than fifteen to thirty minutes. Remember too that many teens will simply be overwhelmed by too many choices. Some will be so compulsive about going over all 50 options and their pros and cons that they will get bogged down in the details and never complete the critical task of implementing a strategy.

4) Next say: "Now we've narrowed down your options. What do you think is the best option for solving your problem with . . . homework completion (coming home on time)? As long as you have a plan, I will leave you alone to solve it. Is there anything I need to do to help you? When do you think is a good time to start work on the plan?" This allows your teenager to assume ownership and responsibility for handling his own problems. Again, he is more likely to follow up on a plan that he selected. Let him attempt to solve the problem on his own, if that's what he wants to do. The plan may include a limited role for you, his parents—perhaps 5) reminding him when to start on homework. You need to figure out how much you need to be involved to ensure that the plan is successful. If the plan is unsuccessful, then make some adjustments until it does work. If you think the original plan was not a good one, 6) try something new.

Teach Time Management. To help your teenager improve his management of time, you might help him develop a schedule for a day or week at a time. Use a weekly or monthly schedule with the hours marked to make the abstract concept of time management more concrete and visual. Then show your teenager how to schedule backward to finish a project on time. For example, if a report on the atomic bomb is due Friday, you might begin by asking your teenager these questions: "How long do you think it will take you to finish it? Do you need to develop an outline (or write a draft)? Are there pictures, models to be built, or library books or articles that you must get?"

Follow a similar process in scheduling chores and leisure time. For example, if your teenager is supposed to mow the yard, but wants to visit his girl-friend Saturday afternoon, discuss the schedule with him. "What time do you want to go see Hillary? How long does it usually take you to mow the yard? How long will you need to take a shower and get dressed? What time do you think you need to get up and start mowing the yard?"

Specific strategies for teaching time management are provided in Chapters 9 and 13, plus in *Teaching Teens with ADD and ADHD,* Summaries 31-36. The graphic organizer in *Teaching Teens* that was developed for completion of long-term school projects may be especially helpful. For teens themselves, helpful written materials and strategies on time management are provided in "I'm Late for …Everything!" in *A Bird's-Eye View*.

Teach Techniques for Dealing with Anger. Your teenager can do several things to learn to handle his anger better. You could say something like this: "Sometimes it's harder for teenagers with ADD or ADHD to handle anger in a reasonable way without blowing up. Anger is a normal feeling, but you need to learn to handle it in a healthy and safe way." There are several things you can suggest he do when he is angry:

1. take three deep breaths;
2. hit something such as a pillow or punching bag, or hammer a nail;
3. do some strenuous exercise such as running or swimming;
4. talk to a friend, teacher, parent, or counselor;
5. do something fun like watch a movie or play a video game to take your mind off the problem; or if you can,
6. look at the humorous side of the situation. Sometimes *you can avoid conflict* with another person who is angry with you by talking calmly, lowering your voice, walking away, or if you are at fault, apologiz-

ing. To *diffuse a tense situation*, you can use humor, stall for time ("let's talk about this later when we're calmer"), or try to negotiate a compromise.

Ask your teenager which of these suggestions might work best for him. You may also help him identify situations that are most likely to upset him or ask him how he could handle an upsetting situation without having an emotional outburst. In addition, you could check to see whether the guidance counselor offers groups regarding anger control and conflict resolution at school.

Keep in mind that low frustration tolerance and impulsivity will contribute to emotional blow-ups even when these youngsters truly wish to stay calm. Medication can be helpful, but in most cases it doesn't last twenty-four hours a day. The reality is that emotional outbursts will still be a problem for some teenagers, especially those with ADHD as opposed to ADD inattentive.

Anger management is also discussed in more detail in *Teaching Teens,* Summary 69. Summary 66 gives tips for teaching conflict resolution, which is another helpful strategy for handling anger.

Teach to Do the Job Properly. Sometimes it is a good idea to begin teaching your teenager certain basic skills by doing them together, or "modeling" the proper behavior. For instance, when teaching him to make his bed properly, show him how to do it. Don't expect perfection in all areas overnight. Praise him for the portions he does well. Talk and enjoy the interaction as much as possible. Set reasonable standards. Perhaps the bedspread isn't smooth or on the bed straight, but at least it is pulled up. As you continue to teach, over time your teenager will come closer and closer to meeting your standards.

Teach Self-Management Techniques. ADD/ADHD education is one of the most important strategies that will help with learning self-management strategies. The more a teen knows about the unique challenges of his attention deficit, the more likely he will be to know how to cope with it. Again, *A Bird's-Eye View* and *Teaching Teens* include advice and information that may be helpful in educating your teenager.

8. Look for the Good; Use Positive Behavioral Strategies

There are several principles of behavior management for parents to keep in mind when interacting with youngsters with attention deficits. For example,

Dr. Barkley has observed that *children with ADHD need positive feedback (reinforcement) more often* than other children do. He also talks about the importance of being *compassionate* and *willing to cooperate* to help these teens be successful. These basic principles are discussed below together with some of my own personal thoughts on these issues. Don't overlook the four additional behavioral strategies that were discussed earlier—giving choices, negotiation, compromise, and depersonalization.

Provide Feedback Immediately. Teenagers with attention deficits are governed by what is going on *right now*—today or this week—not some goal or consequence in the distant future. Feedback that is delayed (such as grades at the end of the six weeks) is not particularly effective in motivating a teenager to do a good job. Feedback may need to be given daily or weekly. For example, if you pay your teenager for chores, paying him immediately after he does them is more effective than paying at the end of the week. Likewise, you should praise your teenager each day for completing chores or homework.

Provide Feedback More Often. Teenagers with attention deficits need feedback more often than other teenagers. Unfortunately, they usually receive more negative feedback than their friends since they are more likely to break rules than teenagers without attention deficits. If important rules are broken, a reprimand or mild punishment may be needed.

Provide Positive Feedback Before Negatives. If you want to change a behavior, don't just punish the problem behavior. Dr. Barkley explains that children with ADHD are already being punished much more frequently than children who don't have ADHD, even though punishment is not working. So try to find a positive way to change behavior. Incentives may work. "If you mow the yard by Friday (on time), I'll let you stay out thirty minutes later Saturday night (or pay you a five dollar bonus)." Chances are, eliminating the fight over the chore is worth five dollars, plus you may be planning to give him extra money anyway. "If you finish your homework on time, I'll let you stay up 30 minutes later (or you can play with your Game Boy or PlayStation for 30 minutes before you go to bed)." But remember: unless the incentive is important to your teenager, he will not work to earn it. Positive comments and rewards should outnumber negatives by at least a two or three to one ratio.

Also try telling your teenager what you *want him to do*, rather than what you don't want him to do. Typically, parents say something like, "I'm sick and tired of you coming in late every Friday and Saturday night." Instead, it may be more effective to say, "I want you to come home by 12:00 or call me if you are going to be later than 15 minutes." Another example may be, "I want you to start your homework each night by 7:00 or 7:30." Then set up the necessary structure and supervision to ensure he does his homework each day. Give positive feedback or rewards when he completes his homework or does as you ask.

Intervene at the "Point of Performance." According to Dr. Barkley, a key element of successful behavioral programs is intervening at the *"point of performance."* That means that you intervene at the time and place where the teenager needs the skill. So if a teen continually forgets his homework assignments and books, then the point of performance is when he must get his books from his locker at 3:00 p.m. when school is dismissed. Telling him at 8:30 in the morning to remember his books and assignments is futile.

Dr. Barkley makes a key point: *"effective treatment does not occur in an office"*; it occurs in the child's environment. Since these students cannot remember key tasks, adults must put visible *external prompts* in place as reminders. For example, place medication beside the bathroom sink so he will remember to take it.

Make Clear Statements. Dr. Barkley teaches parents to make clear commands as opposed to requests. For example, parents will find it more effective to say, "It's time to…. clean your room, do your homework, or come to dinner." Avoid requests like, "Are you ready to do your homework now, hmm?" Leaving a question mark in your voice at the end of the sentence often leaves room for the teen to say no and thus an argument may ensue.

Use Strong, Meaningful Rewards and Consequences. Many teenagers with ADD or ADHD do not seem to be as sensitive to rewards and punishment, nor do they learn from them as readily as teenagers without attention deficits. They do not respond very well to traditional rewards and punishment, so typical parent responses such as praise or negative comments alone may not work very effectively. You may find that stronger rewards are more effective. Examples of positive reinforcers include praise ("Congratulations. You passed your test"), verbal and nonverbal approval

(smiles or head nods), affection (pats on the back or hugs), privileges (driving, TV, phone, Game Boy, Xbox, movies, concerts, sports), and material things (stereo equipment, video game cartridges, clothes, or money).

Money is usually an especially effective reward for teenagers with attention deficits if you are willing to pay them to complete certain tasks. Some parents think it is a great idea since adults receive a paycheck for work they do at the office. Why shouldn't teens be paid for some of their work efforts? Other parents, however, feel guilty or irritated that they have to "resort" to using material rewards with their teenager. They argue that a teenager should contribute to the family without being paid. Some parents may prefer that teenagers do certain chores to earn their allowance.

You may also set up a program where you pay for grades, for example a dollar for every paper with an A, 50 cents for a B, and a quarter for a C. Typically, parents will see an increase in the number of assignments completed plus an improvement in grades. Unfortunately, due to the nature of attention deficits, rewards *must* be stronger and more meaningful in order to work effectively. You must make the judgment call.

"When I was a single parent, I had to pay someone to mow the yard or do other chores. When my son was old enough to mow the yard, I decided to pay him for the job. That allowed him to earn some extra spending money, which I would have given him anyway, and helped me out at the same time."

Rewards must be something your teenager really likes. "When you finish your homework, you can play with your Game Boy." Or, if he can wait a whole week for a reward, "You can go to the movies Friday night with friends when you bring home the note from your teacher saying all your schoolwork for the week has been completed."

Give a Bonus for Good Attitude. Dr. Barkley suggests giving a bonus for a good attitude in addition to rewarding your teen for completion of chores or school work. A bonus can be given for a variety of important behaviors—how your teen treats you, the way he talks to you, or how quickly he does the chore.

Use Behavioral Charts. Behavioral charts come in many sizes and shapes. A basic behavioral chart consists of a list of several behaviors that parents want their teenager to do. The teenager may receive checks each day he does them. Parents may specify that once

Table 8-3   Behavior Chart

TASK	M	T	W	T	F	S	S
Completes homework							
Gets up on time for school							
Mows yard (Friday only)							
Takes trash out (Tuesday only)							
Cleans up room (Saturday only)							
Discusses disagreements in a reasonable, calm manner							

a certain number of checks (points) have been earned, the teenager may have a desired reward—a compact disc, a movie, money, or a trip skiing or to Disney World. Desired behavior should be stated in positive terms instead of negative. For example, "discusses disagreements in reasonable way," instead of "doesn't scream and blow up."

Usually, behavioral charts work best with younger children. However, they may still work for middle or high school students if the reward is strong enough. To be honest, however, behavioral programs can be very difficult to implement consistently, especially if parents also have ADD or ADHD. Take care to avoid making the behavioral program too complex.

By the time your child reaches adolescence, he may feel as though he has been on behavioral programs all his life.

"One teenager with ADHD whose mother is a psychologist said that he felt he had been on stars and charts all his life. He called the rewards, 'Kibbles and Bits,' after the dog food. He must have felt like a 'trained laboratory animal.'"

Be as Consistent as Possible. A basic principle of behavior management is to be as consistent as possible with both rewards and punishment. Your teenager will know what to expect if he behaves a certain way. To put it simply, he will understand that "good things happen when I behave and unpleasant things happen when I don't."

Once you and your spouse agree on a reasonable consequence, try to use it consistently each time. For example, your teenager *can* go to the movies or to the mall on Friday night when *all* his homework is completed. Of course, being consistent is especially difficult if one or both parents also have an attention deficit. Realistically, you should be as consistent as possible,

but try not lose any sleep over it. Also remember that if a consequence just isn't working or if you decide it is too harsh, you can always change it.

Increase Positive Interactions. Although teenagers with ADD or ADHD need a lot of positive feedback, they are more likely to receive negative feedback because of their failure to comply with requests. It is easy for parents of teenagers with an attention deficit to fall into a trap of having mostly negative interactions with their son or daughter. Negative interactions are emotionally draining for everyone involved. Constant criticism is damaging and may drive a wedge between you and your teenager. You may even reach a point where you have difficulty seeing your teenager's good qualities.

Try to increase positive interactions with your teenager. The world can be such a negative place. People complain when something is wrong but say very little when things are done right. Ideally, you should try to get the rate of positive comments and interactions to between 50 and 75 percent. Even if this feels a little phony at first, it will get easier and more sincere with practice.

You may wish to observe your own behavior toward your teenager for a day. Count how often you make positive statements. Can you find good reasons to smile at him, make positive comments, or hug and kiss him? "You did a great job cleaning up your room." "Boy, you must be proud of the 87 you made on your biology test. Keep up the good work." "The yard looks great. Thanks for mowing it."

In contrast, how many negative statements do you make? "You've got to study; you can't watch TV all evening." "Your handwriting is so messy." "You aren't trying." "You've failed the test." "Don't leave your clothes on the floor. You're such a slob." "You did a terrible job cleaning up the kitchen." "You did a sloppy job of making up your bed."

Parents should give praise sincerely and in moderation. Find some part of the job to praise. According to Dr. Dale Carter, Director of Psychological Services for Gwinnett County, GA, Schools, if praise is too flowery, the child may reject it. Many of these children are very perceptive. If parents praise schoolwork as perfect and the teenager recognizes that it is not, he may not respond positively to his parent's praise.

Remember that there are plenty of people in the world who are willing to tear your teenager down. Few people are willing to spend the extra time and energy required to be positive and build your teenager's self-esteem. It will take a strong conscious effort from both parents to become more positive.

Try Grandma's Rule. "Grandma's Rule" teaches a valuable lesson: "First we work and then we play." "When your schoolwork is completed for this week, you can go to the movies or the mall" (or the activity of his choice). Treatment professionals refer to this behavior management technique as the "Premack Principle."

Verbally, you encourage your teenager throughout the week. Tell him that you know he wants to do well and is trying hard. Check up on him at the end of the week and give him a lot of praise if all the work is done. If his work is done, he gets to do the activity of his choice. If he didn't do all the work, tell him you're sorry—he can go to the movies (or wherever) later that evening when his work is finished. Hopefully he'll finish it as soon as possible so he can go. You can be sympathetic and supportive and don't have to be angry, scream, or yell. Exceptions to this consequence, such as when the amount of homework is impossible to complete, are discussed in Chapter 12. If this isn't an effective approach for your teenager, modifications, such as switching to a daily report from the teacher, may be needed.

Start at Your Teenager's Present Level. Avoid putting more pressure on your teenager than he can handle. You need to work with him at his present level of functioning regardless of how low it is. You wish he was responsible and completed all his homework without you having to say a word. But the reality is, he may only remember his assignments once or twice a week and then begrudgingly do his work.

As mentioned earlier, many teenagers with ADD or ADHD may be behind developmentally in their ability to accept full responsibility for their schoolwork and chores at home. Since the ultimate goal for parents is to help their children become independent, responsible adults, you need to help your teenager accept increasing levels of responsibility. To do so, you will need to periodically reassess his progress. As he masters one behavior or task, then you can guide him to the next developmentally appropriate step.

"Shape" Behavior. One behavior management technique, called "shaping" behavior, consists of praising the teen for his effort and for completion of a job that comes close to meeting your expectations. You begin by dividing the skill into three to five smaller steps. Next, start at the first step and teach him skills that move him toward the desired skill. Summary 61 in *Teaching Teens* gives an example of how to shape behavior so that the teen consistently completes his homework. Learning to measure growth in terms of *mastery of small steps* and to be happy with your teenager's progress is important. Many teenagers with ADD or ADHD may need some "coaching" all their lives, and if that is what it takes for them to successfully cope with their attention deficit, what is wrong with that?

Praise the Part of the Job That Is Well Done. Sometimes you may inadvertently undermine positive efforts from your teenager. Most teenagers with ADD or ADHD are not going to do chores as well as adults. They are forgetful by nature and may not pay attention to details. For example, your teenager may mow the yard but forget a section by the porch. The natural response is to complain about the part he forgot. It is more helpful, however, if you compliment him on the 95 percent of the yard he finished.

After a job is finished, thank him for a job well done. For example, after he has mowed the yard, stand on the porch with him and look over the job he did. Then point out a couple of positive things you noticed or tell him how you feel. "Boy, the yard looks great." "I think our home is the prettiest one in the neighborhood, especially right after you mow our yard." "You did a nice job mowing around the flower bed." If he ran over the flowers, say nothing now. Maybe next time, point out where the flowers are and ask him to be careful. Show him how to mow around the flower bed, if necessary. Damaged flowers can be replanted. Damaged self-esteem is much harder to rebuild.

Anticipate and Discuss Potential Problems in Advance. Sometimes parents can anticipate where problems may arise and discuss them in advance. "The grass is growing into the flower bed and it's hard to tell them apart. Let me mow a strip the first time to show you how to do it."

Identify Key Problem Areas. One strategy that can be extremely helpful at school or at home is known as a Functional Behavior Assessment or FBA (see Chapter 14). This is now mandated by federal education law when eligible students with attention deficits are struggling. The school system may call these plans Behavior Intervention Plans or BIPs. FBAs and BIPs are explained in detail in *Teaching Teens,* Summary 63 and Appendix B5. If your teen is struggling at school, you may request an FBA to identify problem areas.

Identify Antecedent Behavior. Sometimes it helps to identify what is known as *antecedent behavior*—what happened just prior to misbehavior that may have triggered the teenager's response. For example, a teenager who has trouble handling change may always misbehave when a substitute teacher unexpectedly takes over a class. Once the antecedent or "trigger" behavior has been identified, you may know how to intervene to prevent the misbehavior. (See suggestions in next section.)

Change the Environment. *If you can't change the teenager, change the environment.* Or, if you are already trying to get your teenager to change several behaviors and another troublesome behavior arises, you may want to change the environment instead of the behavior. For instance, if your teenager always comes home late, try calling or text-messaging him 15 minutes before he is due home or setting his watch to go off 15 minutes before he should return. Or, as described above, if a teenager misbehaves whenever there is a substitute, the environment could be changed by letting him go to his former resource room class for one period when a substitute is teaching. Another option would be to place a teacher's aide in the classroom when a substitute is present. Obviously, if you can, solve this problem

as simply as possible. You might talk to him and actually practice how to act when a substitute is present.

Be Aware of Limitations of Behavioral Strategies. In summary, behavioral programs are not always as effective with teens with attention deficits since they don't easily learn from rewards and punishment. And to be honest, implementing and monitoring a strict behavioral program takes a lot of time, effort, and consistency that many parents don't have. Some parents have found, much to their embarrassment, that their own ADHD or ADD and disorganization prevent them from effectively implementing behavioral programs. Despite the limitations of behavioral strategies, parents are still encouraged to master these important parenting skills and use them to the best of their abilities.

9. Avoid Negative Interactions

Sometimes a simple "No" from parents is sufficient to set limits. Other teenagers with ADD or ADHD, however, are very strong willed, impulsive, and frustrated. They seem to be constantly butting heads with their parents. As you undoubtedly know very well, teenagers with attention deficits do things that are extremely irritating to parents. If you chose to do so, you could spend your whole day correcting your child's behavior. The techniques in this section may help you reduce the number of negative interactions with your teen.

Choose Your Battles. In other words, set priorities and address the most serious issues. These comments from Dr. Barkley about making up beds are instructive:

> *"*M*aking a bed is not a developmental priority. It predicts nothing in adulthood; it has no long-term significance. If you don't like it, close the door. Have them clean their room once a week. To destroy a school morning over an irrelevant battle that has no long-term significance is a waste of time. Focus on what really counts."*

Ignore Minor Misbehavior. Ignoring minor misbehavior is a more effective teaching tool than using constant criticism. If parents criticize everything that teenagers with attention deficits do wrong, they will be exhausted and hostile from all their negative thoughts and comments. In addition, the teenager's self-esteem will suffer. However, if you decide your teenager's behavior is inappropriate and should not be ignored, you should use a consequence immediately. Consequences should be reasonable and not harsh.

"I try to be somewhat laid back about most minor rule infractions. I try not to get 'bent out of shape,' yell and scream, and have major confrontations with my son about his dirty room, dirty clothes, curfew missed by a few minutes, or other less important rule infractions. He faces the logical consequences of the rule infractions but not a ranting and raving mother.

"Part of my reason for this approach is purely selfish. I don't want to be a screaming lunatic, get upset, feel hostile, raise my blood pressure, and shorten my lifespan over the trivial things in life."

Talk about Behavior, Not the Person. When your teenager gets into trouble, talk about the behavior that was unacceptable, not his personality, values, or ability. Give him the message that he is a good person even if you are not pleased with his behavior. You might say, "I am very unhappy that you …came home an hour late (didn't do your homework). That is not acceptable. You must … come home on time or call and let me know you are on your way home (do your homework every night)." Avoid character assassinations, such as, "You're lazy." "You're intentionally being defiant." "You're stupid." "You're just not trying." "You don't care." "You're bad." "You'll never amount to anything." Then develop a plan to ensure that the problem behavior will not occur again.

If your teenager is off-task, try prompting him by making a simple statement about the behavior: "You're getting sidetracked." Don't fuss about not doing homework (finishing a chore) or say anything negative about him ("you're lazy"). Discuss this issue with him before the problem occurs and ask him if you can prompt him when he is off task. For example, you might say, "Teenagers with ADD (ADHD) frequently get sidetracked. Is it okay with you if I remind you when you need to get back to work? My cue will be to say, 'You're getting sidetracked.'"

Avoid Power Struggles. When parents give orders, a power struggle may develop. Avoiding these power struggles is important. It is extremely difficult to "win" power struggles with teenagers. If parents try to prove that they are totally in control, the teenager may work equally hard to prove that parents can't control him. The battle may escalate and erupt into a major power struggle. By winning the battle, you may lose the war. You may win on a specific issue, but overall, family problems may get worse. If serious conflicts build over time, worst case scenarios may include having your teenager run away or move out and live with undesirable friends.

It is an intellectual challenge to talk with a teenager with an attention deficit and get him to do what you want him to do. Sometimes you may be tempted to say, "You'll do it now, because I said do it." Or, "I forbid you to…" This authoritarian approach is difficult to use with these teens without making every interaction a major confrontation.

Some of these teenagers are extremely strong-willed, stubborn, impulsive, and frustrating. If a parent says "no," it is like waving a red flag in front of a bull. The teenager will be determined to do the forbidden activity. If you make a big deal about any issue, such as telling your teenager not to date or run around with certain people, he may embrace the challenge and show you he will do what he wants to do. If the problem is serious and compromise is not appropriate, you can take charge and impose consequences for misbehavior. Possible solutions are discussed in the next section on effective punishment. To avoid a power struggle, you may find it helpful to learn effective ways to say "no" indirectly.

Some teenagers with attention deficits plus complex coexisting problems present a tremendous challenge to their parents. If parents confront them, they throw explosive temper tantrums and parents may fear for their own physical safety. Dr. Ross Green has written *The Explosive Child*, which helps parents understand these youngsters and gives effective parenting strategies. Dr. Green explains that during a crisis, these teens are not in a coherent frame of mind and cannot think or act rationally. They need time to cool down and return to a more rational state. He recommends avoiding confrontations when teens are in this inflexible, explosive frame of mind. Dr. Green classifies problem behaviors and intervention strategies based upon their severity. For more information refer to Dr. Green's book or *Teaching Teens,* Summary 59.

Avoid Badgering. Avoid badgering your teenager about past misdeeds. What's done is done. Focus on the future. Word requests positively. "From here on out, I want you to . . . come home on time . . . complete all your homework assignments." Then come up with a plan to make sure this happens.

Avoid Nagging, Lecturing, and Arguing. In his book *Surviving Your Adolescents*, Dr. Thomas Phelan identifies four "Cardinal Sins," which parents should avoid at all costs:

1. *Avoid nagging.* Nagging usually doesn't work and only causes friction.
2. *Avoid lecturing.* The transfer of words of great wisdom from the parent to the teenager doesn't work in these one-sided conversations. "Transplants of insights," regardless of how well-meaning, don't result in a change of behavior.
3. *Avoid arguing* with your teenager. Rarely is anyone ever argued into submission. If your teenager continues to argue, you can change your own behavior by refusing to argue. Remember that it takes two people to have an argument. State your bottom line position—"You can't stay out all night. I'll let you stay out an hour later, but I *expect* you to be home by 1 o'clock"—then walk away.
4. *Avoid spontaneous discussions* about problems. These discussions typically increase irritability and decrease cooperation. Schedule a time to talk to your teenager about issues such as his chemistry project due after Christmas.

As Dr. Phelan reminds parents, *"Your level of aggravation is not always an accurate measure of the seriousness of the problem."* Sometimes because of "emotional dumping or displacement," parents transfer feelings from one situation to another without even being aware of it. Anger over a fight with the boss may be misdirected at the spouse, the teenager, or the dog. Anger at the other parent may occasionally be misdirected at the teenager.

Dr. Phelan suggests four possible interventions based upon the severity of the problem:

1. do nothing,
2. consult with the teenager,
3. negotiate a compromise or settlement, and
4. take charge when problems are very serious. Obviously, parents must take charge when there are problems with substance abuse, sexual acting-out, pregnancy, truancy, aggression, defiance, and guns. These issues are discussed in detail in Chapter 10.

Redirect Interests; Avoid Saying "No" Directly. You can learn effective ways to get around saying "no" directly: use tact, redirect your teen's interests, suggest substituting another activity, or buy time for things to cool off by saying, "I don't know. Let me think about this." If you later decide that you don't want your teenager to participate in the activity, you can always suggest a different activity. For example, if you find out that the party your teenager wants to attend is unsupervised, you might suggest that he go see a new movie with a friend instead. Occasionally, reverse psychology may work. For middle school students, say something like, "Only very mature and responsible teenagers can mow the yard. I'm not certain you're old enough. Do you think you're ready to accept that level of responsibility?"

Parents can often distract a young child from misbehaving by getting him to substitute another activity for the misbehavior. The same strategy may work with teenagers. For example, if your teenager is picking on his siblings, you may redirect him by asking him to show you his latest video game. You ignore the conflict and never ask him to stop harassing his brother. Likewise, if your teenager is spending time with friends who are a negative influence, you might encourage participation in events with other friends. For instance, if your family plans to attend a sports event or go on vacation and take someone else along, suggest two or three friends for your teenager to choose from. Do not criticize the unacceptable friends.

Tap Their Forgetfulness. Although it is somewhat embarrassing to mention, sometimes parents can take advantage of their teenager's natural forgetfulness to avoid a confrontation. For instance, if your teenager is nagging you about something you don't want him to do—buy a new game cartridge or go to a party—occasionally you can buy time by saying, "Let me think about it." Your teenager may get busy and forget about his request.

10. Punish Wisely

Always try positive parenting strategies first before resorting to punishment, because punishment alone is ineffective. In fact, in parenting classes that Dr. Barkley offers, punishment strategies are not even introduced until the fifth or sixth week of training. Punishment is a last resort and reserved for more serious offenses. When punishment is necessary, however, Dr. Barkley advises that:

1. The key to effective consequences is the *swiftness of the action*—not the length or severity of a consequence. In other words, lengthy or harsh punishment is not going to change your teen's behavior in a positive way.
2. Punishment will not work unless you also *pair it with positive incentives.* So some

good things have to happen to the teen when he complies with your rules and requests.

Here are some additional tips to keep in mind:

Act! Don't Yak. Dr. Sam Goldstein coined this phrase to remind parents not to spend a lot of time talking about an offense. To be effective, consequences for misbehavior must be consistent, immediate, and reasonable.

Use Brief, Reasonable Consequences. For maximum effectiveness, negative consequences should be brief and occur as soon as possible after the problem behavior. When consequences or punishments are too restrictive or severe, teenagers with ADD or ADHD may become terribly angry and resentful. They may become even more aggressive or hostile as a result of harsh and unpredictable punishment. Sometimes when a power struggle erupts, the teenager focuses energy on *getting even* with his parents rather than on *learning from his mistakes.* One goal, however, may be for your teenager to see the consequence as a logical result of his action, rather than as an action you imposed as a punishment.

Some professionals suggest allowing a teenager to face the logical consequences of his actions without any parental intervention, regardless of how severe the consequences. For example, if a teenager doesn't do his homework, he will fail all his classes and theoretically, "learn his lesson." However, this assumption is most always wrong as shown in the examples given in following sections.

Sometimes this approach may be detrimental and unreasonable for a teenager who is having serious academic problems. It will be better to intervene and monitor his schoolwork on a daily basis, rather than allow him to experience logical consequences that are too harsh (failing all his classes). Otherwise, he may experience so much failure that he feels overwhelmed. Remember: teenagers with ADD or ADHD are more easily discouraged. "Digging himself out of the hole he's in" will seem impossible. He may not pass to the next grade level and would then be put in the embarrassing position of being in a homeroom with younger students. He may give up, fail more classes, and possibly drop out of school. It's okay for parents to intervene and assist the teenager with his schoolwork. Until a teenager gets hooked on succeeding in school, he will need more encouragement, accommodations, and support than other students.

Don't Make Consequences Too Restrictive. As a general rule, try to make consequences the least restrictive and intrusive as possible. In addition, take characteristics of your teen's attention deficit into consideration, for example, your teen's impaired sense of time. Since these children do not accurately judge the passage of time, sending him to his room for 15 to 20 minutes may well be as effective as sending him to his room for hours.

In his book *1-2-3 Magic,* Dr. Phelan recommends placing children in time out or sending them to their room for one minute for each year of their age—12 minutes for a 12-year-old. Depending upon the misbehavior, you may elect to send your teen to his room for 15 minutes to half an hour.

Except when serious offenses occur, putting a teenager on restrictions for one day or a weekend seems to work as well as putting him on restrictions for a whole week, month, or grading period. Teenagers with attention deficits appear to remember only that they were punished, not really how long the punishment lasted. In addition, lengthy restrictions are also punishment for the parents, and are less likely to be consistently enforced. Remember, too, a teenager's resentment will build and he will focus on getting even when punishment is too harsh.

Examples of restrictions that may work with your teenager include: no TV, no phone, no dating, no driving, or no Game Boy, Xbox, or PlayStation for one to two days. The restrictions you choose should depend on the severity of the behavior. For example, restrictions for drinking and driving will be more severe than for talking back.

Continue Some Consequences without Increasing Harshness. For some offenses, you may want to repeat the same consequences over and over, even though they don't seem to stop the problem behavior. For example, if your teen continues to forget his homework assignments, you may want to continue having him bring home a weekly report. He will not be allowed to go out on Friday night until the missing homework is completed. With regard to speeding tickets, you should use your own judgment based upon the severity of the problem and risk of danger. Chapter 10 provides guidance on this key topic.

Switching to a harsher punishment will probably not solve the problem either. Perhaps you should simply ask the teacher to email assignments home or check with another student who is in the same class. The consequences *will* sink in eventually, but it may take several years. Remember, even when consequences are imposed, teenagers with ADD or ADHD often repeat the same behavior.

Use Logical Consequences for Minor Offenses. When a "logical consequences" approach is used, the parent allows the teenager to experience the logical consequences of his actions rather than impose an arbitrary punishment. The consequence is the result of his actions. This process treats the teenager with respect and shows him an immediate cause-and-effect relationship.

Although the use of logical consequences has many positive aspects, it also has some significant drawbacks. One major problem is that sometimes natural consequences do not occur quickly enough to be effective. As you know from earlier explanations, immediate consequences are a must for teens with ADD or ADHD.

If possible, let the logical consequences of your teenager's behavior occur rather than punishing him or putting him on extended restrictions. Admittedly, sometimes it is difficult to think up the most appropriate logical consequence for an action, but the effort is usually worthwhile. Here are some examples of using logical consequences that work and some that don't:

Strategies that work:
- The logical consequence for not making a bed is sleeping in an unmade bed.
- If your teenager doesn't put his clothes in the clothes hamper, he will not have clean clothes. He will have to wash his own clothes or wear them dirty. You can be very sympathetic that he doesn't have clean clothes to wear without yelling and getting upset.
- If your teenager isn't ready to leave for school on time, he will have to get dressed in the car on the way to school.
- If he is too sick to go to school, he will need to stay in bed most of the day. Obviously, he must be too sick to go out with friends that evening.
- If your teenager leaves his games or clothes all over the house, you might put them in the "lost and found" box, which may be put away for a few days.
- If your teenager comes home 15 minutes late, have him come home 15 minutes earlier the next night.

Strategies that don't work:
- One logical consequence of failing a class is that your teenager must attend summer school and give up a more leisurely, fun summer. Unfortunately, this consequence is too far removed in time from his failure to complete class work during the regular school year. Plus, it fails to address the underlying problems with executive skill deficits. This consequence may also be punishment for the parents if they have to drive their teenager to and from class. The cost of summer school is also a negative factor, plus family vacation plans may be interrupted.

"When our son failed a class, I thought he would learn a valuable lesson by having to attend summer school. I assumed that would change his behavior—that he would work really hard the next year. Wrong! Even though he hated summer school, by the next fall he was failing another class. I realized belatedly that he had serious learning problems related to his executive skill deficits. Once we identified those and gave him appropriate accommodations, he didn't fail any more classes. The teachers who told us, 'Just let him fail; he'll learn.' were so very wrong."

- Another logical consequence of failing a class is that he may not have enough credits to remain with his peers and may be placed in a homeroom with younger students. The embarrassment of being placed with younger students may push him toward dropping out of school.
- The logical consequence of not making passing grades in high school is that your teenager may not be able to get into the college of his choice.

"I am happy if my son makes passing grades. As he approaches his junior year in high school, I have advised him that he needs to bring his grades up his junior and senior years. Otherwise, he will be unable to get into some universities that he might like to attend. Unfortunately, these natural consequences are too far removed from the present to have a great impact.

"Within the last month, he has expressed concern about the bad grades he has made in the past and talks about improving his grades next year. It is so satisfying to hear him talk this way. However, his grades may be too low to get him in any large universities."

- The logical consequences of receiving speeding tickets is to pay the fine plus any increases in insurance rates. In addition, the teenager's driver's license may be suspended. Unfortunately, delayed consequences may again be a problem. Car insurance rates may not go up for a year, and it may take a year or two for a teenager to accumulate enough points to have his driver's license suspended.

Give a Second Chance. If your teenager breaks your trust and doesn't handle freedom responsibly, discipline him with an appropriate consequence. A few weeks later, give him a second chance. Teenagers with attention deficits must be given numerous additional chances to prove they are responsible until they mature, learn important lessons and can behave appropriately. For example, perhaps he had a party at your house while you were out of town. A month later, you go out of town again but you have an adult stay with him. You tell him then, he can have a second chance the next time you go out of town. But make it clear, there will be no partying. The third time you are out of town, give him a choice of staying by himself with one friend or having another adult stay with him. If he breaks his word again and has a party, an adult will have to stay with him during your subsequent trip.

Don't be afraid to take a humane approach to parenting. Your teenager is going to make mistakes. One of my colleagues says, "They deserve an occasional 'gimme,'" also known as 'give me a break.' Your teenager can learn from a mistake without always having to be punished. Teaching new skills is an alternative to punishment. When a colleague of mine teaches parenting classes, one of his major goals is to help parents remember what it was like to be a teenager. One of the first activities parents do is tell one really stupid thing they did in high school that their parents still don't know about.

11. Weather Each Crisis as It Comes

One important lesson for you to learn is not to overreact when your teenager experiences the typical bumps associated with having ADD or ADHD. *In moments of crisis, his problems may appear exaggerated and overblown.* Address the problem, impose a consequence if appropriate, and nudge him back on the "straight and narrow path." Then be prepared for the next "mini-crisis." Don't be surprised if you have a crisis a day, a week, or a month. If you are lucky, you may experience a crisis only once every six months or so. Learning to live one day at a time is critical.

It is important not to overreact and assume, incorrectly, that your teenager is going to be a delinquent. It may help you keep problem behaviors in perspective if you are aware how common they are among teens with attention deficits. Common problem behaviors of teenagers with ADD or ADHD and more serious behavior problems are discussed in Chapters 9 and 10. Some of the tips below may also help you keep your emotions under control.

"Even though I knew all the right things to do as a parent, everything would just go out the window during a crisis. Then I'd feel badly that I lost my cool and say to myself, 'Why didn't you just stop and get it together and then try it again.' John always knew how to push my buttons. When he was bored, I think he used me as an outlet for his frustrations. He needed to be in a 'debate mode'—he needed someone to argue and fight with."

State Facts and Consequences. When your teenager breaks a rule, calmly state the facts and what the consequences will be. "You haven't finished all your homework this week. When you finish it, you can go to the movies." Avoid placing blame and being angry with him. At this moment, the less talk the better. Later, when things are calmer, a more reasonable conversation may be held to discuss how to avoid the problem in the future.

Manage Your Frustration and Anger. When a teenager with ADD or ADHD is difficult to manage, his parents may become frustrated, embarrassed, or just plain furious. You should try not to lose your cool, but focus on the fact that you are dealing with a child with a disability. Dr. Barkley's advice is helpful: *"ADHD children cannot always help behaving in the ways they do: but the caregivers can."*

"One key lesson that I have learned is that it is very important for me to stay calm when they are upset. If I lose it, the situation quickly deteriorates. If I can stay calm, usually my kids will come around to where they need to be."

Being angry and frustrated with someone who has caused you a lot of grief is normal. Sometimes parents feel guilty for having these angry feelings. The first step in coping with your anger in a healthy way is to admit to yourself that you have these feelings. Sometimes admitting feelings and talking about them to someone you trust (your spouse, a friend, or treatment professional) helps to diffuse and diminish the anger. Holding all the angry feelings inside usually makes things worse.

Don't Say or Do Things You'll Regret Later. Avoid saying things in the heat of anger that you will regret later. Count to ten. Leave the room, but try to avoid screaming and blowing up. Some parents become so angry with their teenager that they tell him he is lazy, stupid, bad, or will never amount to anything, or that they wish he had never been born. Other parents may slap or hit their teenager. Most often, parents don't really mean to react this way. They do so because they are frustrated and don't understand what is going on with their teenager. Unfortunately, angry parental outbursts only increase the likelihood of a teenager's aggressive actions, increase his self-doubts, and damage his self-esteem.

When Frustration Builds, Take a Break. If you and your teenager are working together on chores or a homework assignment that is particularly frustrating, try taking a break to allow things to cool off. The break may help both of you clear your heads and allow you to tackle the problem with renewed energy. You might comment, "We're both tired, this material is really difficult, and I'm feeling frustrated. I'm being impatient with you and I don't mean to be. Let's take a break." By labeling your feelings, you are also teaching your teen to be aware of his feelings.

"Now that my son is in college, I am delighted that I am starting to hear some of my comments about feelings being repeated. Sometimes I help him with subjects such as Spanish that require memorization. During a review for final exams, he commented: 'We're both a little impatient because we're uptight about my final exam. It's not going to help me for you to get angry with me. I'm doing the best I can. I'll just be thinking about

you being angry when I go into my final rather than thinking about the test. Let's take a break and I'll call you back in a few minutes."

Remove Yourself from Conflict; Give Yourself Time to Cool Off. Avoid overreacting when your teenager disobeys you or gets into trouble. If you are enraged, you might say, "This is not acceptable. I am very angry. I want to think about what you did and what your consequence will be. Then I'll come talk with you in a few minutes." Then leave: perhaps go into the bedroom or bathroom to regain your "cool." When you calmly walk away, your teenager no longer has an audience. He may also benefit from having time to cool off and rethink his behavior.

If Your Teenager Blows Up, Lower Your Voice. Especially if your teenager has learning problems, the chances of him becoming frustrated over schoolwork and blowing up are very likely. When this occurs, if you can, stay calm and lower your voice. "I know this is difficult and you are frustrated. Let's take a break." Researchers have found that loud emotional responses from adults result in students becoming more aggressive and producing less schoolwork.

12. Nurture Yourself

Being the parent of a teenager with ADD or ADHD can be very stressful. As Chapter 1 discusses, parents with children who have an attention deficit are much more likely to divorce. Fighting over these teenagers can lead to serious problems in a relationship.

Recognize That Parental Grief Is Normal. Many parents feel a deep level of sadness about their child's attention deficit. You may feel sadness for your child and the struggles he faces as well as sorrow about your own parenting struggles. Initially, parents may go through a grieving process before accepting the diagnosis: denial, anger, bargaining, depression, and ultimately acceptance. But even years later, parents may still find themselves sometimes thinking, "If only he didn't have ADHD" and other "what-ifs." Researchers explain that parents will always have regrets, second guesses, self-doubts, and periodically will grieve again and again over the years.

Don't Ignore Marital Stress and Depression. Parents who experience marital stress and depression perceive their children more negatively than they are and

Table 8-4   Guiding Principles for Parent/Teenager Interactions

The summary of guiding principles for interacting with your teenager should help improve communications within the family and lead to more positive interactions.

1. Give unconditional positive regard
   - Reframe your perception of ADD/ADHD
   - Set fair expectations for girls
   - Keep a disability perspective
   - Write a "healing letter"
   - Enjoy your teenager
   - Nurture with touch

2. Treat your teenager as a partner
   - Give choices
   - Set reasonable expectations
   - Negotiate; consider compromise
   - Depersonalize problems
   - Assume good intentions

3. Maintain good communications
   - Listen when your teenager talks; avoid being judgmental
   - Use active listening
   - Give "I" messages
   - Smooth ruffled feathers
   - Encourage expression of feelings
   - Teach by example
   - Avoid subconscious negative messages

4. Understand ADHD factors influencing behavior
   - Understand the impact of executive function deficits on behavior at home and school.
   - Make accommodations for:
     - impaired sense of time
     - working memory deficits
     - forgetfulness
     - disorganization
     - difficulty planning ahead
     - difficulty planning for the future

5. Provide structure and supervision; be a coach
   - Establish a daily routine
   - Develop rules and consequences
   - Develop a contract
   - Schedule chores
   - Give advance notice and time frames
   - Link responsible behavior to privileges
   - Try creative incentives
   - Set limits; state expectations
   - Provide "developmentally appropriate" supervision; be a coach
   - Encourage teen to do as much as possible for himself

6. Help build self-esteem
   - Build on your teenager's strengths
   - Celebrate strengths
   - Encourage pursuit of interests
   - Select sports carefully
   - Provide support in religious environments
   - Match with good coaches or leaders
   - Make the school environment more positive

7. Teach new skills
   - Teach problems solving
   - Teach time management
   - Teach techniques for dealing with anger
   - Teach to do jobs properly
   - Teach self-management techniques

8. Look for the good; use positive behavioral strategies
   - Provide feedback immediately
   - Provide feedback more often
   - Provide positive feedback before negatives
   - Intervene at the "point of performance"
   - Make clear statements
   - Use strong, meaningful rewards and consequences
   - Give a bonus for a good attitude
   - Use behavioral charts
   - Be as consistent as possible
   - Increase positive interactions
   - Try Grandma's Rule; first we work and then we play
   - Start at your teenager's present level
   - "Shape" behavior
   - Praise the part of the job that is well done
   - Anticipate and discuss potential problems in advance
   - Identify key problem areas
   - Identify antecedent behavior
   - Change the environment
   - Be aware of limitations of behavioral strategies

9. Avoid negative interactions
   - Choose your battles
   - Ignore minor misbehavior
   - Avoid character assassinations; talk about behavior, not the person
   - Avoid power struggles
   - Avoid badgering
   - Avoid nagging, lecturing, and arguing
   - Redirect interests; avoid saying no directly
   - Tap their forgetfulness

(Table 8-4 continued on next page.)

(Table 8-4 continued)

10. Punish wisely
    - Act! Don't yak.
    - Use brief, reasonable consequences
    - Don't make consequences too restrictive
    - Continue some consequences without increasing harshness
    - Use logical consequences for minor offenses
    - Give a second chance

11. Weather each crisis as it occurs
    - State facts and consequences
    - Manage your frustration and anger
    - Don't say or do things you'll regret later
    - When frustration builds, take a break
    - Remove yourself from conflict; give yourself time to cool off
    - If the teenager blows up, stay calm, lower your voice

12. Nurture yourself
    - Recognize that parental grief is normal
    - Don't ignore marital stress and depression
    - Talk with your spouse or a friend
    - Try exercise
    - Seek professional help
    - Practice forgiveness

act more negatively toward them. Emotionally bankrupt parents don't have much love to give to their teenagers. Obviously, parents must take care of themselves both individually and as a couple. *People who are loved and nurtured have more energy to give love and support to others.* You and your spouse should try to schedule a night out regularly and make certain you have fun together. Do something nice for yourself occasionally. Go to a movie. Go out to eat. Buy something new. Have a massage.

Talk with Your Spouse or a Friend. Sometimes you can diffuse your anger by talking with your spouse, another friend, or relative. You can let off steam and regain your composure. If you and your spouse don't agree on discipline, however, your anger may only build if you talk with each other. In this situation, you may need to talk to someone who is not involved emotionally in the problem. Step-parents in particular may first need to talk with a friend to let off steam so that they can talk with the teenager's natural parent in a reasonable way. Usually, natural parents have more tolerance for their teenager's behaviors than step-parents do.

Try Exercise. When you are anxious or upset with your teenager, try jogging, going for a walk in the neighborhood, or walking on a treadmill. Exercise is a natural way to reduce tension and make you feel better. This may also give you some time to develop your strategy and cool off.

Seek Professional Help. Sometimes talking about your feelings with a treatment professional can

help. The professional you choose should be able to offer you two sources of help. First, he or she should help you reduce some of your anger toward your teen by talking about frustrating issues. The professional can also help you learn to avoid conveying anger inappropriately to your teenager. Secondly, you can learn new skills for coping with your teenager and the stresses on your family and marriage.

In choosing a counselor, look for someone who understands ADD and ADHD and the related parenting frustrations. Local ADHD parent support groups may be able to help you find someone who has a good understanding about this challenging condition.

Practice Forgiveness. Dr. Barkley offers parents a powerfully compassionate piece of advice. He encourages parents at the end of each day to forgive their teenager, to forgive others who have misunderstood their child, and last but not least, to forgive themselves for less than perfect parenting. Parents who allow resentment to build up risk losing their self-control and doing or saying things that they may regret later. Some parents may find it helpful to symbolically clean the slate by writing a list of things that went wrong today, and then burning the list.

9

Common Behaviors of Teenagers with ADD or ADHD

"It seemed like I was always in trouble with my parents. Since third grade I felt like I had been grounded my whole life. I forgot my chores a lot. If Dad asked me to bring my dirty clothes to be washed, I forgot to do it. I would forget to clean my room. I felt like my parents didn't trust me. Sometimes I didn't always tell them the truth because I knew they didn't trust me anyway. Medication has helped, but when I'm not on my medicine, I drive real bad. I forget to stop at red lights and sometimes I stop at green lights."

—Shawn, age 16

"Punishment at the time given seems to devastate Lewis but consequences are soon forgotten. If he is on restrictions, it seems like he falls asleep if he slows down. Lewis says he wishes 'he could be in a coma' so that time would go faster.'"

"Sometimes I have trouble getting to sleep at night. I always have so many things I want to do, like work on my car, stereo system, Game Boy, or on anything electronic. I get busy and can't get to bed on time."

—Alex, age 16

Clearly, being the parent of a teenager with an attention deficit is not an easy job. Your teen's impulsivity, inattention, and other classic symptoms of ADD or ADHD can be very challenging. In addition, these symptoms may result in irritating behaviors that are not listed in the official DSM diagnostic cri-

teria. For example, many teenagers with attention deficits act younger than they are, are forgetful, argue or talk back, are hard to wake up, have a messy room, don't learn from discipline, get speeding tickets, or act without thinking of the consequences of their actions.

Since the DSM tells only part of the story about attention deficit disorder, this chapter describes what it is like to live with a teenager with ADD or ADHD on a day-to-day basis. Depending on the severity of the symptoms and the presence of other coexisting problems, your teenager may have a few or many of these characteristics. This chapter offers brief suggestions for coping with these problems, with the goal of helping parents and professionals treat the disorder more effectively. This information should also help parents anticipate and possibly avoid some problems. An easy-to-reference chart of common behaviors and parenting tips is provided at the end of the chapter (Table 9-1). For information on common *school*-related behaviors, see Chapters 12 and 13.

A primary reason for describing these ADD/ADHD behaviors is so that parents will realize how common they are. If your teenager misbehaves, you may be less likely to overreact and believe that the behavior is a sign of laziness, intentional defiance, or budding delinquency. It may also be reassuring to you and your teenager to realize you are not alone.

"When I talked with other parents at our CHADD group, I was amazed at how similar our sons' problems were. I was relieved to know other teenagers with ADHD do the same things."

As a parent of a teenager with an attention deficit, you can always find plenty of problem behaviors to criticize. However, you will be worn out physically and emotionally if you correct every misbehavior. You must pick your battles carefully, use reprimands sparingly, teach compensatory skills, and deal assertively with misbehavior which could harm your teenager or others. Even if your teenager has many of the behaviors described in this chapter, you may be more successful if you pick one or two behaviors that are most disturbing and work on improving those. You can't solve all problems overnight. Plus, punishment is not going to make those behaviors that are a direct result of an attention deficit and executive skill deficits—disorganization, forgetfulness, lack of awareness of time—disappear. Your teenager *can* learn to compensate for these problems as he gets older, but it will take time.

Don't underestimate the impact of executive function deficits. It is critical for you to understand that many of your teen's irritating behaviors are linked directly to deficits in executive skills. This knowledge always helped me keep my son's behavior in perspective and remind myself that his misbehavior typically was not intentional.

ADD/ADHD education is one of the most important things you can do to help your teen understand and cope with her attention deficit, plus improve family relationships. You need to help her learn about the condition so she begins to understand why she does some of the things she does. Then she may be less defensive when you try to teach her to compensate for some ADD/ADHD behaviors. Obviously, you will want

to work jointly with your teen to solve problems. For example, if you organize her closet, she should be involved in suggesting how to do it and where items should be stored.

Helpful Resources

If you need more information on handling difficult behaviors than is covered in this chapter, I suggest you read or reread:

- The general parenting strategies in Chapter 8;
- The list of resources in the Resource Guide;
- The important academic strategies provided in Chapters 11, 12, and 13, as well as in my book *Teaching Teenagers with ADD and AD/HD;*
- The summaries on executive function in Chapters 1 and in *Teaching Teens, Chapter 3;* or
- *A Bird's-Eye View of Life with ADD and ADHD* (my book coauthored with son Alex Zeigler).

A Bird's-Eye View of Life with ADD and ADHD provides teens much needed educational information about this condition. Facts are given about their disorganization, impaired sense of time, and sleep problems and then other teenagers who also have attention deficits give their advice. Often your teen may be more receptive to suggestions from other teens than adults.

For example, with regard to sleep problems, you might read "Night Owls and Morning Zombies." Then say something like, "Most teenagers with attention deficits have major problems falling asleep and waking up. Experts tell us that the brain chemicals don't work exactly right and you can't fall asleep even if you want to. Plus it really is harder for you to wake up. These ADHD related sleep problems have been the cause of our morning fights. Here are several suggestions in this book to help us with these problems. Let's go over these tips and see if you think any of them will help you."

Independence and Freedom

Independence and freedom are high priorities for teenagers with attention deficits. One parent described it as "irresponsible independence." They believe they have perfect, responsible judgment. Frequently, they want more freedom than parents believe they are ready to handle. They don't want anyone to tell them what to do. Dr. Sydney Zentall explains that these youngsters seem to have a greater need to be in control than their peers.

"Cassie had been to Nepal twice and climbed the Himalayas by the time she was twenty-two."

"Alex, at age sixteen, was adamant about going unchaperoned to Panama City, Florida with a group of his friends for a week during Spring Break. He didn't have a clue why I objected."

Encourage Independence; Trust Your Teenager. Try to give your teenager as much freedom as you feel she can cope with successfully. Give her numerous opportunities to make her own decisions. Sometimes, this means trusting her even though you are ambivalent and anxious and may not feel she deserves your trust. You are conveying an important message to your teenager: "I trust you."

Be Observant. Be discreetly observant and intervene when your teenager isn't handling her independence well. It may be necessary to regroup and take away privileges, but extend them again later to give her a second chance. For example, you go out of town for the weekend. You give permission for a friend to spend the night to keep your daughter company. No one else is allowed to be there. Later, you discover empty beer bottles and learn from neighbors that she had a party at the house. You put her on restrictions for a weekend and remind her that she has "broken your trust." After a period of time give her a second chance.

Consider Compromise. Perhaps you can structure the proposed activity so that your teenager is more likely to handle the independence successfully. For example, a brave parent may volunteer to accompany a group of teenagers to the beach for a weekend. This is considered a "win-win" situation. Through this compromise, both the parent and the teenager are happy. The teen is allowed to go to the beach with friends, and the parent is along to provide some level of supervision.

Offer an Attractive Alternative. If your teenager wants to participate in a forbidden activity, try presenting an alternative. Bear in mind that any activity offered as a substitute must interest your child and provide sufficient freedom. For example, suppose you discover that she and some friends have rented a motel room for a New Year's party. After telling her you do not approve, you may offer to let her have a party in your basement with unobtrusive adult supervision. Or, as described below, you might offer to take her and several friends to a nearby lake or the mountains.

You should also anticipate that major events such as a prom or New Year's eve will spark your teenager's need to do something different and exciting. It may help to propose an interesting activity *before* she has ideas of her own. Having a supervised overnight party where the teenagers can stay up all night and play pool, video games, or watch movies may be appealing to them. Other parents may be willing to help supervise the event.

"To celebrate New Year's we took fourteen teenagers to the lake to spend the night. They stayed up all night, watching movies and playing pool. The next day they went for boat rides, and one brave soul put on a wetsuit and went water skiing."

Disobedience; Conflict with Parents and Teachers

Teenagers with attention deficits don't always do as their parents and teachers ask them to do. On the surface, this may look like intentional defiance. Most often, however, their failure to comply with requests is inadvertent.

There are a variety of reasons they may not comply with adult requests. Sometimes they simply forget what was asked of them. Other times they may disobey their parents and teachers because they weren't listening to instructions. Their immaturity and impulsivity may also contribute to this problem. They have trouble focusing on one activity, so they move from one activity to another. Sometimes they become wrapped up in other activities, totally losing track of time. The next thing they know, it's 9:30 p.m. and they haven't started their homework yet. They tend to avoid unpleasant jobs and keep putting off or forgetting to do chores.

Conflicts may be heightened because teenagers with attention deficits often seem oblivious to rewards and punishments aimed at changing their behavior. They often repeat misbehavior even after they are punished. In addition, frustration over other issues such as undiagnosed learning problems or school failure may surface through angry, defiant confrontations with parents over seemingly minor things.

State Rules Clearly. Rules and responsibilities must be clearly stated. Sometimes it helps to post them in writing.

Develop Rules Jointly. Teenagers with attention deficits may be more likely to remember and comply with rules they help develop. A few, simply stated rules are usually better. Examples of rules for homework, dress codes, and curfew are available in Chapter 8.

Immaturity

As explained in previous chapters, teenagers with attention deficits may act younger than they are since their social development is approximately 30 percent behind their peers'. This leads to deficits with regard to acting responsibly and being organized. In addition, if they have learning problems, their communication skills may be somewhat impaired. For example, many teenagers with attention deficits may have trouble following and remembering lengthy explanations or requests (listening comprehension) or finding the right words to answer quickly or in an organized manner (verbal expression). These learning problems must be extremely frustrating to teenagers since their intelligence is usually not affected and they may be very bright.

Your teenager may want the privileges "due a person of her age," yet may not handle them very maturely. Sometimes, you may be deeply disappointed or even infuriated because your child is not as responsible as someone her age should be. But this behavior is part of having an attention deficit disorder.

Adjust Expectations. Parents and teachers should adjust expectations for the teen with ADD or ADHD to a more appropriate age level. Don't be surprised when your 16-year-old continues to forget chores, procrastinates about homework, repeatedly comes home late, leaves her room and the garage a mess, and argues or talks back. Don't take this misbehavior personally. Most likely, she is not intentionally trying to make you miserable. Remember, the symptoms of attention deficit disorder are often the underlying cause of many of these problems.

Ask Her Help Solving Problems. Even if your 16-year-old acts like she is 11 or 12, try some of the suggestions in the preceding chapter that treat her as a respected partner in the treatment process—ask her help in problem solving, teach her the desired behavior, or if needed, impose a reasonable consequence without a verbal fight or character assassination. Remembering your child's actual maturity level, yet treating her without being condescending and with the respect due a 16-year-old, requires a delicate balancing act.

Impulsive Behavior

Impulsivity is a major characteristic of teenagers with attention deficit disorders. If a thought crosses their mind, they may act on it. If they think it, they'll probably say it. Or stated another way, "In one ear and out the mouth." According to Sherry Pruitt, author of *Taming the Tiger*, a teenager with an attention deficit is more likely to say, "Ready. *Fire!* Aim. Oops!," rather than the traditional sequence. Often they wish too late that they could take back their words or actions. They have a terrible time keeping secrets. They live for the moment, and delaying gratification is very difficult for them. They want to open their Christmas or birthday presents early. If they earn money, they want to spend it. Being untruthful may also be a manifestation of their impulsivity.

> *"At age 15, Robert, who had only a learner's permit, took several friends in the family car to McDonald's without his parents' permission. In the excitement, he locked the only key in the car. He had to call his father to come get him."*

Anticipate When Impulsiveness May Cause Problems. Often you can anticipate when difficulties will arise because of your teenager's impulsiveness and plan an appropriate intervention. If she is so excited she can't wait, buy a small gift for her to open the night before Christmas or her birthday. If she is working and earning money, talk with her in advance about putting the money in a savings account. Don't tell her secrets you don't want known.

Avoid Tempting Your Teenager to Act Impulsively. If possible, provide supervision after school or keep your teenager busy with constructive extracurricular activities such as sports. If you suspect that she may be driving the car without permission, put the car keys away so she can't find them. Or note the mileage on the odometer to see if the car is driven while you are gone. If she drives it, you have several options. Don't say anything, but put the car keys away so she's not tempted to take the family car out for a drive. Or say, "I know you drove the car without permission. Don't do it again. You can't drive the car by yourself until you are 16." Or, make the preceding comment, plus put the teenager on restrictions for a day or so.

Medication May Be Helpful. Medication helps reduce impulsive behavior for most teenagers with attention deficits. They are less likely to blurt out comments or act impulsively.

Difficulty Paying Attention

Teenagers with ADD or ADHD often don't seem to pay attention when parents talk to them or teachers are giving instructions. As noted earlier, problems with listening comprehension contribute to their difficulty paying attention. Dr. Robert Brooks, a Harvard psychologist, describes children with attention deficits as viewing the world through a wide-angle lens. They seem to pay attention to everything at once and have trouble selecting what is most important and should receive their attention. For example, they enjoy the thrill of driving and handling the car while being oblivious to their speed or an approaching car or road hazard.

Although they have trouble paying attention in many situations, teenagers with attention deficits can also "hyperfocus"—concentrate on a single activity for hours. Activities such as Game Boy or computer games that are high interest or have a more intense one-on-one interaction can often hold their attention for long periods. Their ability to hyperfocus may be misleading to adults. Parents and teachers may believe the teenager is deliberately not paying attention in other situations.

Are You Listening to Me?

Trying to talk with a teenager with an attention deficit can be an exercise in frustration. While the parent is talking, the teenager may look around, continue to watch TV or work on the computer, or walk away from the parent in mid-sentence. One of the questions parents most often ask is, "Are you listening to me?" Since the teenager doesn't appear to be listening or "showing proper respect," parents can't help being irritated.

"When I tried to talk to Alex, I always wondered if he was listening to me. Getting his undivided attention was almost impossible unless he was on medication. Eye contact was usually brief and I always had the feeling that he was not listening. He always looked as though he was ready to leave, had more important things to listen to, or wanted to be doing something else. This occurred whether I was scolding him for something he did wrong or even bragging on him for the good things he did."

"When Lewis is on his medication, he will actually stand still long enough to listen to what I say. He can carry on a conversation and seems more mature. He seems like he is three years older."

Make Eye Contact; Use Touch. Sometimes, getting your teenager's undivided attention is the hardest part about talking with her. You may not have to use all these steps to get her attention, but here are a few suggestions: Stand or sit in front of her (close proximity). Then gently place your hand on her shoulder or knee (touch). Say her name (sound), and then begin talking. Usually, the teenager will make eye contact with you. Avoid turning this interaction into an unpleasant power struggle. Even if she won't look at you, you most likely have her attention.

Keep Instructions Brief. Many of these teenagers cannot remember more than two or three things at a time and have trouble picking the important points from a parent's lengthy "sermon." The teenager very quickly "tunes out" and begins thinking about other things. When giving instructions, keep them brief and to the point. "Megan, please do two things before you go out tonight. First, clean your room, and second, tell me when it is finished so I can check it out."

Write Instructions Down. As a reminder, either you or your teenager may write down brief instructions.

Avoid Preaching. Sometimes, it is tempting to take this opportunity to preach: "Your room is like a pigsty. You never clean it. You'd walk knee deep in garbage before you'd clean it up." Avoid preaching. Most likely, you'll be wasting your time and energy anyway. You may also be tempted to talk about things that have to be done tomorrow or next week: "Remember you've got to work on your chemistry project tomorrow." By this time, your teenager has already "tuned out" and her mind is miles away. Keep in mind, many of these teenagers have learning problems (inattention, listening comprehension, and memory problems) which make it more difficult for them to understand and follow directions.

Accept Her Listening Style. Sometimes, teenagers do hear what you are saying even though they appear not to listen. You may elect to ignore your teenager's restlessness and apparent inattention and accept her unique listening style under certain conditions. For example, if she continues to play video games and can repeat your instructions, then she may not need to look at you or write down instructions. However, if she does not follow through with instructions or does not answer questions, then try the suggestions above.

Forgetfulness; Doesn't Do Chores

Having to constantly remind your teenager to do her chores can be a major frustration. Actually, forgetfulness and inattention may be combining to cause problems with compliance. Sometimes forgetfulness can give the appearance of intentional disobedience. In reality, the teenager may not be paying attention, hears only a portion of the instructions, fails to recognize the key words of instruction in the sermon about a dirty room ("clean your room"), or procrastinates and then forgets what she was supposed to do. Furthermore, difficulty getting started or *activation* is another problem linked to deficits in executive skills. It really is harder for our teens to get started on work and projects than other teens.

Make a Written List. Making lists of chores or other responsibilities such as a doctor's appointment may provide a helpful reminder for your teenager. Try putting "Post-it" notes in a conspicuous place as a reminder. A note may be placed on the bathroom mirror, door to her room, top of her books, or jacket. A reminder placed on the steering wheel of the car she drives may help her remember to turn in the note for her excused absence or to ask about make-up work.

"Now that she is a teenager, sometimes I make a list of things she has to do before she can go out with friends. She can't remember all her chores if I just tell her. It's better to make a list."

"The most wonderful thing happened last week. I walked into my son's room and saw a list of 'things to do' that he had written. I think that must be the first list he has ever made for himself. He's eighteen now and a freshman in college. I was elated!"

Quite frankly, it would be nice to tell your teenager with an attention deficit to do something only once and have her remember to do it. However, don't hold your breath. You will need to remind her frequently if tasks are to be completed.

Help Get Started; Show How to Do the Task. You may need to help your teenager get started on her chores. You may also have to do some chores with her to show her how they should be done or how to get organized to complete a job. For example, when cleaning the garage, have your teenager pick up the largest things and put them away. Next concentrate in one area, maybe one-fourth of the garage, until it is all cleaned up. Anything you can do to make an abstract task, such as cleaning the garage, more concrete and visual will be helpful. For example physically mark off the area into sections with rope or plastic strips so that the teen can "see" what needs to be done. The teen may do one area and take a break. Breaking the task into smaller segments may be less overwhelming for her.

Ask What Would Help. On one of your more patient days, talk with your teenager about chores. "You haven't cleaned up the garage yet. Is there a problem? Do you need some help?" As you talk with her, you may realize she feels overwhelmed, doesn't know where to start, and has trouble making herself begin the job. Because of her impaired sense of time, she may feel like the task or assignment will take forever anyway, so why even start?

Their ability to concentrate and pay attention to high interest activities combined with their poor memory contributes to some interesting contradictory behavior.

"Frequently, they can't remember their chores or other requests. They may forget to feed the dog, take the garbage out, mow the yard, or bring down their dirty laundry. They may not remember their homework assignments. They forget major semester projects that are due after the Christmas holidays. . . . But they can remember every verse to every rock and roll or rap song."

"Getting started and finishing classwork and homework is especially difficult for these teenagers...but they can play Game Boy for hours."

Disorganization; Losing Things

Many teenagers with attention deficits are disorganized in their personal lives and at school. They lose things such as clothes, shoes, jewelry, games, books, or tools. Messy rooms are another manifestation of their disorganization. They take electronic devices apart and somehow never manage to put them back together. Some teenagers seem to live out of their cars. Missing clothes, books, homework, and tools may be found in their cars. Of course, these behaviors are linked to their executive function deficits and should not be totally unexpected. Strategies for dealing with disorganization at home are discussed below; for disorganization at school, see Chapters 11 to 13, plus *Teaching Teens*, Summary 29. With regard to tips for teens to review, you may want to have them read "Chaos and Clutter" in *A Bird's-Eye View*.

"My husband is the most patient person I know, but the one thing that drives him crazy is the constant mess in our garage. Tools are strewn all across the garage from when our son has worked on his car. When he cleans out his car, he sets papers and clothes on the floor. He never puts the trash in the can or puts his cleaning supplies back on the shelf after he washes his car. We have had water hoses run over and ruined because they were left in the driveway after the car was washed. We can never find the hammer or screwdriver when we need it. We must have bought hundreds of screwdrivers over the years and they always disappear. About once every six months we all go down and clean out the garage."

"My son has lost coats, clothes, shoes, and his high school senior ring. He stays overnight with friends and leaves his clothes. He doesn't even remember they are missing, let alone where he left them."

Put Her Name on Possessions. Put your teenager's name on her clothing and books with a permanent marker or on other possessions with an engraver.

Purchase Less Expensive Items. Until your teenager is more responsible with possessions, you might want to purchase less expensive items of clothing or other possessions. If losing things is a frequent occurrence, you might have your teenager buy replacement items herself or do without. You may also have her visit the school "Lost and Found" to look for her things.

Help Your Teen Be Organized. You will probably spend a lot of time helping your teenager with organization. Encourage her to have a specific place for her belongings. School books are placed on her desk. Game Boy cartridges are placed in a special rack. When homework is finished, follow a routine for getting all books and assignments together and ready for school the next morning. You can help by providing storage areas that will help your teenager be organized—plenty of open shelves, a desk, stack baskets with labels for schoolwork. Organize her closet too; provide some shelves, see-through baskets, and label everything to help her remember where her things should be placed.

Serve as a Coach. Coaches are helpful, even for adults, to improve organization and give reminders about important responsibilities. Parents often serve in this role as a coach for their teenager.

List Steps for a Clean Room. Don't assume your teenager knows what you mean when you say "Clean your room." To her, it may mean pushing everything under the bed or in the closet. Make a list of key activities:

1. make up bed,
2. hang up clothes,
3. pick up things off floor,
4. put them in closet, and
5. vacuum.

Most likely, your teenager is not going to make her bed as well as an adult. For starters, just pulling up the bedspread may be a great improvement.

Help with Cleaning and Organizing. You may want to work with your teenager to straighten the room or garage on a weekly or monthly basis as you teach her how to keep things in order. Make this learning opportunity as pleasant as possible. Listen to music, talk about hobbies or her plans for the evening. In the process, your teenager learns that everything has a place. If clothes or games are put away in their proper place, they can be found the next time she wants them.

"I keep thinking that the logical consequence of never being able to find anything in his room will hit him one day. So far, it hasn't worked. He still doesn't clean up his room. Occasionally, I remind him that if his room were clean he would be able to find things. I state it matter-of-factly, not sarcastically. I hate to admit it but one of the most frustrating things is that often he can actually find things in the chaos. I guess it's his

strong visual memory—he can 'see' where he used the tool last and can find it immediately."

Close the Bedroom Door. You may elect to close the door to your teenager's room so you don't have to look at the mess. Remember, failure to make a bed doesn't predict a child's success as an adult. Or, when it gets so bad you can't walk safely across the floor, work with your teen to clean up her room. Teenagers with ADD or ADHD give their parents plenty of other reasons to be angry. You must pick your battles and decide which behaviors are most important to try to change. You may decide to save your reprimands for other issues.

Lack of Awareness of Time

Teenagers with attention deficits are often late for meals or family events because they lose track of time. Again, this is not simply a matter of choice, but a characteristic of their deficits in executive skills; they don't accurately judge the passage of time. In other words, they have no sense of time, so they think that have more time than they do.

Time impairment is actually linked to problems with neurotransmitters. One researcher reported that you can't accurately measure the passage of time unless you have enough dopamine in certain parts of your brain. These teens also have difficulty estimating time; that is, guessing how long it will take to finish a task. For example, if they are getting ready to go somewhere, they may not allow enough time to get dressed, plus they may not check ahead to see if all the clothes they need are ready.

"We hosted a brunch to celebrate the high school graduation of six teenagers who had ADHD. As you can guess, they were late. Of course, their car broke down and they forgot to call and tell us. But I had already anticipated all the scenarios of what could go wrong. I didn't start cooking the eggs until they arrived at my house. They were two hours late, but I didn't get upset. I enjoy them and their enthusiasm! Life is never dull when they are around."

Dr. Barkley reminds us that *"time is the enemy of anyone with ADHD."* He explains that the longer an academic task must be organized over time, the more disabled the teen will be. That explains why long-term projects are such a nightmare for these children and their families. Barkley uses these terms to describe this process: *ERO*, Event, required Response, and Outcome or product. As long as the E, R, and O occur close in time, our children can perform, but when you plug in a time lag between E, R, and O, you disable the child. Obviously, long-term projects interject days and weeks in between the E, R, and O.

Having an awareness of time is critical for planning ahead to complete chores or major school projects. Dr. Barkley describes time awareness in a couple of ways: 1) as a developmental skill that is significantly delayed, and 2) as a "window on time." The average teenager is able to plan ahead for three to five days. Unfortunately, teens with ADHD often have a twelve-hour window on time as evidenced by their forgetting major projects until the night before they are due.

For most of us, an "instant message" will suddenly dart into our head, reminding us that we have a doctor's appointment in a couple of days or that a major deadline is near. This reminder from our brain keeps us from forgetting important details. Unfortunately, these reminders come too late or not at all to be of help to teens with ADD and ADHD. The good news is that their time awareness does improve with age, but during the teen years this is a source of major conflict in families.

Clearly, the inability to accurately judge the passage of time can cause major problems, especially in the school setting and in planning ahead for the future. Our present society worships time and time management, which makes this deficit even more disabling in today's world. Since these teens are unable to judge passage of time in their head, you can help them by *externalizing time.* In other words, make it visible or provide them prompts. Here are several helpful tips.

Set a Wristwatch Alarm for Key Times. Your teenager can set her alarm for two or three important events that she must remember: time to leave for school, time to take medicine, time to do homework, time to get ready for bed, or time to leave a friend's home, a party, or a dance. With the alarm set, she can relax and enjoy herself without worrying that she will be late. You may need to remind her to set the alarm before she leaves the house. Some wrist alarms will go off each day at the same time without being reset.

Use a Talking Timer. A "Talking Timer" is available from Tel-Time that counts down time and calls out the minutes left before a deadline. Initially it may call out "30 minutes" then again when it reaches 10, then 5, and every minute after that. Contact information: www.maxiaids.com; 800-522-6294.

Buy a Cell Phone. This idea might not be for everyone, but it solved one family's problems of having their son lose track of time and come home late.

"We finally bought our son a cell phone so that we could find him when we needed him. Dinner time seemed to sneak up on him. He would be somewhere and lose track of time. He wouldn't be home when we were ready to eat. Now I call or text message him about 15 minutes before dinner and he is home on time. If he is running late coming home from a date, I may call and remind him of the time. Sometimes when we are out of town, we text message with a code, which is his birth year, to remind him to take his medication."

Discuss Strategies for Being on Time. As Alex explains in *A Bird's-Eye View*, add in "get ready," "travel," and "oops" time. Your teen may need an hour to get ready, 10 minutes to gather up school supplies and get in the car, 20 minutes to drive to school, 15 minutes to find a parking space and go by her locker. Then add in an extra 10 minutes just to be safe. Schedule backwards to see what time your teen must get up and leave your house if she is to arrive on time to school. You can't assume your teen knows how to do this; you must teach and practice this skill.

Break into Segments. Breaking a project into smaller segments with more frequent due dates is very helpful. Summary 36 in *Teaching Teens* should help you understand how to break projects into smaller segments and schedule them backwards over time.

Teach Awareness of Time. Time management is discussed in Chapter 13 and in *Teaching Teens,* Summaries 31-36.

Procrastination

"I'll do it later" is a favorite refrain of many teens with attention deficits. This is especially true of hated tasks such as cleaning up their room or completing a school project. These tasks often seem overwhelming and our teens have difficulty figuring out where to begin and how to do the task. Getting started is also a huge challenge for them. Their impaired sense of time may contribute to their procrastination; they believe the task will take forever, so why bother to start? As you can see, their avoidance is often linked to aspects of their executive skill deficits.

Jump Start Your Teen. Strategies for helping your teen get started such as calling a friend for clarification, walking around while reading, or using Post-It notes to brainstorm are discussed in *Teaching Teens,* Summary 34.

Difficulty Planning Ahead

Teenagers with attention deficits may have trouble planning ahead when it comes to schoolwork or social or family events. They prefer to do things on the spur of the moment. Trying to get them to make a commitment to participate in a future activity is often very difficult.

Teach Planning and Time Management. Actively work with your teenager to help her get in the habit of planning ahead. For example, include her when planning for family activities, if possible. Using a weekly calendar to help with time management plus making a "to do" list may be helpful. Plan backward from the final day and estimate time required for each step. For example, help your teenager write on the calendar the individual steps involved in planning for a school trip: May 15 - leave for Florida; May 14 - pack; May 13 - select clothes to take on trip; make sure they're clean; May 10 - get traveler's checks, buy swimsuit; May 1 - last day to bring in permission slip and deposit.

Difficult to Discipline

Traditional punishment doesn't seem to work as effectively with teenagers who have ADD or ADHD. They don't seem to learn from their mistakes or parental punishment as easily as most teenagers do. Some parents say that their teenager doesn't respond to discipline. No matter what the parent does, it never seems to make a lasting difference. The teenager will repeat the misbehavior or she may repeatedly do something dangerous. Sometimes, these young people don't seem to make a connection between their misbehavior and consequences.

"When I'm not on Concerta, I forget why I was grounded and feel like my parents are just being mean to me. It doesn't connect in my mind that I really did something wrong. Punishment doesn't work a lot of times because it doesn't connect in my mind."
—Shawn

Because traditional punishment doesn't seem to work, parents may resort to using harsher discipline than they feel should be necessary. The teenager's behavior is exasperating at times and it is easy for parents to lose control of their emotions. Chapter 8 offers suggestions for more effective parenting strategies.

As explained earlier, many experts believe that biochemical deficiencies are to blame for the difficulty these teens have following rules and their reduced sensitivity to rewards and punishment. A key point to remember is that *most of their misbehavior is not malicious, intentional defiance of parents or other authority figures, or a flagrant disregard of the rules.*

These factors should influence how you discipline your teenager. If symptoms of the attention deficit appear to be the major reason for the problem—coming home late—you may decide not to punish but to teach your teenager a system for remembering to come home or simply text message her 15 minutes before she is due home. Avoid frequent hostile interactions with your teenager since it may result in even more serious problems later on.

"*No punishment was ever effective! Shawn got to the point that he didn't care when we punished him. As a young child when we took away his toys, he'd play with toothpicks, or make shadows with his fingers. At first, grounding Shawn when he was in high school seemed to work, but eventually he got to the point that he would say, 'I'll be grounded the rest of my life—but it won't make any difference.'*"

"*When he was younger, Alex told me somewhat apologetically, 'I'm sorry, Mom, but when you punish me, it just doesn't seem to work.'*"

Many times the teenager seems genuinely sorry when she does something wrong, but has trouble maintaining her good intentions.

"*Our sons would appear extremely remorseful about something they did wrong, such as not doing homework, would make a commitment to do better, but could not maintain their good intentions. They sincerely wanted to do better but had great difficulty following through on their promises.*"

Since some teenagers act out impulsively without forethought or planning, they are more likely to get caught by parents or the police. Dr. Robert Brooks describes this as "malice without thought" as opposed to "malice with aforethought."

"*My son may be the only person in the country to have received a ticket for bridge jumping. He and several friends were jumping from a bridge that is under the jurisdiction of the federal government. He was the only one to get caught and get a ticket.*"

Some parents may find it difficult to decide which disciplinary style works best for their teenager. A number of different behavior management strategies that were discussed in Chapter 8 *may* be helpful.

Low Frustration Tolerance; Emotionality

Many teenagers with attention deficits become frustrated easily and respond more emotionally than other teenagers. Some may seem irritable or moody, especially when they are not on medication. Sometimes their moods are pleasant and at other times hostile. Many are oppositional, arguing with their parents and teachers over the smallest issues. Parents are never quite certain what mood to expect when they greet their teenager.

"Teenage males with ADHD seem to have a bad case of testosterone poisoning" (testosterone is a male hormone linked to aggression).

Girls with attention deficits are described as being very emotional during the teenage years, especially when you factor in hormonal changes and premenstrual syndrome (PMS). Several strategies for helping them are provided in subsequent sections.

Teens with ADD or ADHD may respond to stress with angry outbursts and aggression. Anger may be directed at their peers, parents, or inanimate objects. Sometimes when a teenager does something wrong, rather than apologize or accept a punishment, she gets defensive and becomes angry at the person correcting her. They don't always seem to understand what they have done wrong or why their parents are punishing them. Dr. Steven Evans and his colleagues have found that these teenagers also may have a distorted sense of fairness. They blame some of their anger on "unfair" actions by their parents and others. Often this anger is directed more at parents than at other adults. Paradoxically, they may direct their anger at the person they love the most and with whom they feel safest.

"My son has gotten so angry he punched a hole in the wall in the garage. He was failing all his classes and was extremely frustrated. Thank goodness he didn't hit another teenager or adult."

"I got a call to come pick up my son from middle school. He was so frustrated that he hit the brick wall in his room and his knuckles were bleeding. I suggested to teachers that when something like this happens again to try to find out why he is frustrated. He incorrectly assumed that he was going to be punished for earlier misbehavior and would not be allowed to attend the school dance."

Many teenagers with attention deficits seem extremely sensitive to criticism or disapproval from their parents or teachers. They have a tremendous fear of being embarrassed. Some of them overreact or are overly sensitive to crises in their lives. If they fail a test or a teacher embarrasses them in class, they become very upset. They may become distraught if they break up with a girlfriend or boyfriend or receive a speeding ticket. Their reaction seems more intense than would generally be expected for teenagers. They may also become anxious or depressed.

"My son went up after class to ask his teacher if there was any homework assigned. The teacher must have forgotten about his ADD because he gave him a look like 'you must be stupid' or 'where have you been for the last hour?' Now my son is very reluctant to approach the teacher to ask him anything. He is very sensitive and hates to look foolish."

Your teenager may also be experiencing the normal adjustments related to adolescent hormonal changes. During these years, most teenagers feel different. At times, they may feel extremely lonely and isolated, even in a crowd. They are seeking answers to difficult questions: "Who am I? What are my values? What do I have to do to be accepted by my peers? Am I attractive to members of the opposite sex?" In addition to the usual stress of growing up, teenagers must find their attention deficit and heightened emotionality even more puzzling and frustrating. They wonder if they are the only one who has felt this confused. They may also wonder if they are going crazy or if they are bad.

Sometimes it is very hard for parents to cope with their teenager's emotionality and "talking back." Parents get weary of being the adult and trying to stay calm and keep family interactions peaceful. Ignoring minor blow-ups or using "active listening" is difficult to do in highly charged emotional situations.

Be Supportive; Be a Role Model. Most teenagers seem sensitive during their adolescent years, but teens with attention deficits seem even more so. Treating your teenager with respect is very important. She is learning from her parents and family and will model your behavior. If you are patient and listen, your teenager will learn to be patient and listen. You can be supportive by encouraging your teenager, bragging about things she does well, helping her develop strategies for coping with her schoolwork, and being her advocate with her teachers.

"I followed the 3Rs with Jeremy: be respectful, responsible, and reasonable. I made myself follow those same rules too. One of the hardest things I think parents have to do is practice what you preach. You have to keep your own emotions in check and not scream and yell. If you lose your cool, you can't expect your child not to do the same thing. After all, you are showing him by your actions how to handle stressful situations. I constantly had to challenge myself to follow my own advice. And I have to confess I didn't make it every time."

Help Teens Understand Their Emotionality. Joan Helbing, a Wisconsin ADD consultant and parent, gives several excellent tips:

"Understanding and talking about the fact that girls are pretty emotional anyway, plus are more challenging when you add hormonal and PMS problems, is really important! You might say something like, 'This might be why you're feeling so irritable this week.' Next, problem solve around the issue. In our family it is critical for us to treat each other with respect. So we always sit down and talk about problems.

Some of the strategies we use with our daughter during these emotional times include:

1. ***Slowing things down for her.*** *We make certain that she is not involved in 452 things a week. We build in more down time.*
2. *We do things to **take pressure off her**. We let her set her own eating and sleeping time within reason.*
3. *We try to **be more flexible**. We ask her, 'What will help you right now?'*
4. *We **give her feedback** in a positive way about what works. 'That seemed to be a good strategy.'*
5. *We **ask questions** to help her identify issues and come up with her own solutions. 'Did you need more sleep this week?' This way she can make the connection between her lack of sleep and irritability.*
6. *Finally, we also **give her the option** of saying, 'I don't feel like talking right now,' which she does say occasionally."*

Verbal Fights and Arguing

Parents often complain that their teenager with an attention deficit argues, talks back to them, uses profanity, and treats them disrespectfully. Family fights may erupt when parents press the teen to complete homework assignments or try to discipline her.

Teenagers are struggling to grow up. As they discover who they are, they experiment with different clothes, haircuts, earrings, actions, and/or profanity. Sometimes they try to shock parents to get an angry reaction and draw them into a power struggle. Being a parent and not responding angrily in return is not easy.

Overlook Minor Infractions. If the misbehavior is minor or you suspect your teenager is intentionally trying to get a rise out of you, try ignoring the behavior.

Walk Away from Conflict. Sometimes you may respond to profanity by calmly telling your teenager, "I know you are upset, but cursing is not acceptable. I will not stand here and listen to you talk that way. I will come back later and we will talk when you have calmed down or when you can talk without cursing." Then leave the room. Ten or fifteen minutes later, come back and resume the conversation.

Give Your Teen Space When Angry. These teenagers seem to need time alone when they are angry or have had an emotional blow-up. Otherwise, they are more likely to say or do something impulsively that they later regret and that may only make matters worse.

"Elizabeth says, 'Mother, you don't give me enough space when I'm upset and you make it worse.' I think she is right. But my overwhelming need to fix it and help her out of her pain sometimes makes things worse. It is hard for parents to hit the fine line."

Impose a Consequence. If you find profanity deeply offensive, you may send your teenager to her room or place her on restrictions. Some teenagers will accept their consequences without question. With others, this situation may escalate into a power struggle, resulting in a battle that is worse than the initial confrontation over the profanity. As mentioned before, you must pick your battles carefully. Your family situation will be incredibly hostile if you correct your teenager for everything she does wrong.

Adjust Medication. In a few instances, irritability may occur because of hypersensitivity to stimulant medication or a dosage that is too high or too low. Or it could be an adverse reaction to medication. For example, a child with bipolar disorder can experience a manic reaction to being given an antidepressant. So you must be alert and monitor your teenager's response to medication. You should also be aware that as stimulant medication is wearing off, some youngsters experience "rebound." They may be more active or more irritable as the medication level drops. As a result, they may be more argumentative or grouchy during this period.

Consult your doctor if you think a medication adjustment may be in order. The doctor may adjust the current medication dosage, consider switching to another stimulant, or consider adding a different medication, such as Strattera, Clonidine, or Zoloft, if aggression or defiance become major problems.

Difficulty Accepting Responsibility for Their Actions

Sometimes teenagers with attention deficits have trouble admitting they have done something wrong. They may blame someone or something else for their actions. "It was my teacher's (friend's) fault." Sometimes they also have trouble saying they are sorry.

Deal with the Problem Behavior. Deal with the problem behavior rather than trying to assess your child's degree of guilt or accept excuses. If a pattern of problems develops, you and your teenager may set consequences for specific misbehaviors, such as skipping school:

"You skipped school. That is not acceptable. I don't care if Mike (your ride home) left school at lunchtime. You didn't have to go with him. You should have called me to come get you. You have to be responsible for your behavior. You made the decision to leave. You can't blame anyone else. I am really sorry to have to do this, but you knew the consequences for skipping school. You won't be able to go out Friday night and you will have to make up work you missed at school."

I Hate to Say It, But . . . They Don't Always Tell the Truth

Teenagers with attention deficits aren't always truthful. For instance, they may say that they don't have any homework, when in fact they do. Many times, they have honestly forgotten something and are not lying intentionally. Other times, lying is prompted by impulsivity and a desire to avoid punishment or unpleasant work, especially homework.

Parents often cringe at the thought that their teenager would lie to them. Most parents believe that honesty is a very important value to teach their offspring. But, just because your teen lies, don't assume that it is an indication of a serious moral defect. Although lying is a worrisome behavior, avoid overreacting. Typically, as teenagers mature and achieve more successes at school and home, they are more likely to be truthful. Try to reduce the stresses that may result in your teen resorting to telling a lie.

If You Know the Answer, Don't Ask. Don't create opportunities for your teenager to lie. If you know for a fact that she did something wrong, don't ask her if she committed the misdeed. For example, don't ask if she finished her homework if you know she hasn't done it. This is not the time to "test her honesty." If you observed the misbehavior firsthand, you should state the facts you know, and simply impose consequences without badgering or yelling . . . as much as possible.

"You know your curfew is 12:30 on weekends. It's 1:30 and you didn't call and let me know where you were or if anything was wrong. You'll have to come in an hour earlier tonight. Call me if you're going to be late so I won't worry."

"You hit your brother first when he wouldn't give you the remote control. That behavior is not acceptable. Now, I'm going to turn off the television for 15 minutes. Maybe next time you will remember to take turns and come up with a better solution than fighting."

Eliminate Some Punishment. If you believe that your child is lying to avoid punishment for a behavior such as not finishing homework, Dr. Sydney Zentall suggests that you eliminate the punishment. Then:

Develop a Plan to Solve the Problem. Of course, you must develop a plan to deal with the problem that your teen has been lying about—for example, not completing homework. You may need to teach your teenager new skills or supervise her homework more closely. Homework assignments may need to be modified or accommodations made for class work.

Impose a Consequence. You may decide to impose an appropriate consequence if your teenager has been dishonest.

"You told me you were going to spend the night with Rosa and then told Rosa's parent's that you were staying here. Then you both stayed out all night and partied. That kind of behavior is not acceptable. I am putting you on restrictions this weekend."

Difficulty Participating in Family Events

Taking teenagers with ADD or ADHD out to eat, to church, to sports events, or to public events where they are required to sit still for an hour or more may be very difficult. Because of their restless nature, they are often ready to get up and walk around after about half an hour or so.

Keep Outings Simple. Don't ask your teenager to do more than she is capable of. Keep family outings simple without demands to "perform" as a perfect angel. For example, at a large family Thanksgiving meal, perhaps the young people may eat at a separate table so that "bad manners" or restlessness are less noticeable. If the family event was previously a negative experience because your teenager was not accepted or was put down by cousins, don't make her attend the family lunch. Perhaps she can drop by briefly but plead having other plans, such as eating with her boyfriend's family. Or she may bring a friend along so she has someone whom she enjoys.

Keep Outings Brief. Brief outings may be better. If possible, provide a "safety release valve" that will allow your teenager to get up and move around. You might allow her to sit in the car and listen to the radio after the restaurant meal is over and the adults want to sit around and talk.

Find Creative Solutions. If sitting still in concerts or church is a problem, providing an outlet for restlessness may be more difficult. Some teenagers may be interested in helping with the nursery at church or may find interesting church materials to read during the service. If your teenager is not interested in going with the family to an activity such as the Nutcracker ballet, then it may be better not to take her.

Medication May Help. Remember, too, that teenagers on stimulant medication can usually sit still and participate more fully in family activities.

Difficulty Participating in Sports

Inattention and distractibility may make it harder for teenagers with attention deficits to take part in organized sports and physical education classes. They may have difficulty listening to the coach's instructions, following the rules, staying calm when frustrated, watching the ball, or keeping up with what is happening in the game. In addition, 50 percent of teenagers with ADHD have poor motor coordination and may be awkward and clumsy.

Although finding a sport that your teenager enjoys can be difficult, it is definitely worthwhile. Exercising is helpful on many levels. It is an effective way to reduce the symptoms of ADHD such as hyperactivity or restlessness. It also is a excellent way to reduce stress.

It is also good for the heart, helps people sleep better, and increases the production of neurotransmitters.

Pursue Gross Motor Sports. Some teenagers with attention deficits have problems with hand-eye coordination. Catching or hitting a ball may be highly challenging. Comparatively speaking, their gross motor skills may be better. Consequently, they are usually more successful in activities such as swimming, soccer, or track, which require large muscle coordination. Both swimming and soccer have the added benefit of requiring a lot of physical energy, which is good for these teenagers. Wrestling and karate may also be sports in which they excel, and, at the same time, develop self-discipline.

Baseball or softball can be a more demanding sport for some teenagers with attention deficits, since it requires concentration and good hand-eye coordination to hit or catch a ball. Players must spend long periods waiting—to take their turn at bat or for a ball to be hit or thrown to them. Since playing a position in the outfield is less demanding, many children with ADD or ADHD are assigned to play those positions.

"My son played baseball when he was in elementary school. He would get distracted by other things during the game and forget to watch the ball. One day he was standing in right field having a great time throwing dirt in the air. He had filled his pockets with dirt earlier when his team had come in to bat. I prayed that the batter wouldn't hit the ball to him while he was throwing dirt."

Play a Position That Requires Full Attention. If your teen is well coordinated, sports positions such as pitcher, catcher, or quarterback, which involve higher activity levels, are more likely to hold his or her attention and focus. On the other hand, playing goalie on a soccer, lacrosse, or field hockey team may *not* be such a good idea, as it requires waiting and paying attention to prevent a score.

"My son played catcher in baseball. That was the only way he could pay attention. He was so busy catching and throwing the ball, he had to concentrate."

Consider Medication. Medication may help improve performance in most sports. Many parents are cautious about giving medication, especially late in the afternoon, for fear of disrupting the teenager's sleep. However, some teens take a short-acting medication just before game time. The medication improves their concentration and ability to focus on the game. Since they also have a good physical workout, the medicine usually doesn't interfere with sleep.

"Robert and Lee are both state high school championship wrestlers in their weight class. Neither one of them takes their medication when they are wrestling, but they do when they play football."

"Will says he can concentrate better and his golf game improves by a few strokes when he takes his medicine."

Restlessness; Easily Bored

As children with ADHD reach adolescence, their hyperactivity declines. Their hyperactivity may be replaced by feelings of restlessness or sometimes rebelliousness. Both hyperactive and nonhyperactive teenagers may appear restless and complain of being bored and having nothing to do. *Most of these teenagers want to be doing something or be going somewhere constantly.* They are often not satisfied with staying home. Try to recognize and accommodate this need as much as possible.

Encourage Involvement in Community Activities. If your teen's time is unstructured, he will find something to get into, and it may be something undesirable or dangerous. Encourage her to take part in structured, positive activities. Involvement in physical activities or organized sports, for example, helps teenagers release pent-up energy in positive ways. You might also encourage your teen to join the YMCA or religious groups and participate in "overnight" parties or weekend activities such as ski trips. Sometimes, the YMCA sponsors overnight events during which the teenagers are "locked in" and supervised, yet get to stay up all night and be with friends. Volunteer work may interest some teenagers.

Plan Interesting Family Outings. Schedule family events that allow your teenager to be very active. Visit a science or activity-oriented learning museum, or go hiking, canoeing, camping, or to an amusement park. Ask your teenager for suggestions. Planning a family vacation around the teenager's interests is another option—visiting Civil War battlefields or the Space Center in Florida.

Encourage Hobbies and Interests. Many teenagers with attention deficits pursue unusual hobbies, interests, or pets. As discussed earlier, these youngsters are drawn to novel and exciting activities.

"In middle school, our son volunteered to keep the school snake for the summer. He fell in love with the snake and we ended up buying one for him. He loved to take it to school and show it to other students. One day when he brought the snakes home in a shoebox he forgot to put them back in their aquarium. They got loose in the house. The older lady who had watched him after school for five years quit on the spot when I told her two snakes were loose in the house. My dog found one snake in the closet but we never did find the other one."

"My teenaged son has pursued interests in photography, a blow dart gun, scuba diving, and flying lessons. He was not especially interested in team sports."

You can help your teen discover her interests by exposing her to a variety of activities. Most of us, teenagers included, like to do activities we do well. *Play to her strengths.* If she is a strong swimmer, a swim or diving team, scuba diving, or life guarding may be interest areas to consider. If she is good with computers or video games, consider a summer computer class. If she is interested in space flight, engineering, and computers, the Space Camp in Huntsville, Alabama, offers exciting activities for teenagers.

If your teenager constantly complains of boredom and seems at a loss as to what to do, you could discuss options and then let her pick one out. Sometimes the options may be very simple—inviting a friend over to use the PlayStation, watch movies, or go swimming. Encourage her to be responsible for finding something to do. But occasionally, she may need help selecting an activity.

Make Special Plans for Holidays. Arranging for your teenager to participate in structured activities during the holidays may help her avoid boredom, plus make the time pass more quickly. The YMCA may have a program of activities when school is out but parents are still working. If finances are an issue, some religious groups may offer reduced prices for these programs. Some older teenagers may want to get a part-time job during the holidays.

Materialistic Behavior

Youngsters with attention deficits have an intense interest in acquiring material possessions, according to Melvin D. Levine, M.D., a professor at the University of North Carolina School of Medicine. Many of these teenagers have difficulty feeling satisfied with their activities or possessions. They constantly want something new or something different. They may be bored with their presents after a few days and want something else to play with or something else to do. On the surface, this behavior appears to reflect a lack of appreciation for others' generosity. But it is more likely related to her symptoms of ADD or ADHD—short attention span, restlessness, and need for new and different stimulation.

Allow Your Teen to Earn Money. If your teenager is interested in material possessions, you can use that knowledge to your advantage. Depending upon her age, help her get a job during summers or holidays or allow her to do extra chores around the house to earn money. Your teen may also respond to money as a reward for appropriate behavior or completion of tasks.

Plan for Holidays or Birthdays. Holidays and birthdays are times when the importance of material possessions to teenagers with attention deficits is very obvious. Children and younger teens may become upset if they have only two or three presents to open at Christmas, Hanukah, or birthdays. You may try buying a number of less expensive gifts instead of two or three expensive items. If your teenager is bored after gifts are opened, she may want to visit friends or relatives and enjoy trying out their new gifts too.

Teach to Express Gratitude. Although all adolescents must be taught good manners and expression of appreciation, teaching these teens takes a lot of patience and repetition. You may tactfully prompt your teenager to say thank you for gifts from relatives or friends.

Sometimes you may need to dial the phone number and hand the phone to your teen to say thank you. Even though you may have learned that "real" thank you's are handwritten and mailed, if she is willing to email a thank you, that is better than doing nothing.

Self-Centered Attitude

Some teenagers with attention deficits appear somewhat self-centered. Because of their developmental delay (immaturity), difficulty delaying gratification, impulsivity, forgetfulness, and need to acquire material possessions, they may overlook the needs of others. For example, they may forget to buy gifts for birthdays or holidays. Sometimes they seem unaware of others' misery or problems because they are too wrapped up in themselves. They may say something that hurts someone's feelings without even realizing the significance of what they said. Over time, these teens become less self-centered, but they must be taught to be thoughtful of others.

"I remember one Christmas when my son was in high school, he forgot to buy me a Christmas present. We are very close and I know he loves me. But Christmas Eve came, all the stores were closed, and he was horrified that he had forgotten me. I had an apropos gift for him to give me, an intricately carved wooden plaque that had the inscription, 'Love bears all things.' I had reminded him to buy gifts for all the other family members, but no one had double-checked to make certain that he had bought one for me."

"Now that my son has a girlfriend, he is much better about remembering when gifts should be purchased. I am pleased that he will buy her a rose occasionally, for no special reason. It makes me feel good for him to be thoughtful of those he loves."

Sometimes teens with attention deficits exhibit the exact opposite behavior also. They may be generous to a fault. They may literally give a friend the shirt off their backs or lend them more money than they can afford. Sometimes they give away their parent's money. One teenager gave her parent's ATM bank card to a needy friend to withdraw 20 dollars.

Remind of Special Occasions. Remind your teenager about upcoming gift-giving occasions. So often during the holidays she is thinking of what she wants and does not give much thought to what she will buy other family members. One way to teach her to think of others is to discuss her holiday gift list. You might also invite her to go shopping with you, or encourage her to go with her boyfriend or another friend when she shops. Finally, you may need to double check just before the occasion to ensure a gift was purchased.

Encourage to Do Things for Others. Encourage your teenager to volunteer during the holidays to help gather food for less fortunate families, to write a brief personal letter to distant grandparents complete with pictures of herself, or to sing Christmas carols in a nursing home.

Accident Prone

Sometimes in their excitement, these teenagers may break things. Typically, it isn't malicious destruction. They act impulsively without considering consequences, or don't pay attention to what they are doing. Some may also have poor motor skills that contribute to their accidents.

"One visiting athletic teenager with ADHD has broken a chair, our son's bed, a boat paddle, and a door, and has dented the top of our car."

Since they don't anticipate consequences, they may not take good care of their possessions. For example, they may run a battery-operated car through water without a thought that this may ruin the toy. Eyeglasses may be left on the floor, then accidentally stepped on and broken.

Handle Accidents Philosophically. One way to approach this issue is to remember that accidents happen and not a lot can be done to avoid them. Broken objects can be replaced; "broken self-esteem" is extremely hard to repair. Parents inadvertently damage their teenager's self-esteem if they constantly tell her: "You're a real a klutz." "You don't ever use your head." "I can't believe you were so stupid to leave your glasses on the floor." You may think things like this, but try not to say them or show her how you feel.

Treat Your Teenager as You Would an Adult. Imagine how you would handle an accident involving an adult. How would a mother handle a situation if the father broke an object or spilled tea? Most likely, the father would apologize. The mother would bite her lip and tell him it was okay. It was just an accident. Why not handle a teenager's accident the same way? If she spills a glass of tea, calmly help her clean up the mess without making a big issue of the accident. If similar accidents happen often, take some precautions—for example, move the glass away from the edge of the table or set the glass further away from the plate.

Discuss Your Teenager's Physical Strength. If your teenager is strong and prone to break things, sit down and have a talk with him or her about her strength and the need for more caution.

Put Expensive Possessions Away. Keeping more expensive family possessions away from your teenager is also a possibility. Do not be too obvious about doing this, though, or she will sense your lack of trust. Avoid telling her that she is clumsy or that she will probably break the object if she uses it. Try to subtly divert her to another activity or object. If she is on medication, she may be less impulsive and less likely to break things.

Our Daring Little Darlings; Broken Bones

As mentioned above, teenagers with attention deficits frequently act without thinking of the consequences of their behavior. Many teenagers, even some without hyperactivity, seek excitement, and the more daring the activity, the better they like it. In fact, researchers tell us they have actually discovered a gene that is linked to risk-taking behavior. Their daring activities may result in injuries or broken bones. Inattention probably plays a major role in causing their accidents. That trait, together with impulsiveness and an inability to anticipate consequences of their actions, frequently means that teenagers with ADD or ADHD don't avoid dangerous situations.

"Alex had 5 broken bones in a 3-year period (ages 13-16). He broke his leg twice—once while riding a dirt bike and once when jumping off railroad tracks. My husband and I were both out of town on business when he broke his leg the first time. The doctor couldn't administer medical treatment until the hospital finally contacted us for consent. After that, we wrote up a notarized letter giving medical consent for treatment for him to carry in his wallet."

"One of Lewis's and Alex's favorite summer activities is riding their bicycle off a ramp into the lake . . . also known as 'lake jumping.' They built a four-foot ramp on the end of our boat dock. They ride their bicycle down the hill, across the dock, up the ramp, and into the lake. Their 'flight' takes them 25 feet in the air and about 20 feet out into the lake. The first ramp they built was only two feet high. It wasn't challenging enough, so they began diving over the handlebars in midair. To escalate the challenge, they began doing one and a half somersaults over the handlebars. Some of their friends with attention deficits are more cautious and won't even try lake jumping.

We jokingly say that this is the only true diagnostic test for ADHD. Anyone who will do this jump has ADHD. In fact, the only person who ever got hurt lake jumping didn't have ADHD. We had to take him to the hospital to get seven stitches in his leg. He was too cautious."

"Shortly after our son took his first snow skiing lesson, we told him not to go down the 'expert slope' just behind our cabin until he was more experienced. He quickly replied that he had already gone down the slope the day before."

Climbing is a favorite pastime for many children with attention deficits and may continue into adolescence. Their lack of fear probably plays a role in this behavior.

"A neighbor called telling me to come quickly because Cassie, at age four and a half, had climbed to the top of the three-story gas well in their back yard. Her husband wouldn't even climb it because he is afraid of heights. Sure enough, there she was sitting on top taking her shoes off."

"When my son was in high school, I found out he had climbed a radio tower one night so that he could take a time-release photograph of the cars driving in the city. It made a beautiful picture but scared me to death."

Some of the "stunts they pull" are humorous but harrowing. Because they are inattentive or do not anticipate consequences of their actions, they seem unaware of their surroundings or potentially dangerous situations.

"When he was young, Lewis vacuumed all the water out of the toilet one day. He used a regular vacuum cleaner. I was just grateful that he didn't get electrocuted."

"Alex has always been a strong swimmer, so taking scuba diving lessons when he was in high school was a natural choice for him. During his final check-out dive, he and a partner were diving around a sunken ship. Alex was so excited he was breathing deeply and forgot to check his air supply. He ran out of air! He calmly tapped his partner on the shoulder, indicating his predicament, and they shared the air 'octopus' as they ascended to the surface. His partner was more nervous than Alex was. Most likely he had forgotten to take his medicine before the dive."

Regardless of their age, some youngsters with ADD or ADHD seem to know no fear.

"My son put a decal on his car that says 'No Fear!!' It seems to convey his attitude about life."

Encourage Safe, Stimulating Activities. When possible, guide your teenager into satisfying activities that are not as risky. For example, wind surfing, sailing, and water or snow skiing have a high excitement level, but are somewhat safer than hang gliding, cave diving, bridge jumping, or riding motorcycles. Trying to teach about the dangers of certain activities may help some but probably not a lot.

"The world needs people who are daring; people who are brave enough to land jets on the decks of aircraft carriers or rescue others from danger. I could never do these kinds of things, but my son certainly could."

Monitor the Danger Level of Activities. While accepting your child's need for challenging activities, you can also monitor the danger level. If it is too dangerous, you may need to take charge and state limits as described below.

"The original ramp for lake jumping was almost five feet high and had a slope that was nearly vertical. We watched the boys jump one time and made them cut the ramp down to four feet and decrease the slope."

Provide Supervision. Providing closer supervision sounds like a great answer. But closely supervising teenagers is not very easy. Your teenager may impulsively participate in dangerous activities and never tell you. Still, it doesn't hurt to try to keep tabs on her activities. Subtlety is best if you don't want your teenager to feel as though she is experiencing an inquisition. You can find out a lot about your teenager's plans if you just listen to casual conversations between her and her friends. Remember, though, if you "eavesdrop" and intervene too often, your teenager may become more secretive but continue to pursue daring activities.

Negotiate a Compromise. If you don't approve of her plans, talk with her. Negotiate a reduced level of danger, substitute another activity, or tell her she can't go. Of course, even if you say no, your teenager may go ahead and do it anyway without telling you. If you can negotiate a safer compromise, you may be better off. For example, she can go scuba diving but only if she takes a partner with her.

Ask Others for Help. If your teenager is taking lessons or classes to learn an exciting hobby such as scuba diving, you may need to talk confidentially to instructors to make them aware of the symptoms of the attention deficit plus the importance of taking medication. Discuss with your teenager first. If your teen's class takes a trip, you may make the trip contingent upon having the instructor discreetly check to see if she takes her medication. A responsible sibling or friend may also keep an eye on your teenager and make sure she doesn't do anything too dangerous.

Difficulty Sleeping

As Chapter 7 discusses, slightly over half of all youngsters with attention deficits have problems related to sleep. They may have problems falling asleep, waking up, or both. Half also report that they feel tired when they wake up, but others appear to need less sleep. Some also have frequent night waking, nightmares, or restless sleep in which they move all around in the bed. Many of these teens have a *delayed sleep cycle*—that is, they want to sleep from 4:00 a.m. until noon.

Researchers are not yet sure why these teens have sleep problems. It may be, however, that their biochemical problems and reactions to stressful situations make it difficult to fall asleep and to get a truly restful night's sleep. Serotonin, which is essential for sleep, is thought to be deficient in some children with ADD or ADHD. It is also possible they get distracted by one activity after another, which prevents them from getting into bed and falling asleep. Sometimes teenagers with attention deficits feel as though they can't turn their brains off when it is time for bed. They think, and think, and think some more. They hear every sound and creak the house makes.

"Our 'night owl' son with ADD inattentive has periods when he has difficulty sleeping. He has always needed less sleep even in infancy. Occasionally, he can't fall asleep before two or three o'clock in the morning. Sometimes these sleepless periods seem to be related to stressful events such as receiving failing grades, speeding tickets, car accidents, and losing money."

Helpful reading material and tips for teens on falling asleep and waking up are available in "Night Owls and Morning Zombies" in *A Bird's-Eye View*. Chapter 7 also identifies key facts about sleep disorders.

Establish a Reasonable Time for Bed. Discuss and set a reasonable bedtime with your teenager. "I've observed that you need at least seven hours sleep or you are tired and have trouble getting up. That means that if you get up at 7:00, you must get in bed no later than midnight. What time do you think you should go to bed?"

"Because of the early starting time for high school, we realized that getting ready for bed beginning at 11:00 P.M. was too late. Our son was getting up at 5:45 A.M. so he could shower in the morning. He was attempting to function at school with only six hours sleep. We encouraged him to start getting ready for bed at 10:00 or 10:30 p.m."

Establish a Bedtime Routine. First, encourage your teenager to establish a good bedtime routine. Because your teenager is easily distracted, it may take longer to prepare for bed. Establishing a nighttime routine that begins a half hour to an hour before bed may be helpful. You may have her set an alarm or verbally prompt her when to start getting ready for bed. She may wish to take a hot bath or shower at the same time each evening and read or listen to music for a while before turning out the light. Listening to music, reading, or other calming activities may also help. She might also eat a snack and drink a glass of milk. Your teenager may need to avoid soft drinks with caffeine in the later afternoon, but soft drinks don't seem to interfere with sleep for many teenagers.

"Our son wanted to stay up extremely late on the weekends and had difficulty getting to sleep Sunday night. Our doctor suggested going to bed at a reasonable hour even on weekends plus establishing a bedtime routine. He pointed out that it is important to establish a more consistent sleep schedule throughout the whole week, including the weekend. Midnight or one o'clock would have been acceptable, but our son liked to stay up until four or five in the morning on the weekends. His schedule was terribly out of balance."

Don't Start Projects after a Set Time. Come to an agreement that your teenager will not start any personal projects until her homework is finished or within an hour of bedtime on school nights.

"Our son loses track of time and the first thing he knows, it's 11:00 and he hasn't done his homework. Or he gets sidetracked wiring his stereo system and suddenly it's two o'clock in the morning. He is impulsive and may start wiring his stereo system at 10:30 p.m. He doesn't think ahead and figure out how long it will take or if he can finish it by bedtime. He is so intensely wrapped up in the project, he will work on it until it is finished, regardless of the time. 'Just give me 15 more minutes.' Then, an hour later, he still hasn't finished."

Compromise May Be Necessary during a Crisis. Sometimes during a crisis or unusual situation, you may need to work out a compromise with your teenager. An example of an unusual situation which required a compromise is discussed in the following paragraphs. You can't go wrong by applying good common sense in these situations.

"During one particularly difficult sleepless period when our son couldn't fall asleep before three o'clock in the morning during the school week, I let him go back to sleep and go to school after second period. Realistically, I knew that if he went to school at 7:30, his school day would be wasted anyway. He could not think clearly, would probably sleep through class,

would be grouchy, might fail a test, and perhaps have cross words with a teacher.

"I wouldn't want to make this a habit, but I felt the circumstances warranted this unusual approach. We worked as quickly as possible to change his 'environment' to normalize his sleep schedule. He drank milk, ate cookies, took a warm shower near bedtime. Sometimes I would give him a facial massage to help him relax. Our son decided to take his medication (Tofranil) earlier— 10:00 p.m. rather than 11:00, take a shower, and maybe watch TV or listen to tapes just before bedtime."

Encourage Exercise. Researchers tell us that children with attention deficits derive significant benefits from regular exercise. Physical exercise earlier in the day may help your teen sleep better at night. Avoid exercise too late in the evening, however, or it may actually interfere with sleep.

Confer with a Physician. Some teenagers have difficulty sleeping because of the effect of stimulant medication. If sleep problems arise *after* your child begins taking medication, talk with her doctor. It may help to adjust the time at which the medication is administered, reduce the amount of the second dose in the afternoon, or try another stimulant medication. Sometimes it helps to take medication earlier in the day. Together, you, your teen, and the physician can determine the latest hour (between three or six o'clock in the afternoon, for example) that she can take medication and not disrupt her sleep pattern.

Some physicians suggest using antihistamines such as Benadryl™ to help teenagers fall asleep more easily. However, researchers recently reported that long-term use of Benadryl may impair memory. Other medications that doctors may prescribe include Tofranil, Trazadone, or Clonidine. Sometimes small doses of Clonidine (.05 to .1 mg, 1 to 2 hours before bedtime) are prescribed for teens who are having serious sleep problems. Although Clonidine is usually prescribed to help reduce anger or aggression, one side benefit is that it also helps some teenagers fall asleep more easily. Dr. William Larsen, a pediatrician in Anchorage, Alaska, prescribes a low dose of Tofranil (25-50 mg) to help his patients fall asleep and wake up more easily. However, since there is a risk of overdose, either accidental or intentional, it is extremely important to control the dispensing of these medications.

"Both Adderall and Tofranil were prescribed as the best medication regimen to meet our

son's needs. One of the side benefits is that he can fall asleep more readily, plus he has been easier to wake up since he began taking 50 milligrams of Tofranil at bedtime. The second morning after he began taking the medication, he opened his eyes when I turned on the bathroom light. I was shocked. It is wonderful to be able to wake him up without having a major yelling, screaming family fight."

Trouble Waking Up

Extreme difficulty waking up may be indicative of a sleep disturbance. Many parents hate waking up their teenager because it is such a battle. The teen may say and do things that she does not remember later. Parents and teenagers may scream at each other, starting off the day on a terribly negative note. If parents are busy trying to get ready for work, it is a major hassle to keep checking on the teenager to make certain she has gotten up. Parents may arrive at work feeling frustrated and angry. By the time the teen gets to school she may be so angry she may snap at other people. Sometimes it may be difficult to determine if the ADD, ADHD, or depression is responsible for the sleep problems.

"Waking up our 16-year-old each morning is a battle. I hate it. You can shake him and yell at him and you can't wake him up. He can sleep through alarms, loud music, and lights on in the room. Finally, he will talk to you, promise to get up, and then fall back asleep. Later he will have no memory of what he said or did."

Buy an Alarm Clock. Try buying your teenager an alarm clock and telling her she is responsible for getting up and going to school on her own. If she oversleeps, then she will have to go to school late and will miss some of her classes. If she enjoys going to school, then she will be upset that she didn't get up on time and will try harder to wake up. This idea probably won't work if she dislikes school. Really loud alarm clocks are available at the truck stop plazas along the interstates. You might also consider an alarm clock that rolls off your table and hides if you don't turn it off in time (www.clocky.net).

"Lewis sleeps like a dead person. He is so hard to wake up, it is incredible. He will talk to you and not remember a word he has said half an hour later. Somehow, he has learned to get up on his own when his alarm goes off. He is a senior and enjoys school."

Connect Lights and TV to a Timer. If an alarm clock doesn't work, try connecting the lights and TV to a 24-hour electric timer, such as the ones people use when they're away on vacation. When the timer reaches a set time, lights and the TV will turn on. The novelty may work for a while.

Try Positive Incentives. If your teenager hates school and is doing poorly, she would probably be happy to stay in bed half the day. Other measures must be tried. Try positive incentives first. "The fights we have every morning about your getting up for school upset me and my day starts out on a bad note. If you will get up on time for five days, I'll rent you an extra video game or movie Friday night . . . or I'll pay you a dollar for each day you get up on time."

If these ideas don't work and she claims illness, you may say, "If you are sick and don't feel like going to school today, then you need to stay in bed so you'll feel better tomorrow." Or, "I expect you to go to school every day and be on time. If you don't go today, then you can't have the car and go out tonight."

Have Someone Important Call. *In A Bird's-Eye View*, Alex suggests that you have someone like a girlfriend or your best friend call and wake you up. Or get the teen to tape record her own voice or her grandfather's with a special morning greeting.

Consider Medication as a Last Resort. If major fights are erupting each morning and everything else has failed, consider discussing medication with your child's physician.

Look for Other Causes. Sometimes attention deficits alone are not to blame for a teenager's sleep difficulties. A good physical examination can pinpoint any health problems that may be causing sleep problems. If life is not going well at home and school, your teen may also be depressed. If she is depressed or anxious, she may not be getting truly restful sleep. If this is a major problem, talk with a mental health professional or physician. For more information on depression, see Chapters 6 (use of antidepressants) and 7 (diagnosis of coexisting conditions).

Morning Battles

The morning routine of getting dressed for school may be a nightmare because of a sleep disturbance or distractibility. Teenagers with ADD or ADHD often start getting ready, then get sidetracked on something more interesting. If mornings are a terrible battle, develop a plan to change whatever is bothering you. Otherwise, if your teenager misses the bus occasionally, drive her to school when she gets ready.

Allow Enough Time. If your teenager is slow moving each morning, you may need to build in 15 extra minutes for her to wake up and become alert enough to get ready.

Use Logical Consequences. If she misses the bus frequently, you can try a couple of approaches. For example, ask her help in solving this problem. "These battles each morning really bother me. Please help me come up with a solution to solve this problem. You need to get up on time to ride the bus." Or, subtract her late time from some event she really likes. For example, she loses 15 minutes Game Boy time or her curfew is backed up by 15 minutes. Or if she lives close enough and especially likes school, she can walk even though she will be really late. Don't try this approach if she has a very low frustration tolerance and you suspect that she will blow up and have even more serious problems at school.

Leave On Time; Dress in the Car. If your teenager rides to school with you, plan to leave for work and school at a set time and tell her in advance. If she isn't ready, she has to finish dressing in the car. You may tell her, "I am leaving for work at 7:00. If you are not ready to leave at 7:00, you will have to take your clothes and get dressed in the car." It may help to warn her ten minutes before you are ready to leave. Finally, say, "I am ready now and I am going to the car." After she has to dress in the car a couple of times, she will probably make a greater effort to be ready for school on time.

Obviously, this is not going to work with all teens. If your teen is pretty compliant with your requests and wants to go to school, she may actually take her clothes to the car and get dressed there. But if your teen has oppositional defiant disorder, you probably will just create another unpleasant, unproductive power struggle by using this strategy.

Take Away Driving Privileges. If being late is a major problem for a high school student who is driving herself to school, one logical consequence is to take away her driving privileges. Remember, immediate consequences work best. "If you are late to school today, you cannot drive to school tomorrow." Or to state the same concept in a positive way, "Each day you leave for school on time you earn the privilege of driving your car to school the next day. Otherwise, if you are late, you cannot drive to school the next day." It shouldn't take too long to change this behavior, unless depression or sleep disturbances are a major problem. If these problems are severe, medical treatment may be required.

Get Ready the Night Before. Your teenager could take a shower the night before and lay her clothes out in preparation for the next morning. However, night time showers may not work for some teenagers, since they need their morning shower to wake up and function at school.

Consider Giving Medication Early. If mornings are really a battle, one fairly simple solution is to talk with your doctor about giving a short-acting medication like Ritalin, Focalin, or Dexedrine as soon as your teenager wakes up. You could wake her up a few minutes early, give her her medication, and let her stay in bed 20 to 30 minutes. Once the medication takes effect, it may be easier for her to get up and get dressed. One drawback is that she may not be hungry at breakfast.

"For the last two mornings I've tried the technique of waking the kids up 30 minutes early to give them their meds and letting them go back to sleep. We were on time for church Sunday (I was afraid that everyone would stand and applaud) and Natalie made it to safety patrol this morning early! These are both firsts! Even better, the mornings have been amazingly calm—no screaming and hollering (nor wailing and gnashing of teeth)."

Birds of a Feather Flock Together

Subconsciously, teenagers with attention deficits may seek out friends who also have ADD or ADHD and act the same way they do. This may occur more often in urban areas where families are more likely to move and teenagers are less likely to have childhood friends with whom they have grown up. If your teenager has friends from early childhood, they are more likely to include a broader range of personality types, not just other teens with attention deficits.

"Several of our youngest son's friends 'hang out' at our home. We observed that a few of them seemed to exhibit characteristics of ADHD. At first I couldn't explain this phenomenon and wondered if I was projecting these behaviors on everyone else.

"It was not my imagination. At least five of my son's teenage friends have ADD or ADHD diagnoses confirmed by a physician. I suspect they tend to be drawn to each other because they exhibit similar behavior, are having difficulty at school, and feel more comfortable with teens who are more like themselves."

"I think part of the attraction is that they are very bright and have many varied interests. None of them do very well at school. Therefore, they don't seem to care about grades. They don't see grades as being a measure of their intelligence or worth."

Having friends who have ADD or ADHD in itself is not bad. However, if her friends have severe cases and are always doing reckless things, this could be dangerous.

Refer Other Teenagers for Treatment. As a matter of self-defense, consider referring other teens you suspect of having attention deficits for treatment. Otherwise, several very impulsive, daring teenagers who are doing poorly in school may be influencing each other to try new and daring adventures.

If your teen suspects that one of her friends has ADD or ADHD, she could talk with her about the characteristics of the disorder. Your teen may describe her own behavior and how her attention deficit was diagnosed. She may also explain how much better things are going now that she is being treated. If she has a good relationship with her friend, she may show her a list of behaviors from DSM that are characteristic of ADD and ADHD and ask, "Does any of this sound like you?"

You may be able to help your teenager educate other parents. If you also suspect that one of your teenager's friends has ADD or ADHD, be tactful in raising the issue with the friend and his or her parents. You might tell the parents what a difference treatment has made in your daughter's life. If the other parents volunteer that their teenager isn't doing well in school, you may offer them materials to read about attention deficit disorder. If the parents and their teen seem interested, discuss the issue in more detail. However, if the other parents are reluctant to talk about it, drop the subject. Sometimes you can be very helpful by simply planting a seed for parents to think about. After they have had some time to think things over, they may come to the same conclusion about the attention deficit. Some parents may view outside intervention as meddlesome.

Encourage Other Friendships. Consider encouraging your teenager to associate with a variety of friends, including some who don't have ADD or ADHD.

You might invite different friends to do things with your teenager—spend the night, go to amusement parks, or participate in sports.

Unique Challenges of ADHD vs. ADD Inattentive

Although teenagers who have ADHD or ADD inattentive share many common characteristics, they may also show some distinctly different attributes. Teenagers with ADD inattentive may have problems with low energy, daydreaming, or spaciness. Teenagers with ADHD may be attention seekers, intrusive, or have more difficulty making and keeping friends.

Low Energy

Many teenagers who have ADD inattentive may have low energy levels and seem sluggish. At times they may even be lethargic and have trouble getting started on projects. Researchers sometimes refer to problems with drowsiness, lethargy, and under activity as *sluggish cognitive tempo*. They may also be more likely to become depressed than teens with ADHD. They may prefer sedentary activities such as watching TV or playing video games to physically strenuous activity. Even though they may be sluggish, restlessness may also be present, just as in teens with ADHD, and should be channeled into positive activities. Sometimes aggression may also surface as the result of the teenager's frustration or depression.

Encourage Pursuit of Physical Activities. If your teenager enjoys any physical activities, encourage her to participate in them. Physical activity will help relieve depression, direct her energies in positive endeavors, and may also help build her self-esteem if she excels in a sport. As discussed earlier, individual sports such as karate, gymnastics, swimming, or wrestling may hold greater interest for some teenagers than traditional team sports. Skills required for team sports such as social interactions, team play, and sensitivity to cues from teammates are not always strengths of teens, especially those with ADHD. Plus, they like novelty, and individual sports may allow more individuality. If you expose your teenager to enough activities, you will usually find one she enjoys. For example, horseback riding, riflery, modeling, motorized dirt bike racing, fencing, archery, hiking, ice skating, or scuba diving are less traditional activities that your teenager may enjoy.

Consult Your Physician. A change in medication may help if lethargy is a major problem. If your teenager has ADD inattentive, Adderall, Dexedrine, or Strattera may improve both her attention and energy level. All three of these medications affect norepinephrine, plus Adderall and Dexedrine also affect dopamine.

Deficits in serotonin are linked to depression and sleep problems. If your teen with ADD is also depressed, has emotional ups and downs, or is aggressive, medications such as Zoloft, Celexa, Effexor, Lexapro, or Tofranil, which increase serotonin, may also be prescribed. See Chapter 6 for more information on medications, especially the FDA warning about antidepressants.

Get a Physical. A good physical examination is important to rule out other health problems that may be causing the lethargy. For example, anemia or mononucleosis may cause reduced energy or depressive symptoms. Teenagers with attention deficits seem more prone to have allergies, which may also contribute to feelings of low energy.

The Absent-Minded Professor

Some teenagers who have ADD inattentive may have a spacey or "absent-minded professor" quality to their personality. Daydreaming in class is common. They may become confused easily and lack awareness of their surroundings, instructions, or consequences. They may get lost when they are driving or have trouble following travel directions. When they are shopping, they could unthinkingly put a small item in their pocket or purse and forget to pay for it. If observed by store security, they could be stopped for shoplifting.

"My son was driving home from college and totally missed his exit off the interstate. If his roommate hadn't been watching, they would have ended up in another state. He has driven that route hundreds of times but was oblivious to road signs."

"A college student with ADD was told that if he had a 90 average for the semester, he didn't have to take a final exam. He didn't take the exam because he thought his average was 90, but it was actually 87. He remembered taking only two tests and receiving grades of 90 on each. He had forgotten that he had a third exam and had made 80."

Help with Organization. Issues regarding disorganization have been addressed elsewhere. See the earlier section on "disorganization" plus Chapter 13 for tips on planning ahead with regard to schoolwork. In addition, numerous suggestions to help with organizing school issues, including long-term projects, are provided in *Teaching Teens,* Summaries 29 and 36. Helpful tips are also given by teens in "Chaos and Clutter," *A Bird's-Eye View.*

Anticipate Problems; Make Adjustments. If getting lost is a problem, figure out what works best for your teen. Mark the route on the map and review it with her. Write out the directions or hand draw a map. Or encourage her to take a friend along who can help follow the map.

Medication May Help. Stimulant medication may help improve your teenager's ability to pay attention and plan ahead.

Slow Processing Speed

Slow cognitive processing speed is more likely to be characteristic of teenagers with ADD inattentive. This can have a major impact on school performance. These students may read and write very slowly. They may feel overwhelmed by their schoolwork. They may also have problems understanding instructions from parents and, as a result, may not do chores correctly.

Seek Accommodations. Remember to keep this problem in mind when you talk with your teenager. For example, keep instructions brief and write them down. Accommodations, such as extended time on tests or shortened homework assignments, may also be needed at school. See the suggestions in Chapter 13 on accommodations. Again, numerous suggestions are given in *Teaching Teens* that will help your teen be more successful in school.

Attention Seekers; Class Clowns

Many teenagers who have ADHD love to be the center of attention. They may monopolize the conversation at dinner or family outings or be the class clown. Because they like attention, if a new fad comes along they will probably try it. Sometimes conflicts also erupt over clothing and jewelry teenagers want to wear.

Give Opportunities to Be Center Stage. Provide opportunities for your teenager to be the center of attention. At dinner, ask her to tell about school or a recent activity. Praise her successes and recognize her accomplishments. After she has told of her adventures, draw siblings into the conversation. Each should have a turn to share their joys and successes.

Encourage Pursuit of Activities That Give Recognition. Encourage your teenager to purse activities which allow her public success and recognition. For example, she may enjoy activities like theater, music, debate team, or stand-up comedy. You can help her find out if these activities are offered at school, the YMCA, or through other community groups.

Discuss Inappropriate Attention Seeking. Occasionally, your teenager may alienate teachers or lose friends because of inappropriate attention seeking. Try discussing this situation with her. "Sometimes teenagers with ADHD become the class clown and some teachers don't like that. Your history teacher, Mrs. Smith, is less than thrilled with your behavior. On the other hand, Mrs. Duncan enjoys your entertainment. Can you clean up your act and cut out the clowning in Mrs. Smith's room? One of the lessons we all have to learn in life is to adjust our behavior to the situation."

Ignore Some Behavior. If possible, ignore attention-getting behavior such as unusual haircuts, body piercings, or earrings (on boys). Or compromise—ask your teenaged daughter to take out her nose ring when she visits her grandfather. These behaviors usually run their course and disappear. Frequently, teenagers reach an age when they decide on their own to cut their hair or take out their earrings. Sometimes their behavior also changes when they learn that unconventional hairstyles and earrings don't make a good first impression at most job interviews.

Intrusiveness

Sometimes teenagers with attention deficits, especially with hyperactivity, have difficulty understanding boundaries of space and communication. They may intrude on parents who are trying to spend time alone, go into their parents' room, or get into others' possessions without permission. They may also interrupt others when they are talking.

Set Boundaries. Obviously, the more rules you have, the more rules there are to break. There is no need to declare a room off limits unless your teenager is causing problems because she is getting into things that don't belong to her.

One potential area of conflict is when your teenager borrows things from her brother or sister and breaks them or never returns them. If this happens, you may decide to make certain areas "off limits." Tell her which room is off limits and ask her to leave if you find her in the room. If necessary, put her on restrictions or have her pay for lost or damaged items. To avoid potential accidents, keep fragile, expensive items such as a video camera in your space and not in "shared spaces."

Teach Your Teenager to Wait. If your teenager interrupts people who are talking, teach her to wait until the conversation is finished and she is recognized. If she interrupts *you,* you can try ignoring her. However, teens with ADHD may be pretty difficult to ignore. It will probably work better to explain, "I am talking with someone right now. I'll be finished in a minute and I can listen to you then." Later, explain the procedure you want her to follow. "When I am talking on the phone, I don't like to be interrupted unless it is urgent. Please tap me on the shoulder. When I get off the phone, I will come find you or I will pause and talk with you briefly."

Difficulty with Relationships

Teenagers with attention deficits, especially those who are hyperactive, may have trouble finding and keeping friends. Experts tell us that 50 to 60 percent of children with ADHD have problems with peer relationships. Some teens may have difficulty establishing close relationships because they have trouble focusing or concentrating long enough to communicate with their friends. Many teenagers with ADHD also appear to miss social cues in their communication with others. They may say something harsh or blunt and have no clue that they have insulted someone or hurt their feelings. Sometimes they miss the meaning behind subtle facial expressions or body language and may not accurately interpret others' reactions to them. They may interrupt others and monopolize conversations. They may be aggressive and bossy. As a result of their poor social skills they may be susceptible to bullying, either as a victim or perpetrator (see Chapter 10). Ultimately, executive skill deficits that contribute to lack of self-control are a key underlying cause of their social problems. Teens with ADD inattentive have fewer problems in these areas.

Experts also tell us that having at least one good friend helps our children cope more successfully with life and their attention deficit. So it is important to provide interventions aimed at enhancing friendships by teaching needed skills. (Interested readers can find out more about this topic in the chapter on "Social Skills" I contributed to the CHADD *Educators' Manual).*

"Jeff was so unaware of how others reacted to him. He really didn't see himself as any different from the other boys. I sat and watched him stand in line for warm ups at a basketball game. He could never be still. He was in his own world, bumping into other boys. He never saw the dirty looks other boys gave him. He didn't hear their comments to 'leave me alone.' It hurt me so much to watch this happen. I'd say afterward, 'Son you've got to learn where your space is or people won't want to be around you.' He thought I was way off base. He said, 'Mom, you don't understand. We boys just got it going on.' He didn't even know he was being obnoxious and a pest."

Social Issues and Girls with ADHD. Although girls with attention deficits may not cause as many discipline problems as boys, the problems they face are just as serious. Girls are more likely to have trouble with social relationships than boys do. The Shaywitzs have found that girls with ADHD are more likely to be rejected by their peers.

Invite Her Friends on Outings. Try placing your teenager in the center of activities by being the parent who is willing to take several teenagers on fun outings. Let your child invite one or two friends to go along on a special activity such as going to an amusement park or to the lake or beach. Taking one friend along may be best, because otherwise there is a risk that the other two friends may pair off and exclude your teen.

Provide Tips on Relating to Friends. If your teenager is receptive, you or a teacher or counselor may give her hints on how to interact successfully with his friends. Identify one or two major behaviors that cause trouble with her friends and work on those. Be gentle, subtle, and loving. Don't blast the teenager as she learns new skills. For example, avoid putdowns: "You're a loud mouth. You're so bossy. You talk too much." It may help to review the gender-related desirable social skills such as activities (sports) for boys and friendliness and appropriate dress for girls, as described in the CHADD *Educators' Manual.* Then you might give your son brief updates on the win-loss standings of a popular sports team. Or it might be helpful to advise your daughter to greet friends in passing at school or experiment with more fashionable ways to dress. Increasing the knowledge base of both boys and girls about "hot topics" being discussed by their desired peer group can be helpful.

Wait for a Teachable Moment. If your teen complains that no one likes her or she doesn't have any friends, listen to her talk. Then say, "Sometimes teenagers with ADHD (ADD) have trouble getting along with friends. There are some things you can do to get along better with your friends." If she seems interested, offer one or maybe two suggestions about behaviors that may be turning people off: "When someone else is talking, they like other people to listen to them. Try not to interrupt your friends." Don't overwhelm her with all the negatives at one time. Over time, share tips such as: "Most people like to hear themselves talk. Give everyone a chance to talk. Don't monopolize the conversation." "Try talking less and listening more." "Most people don't like to listen to a person who brags all the time. If you are proud of something, tell your best friend or someone in our family." In addition, some schools offer social skills groups that may benefit your teenager.

Seek Social Skills Training. The role of social skills training is discussed in Chapter 5. Generally, researchers report that it is not that effective. However, it is definitely worth trying as long as parents have realistic expectations that it will not miraculously change their child's behavior. Social skills tips are also provided in *A Bird's Eye View* and the *CHADD Educators' Manual* (Chris Zeigler Dendy, editor). Dr. Rick Lavoie's book, *"It's So Much Work to Be Your Friend,"* also has a lot of helpful information. Lavoie utilizes a unique strategy known as a "Social Skills Autopsy" in which the teen and adult discuss the social faux pas and identify strategies for correcting it, and then the teen practices the proper response.

Ensure Success in School. One interesting study found that social skills improved more when students had tutoring than actual social skills training. Perhaps this occurs because children who are successful in school are less likely to be teased or bullied.

Coach Her Team. Depending on your relationship with your teenager, you may want to sponsor or coach an athletic team, scout troop, or religious group. A major question is "Does your teenager want you to help coach the team or will it be an embarrassment?" There may be some advantages to being a parent/coach—you know your teenager's strengths, her strongest and weakest skills, and how her attention deficit affects her playing ability. As a result, you may be a more patient and effective coach. On the other hand, some parents may be more impatient with their own child than someone else's. Do what works best for your family.

Medication May Help. Medication often seems to help reduce impulsivity and behaviors that can be offensive to other teenagers and coaches. Researchers tell us it will help them focus on the game, be better team players, and get along better with their teammates.

Encourage Having Friends in Addition to Boyfriends (Girlfriends). Some teenagers with attention deficits have intense, short-term relationships with members of the opposite sex. Relationships may last for a couple of weeks or a month at most. Others may have long-term relationships based on an unhealthy dependency.

For some, a girlfriend or boyfriend may be a very positive influence. If your teenager is a good student, his or her schoolwork may improve. The friend may share your role as "coach" in reminding your teen of homework assignments. So even though they are dependent on each other, the relationship may be good for your teenager. You should use common sense in looking at relationships. If the benefits are primarily positive, don't intervene.

If your teenager is too dependent on a girlfriend or boyfriend, you may have to let the relationship take its natural course. Trying to force a couple to break up seldom works. One thing you can do is to encourage your teenager to do things with other friends too. Also, let her make as many decisions as possible about things that affect her life. Hopefully, as she makes more and more decisions on her own, she will become increasingly independent.

Conclusion

Living day-to-day with ADD or ADHD can be very trying for parents. Forgotten chores, unfinished homework, chronic lateness, and repeating the same misbehavior are enough to give parents gray hair or ulcers. For best results, target one or two problem areas and work on those. Select interventions based upon your family's unique needs. Remember, too, that consequences may be effective for only a limited time; when one intervention ceases to work, you will need to try another one. The easy-reference guides at the ends of Chapters 8 through 13 can help you select interventions appropriate for specific behaviors and school problems.

One last thought: it is easy for outsiders to have all the answers—to tell you how to properly discipline your son or daughter with an attention deficit. However, most professionals will acknowledge that it is easier said than done. Outsiders don't live with your teenager 24 hours a day; you do. Parents can only do so much, and regardless of how "perfect" your parenting is, crises will inevitably occur. When parents blow up and "lose their cool," they tend to "beat themselves up" for their lack of parenting skills. It is far better to simply do your best, learn new parenting techniques, and be forgiving of yourself and your teenager.

Table 9-1   Common Behaviors of Teenagers with ADD and ADHD

Easy Reference Guide

A summary of common behaviors of teenagers who have attention deficit, plus possible interventions, are listed below. Most teenagers with ADD or ADHD will have some but not all of these behaviors. After reading the detailed information on particular behaviors and interventions in this chapter, this easy reference guide should serve as a helpful refresher of possible interventions. As you become more familiar with using these strategies, you will find that you can often use them to handle more than one problem situation.

CHALLENGING BEHAVIORS	POSSIBLE INTERVENTIONS
Independence; "pushes limits"	■ Encourage independence ■ Trust until proven not trustworthy ■ Be observant of activities & friends ■ Consider compromise ■ Set up win/win situations ■ Offer an attractive alternative
Disobedience; conflicts with adults	■ State rules clearly ■ Involve in developing rules ■ Write down rules; post them
Immaturity; acting younger	■ Adjust expectations ■ Ask her help in solving problems
Impulsivity	■ Anticipate problems ■ Avoid tempting your teenager ■ Consider medication
Inattention; doesn't seem to listen	■ Make eye contact; use touch ■ Keep instructions brief and simple ■ Write instructions down ■ Avoid preaching ■ Accept her listening style
Forgetfulness; doesn't do chores	■ Make a written list ■ Use "Post It" notes ■ Help get started; show how to do tasks ■ Ask how you can help
Disorganization; loses things	■ Put name on possessions ■ Purchase less expensive things ■ Assist in being organized ■ Serve as a coach ■ List steps for a clean room ■ Help clean & organize room, garage ■ Close the door to a messy room

Impairment of sense of time; lateness	■ Use a wrist watch alarm ■ Use a "Talking Timer" ■ Rent or buy a beeper or cell phone ■ Discuss strategies for being on time ■ Break projects into segments ■ Teach awareness of time
Procrastination; difficulty getting started	■ Jump start your teen
Difficulty planning ahead	■ Teach planning ■ Teach time management
Difficult to discipline	■ Use positive reinforcement (See Chapter 8) ■ Use logical consequences ■ Reward or punish immediately ■ Be consistent ■ Create new consequences/rewards ■ Use behavioral charts ■ Use rewards; may include money ■ Try "Grandma's Rule" ■ Avoid power struggles ■ Redirect interests ■ Give a second chance ■ Be humane; practice forgiveness
Low frustration tolerance; irritability	■ Listen; be supportive ■ Use active listening (See Chapter 8) ■ Teach teen strategies for coping ■ Teach problem-solving skills ■ Teach anger control ■ Help teen understand emotions
Argumentative; talks back; argues	■ Ignore minor infractions ■ Walk away from conflict ■ Give space and time to cool off ■ Impose a consequence ■ Adjust medication
Difficulty accepting responsibility	■ Deal with problem behavior
Dishonesty	■ If you know the answer, don't ask ■ Eliminate some punishment ■ Develop plan to deal with problems ■ Impose a consequence
Difficulty with family events	■ Keep outings simple ■ Reduce demands ■ Keep outings brief ■ Find creative solutions ■ Consider medication

Difficulty participating in sports	■ Play large muscle sports ■ Play an active position ■ Consider medication
Restlessness; easily bored	■ Get involved in activities and sports ■ Plan interesting family outings ■ Encourage hobbies & interests ■ Make special plans for holidays
Materialistic	■ Allow to earn money ■ Plan for holidays or birthdays ■ Purchase fewer, less expensive gifts ■ Teach to express gratitude
Self-centered	■ Remind of special occasions ■ Invite to shop for others with you ■ Encourage to do things for others
Accident prone	■ Handle accidents philosophically ■ Treat as you would an adult ■ Discuss physical strength ■ Put expensive possessions away
Daring; break bones; climb the unclimbable	■ Encourage safe, stimulating activities ■ Monitor the level of danger ■ Provide supervision ■ Negotiate compromise ■ Ask others for help
Sleep disturbances; can't fall asleep	■ Establish reasonable bedtime ■ Prompt to get ready for bed ■ Establish bedtime routine ■ Don't start projects after a set time ■ Consider compromise during crisis ■ Encourage exercise ■ Consider medication; confer with Dr.
Can't wake up	■ Buy an alarm clock ■ Connect lights and TV to timer ■ Try positive incentives ■ Ask someone important to call ■ Consider medication as last resort ■ Look for other causes
Difficulty with morning routine	■ Allow enough time (See Chapter 7) ■ Ask her help in problem solving ■ Use logical consequences if late ■ Give 10 minute warning ■ Take away driving privileges ■ Get things ready the night before ■ Give meds immediately upon waking

Birds of a feather flock together	▪ Refer friends for treatment
	▪ Approach other parents with tact
	▪ Tell of treatment benefits
	▪ Encourage other friendships

BEHAVIORS UNIQUE TO TEENAGERS WITH ADD or ADHD:

ADD Inattentive

Low energy	▪ Encourage physical activity
	▪ Consult your physician
	▪ Get a physical exam
	▪ Check for depression
	▪ Consider meds if needed
Absent-minded; spacey	▪ See suggestions re: organization
	▪ Anticipate problems; make adjustments
	▪ Consider medication
Slow processing speed	▪ Seek accommodations at home and school
	▪ See suggestions for school (Ch.13)
	▪ Reduce amount of writing

ADHD

Attention seekers; class clown	▪ Give opportunities to be center stage
	▪ Participate in activities allowing recognition
	▪ Discuss inappropriate attention
	▪ Ignore some behavior
Intrusiveness	▪ Set boundaries
	▪ Identify parent's & sibling's space
	▪ Impose consequences
	▪ Teach teen to wait
Difficulty with relationships	▪ Be aware of unique issues for girls
	▪ Invite friends on outings
	▪ Provide tips on relating to friends
	▪ Wait for teachable moments
	▪ Seek social skills training
	▪ Seek "bullying prevention" program
	▪ Ensure school success
	▪ Coach your teen's team
	▪ Consider medication
	▪ Encourage having friends in addition to opposite sex friends

10

When Teenagers Continue to Struggle

Many teenagers do well at home and school after their attention deficit is diagnosed and treated. Often, using suggestions such as those given in Chapters 5 through 9 is enough to help parents bring their teen's behavior within manageable limits. Some adolescents, however, continue to struggle. Perhaps learning problems have not been properly addressed, the best medications have not yet been identified, or outside stresses are compounding the problem. For a variety of reasons, these teenagers may be unsuccessful and unhappy, and as a result of their pain, lash out at the world. They may make poor decisions that endanger themselves or others.

More serious behaviors that parents may worry about include *defiance, aggression, excessive drinking, drug usage, speeding tickets, car accidents, sexual acting out, pregnancy, shoplifting, running away from home, a suicide attempt, purchase of a handgun, or brushes with the law.* Most parents hope they will never have to deal with any of these stressful problems. However, since some teenagers with attention deficits have a tendency to be impulsive and daring and fail to anticipate the consequences of their actions, you may be faced with some of these frightening events.

"My son and a friend sneaked out of the house one night to buy cigarettes. Since they were out after the local curfew, a police officer brought them home. I was horrified—it was so embarrassing."

"My son's friend, who is really a great kid, was picked up for attempted shoplifting. He was at a local store with some friends who suggested they take some things. Impulsively, he did. He had to go to juvenile court and participate in a community service program. There have been no more problems with shoplifting."

"At least three of my son's friends who have ADHD were pregnant or got a girl pregnant when they were in high school."

"One mother told me about her daughter's suicide attempt. Her teenaged daughter's ADD inattentive was not diagnosed until she was placed in a psychiatric hospital after the suicide attempt. This poor mother felt so guilty because she didn't recognize the ADD and had taken the school's side when the girl had not been doing well in school."

If your teen is undergoing any of the difficulties described in this chapter, you are probably experiencing a wide range of feelings. You may be frightened, and justifiably so, for your teenager's life and safety. You may be angry that your teenager is making your life so difficult. Or you may feel powerless because it seems as though you have very little control over your teen. Feelings of isolation are also common since you may be facing this frightening time alone. Besides handling your misbehaving teenager, you may also find yourself grappling with a punitive world governed by school administrators, police, probation staff, and juvenile court judges who may blame you for your child's problems. You may feel helpless, overwhelmed, and depressed because you can't find the assistance you need.

"I remember being so frightened for my son. His judgment during the teenage years was not the best. He was angry at the world and ever so daring. I was so afraid that something terrible might happen to him and that he would die or that he would impulsively do something stupid and end up in jail. No formal accommodations were made in high school for his learning problems. Finally, when the proper accommodations were made in college, he began to succeed academically. Next we found the right medication combination and he was so much happier and on an even keel emotionally."

Behaviors That Worry Parents Most

Teenagers of today face challenges that their parents never had to confront. Illegal drugs, guns, and AIDS are just some of the dangers young people must evade on their way to adulthood. It is not an easy time to grow up, and for that matter, not an easy time to be a parent—especially of a teenager with an attention deficit. No parent wants their teenager to smoke, use drugs, get drunk, or engage in premarital sex. Yet many parents are faced with teenagers who are doing these things.

To help parents put these problems in perspective, statistics are included from studies by the Centers for Disease Control and Prevention (CDC) in Atlanta. Many teenagers of today engage in more risky behaviors at an earlier age than we did. It should help parents to compare their teenager's behavior with "typical" adolescent behavior. As you can see from the CDC study on page 205, experimenting with cigarettes, alcohol, drugs, and sex is fairly common among teenagers today, not just those with attention deficits.

Sometimes these problems are linked to each other. For example, a teenager who drinks excessively may also be more sexually active, have a car wreck, or attempt suicide. The importance of one condition—depression—in these high risk behaviors is sometimes overlooked. As discussed in Chapter 7, some researchers believe that acting out behaviors such as delinquency, sexual promiscuity, or alcohol and drug use are actually symptoms of depression. This is significant. *By treating the depression, some of these problems may disappear.*

Unfortunately, there are no easy answers for resolving most of these behavior problems among teenagers with attention deficits. Generally speaking, keeping your teenager busy with activities, helping him succeed in school, giving him a sense of hope, providing supervision, and seeking treatment for his attention deficit and coexisting problems such as depression, sleep disturbances, and learning problems should be helpful and also strengthen self-esteem. Teenagers with high self-esteem are more confident, less likely to be pressured into doing things they don't want to do, and better able to withstand disappointments.

The suggestions given below are offered as broad guidelines only. If your teenager is having serious problems, you should talk with a treatment professional to develop a strategy for coping with these issues. Licensed counselors, social workers, physicians, psychologists, or psychiatrists—especially those who specialize in treating ADD and ADHD—should be able to help your family.

Defiance and Aggression

Teenagers who are very aggressive and defiant may be diagnosed with an emotional or behavioral disorder in addition to their attention deficit. As discussed in Chapter 7, oppositional defiant disorder (ODD) and conduct disorder (CD) are not uncommon in teenagers with attention deficits. Clearly, their difficulty regulating their emotions is a contributing factor in their problem behaviors.

The higher rates of conduct disorder or law breaking behaviors reported in earlier years are very frightening to parents. Parents, however, should be greatly encouraged by research from the MTA study that showed a reduction of conduct disorder when children received proper treatment.

According to the CDC study, fighting, one form of aggression, is common among all high school students. Approximately 33.2 percent had been in a fight in the preceding 12 months. Teenagers of today are some-

Table 10-1   CDC Youth Risk Behavior Survey—2001

All Children Grades 9 through 12
Percentage Who Engaged in Health-Risk Behaviors

Behavior	Percentage
Tried Cigarettes	63.9
Smoke cigarettes regularly	28.5
Use smokeless tobacco	8.2
Tried alcohol	78.2
Drank alcohol; once in last 30 days	47.1
Occasional heavy drinking	29.9
Tried marijuana	42.4
Smoked marijuana; once in last 30 days	23.9
Tried cocaine	9.4
Used cocaine; once in last 30 days	4.2
Used inhalant; once in last 30 days	4.7
Tried heroin	3.1
Tried methamphetamine	9.8
Offered, sold, or given illegal drug at school	28.5
Rode with a drinking driver	30.7
Drove after drinking	13.3
Rarely used seat belts	14.1
Involved in a fight	33.2
Carried a weapon	17.4
Carried a gun	5.7
Had sexual intercourse	45.6
Had sexual intercourse; once in last 90 days	33.4
With more than 4 partners	14.2
Used a condom	57.9
Used some other form of birth control	18.2
Dating violence; was hit, slapped, or hurt	9.5
Forced sexual intercourse	7.7
Seriously considered suicide	19.0
Developed a suicide plan	14.8
Attempted suicide	8.8

Leading Causes of Death among Young People (15-24)
National Center for Health Statistics—2001

Cause of Death (Total)	Percentage
1. Accidental Death (13,871 total; 10,259 from car wrecks)	34.7
2. Homicide (5,126)	12.8
3. Suicide (3,854)	9.6
7. HIV (227)	0.6

times frightened for their own safety. As a result, they foolishly, may carry a weapon to school (17.4 percent). Some have even carried guns to school (5.7). Weapons are discussed later in this chapter.

Causes. There are several theories about the causes of ODD and CD. The underlying causes of these problems most likely are linked to a combination of biochemical problems plus constantly hostile or abusive family interactions. Although a disorganized, chaotic, and disturbed family situation does not cause ODD or CD, it can make it much worse.

Many researchers believe that some cases of conduct disorder are linked to a deficiency in neurotransmitters. In fact, Dr. Biederman reports that, on average, children who are diagnosed with conduct disorder have more than three other coexisting conditions such as depression or bipolar disorder. The related deficiency in neurotransmitters often results in decreased sensitivity to punishment, making it harder to learn from punishment or rewards. These youngsters repeat misbehavior even after being punished. On the surface, it often looks as though they are maliciously disobeying or defying their parents and other authority figures.

Studies in California, Canada, and Finland have provided additional evidence that there is a biochemical basis for aggression. Researchers were able to increase aggressive behavior in both people and monkeys by reducing the levels of the neurotransmitter serotonin. According to these studies, when the levels of serotonin are low, both people and animals are more impulsive, aggressive, violent, and even suicidal. Studies at the National Institutes of Health also have identified a faulty gene that makes people predisposed to aggression. However, low levels of serotonin may be the result of both inherited and environmental factors. For example, violence or neglect in childhood or excessive alcohol can also trigger lower serotonin levels.

The parenting strategies discussed in Chapters 8 and 9 should help parents cope more effectively with their teen's anger, defiance, and aggression. One key treatment intervention is worth restating here: a second medication such as Clonidine, Zoloft, or Tofranil may help reduce aggression and defiance. Dr. Ross Green's book, *The Explosive Child*, or Dr. Harold Koplewicz's, *It's Nobody's Fault,* may be especially helpful for understanding and dealing with challenging teen behaviors. At school, students with serious problems of aggression and defiance may be placed in special education classes for students with emotional and behavior disorders (ED).

BULLYING

Bullying, a serious form of aggression, is a significant issue for some adolescents with attention deficits, either as a victim or in the role of the bully. The *Journal of the American Medical Association* reported that roughly 30 percent of all students reported involvement in bullying either as a bully (13 percent), a victim (11 percent), and as both (6 percent). A person is being bullied when "he or she is exposed, repeatedly over time, to negative actions on the part of one or more students." Regrettably, students with both ADHD and low self-control are more likely to bully or be the victims of bullying.

Bullying may get worse in early adolescence, especially in middle school. One of the major reasons reported for bullying is to try to "fit in" the new school environment. Unfortunately, these young teens have not yet learned how to interact positively to fit in with their peers. At this age, gaining social status and popularity is critically important. Consequently, many teens unknowingly play a major role in promoting bullying and victimization by either reinforcing the aggressor, failing to intervene to stop the victimization, or "hanging out" with students who bully.

In middle school, boys gain status through toughness and aggressiveness, while for girls, appearance is the major consideration. Bullying among boys is typically physical, including pushing and hurting other children. Girls are more likely to use name calling, taking friends away, or sending abusive email messages. Intentional exclusion from parties and sleepovers is extremely painful for both boys and girls.

Signs that your teen may be being bullied include becoming quiet or withdrawn, becoming aggressive with siblings, exhibiting anxiety or insomnia, doing worse in school, or becoming emotional and dreading going to school. On rare occasions, bullying can be so severe and damaging to teens they resort to extreme violence toward themselves or others. Researchers report that untreated aggression in adolescence such as bullying may well continue into adulthood. So, the importance of preventing bullying is obvious.

Talk with Your Child. Reassure your child that he or she is an okay person and that the bullies are wrong for acting the way they do. Some teens are reluctant to tell parents about bullying, so be certain to encourage them to always tell you about it. If the situation is serious—for example, there have been fights or a risk of school suspension—then let him know that you are going to do something about the problem by talking with school officials.

In the meanwhile, give your child a few tips for coping with the bullying until you can resolve this issue. For example, always tell someone when you have been bullied, don't hit back because you might get hurt or get in trouble, avoid eye contact with bullies, don't react and let them know they are upsetting you, stand tall and look confident, and avoid being around bullies. You may find several helpful websites, for example, www.addconsults.com, with tips from Terry Matlen, a respected ADHD consultant.

Educate Yourself about Bullying. Read more about bullying so you understand the seriousness of the issue and have some facts to support your concern. Several ADHD magazines, including CHADD's *ATTENTION,* ADDA's *Focus,* and *ADDitude,* have all carried articles on bullying. Audio tapes or videos may be available from CHADD's past conferences (www.chadd.org).

Talk with School Officials. You may need to talk with school officials and report the problem. Some school officials may not be very sensitive to the importance of this issue, so you may have to educate them.

Encourage School Officials to Implement a School-wide Bullying Prevention Program. The Olweus Bullying Prevention Program has been endorsed as a model program by both SAMSHA (Substance Abuse and Mental Health Administration) and the OJJDP (Office of Juvenile Justice and Delinquency Prevention). This program was initially developed in Norway by Dan Olweus, Ph.D., who is generally recognized as the world's leading authority on bully/victim problems. In the U.S., information on the Olweus program is available from Marlene Snyder, Ph.D., at Clemson University, www.clemson.edu/olweus; nobully@clemson.edu and from www.modelprograms.samhsa.gov.

Substance Abuse

Research done from two different perspectives—on children with ADHD and separately on substance abusers—sheds some light on the issue of drug abuse among teens with ADD or ADHD. 1) ADHD alone does not appear to put a teenager at greater risk for drug use than his non-ADHD peers. 2) However, ADHD in combination with high levels of aggression and hyperactivity—such as is found among those with conduct disorder or bipolar disorder—does.

Cigarettes are the substance most often abused by these teens, with alcohol a close second. Some teens with attention deficits may experiment occasionally with substances, while others may *abuse* them (use them to excess). Those who abuse substances usually do so as a misguided way to cope with other stresses of life, such as family problems, school problems, feeling like an "outsider," or hormonal changes in puberty. Teenagers don't abuse drugs to intentionally punish their family. Current thinking about causes of addiction are provided in Chapter 6.

Many experts think that teenagers with attention deficits may use alcohol or drugs to "self-medicate" to deal with school failure, hostile fights with parents, and anger directed at themselves. Drugs may help ease the pain of coping with the disorder. This may be especially true when the ADD or ADHD is undiagnosed or not properly treated.

If a teenager becomes addicted, he may not be able to stop even if he tries. Begging or telling him to stop is not going to work. Addiction involves both physical (the body craves the substance and experiences withdrawal symptoms) and psychological dependence (the teen thinks he needs the drug to function normally).

Addiction problems cause a range of contradictory feelings for parents: fear, rage, depression, and self-blame. Teenagers who are addicted need more love, understanding, and support at a time that it is most difficult for a family to give it. Parents may be so upset that they don't have any emotional energy left to give their teenager. If so, a counselor or Al-Anon or other groups may offer family members information and support regarding substance abuse problems.

Dr. Tim Wilens has made several important observations about substance addiction among young people with attention deficits:

1. The onset of substance abuse is earlier.
2. The period of transition from use to abuse is shorter.
3. The duration of the abuse is longer.
4. Alcohol use is basically the same for adults with and without ADHD
5. Marijuana use is higher for ADHD vs. non-ADHD adults.

FACTS ABOUT SPECIFIC DRUGS

Early experimentation occurs around the ages of 11 to 14. The first drugs that teens may use are most often tobacco, alcohol, and/or inhalants. Some may move on to marijuana or LSD and then may try club drugs like Ecstasy. The use of cocaine/crack and methamphetamine/ice is more likely after high school, due in part to the expense. It should be noted, too, that

Table 10-2   ADHD/Substance Abuse and Addiction Data

	ADHD	non-ADHD
Age of onset	19	22
Transition from use to abuse	1 year	3 years
Adults with substance abuse	52%	25%
Adults who smoke	75%	30%
Duration of substance abuse	12 years	5 years

heroin has made a major comeback. It may be added to marijuana and smoked (some users mistakenly think it's not as addictive smoked as it is when injected). This section covers a few key points about the substances teenagers most often abuse.

Cigarettes. Although alcohol, marijuana, cocaine, and heroin are probably the most common drugs that come to mind when substance abuse is mentioned, we tend to forget that nicotine in cigarettes is also highly addictive. Smoking is a very serious form of substance abuse, because it is so bad for your physical health. In addition, girls who smoke during pregnancy are two and a half times more like to have a child with ADHD. Unfortunately, teens tend to self-medicate with nicotine since it helps them stay more alert, concentrate and calms them down. Ironically, nicotine improves memory so well that one of the major drug companies is currently doing research on it in hopes of creating an effective treatment medication.

Inhalants. Use of inhalants can also be a problem, since they are readily available at home. Inhalants such as gasoline, aerosol sprays, airplane glue, nail polish remover, lighter fluid, and sprays for waterproofing fabrics may be used to get high. Inhaling too much may result in blurred vision and hallucinations or even permanent damage to the brain. Inhalants can be deadly.

Cocaine. One of the most dangerous drugs, cocaine poses special risks of addiction and possibly death. Parents should learn more about the drug and share that information with their teenager. Two points you may want to make include: "Cocaine damages your heart. The heart muscles lose their elasticity, possibly causing a heart attack. Second, cocaine permanently alters your brain chemistry. The full implications of this are not clear, but it seems to make it harder for teenagers to be happy doing normal things. They may have to take illegal drugs in order to feel good."

Cocaine comes in two major forms: a white powder, which is snorted through the nose, and crack cocaine, a more potent form, which is smoked. Some experts believe that three of four first-time users become instantly addicted to crack cocaine. The "high" from cocaine doesn't last very long, only fifteen minutes or so, and then the user "crashes" and becomes depressed. When teens stop taking the drug, they have withdrawal symptoms that include severe depression and craving for the drug. Withdrawal from crack cocaine may also cause shakiness, extreme anxiety, and fatigue.

Additional side effects of cocaine include rapid heart beat, possible high blood pressure, respiratory problems, and decreased appetite. Over time, the highs don't last as long. A tolerance to the drug may develop and more cocaine is needed to get high. John Belushi, the well-known comedian and actor, died of a cocaine and heroin overdose, and Len Bias, a star basketball player, died from a heart attack triggered by cocaine.

Heroin. Heroin is also extremely dangerous, but fortunately most teenagers seem to know this and avoid the drug. Withdrawal from heroin is very painful. Ultimately, people don't take heroin to get high but take it to keep from experiencing the terrible symptoms of withdrawal. Tolerance develops over a period of time and more heroin must be used to achieve the same high. The risk of HIV is also a major problem with any drugs like cocaine or heroin that may involve use of shared needles.

Marijuana. Marijuana or "pot" causes a psychological dependence—that is, smokers may feel as if they need to smoke it to feel good. Although it has not traditionally been thought of as being physically addictive, some substance abuse experts now believe differently. The marijuana cigarettes, or "joints," smoked today are significantly stronger than were smoked during earlier generations, and sometimes cause addiction problems. Only one "hit" or puff can make a teenager high for two to six hours. Parents and grandparents who grew up during the 1960s through the 80s may have a fairly tolerant attitude toward smoking marijuana. However, the more potent "pot" may pose problems for our teenagers.

Smoking marijuana can impair coordination, which may lead to accidents. Furthermore, smoking pot is more damaging to the lungs than smoking cigarettes. Marijuana impairs memory, reasoning, attention, and coordination. In one test of short-term memory, three objects are named such as cup, plate, and fork, and then the teenager is asked to remember them five minutes later. Many marijuana smokers are unable to remember these three simple items. Because short-term and working memory are already problems for many teenagers with attention deficits, the additional memory loss from smoking pot may cause more problems at school.

Stimulants. Although stimulants such as Ritalin can be abused, leading treatment professionals of ADD and ADHD state that they have not seen abuse of these medications among their patients. Teenagers who do abuse stimulants may crush and snort them. They may even hoard them and then binge—taking one after another so that they don't sleep and are even more hyperactive and aggressive. However, when teens take the medication as prescribed, they do not get a drug "high." In fact, most teenagers with attention deficits would prefer not to take their medication. Although teens with the prescription are not the ones who abuse the stimulant, they may, however, give or sell it to others. Often, the teen's intentions for giving Adderall or Concerta to a friend may be good. For example, they may occasionally give a friend with a suspected attention deficit one of their pills to "help" them study and do better in school. However, when teens want to help their friends, make sure they know that the best way to do so is to send them in for treatment.

Alcohol. After nicotine, alcohol is the illegal substance used most often by teenagers. A major concern about alcohol is that it greatly impairs the ability to drive. In fact, alcohol-related accidents are the leading cause of death among 15- to 24-year-olds, according to the Department of Health and Human Services. In addition, girls who both smoke and drink during pregnancy are five times more likely to have a child with ADHD. Facts about alcohol that you might want your teenager to know include:

1. one 12-ounce beer has as much alcohol as a 1.5-ounce shot of whiskey, a 5-ounce glass of wine, or a 12-ounce wine cooler;

2. you get drunk quicker when drinking on an empty stomach; food slows the absorption of alcohol;

3. it takes about two hours for the effects of the alcohol in one drink to wear off; you can't make it leave the body any faster.

Methamphetamine. Methamphetamine, Ecstasy, and Rohypnol are three drugs that parents hear about more often nowadays. Methamphetamine, also known as *speed,* gives the teen an intense "high energy" boost. Unfortunately, because it is often made from hazardous materials like battery acid, drain cleaner, lantern fuel, and antifreeze, there is a serious risk of brain damage. *Ecstasy* can cause both a "high" or "rush" and hallucinations. Long-term damage can be done to a teen's thinking and memory even from short-term use. Rohypnol or the "date rape" drug may sometimes be slipped into an unsuspecting teen's drink. This drug acts as a sedative that may later cause a type of amnesia.

STRATEGIES FOR PREVENTING SUBSTANCE ABUSE

According to researchers, these six strategies are thought to help prevent later substance abuse:

1. Educate about Drugs and Alcohol. The better informed your teen is, the more likely he'll steer clear of drugs. Since most children experiment with substances at young ages, the importance of early education is clear. In one study of high school students in general, the average age for first smoking cigarettes was 11, for drinking alcohol 12, and for smoking marijuana 13. NIDA has developed educational materials for children as young as second grade and a website just for teens (www.teensdrugabuse.gov).

Learn to Recognize Drugs Yourself. Many parents wouldn't recognize these drugs if they found them. You need to know what these substances look like. For example, one drug education instructor uses a small chunk of Ivory soap to show what crack cocaine looks like. Tiny 1/8 inch squares of paper, some plain and others with innocent looking blue stars or dots, may actually be "hits" of LSD. These squares are placed on the tongue and the LSD is absorbed into the body. The "hits" are usually kept in plastic bags or cellophane. Some websites may have pictures of these drugs so that you can recognize them.

Be aware of potential abuse of inhalants and keep them stored away. Or at least pay attention to how frequently they are used. Do the cans quickly become empty? Do you find them on the floor in your child's room? You may also notice drug paraphernalia such as a glass pipe for smoking cocaine, a "roach" clip (tweezers) for holding a marijuana cigarette, or cigarette papers for rolling marijuana "joints."

Use Fact Sheets. Fact sheets about the effects of alcohol and drugs are available from the sources listed later in this section. The fact sheets from *NIDA for Teens* are written specifically for adolescents. You could go over a fact sheet with your preteen or teenager and say, "It's important that you wait until you are twenty-one if you are going to drink. But I want to start educating you now. Here are some things you should know about alcohol. Look over this fact sheet. (Mention one or two facts.) Let me know if you have any questions."

Advise teens that if they use illegal drugs, there are some careers that they will not be able to pursue as an adult. For example, one young adult who wanted to go into law enforcement was told that some local agencies give polygraphs to recruits and that anyone who has used LSD even once will not be accepted under any circumstances.

Make Teens Aware of Dangers of Mixing Alcohol and Medication. A couple of things make it very difficult to determine the impact of taking stimulants and drinking. First, according to Dr. Theodore Mandelkorn, a Washington pediatrician, there is no research on the medical risks of mixing Ritalin and alcohol. Actually, if teenagers drink at night, stimulant medications are typically no longer in the blood stream. However, drinking excessively may result in increased impulsiv-

ity and risk taking, whether or not the teenager is taking medication. This, in turn, could lead your teenager into dangerous situations. Some teenagers are afraid of mixing their medications and alcohol, so they may give up their Adderall or Concerta rather than alcohol.

Clearly, excessive drinking in combination with certain antidepressants is dangerous because the effect of alcohol is intensified. One drink (or one marijuana cigarette) plus an antidepressant may produce the effects of two or three drinks. The combination of higher dosages of antidepressants, such as Tofranil, and excessive alcohol has the greatest potential for causing an accidental overdose. An overdose may result in an irregular heart beat, or the heart may actually stop beating.

Use Teachable Moments. TV programs, newspaper articles, or things that happen to your teen's friends may offer a springboard for discussion. "I read in the paper about a teenager at your high school who was injured in a car wreck caused by his friend who was driving drunk. Did you know them?" Pose hypothetical situations and ask how your teenager would handle them. "What would you have done? What would you do if you were riding with a friend who was drinking and driving?" You know your teen best, so trust your instincts about the best time and manner in which to present a teachable moment.

Don't Teach the Wrong Information. Potentially, there is a down side to drug education. Don't inadvertently teach your teenager how to use drugs. For example, don't name specific inhalants such as airplane glue or water repellents. Or don't talk about different ways to snort or smoke cocaine. Realistically, your teenager may be exposed already to much of this information from friends and the media. But, don't take a chance of adding to his knowledge of ways to abuse drugs.

Avoid Scare Tactics. Sometimes we describe the side effects and dangers of drugs in hopes of scaring our teenagers away from them. Be cautious when using this approach. Side effects of drugs that alarm us, as parents, may not scare our teenagers. For example, a teenager may not worry much about getting high and being impulsive when using cocaine. In addition, if you exaggerate the negative effects of drugs or alcohol, and your teenager finds out you're wrong, you lose credibility.

Make certain your information is accurate, so your child will trust your advice. Try contacting your local drug prevention program first. Librarians, media specialists, high school guidance counselors, or mental health center staff may also help you find appropriate materials on a variety of substances. The Drug Free

School Coordinator in each local school system should also be a helpful resource.

Reliable Information on Substance Abuse. These three organizations have extensive information that is easily available from their websites or free copies may also be mailed to families. Facts sheets about drugs and drug research studies are also available. Street names of drugs plus effects and health hazards are stated. Some facts sheets are written specifically for teens. Spanish translations of some documents are also available. For more information, contact:

> National Clearinghouse for Alcohol and Drug
>   Information (NCADI)
> 800-729-6686
> www.store.health.org
>
> National Institute on Drug Abuse (NIDA);
>   NIDA for Teens
> 301-443-1124
> www.nida.gov or
> www.teens.drugabuse.gov
>
> Al-Anon/Alateen Family Group
> 888-425-2666 (4al-anon)
> www.al-anon-alateen.org

Convey a Sense of Concern. It is important to convey a sense of concern and trust. For example, "I think it is important for you to have information about the effects of drug use. I believe once you have that information you will make responsible decisions. Some drugs like cocaine are highly addictive and can kill you. I love you so much and would be devastated if something bad happened to you. Please stay away from drugs. If you have any questions about drugs, ask me. I may not know the answers but we'll find out together."

2. Provide Supervision. Knowing where teenagers are and with whom is important. If they are going to a party, is it supervised? Ask whether adults will be present and tell them you will need to confirm it. If necessary, call and talk with the parents who will be chaperoning. "Hello. I'm Robert's mother. He said he has been invited to a party at your house. I was just calling to make certain that you or another adult will be supervising the party."

Establish Curfews. Curfews are still appropriate for high school students. Curfews should be reasonable and not too different from the majority of your child's friends. Obviously, older teens may be allowed to have later curfews. The main issue is not to allow your teen to stay out all night without any supervision. Late curfew may be allowed on special occasions. Greeting your teenager and his friends when they return home is often informative. In addition to listening to their adventures for the evening (if they are in a talkative mood), you can see for yourself if they are drinking or using drugs.

Establish Rules about Drinking and Driving. Approximately 60 percent of all teenage drivers (not just those with attention deficits) who die in car accidents have been drinking. The youngest drivers, age 16, are responsible for 40 percent of all teenage car accidents involving alcohol. Of even greater concern, Dr. Barkley reports that teens with ADHD drive worse than their peers even when they drink just a little alcohol.

Make it clear that drinking and driving will not be tolerated. Driving privileges will be taken away for several weeks. Typically, two to four weeks is an eternity for a teenager, especially one with ADD or ADHD. Include a statement about the consequences of drinking and driving if you draw up a contract regarding rules for driving.

3. Ensure Success in School. Chapters 11-14 provide guidance for identifying learning problems and ensuring that additional support and accommodations are provided if needed.

4. Seek Help to Control Aggression and Hyperactivity. Seek treatment for aggression and hyperactivity and ensure that they are brought under control. Medications are extremely effective in reducing aggressive, self-destructive behavior.

5. Keep Your Teen Busy with Positive Activities. Participating successfully in after school activities like sports, band, or clubs with positive peer role models should also help build confidence and self-esteem. Engaging your teen in community service such as volunteering at school or church often provides a much needed sense of self-worth and connection. *Additional strategies are provided in Chapter 8.*

6. Tactfully Influence Selection of Friends Who Are Positive Role Models. If you suspect that some of his friends are abusing drugs, encourage your teenager to do things with other friends who are not. Tactfully steering him away from friends who are a bad influence will be more effective than a volatile confrontation. Try the indirect approach first. If that is not successful, try making more direct statements.

"I've heard that your friend John uses drugs pretty heavily. If you hang around with him, your friends will think you are using drugs too. Your other friends may start to avoid you. Drugs are serious business. They're illegal, and penalties are stiff. If drugs are ever sold on our property, technically our house or car could be seized and sold by law enforcement. We cannot allow drug use in our home."

Sadly enough, these teenagers are sometimes rejected by the very friends you would like them to have. They then turn to less desirable friends to find acceptance and approval. To guard against this happening, keep them busy after school. For example, sign them up for after school sports or classes. Suggest that one or two friends join them for special activities. Or let them go to a parent's office and help after school. See if they will agree to stop seeing the undesirable friend for a while, maybe two weeks. During that time, try to get them interested in other friends or activities.

"Our son was shunned by one of his friends because he was hanging out with someone who used drugs. He learned that if you hang out with drug users, other people automatically assume you are also using drugs. He asked a friend to spend the night and was told he couldn't because he was going out of town. Well, as luck would have it, we ran into him at the mall the next day. The truth came out that he was avoiding my son because of possible drug use. In a way we were very lucky. It made a big impression on my son."

IF YOU SUSPECT YOUR TEEN IS ABUSING SUBSTANCES

1. Find an Approach That Works for Your Teen. If your teenager is using substances, you can try one of several approaches. Your main goal is for him to learn from his mistakes and to stop inappropriate behaviors. Sometimes different approaches are needed. If it is a first offense, you might try just talking to him. The simplified message, in your own words, should be: "Using drugs is not acceptable. Please stop. I love you and am afraid of what will happen to you if you become addicted to drugs. How can I help you?"

If problems continue, next use restrictions or loss of privileges (driving) to try to change behavior. Remember, reasonable consequences are most effective. If restrictions are too harsh, teens may react in a volatile manner and the conflict may get worse. They may drink even more to get back at you (or to drown their sorrow). Obviously, if they are out of control, you should seek professional treatment.

2. Should You Consider Drug Testing? If your teenager is experiencing serious problems, you might consider having a drug test done to see if drugs may be a factor in the misbehavior. There are pros and cons to testing. In deciding whether or not to seek drug testing, ask yourself a few important questions: First, what is the purpose of a drug test? Second, how will it help my teenager? And third, what will I do after I obtain the test results?

The American Academy of Pediatrics issued a policy statement in 1989 *opposing random drug testing* of teenagers. So if you can take action without the results of a drug test, try that approach first. If you suspect serious drug use, you can seek treatment from a substance abuse counselor without ever having your teenager undergo testing. Later, as part of their evaluation and treatment, they may do a physical examination, including a urine test, for drug use.

The primary advantage to testing is that it will confirm the presence of most, but not all, drugs. Also, if your teenager adamantly denies drug use and refuses treatment, a positive drug test may give you some leverage to push him into treatment. Then you can say with certainty, "You are using drugs. Your grades have dropped and I believe you need help."

One drawback is that teenagers the test may not pick up drug use. Ask the doctor what drugs will be identified by the test. Alcohol is excreted from the body rapidly and will not show up in most of these tests. Many people believe that LSD does not show up in drug tests. However LSD can be identified if the urine sample is handled properly. Evidence of cocaine use may only be present in the body for 24 to 48 hours. Marijuana is easier to pick up, since traces are present in the body for approximately two to four weeks.

"My son had a urine test for drugs as part of his annual physical exam. The test came back negative, but he later told me he had used LSD. Initially I felt guilty because I had 'wrongly suspected' my son. Boy, did I feel stupid when I realized he had been using LSD and the test didn't even pick it up."

The worst part of having your teen take a drug test is that it may further damage your relationship with him. One option is to simply ask if he is using drugs. He may say "yes," thus saving you the time and expense of a drug test, plus preserving some element of trust in the relationship. Sometimes teenagers will tell their counselor whether or not they are using drugs. If they are 18 or older, federal and state confidentiality laws forbid the counselor from sharing this information with anyone else, including you. Even though your curiosity may kill you, the good news is that at least they *are* in treatment.

3. Seek Treatment. Several treatment strategies, outlined in Chapter 7, are available, but just remember it will not be easy.

4. Contact Alcoholics Anonymous and Narcotics Anonymous Groups. Participating in AA or NA groups may be helpful. Unfortunately, you may have trouble finding a group specifically for adolescents. You might also encounter philosophical differences over treatment of attention deficits. Some members of AA and NA believe that alcohol and substance abuse should be treated without any medication. Since teenagers with ADD or ADHD benefit significantly from stimulant medication, this may be a major point of disagreement between your family and these organizations. Even if you ultimately decide not to send your teenager to AA or NA, however, you may still choose to attend Al-Anon for family support.

5. Consider the Message Your Own Behavior Sends. Many parents who drink alcohol socially may face a dilemma when deciding how to handle the problem of teenage drinking. A teenager who sees his parents drinking may think it is okay for him to drink too. Once your child reaches legal drinking age, it will be up to him to decide about using alcohol responsibly. Obviously, until that time, the best advice for parents is not to encourage your teenager to drink. *The Link Between ADD and Addiction,* by my colleague Wendy Richardson, MA, may provide helpful insights for understanding substance abuse.

According to Ari Russell, director of the GUIDE substance abuse prevention program, teenagers who are allowed to drink *regularly* at home are more likely to believe they can drink everywhere else too. She notes that successful lawsuits have been won against host parents who allowed underage teenagers to drink, even at social functions such as wedding receptions.

Parental opinions on this topic are diverse. Some parents see drinking moderately as a way to model responsible drinking habits. These parents may view underage experimentation with alcohol as an unavoidable, age-old "rite of passage." Others are totally against allowing their teen to have any alcohol.

"During the ages from 16 to 18, we have let our son have an occasional beer or glass of wine at home, provided he doesn't drive afterwards. We have an occasional social drink and are trying to teach our son that if he is going to drink to do it responsibly and in moderation. I believe it takes away the glamorous appeal of a forbidden activity and avoids unnecessary power struggles."

If teenagers are determined to drink alcohol, *they will,* regardless of their age and what you do. If they have to sneak off somewhere to drink, the consequences may be even worse. They may end up driving home under the influence of alcohol. Some parents prefer that teenagers drink at home, if they are going to drink. Parents can monitor their children's consumption and make certain they don't drive. In a few states, it is legal for teenagers to drink under the direct supervision of their parents in their own home. However, it is illegal for anyone else's child to drink there. Laws change, so don't just guess about what is true in your state; if you are curious, ask about laws in your state. A good starting point may be www.youthrights.org/dastatelist.shtml.

"We locked up our liquor in a cabinet when our son was in high school. This became a challenge for him. Sometime later he told us that he took the hinges off the cabinet door. I don't think he really drank that much but he couldn't resist the challenge of showing us that we couldn't control his behavior by locking the cabinet."

Key Strategies for Handling Substance Abuse

1. Don't be judgmental or preachy; remember, alcoholism and drug abuse are diseases.
2. Be willing to listen.
3. Voice your concerns about his drinking or drug use, but don't do it when he is under the influence.
4. Offer your help; get educational materials.
5. Be encouraging and positive if he tries to stop drinking or using drugs.

Sadly, addictions are incredibly powerful and difficult to break. Parents must understand that *relapse* is often part of the recovery process. The average number of tries to successfully achieve sobriety is eight attempts. So don't be discouraged if your teen attempts to stop and then stumbles. Don't give up.

Driving, Speeding Tickets, and Car Accidents

Perhaps because of their impulsiveness, daring, and difficulty anticipating the consequences of their actions, children with ADD or ADHD may attempt to drive a car long before they are legally old enough, sometimes as early as age two or three. Never leave a child with an attention deficit alone in a car with the motor running, even if you are going into a store for only a few minutes.

"Michael, our two-year-old son, found our car keys and tried to drive our car. He put the keys in the ignition and began turning the steering wheel back and forth. He turned the ignition just enough for the car to slip in gear. The car rolled backward down the driveway and hit a tree. Try explaining to your car insurance agent that the driver of the wrecked car was your two-year-old son."

According to Dr. Barkley's research, many teenagers with attention deficits do in fact drive before they are legally old enough to drive. When your child reaches his early teenage years, stay alert and pay attention to your car. Has it been moved? Have the windows been rolled down? Does the car smell like smoke from cigarettes? Clearly you need to keep car keys away from him.

More Speeding Tickets. In a survey of 16- to 22-year-olds, Dr. Barkley found that *teenagers with ADHD had almost four times as many traffic citations as non-ADHD teenagers.* Speeding was the most frequent traffic citation.

"Both of our sons have received numerous speeding tickets. Their lack of awareness and concentration, impulsiveness, and daring nature seem to result in their being oblivious to speed limits. Frequently, they don't see the police sitting with their radar guns until it is too late. One police officer reported that he had his blue lights on and was chasing another speeding car, when our son passed him at an even faster rate of speed. The first six months our son was driving, he was stopped seven times for speeding and 'totaled' his car. Obviously, I am worried sick about him."

Speeding tickets often continue to be problematic even in adulthood

"As a young adult, my father (undiagnosed ADHD) was stopped for speeding. When the highway patrolman sarcastically asked to see his 'pilot's license,' my father promptly handed his real airline pilot's license to him. The patrolman threw the pilot's license back in the car window, gave him a warning, and told him to get back home to Georgia. Later in his life, he was a respected attorney and judge."*

Impact of Executive Function Deficits on Speeding. Because of their disorganization, impaired sense of time, and failure to plan ahead, teens with ADHD are often running late which may also contribute to their speeding. Their impulsiveness and attraction to exciting, daring things may also play a role.

"Our daughter was explaining about the two broken headlights on her new car. 'Dad, the light was green. But the truck in front of me didn't go.'"

"When our son was 18, his driver's license was suspended because he received so many speeding tickets. He was devastated! He took a defensive driving course and his license was returned. Hopefully, he has learned an important lesson."

In addition, these teens, especially those with ADHD, may be more likely to drive aggressively, for example, tailgating, blowing their horn, flashing lights, making obscene gestures, cutting people off. Road rage may also be a problem.

Again, I emphasize, not all teenagers with ADD or ADHD are alike. Some teenagers with this disorder are very cautious drivers and do not speed. However, they still may have problems paying attention to stoplights and concentrating on their driving unless they are on their medication.

"Before Shawn's ADD was diagnosed, we were so worried about his concentration that we wouldn't let him get his learner's permit for a year. When he hasn't taken his medicine, he'll stop at green lights, go through red lights, weave from side to side of the road. We don't worry about speeding; we worry about his inattention. With the medicine, he is a very good driver.

"Sometimes Shawn starts driving too soon before his medicine has taken effect. We have to remind him to be careful and wait until the car is stopped to turn the radio off or on, turn up the volume, or change stations."

More Accidents. Because teenagers with attention deficits have more difficulty concentrating and paying attention, they may be more likely to have car accidents than teenagers who don't have the disorder. According to Dr. Barkley's survey, *teenagers with ADHD had four times as many car wrecks and were more than seven times as likely to have had a second accident.* In addition, they were more than four times as likely to be at fault in the accident. The cost of damages was also more than twice as high as for non-ADHD drivers. Inattention was the most common reason given for the accident. Dr. Barkley has also found that they are less likely to use good driving habits. They are also four times more likely to have their license suspended (21.9 percent). Unfortunately, risk-taking behavior in an automobile can be fatal.

"The issue of safety was absolutely nonnegotiable where Jeremy was concerned. When he got his learner's permit, he took the family car without permission and drove off the side of a mountain. I went to the Department of Motor Vehicles and pulled his learner's permit immediately. I didn't argue about it; I just did it. He didn't drive for two more years and when he finally did, he totaled our car with our three-week-old son in it. I knew then I had done the right thing to have his license revoked. The consequences of poor driving are just too serious to take lightly."

"Our son has had two major wrecks in the three years he has been driving. He was driving about thirty miles an hour when he hit a solid brick mailbox in our neighborhood and totaled the car. His medication hadn't taken effect yet. He leaned down to pick up something from the floorboard and hit the mailbox. His second wreck occurred during a terrible rain storm. He hydroplaned across three lanes of traffic, barely missing an eighteen-wheel truck and struck the guardrail head-on. He had on his seatbelt and walked away without a scratch. The good Lord was watching over him that day. We were lucky."

Send to Driver Training. Some states require that teenagers take driver education training or a defensive driving course before they can be licensed. If this is not required in your state, consider sending your teen for training anyway. Specialized training should be very informative and help improve your teen's driving skills. Some insurance companies discount their premiums for teenagers who have completed such training.

Provide Extended Supervision. Some states require that a student with a learner's permit must drive a minimum of 50 hours under the supervision of an adult driver. Consider doing this even if it is not a state requirement.

Try a Video Driving Game. "Streetwise," a video game that was created to help improve teen driving skills, is available from Daimler Chrysler at www.road-readyteens.org. This game may appeal to teens since it was developed by a leading video game maker.

Gradually Increase Driving Privileges. As your teen moves from a learner's permit to a driver's license and drives responsibly, gradually increase his driving privileges. You might allow him to drive only during the day during good weather for a couple of months. If there are no problems, he can graduate to driving some at night, in good weather. Next, let him move to driving during the day in bad weather, first with a parent and then on his own. He can then drive at night in bad weather. This provides more practice time to gain experience driving in increasingly difficult situations.

Purchase a Slow "Tank." If you buy a car for your teenager, consider a larger, heavier car that offers more protection in the event of an accident. For some teenagers, a pickup truck may be the perfect choice. Instead of having six or eight people crammed into a car for the teenaged driver to impress, only one or two passengers can ride in the cab. Purchasing a car with a four- or six-cylinder engine may also decrease the risk of speeding. Some cars with smaller engines, however, can achieve a high rate of speed very quickly. So, make an informed decision.

Consider Taking Medication When Driving. According to Dr. Barkley's research, teens' driving skills do improve when they are taking a stimulant medication. If you anticipate a problem with accidents or speeding tickets, or if your teenager has already received several tickets, ask your physician about taking Strattera or a short-acting medication

(Ritalin, Focalin, or Dexedrine) at 6:00 or 7:00 in the evening when he drives on the weekend. If taken at 7:00, these medicines should wear off by 11:00 or so. This runs counter to the general medical advice not to take medication too late in the day to avoid sleep problems. However, most teenagers stay up late on weekends anyway, so sleep difficulties caused by taking one of these medications should not be a major problem. Medication should help improve their concentration and reduce impulsiveness.

Use Positive Incentives to Avoid Problems. If you want to try positive incentives for your teen, remember that privileges must be given immediately, within a week or so to be effective. You must figure out what motivates your teen and then use that as part of a reward. For example, you might say, "Each week that you drive without getting a ticket, I will give you $5 extra in your allowance."

"One incentive I tried was to say, if he could drive for a whole year without getting a ticket, I would pay him $200. I figured we'd save at least that much in insurance costs. Unfortunately, it didn't work—the reward was too far in the future."

Develop a Contract for Driving. You may want to develop a contract clearly stating rules for driving. A model contract is included in Appendix 2. Include statements about your teenager's responsibilities: seatbelt use, maintenance, who will pay for gas and insurance, few or no friends riding with him, who else may drive your car, and when to call for help. Getting your teen to fulfill the contract can be difficult; frequent reminders may be needed. For example, although wearing a seatbelt is critical, only about a third of all high school drivers wear them. Students Against Driving Drunk (SADD) included these paragraphs in their model contract:

> "Teenager: I agree to call you for advice and/or transportation at any hour, from any place, if I am ever in a situation where I have been drinking or a friend or date who is driving me has been drinking."

> "Parent: I agree to come and get you at any hour, any place, no questions asked and no arguments at that time, or I will pay for a taxi to bring you home safely. I expect we would discuss this issue at a later time."

If your teenager is responsible and you don't think he will use too much gas when driving, you may not need to set limits on miles driven. However, if gas use is excessive or you anticipate that it could be, you might give a monthly gas allowance. If he exceeds the allowance, he or his friends must pay for gas themselves.

For More Information. Read *AD/HD and Driving: A Guide for Parents of Teens with AD/HD* by Marlene Snyder, Ph.D. This helpful book gives twenty strategies for helping your child be a safer driver. Tips address issues like supervision, graduated privileges, and earning driving time. Visit www.whitefishconsultants.com for more information.

DEALING WITH SPEEDING TICKETS

Ideally, through careful training, supervision, and having the teen take medication while driving, parents will be able to avoid major driving-related problems. Obviously, if your teen receives speeding tickets or has accidents, you must impose consequences immediately if they are to be effective.

Teens with attention deficits may get tickets for a variety of different reasons: some they deserve and some are more by chance. Our teens do drive faster and have more wrecks. They are often late and may speed because they are trying to make up time. On the other hand, they may get more tickets by virtue of where they live. Larger cities often rely on revenue from speeding tickets. Teens are more likely to drive late in the evenings, especially on weekends and to drive cars that have been "souped" up and are attention getters. Unfortunately, the car gets the attention of law enforcement too.

In contrast, the teen in a smaller town may know the police or deputies and may be more likely to get a warning instead of a ticket. Some girls may be less likely to be given a ticket when they are stopped for speeding by male police officers. Of course, you must keep in mind that you are legally liable for any accident or injuries caused by your teen. That is a sobering and frightening thought. So regardless, if speeding tickets become a problem, here are several strategies to try:

Consider Medication. As suggested in the preceding section, hopefully the teen is taking his medication regularly and it is working effectively.

Identify the High Risk Time of Day. Determine whether your teenager receives speeding tickets during the same time period. Then develop a plan to deal with the problem. For example, consider letting a friend drive during this time or have him take medication when driving.

> *We warned our son that his 'danger zone' (getting tickets) was between 10:00 P.M. and midnight on Friday and Saturday nights when his medication had worn off. We encouraged him to let his girlfriend drive during those hours."*

Impose Consequences. Tell your teenager in advance what the consequences for speeding tickets will be and stick to it. "If you get a speeding ticket, you will have to pay for it." Or, limit the teen's driving privileges based upon the severity of the ticket.

1. Your teen can drive only with a parent.
2. He can drive only to school and come straight home.
3. You take driving privileges away for a week or more.

State the consequence in the contract. If your child accumulates many tickets, reassess the consequences you are using. Consequences are more effective if they occur soon after an offense.

Stricter State Laws Are Addressing Speeding Teens. Parents may not have to impose consequences; the state may do it for them. Recently, many states have enacted stricter laws aimed at curtailing teen speeding. In Georgia, if you are 18 or younger and receive even one ticket, your driver's license will be suspended for 6 months and you have to take a class. If there is a second ticket, the license will be taken away for a year. Teens are not allowed to drive from midnight to 6 a.m. In addition, they can't have more than three people in the car if they are all under 21.

These new laws may help keep your teen safe but they may also create major conflict between parents and teens. Parents are then faced with enforcing stiff punishments imposed by state law. Unfortunately, a few parents may then face an angry, irate teen who sneaks and drives in spite of having a suspended license. Or worse yet, knowing his license will be suspended, the teen may impulsively try to outrun the police.

Basically, state action takes control of this issue out of the parents' hands. Our teens quickly tell us about the unfair aspects of these laws; teens receive stiffer consequences than adults for committing the same offenses. Unfortunately, being charged with driving with a suspended license may result in unpleasant contact with the juvenile justice system. Regrettably, a few of our teens will not learn easily from these puni-

tive consequences from the court and may drive again, with a suspended license.

Consider a Computer Monitor. Davis Instruments, a California company, has invented a computer program known as *DriveRight* that can record your teen's speed. The device records their highest speeds, date, and time for up to ten days. This information can be printed out or you can view it on the screen in the car. An optional beeper that squeals is also available when the driver exceeds a certain speed limit. Visit www.driveright.cc for more information.

Is a Speed Governor a Viable Option? Another option that some parents may consider is installing a speed governor, a mechanism that limits the car's top speed. Of course, there are some serous risks involved. If your teenager is passing someone and needs additional speed because of an oncoming car, he could have a disastrous wreck.

Teach Your Teen Ways to Avoid Being Late. As you know, our teens have an impaired sense of time, including problems with time estimation, and are often late. There are several excellent time management tips in our book *A Bird's-Eye View* that may help teens allow adequate time for arriving promptly so they won't have to speed.

> *I suspect that there were several reasons my son was always getting speeding tickets: he was so disorganized, has an impaired sense of time, was always late, and didn't allow enough time to get to his final destination."*

Ride with a Police Officer. One set of parents elected to use a somewhat unusual approach. They allowed their teenager to ride on duty with a police officer so he could see the dangers of speeding from another perspective. Although this arrangement can be a good learning experience, it is also potentially dangerous for the teenager. Liability issues may also make most police departments reluctant to allow teenagers to ride on duty with them.

> *Our son was stopped twice in one week for speeding by the same police officer. The officer was very kind and came to our home to talk to us. We suggested that our son ride on patrol with him one night. We hoped he would see the potential danger of speeding. My son established a good rapport with the officer and saw*

him as a human being, not just a man in a uniform. He developed a new respect for the police. Previously, he was negative toward them because he had been stopped for speeding several times. He really seemed to want to curb his speed. One night things got a little too exciting while they were on patrol. They were the first car on the scene to investigate a stabbing at a local fast food restaurant."

Visit a Spinal Center. A few parents have taken their teen to visit a treatment center to talk with other young people who have driven carelessly and been paralyzed. You may even consider taking your preteen for a visit of this sort well before he is old enough to drive.

Have Your Teenager Pay for His Own Insurance. If teenagers have to pay for part or all of their own insurance, they will definitely experience the natural consequences of getting speeding tickets or having accidents. If they get several tickets, they may not be able to afford the insurance. If you pay for their insurance, consider having them pay for any rate increases. Also, remind them that once they are out of school they will have to pay for their own insurance.

"We found that this consequence was not very effective. The consequences were too far removed in time from the speeding ticket. By the time we were notified of the insurance increase, it was nearly a year after he received the ticket. Plus, my husband had received a ticket and we weren't certain who really caused the rate increase."

Warn Your Teen That Insurance May Be Canceled or Be Cost Prohibitive. If your teenager has a major accident, plus has received several speeding tickets, insurance costs may be prohibitive. Insurance companies may even cancel the family's insurance or continue the policy for the parents while refusing to reinsure the teenager. If this happens, insurance coverage to protect the parents' assets in the event of a lawsuit may be purchased from a high-risk pool, but will be more expensive. Discussing the potential consequences of a poor driving record for you and your teenager in advance may be of some help.

"We were notified that our insurance company would no longer provide automobile insurance coverage for our son because he had so many speeding tickets. We had to sign an agreement that he couldn't drive our car at all. We were able to obtain coverage for our son (liability: $50,000 per person, $100,000 per accident) in a high-risk pool for approximately $3,000 annually."

IF YOU DECIDE TO GO TO COURT

Here are a few tips if your teen must go to court for a traffic ticket. There may be an occasion when you think it is in your teen's best interests to go to court and appeal the ticket. You may elect for just the two of you to go or you may hire an attorney. In addition, please read the section regarding brushes with the law. Suggestions are given for ways to dress, mentally prepare, and to address the judge. Furthermore, it is usually better for you to have implemented a consequence before you go to court because the judge will probably ask you what you have done.

Check Tire Size and Speedometer. If teens don't think they were speeding when they were given a ticket, they may be right. Have the speedometer checked; it may not be accurate. Some teenagers with attention deficits love to customize their cars and trucks. Sometimes they buy oversized tires. Larger tires will cause the speedometer to read incorrectly, so the teenager will actually be driving faster than the speedometer shows. An authorized speedometer repair service can fix any problems with the speedometer and issue a statement about any speedometer error.

Appeal the Speeding Ticket. If you or your teen obtains a certified statement from the repair service, you can usually appeal a speeding ticket in traffic court...once. The judge's response will vary. He may dismiss tickets or allow the teen to plead guilty to a lower rate of speed. Pleading guilty to a lower rate of speed may eliminate the addition of any points to his driving record. But he will still probably have to pay a fine.

Plead Nolo Contendere. Sometimes a teenager cited for a traffic violation may plead *nolo contendere* in court, which means, "I agree to pay the fine, but I am not admitting my guilt." In some states, if a nolo plea is entered, no points are added to the driving record. However, a state may limit use of nolo pleas to only once every five years or so, so use this option wisely. If you believe your teenager's driving skills are improving and he or she should be allowed to drive, you may want to consider this option. Just because your teen pleads nolo doesn't mean you condone or will not punish your child.

Take a Defensive Driving Course. In some states, teenagers may take a defensive driving course and have the number of points on their driving record reduced. If appropriate, keep up with your teen's record of points so he or she can take the class and reduce the points before the license is actually suspended.

Consider Hiring an Attorney. For more serious offenses you may wish to hire an attorney. Do your homework so you get someone who carefully prepares and is effective in court. You may visit juvenile court before your teen's court date and see if there are any attorneys there who seem to be especially competent and have a good relationship with the court.

"When our son was about to lose his license, we hired an attorney. He was in college then and had been driving much better of late but his poor driving record from his younger teenage years finally caught up with him. The attorney was also a part-time traffic court judge in a neighboring county and knew the traffic laws cold. He also knew to check things like seeing if the highway patrolman's radar gun had been properly certified."

Driving Problems Are a Lifelong Challenge. Unfortunately, experts tell us that poor driving records that include speeding tickets and license suspensions are a lifelong problem for many people with attention deficits. It is not just a problem of adolescence. So teach your teen well now. Although that is no guarantee that it will solve driving problems, at least you can help him survive his adolescence. Teach him tips for prompting himself not to speed and especially to take his medication when driving.

Sexual Behavior

To date, Dr. Russell Barkley is one of the few researchers who has actually gathered data on sexual activity among teens with ADHD. His results are of serious concern. To begin with, our teens begin having sex a year earlier than their peers and they have more partners. Their relationships are also shorter in duration. In addition, they are less likely to use contraceptives, more likely to have a sexually transmitted disease, or be involved in a pregnancy. The teens in Barkley's study had a pregnancy rate 9 times higher than their peers. Fifteen of the 21 girls in the study (68 percent) had had a child by the age of 19. These girls were more likely to use poor judgment or experience sexual abuse. However, keep in mind that the teenagers in this study typically had more serious problems than the average teen with ADHD. Unfortunately, the sexual behavior of teenagers with attention deficits may be influenced by

their impulsivity, tendency to take risks, or excessive alcohol or drug use.

"I was really worried when Jeff's girlfriend got pregnant. I know what the statistics are and I was so afraid that the baby might have a really bad case of ADHD or bipolar. At first, he told her he wanted to give it up for adoption. He also said that he wasn't ready to be a dad. He even told her that they were finished if she kept the baby.

"I had no clue they were going to keep the baby until the day he was born. My son called and simply said, "He's cute. We're going to keep him." Of course, I worry about them all the time. When the baby was born, they had no jobs, no car, and no place to live. Thankfully, things are better now.

"Unbelievably, my grandson has been one of the greatest joys of my life. Jeff's son is a beautiful vision of what my hopes and dreams were for him as a baby. So far he has been a wonderful, happy baby and looks perfectly normal."

According to the Youth Risk Behavior study by the CDC, 45.6 percent of all high school students have engaged in sexual intercourse. Roughly 7 percent had sexual intercourse for the first time before age 13. Fourteen percent of the teens in the CDC study had sex with 4 or more partners within the last 3 months. When drugs or alcohol are combined with these characteristics, girls with ADD or ADHD may be more likely to put themselves in dangerous situations which could result in rape or assault. Rape brings not only the emotional trauma of the rape itself but also the risk of AIDS.

"I was shocked when my son told me he was only 12 years old the first time he engaged in sex with a girl."

There is some good news in the most recent CDC data. The number of young people who are engaging in sexual relationships dropped by roughly 9 percent between 1991 and 2001. There has also been a drop in the number of teens who have multiple sex partners.

Provide Appropriate Sex Education. It is your responsibility to ensure that your teenager receives appropriate sex education. Do not assume that someone else will teach your teen what he needs to know about sexual relationships. The emergence of AIDS is forcing us as parents to change the way we approach sex education with our children, especially impulsive teenagers with attention deficits. Being sexually active in this day and age can be deadly. We can no longer permit our children to learn about sex from their friends and through experimentation.

Sexual behavior is such an emotionally charged issue, each family will approach it differently. You should select an approach to teaching about sexual issues that you feel comfortable with and that is consistent with your values.

Since teens with attention deficits may experiment early, most will need information early in their teenage years. Actually, the foundation of sex education really begins well before the teenage years. In fact, one resource suggests that the first "big talk" should occur around age 9. During early adolescence, more specific information about sexual intercourse, birth control, and protection from disease may be provided. However, if you have a teenager and are just now getting started teaching sex education, that's okay too. Better now than never.

Arrange for a Sex Education Class. Children and teenagers are often embarrassed to talk about sex with their parents. So they may be more receptive to taking a class at their church, synagogue, or school. Even then, they may feel more comfortable if they are allowed to write down their questions rather than ask them aloud. If your teen does attend a class, you should still provide reading material at home, including a reference book, and be available to answer questions.

The availability of good sex education programs varies across the country. Some areas offer only cursory sex education. Some programs place an emphasis on responsible decision-making skills, including identifying choices, weighing decisions, and evaluating outcomes. Other programs have older teens talk with younger ones to help them withstand peer pressure to have sex. These teens serve as role models who are attractive and popular yet are not sexually active.

Provide Reading Materials. Make reference materials available to your teenager. This way he or she can look things up in a book without having to ask questions. Several books that may be helpful are listed in Resources. You could also suggest that your teen write down any questions he has and give them to you. This may be a less embarrassing way to handle sensitive sexual questions.

Local churches, synagogues, chapters of the Red Cross, AIDS organizations, Planned Parenthood, or health departments have information and materials to help educate about sexual issues. Libraries, too, often have good sex education materials.

Various sites on the Internet provide helpful resources. The philosophy behind these sites varies. Some are what may be termed conservative and advocate abstinence. Others are more liberal and may provide education on contraception. Visit these sites yourself and select the one you find most helpful. Some representative websites are listed in the Resources.

Discuss Values Related to Sexual Relationships. If you have a comfortable relationship with your teenager, discuss important elements of sexual relationships with him. Basic anatomical differences between men and women are often taught in biology or science classes. However, other important issues must be addressed at home or through classes: love, commitment, making decisions, responsible relationships, sexual intercourse, birth control, protection from disease, and pregnancy. Sometimes it is nice to have spontaneous discussions on these topics. Again, teachable moments are important. For example, a TV program, newspaper article, or a family discussion may provide an opportunity to share your values regarding sexual relationships and ask what your teen thinks about the topic.

Any discussion should be a two-way, open exchange of information. Listen to your teenager's opinions. If you disagree, avoid arguing or putting him down. His ideas may change with time, but for now may be different from yours. Briefly, explain the reason for your beliefs. You may well be influencing his thinking, although he may not show it at the time.

Avoid Tempting Your Teenager. You and your teenager may develop rules for having someone of the opposite sex come for a visit. For example, the couple cannot be home alone. When you are home, however, his friends are always welcome. Know where your teenager is going and whether or not the activity will be supervised.

Avoid Overreacting. If you come home and find your teenager involved in heavy kissing and petting, don't jump to the conclusion that he or she has had sexual intercourse. Try not to overreact and attack your teen. ("You're promiscuous. You'd have sex with anything that moves.") If parents do so and impose a harsh punishment, teenagers may respond just as angrily. They may think, "Since my mother already thinks I'm having sex, I may as well go ahead and do it." A more helpful approach may be an open discussion and an agreement on rules regarding being at home without parental supervision.

Teach Your Teen It's Okay to Say No. Knowing the reasons why teenagers have sex may help you prepare your teen to say no to sexual activity. "You may be pressured by your friends to be sexually active before you are ready. You might get a lot of peer pressure ('Everyone is doing it'). Or you might want to be popular or be curious about what it's like. Someone might use guilt ('I've spent a lot of money on you') or make threats ('I won't date you anymore unless you have sex with me'). You may even feel as if you need to rebel against Dad and me because we're too strict. Anticipate these pressures and try to figure out in advance how you will respond to them. If you like, I'll help you figure out what to say."

Emphasize that it is okay to say no. Explain that people may try to pressure him into being sexually active by bragging about their own "manly" conquests, calling him names, saying he must be gay, or daring him. According to Dr. Marion Howard, there are several steps your teenager may take: 1) Make a direct statement. "No. I don't want to do that." 2) Turn the pressure around by asking, "Why are you trying to pressure me into doing something I don't want to do?" 3) Put them on the defensive by saying "You're making me angry by pressuring me to do something I don't want to do." 4) If the pressure continues, leave or ask to be taken home.

Discuss the Impact of Pregnancy. You may want to talk with your teenager about the responsibilities of being a parent. Since teens with attention deficits tend to think in concrete terms rather than abstract ones, discuss the impact in specific details. Look for a teachable moment when the issue of pregnancy comes up. You might ask, "What would you do if your girlfriend (or you) were pregnant like her friend Sasha? How would your life change?" After your teen responds, share a few more ideas. For example, "Have you thought about how much time a baby will take? You don't sleep very well because they wake up every three or four hours at night. Babies are totally helpless. You have to feed them, give them a bath, change their diapers, put on their clothes, and take them to the doctor. You can't go out at night without getting a babysitter. Babies are expensive too. The hospital and doctor costs of having a baby range from $3,000 to $10,000, or even more. You have to buy them clothes, diapers, food, medicine, and pay for child care."

For boys you could also add, "If your girlfriend gets pregnant, you may have to pay $100 to $200 a month child support." For girls, "Your body changes, you can't wear your clothes, your friends may avoid being with you, and you can't go out unless you find a babysitter. Having a child is wonderful, but you will be able to handle it better when you are older, in love, married, and you and your spouse want children."

"One teenage father with ADD had to pay forty dollars a week child support while he was in high school. After he graduated from high school, he had to pay eighty dollars a week. Three hundred twenty dollars a month is a lot for a teenager to have to earn. He had to work while he went to college to pay child support."

"A teacher in one sex education class had her students carry around an uncooked egg for a week so they would begin to appreciate just how fragile and time consuming a baby could be. Students had certain rules to follow about how to care for it, feed it, and when they could leave it alone."

Consider Birth Control. If you learn that your teenager is sexually active, you will have to struggle with the decision of whether to assist in obtaining birth control supplies. Although this may conflict with your family values, the alternatives risks, pregnancy or AIDS, are frightening. If your daughter does take birth control pills, she will probably need help remembering to take them.

Educate about the Risks of Unprotected Sex. Sexually transmitted diseases (STDs), especially AIDS, pose tremendous health risks for anyone who is sexually active. Presently, slightly less than 1 percent of the population has AIDS. It is the seventh leading cause of death among teenagers. However, this low percentage rate is misleading, since a teenager who is exposed to AIDS when he is 13 will not show symptoms for 8 to 10 years, at age 21 or 22. Other diseases such as syphilis, gonorrhea, genital warts, herpes, and chlamydia can cause serious problems. Most of these diseases show symptoms and respond to treatment. However, chlamydia does not have any symptoms and, untreated, can cause infertility. Herpes cannot be cured, but is not fatal.

Some AIDS information you may want to share with your teenager includes: "AIDS is caused by the human immunodeficiency virus, HIV, which weakens the immune system. As a result, the body is unable to fight off disease and infection. AIDS is spread through the exchange of body fluids (blood, semen, vaginal secretions, saliva, tears, urine). The two most common ways the virus is passed from one person to another is unprotected sexual intercourse, both vaginal and anal, and blood on shared needles used for illegal drugs. You can't get AIDS from coughs, shaking hands, or toilet seats. People who have AIDS don't show symptoms for several years so you can't tell by just looking at someone whether or not they have AIDS. Furthermore, a person may not even know he has AIDS, and may unknowingly give it to you. Anyone can get AIDS even if it's their first time to have sex."

AIDS can strike anyone regardless of age or wealth. Remember how stunned everyone was to learn that Magic Johnson, one of the greatest basketball players of all times, had the HIV virus. Although he had not developed any obvious symptoms of AIDS, he retired from playing basketball. The CDC has a toll-free telephone hotline to answer your questions about AIDS: 1-800-342-AIDS.

Suicide Risk

According to the CDC, suicide is the third leading cause of death among young people between the ages of 15 and 24. Among this age group, approximately 3,854 or 0.6 percent committed suicide in 2001. The percentage of teens who attempted suicide was 8.8 percent. A study of ADHD found that the number of youngsters with ADHD in a clinical sample who *attempted* suicide (10 percent) was higher than for youngsters without the disorder. In this study, none of the children without ADHD attempted suicide. As explained earlier, research statistics on ADHD tend to be higher since they are collected on children in clinical samples with more serious problems. However, if even a 5 percent rate is accurate, the high risk of suicide for children with attention deficits is of serious concern.

Suicidal thoughts and planning among all high school students are alarmingly common. Approximately 19 percent in the CDC study had thought seriously about committing suicide. Roughly 15 percent have actually gone so far as to develop a plan. According to the Surgeon General's Report on Children's Mental Health, girls are twice as likely as boys to attempt suicide, but four times as many boys die as a result of their attempts. Boys tend to use more lethal methods, such as guns, to attempt suicide. However, suicide rates among females are starting to change since girls are also using more lethal methods. Guns account for 60 percent of teen suicides.

Hispanic, Native American, and Alaska Native youths are at a proportionally higher risk to attempt suicide. However, in actual numbers, white male teens, primarily from middle to upper-middle class families, constitute the majority of all teenage suicides.

Although teenage suicides more than tripled between the late 1950s and early 1990s, here is some good news: the percentages for both suicides and homicides have actually dropped over the last ten years. Hopefully that means that some of the suicide prevention efforts are paying off.

WHY DO TEENS CONSIDER SUICIDE?

When we look at the fact that 3,854 young people were so distraught during 2001 that they committed suicide, we must ask ourselves why? Perhaps our achievement-oriented, highly competitive society has contributed to these grim statistics. Failure and lack of achievement is very painful for adolescents with attention deficits. Even when they appear indifferent, most desperately want to succeed. Some of these teenagers may develop feelings of hopelessness about their ability to be successful. They may think, "If I'm having such a difficult time passing high school classes, how can I ever succeed in college or life?"

Key stress factors that may lead a teenager to consider suicide include: depression, feeling alienated from the family, loss of a parent (death or divorce), feelings of hopelessness about the future, feelings of worthlessness, and employment problems. Other factors that may trigger an attempt include: loneliness, breaking up with a girlfriend or boyfriend, a fight with parents, pressure to succeed at school, receiving bad grades, failure in academics or athletics, not getting accepted into college, poor health, or physical awkwardness.

Teenagers who consider suicide tend to have low self-esteem and feel unworthy, abandoned, and unloved. They are deeply angry with themselves and those around them. Their depression, manifested through delinquency, drug addiction, and alcoholism, may actually be a "cry for help" and an indicator of suicidal risk. Researchers from the CDC were surprised to learn that many teens who attempted suicide were not depressed but rather were angry, in trouble, or feeling hurt over some rejection.

Other factors may also contribute to suicidal risk. According to the American Psychiatric Association, 53 percent of all adolescent suicide victims used drugs or alcohol just before they died. Some teenagers may seem to have a "death wish" by drinking excessively and speeding. The availability of guns also increases the risk of suicide. Suicides are five times more likely to occur in homes where guns are present. Teenagers who are gay are at greater risk for suicide attempts. While only 10 percent of all teens are gay, they account for 30 percent of adolescent suicides. For girls, the end of their first sexual relationship is a high risk time for suicidal thoughts.

To add to these risks, teenagers with attention deficits tend to be more emotional and impulsive. Their impulsivity, risk-taking behavior, and failure to recognize the consequences of their actions may also increase the risk of having a suicide attempt or serious accident.

Suicide is a very difficult, emotional topic to discuss. No parent wants to think that his teenager might attempt suicide. But, parents must be alert and watch for signs of serious depression or comments that teens are wishing they were dead or want to kill themselves. Most people who are considering suicide give warnings about their intentions. Table 10-3 shows potential warning signals, as listed by the American Academy of Child and Adolescent Psychiatry (AACAP).

Other possible indicators include experiencing a recent loss such as the death of a family member, break-up with girlfriend or boyfriend, moving away from friends, poor health, or loss of respect. Parents should also take note if their teen is experiencing several of these symptoms plus makes an unusual purchase such as a gun, knife, or rope. Obviously, parents should be vigilant if their teen has made a previous suicide attempt.

Take All Suicidal Statements Seriously. AACAP fact sheets emphasize *that any comment by teenagers that they are going to kill themselves or want to commit suicide should be taken seriously.* It is also critical to know that someone who has been depressed for a long time but suddenly no longer seems depressed may, in fact, have decided to commit suicide. The sudden mood change may be a warning sign that such a decision has been made.

Frequently, teenagers are undecided about living or dying. In some ways it is a form of Russian roulette. They leave it up to fate or others to save them. Asking questions and providing supervision, when warning signals are observed, could save their lives.

Ask about Suicidal Thoughts. "You seem really stressed out. Are you okay? Tell me what's going on." If you are concerned, ask your teenager straight out, "Are you considering suicide?" Or, "Are you thinking of harming yourself?" Asking these questions provides assurance that somebody cares and gives teens the opportunity to talk about their problems.

Listening Is Critical. Listen to what your teenager has to say. Assure him that you love him and that you will help him work through this difficult time. Listening and responding to him in a loving way are the two most important things you can do. Don't argue, criticize, or make him feel guilty. Offer support but don't make judgmental comments. Don't say, "Things are not as bad as you think." Or, "Things could be worse." If you listen to what he says, often he will tell you why he wants to commit suicide. You won't have to ask. If he won't talk or denies he is considering suicide, talk in confidence with one of his friends. Ask if they have observed any of the warning signs of suicide included in Table 10-3.

Table 10-3 Warning Signs of Suicide Risk

- Change in eating or sleeping habits
- Withdrawal from friends, family, and regular activities
- Violent actions, rebellious behavior, or running away
- Drug and alcohol use
- Unusual neglect of personal appearance
- Marked personality change
- Persistent boredom or difficulty concentrating
- A decline in the quality of schoolwork
- Frequent complaints about physical symptoms, often related to emotions, such as stomachaches, headaches, fatigue, etc.
- Loss of interest in pleasurable activities
- Not tolerating praise or rewards
- Complaining of being a bad person or feeling "rotten inside"
- Giving verbal hints with statement such as: "I won't be a problem for you much longer," "Nothing matters," "It's no use," and "I won't see you again."
- Putting his or her affairs in order, for example giving away favorite possessions, cleaning his or her room, throwing away important belongings, etc.
- Becoming suddenly cheerful after a period of depression
- Having signs of psychosis (hallucinations or bizarre thoughts)

Show Concern and Affection. Don't be afraid to show your child love and affection during this time. Hug him, pat him on the shoulder, hold his hand if it seems appropriate. Tell him how much you love him and that you will always be there when he needs you. Don't be afraid to cry and laugh together.

"Once my teenaged son was very depressed and I feared a suicide attempt. He said he just wanted to go to sleep and never wake up. We talked and cried together. I told him how much I loved him and that I would be devastated if something happened to him."

Take Action to Reduce Depression or Anger. Depression or anger, at times key factors in suicidal risk, may occur when people feel they have no control over their lives. One way to combat depression and anger is to identify one or two critical areas of concern to your teenager and develop a plan to resolve them. Ask him what you can do to help. Then develop a plan together. For example, if he is upset about failing a course at school, plan to work with him or get a tutor to bring up his grades. If he or she has broken up with a girlfriend (boyfriend), would it help for him to talk with his best friend, take a special trip (supervised, of course), or work on a special hobby? Buying a new computer game or going on a trip may help him keep focused on more positive things. By taking action, teenagers feel they again have some control over their life and future. They also gain experience coping with disappointments in life and problem solving.

Talk with your teenager about the need to see a treatment professional and the possibility that medication such as an antidepressant may help him feel normal again. If he is resistant, explain how the antidepressant works. "When depression or anger is present, the neurotransmitter serotonin is often low. Antidepressant medications help increase production of serotonin, and can help you feel better and be less angry." More information on antidepressants is provided in Chapter 6. Of course, parents must work closely with their doctor to monitor any use of antidepressants.

Remove Weapons and Dangerous Medications from the Home. Remove any potentially lethal weapons and dangerous medications from the house. As mentioned earlier, the risk of suicide increases significantly when guns are available in the home. Antidepressant medications such as Tofranil or Norpramin (tricyclics) in large quantities also pose the risk of a fatal overdose.

Seek Professional Help. If your teen admits he is considering suicide or shows the warning signs, call your doctor, a psychiatrist, or a psychologist immediately to discuss the risk. If he has already developed a detailed plan for suicide, seek help as quickly as possible. The psychiatrist or psychologist can decide whether your teen should be brought in for an assessment. If it is an emergency and you don't have a psychiatrist or psychologist, call your local community mental health center (CMHC) or hospital emergency room. These staff have received crisis training and know how to deal with potential suicide attempts.

Provide Supervision. If your teenager is extremely depressed, keep him busy and provide supervision and companionship 24 hours a day. While you are deciding if you should seek professional help, make certain he does not spend time alone. Explain your concerns to a brother, sister, or friends and enlist their help keeping him busy.

Supervision will still be needed even after a suicidal teenager begins to feel better. Some research has shown that many suicides occur within three months after a person starts to feel better. By that time, teens may have found the energy to carry out a suicide plan.

Weapons

Many teenagers—whether or not they have ADD or ADHD—seem to be enamored with guns and other weapons. Roughly 6 percent of high school students have actually carried a gun for protection or self-defense. Seventeen percent have recently carried a weapon of some sort—a gun, knife, or club. Nightly news programs tell of teenagers being shot at school over trivial issues that were resolved through fist fights a generation earlier. Guns are easily accessible to young people today, and some teenagers feel they need them for protection. Some teenagers with attention deficits are also drawn to knives or novel weapons such as oriental nun chakus or brass knuckles. For our teens, impulsivity and risk-taking behaviors may make the combination of weapons and attention deficits extremely dangerous, not only for others, but the teenager himself.

It's frightening to think that homicide is the second leading cause of death among teens. According to the Child Trends DataBank, guns were used in over 80 percent of teen homicides and 60 percent of teen suicides. In some parts of the country, interest in guns is a family matter, since hunting is a major activity for teenagers and their fathers. Often children are carefully trained in the proper use and care of guns starting at a fairly young age. However, they will still need close supervision when guns are used because of their impulsiveness.

Remove Guns from Home. If you are concerned about your teenager's impulsivity, aggression, or risk of suicide, remove all guns from the house. Storing them at a friend's or relative's house would be ideal. If you keep guns in the car, chances are the teenager can still get to them.

Lock Up Guns. You may decide to leave guns in your home if you feel that your teenager is responsible and that impulsivity and aggression are not problems. The guns should be locked up, however, and only the parents should have a key.

Provide Safety Training. If your teenager is determined to be involved with guns, you may offer him the opportunity to participate in gun safety classes, hunting trips, or visits to shooting ranges so he can learn the proper way to shoot guns. This may also satisfy his need to have and shoot a gun in a safer, structured environment. You could take him to a firing range to practice his marksmanship. If you let him participate in a "forbidden" activity under safe, supervised conditions, some of the appeal of the forbidden may be removed.

Set Limits. If a discussion of gun ownership comes up, make it clear to your teen that he will not be allowed to have a handgun until he is legally old enough to buy one (21 in many states). However, teenagers often can legally own shotguns or rifles. If you think your teenager will take it as a personal challenge to go out and buy a gun, don't bring this issue up spontaneously. Discuss it naturally when the issue comes up on TV or in the newspaper.

Take Guns Away. If you find a handgun, either lock it away in a safe place or give it to the police. You should first find out, however, what the police will do. Will they press charges against your child, attempt to find the person who sold the gun, or accept the gun with no questions asked? If you have a family friend who is a policeman, an attorney, or judge, you may ask them how these matters will be handled. For most teenagers, this may be their only involvement with guns. However, if your teenager buys another gun, again take it away and lock it up or otherwise dispose of it.

"I couldn't believe my wonderful son had bought a gun. I was terrified and felt totally incompetent. I stood facing him crying and yelling at the same time. 'I will not let you have a gun. I am afraid you'll get killed or hurt someone else and be in jail for the rest of your life. I love you too much to let you have a gun.'"

If your teenager flies into a rage when he discovers you have taken the gun, leave him alone to cool off. If you are afraid for your physical safety, leave the house. You should talk with your treatment professional about how to handle issues with guns.

Discuss the Issue with Your Teenager. Afterwards, you need to talk with your teenager. Make it clear he will not be allowed to have a handgun in your home under any circumstances. It is illegal and dangerous. "I love you too much to let you have a handgun. I am not going to take a chance that you will get killed with it or accidentally hurt someone else. Most people who are shot at home are killed with their own gun."

You could also say, "I assume you feel you have a good reason for getting a gun. Why don't you tell me about it?" If he has a valid reason for concern, help him find another way to solve the problem.

"One teenager who bought a gun had been beaten up twice by a bully at school. These attacks were unprovoked and his fears justifiable. His parents decided to help reduce his fears by making school officials aware of the other student's aggressiveness. It turned out that the boy had been expelled from school and was hanging out illegally on school grounds. In addition, the parents offered to sign their son up for a self-defense course, plus gave him mace to carry in his car."

Brushes with the Law

Teenagers with attention deficits may occasionally get in trouble with school officials, law enforcement agencies, or courts. They may be suspended from school, given a ticket, taken home, or arrested. Usually, their misbehavior is not malicious but done impulsively without thought of consequences. Nonetheless, these problems worry parents sick.

Thinking back about all the teenagers with ADD or ADHD I have known, I can remember these examples of impulsive, hair-brained, and sometimes dangerous behavior:

- getting stopped for speeding and impulsively arguing with a police officer;

- sneaking out of the house at night to buy cigarettes and being brought home for breaking curfew;
- being arrested for public drunkenness;
- having police called to a loud party at the home of a teenager whose parents are out of town;
- jumping off a bridge and getting a ticket for trespassing;
- stealing an item in a store on a dare and being arrested for shoplifting;
- being caught with drugs or a weapon at school;
- being arrested for possession of a gun;
- fighting at school; police were called;
- being given a ticket for water skiing after sunset;
- running away from home and stealing money to buy food to eat;
- drinking underage and being caught by police;
- drinking too much and being raped; having to undergo AIDS testing and testify in court;
- making an unsuccessful suicide attempt.

DATA ON YOUTH WITH ADHD IN THE JUVENILE JUSTICE SYSTEM

In their long-term study, Drs. Salvatore Mannuzza and Rachel G. Klein found that 9 percent of young adults with ADHD had been incarcerated. Although this data is worrisome, Mannuzza and Klein explain that ADHD with hyperactivity alone was not predictive of brushes with the law, but conduct disorder or antisocial behaviors were.

The results of another study showed that 54 percent of youths in the juvenile justice system had ADHD. This data was also echoed by juvenile justice staff at a statewide conference where I was presenting. When asked, participants said that roughly half of the young people they served had ADHD. Of course this data is frightening. But remember that doesn't mean that half of all young people with ADHD will become delinquents. Rather, it means that of the smaller population who are within the juvenile justice system, roughly half have been diagnosed with ADHD. But the message is still clear—our children are at risk for serious problems and parents must be alert and actively involved in guiding their teen's future. The best strategy for parents to pursue is to intervene early, ensure school success, treat aggressive behavior, and make certain that medication is right.

Learn about Factors Contributing to Delinquency. Dr. Scott Henggeler, professor at the Medical University of South Carolina, explains that the number one predictor of delinquent behavior (vandalism, burglary, assault) is having "deviant" friends who are breaking the law. Not surprisingly, delinquency is also linked with substance abuse. Clearly, it is important for you to subtly encourage your teen to make friends with classmates who do not use drugs or engage in delinquent behavior and can be a positive influence.

According to Dr. Henggeler, other factors contributing to delinquency include: parents with problems such as alcoholism, drug abuse, or mental illness; poor family relations, including a lack of love in the family; lack of supervision and structure; and poor performance at school. Another interesting tidbit of information is that the peak time for juvenile crime is 3:00 p.m.—right after school.

HOW TO HANDLE UNLAWFUL BEHAVIOR

Impose Consequences But Don't Overreact. Obviously, behaviors such as those listed above are totally inappropriate. When they occur, we are embarrassed and horrified that this may mean our teenager will be a "juvenile delinquent." Even though some of these offenses are very serious, it does not mean that the teenager cannot grow up to be a productive adult. Dr. Henggeler notes that nationally, 70 percent of first-time offenders have no further brushes with the law. I don't want to understate the seriousness of these problems, but I urge parents not to give up on their teenager. You should continue to believe in your teenager, while addressing each problem as it comes up.

Avoid Court Involvement. Sometimes parents feel so overwhelmed that they petition the court to help control their teenager's behavior. However, sending a teenager to juvenile court is not going to magically make him behave. Usually, the court imposes a consequence—community service, a fine, a curfew, or a loss of privileges. The court may also place the teenager on probation and monitor his behavior. What most courts can't do, however, is provide treatment.

My cousin, the late Judge Billy Shaw Abney, Walker County, Georgia, was a juvenile court judge for over thirty years. He believed that in 95 percent of the families who came before his court, the parents were more concerned than anyone else. If the court stayed out of the picture and gave parents a chance, most parents corrected the problem at home. He reported that only 17 percent of the children seen in his court returned a second time. Judge Abney had serious reservations about locking them up with other delinquent youngsters. In fact, research shows that being with other delinquents often teaches someone how to "be a better delinquent."

In addition, juvenile court records of delinquency can come back to haunt a teenager as an adult. For example, a teenager may not be accepted into or may be released from the military if he has a court record other than traffic offenses, even though minor. Although in many states juvenile records are confidential, the military and other organizations may ask the teenager to sign a release that allows access to his records.

Sometimes parents may report a teenager who is out of control to the court system. The judge may intervene and mandate treatment. This may or may not be an effective strategy, as noted in "File a Petition," below.

Intervene Early; Provide Supervision and Structure. During his twenty years in Newton County Juvenile Court (Georgia), Judge Virgil Costly saw many parents who didn't spend enough quality time with their children. He observed that parents may see problem behaviors early but don't intervene. They don't seem to know how to help their teenager.

According to Judge Costly, keeping teenagers involved in activities or providing supervision after school is critical. Parents may have to make adjustments in their activities and lifestyle to provide adequate supervision for their child. Sending the teenager to a psychologist an hour a week and expecting that to solve all the problems is not a realistic solution. Parents need to work together with their teenager to come up with solutions to their family's problems. Parents may also have to look at their own behavior to see if they can change some of the strategies they use to reduce or diffuse their teen's behavior problems.

PREPARING FOR COURT

If your teenager has broken the law and must go to juvenile court, the following information may be helpful. Most state laws give juvenile court judges greater latitude in dealing with teenagers under 18, allowing them to take into consideration the "foolishness of youth." Typically, an attorney will not be needed except for the most serious charges.

Be Aware of Verbal Expression Problems. You may need to help your teenager present his case. Court may be difficult for him if he has verbal expression or slow processing speed problems. Most judges are not aware that many of these youngsters have difficulty organizing their thoughts and expressing themselves clearly. Teenagers who process information slowly may have little to say or respond slowly, which may come across as insolence or lack of remorse. They may appear confused at times. Or they may not respond at all because it is so difficult for them to quickly articulate thoughtful answers for the judge.

Dress Conservatively. Conservative dress—no wild tee shirts with profanity—plus a decent haircut will make a more favorable impression on most judges. Leaving the nose or tongue ring at home may also be a good idea. Encourage your teenager to speak respectfully to the judge and look him or her in the eye when talking. Be certain he takes his medicine before going to court so he can listen and pay attention.

Review What You Will Say. Help your teenager think ahead and practice what he will say. For example, ask, "What will you say if the judge asks you why you…?" Present him with a few hypothetical questions you think the judge may ask. When you and your teenager are allowed to speak, make brief but methodical comments. By watching the people ahead of you in court, you may get a better feel for how to speak to the judge. Your teenager will probably speak first and admit or deny the allegations, mention if it is his first offense, describe consequences already imposed by parents, and express his regret. You will also probably have the opportunity to speak and may mention anything the teen left out: his good character, his attention deficit and impulsiveness, his good grades (if true), community activities (religious or sports), this one-time lapse in good judgment (if true), consequences already imposed, and the amount of structure and supervision usually provided.

Consider Whether to Mention Mitigating ADHD Factors. Don't make a lot of excuses, but if the judge seems receptive, mention extenuating circumstances (medication had worn off, change in medication, death of relative, learning disabilities, or new undesirable friends); explain disciplinary steps you have already taken; mention a counselor or doctor you are already working with; and give additional suggestions. If the judge is interested, give information about attention deficit disorders. Or preface remarks with a comment such as, "I know that the ADHD (or medication wearing off) is no excuse for misbehavior (shoplifting), but it does contribute to this problem. He has signed up for karate class after school and we are encouraging him to spend more time with different friends (or giving him an afternoon dose of medicine to reduce impulsiveness) to correct this problem."

Describe Previous Intervention Strategies. Judge Costly asked parents to explain how they have handled past misbehavior, what consequences worked, and what suggestions they may have. That is more helpful than parents blaming their child, saying he's bad, "throwing up their hands in defeat," and saying they have no idea what to do. Court-imposed consequences are often tailored to suit each child or offense and may include things like having to ride the school bus instead of riding with parents or driving themselves, volunteering at the animal shelter, or picking up aluminum cans. Based upon other cases you have heard in court, be prepared, if asked, to make a suggestion for a reasonable consequence if you have any good ideas. It may forestall the judge imposing a harsher punishment.

Understand ADHD in the Juvenile Justice System. In an article in *Attention* magazine (12/02), Judge Gerald Rouse, a veteran family court judge, provides an overview of ADHD and the juvenile justice system. His astute observations are instructive to all juvenile court officials:

> "*One* *ne of the most exciting discoveries I have made as a judge is that children may have understandable reasons for doing things that seem to make little or no sense to most authority figures.*"

Once he came to this realization, Judge Rouse was able to put strategies in place that addressed many of the special needs of these children. For example, he makes it clear that learning disabilities or mental health issues such as attention deficits should be taken into consideration by the court system. He also reminds parents that their teen has a right to remain silent and the right to legal counsel. Parents should tell their teens not to answer questions of law enforcement officers without their parents or an attorney present. Teens also should not agree to a search of their car, room, or house.

Seek Professional Help Before Court Involvement. If you still have a fairly decent relationship with your teenager, seek counseling first before court action. The reasons for avoiding court involvement are discussed in more detail in this section. A treatment professional may be able to help you and

your family work out a solution to conflicts. If possible, seek help from a treatment professional or family friend who is also respected by your teenager.

Even if the court gets involved, the underlying problems will be there until your teenager receives proper treatment. If you are lucky, the judge will understand this. Judge Costly, for example, saw his role as helping parents find an effective treatment source. In his county, the local mental health center assigned a counselor to his court. You may seek counseling for yourself as you learn to use consequences more effectively, find activities to build your teen's self-esteem, help him find a more positive peer group, or improve family communication skills. Or seek treatment for your teen, especially if depression or suicide is a risk (see Chapter 5).

Should You File a Petition Declaring Your Child as Unruly or Ungovernable? Sometimes, parents file a petition with the court to have their child declared unruly or ungovernable. Depending upon your teenager, this may or may not be helpful. Court involvement gives the parent some legal leverage to enforce certain rules such as curfews or school attendance. However, on the down side, if teens still refuse to comply, they may become further entangled in the legal system. One parent who did this expressed deep regret because now every time her daughter does something, even minor, she sinks further into the bureaucracy. The mother has now lost custody of her teenager. Probation staff, against the recommendations of mental health professionals and the parent's wishes, are attempting to remove her from home and place her in a residential treatment program.

Seek Other Successes for Your Teen. In addition to addressing the specific problems described in this chapter, you can also help resolve these issues indirectly. One of the best ways to do this is by helping your teen achieve some sense of normalcy, self-esteem, and joy by getting him involved in special activities—computer class, karate, or whatever his interests are.

Chapter 8 contains more information on helping your teenager find other successes.

Seek Help from the Court. Ultimately, if your teenager is totally out of control and a potential danger to himself or others, you may have no other choice but to ask the court to be involved. Sometimes courts can be helpful by mandating that your teenager and your family seek treatment. If you decide you need help from the court, call your local county juvenile court for advice.

Be Positive; Expect Good Things. Judge Abney believed that a self-fulfilling prophecy is a major factor in helping youngsters who get into trouble with the law. They will act as we expect them to act. No child left his court without hearing something positive from the judge. Children make mistakes and should not have to pay for them for the rest of their lives. In his thirty-plus years as a judge, he saw youngsters in his court who broke the law and grew up to be highly respected leaders in the community.

Skipping School/Dropping Out

Students who enjoy and are succeeding in school don't have problems with truancy. However, some students with attention deficits experience so much failure in school that they may skip classes. According to Dr. Barkley, approximately 21 percent of teenagers with ADHD repeatedly skip school. They also have a high risk of dropping out of school (35 percent) or being suspended (45 percent).

Provide Accommodations at School. After learning problems have been identified, it is crucial to provide accommodations to help your teenager succeed at school. See Chapter 13 for detailed information about accommodations, as well as our companion guide, *Teaching Teens with ADD and ADHD.*

Running Away

A few teenagers with attention deficits become so unhappy, angry, and depressed that they run away to escape their pain and ease their frustration. Dr. Barkley's study found that running away from home (twice or more) was a significant problem for only 5 percent of teenagers with ADHD. When they do run away, the length of time they are gone varies from a few hours to several days or weeks.

Watch for potential problems—breaking up with a girlfriend or boyfriend, school failure, or family fights—and try to help your teen cope with the crisis before the situation gets so painful that he runs away to avoid it.

Maintain Open Communication. If possible, keep lines of communication open with your teenager while he is away from home. Avoid arguing or threatening him during telephone conversations. The most important thing is to get him back home, safe and sound.

Try to Find Your Teen. Ask some of your teen's friends to help you find him. They may know where he is staying. If he is missing for several days or you suspect he is in danger, call the police. Some police will begin looking immediately. But others won't take any action for several days until it is clear that your teenager has run away. The National Runaway Switchboard (1-800-RUNAWAY or www.nrscrisisline.org) offers parents of runaways guidance on searching for a missing teen.

Conclusion

Helping your teenager navigate the troubles described in this chapter can be very stressful and emotionally exhausting. You may shed many tears and spend many sleepless nights worrying. At times, you may wonder whether there is really anything useful that you, as a parent, can do. The answer is "yes." You can show your teenager you believe in him by supporting his success at home, at school, and in the community. As discussed in earlier chapters, helping teenagers get involved in activities they like and can excel in is one excellent support strategy. A teenager who is doing well in school, sports, or other community activities and is taking medication is less likely to become involved with drugs, have need of a handgun, or otherwise get into trouble.

It is important to avoid power struggles if your child has any of the problems described in this chapter. The forbidden has tremendous appeal for teenagers with attention deficits. If parents make a big deal about any issue, teenagers may embrace the challenge and show you they will do what they want to do.

Often teenagers with attention deficits have serious learning problems that have been overlooked by school personnel. So parents absolutely must ensure that their teen's learning problems are addressed. Helpful strategies are discussed in Chapters 11, 12, and

13. Furthermore, *Teaching Teens,* the companion guide for this book, offers roughly 350 pages of strategies for ensuring school success.

In addition, Drs. Russell Barkley and Peter Jensen have made us aware of how critically important it is to educate each teen about his or her ADD or ADHD. Believe it or not, education about attention deficit disorders can be more effective than regular counseling. The better teens understand themselves the better they will be able to cope with their attention deficit. Be sure to educate yourself first by reading books and watching videos.

Finally, do not hesitate to seek professional help for yourself when your teenager is experiencing serious problems. You may learn new skills that will enable you to help your teenager cope with this difficult time in his or her life.

Table 10-4   Problem Behaviors of Teenagers with ADD and ADHD

Easy Reference Guide

A summary of the behaviors discussed in this chapter, as well as helpful interventions, is provided below. As you become more familiar with these suggestions, you will find that you can use many of them for more than one challenging behavior. Your teenagers may have some but not all of these behaviors. Use common sense in dealing with these issues. If your teenager's problems are serious and these interventions are not working, seek professional help. Find a counselor, social worker, physician, psychiatrist, or psychologist who understands attention deficits and works well with your family.

CHALLENGING BEHAVIORS	POSSIBLE INTERVENTIONS
Defiance & aggression	■ See criteria for ODD/CD (Chapter 7) ■ Seek treatment (Chapter 5) ■ Consider medication (Chapter 6) ■ Teach anger control (Chapter 8) ■ Consider special education services (Chapter 14)
Bullying and being bullied	■ Reassure your child ■ Educate yourself about bullying ■ Talk with school officials ■ Seek a "bullying prevention" program
Substance abuse	1. Educate yourself and child about substances ■ Learn to recognize drugs ■ Use fact sheets ■ Provide an overview ■ Convey concern and trust ■ Be aware of dangers of mixing drugs & meds ■ Use teachable moments ■ Don't teach wrong information ■ Avoid scare tactics ■ Seek reliable information ■ Absolutely no drinking and driving ■ Develop a contract for driving 2. Provide supervision ■ Establish curfews ■ Establish rules re: drinking & driving 3. Ensure success in school (Chap. 11-14)

4. Seek help to control aggression & hyperactivity

5. Keep teen busy with positive activities

6. Influence selection of friends

7. Watch for signs of substance abuse (Chap. 7)

8. How you can help
   - Find what works for your teen
   - Impose consequences
   - Seek drug testing, maybe?
   - Seek professional help
   - Contact AA or NA
   - Consider your own drinking habits
   - Review general strategies in this section

Driving accidents	■ Send to driver training
	■ Provide extended hours of supervision
	■ Gradually increase driving time
	■ Purchase a slow tank
	■ Consider medication
	■ Use positive incentives to avoid problems
	■ Develop a contract for driving
	■ Educate yourself about driving issues
Speeding tickets	■ Consider medication
	■ Identify high risk time for tickets
	■ Let others drive
	■ Impose consequences
	■ Consider a computer monitor
	■ Consider a speed governor
	■ Teach teen to avoid being late
	■ Ride with a police officer, maybe?
	■ Visit a spinal center
	■ Have teen pay for tickets
	■ Have teen pay for insurance
	■ Warn of insurance cancellation
Court appeals of driving offenses	■ Check tire size; speedometer calibration
	■ Plead nolo contendere
	■ Take a defensive driving course
	■ Consider hiring an attorney
Sexual behavior	■ Provide sex education
	■ Arrange for sex education class
	■ Provide reading materials
	■ Discuss values re: sexual matters
	■ Avoid tempting your teen
	■ Avoid overreacting
	■ Teach it's okay to say "no"
	■ Talk about impact of pregnancy
	■ Consider birth control
	■ Educate about AIDS/unprotected sex

Suicide Risk	■ Watch for warning signs of suicide
	■ Take all suicidal statements seriously
	■ Ask about suicidal thoughts
	■ Listen to teen
	■ Show concern and affection
	■ Take action to reduce depression or anger
	■ Remove weapons & medications from home
	■ Seek professional help
	■ Provide supervision
Weapons	■ Remove guns from home
	■ Lock up guns
	■ Provide safety training
	■ Set limits
	■ Take guns away
	■ Discuss weapons with your teen
	■ Address his fears

Brushes with the Law

1. Avoiding brushes with the law
   - ■ Be aware of factors contributing to delinquency
   - ■ Promote positive friends
   - ■ Ensure success in school (Chaps. 11-14)

2. Handling unlawful behavior
   - ■ Impose consequences but don't overreact
   - ■ Avoid court involvement
   - ■ Intervene early
   - ■ Provide supervision & structure

3. Preparing for court
   - ■ Be aware of verbal expression deficits
   - ■ Dress conservatively
   - ■ Review what you will say
   - ■ Consider mentioning ADHD mitigating factors
   - ■ Describe previous interventions
   - ■ Learn about ADHD in the JJ system
   - ■ Seek treatment
   - ■ Consider declaring child unruly
   - ■ Seek other success for teen
   - ■ Seek help from court
   - ■ Be positive/expect good things

Skipping school; dropping out	■ Identify learning problems
	■ Make accommodations at school (Chap. 11-14)
Running away	■ Maintain open communication
	■ Try to find your teen
	■ Seek professional help rather than court involvement

11

The Parent's Role in Eliminating Academic Agony

"The memories of those early school years came flooding back as I read your book, and tears sometimes filled my eyes. Scott's kindergarten teacher loved him but she told us at his graduation that he marched to the beat of a different drummer and he would have a difficult time with school. Truer words were never spoken.

"It was the beginning of 12 years of agony for us all. How Scott survived with a desire to go on to college is a miracle. His ADD was not diagnosed until he was 18."

For many teenagers with an attention deficit disorder, attending school is truly academic agony. As many parents might expect, the teenager's inattention and impulsivity usually make it more difficult for her to succeed in middle and high school. Another debilitating, often hidden factor may also have a profound impact on her school performance—executive function deficits. As explained in Chapter 1, these deficits manifest themselves in a variety of ways: *disorganization, forgetfulness, slow reading and writing, difficulty with math computation, poor working memory, difficulty memorizing, difficulty writing essays and reports, difficulty getting started on work, controlling emotions, and poor analytical and problem solving skills.* In addition, their lack of maturity—the 30 percent developmental delay—that typically accompanies deficits in executive skills is a key factor in academic difficulties.

"As a young teacher and school psychologist, I assumed that any child with a high IQ could do

well in school, if they worked hard enough. Now I know that IQ is simply a measure of what a student knows. The true predictor of academic achievement is executive functioning. Without these key skills, the teen's true intellectual potential will never be realized."

In turn, frustration with learning problems and executive skill deficits may lead to behavior problems. Indeed, coping with the academic frustration that sometimes accompanies ADD or ADHD can be emotionally upsetting to the whole family. All these factors, plus the defiance and anger present in some of these teenagers, may make the middle and high school years exasperating for all concerned.

For most teens with attention deficits, medical treatment and academic interventions are critical for success in school. If their ADD or ADHD remains undiagnosed or improperly treated, some teenagers will achieve only marginal successes at school. Others may suffer through years of failure, discouragement, and underachievement in school, hating the hours they are "trapped" in classrooms. They may become extremely discouraged and eventually drop out of school. There is little or no joy in learning for these teenagers.

Dr. Barkley reports that roughly 35 percent of our teenagers drop out of school. Even more disturbingly, of the 65 percent who do graduate, only 5 percent go on to graduate from college. Even though this is research on children with more serious problems, it is still very disturbing news. If you don't want your teen to become one of these sad statistics, you absolutely must address both academic and executive function deficits.

Obviously, many problems at school can contribute to problems at home. This chapter discusses typical school-related problems, including developmental delays and learning disabilities, and suggests ways to work effectively with school officials. If your teenager continues to struggle even after treatment has begun, reassessing her academic needs must be a top priority. Specifically, have your teenager *evaluated for learning problems*, including executive function deficits, as described in Chapters 3 and 13. Then, in partnership with school personnel, *develop a plan* to meet the academic needs of your teenager at home and school (Chapters 11-13). Remember also that *Teaching Teens with ADD and ADHD,* the companion guide for this book, is devoted entirely to providing you with specific suggestions to help your teen be successful in school.

The Educational Endurance Test

For some of these teenagers, school represents an unpleasant educational endurance test. It is as if they are forced into "careers" (school) for 12 years that they strongly dislike and in which they have difficulty succeeding. Most adults avoid or quit unpleasant endurance tests. Adults usually do not enter careers or participate in sports they hate or in which they cannot excel. Teenagers do not have the same luxury where school is concerned, however.

"Even though he was very bright, most of Alex's school experiences have been negative. As a result, he hates school. He attends school because it is statutorily required and thankfully because he is a teenager and girls are now a major interest. The few joys he has gained

from school are the social interactions with friends, physical education, computer, and industrial shop classes."

Reason for Concern

Researchers have confirmed what parents already knew: there are good reasons to be concerned about their teenager's potential academic problems. The key word here is *potential.* The information shared in this chapter is intended to alert parents to *possible* problems their teenager may face. It is not intended to frighten you, but to make you aware that many school-related problems can be avoided through early intervention.

Most adolescents with attention deficits are ill prepared for high school, according to Dr. Gabriella Weiss, a Canadian researcher who has done long-term studies on ADHD. For many, learning disabilities, executive function deficits, and attention deficits together add up to major problems at school.

However, one of the positive trends that I have observed over the past ten years is that parents have become better-educated advocates on behalf of their children, plus teachers are doing a better job of providing needed accommodations. As a result, more of our children are being successful in school.

Understanding Major Learning Challenges

Learning Disabilities

A significant number of teenagers who have attention deficit disorders also have a disorder that impairs learning in one or more academic areas. You may hear a number of different names for these learning problems: learning disability (LD), specific learning disability (SLD), learning disorder, or learning deficits. The meaning of these labels is basically the same. For a variety of reasons, these students have more trouble learning than their peers, even though they have average or above average intelligence.

The criteria used in determining whether a student qualifies as having a specific learning disability are spelled out in a federal education law called the Individuals with Disabilities Education Act (IDEA). These criteria are somewhat different than those the American Psychiatric Association has established for learning disorders in the *Diagnostic and Statistical Manual (DSM).*

If your teenager has a learning disability, the label she is given—SLD or something else—matters for only one reason. If she qualifies as having SLD, that means she is eligible for special education services under IDEA. If she is considered to have problems learning, but does not qualify for SLD, the process of obtaining special education services is not usually as clearcut. There are, however, other avenues for obtaining help—for example, 1) by qualifying under *Other Health Impairment* (OHI), the preferred eligibility category for ADD/ADHD under IDEA, and 2) by qualifying for assistance under federal civil rights law such as *Section 504* of the Rehabilitation Act of 1976. See Chapter 13 for more information.

When eligibility criteria are defined conservatively, researchers tell us that the number of students with ADHD and specific learning disabilities is probably between 20 to 25 percent. In 2002, however, the Center for Disease and Control conducted a survey of families that reported a higher rate of learning disabilities—50 percent. A student may have a specific learning disability in one or more of seven academic areas:

1. Oral Expression
2. Listening Comprehension
3. Written Expression
4. Basic Reading Skills
5. Reading Comprehension
6. Mathematics Calculation
7. Mathematical Reasoning

Exactly how a student is determined to have SLD varies from state to state. Until 2005, evaluators looked for a *major discrepancy between ability and achievement.* More recently, however, states are broadening the criteria for eligibility to include: problems with slow processing speed, specifically reading, writing, and spoken language deficits. Current classroom performance is also assessed. For example, samples of written work and the status of daily grades and class failures may be checked. Chapter 13 explains how students are evaluated to determine what is causing their academic struggles.

Developmental Delays

Parents and teachers are often unaware that many teenagers with attention deficits lag behind their peers *four to six years developmentally.* As explained earlier, a 16-year-old may act more like a 10- or 12-year-old with regard to obeying her parents and completing chores and schoolwork.

Frequently teacher and parent expectations are based upon what are often referred to as *developmental norms.* These norms are based upon the average age that most students master important skills. Developmentally, most children are using working memory and visual imagery by age 5. By 7, they're developing a sense of time and by 9, they've internalized language and are beginning to use it for self-control. By 12, they handle their emotions better, plus begin problem solving. So by the ages of 11 to 13, most middle school students *can* successfully keep up with their homework assignments and complete and submit them on time. In contrast, most students with attention deficits cannot complete these tasks without help from teachers and parents.

Unfortunately, we adults sometimes act as though these developmental norms are etched in stone. So, if students with ADD or ADHD don't remember their assignments by the time they are in middle school, they are often viewed as simply being lazy or not trying. Sometimes both parents and teachers fail to recognize that their brains aren't mature enough for teens to master these skills! Getting angry and punishing the student is ineffective—these actions will not grow more white matter in the brain or produce more neurotransmitters.

Dr. Barkley often describes ADHD as a *developmental disability* because of this delay in developing key skills. According to Barkley, this developmental delay tells us the maximum we can expect this child to do at certain ages and no more. Unfortunately, parents and teachers frequently have unrealistic expectations, especially with tasks such as independent completion of homework. For obvious reasons, these teens are not going to be as mature or as responsible as their peers.

Furthermore, for an 18-year-old to be successful in school, parents and teachers must provide the supports, prompts, and accommodations that would be appropriate for a younger child—in other words provide *"age appropriate developmental supervision."* The fact that so many adults are unaware of this significant developmental delay is the source of many major conflicts between these teens and their teachers and parents.

"A doctor friend of ours has ADHD and takes Adderall. He is always preaching at us, 'Give Abby time to grow up!'"

It is important to remember that their brains have not finished maturing. And in fact, there may be certain skills that they will never master because their brain chemistry doesn't allow them to do so. So even in adulthood, many people with ADD or ADHD will need an "ADHD coach," assistant, or spouse to pick up the slack caused by the symptoms of their attention deficit.

Other Common Problems at School

Common Learning Problems. Children with attention deficits often share several common learning problems that stop short of meeting the criteria for SLD. These are discussed in detail in Chapter 14. Briefly, researchers estimate that approximately one-third of teenagers with ADHD have *serious reading, spelling, and/or math disabilities.* Until recently, most tests did not assess written expression skills. In 2000, Drs. Susan Mayes and Susan Calhoun found that 65 percent of students in one study had a learning disability in *written expression.*

Executive Function Deficits. Deficits in executive skills, especially *working memory*, have a profound impact on a student's school performance. *Reconstitution*—the ability to analyze, organize, sequence, and produce a work product—is also a major problem area. Academically, strong executive skills are key for writing essays or doing algebra. Suggestions for dealing with academic issues related to executive function deficits are provided in Chapter 13. Chapter 3 in *Teaching Teens* is devoted to a discussion of this topic. In addition, an in-depth discussion on writing essays and completing math problems is also available in *Teaching Teens*, Summaries 14-21.

Inattention and Impulsivity. The key characteristics of attention deficits—inattention and impulsivity—can also adversely affect schoolwork. Obviously, students who can't pay attention in class will have great difficulty being successful in school. Teens with attention deficits may not listen in class, daydream, forget homework, and impulsively take short cuts in schoolwork.

School Failure. With all the potential academic problems these youngsters face, it should come as no surprise that teenagers with attention deficits are more likely to fail a grade or drop out of school. Also not surprisingly, they have lower self-esteem than other students. According to a study on teenagers with ADHD by Dr. Barkley, approximately 30 percent of them had failed a grade. This rate was three times higher than for teenagers in a control group who did not have ADHD.

"*Each year, school has gotten worse and worse. Elementary school was a breeze but by 7ᵗʰ grade, we knew Emily had some issues. We monitored her homework carefully and insisted she did not fall behind. I had*

her teachers sign a report at the end of the week that she was caught up with everything. It worked pretty well.

"*In high school, she didn't want us 'intruding' on her school work. She got one incomplete, two C's, and two D's. She 'forgets' homework. Forgets to write it down. She thinks she's current. She thought she had a B in one subject, but she had a D. She started to fall further and further behind until she gave up completely. Finally, things got better after we diagnosed her ADHD.*"

Grade Retention. Research has clearly shown that there is no benefit to students who are retained and in fact this practice is often harmful to the child. Students who fail a grade show a dramatic drop in motivation to learn, give up more easily, and are more likely to drop out of school. In addition, they show an increase in antisocial, oppositional, and aggressive behavior, are rejected by peers, and show disrupted relationships with their peers.

School Dropouts. Researchers tell us that high school dropout rates for students with attention deficits are around 35 percent. Dropout rates for students with serious emotional problems who are in ED (Emotional and Behavior Disorder) classes are even higher, 48 percent.

"Behavior Problems." Teenagers with attention deficits are more likely to get into trouble at school by misbehaving, being defiant, or skipping school.

Researchers have found that students with ADHD have significant problems with "stubbornness, defiance, refusal to obey, temper tantrums, and verbal hostility toward others." They may impulsively talk back to teachers or say things before they think.

Suspensions and Expulsions. Because of their behavior, students with ADHD are 10 times more likely to be suspended from school and 7 times more likely to be expelled. Of the teenagers with ADHD in Dr. Barkley's study, 46 percent had been suspended and 11 percent expelled. On average, these teenagers had been suspended from school 4 times. According to Dr. Barkley, rates of truancy were reported at 21 percent.

Keeping Statistics in Perspective

Now that every parent's worst nightmare has been described, a word of caution about research studies may alleviate some anxiety. Most of these studies have been done on a narrowly selected group of youngsters with ADHD (a "clinical sample") who were referred to a clinic for treatment due to more serious problems. Consequently, the results of these studies are skewed negatively when compared to studies that would be conducted on youngsters with attention deficits who have adjusted fairly well and are receiving services primarily through their local pediatrician or adolescent medicine specialist (a "community or epidemiologically derived sample").

A community sample study by Dr. N. M. Lambert confirms that youngsters served in traditional settings do not have as serious problems as those in clinical samples. These youngsters had *less than half* the academic problems, antisocial behavior, and ADHD symptoms in adolescence of those in clinical samples. My advice is to apply a "one-half rule" to research studies. If statistics you come across were collected on a clinical sample, cut the figures in half. Obviously, it is important to keep study results in perspective, especially those that are negatively skewed. Otherwise, parents may give up or expect the worst and get it (a negative self-fulfilling prophesy).

At this point, perhaps you are feeling overwhelmed. Or you may be somewhat relieved to know that your adolescent is not so different from others with attention deficits. Then again, you may consider yourself extremely lucky because your teenager has had only minor problems. Regardless, don't be discouraged by anticipating what may happen in the future. Some teenagers with ADD or ADHD do extremely well in school. And if yours does not, you're educating yourself now so you can take steps early to avoid potential academic pitfalls.

Success in School Is Critical

Teenagers with attention deficits must succeed in school if they are to build strong self-esteem and become healthy, productive adults. The more academic successes a teenager achieves, the more likely her problem behaviors will decline significantly. If you must make a choice between working on problem behaviors or academic problems, Dr. Sydney Zentall strongly recommends you address the academic problems *first*. Teenagers who are successful and happy in school are less likely to be angry and aggressive toward teachers and other students. Here is one of my favorite sayings:

"One of the most therapeutic things that can happen to a child or teenager is to succeed in school!"

Parents Must Pave the Way

Parents must be *actively involved* to ensure school success. If your child's problems are less serious, she may be able to succeed academically with accommodations at school and minimal involvement from you. If, however, she continues to struggle, you must be *her advocate* at school to ensure appropriate accommodations and supports are provided. Frequent communication between you and the school may be necessary. Even when accommodations are made, you may still need to be your teenager's *academic tutor or coach*. When your teenager forgets to follow up on a specific task, you may have to remind her. You may have to talk directly with the teacher to find out if she is failing a class or to discuss accommodations. Sometimes you may be much more involved in schoolwork than you would wish.

Determining Your Level of Involvement. One major question to resolve is how willing and capable are you of helping your teenager succeed academically? This is a hard decision to make, since other well-meaning adults may tell you that you are overprotective, overinvolved with your teenager's schoolwork, or codependent. Or you may be criticized for not being involved enough! It may be a no-win situation. Yet if you don't get involved, your teenager may fail her classes. This could lead to even worse problems such as dropping out of school, running away, or using illegal drugs.

Consider Getting a Coach. Having a coach to help with academic and other activities can be extremely helpful. Some parents will be able to serve as a coach and others will have to find someone else to do this job. If you or your spouse have an attention deficit and problems with disorganization and inattention, it will, of course, be difficult for you to monitor progress and help your teenager be more organized. This is not often discussed, but 40 to 50 percent of all youngsters with attention deficits have at least one parent with the disorder. You might consider getting treatment for yourself so you can help your child. Even if it is hard, you may have to help your teenager, especially if no one else is available. You and your spouse could also work as a team, sharing responsibility for helping your teenager with her schoolwork. You can also help your teen by sharing tips you have learned for compensating for your own attention deficit.

Become an Effective Advocate for Academic Success. To advocate successfully, parents must learn new skills. If your teenager is struggling at school, you must understand her learning problems, her learning style, needed accommodations for homework and school, and ways to maximize her strengths to teach her most effectively. Once you understand her educational needs, you can share specific suggestions with teachers who may not know much about teaching teenagers with attention deficits. You can also use many of these same teaching strategies when helping your teen with homework.

Find and Coordinate Outside Help. If your teenager's problems are more complex, you must take charge, become the "case manager," and coordinate an individualized treatment plan with key professionals. This may be the case if your child has serious learning disabilities, depression, or aggression, or is not on a proper medication regimen. As discussed in Chapter 5, it would be nice if you could schedule a meeting and invite all key people—physician, treatment professionals, school psychologists, teachers—who are involved to develop a treatment plan. In reality, you may have to do it piecemeal. Some school Child Study Teams do a nice job of coordinating a student's educational plan. If necessary, you may have to meet with individual teachers to develop the educational portion of the treatment plan.

General Strategies for Ending Academic Agony

Providing each child with individualized instruction that meets her special needs is critical for school success. Many students with attention deficits need creative accommodations in the classroom to help them learn. *So, if you can't change the child and her "ADD behavior," change the environment.* Some accommodations, such as a weekly report, may be needed only for a short period until the student masters key skills. Other accommodations, such as extended time on tests, may be needed throughout a student's school career. Use common sense when developing accommodations. If your teenager can't learn her multiplication tables, then let her use a calculator.

Although learning problems make school difficult, these teenagers know that they must still master academic skills. They don't want teachers to lower expectations, but to make adjustments to the classroom that will "level the playing field." These students want and deserve an equal chance to succeed in school.

Another critical element is "working smart" as a parent. Use the parenting approaches such as those discussed in Chapter 8, which have a greater chance of being effective with these teenagers.

1. Work in Partnership with Your Teenager

First of all, it is critical to include your teenager as a respected partner in the process of pursuing her academic success. You must give her the message that she is a good person even if you are not pleased because she is not doing her schoolwork. Separate the unacceptable behavior from the child. Make statements about the behavior, such as, "I'm not happy you didn't complete your homework last night," but not about your teenager's personality. Praise her effort to complete tasks.

"When I left on a business trip and we were anxiously awaiting my son's progress reports, I left a message taped to the Coca Cola cans in the refrigerator that read: 'Hope you did well on your report card today. But just remember I love you because of the neat person you are, not because of the grades you make. If you have any problems, we'll work them out together.' Yes, there is life after graduation from high school and my son's self-esteem is more important than making straight A's."

Avoid character assassinations of your teenager when she has difficulty with schoolwork. Don't say: "You're lazy"; "You just don't care"; "You're bad"; "You'll never amount to anything." Continue to work with her so that she experiences success at school and it comes naturally for you to give her approval for completing her schoolwork.

By learning new parenting skills such as those discussed in Chapter 8, you can avoid saying and doing things that are likely to escalate problems and make the situation worse. Specific tips for deescalating problem situations, avoiding confrontation, and shaping desired behavior are provided in *Teaching Teens*, Summaries 59-61.

Involve your teenager in the decision-making process regarding school issues. This way, you convey a message of respect and indicate that you are partners working together to solve school problems. One way to involve her is to ask her opinions on the problems and solutions: "Why do you think you are failing algebra? How can I help you?" Some of these teenagers have listening comprehension and slow processing speed problems and may not be able to quickly articulate an answer. Give your teen time to respond to each question before asking another one. If she has no answer, try prompting her by asking, "Does it seem like _____ (not competing homework) is the biggest problem?" If she has no suggestions, say, "Why don't we try _____ (working on algebra every night) for a few weeks?" Then ask her or the teacher if she is completing more homework.

Here is an example of how you might respectfully discuss school-related issues with your teenager over the long term:

"Rachel, as long as you are being responsible about your homework and are passing all of your classes, I will not intervene in your evening study routine."

(A few weeks later) "You got a mid-term academic warning that you are in danger of failing algebra. According to this note, you have not been turning in your homework. I know you want to do well in school. I also know school is harder for you because of your ADHD. What do you think is causing the problem? Maybe we can make some accommodations at school that will help us solve the problem. How can I help you get more organized to complete your work? Do you need for me to work with you to set up a study routine? (If the answer is no) I'll give you one week to try your ideas first. If you are responsible and turn in homework, I won't intervene."

(Later still, homework is not being turned in) "You haven't been turning in your homework and are still failing algebra. Let's work together to set up a study routine. What are your ideas? I have a few suggestions too." (Implement a strategy. Give choices as described earlier.)

Bear in mind that you may need to intervene earlier than in this example. For instance, if your teenager usually makes borderline grades and is at risk for failing a class, you may have to intervene after only two or three weeks and find out what her class average is. Obviously, you should not pepper your teen with all these questions at once but rather select the ones that seem appropriate for your child. Keep in mind that possible expressive language problems may make it difficult for her to easily answer your questions.

Your teenager may recognize the need for help and willingly accept your assistance. Or she may not want much assistance because she doesn't want to be different from her friends. A few teenagers may be very hostile and reject any parental involvement. If this happens, perhaps you might have the other parent or a relative talk with the teenager to see if she will accept help from them.

If your teenager acts responsibly and is willing to work with you on a plan to improve performance in school, involve her in more strategies to take charge of her life. Encourage her to assume as much responsibility for schoolwork as possible, depending on her ability and learning problems. If, however, she is failing classes and is defiantly refusing to complete schoolwork, you may need to talk with a treatment professional about ways to reduce the conflict. For example, you may have to make driving privileges contingent upon her completing her homework. "You can drive the car to school tomorrow (next week) if you do your homework tonight (each night this week)."

Be aware of the subtle messages behind your words. The values behind the statements in the sample conversation above convey several important subtle messages to the teen:

- I believe you want to do well in school.
- I know you are not intentionally being noncompliant.
- I respect your opinion.
- I want you to be involved in deciding how to solve the problem.
- I believe you can handle your homework problem.

- I know sometimes your attention deficit makes school harder, but together we will figure out and solve the problems.
- You may need help from me for a while but ultimately, you'll take charge of your homework routine again.
- Things may be difficult, but I'll work with you. Together, we can make it.

This approach may be difficult for many parents because we have been conditioned to assume that if a student doesn't do well in school, it is because she *doesn't want to, doesn't care, or isn't trying.* If your teenager is discouraged or depressed, she probably acts like she doesn't care. But her attitude will usually change for the better when you intervene and her grades improve. Sometimes it is hard for adults to believe that their teenager wants to do well—and instead they assume they have to *make* their teenager do well in school. Unfortunately, some parents approach this situation with a baseball bat instead of mutual respect and decision-making.

Encourage your teenager to ask for help. Dr. Zentall has found that *students with ADHD are less likely to ask teachers for help.* Many have experienced so much failure and negative feedback from teachers, they may understandably be reluctant to approach their teachers. They may fear that the teacher will not listen to them or believe them about the learning problems they are having. Requesting a teacher conference that includes your teenager may identify the problems and empower her to ask teachers for assistance. Furthermore, by asking her opinion during the conference, you can show the teacher how to treat her as a respected partner.

There may also be other reasons why teenagers have difficulty asking for help. They may forget to ask later (memory problems), be embarrassed (afraid the teacher answered the question when they weren't lis-

tening), have trouble waiting for a response, and/or be unwilling to wait until after school to ask the question (impulsivity and difficulty waiting).

2. Give Your Teenager Choices

Dr. Sydney Zentall has observed that these youngsters have a high need for control. One reason may be that they feel as if they have very little control over their grades and most events at school. Giving them choices gives them a sense of control and ownership in completion of their schoolwork. According to Dr. Zentall, youngsters who are given choices pay attention better, complete more schoolwork, and are less disruptive and aggressive in the classroom. They also work longer and are more likely to do as adults ask.

It is probably best to limit your teen to two or three choices. You might give her choices about assignments to be completed, time for starting, length of work sessions, rewards for completion of work, or selection of essay topics. If she has trouble selecting one, talk through her choices with her. "You like the ocean and scuba diving. Maybe it would be more interesting for you to write an essay about coral reefs." Narrowing down choices or selecting an essay topic can be a major challenge. You might help her narrow down her choices by flipping a coin, telling her to eliminate one topic, or picking an assignment for her.

3. Start at Your Teen's Current Level

By starting at her present level, you can avoid putting more pressure on your teenager than she can handle. Remember that developmentally she is significantly behind in her ability to be organized and accept full responsibility for her schoolwork and chores at home. Since the ultimate goal for parents is to help their child to become an independent, responsible adult, you need to help your teenager accept increasing levels of responsibility. As she masters one behavior or task, then you can lead her to the next developmentally appropriate step. This technique is known as "shaping" behavior and is discussed in Chapter 8 and in *Teaching Teens,* Summary 61.

4. Provide "Developmentally Appropriate Supervision"

If you embrace this philosophy, then you must also be prepared to *give yourself permission* to be more involved in your teen's life and for longer than you really want to be, or for that matter, longer than you think you should be. Perhaps educators have told you that your teenager should "take full responsibility for her schoolwork" and experience the negative consequences of not doing so. If your teenager can manage an adequate level of organization, that is wonderful! However, if she is extremely disorganized and doing poorly academically, you should not feel guilty about helping her succeed in school.

"My son passed all his classes his sophomore year in high school. His sophomore year was an improvement over his freshmen year, when he failed 3 of 12 classes. He started out the school year with no intervention from me. After his midterm report, we identified those classes that he was in danger of failing, and weekly reports were introduced for those subjects. Once his grades were passing for a grading period, weekly reports were dropped."

You must remind yourself that she is developmentally behind her peers. Give yourself permission to be involved as much as necessary to help her succeed in school. Trust your instincts about your level of involvement. Obviously, the bottom line goal is to continually reduce your level of involvement in your teen's life, but you have to do it gradually over time. And trust me, it will take longer than you want it to take.

If teachers challenge you regarding your level of involvement, you may make them aware of the developmental delay typically found among those with attention deficits. If teachers are interested, follow up by giving them brief reading materials on developmental delays from this book or *Teaching Teens*. Using the term, "providing developmentally appropriate supervision" may help the teacher understand what you are doing.

"The feeling among many psychologists is that these children need to "take responsibility for their lives and for their actions. One psychologist I saw told me, 'You're micromanaging Bill's life. He's making mostly As and Bs and is in the honor society. What more do you want?'

"Her implication was that I was meddling in his life and should just leave him alone because he was doing so well. The message I got from her was 'Let your child sink or swim on his own. He's got to take the initiative on his own.' What she failed to realize is that he wouldn't be achieving any of this if I didn't work so closely with him.

"I've watched other friends as they let their children with ADHD fail. Their children became angry, frustrat-

ed, and more dependent on their parents for daily needs. Their kids didn't learn from failure; they just continued on their downward spiral. I figured, 'What did I have to lose if I helped my son?'

"What the psychologist did not understand was my deep down desire to have Bill take over his life. He will one day, but he and I know that is not possible at this time and I refuse to neglect my parental responsibility. My son is brilliant and he is going to graduate from college. If he needs added assistance, I am going to provide it.'

5. Use Legal Leverage to Obtain Needed Services

Two important laws, IDEA and Section 504, are described in detail in Chapter 14. Provisions in these laws guarantee that children with learning problems receive needed help from their school. Because system change comes extremely slowly, knowledge of the educational rights and possible classroom accommodations mandated for students with attention deficits may not be widespread among rank-and-file teachers and some mid-level administrators. You may therefore have to help educate teachers about ADD or ADHD.

Following the strategies outlined above won't guarantee that interactions between you and your teenager will always be pleasant. But then, what teenager always gets along with her parents? The key is to remember that there is no single method that works with teenagers who are struggling academically. You will have to alternately push and pull your teenager, use reason and logical consequences, try behavioral interventions, treat her with respect, give her choices, and involve her in the decision-making process as much as possible. Try one intervention and when that stops working, shift to another. Eventually, you *will* see the light at the end of the tunnel. Between the ages of 17 and 21, life usually seems to improve and be on more of an even keel for these teens. The good news is that improvements will continue into the early 30s when executive skills finally reach full maturity.

Suggestions for Making School More Positive

Several possible strategies for making school more positive are discussed in this section. Depending on the complexity of your child's attention deficit, you may use only a few or most of these suggestions.

1. Work in Partnership with the School Officials and Teachers

Working in partnership with the school to identify learning problems and implement accommodations is crucial. If learning problems are serious, teachers or parents must work together to help the teenager succeed. Parents and teachers must be familiar with common learning problems, effective teaching strategies, and possible accommodations teachers can make in the regular classroom. This information is discussed in Chapter 13 and summarized in Table 13-1. Detailed information to ensure school success is also provided in *Teaching Teens*.

When a teen is struggling, parents and teachers must communicate on a regular basis, perhaps daily or weekly. Usually, the teacher must monitor the teenager's work more carefully, make certain assignments are made known, and make accommodations in the classroom. At home, parents must ensure that homework is completed and returned to school. They must also double check to see that missed assignments and tests are made up. Otherwise, the student may find herself facing academic failure. Of course, she should be encouraged to do as much as she can for herself, but she will need help from the adults around her.

Build a Positive Relationship with School Officials. Building a positive working relationship with school personnel *before a crisis* arises is a good strategy. Some parents volunteer at school to help classroom teachers or in the school clinic. Volunteering to serve as an officer of the PTA or work on PTA projects is another way to build strong relationships with the school. Being present at school in a neutral or positive role will increase the odds that teachers will be more positive with your teenager and work with you if there are problems. If you need help, you will be talking with school officials you know rather than strangers.

Educate Yourself about School System Philosophy and Policies. It may also be helpful for you to understand the educational philosophy endorsed by the superintendent and board of education. Call the superintendent's office and ask for a copy of the school system's mission statement and student handbook. (This information might also be posted on the school system's website.) Frequently these documents contain comments about what services and accomplishments will be provided for "all children." Any or all of this information might support your request for services or accommodations.

Treat Teachers with Respect. Respecting teachers and treating them with tact is always important. Teachers are human just like we are: they want to be competent in their jobs and they fear failure. Initial discussions with the teacher may center on your teenager and her learning problems. Give the school a chance to tell you what they can offer based upon the issues you identify. If the school year is in progress, find out what interventions the teacher is currently using or has tried previously. If appropriate suggestions are not made, you might tactfully introduce some new ideas. For example, "In the past, my son has had difficulty with. . . ." "Other teachers have found it effective to. . . ." Or, "Here is some material that you may find helpful." Teachers are very busy, so give them a few pages of material at a time. Otherwise, it may go unread. Be positive with school personnel and avoid hostile confrontations.

Find the "Voice of Reason." If your teenager has an uncooperative teacher who doesn't understand attention deficits, or if you have problems with one school official (the teacher or a vice principal in charge of discipline), look for another school official who may be helpful and supportive.

Parents can usually find at least one *Voice of Reason* at school. This educator can see the good beneath the adolescent's sometimes aggravating and frustrating behavior and is willing to work as an ally with the parents and teenager. This may be a person who understands ADD and ADHD or who simply realizes that teenagers have different learning styles. He or she may be a teacher, former teacher, principal, guidance counselor, school psychologist, social worker, or special education teacher.

Work through the Guidance Counselor. Since students have several teachers in high school, it may be easier for you to work through one person, typically the guidance counselor. Counselors can advise all teachers of your teenager's learning deficits and needed supports and accommodations. And teachers could also notify the guidance office first if problems arise, although some teachers call or email parents directly. However, if your teen is having problems in only one or two classes, you may prefer to work directly with each teacher.

Express Appreciation! If teachers or school personnel have gone out of their way to help your teenager, don't forget to express appreciation. Writing letters or personally thanking the principal, superintendent, or school board for the work of outstanding teachers or school administrators will be helpful. If appropriate, say "Thanks" at the end of conferences or at the end of the school year. Teachers talk to each other, and this will enhance the reputations of you and your teenager. If confrontations occur in the future, school personnel may have heard positive things about you and may be more willing to work with you.

What If School Officials Aren't Responsive? If help is not forthcoming from the school, you may hire an *outside expert* such as a psychologist, educational consultant, or social worker. School officials will sometimes listen to outside experts or their peers when they won't listen to parents. This person may observe your teenager, consult with the teacher, make recommendations, or go to the classroom on a regular basis. To control costs, a *classroom or behavioral aide* may be trained to help in the classroom instead of a psychologist. Another option is to *hire a private tutor* to help with specific academic deficiencies, teach study and organizational skills, and help your teen keep up with assignments. The tutor may talk periodically with the teacher about daily assignments or academic problems that need work.

"I have found it helpful to have a professional attend school conferences to help educate school personnel. Information I presented to teachers, school psychologists, and/or guidance counselors was sometimes considered suspect since I was 'just the student's parent' and might be 'making excuses for my son.'"

2. Address Academic Issues

Researchers recently reported an exciting new finding: *both the academic performance and behavior of students with attention deficits who received only tutoring improved!* In contrast, the academic performance of students who received only behavioral interventions did not improve. The implication here is to ensure that your child's academic challenges are addressed. If you do, your teen is much less likely to have behavior problems at school. Detailed strategies for addressing academic challenges are available in Chapters 12 to 14 and in *Teaching Teens with ADD and ADHD.*

Schedule a School Conference. Meet with school officials to notify them about your teen's diagnosis of ADD or ADHD. Try to schedule the meeting before school begins, or as soon as possible after school starts. Don't wait until mid-term when you are notified of failing grades. As one parent explains, "Be proactive, not reactive."

If your teenager needs extra help, it is critical to *have the ADD or ADHD documented in writing* in school records and/or in the Individualized Education Program (IEP). Otherwise, you end up in the middle of an unexpected crisis, and the principal looks at you and says, "We have no record that your daughter has ADHD." It's difficult to get special consideration during the midst of a major crisis.

If the attention deficit hasn't already been documented with school officials, ask your physician/psychologist for a letter confirming the diagnosis and take it to the meeting with you. The letter should include the diagnosis of ADD or ADHD, academic or intelligence test results, identification of any learning problems, and suggestions for classroom accommodations. Once the attention deficit has been documented at school, you have more options available:

1. If your teenager has *occasional minor problems* at school, just dropping by the teachers' rooms at the first PTA meeting may be enough. Advise the teachers of your teenager's attention deficit and assure them that she wants to do well in school. Ask the teachers to call if there are any problems.
2. If your adolescent *needs extra help* but has no major problems at school, informally ask the teacher for needed classroom accommodations.
3. If she is *experiencing significant difficulty* (in danger of failing classes without accommodations or suspension/expulsion because of behavioral problems) or you *anticipate serious problems* in making the transition to middle or high school, consider requesting services under the federal laws.
4. If your child is *eligible for special education,* give additional accommodations in the regular class or have her participate in special education classes.

Seek Help under Federal Laws If Necessary. You can help your teenager succeed in school by ensuring that learning deficits are identified and appropriate classroom accommodations are made. If she is struggling, then be tenacious—seek help from school officials. As discussed in Chapter 14, two federal laws—IDEA or Section 504—may ensure provision of needed help. If your child needs special services or accommodations in the classroom, it is essential to know what she is entitled to under the law. These issues are also discussed in detail in *Teaching Teens,* Summaries 39-47.

Identify Major Learning Challenges. Work with school officials to identify your teen's learning problems and accommodations that might be helpful. Chapter 13 and Table 13-1 should be helpful with this task. The more knowledgeable you are and the more knowledgeable you sound, the more likely school officials will listen to you. Blank forms are provided in Chapter 16 so you can develop a draft accommodation plan for your teen.

Request Accommodations. Most adolescents with attention deficits can be served effectively in their regular classroom through minor changes in their present instructional program. In most cases, there is no magic academic benefit associated with being placed in a special education classroom. Teens say that one of the most helpful accommodations they receive is extended time on tests and occasionally on essays or long-term projects. Of course, not all teens with attention deficits will benefit from extended time, but most students will.

Ask That Assignments Be Modified, If Needed. Some teenagers with attention deficits struggle and spend more time than their peers on homework due to slow reading and writing, poor organization skills, slow processing speed, or poor working memory. These students may need shortened assignments. Teachers can assign half the problems and still teach mastery of key concepts.

Make it clear, however, that you're not trying to use the attention deficit as an excuse for these behaviors, but rather want to identify them as symptoms of the condition that must be addressed with accommodations.

If a teacher is reluctant to reduce the amount of homework, justify your request by stating the reasons why your child needs reduced written work: for example, slow processing speed, limited working memory capacity, and poor fine motor coordination. In addition, you might show the teacher advice from Drs. Sam Goldstein and Sydney Zentall in *Teaching Teens,* Summary 24. They explain that most teachers underestimate how much time students with learning problems will require to complete assignments. Consequently, teachers may think that the assignment will take only thirty minutes, yet it may take your child over an hour. Teachers may be totally unaware that homework assignments are too long.

Goldstein and Zentall offer a wonderful suggestion: The teacher writes on the student's paper the time she expects it should take to complete an assign-

ment. Next the student and parent write down how long the assignment actually takes. Then the two compare notes and make adjustments if there is a significant time discrepancy between what is expected and the actual time required.

Monitor School Work and Progress. Teachers alone can't ensure your child's success at school. You must be involved in monitoring assignments, completion of homework, make-up of missed homework and tests, completion of long-term projects, and mid-term checks to ensure that she is not in danger of failing any classes. Ensure that homework is completed and placed back in the notebook before bedtime, since non-completion of homework may be one of the major reasons for school failure.

Parents or their treatment professional might be interested in MyADHD.com., an innovative program that enables stakeholders such as parents, educators, health care providers, and adults with ADHD to stay connected with one another. This program via its website contains dozens of behavior rating scales (in English and Spanish) and history forms that can be completed electronically and stored in the subscriber's secure private account. A doctor, for example, can send a rating scale to a teacher's email for completion and when filled out online the completed form is sent back to the doctor's private MyADHD.com account. The site (www.MyADHD.com) also contains many treatment tools for behavior management, family communication, study strategies, cognitive therapy, and tools for adults to better manage their ADHD symptoms. MyADHD.com was founded by Harvey Parker, Ph.D., who also co-founded CHADD. If a student is struggling, teachers might suggest that parents talk to their treatment professional about this resource.

Phase Out Interventions Over Time. One of the ultimate goals for adolescents with attention deficits is to *take full responsibility for schoolwork*. Extra supports that most of these teens require can be phased out over time. For example, your teenager may no longer need weekly reports, homework reminders from teachers, or graph paper for math problems when she begins turning in all her assignments. However, some accommodations, such as untimed tests, written homework assignments, or modified assignments may need to be continued throughout her school career.

Consider Giving Medication to Enhance Academic Performance. Taking medication, such as Adderall, Concerta, or Strattera has been found to significantly improve academic performance by reducing impulsivity, improving concentration and attention, and increasing accuracy and amount of work completed. Secondary benefits of taking medication include: better monitoring and controlling their own behavior; working harder and complying with requests; being less physically and verbally hostile; having fewer negative behaviors and therefore less likely to get into trouble; and being less physically active.

Other medications might also be prescribed for teenagers who have greater problems controlling emotions, disrupt class, or are aggressive, putting them in danger of suspension from school (see Chapter 6).

3. Educate School Personnel about ADD or ADHD

Some teachers who are unknowledgeable about this disorder see the actions of these teenagers as willful disobedience, disrespect, and laziness. Teachers may show their disdain in subtle ways, many times without their full awareness—through dirty looks, sarcasm, negative comments, and lack of positive approval. Such negative attitudes from teachers can spell "academic agony" for teenagers with ADD or ADHD. Teachers who are educated about attention deficits can be more understanding and are more likely to make needed classroom accommodations.

Let teachers know about common "ADHD behaviors." For example, remind them that forgetfulness and losing things are both diagnostic criteria for having an attention deficit disorder. You may also mention strategies you have found to be effective with problems such as forgetting homework and losing papers.

Advise teachers about your teenager's problems with awareness of time. For example, explain that she typically will *underestimate* how long it will take to complete a complex project. She may also be more likely to be late to school or class. Or her impaired sense of time, combined with forgetfulness, can cause problems such as forgetting to do a class project or to staying after school for a scheduled meeting with the teacher.

Provide Brief Materials to Teachers. Some teachers are very knowledgeable about attention deficits and are making appropriate accommodations. Sometimes, however, parents must educate teachers and other school officials about the disorder. If possible, give them brief, one-page summaries on various aspects of dealing with ADD or ADHD. Several "ADHD fact sheets" are available from CHADD (www.chadd.org and www.help4adhd.org). In addition, you might photocopy relevant sections of this book or *Teaching Teens* and give them to teachers. You may also find it helpful to give them the summary entitled "ADD/ADHD: Impact on School Performance," which was developed for parents to give their child's teachers (Appendix 3).

Seek Countywide Training for Teachers. Another option is for local parent support groups to talk to the principal, superintendent, or board of education members about sponsoring a countywide workshop on attention deficits. Even though training may have been provided a few years ago, due to the availability of important new information on ADHD, teacher turnover from retirement and arrival of new teachers, teacher education about attention deficits must be ongoing if it is to be effective. Parents, teenagers, clinicians, and educators could all be on the program. Topics may include characteristics of ADD and ADHD, their impact on school performance, identification of common learning problems in these students, classroom accommodations, tips for coping at school with their impulsivity, disorganization, forgetfulness, and poor memory, and tips for parents on helping at home. On several occasions, I have been invited to do training on ADHD for teachers, because a local parent took the initiative to suggest it to school officials.

As a former teacher and school psychologist who provides workshops for teachers across the country, I have been impressed with the number of dedicated educators who are eager to learn new information. Simultaneously, I am still amazed that with all the new scientific information available, so many teachers are not aware of the basics about the impact of attention deficit disorder on student learning.

4. Change the Environment...If Needed

If you can't change the ADHD behavior, change the environment. For example, request teacher assignments well in advance or change a teacher who has a major personality clash with your teen. Or you can also attempt to teach your teen coping strategies for dealing with difficult teachers.

Teach Your Teen to Cope with the Teacher. Before you request a teacher change, you may try teaching your child to cope with a difficult teacher. After all, we know that our teens are going to meet challenging adults throughout their life. Here are some excellent tips from Joan Helbing, an ADD consultant in Appleton, WI:

"Every year, at least one teacher describes my daughter as disruptive or thinks she talks to much. But Katie is Katie; she's the same in every class. So when we find a teacher who thinks Katie's a challenge rather than a joy, we problem solve with Katie around why that is true in this particular situation. Typically the challenge has to do with the teacher's personality and style, not Katie. Katie communicates very openly and directly; she has opinions and wants to express them. When a teacher doesn't see her in a positive light, then we discuss why that is and focus on how make things better for Katie. We help her understand her teacher's style and then discuss what she needs to change to be successful in that classroom.

"Katie's perception is usually accurate. She can tell who the good teachers are by the second day of school. We've learned that if we hear anything negative early on, we talk about it right away. Otherwise, she can quickly get feisty around her frustration in these situations."

Request a Change in Teachers. If your teen has tried, but is miserable and in danger of failing, you may have to request a teacher change. Additionally, if she is placed in a teacher's class a second grading period, and you know it will be a negative experience, *ask for a class assignment change.* If your request is not sufficient, ask your child's psychologist or physician for a letter making the same request.

"I once requested a class change for my son because he was scheduled to have the same teacher for a second semester in algebra. This teacher was very negative and had a personality conflict with my son. The straw that broke the camel's back was when she said very angrily to my son in front of other students, 'Your mother may overprotect you, but I'm not going to.' The principal would not make this change on the basis of my request alone. However, he accepted the same request from my son's doctor. The doctor submitted a two-sentence request written on a prescription pad."

Occasionally, a teacher may inadvertently contribute to the teen's academic problems. In these situations, changing the teacher, teaching your teen tips for coping with the teacher, or talking with the guidance counselor about getting help for the teacher may be effective strategies.

"One year Katie had problems in Science class. The teacher was very disorganized and was often unclear about when assignments were due. He would arbitrarily change due dates. He gave instructions orally, and provided no written expectations about what projects should look like. Sometimes on tests the teacher would stick in a question that wasn't even covered in class. It was like a "gotcha game." If Katie knows up front what to expect, she will do well on tests. Because I work for the school system, I knew this teacher was struggling and in fact was on probation. Katie needs the teachers in her life to be organized. "

Request Teacher Assignment...In Advance. One way to avoid problems is to request a teacher assignment six months in advance for the next school year. Teenagers with ADD or ADHD are more likely to be successful with a teacher who is patient, firm but supportive, flexible, and respectful to students. These students also tend to do better in a class if they like the teacher. If your adolescent is struggling, don't be afraid to request teachers who are more flexible and work well with students who have learning problems. Find out exactly what time of year class assignments are made. The principal may not grant a request for a specific teacher by name, but you could say, "My daughter will do best in a classroom with a teacher who is supportive and flexible like Mrs. Smith." Work with the school counselor to avoid having your teenager assigned to teachers who may be rigid or inflexible.

5. Anticipate and Avoid Crisis

Parents can often predict which events will upset their teenager and cause problems at school. If you know that your teenager is going to school upset and could possibly get into an explosive situation, you might suggest she talk with the guidance counselor first thing that morning. You may also call the counselor and say, "Jessica broke up with her boyfriend and is really upset. Can you talk to her? I'm afraid she may be planning to fight his new girlfriend." Having a back up "crisis plan" in place is also important. For example, if your teen is extremely upset and might blow up, she

has permission, given in advance, to go speak with the guidance counselor.

Develop a plan for handling crises or infractions of school rules. Federal IDEA guidelines require the school to develop a plan for dealing with problem behaviors that are related to a child's disability. Conducting a functional behavior assessment (FBA) to identify the "trigger" for problem behavior, and the subsequent development of a behavior intervention plan can be invaluable. In other words, behaviors that frequently get your child in trouble must be identified and a plan developed to deal with them. See Chapter 14 and *Teaching Teens* for more information on FBAs.

Conclusion

Unfortunately, working with educators to find the best way to teach your teenager is not something you do once and never have to do again. As parents of children with attention deficit disorders, in many respects, we are all "trail blazers." The best practices for teaching our children and teens are still being discovered. Because you "live and breathe" attention deficit disorder, you may be better informed about this condition than many teachers. Most likely, you will have to work with each new teacher as your teenager progresses through school. Other children will benefit from laying this educational groundwork. The suggestions in Chapters 12 through 14 and in *Teaching Teens* should make this process a little easier. During those years when you have excellent teachers, enjoy your good fortune. For there will be other years when you must find the patience to educate and forgive the few skeptical and uninformed teachers you will undoubtedly run across.

Working on the Home Front

"I can picture my son sitting at the kitchen table, starting his homework while I cleaned up the dishes after dinner. 'Starting' his homework is probably not a very accurate description. Typically, the scenario played out like this: 'It's time to start your homework.' 'Okay Mom, I'll be right there.' Ten minutes later, he has not yet begun writing. Then he has to go to his room twice. The first trip is for his book. Next he has to return because he forgot his pencil. He cannot resist stopping to watch his snake crawling under a rock in the corner of the aquarium. Another delay occurs because he doesn't remember his homework assignment and has to call a friend. Now I heave a sigh of relief because the first part of the battle has been won. I have him at the kitchen table ready to begin.

"He is tapping the table with his pencil and looking out the patio door at the dog drinking water. Patiently, at first, I say, 'Dear, it's time to get started.' Fifteen minutes later, one problem has been completed. Impatiently, I stop doing the dishes, walk to the table, put my finger on a specific line on his paper, and scream, 'Right here, right now, put your pencil on the paper and write something, I don't care what.' He works hard for a few minutes and then is distracted by something else. This process continues throughout the next hour with both of us feeling increasingly angry and frustrated."

Failure to complete homework is one of the biggest sources of conflict between parents and teenagers who have an attention deficit. Parents often get so an-

gry and upset that they completely lose their patience with their child. Parents from across the country have expressed similar concerns about their teenagers and their homework: they're disorganized, don't have the right books or don't remember their assignments, put off getting started, argue, refuse to complete their work, yell, or accuse their parents of nagging and then forget to turn in their homework. Or, parents may hear two of their more famous lines: "No, I don't have any homework." Or, "I finished it all at school."

You and your teenager may face many challenges as he attempts to succeed in school. As discussed in Chapter 11, you should give yourself permission to "do whatever it takes" to help your teenager succeed at school. If your child is struggling academically, you should not feel guilty about helping him. Once a routine of successful school performance is achieved, you will be able to reduce your day-to-day involvement. The key is to teach your teen the skills or compensatory strategies needed so that he can accept increasing levels of responsibility for his schoolwork.

This chapter discusses common school-related problems that parents and teenagers can work on together at home to resolve. They include: battles over homework, forgotten assignments, books, and weekly notes; failure to complete homework; not turning in homework; getting too many zeros; failing classes; sleep problems; and school avoidance. A summary of intervention strategies is provided in Table 12-2 at the end of the chapter.

The Bloody Homework Battles

If your teenager with an attention deficit takes full responsibility for his schoolwork, you are lucky. Many parents must regularly check that their teen has completed his homework, especially if he is in danger of failing classes. Because homework sessions can be extremely exasperating, many parents dread evenings and the looming battles over homework.

Sometimes, anger and frustration over homework battles lead to a great deal of guilt and depression for both the parents and the teenager. If parents aren't careful, love for their teenager may become conditional, contingent upon good academic performance. Inadvertently, parents may send the unspoken message, "I love you *only* when you do well in school."

"We reached a point where our interactions were a constant battleground over his academic work. In my frustration and anger, I would lose my cool and find myself screaming. I would guiltily think, 'I am a well-trained, compassionate professional. I should know how to deal more effectively with my own child.' Without realizing it, my unspoken message to my son was that my love and approval were contingent upon his school performance. The subtle messages I had been unwittingly giving him were: 'You are not okay. You are not 'good' unless you complete all your homework. We don't like you when you do not complete your homework.' When I came to that realization, I began changing ways I interacted with my son and the kinds of statements I made to him."

Avoiding bloody battles over homework is important. If homework becomes a constant battleground,

your teenager may associate learning with negative experiences that are to be avoided at all costs, along with *you,* the "slave driver" who is forcing him to do all this "stupid schoolwork." Although the reactions of both you and your teenager are understandable, allowing battles over school to continue can damage the long-term parent-child relationship. Frequent hostile interactions may cause even worse behavior problems. The best way to end the fighting is to ensure that learning and deficits in executive skills are identified, accommodations are made in the classroom, and, if needed, medication is taken during homework sessions.

If you end up battling your teen when you try to help with homework, recruit someone else for the job—your spouse, a friend or relative, or a paid professional. If you are working, you may even find an adult who can help on two levels: supervising your teen after school and helping with his homework.

Parents grow weary of constantly repeating statements and questions about schoolwork: "What is your math homework? Your math teacher always puts the math assignments on the board. Write them down every day! Do you have your math book? You don't have it? Well, let's get in the car and go back to school and get it." Sorry, but repetition, ad nauseam, goes with the ADD/ADHD territory.

Here are a couple of suggestions for where you may find additional help on homework. For example, Chapters 11 and 13 provide helpful information to reduce homework battles. In addition, *Teaching Teens* offers homework tips plus even greater detail about topics such as writing essays, doing math, and addressing executive function problems. See Summary 24 for specific information on what constitutes good homework. *A Bird's-Eye View* also offers easy-to-read homework strategies for teens.

Avoiding Bloody Homework Battles

The following suggestions will help you provide structure for your teenager when he is doing homework. These suggestions are summarized at the end of the chapter in an easy reference chart. One key tip here: use as few words as necessary to get your point across about homework. With fewer words, confrontations are less likely. For example, point to the clock to indicate that it is time to start, raise your eyebrows, or give your teen "the get started look."

1. Establishing a Study Routine

Set a Specific Time to Do Homework Each Evening. Many teenagers with attention deficits have poor organizational skills and also lack an awareness of time. *Getting started is frequently the biggest challenge.* As discussed earlier, the ability to initiate work, or in other words get started is a critical executive skill. The opening vignette in this chapter is typical of many youngsters with attention deficits—especially before diagnosis of their ADD or ADHD and use of stimulant medications during homework sessions. Of course, even with medication, starting work can still be problematic. Usually, these teenagers can also benefit from the structure of having a set time to start homework each evening.

Involve your teenager in selecting his starting time for homework. For example, you might give him limited choices: "Would you like to start your homework at 7:00 or 7:30?" He may set 7:00 as the starting time. Wait and see if he starts his homework on his own. If he doesn't start his assignment by a set time, then discuss in advance how it will be handled. "How do you want me to remind you if you don't get started right away: "Walk to your bedroom door and give a signal (use no words) or just tell you?" If he doesn't know what his assignments are, let him call a friend or have him look it up on his weekly assignment sheet.

Set an Alarm to Announce Homework Time. A wristwatch with an alarm function may be a wise investment. The teenager (or parent) can set his wristwatch, a kitchen timer, or alarm clock to announce when it is time to start homework. The digital timer on the microwave can also be used as an alarm. The alarm ring announces it is time to start, not the parent. Your teenager may enjoy the novelty, at least for a while. Let him select which alarm system to use.

Minimize Distractions. Find a place to study that is relatively free from distractions. The kitchen table or a desk may be a good choice, unless there are objects on them that distract your child. If the desk in his room is covered with papers and other items, it may not be the best place to study. However, as long as he is completing his work, give him a choice of study location.

Find a "Study Buddy" or Establish a "Study Circle." Your teenager might ask a student who is in the same class to study with him. Afterwards, the teens can spend time together on recreational activities. This "study buddy" system works best if the other teenager doesn't have an attention deficit and remembers the homework assignments. If his friend has ADD or ADHD, you'll just have to provide a little more supervision. Your teenager may find the terms offensive, so you may not want to use the labels "study buddy" or "study circle."

When two teenagers study together, they often review the material verbally. If your child has learning difficulties, this can be very helpful, as the more senses he uses when doing his homework, the more likely he is to learn the material. Instead of just reading and writing his assignments silently, he will also be discussing them out loud.

> *"Cassie thinks her 'Study Circle' of friends has helped her make better grades."*

Consider Medication When Doing Homework. If your child has great difficulty completing his schoolwork, consider having him take medication during this period. Frequently, by the time teens begin working on homework, all the effects of the morning dose of stimulant medication have worn off. If medication has worn off, your doctor may prescribe a small dose of a short-acting medication such as Ritalin, Focalin, or Dexedrine as described in Chapter 6. You and your teenager need to determine the latest time in the afternoon that stimulant medication can be taken without interfering with his ability to fall asleep. For example, if he takes regular Ritalin or Dexedrine at 5 p.m., the medication will wear off by approximately 9 p.m., so homework must be complete before then.

> *"A few days after a big fight over homework, I found myself reflecting on the conflict between my son and me. This can't be normal. He wants to do well in school but something is going on internally that makes school extremely difficult for him. I reasoned, if he could get started and complete his work promptly, he would, simply to avoid years of ranting and raving by an enraged mother.*
>
> *"My son's ADD was diagnosed a few years later. Since we were reluctant to give him stimulant medication during the evenings, problems with homework completion continued into high school. If I had it to do over again, I would definitely let him take medication while he worked on homework."*

> *"Since my son began taking Ritalin when he studies at night, his memory of what he has studied has increased and his test grades have improved."*

2. Ensuring Homework Assignments Are Known

Call a Friend to Confirm Homework Assignments. Parents may set up a daily routine of asking their teen what his assignments are for any subject he is in danger of failing. If he can't remember, he should have phone numbers of other students in his class to call for the assignment. Be sure to obtain phone numbers for other students early in the grading period. Otherwise, your teenager may need a number and he won't remember last names or addresses.

Call the School Homework Hotline or Visit the School Webpage. Find out whether the school has a homework or tutoring hotline or a webpage that students or parents may use to either find out homework assignments or to receive assistance in a specific subject.

Request That an Email Be Sent Home. Some teachers will email assignments to your home email address or ask your son to send home his own assignment via email. Some teachers might allow the student to call home and leave a homework message on the home phone.

Ask That Assignments Be Posted on an Outside Classroom Window. One of the more creative strategies one teacher used was to post homework assignments on a window, facing the outside, so that parents could come by after school or at night, if needed.

Use a Color-Coded Monthly Calendar. Mary Kay Clyburn, a learning disabilities teacher, suggests having teenagers with ADD or ADHD keep a monthly calendar, perhaps hanging on the wall. Color code this calendar for tests, quizzes, and projects, with reminders for when to start preparing for a test. For example, if a test is scheduled for Friday, write a reminder on the calendar to begin studying a couple of days before the test. Otherwise, your teenager may not think about it until Friday morning.

Find Out the Routine of Homework Assignments. Many teachers establish daily and weekly routines for assigning homework. For example, one section of history questions may be assigned for homework each night, Monday through Thursday. The "Bioquiz" questions at the end of the biology chapter may always be assigned Tuesday and Thursday. It may take two weeks to complete one chapter. So expect a test every two weeks. By learning assignment routines, it will be easier to monitor your child's completion of homework. For example, you may say, "Your biology questions are due tomorrow—it's time to start work on them." Or, if an algebra test is scheduled every two weeks: "Don't forget you're supposed to have an algebra test tomorrow." The implied but unspoken message is that you should study tonight.

Find Out When Special Projects Are Due. Teenagers with attention deficits frequently forget special assignments. This can be an academic disaster, since long-term projects usually represent a major grade. If you know that your teenager frequently forgets these projects, ask teachers at the beginning of the semester about any major class projects and due dates. This can be accomplished at the first PTA meeting of the year when you have a chance to meet all of your child's teachers. You may also find the tips and sample graphic organizer in *Teaching Teens* helpful for completing these often monstrous long-term projects (Summaries 35 and 36). Some parents incorporate a statement into the IEP or 504 Plan that they will be notified of due dates of any major projects.

3. Tackling Homework

Divide Homework into Smaller Segments. Some students become overwhelmed by the length of a major assignment or test. Breaking the assignment into shorter segments can make it seem more manageable. You or a teacher might cut a worksheet or fold it into sections for younger teens. Your teenager can give you each section as he completes it and pick up the next worksheet or assignment. This allows him to get up and walk, releasing some of his energy and giving him a little break. For assignments in a textbook, you might ask him to complete one-fourth of it and bring it to you when he is finished. Then you give him the next portion of the assignment. Sometimes using a timer and making a game of it may add more interest. For example, ask him to see how many problems he can complete before the timer goes off in ten minutes. Some teens may enjoy this "game." Other teens may think it's stupid.

Let Your Teen Use a Computer. Since many of these teenagers have problems with limited working memory capacity, weak verbal expression, slow processing speed, and poor fine motor skills, writing assignments may be time-consuming and laborious. If your family has a computer, it will be extremely helpful for completion of homework. Plus, having a copy of all completed work is wonderful insurance for teenagers who often lose their schoolwork before it is ever turned in to the teacher.

Have Your Teenager Dictate Essays or Reports. As an alternative to using a computer, he could dictate an essay or report to you to type. Afterwards, you can give him the rough draft to edit and correct. Even for math, you can write the problems down as your teenager explains what needs to be done. This might be helpful if your teen has major visual-motor problems or finds math so aversive that he refuses to do any math problems. Later, you and your teen can alternate writing the math problems. Eventually, the teen will do all the problems independently. Ultimately, you are "shaping" your teenager's behavior by moving him toward completing all his work on his own.

"My daughter has to write a major term paper and was told she would have to handwrite it or type it herself. My question is, what are we grading and teaching here: writing or typing?"

The limited working memory, slow processing speed, and fine motor problems some students have affect their typing skill and speed.

"My son took keyboarding, which I assumed would be a fairly easy A . . . wrong. His typing was so slow, he really struggled just to get a C in the class. Because of slow processing skills, it took him so much longer to finish his typing assignments than other students."

Use White Noise or Play the Radio. If your teenager is too easily distracted by other noises, "white noise" in the background may help block out distractions and help him concentrate better. You might purchase a recording of ocean sounds. Some students use fans to provide a background noise. Or the teen may wear headphones that simply block out noise.

Some teenagers and adults with attention deficits say they can study better when the radio is playing. One adult said it helped her stay on task by keeping her from daydreaming. She always likes to do two or three things at a time.

"Beth has always preferred to do homework while listening to the radio and sometimes while watching television. She tells me that she can concentrate better when she studies. This was especially true before her ADHD was diagnosed and she started taking medi-

cation. Although I cannot study this way, my daughter seems to be able to do so. Usually, if she turns the TV on while studying, I suggest she watch a program that does not involve a plot or story line she needs to follow."

Limit Time Spent on Homework. Homework, when completed and done correctly, may take forever for some teenagers, especially if they have learning problems such as poor working memory, slow reading or writing, a written language deficit, poor reading comprehension, or poor organizational skills. A teenager with working memory and memorization problems will have trouble working basic math calculations quickly. Consequently, math homework assignments may be very time-consuming. While a student who works quickly can complete the assignment in 30 minutes, a teenager with ADD or ADHD may take an hour or more. If homework takes too long, the student may soon avoid and hate doing homework.

"As a junior in high school, my son spent two to three hours at least three nights a week on homework. He worked so slowly, it took him forever to finish his work. Prior to starting on medication he could never have worked that long. We probably should have had the amount of homework reduced so that he could finish one assignment in an hour. He understood the math concepts but he just couldn't produce the volume of work necessary."

"You cannot rush our son who has ADD but is not hyperactive. Even though he is very bright, he processes things slowly, reads slowly, works slowly, writes slowly, and has only one speed—slow. Great patience is needed to work with him."

How much time should be spent on homework? As a rule of thumb, high school students should generally be able to finish most homework assignments in all subjects in an hour or two. An average high school student doesn't spend more than one to two hours total on homework each night. If homework takes more than two hours almost every night, parents will need to work with teachers, a guidance counselor, their treatment professional, or physician to develop a plan to modify homework assignments. Sometimes having your treatment professional or physician write a letter requesting an accommodation may help.

General guidelines from the PTA (Parent Teacher Association) and NEA (National Education Association) suggest that students should spend no more than roughly ten minutes per grade each night on homework. So that means a ninth grader could spend up to a total of an hour and a half (90 minutes) on his homework for all his subjects.

Rarely, you might elect to limit time spent on homework even if your teenager has not finished the assignment. Sometimes if a student is not on medication, or is extremely upset, angry, in crisis, or struggling with a difficult assignment, he may not be able to concentrate. Rather than have him sit for hours staring at a book, stop battling an impossible situation. He probably won't be very productive anyway if more than two hours is required for homework. If you limit his homework, send a note to the teacher asking for a delay or modification of the assignment so that he won't get into trouble at school. You might even consider adding a statement to your child's IEP stating that the parents will limit homework if need be.

Watch Out for Hasty Errors. Some teenagers rush to get homework over with as quickly as possible. It doesn't matter to them if it is finished or if it is correct.

"Steven (ADHD) had difficulty working more than fifteen minutes on homework, so he tended to rush through his work. He would come out of his room talking about how hard he had been working and my husband and I would just look at each other with questioning glances. Later, during discussions with my doctor, our son's comments began to make sense. Since it is so difficult for him to concentrate and stay on task, he has to work harder than the average student. Fifteen minutes study time must take tremendous energy for these teenagers and must seem like an eternity."

If your teen has a tendency to rush through homework, you may have to review it when he is finished. You can mark mistakes and then have him correct his errors.

If you don't know much about the subject yourself, you may only be able to check to see if he has at least answered all the questions. Sometimes answers are found in the back of the book. Or have your son work with a friend and they can double-check each other's answers.

Teach Your Teenager That School and Homework Must Be Done, Either Now or Later. Sometimes students may learn the wrong lesson.

"What my son had learned regarding homework was that if you don't do the work when it is due, you'll get a zero but never have to do the assignment."

To correct this problem, tell your teenager he must make up any schoolwork he doesn't complete during the week. The work must be done even if it is late and he will receive partial or no credit. You will need to review the weekly report (see Table 12-1) at the end of the week to see what work your teen missed. Then you can calmly tell him that when the schoolwork is done, he can go to the mall, or do whatever activity he likes. If he finishes the schoolwork at 7:00 p.m. Friday night, let him go to the mall. The lesson learned speaks for itself and you have no need to preach, nag, or punish. Your teenager will learn that he has to do the work regardless. So, he may as well do the work when it is assigned.

Of course, you must use common sense when using this approach. Avoid overwhelming your teen with an impossible task, such as completing all makeup work from four or five classes. When you implement this strategy, start with a clean slate and tell the teenager "We will start next weekend, so please do your homework all week so you can go out Friday night." This intervention will be easier to monitor if only one or two subjects are involved. You may need to start with only one or two of his most important subjects. If the work missed is in classes where the teacher will not give any credit for late work, you might ask him just to do a few problems that will ensure that concepts are mastered for the next test. Or you may discuss this at the IEP or 504 meeting to see if teachers will give credit until the student is consistently completing work in a timely manner.

Ensure Completed Homework Is Placed in the Notebook. Finally, your teen may have done the work, but double check to make certain that it is in his notebook ready for the next day. You may also check through his notebook for notes from the teacher. You should probably ask your teen's permission to look through the notebook for assignments or notes. Do this when your teenager is present so that he doesn't feel that you are sneaking around spying on him.

Keep Extra School Supplies on Hand. Parents often find it helpful to keep extra poster board, report covers, and markers on hand for the forgotten project. You may also want to keep duplicates of items such as a calculator that may be easily lost.

> *"Recently Barry lost an expensive calculator. Thankfully, I always keep a back-up calculator at home, just in case of an emergency. One semester he lost his calculator the day of his math final exam. We were in the store parking lot stuffing batteries in the new calculator at 9:15 that morning so he could make it to school and take his final exam at 10:00."*

Clean out Notebook Periodically and Save Old Papers. Often, your teen's notebook is so messy, he can't find important papers. After cleaning out the notebook, place current assignments in the proper section. Be sure to hang onto old papers. Otherwise, you may find out that you have thrown away assignments your teenager completed but failed to turn in. If grades are missing and the teacher will accept homework late, find the completed papers and turn them in.

> *"Bart would do his homework and forget to turn it in. Days later we would find out that he was missing some grades. The teacher never received the homework. We would usually find it in his bookbag and turn it in then."*

4. Ensuring Good Communication with the School

Use Daily or Weekly Reports. Using a weekly report is one of my favorite tools for ensuring that students consistently complete and turn in homework. Under a weekly report system, your teen brings home a signed note from his teachers that describes his academic progress that week. The report may indicate whether all homework was completed and list his test and daily grades. Limiting this to only those subjects that your teenager is failing or in danger of failing is probably a good idea. You might make participation in a weekend activity that he likes contingent upon bringing home a satisfactory "weekly report." The teacher may send the report home each week, fax or email the note home or to your office, or have the school secretary call. Or if teachers are willing, they can email or call each day and leave a message on the answering machine.

Some schools have developed their own weekly report forms or may use an online grade reporting system such as Edline (www.edline.net). Online grade reporting of grades and missing homework can be a lifesaver for our forgetful children. If your school does not have its own report, you can design your own. A sample report is provided in Table 12-1 on the next page. Anything you can do to make the process quick and easy will be greatly appreciated by teachers. They are also more likely to follow up on your request. Keep things simple: decide what information you need (test grades, completion of homework) and include that on the form. You may request the teacher's signature rather than initials. Of course, no student with an attention deficit would ever think of forging a teacher's initials, but just in case, it's harder to copy a name than initials.

> *"I found that I didn't need to demand A's or B's or passing grades on all my son's work in order for him to go to the mall. All I had to ask for was completion of all his assignments. Because he was so bright, if he did his schoolwork, then he passed the tests and made good grades on daily assignments. Weekly repots were the perfect thing for us!"*

If your teenager is struggling and the weekly report isn't effective, then try a daily report until he begins to consistently complete home- and schoolwork on a daily basis. A daily report may include the homework assignment, any uncompleted class work that must be done that night, or any grades for the day—so you can praise him for his good work. Then you can drop back to a weekly report and hopefully eliminate both reports eventually. To learn more about how to successfully use weekly reports, read *Teaching Teens,* Summaries 26 and 27. Dr. William E. Pelham, Jr., has created an excellent "school-home daily report card" for his Summer Treatment Program in New York.

Forgetting to Bring Home the Weekly Report. Remembering to get the weekly report signed and bringing it home, seemingly simple tasks, are two major hurdles for students with ADD or ADHD. After all, *forgetfulness* is one of the diagnostic criteria for ADHD. Use common sense in monitoring the weekly report. If your teenager is failing a class but homework and class work grades have improved, don't have a heart attack if he forgets the weekly note. He may have done his homework (the primary goal), but simply forgotten the note. Work on setting up a system to ensure that the note makes it home in the future. Regardless, if you set up this kind of program, you must receive the report on

Table 12-1   Daily/Weekly Report

NAME:_____ DATE: _____

PERIOD____: _____ (CLASS)

	M	T	W	T	F
homework turned in					
classwork completed					
grades					

Comments: _____

_____

_____

Unfinished assignments (Optional): _____

Teacher Signature: _____

Friday to determine if he has earned the right to go out on Friday and Saturday nights. Remember, to be effective, feedback must be immediate, not delayed.

The teenager who forgets a note may be in "hot water" twice: First for not doing the work, and second, for not bringing home the note. Obviously, even if your teenager finished his homework but forgot to bring the note home, positive interactions with parents did not increase.

"Until recently, I had always been blessed with an excellent memory. I was not very sympathetic to those who did not remember things and assumed my memory was better because I chose to be that way. During a recent illness, my memory was affected. Plus, I must reluctantly admit that perhaps the aging process is having some effect on my memory. I totally forgot a teacher conference I had scheduled. For the first time in my life, I can identify with my son and his forgetfulness. Being forgetful isn't any fun and it's embarrassing."

Set Up a Reminder System about the Report. Remembering the note is likely to be problematic. Obviously, we can't easily change this ADD behavior (forgetfulness), so why not change the environment? Have a teacher or a friend remind your teen to get the weekly report. Or he could set a wristwatch alarm, computer, or Palm Pilot to remind him about the note.

Take or Send Him Back to School for the Weekly Report. If necessary, take him back to school to get the note or call the teacher. If your teenager continues to forget to bring the weekly report home even though he experiences the logical consequences of not going to the mall, adjust the plan. For example, you might switch to a daily report and check to see that he completes his work each day. Or have the teacher or school secretary call or email or fax the information to you. Or with her permission, call the teacher at home.

Teach Key Skills First; Let Others Slide. Your teenager can't learn every skill you want him to learn overnight. The most important issue or skills must be identified and taught first. Right now, the most important issue may be the academic one—completion of homework. After he learns to finish his work consistently, you can work on other issues, such as remembering to bring his weekly report home. In truth, he may never consistently remember to bring the report home each Friday. But the major issue—completion of homework—should improve.

5. Avoiding Emotional Blow Ups over Homework

Identify Parenting Strategies to Keep Homework Time Peaceful. Several strategies are discussed in Chapter 11 about effective ways to interact with your teenager that should make homework sessions more positive. For example, establish a homework routine, give choices, make certain medication is working, and if you can't change the ADD behavior, change the environment. Here are a couple more tips that may be helpful:

- If frustration builds during homework sessions, take a break to allow things to cool off.
- If your teenager blows up, stay calm and lower your voice. A loud emotional response from you may result in your teen becoming more aggressive and producing less schoolwork.

Give Time to Unwind Before Bedtime. Your teenager may need time to unwind after the harrowing homework battles. He may want to take a shower, get ready for bed, listen to music, and have a few minutes to himself.

Additional School Challenges
1. Making Too Many Zeros

Many students with attention deficits often make good grades if, and when, they complete and turn in school assignments. Unfortunately, more often than not, they have a terrible time remembering to complete and turn in their homework. Consequently, they may have lots of zeros averaged into their grades. Zeros on homework, major projects, or missed make-up tests may result in the youngster failing a class. Strategies must be put in place to help your teen compensate for forgetfulness.

"One year, my son Tyler, who has ADD, failed math. He was so frustrated and overwhelmed that he just shut down. Not turning in homework was a huge problem. It was so frustrating to me because if he simply turned in his homework, he got 10 points added to his grades. But if he didn't, the teacher actually subtracted 10 points. I consider this an easy, "effort" grade.

"It makes me so mad at him when he doesn't even try. Some days, we have had knock down, drag out discussions. His good intentions last only a couple of days. Then he stops turning in his work again. I tell him that if he would just try, they won't fail him. I have taken privileges away many times, but the results are always the same. He simply gets overwhelmed and shuts down."

Monitor for Zeros in Subjects in Danger of Failing. If your teen is receiving a lot of zeros and is in danger of failing a class, consider monitoring his progress through daily or weekly reports, homework checks, or a telephone conference with the teacher. Also double check to see if make-up assignments and tests are completed after absences.

"The grades Shawn receives for completed work are usually pretty good. But he has gotten more zeros than I can count. I remember once when Shawn was in the fifth grade, he had to turn in a composition at the end of each week. One week he spent two and a half hours and wrote a beautiful paper . . . on the wrong topic. When he realized that it was the wrong subject, he just threw his composition away.

"His teacher sent a note home indicating he received a zero. I wrote back and said I hope she had praised him for the report he wrote even though it was on the wrong topic. She wrote back and said, 'What report?' She never even saw the paper.

"If he received a 90, he seemed to take a vacation. He wouldn't do any work for a few days and he would get a few zeros. He never seemed to understand that zeros bring your grades down significantly."

"When my daughter's out sick, the last thing she does is organize herself before she goes back to school. The thought of what will we be doing at school never enters her head. She is concentrating on getting her body to school."

Ask Teachers to Be Flexible with Make-up Work. Sometimes these students forget to do their homework, or complete it but forget to turn it in. Or, because of their listening comprehension and memory problems, they may do an assignment incorrectly. Teachers can be most helpful if they are willing to allow some flexibility in completion of assignments and determining grades, at least until an effective plan is implemented and the student is more successful in school. Ideally, his teachers will allow him to turn in work late for full or at least partial credit so he doesn't get so many zeros.

"One mother told me of her son's beautiful work drawing a timeline of major history events. He spent hours on the project. The teacher gave the student a failing grade because he put approximate dates rather than exact dates. Since his ADHD and listening comprehension problems resulted in not completing the assignment correctly, the teacher should have been willing

to be more flexible in grading. The teacher should also ensure that the teenager is clear on future assignments."

Understandably, high school teachers are trying to instill a sense of greater responsibility in teenagers. They set deadlines and expect them to be met. However, many students with attention deficits have major challenges to overcome—weak organization skills, poor memory, poor work habits, knowledge gaps, an impaired sense of time, and a developmental delay. Plus, they don't learn from negative consequences (failing a test or class) like other students do. They may feel badly about failing, but even their good intentions will not always change their behavior. This is a major difference in these teens that may be difficult for both parents and teachers to understand and accept.

Depending on your teenager's confidence and how positive and receptive the teacher is, he may ask to turn in work late himself. If teachers are negative, you or the guidance counselor may have more success explaining the issue and asking them to cut the teen some slack.

Flexibility in turning work in late should be used sparingly for a limited time. You must work with your teenager to improve completion of his homework. Once

he begins to turn in assignments regularly, he may become hooked on success. The accommodations may then be phased out over time.

Have Your Child Average His Grades. Asking your child to average his current grades may make him more aware of what grade he is earning for the grading period. In addition, to teach him how damaging zeroes can be, you might ask him to determine how many 100's are required to bring a zero up to a passing grade. Or, more realistically, how many grades of 85 does it take to bring one zero grade up to a passing score? The answer: 5 grades of 85 are required. Here is some advice from an expert—a teenager who knows about zeros.

"Don't ever let yourself get a zero. Turn in something even if it's not up to your standards. Zeros averaged in with other grades are too hard to bring up to a passing grade."

—Amelia, age 18, *A Bird's-Eye View*

2. Failing Some Classes

Because of the factors discussed in previous sections (learning problems, working memory deficits, forgetfulness, failure to do homework, and averaging zeros) teenagers with attention deficits may fail a class.

Many of these students have no idea whether they are passing their classes or failing. They may remember passing grades on tests, but forget about zeros on homework. They may be shocked when they fail or receive a low grade. They feel confused and may decide that regardless of how hard they try, they are going to fail anyway. Or, they may start off a new grading period with the best intentions and sincere promises of making better grades. Then their grades begin to slide and it is a struggle to pull out passing grades by the end of the period.

"We referred to this period as 'The Agony and Ecstasy.' The teenager starts off great, goes downhill fast, and then you have to race like crazy the last week to get A's to bring F's up to C's."

Discuss the Full Impact of Failing a Class. These teenagers often don't understand the full ramifications of failing eighth grade (having to stay behind when peers leave for high school) or failing subjects in high school (not being in a homeroom or classes with friends of the same age, being ineligible for extracurricular activities, having to attend summer school, or not graduating with classmates). Discussing these consequences of school failure may impress your teen with the importance of maintaining passing grades. On the other hand, because of his attention deficit, even understanding the implications of failing may not change his behavior.

"Alex failed a class his freshman year in high school with a grade of 69. (70 was passing.) He had no idea that he was failing the class. He made 87 on the final exam but forgot to make up two tests that he missed. Consequently, two zeros were averaged in with his test grades. If the educational goal was to teach students the material, my son met that goal by passing the final exam with an 87. However, the secondary goal of being organized and completing and turning in all homework was not met.

"He was allowed to make up the missed tests, but still failed the class by one point. The teacher didn't like him and didn't want to let him make up the tests. Higher-ranking administrators authorized the make-up tests, against the wishes of the classroom teacher. I wouldn't be surprised if the teacher gave my son an impossible 'ringer' test (for advanced classes). The teacher wasn't willing to give him a break."

"Due to 'no pass, no play' legislation in our state, our son couldn't swim on the swim team. He was the fastest swimmer on the team. Swimming was one of the things in which he excelled. School was a terrible experience for him. He needed to swim. He needed to be successful."

Monitor Progress If Your Teenager Is Struggling. If your teen is often on the verge of failing a specific class such as algebra, monitor progress early, after two or three weeks, so you can intervene if necessary. Ask your teen to check with teachers to find out how he is doing, or failing that, call yourself or email the teacher for an update. Also check the midterm academic progress reports the school sends home. You may also ask teachers to write weekly progress reports, as described earlier in this chapter.

"When my son started high school, I decided to let him tackle his classes on his own and did not monitor his school progress. He received notices midterm that he was in danger of failing some of his classes. He ended up failing two classes and had to attend summer school.

"I learned two lessons. First, I needed to monitor his academic progress more closely, even though he was in high school, and make certain he did his homework. Teachers began sending home weekly reports regarding completion of homework. Weekend privileges were contingent upon completion of homework. Second, the logical consequence of having to attend summer school was not effective. Unfortunately, the consequence (summer school) was too far removed in time from the problem behavior (failing a class)."

Help Your Teenager Graph His Grades. Helping your teenager chart daily grades on graph paper may give him the visual aid he needs to realize what the grades actually mean. You can encourage him to decrease the distance between the high and low points of his grades on the graph. If necessary, quizzes, tests, and daily grades may be color coded to show him the specific areas needing improvement. Your teen can visually observe improvements in his grades and this provides concrete positive feedback.

Obtain Factual Information Regarding Grades. Don't take for granted that your teenager knows what a passing grade is. Find out actual grades or requirements by asking teachers or by reading written information sent home by the school. Ask the teacher how final grades are obtained. Some grades such as test scores may be weighted differently than homework. The student may think he's failing when he's not and feel overwhelmed without fully knowing all the facts. Recently, greater emphasis has been placed upon test scores so grades for homework may be of less importance. For example, in one Maryland school district, grades on homework are only 10 percent of the final grade, classwork 40 percent, and test scores 50 percent.

Find Innovative Ways to Make Up Needed Credits. If your teenager has failed some classes, he may not have enough credits to graduate with his friends. Graduating with friends is critically important to many teenagers and they may be willing to work hard to accomplish this goal. Typical ways to do this include taking additional credits during the regular school semester, attending summer school, or attending alternative public high school, possibly at night. Some public high schools may have a modified semester system for night school in which a student can earn a full semester's credit in eight weeks by attending class eight hours a week. An educational consultant found an innovative way to help her teenager with ADHD graduate on time by earning the dreaded science and algebra credits through a correspondence class.

If your teenager has poor organizational skills, you may have to take the initiative to make arrangements for these courses. But your teen has the hardest job: he has to do the class work.

"Katie lacked two semesters of physical science to graduate from high school with her classmates. She desperately wanted to finish and walk at graduation with her friends. I did a lot of research and found out that she could earn high school graduation requirements through a correspondence program offered at a university in another state. The critical requirement was that the course content had to meet the credit requirements established by the state.

"I was so proud of my daughter—in addition to her regular high school classes, she completed both classes. Each class required eight weeks to finish. Staff at the University of Texas said they had never done anything like this before but they were willing to work with us. It was wonderful to have the cooperation of all those involved to help her graduate with her class. I had to do all the leg work required, including linking with the University and the State Department of Education, but she did all her own schoolwork."

"Kenosha, Wisconsin schools offer a special program to make up credits toward graduation. Since many of these students have already failed the class previously, the program is a self-paced instructional software program from the Plato Company, which allows the student to move at his own pace as he masters the material."

The University of Nebraska (UNL) has offered correspondence courses for earning credits toward high school graduation since 1929. This service was started years ago to help youngsters who lived and worked on isolated farms and ranches across the state. The University offers a broad selection of courses: 164 correspondence courses and 33 web-based courses. UNL is a nationally recognized leader in the area of distance learning courses. Consequently, other states are now contracting with them to offer virtual high schools on-line. Visit the website of the University of Nebraska (www.distance.unl.edu) and read about distance learning. The site also has a catalog listing of their courses. Parents who are home schooling their children have also used some of these courses to enrich their child's education.

If you or your teenager is interested in pursuing correspondence courses, you may also check with the nearest state university and their student services or Section 504 coordinator if such courses are offered. You may call your state department of education and ask for the coordinator of special education or Section 504. Be persistent, since several telephone calls may be required to track down the right person who can give you the necessary information.

3. School Avoidance

Because school is such a negative experience, some teenagers with attention deficits may not want to attend. For these teenagers, the emotional trauma of having to go to school may be enough to make them physically sick some mornings. When they get up, their stomachs may be upset, their heads and muscles may ache. Others may not have physical symptoms but are emotionally fed up with school. They may skip school rather than face failure in an unpleasant learning environment.

"Although our daughter didn't have allergies, as a high school student, she developed severe muscle spasms. I'm sure it was from anxiety. Once we even had to go to physical therapy."

For some, school avoidance may not be a conscious action but reflect anxiety about attending school and a desire to avoid a negative experience. As adults, we should understand this feeling, since most of us avoid things we do not do well.

If these students miss a lot of school, they often fall behind academically. Because of their lack of organization and follow-through, they may not complete make-up work. This puts them in danger of failing classes. Frequently, a sense of despair overwhelms them when they get too far behind in their schoolwork. They may see no way out of their predicament. Doing regular homework plus make-up work seems like an impossible task. They may give up. These problems create the perfect scenario for producing an extremely depressed teenager.

Set a Standard for Attending School. You must take care not to allow a major problem with school attendance to develop. Set standards and limits for the circumstances under which you will allow your teenager to stay at home. For example, you might let him stay home from school if he has a fever. Make it clear that if he misses school, you expect him to turn in make-up assignments. You may email, call, or go by school the day he is absent and ask for assignments. If he is feeling better by evening, he can work on assignments then. Most of the time you don't need to be this compulsive unless your teenager gets behind easily and has trouble catching up with assignments or is failing a class.

Some teenagers with attention deficits simply refuse to go to school. Obviously, it is difficult to physically make an older teenager go to school. You may have to try the strategies below to resolve the problem.

Have a Physical Examination. A good physical exam should be conducted to rule out any medical problems or allergies. According to Dr. Nadine M. Lambert and Dr. Carolyn Hartsough, approximately one-third to one-half of youngsters with ADHD have chronic health problems such as recurring upper respiratory infections, allergies, or asthma. During certain seasons, sinus drainage and infections may make some teenagers feel nauseated each morning before school. Headaches may be a problem too.

"Allergies were a major problem for my son and contributed to poor behavior and frequent illnesses starting at four months of age. He was tested for cystic fibrosis at fifteen months. The red dye in some medications made things much worse."

If no other medical problems are found, but week after week your teenager complains of being sick or frequently wants to stay home, you need to take other steps. These could include developing a comprehensive strategy to increase successes and make school less aversive, working to resolve sleep problems, or adjusting present medications. You may also need to use logical consequences, as described below.

Logical Consequences. If your teenager refuses to go to school, try logical consequences. "If you are sick, you stay home all day with no company." You might also take him to the doctor, and if he is not sick, then back to school.

"We had a rule that if Cooper stayed home from school, he couldn't leave the house that day or have company. 'If you are sick enough to stay home, you won't feel well enough to do these other things.' Our pediatrician also helped by saying, 'If you are sick enough to leave school, come straight to my office. If I can't find anything wrong, then you go right back to school.' It worked! He only tested us twice."

Hopefully, you can find a positive solution to school attendance problems using logical consequences alone.

If necessary, however, you may need to make privileges such as driving the car contingent upon school attendance. "When you don't go to school, you can't drive the car." Or you can phrase this more positively by saying, "For each day you attend school, you can earn the privilege of continuing to drive the car to school."

Seek Professional Help. If school avoidance is a major problem for your teenager, you may need to work with the classroom teacher, school counselor, or school psychologist to improve the school environment. Although there is no official diagnostic category, this pattern of school avoidance or refusal in children is sometimes referred to as a *school phobia*.

Make School More Positive. If your teenager is avoiding school, there is probably a good reason. For example, he may be failing classes because he has undiagnosed learning problems or executive function deficits. As Chapter 13 discusses, there are many accommodations that can be made in the classroom that will make school more positive.

Of course, there are always exceptions. Some teenagers with ADD or ADHD love to go to school. Most teenagers who like school say they love to visit with their friends. Favorite classes are usually nonacademic ones such as P.E., art, music, drama, and shop.

"Lewis has always loved school. He loves to socialize. He never missed much school."

"We never had any problem getting Shawn to go to school. He liked being with his friends. Even in elementary school, he'd tell me the only good thing about school was lunch and gym."

Work on Resolving Sleep Disturbances. As mentioned earlier, roughly half of all teenagers with ADD or ADHD have problems falling asleep and/or waking up. Since over half of these teenagers wake up feeling tired, they may not feel like going to school. The potential for sleep disturbances to undermine a student's school performance is obvious. If a student attends class with less than six or seven hours of sleep, he is not going to have a particularly productive day at school. Sleep deprivation may result in irritability, poor concentration, poor memory, and possibly falling asleep in class.

"Since high school classes start at 7:20 a.m., staying awake all day in class with only four or five hours sleep is very difficult. This presents a real dilemma for our son and his teachers. Most teachers aren't aware of his sleep problem. All they see is a student who sleeps through their class. Understandably, most teachers don't feel much sympathy for this behavior unless they are aware of the sleep disturbance problem."

"The alarm goes off, the TV, radio, and lights all come on automatically, and I yell but my son can still sleep through all the noise. Thirty minutes later he can't even remember that we had an ugly exchange of words."

Since many teachers may not realize how common sleep disturbances are for these youngsters, you should explain this problem to them. Teachers need to be aware that teenagers with sleep disturbances may be coming to school exhausted. Also explain that if your teen fights with you about getting up, he may feel as though he has been through a major war before ever arriving at school. He may be in an extremely hostile mood or may sleep through classes. Suggestions for reducing sleep-related problems are provided in Chapter 9.

It is also critical that your teen understand why he has such a terrible problem with sleeping and waking up. You may want him to read "Night Owls and Morning Zombies" in *A Bird's-Eye View*.

Consider Medication. As a last resort, some doctors prescribe medications such as antidepressants that increase levels of the neurotransmitter serotonin, which is essential for sleep. This medication may enable the teenager to get more restful sleep, wake up more easily each morning, and feel more alert. See Chapters 6 and 9 for more information.

4. Uneven Academic Performance

Teachers and parents often notice great variability in homework, test grades, and class performance. Students with attention deficits can do the work one day, but not the next. Because of this unevenness, teachers may comment that "the teenager could do the work if he just wanted to." These behaviors, although often linked to deficits in executive skills, may be viewed as "laziness" and are a source of puzzlement and frustration for both parents and teachers. Parents should let teachers know that uneven school performance is a hallmark characteristic of both ADD and ADHD.

School Problems Related to Specific ADD/ADHD Symptoms

Please keep in mind that one of the most effective interventions for symptoms related to ADHD and ADD is medication. For example, make certain that your teen's medication is effective during homework time, even if it means taking a short-acting medicine like Ritalin just before beginning work. See Chapter 6 for more details.

1. Restlessness, Previously Hyperactivity

By adolescence, very few children with attention deficits are extremely hyperactive. Typically, most parents will be dealing with restlessness instead of hyperactivity. If your teenager *is* still hyperactive, however, his hyperactivity may affect his ability to complete homework.

Accept His Study Style. If your teenager literally can't sit still, don't worry about appearances. As long as his work is completed, let him choose how and where he sits. Let him sit on his feet, or lie on the bed or floor.

Give Study Breaks. Most people, not just students with ADD or ADHD, work more effectively when they take breaks every 30 minutes or so. Breaks may need to be more frequent—every 20 minutes—for these students. During his 5- or 10-minute break, he might listen to music, play with the dog, or eat a snack. Of course, discuss this issue with your teen and give him a choice. Some teens may actually prefer to work straight through and finish the assignment once they get started.

Reward Completion of Work. After he has finished one subject, you might give him a break as a reward. For instance, after he has completed his math homework, he can play video games for 20 minutes, take a bath, or watch TV. This approach may not work if it is too late in the evening, medication has worn off, and your teenager cannot refocus on his remaining homework.

2. Lethargy or Low Energy

Some teenagers with attention deficits daydream, yawn a lot, appear bored, or even sleep in class or while doing homework. Attempts to concentrate seem to take tremendous energy. Schoolwork seems to wear them out mentally even though they may work for only 15 minutes to half an hour without completing very much material.

Although lethargy can be a problem for both teenagers with and without hyperactivity, it is more common in those who have ADD inattentive. These teenagers often feel drowsy when they work on tasks even when they have had a good night of sleep. Dr. Thomas E. Brown, a Yale psychologist who specializes in treating attention deficits, believes that some appear to be borderline narcoleptics. Although they may not meet diagnostic criteria for narcolepsy, some do report "micro-sleep"—dozing at long stoplights or while listening to long lectures.

"Frequently, when my son who has ADD sits down to start his homework, he gets very sleepy. His physical appearance actually changes. His eyelids look heavy and he can hardly keep his eyes open. He has also told me he has to fight off sleep sometimes when he drives. Apparently, he has dozed off a few times while driving. I wonder if he drives fast to provide enough stimulation to keep himself awake."

Have a Physical Examination. If your teenager is lethargic, a good medical check-up is critical to rule out other illnesses.

"Our son frequently seemed tired and looked anemic. We had him checked for mononucleosis. The last blood test the doctor ordered showed that he had an iron deficiency.

"Our son began taking ferrous gluconate, an iron supplement that is more easily absorbed by the body, and began to look and feel better. He also takes vitamins along with his Adderall. He seems to have more energy and doesn't seem to be sick as often. We had his blood level checked again later and found it was too high. He cut back on the iron and began taking it every other day."

Check Lab Results. Be sure to discuss the results of any laboratory tests with the doctor's staff. Ask if there is anything you need to follow up on. Or better yet, ask for a copy of the results so you can check them yourself.

"Sometimes it is a good idea to follow up on blood or other laboratory test results. The doctor's office was supposed to call us and tell us if there were any problems with the test. As a precaution, I called and asked for a report on the blood tests. The doctor's staff had accidentally overlooked the low iron problem. If I hadn't called and asked about the test we would not have picked up the iron deficiency."

Consider Vitamins. Talk with your doctor about giving your teenager vitamins that may help him shake off his lethargy. Sometimes teenagers with attention deficits do not have good eating habits. They may forget to eat regularly, plus stimulant medications may curb their appetite. Vitamin supplements may ensure they receive all necessary vitamins and minerals.

Encourage Exercise. Researchers tell us exercise can also be extremely helpful for these students. Not only can it help hyperactive teenagers release extra pent-up energy, but it can also give depressed teenagers more energy. Simply put, exercise helps the brain work better. Exercise may also help them sleep better. In addition, increased athletic skills bring enhanced self-esteem.

"Exercising has been great for Tyler and Katie, who both have attention deficits. They have begun working out three times a week with an exercise trainer and it has helped them tremendously. My son says he can tell a difference in how his brain works. Tyler is in college now and by exercising frequently, he has actually been able to keep up with his school work."

3. Depression, Anxiety, Hostility, and Self-Doubt

After a few years in school, teenagers with attention deficits may show signs of depression or anxiety. They may have tremendous feelings of self-doubt and feel overwhelmed. They may get discouraged and give up easily. Not surprisingly, they are more likely than other teenagers to believe the negative things adults say about them. Hostile feelings emerge and by the time a teenager reaches middle and high school, he may exhibit a tough, "I don't care" veneer to cover years of discouragement and failure. Loving, patient parents and teachers can penetrate that veneer and help these teenagers lead happy, productive lives. You can read more about the treatment of depression and anxiety in Chapters 6 and 7.

"It took only a few months, not years, for my son to become dejected, depressed, and hostile. By the time he reached the second grade, a referral was made for placement in a class for students with emotional problems. We would not give permission for him to participate. He just needed appropriate accommodations in the regular classroom."

"Last year, I suspected that one of my son's friends had ADD inattentive and referred him to a physician. The teenager was tested and my suspicions confirmed. When I asked the teenager why he thought he had done so poorly in school he said, 'I just thought I was lazy.' He had begun to believe what the adults in his life were saying about him."

There are many ways parents can help their teenager feel better about himself. A few are noted below. In addition, see the sections on building resilience (Chapter 4) and self-esteem (Chapter 8) for more information about pursuing successes outside of school.

Help Your Teenager Succeed in School and Other Environments. Building your teenager's self-esteem through success in school and other settings is critical. Identifying learning problems including deficits in executive skills, asking for accommoda-

tions, or doing whatever it takes to keep him on track in school is critical. Participation in sports or other activities may present additional opportunities for achieving successes.

Provide ADHD Education. Educating yourself and your teen about attention deficits should enable you both to understand the condition better and also to help you develop realistic expectations. For example, your teen will realize that disorganization and forgetting things is part of his challenges with executive skills, not because he is lazy or dumb. Hopefully he will be open to developing compensatory skills. Resources like *A Bird's-Eye View* should be helpful for teens.

Don't Pressure about Grades. Many teenagers with attention deficits seem very sensitive to pressure and may give up more easily than other students. If you tell your teenager that he has to keep an A or B average, it may make him very anxious. If he is doing his best, but is just getting by with C's and D's, he will be extremely frustrated if you demand that he do better. Particularly if your teenager was older when ADD or ADHD was discovered, he has experienced a lot of failure at school. He may be terrified of more failure. If he thinks a goal is too difficult to reach, he may not even try to accomplish it.

"Although I was a straight-A student in high school and had an A average in college, having my son make straight A's is not that important to me. Having him feel good about himself is much more important. Of course, it would be nice if he made higher grades, but we are pleased that he has passed all his subjects and improved his grades his sophomore year in high school. He failed two of twelve classes his freshman year.

"The major expectation we have of our son is that he pass all his subjects. He is bright enough that he will pass his high school classes if he does his homework. Requiring completion of homework on a daily or weekly basis is critical for him to obtain passing grades."

Avoid Issuing Challenges. Sometimes it is tempting for parents to challenge their teenager to *prove* that he can do better academically. Many of these teenagers, however, will feel overwhelmed with the challenge and may give up completely. The failure further compounds their damaged self-esteem. Most teenagers with ADD or ADHD respond better to encouragement and support from the family and school.

4. Defiance, Emotionality, and Low Frustration Tolerance

Teenagers with ADD or ADHD may become upset more easily than other adolescents. As mentioned earlier, as many as 65 percent of them have significant problems with stubbornness, defiance, refusal to obey, temper tantrums, and verbal hostility toward others. Oppositional behavior is more common in teenagers with ADHD. For some adolescents, frustration has been building for years while they have been struggling unsuccessfully in school. They may be overly sensitive to criticism and failure. They may get into trouble for impulsively talking back to teachers or administrators. They may get upset and end up fighting at school. Parents may see angry temper outbursts, aggression, or what appears to be defiance. Remember, as was explained in Chapter 7, aggression and defiance may really be symptoms of depression.

These behaviors are also more likely to occur as medication is wearing off. Suggestions for coping with these problems discussed in this chapter and Chapter 6 include: listen, be supportive, use active listening, give choices, teach problem solving skills, teach anger management, lower your voice, overlook minor infractions, and give your teenager space and time to cool off. Specific tips on anger management are provided in *Teaching Teens,* Summary 69. Tips for teens are available under "Short Fuses" in *A Bird's-Eye View.*

Conclusion

In a CHADD conference presentation entitled "Help Me, I'm Losing My Child," Dr. Russell Barkley tells of a distraught mother who came to him for help because her son had started withdrawing emotionally from her. Through her intensive efforts, her son's grades had improved significantly. However, she was devastated when she realized that he was intentionally avoiding her. The spontaneous joy and love in their relationship was dying. Fortunately for them, it was not too late to rebuild their former relationship.

For your family, too, academic success at any cost may not be worth it. Driving a teenager with ADD or ADHD to achieve high grades is usually not realistic. The high grades become grades that you, the parent, have earned, not the teenager. *You need to keep your lifetime relationship with your child in perspective!* If your interventions are too intense, controlling, and negative for too long, you risk damaging your parent-child bond and doing irreparable harm to your relationship. Ideally, you will be able to forge a cooperative partnership with your teenager and avoid a protracted, hostile power struggle. Love and accept your teenager for who he is, not for his grades or his accomplishments, and not for who you want him to be.

Table 12-2   Avoiding Bloody Homework Battles

This table contains suggestions for parents to try at home that should help the teenager improve his performance with homework and at school.

Homework Challenges

1. Establishing a Study Routine
   - Set a specific time to do homework each evening
   - Set an alarm to announce homework time
   - Minimize distractions
   - Find a "study buddy" or establish a "study circle"
   - Consider medication when doing homework

2. Ensuring Homework Assignments Are Known
   - Call a friend to confirm homework assignments
   - Call the school homework hotline or visit the school webpage
   - Request that an email be sent home
   - Ask that assignments be posted on an outside classroom window
   - Use a color-coded monthly calendar
   - Find out the routine of homework assignments
   - Find out when special projects are due

3. Tackling Homework
   - Divide homework into smaller segments
   - Let your teen use a computer
   - Have your teenager dictate essays or reports
   - Use white noise or play the radio
   - Limit time spent on homework
   - Watch out for hasty errors
   - Teach your teenager that school and homework must be done, either now or later
   - Ensure completed homework is placed in the notebook
   - Keep extra school supplies on hand
   - Clean out notebook periodically and save old papers

4. Ensuring Good Communication with the School
   - Use daily or weekly reports
   - Set up a reminder system about the report
   - Take or send him back to school for the weekly report
   - Teach key skills first; let others slide

5. Avoiding Emotional Blow Ups over Homework
   - Identify parenting strategies to keep homework time peaceful
   - Give time to unwind before bedtime

Additional School Challenges

1. Making Too Many Zeros
   - Monitor for zeros in subjects in danger of failing
   - Ask teachers to be flexible with make-up work
   - Have your child average his grades

2. Failing Some Classes
   - Discuss the full impact of failing a class
   - Monitor progress if your teenager is struggling
   - Help your teenager graph his grades
   - Obtain factual information regarding grades
   - Find innovative ways to make up needed credits

3. School Avoidance
   - Set a standard for attending school
   - Have a physical examination
   - Logical consequences
   - Seek professional help
   - Make school more positive
   - Work on resolving sleep disturbances
   - Consider medication

4. Uneven Academic Performance
   - Identify and accommodate hidden learning problems including deficits in executive skills
   - Double check effectiveness of medication

School Problems Related to Specific ADD/ADHD Symptoms

1. Restlessness, Previously Hyperactivity
   - Accept his study style
   - Give study breaks
   - Reward completion of work

2. Lethargy or Low Energy
   - Have a physical examination
   - Check lab results
   - Consider vitamins
   - Encourage exercise

3. Depression, Anxiety, Hostility, and Self-Doubt
   - Help your teenager succeed in school and other environments
   - Provide ADHD education
   - Don't pressure about grades
   - Avoid issuing challenges

4. Defiance, Emotionality, and Low Frustration Tolerance
   - Lower your voice
   - Use active listening
   - Give choices
   - Teach anger management

13

Success, Not Just Survival in School

"The most painful vignette for me to recall about Alex's school experience occurred when he was in the first grade. He had just received his first progress report in school and I eagerly asked to see it. As I read the report, he began crying and said, 'Please don't read my report card. My teacher thinks I'm bad.' As I listened to my child's distressed plea, tears flooded my eyes. The first hint of the academic agony ahead had surfaced.

"Alex could not read or understand the passing grades and positive words written on his first-grade report card. But at the young age of six he was extremely perceptive about his teacher's negative attitude toward him. He was right—the teacher thought he was 'bad.' Alex struggled through six difficult and bewildering years of school until a school psychologist diagnosed ADD inattentive when he was twelve."

Although children with attention deficits may start school with great expectations and willingness to do their work, their inattention, impulsivity, and learning problems can make it difficult for them to do well academically. Over the years, the struggle to succeed at school may quickly become an overwhelming challenge. Unless parents and teachers intervene—both at home and at school—teenagers with ADD or ADHD may give up trying to succeed academically.

The importance of school success is profound! After all, continuing school failure is often linked to dropping out of school and subsequent drug use and brushes with the law. Upon coming to this realization, I felt the four chapters on educational issues that I wrote for the first edition of this book were inadequate. So I spent four years gathering information and writing a companion guide to give both parents and teachers additional detailed information on critical school-related topics. This guide, *Teaching Teens with ADD and ADHD,* is rich with academic tips for parents and professionals alike to utilize. It contains 75 detailed summaries that provide invaluable information that will help at school and home.

Initially, I considered deleting this chapter since *Teaching Teens* is now available, but the chapter was retained for several important reasons: to help parents recognize:

1. major academic challenges for our students,

2. best practice teaching strategies for students with attention deficits,
3. a good teacher when they see one,
4. potential ways teachers can help their child with a specific problem,
5. teacher characteristics to look for when requesting a teacher placement for your teen, and
6. teaching strategies to be incorporated into the IEP or 504 Plan, if needed. If parents know this information, they can share it with their teenager's teachers.

The key concepts in the chapter were retained, but in a much shorter format, listing only two or three strategies under each academic challenge. Table 13-1, however, is available in its entirety from the 1995 edition to make parents aware of the full range of strategies. You may find it helpful to skim over the chart before reading the rest of the chapter. The techniques in the table are discussed in more detail in *Teaching Teens*. Additional resources that can help you to ensure school success for your teenager, include:

■ Chapters 11 and 12, which discuss interventions parents may try at home; Chapter 14, which offers advice for success after high school graduation.
■ *A Bird's-Eye View.* Your teen may be more willing to listen to tips for school success from other teens instead of adults.

Dr. Barkley on the Academic Challenges of ADHD

Dr. Russell Barkley summed up the challenge of educating students with attention deficits during a keynote address at a national CHADD conference. As a result of their attention deficit, many of "these youngsters, unlike other children, do not have a natural love of learning, the desire to be the best, to master a skill, or make the highest grades in the class." Even though students with attention deficits may be bright, parents and teachers must use a variety of techniques at home and school to help them succeed academically.

Since I originally quoted this statement ten years ago, the good news is that the truth about attention deficit disorders is changing. When we provide appropriate accommodations, many of our students come to love learning and are successful in school.

Linking with the School

Working with school officials to ensure that your teen is successful academically is critical. Here are several helpful strategies for parents:

Determine Whether Effective Teaching Strategies Are Being Used. If you know what to look for, you can recognize when teachers are doing a good job and notice areas where you might make tactful suggestions for working with your teen. Referring teachers to specific sections of *Teaching Teens* as noted below may also be helpful.

Effective Teaching Strategies for Students with ADD and ADHD. A few effective teaching strategies from Summaries 13A-E of *Teaching Teens* are listed below.
■ *Modification of teaching methods and provision of accommodations* (active, hands-on learning)
■ *Modification of assignments* (reduce the length)
■ *Modification of testing and grading* (shorten or give extended time)
■ *Modification of the level of supervision* (increase the amount)
■ *Use of technology* (computer or calculator)

Here is a description of what I mean by "teaching methods and accommodations." If your teenager has trouble paying attention in class, teachers may be more effective by varying the way they present information in class. Educators may use a multisensory teaching approach by providing more visual cues or increased class participation. For example, students who are actively highlighting key facts in color are more likely to pay attention and remember what they read.

Effective Classroom and Behavior Management Strategies. Effective strategies include providing a structured classroom, developing simple rules and stating them clearly, keeping instructions brief and simple, using positive behavior supports, and providing more support and monitoring work completion.

This is what I mean by providing a structured classroom. Students with ADD or ADHD perform better when teachers provide a positive and orderly classroom. External order, routine, and structure provide a sense of security that students who lack self-control need. Having a routine helps students know the class procedure and what is expected of them. If teenagers forget their book, they know where to find an extra one to borrow.

Remember, providing structure is *not* the same thing as being rigid. When a teenager is struggling, having a teacher who will work with her and allow some flexibility is wonderful. For example, occasionally letting students turn an assignment in late is very helpful and may make the difference in them passing or failing a class. Of course, the next step is to teach teens compensatory strategies so they can remember to turn in assignments.

Effective Strategies for Parents. Furthermore, parents can facilitate success at school by taking several actions at school. Key suggestions are listed in detail in Chapter 11, "Suggestion for making school more positive."

Common Learning Problems and Classroom Accommodations

Learning problems that are common among teenagers with attention deficits are discussed in Chapter 11 and in Sections 2 and 3 of *Teaching Teens*. Another profound challenge, the deficit in executive skills, is discussed in Chapters 1 and 2 of this book and in Section 3 of *Teaching Teens*.

Several characteristics commonly associated with attention deficits contribute to problems at school and must be addressed. Common symptoms of ADD and ADHD that cause problems include *inattention, distractibility, impulsivity, disorganization, forgetfulness, and for some hyperactivity.* A variety of other less obvious factors linked to attention deficits can also have a significant effect on academic achievement: *sleep disturbance, low energy, emotionality, low frustration tolerance, defiance, aggression, depression, anxiety, or medication wearing off.* In addition, teens may have difficulty maintaining effort on academic tasks, resulting in *uneven school performance,* a hallmark characteristic of attention deficits. Some days our teens do well and other days they can't.

Further compounding their academic difficulties, as reflected in research by NIMH, approximately one-third to one-half of all teenagers with attention deficits also have one or more of these learning problems:

1. language deficits (poor listening comprehension and poor verbal expression),
2. poor written expression,
3. poor reading comprehension,
4. poor math computation skills,
5. poor organizational skills,
6. poor memory,
7. slow processing speed, and
8. poor fine-motor skills.

Failure to make accommodations for learning problems and executive function deficits may be one of the major reasons why many students who are being treated for attention deficits continue to do poorly in school. One other key point: continuation of extrinsic or external motivation (rewards) and certain key accommodations must be maintained throughout the academic career of many of our children. Sometimes after a child has been successful with a reward system or specific accommodation, school officials want to phase it out. But Dr. Barkley reminds us these supports for teens with attention deficits, such as shortened assignments, are much like a ramp for a child in a wheelchair; they may need it forever.

Inattention

Inattention can cause major problems at home and in the classroom. Students may have trouble staying "on task" to complete schoolwork and homework. They may be distracted by things in the room or by their own internal thoughts and may not be listening to instructions. They may forget to take home the necessary books, or lose or misplace their homework, notebooks, or notes.

Sometimes behaviors caused by inattention or forgetfulness can be mistaken for laziness or defiance. For example, a teenager who forgets to do her schoolwork or chores or to stay after school for detention may seem to be acting willfully. Once confronted by adults, teens may become defiant. Their defiance may actually mask their embarrassment over their failures. As we discussed before, many teens would rather be seen as "bad" than appear stupid. This lack of education about "ADHD behaviors" may cause misunderstandings that can lead to major conflicts at home and at school.

Dr. Sydney Zentall is one of the few educational researchers who has studied techniques for teaching students with ADHD. She prefers to describe these students as having an "attentional bias" instead of an attention deficit. She explains that these students seek out tasks that are high interest, new, or presented in a different way. Problems with inattention are more likely to occur when the material being learned is uninteresting, familiar, and repetitive. Unfortunately, this description sounds like most traditional schoolwork.

Several common problems related to student inattention are discussed below:

1. DIFFICULTY COMPLETING SCHOOL AND HOMEWORK

A major complaint from parents and teachers is that students with attention deficits have trouble completing their class- or homework. These students get distracted by things that they find more interesting than schoolwork. They focus on people talking in the hall or the air conditioning unit turning on instead of on their work. They impulsively move from one task to another. Many have difficulty concentrating when they read school material. Some suggestions for dealing with these problems are outlined below.

Monitor Completion of Schoolwork. Make certain that your teen knows his assignments. Some schools make this information easily known through email or homework hotlines or by posting assignments on a school webpage

Use Weekly Reports. Make participation in fun activities on the weekend contingent upon receiving a "weekly report" indicating satisfactory completion of assignments.

2. TUNING OUT AND DAYDREAMING

Another common complaint is that teenagers with attention deficits don't seem to pay attention in class. When they do listen, their attention span may be short. Since they pay attention only briefly, they may have difficulty following instructions. Some students also may have learning deficits related to poor memory or listening comprehension, which can further compound their problems following teacher directions.

" Sometimes they don't realize they are off-task until the teacher calls on them. Then anxiety grips them."

"Are you listening to me?" is a question frequently asked by parents and teachers alike. This issue was discussed in Chapter 9 because it is also a common problem at home. The discussion of "poor listening comprehension" skills in the next section may also help adults understand why these students don't always know what is said to them or follow directions.

An "absent-minded professor" quality, as reflected in a lack of awareness of time, grades, or assignments, or a lack of attention to detail, may also be observed, especially in children with ADD inattentive. Teenagers with ADD may sit, daydreaming in a world all their own. They may seem confused or appear to be "in a fog."

These teens are often described as bored or restless, whether or not they were hyperactive as children. While daydreaming, they may fidget, tap their foot, drum their fingers on the desk, tap their pencil, or stare into space. There is some speculation, although no scientific proof, that *physical activity may actually prime mental activity.* In other words, fidgeting may help these teens stay alert so they can pay attention.

" I was a daydreamer in school. Through college, my daydreaming usually dealt with hunting. In high school, it dealt with cars and girls. In middle school, I daydreamed about bicycles. I was also a doodler. I still doodle a lot.

"The best way I can describe how my medicine affects me and my daydreaming is by telling this story. When I am sitting in class and my stomach starts growling, before I started taking Adderall, I would sit there and think, 'When I get home, I'll have me a ham sandwich, with mayonnaise and mustard, two slices of cheese, lettuce, some Fritos, and I'm gonna watch TV.' I visually built the sandwich in my mind. Then I would realize I had just missed 30 minutes worth of notes. Adderall keeps me focused." —Steven

Effective teaching strategies such as keeping instruction brief and simple, whether used by parents or teachers, make a huge difference in helping students pay attention and reducing daydreaming.

Use Cues to Get Attention. When making an announcement about homework or a test, teachers might start off with an attention-getting statement such as, "Listen carefully. This is important!" or "Write this down. It will be on the test." Or they might give a signal by tapping their desk or clapping their hands to get the student's attention. Once assignments are made, the parent or teacher should state clearly that a new topic is being addressed before going on to the next subject. A teacher may also say, "Marcie, I am going to call on you next. Be thinking about this question." This gives her time to collect her thoughts. There is no need to embarrass her by calling on her when she is not listening.

Ask for a reminder. Teens can ask a friend to remind them to pay attention or nudge them when they seem to drift off. Make certain the teacher knows about this arrangement so the two students don't get in trouble for whispering in class.

3. LACK OF ATTENTION TO DETAIL

Students with attention deficits often make what appear to be "careless errors" in their work and on tests. Typically, they don't double-check their homework or tests for mistakes. Even if they do double-check, they may still overlook the error. Sometimes when working math problems, they don't notice changes in signs. For example, they may add all the problems, never noticing the change from addition to subtraction. They may overlook errors in spelling, capitalization, grammar, and punctuation. They may not do well on tests that use bubble sheets, since they may lose their place and mark the answer sheet incorrectly.

Use Color to Aid Learning. Dr. Zentall has found that using color adds an element of novelty that is effective in teaching these students. Usually, a skill is taught first and then color is used to increase the student's awareness of potential problems. For example, if a student doesn't notice sign changes in math (+ or -), a highlighter could be used to mark all math signs on an assignment or test. Or if she consistently misses a letter in spelling words or at the end of foreign language verbs, highlight the correct information in color. The student may also be asked to highlight directions for homework or a test.

Have the Student Read Aloud. Researchers have confirmed that some teenagers overlook grammatical errors when they read silently. If students read the material aloud, they find the errors more easily. If your teenager is having problems in Language Arts, she could read her homework answers aloud and record them on tape. For example, sentences which require selection of proper subject-verb agreement, plural vs. singular, or verb tense could be recorded. Or read the material aloud to another student, who writes down the answers. Occasionally, a student may do better when she takes tests orally. If this is true for your teenager, the school can find someone to be a "reader" for the test and record your teenager's answers.

4. LACK OF AWARENESS OF GRADES

Many students with attention deficits are clueless about their grades, as explained in Chapter 12. Some are also oblivious to their past academic performances. When a grading period is over, they do not seem to remember that they barely squeaked through the class, thanks to their parents pushing them. They only remember that they passed the class. Factors such as inattention, poor organization, and poor memory probably play

a role in their lack of awareness of grades. Several intervention strategies are recommended in Chapter 12.

Impulsivity

Acting or speaking impulsively may cause problems at home and school. Teens may begin schoolwork without waiting for instructions, make careless errors in their work, take short cuts in homework, interrupt others, talk back to teachers and parents, or impulsively break rules. Usually, they are not acting maliciously but simply acting before thinking of the consequences. Delaying gratification is also extremely difficulty for them. Unfortunately, success in most school systems is based upon the ability to delay gratification: students must wait nine weeks for a grade; earn credits to graduate from high school four years later; and do schoolwork to learn information that will help them get a job years later.

1. GETTING INTO TROUBLE AT SCHOOL

Impulsive behavior is probably one of the major reasons that these teenagers get into trouble and may be suspended or expelled. Noncompliance, forgetfulness, lack of awareness of school rules, and academic frustration also contribute to their problems. Common

behaviors that make school administrators angry or are grounds for automatic suspension or expulsion include: talking back to teachers, walking out of class without permission, refusing to do as asked, skipping school, smoking in the restroom, leaving school grounds, forgetting and carrying a pocket knife to school, or getting into fights. As noted earlier, approximately half the students with ADHD in one clinical study had been suspended and approximately 10 percent expelled. Here are some helpful tips.

Ask about a FBA and BIP. The Individuals with Disabilities Education Act (IDEA) recommends two very helpful tools for identifying and preventing future behavior and academic problems. A Functional Behavior Assessment (FBA) can be conducted to determine what triggered a problem and then a Behavior Intervention Plan (BIP) can be implemented to prevent the problem in the future.

Request a Classroom Aide. Classroom aides can provide assistance for teenagers who have more serious academic or behavioral problems. Students who are eligible for special education services under IDEA

FBA: Functional Behavior Assessments

Functional Behavior Assessments (FBA) can be very helpful in gathering needed facts about the "who, why, when, and where" of a student's academic difficulties or misbehavior. By identifying the cause or trigger for school failure or misbehavior, the school is then able to develop an effective intervention plan. Most schools know how to conduct these assessments. Unfortunately, IDEA mandates FBAs be conducted only when students have shown a pattern of disruptive incidents at school, especially if they place the student at-risk of a school suspension.

Parents may request an FBA, especially if the child is in danger of failing, but the school may not agree to conduct it. Some parents may decide to review this process and attempt to do some of this "detective work" or assessment on their own. You may be able to identify potential underlying problems, or at least lead school officials in the right direction. You can read more about this process in Chapter 14 and even more detail in *Teaching Teens,* Summary 63 and Appendix B5.

---

are more likely to get this service. To avoid embarrassment, other students would not have to know that the aide was assigned to a specific student. She could work with one or two other students at the same time.

"One school system was refusing to take a student in special education on a class field trip because she needed one-on-one supervision. Under IDEA and Section 504, however, the school must allow students in special education access to the regular education curriculum. The parents were unable to go along on the field trip, so they talked with school personnel. Arrangements were made for someone to accompany the teen on the trip."

Shorten the School Day. If your teenager is on the verge of being suspended or expelled, consider discussing a shortened school day with school officials. For example, your teenager could go home after lunch each day for a few days until the crisis is resolved. If appropriate, check to see what the assignments are, so she can work on them when she gets home. Certain times of the year are more difficult than others. Most students are keyed up just before winter break and at the end of the school year.

2. IMPULSIVE LEARNING STYLES

Teenagers with attention deficits may also have impulsive learning styles. Often, they start assignments without first reading the instructions or examples. They may answer multiple-choice tests impulsively without reading each choice carefully. Rushing through homework and not double-checking their work are also common occurrences.

Highlight Instructions. You or the teacher can have your teenager highlight key words in the instructions before starting assignments. Tell her, for example, "Read the directions for your assignment and mark the key words with a yellow highlighter." Then check to make certain she did it right. Erasable highlighters are available from Crayola at www.crayola.com.

Mark Out Wrong Answers on Multiple Choice Tests. Dr. Zentall recommends having students with ADHD mark out the wrong answers first. This lets them satisfy their need to mark something immediately. On multiple-choice tests, this may prevent giving impulsive wrong answers. Ask your teenager if she thinks this idea will help.

Executive Function Deficits

On the surface, teenagers with ADD or ADHD may appear to be "lazy or unmotivated students" who don't want to do schoolwork. In reality, their executive skill deficits greatly interfere with their ability to be successful in school. (The key components of executive skills are discussed in Chapters 1 and 2.)

These deficits may manifest themselves as disorganization, limited memory capacity, tardiness, reduced productivity, poor analytical and problem solving skills, weak written expression, poor math performance, and difficulty controlling emotions. In addition, these teens typically tend to live in the here and now. Weak organizational skills and limited working memory capacity make it extremely difficult for students to plan ahead, remember tasks, get started, and organize and finish assignments. Language processing deficits are also likely to contribute to their poor organization. If a teenager doesn't understand instructions correctly, then she won't follow through on assignments. Or she won't be able to organize her thoughts into a coherent, logically sequenced essay.

Poor Organizational Skills

1. DISORGANIZATION

Learning to be organized is one of the most difficult challenges facing our teenagers. In fact, disorganization is one of the key criteria for diagnosing attention deficit disorder. Disorganization makes it incredibly difficult to complete schoolwork and chores. In addition, organizing materials and keeping a notebook containing assignments in sequential order are almost impossible tasks for these teenagers. Realistically, someone must work one-on-one with them, teaching them to order their papers and record grades.

"A high school biology teacher required that each student keep a notebook containing all homework, class work, and tests in sequential order. A cover sheet with three columns had to be kept noting the date, the assignment/test, plus the grade. My son with ADHD didn't have a prayer in a class like that."

Find a Tutor or Academic Coach. Teenagers with attention deficits may or may not need tutors for academic purposes. Often, however, they need an "academic coach" to help them learn how to be organized, learn how to study, and to monitor completion of schoolwork and due dates for assignments. This assistance could be split among several adults or peers. For instance, a teacher or guidance counselor may be able to teach organizational skills to your teenager. Another student or girlfriend, rather than a teacher, could help monitor assignments.

The school may also be able to provide tutoring if needed. If not, consider hiring a tutor to teach study and organizational skills to your teenager or try teaching her yourself. If monitoring your teenager's homework is a battle almost every night, find someone else to do this job. However, finding a tutor who is familiar with or willing to learn the unique aspects of tutoring students with ADD or ADHD is often difficult.

"In some ways our son's broken leg was a blessing in disguise. The school system assigned a 'homebound' teacher, who came to see him three times a week. She was the most patient woman I have ever met. She sat with him, waiting patiently, while he figured out which assignments were due when and developed an outline for the assignments due for her next visit. She taught him how to study and be better organized."

Keep an Assignment Notebook or Use a Palm Pilot. Your teenager knows that she *should* write down her assignments each day. Either you, a teacher, or another student can check to see that she actually did write them down. Using a Palm Pilot is a great idea if your teenager can remember to write assignments down or keep up with the notebook. An alternative is for the teacher or another student to write down homework assignments.

2. LOST POSSESSIONS

Because of their disorganization and forgetfulness, teenagers with attention deficits regularly lose possessions—schoolwork, homework, assignments, books, pencils, coats, games, and tools. Notes from the teacher don't always make it home. Remember too that losing things is also one of the diagnostic criteria for attention deficits.

"Barry was always losing things. When he was little, he was always the last to come out and play because he couldn't find his shoes. If he wore a jacket to school, he often lost it. I actually started a jacket collection. If I found any jackets on sale for under $25, I bought them."

Put Name on Possessions. It may help to put your teenager's name on books, notebooks, papers, coats, and gym clothes. To make this more fun, consider buying a name stamp.

Check Lost and Found. When possessions are missing, have your teenager check the lost and found at school. Or go by the school and check for yourself. In truth, you'll spend a fair amount of money buying replacements for lost items.

3. DIFFICULTY BEING PREPARED TO DO SCHOOLWORK

Teens with ADD or ADHD have difficulty gathering all the supplies they need to complete school and homework assignments—the right book, paper, rulers, pens, correct assignments, and due dates. Completed papers are lost or crumpled in the bottom of the locker. Or the assignment is left on the kitchen table where they worked on it the night before.

Request Flexibility from Teachers. If your teenager is having problems with organization, teachers may help by being flexible and shaping her behavior as she masters this skill. For example, the teacher may tell her in advance where she can find a pencil or book if she forgets to bring one. If necessary, buy a pack of pencils and give it to the teacher.

Make Certain Homework Is Submitted. The first step is to ensure that the completed homework is put back into the notebook, ready for the return to school. Some teachers accept finished homework at the end of class, so that the student doesn't have the opportunity to take it home and leave it.

Related Organizational Problems

4. DIFFICULTY GETTING STARTED

Getting started on schoolwork can be extremely difficult for teenagers with attention deficits. They may get sidetracked talking to friends, doodling, looking out the window, reading a magazine (even during class), or thinking about what they are going to do after school. This difficulty initiating activities requested by parents and teachers is linked to deficits in executive skills.

Prompt to Start Working. Teachers can get your teenager's attention without calling out her name or otherwise embarrassing her when she is not working. When the teacher notices that your teen has not started working, she could walk near your child's desk and place a hand on her shoulder or desk. This cue should be discussed in advance with your teenager so she knows it means it is time to get started.

Monitor Getting Started: "Jump Start" Your Teen. Teachers may need to monitor the starting period. Remember, transition periods such as beginnings and changing from one activity to another are very difficult for our teenagers. Monitoring and prompting may be done unobtrusively with minimum embarrassment to the teen. Tips for "jump starting" students include dividing the assignment into smaller segments and using physical activity, such as playing with a pipe cleaner or "Wikki Stix" to "prime mental activity."

5. PROCRASTINATION

Many teenagers procrastinate when it is time to do schoolwork and chores. They do not start work on assigned reports or projects until the last possible moment. Poor organization, forgetfulness, lack of time awareness, difficulty getting started, and distractibility may also contribute to procrastination. Of course, the fact that schoolwork is often unpleasant also means that they may avoid it as long as possible.

Prompt Regarding Assignments and Due Dates. To help your teenager remember due dates on reports, essays, or projects, try writing a reminder for a class project on a "Post-it" note and sticking it where she does her homework. Also review the monthly calendar with her on a regular basis and bring special projects to her attention. "Your science project is due next week. When do you want to start?" Of course, she could also use an automatic prompting system from her computer or Palm Pilot.

Try using *depersonalization* in advance to avoid making her angry or defensive: "Students with attention deficits often forget assignments. One way to handle that is for someone to remind you. Would you like for me to just tell you or write it on a Post-it note?"

6. MESSY DESKS AND NOTEBOOK

These teenagers' desks and school lockers may be crammed to overflowing with papers and books. At home, their room may be a wreck and they may have trouble finding their possessions when they want them.

"My son's locker at school looks like a squirrel's nest. There are papers stuffed in his locker and his notebook. He may have his completed homework in his notebook and never even find it. A month's supply of dirty gym clothes may also still be in the locker."

Work with the Teen to Organize the Locker. Give her tips on organizing it, for example designating a part of the locker for books to take home.

Clean Out Locker Periodically. You or one of your child's teachers must supervise the periodic cleaning out of her desk or locker.

7. DIFFICULTY MANAGING AND BEING AWARE OF TIME

These teenagers have difficulty managing time, knowing where they need to be at a certain time, or anticipating how much time is needed to complete a task. According to Drs. Barkley and Zentall, they actually have an altered awareness of time. Dr. Barkley explains that slightly over half of these students *don't accurately judge the passage of time.* Time may creep along slowly for them unless they are interested in a task. Adequate amounts of the neurotransmitter dopamine are essential for an accurate awareness of time.

Give Reminders for Key Times. Your teenager can set a reminder on his wristwatch alarm, computer, or Palm Pilot for important events: time to leave for school, time to take medicine, time to stay after school and meet with a teacher. With the alarm set, she can relax and enjoy herself without worrying that she will forget something. You may also ask teachers to give written reminders about upcoming tests, appointments, or projects.

Provide Accommodations for Long-Term Projects. Breaking the project into smaller segments with more frequent due dates will be helpful. That means less time intervenes between the time the assignment is given and when it is due, thus increasing the likelihood the assignment will be completed. The long-term project graphic organizer in *Teaching Teens* should help you understand how to break projects into smaller segments and schedule them backwards over time. The IEP or Section 504 Plan may need to include a statement that the parents will be notified of due dates for long-term projects.

Practice Time Awareness. To be honest, teaching compensatory strategies will be more beneficial than practicing time awareness. But at a minimum, teachers and parents must help teens understand that this difficulty is part of her attention deficit. Parents and teachers can work together to teach the concept of time management and awareness. You can also practice developing timelines for completion of a project. Some

teens may even practice estimating how much time it will take to do their homework. Remember, however, that even with practice, this will still be a huge problem area for many of these teens. There is no magic that will change brain chemistry overnight.

Language Deficits

Several language-processing problems are common among teenagers with attention deficits: difficulties with *listening and reading comprehension* and *spoken and written language production.* Although the reasons for these problems are not fully understood, the brain appears to have difficulty translating symbols (letters of the alphabet) into words, interpreting words seen and heard, identifying corresponding meanings, and then quickly giving a verbal or written response. Often these language deficits are related to several problems: inattention, limited working memory capacity, slow processing speed, and or an auditory language processing deficit.

Note: Asterisks (*) in this section are used to indicate the category of Specific Learning Disabilities (SLD) recognized under the Individuals with Disabilities Education Act (IDEA). (See Chapter 14 for an explanation of SLD and other IDEA categories.)

Dr. Barkley also reports these statistics from recent research: Roughly one in four of children with ADHD may also have dyslexia, a nonverbal learning disability, a math disability, or central auditory processing disorder. However, Barkley has expressed concern that CAPD should be more narrowly defined as a language processing disorder, not just inattention on listening tasks.

Poor Listening Comprehension

Some teens have trouble understanding spoken messages. They may appear confused by verbal instructions and have difficulty following them. Dr. Zentall explains that they have even more problems listening and comprehending if irrelevant details or lengthy descriptions are added or if interesting conversations of others compete for their attention. If instructions (homework assignments or chore requests) are imbedded within a much longer discussion, the teenager may not "hear" (selectively pick out) the instructions. For most of us, listening seems like such a simple task. However, Dr. Zentall reminds us that listening is a complex skill that "requires the ability to select out and attend to a message while ignoring competing information." Several related problems are discussed in subsequent paragraphs.

1. DIFFICULTY UNDERSTANDING INSTRUCTIONS

If an assignment has many steps or is given during the context of a general discussion, students with attention deficits may not understand and may miss the assignment totally. They have difficulty following several instructions at one time and may become confused. Many are too embarrassed or shy to ask questions to clarify their confusion or misunderstanding.

State Instructions Clearly. Teachers should give clear instructions. Numbering the directions may help. "First, do all odd problems on page 37. Second, do all five word problems on page 38." Of course, check to be certain that you have the teen's attention first.

2. DIFFICULTY FOLLOWING INSTRUCTIONS

Teenagers with attention deficits may have trouble following verbal instructions given in class due to auditory processing problems. They may miss assignments and never "hear" the teacher when an assignment is made. Even when assignments are written on the chalkboard, they may not "see" them or remember to copy them down.

Ask the Student to Repeat Instructions. Parents or teachers may ask students to paraphrase the instructions.

Give Written Instructions. Another student may write instructions or assignments on "Post It" notes and put them on the student's desk. She may never see the assignment on the board but she is more likely to see the "Post it" note. The teacher may number and simplify the instructions and write them on the board. For example, "1) Do odd problems on page 27. 2) Swap papers with a neighbor and check answers. 3) Put your finished paper on my desk."

3. DIFFICULTY LEARNING FOREIGN LANGUAGES

Teenagers with attention deficits have enough trouble paying attention when the teacher speaks in her native language. Imagine how much harder the subject may be if the teacher speaks nothing but a foreign language during class. Besides auditory processing problems, inattention, and limited working memory capacity, poor strategies for memorization also contribute to difficulty with foreign languages.

"After the first day of class my son's teacher spoke nothing but Spanish. Of course, his language labs required good listening comprehension since he had to listen to tapes in Spanish. He got lost when he listened to tapes because they speak too rapidly. Fortunately, they allowed him to use a computer program instead of the auditory tapes. Since he is a visual learner, he found the computer more helpful."

Use Tips on Memorization. Suggestions for improving memorization are provided in subsequent sections.

Seek a Waiver. If your teenager has major problems with listening comprehension and memorization, some subjects, such as a foreign language, may be extremely difficult for her to pass. She may give her best effort and still fail the class. Because her ability to learn is adversely affected by ADD or ADHD and her learning problems, you may be able to use federal laws to exempt the class as a requirement for high school or college graduation. If she is unable to achieve passing grades after intensive intervention, the evidence should be pretty clear that she will be unable to pass it.

"My son's counselor in college said that his language problems were so serious he would never be able to learn a foreign language. She requested an exemption from having to take the class. Another class was substituted instead."

A few parents of high school students have successfully obtained a waiver, but this is still a new experience for most school systems. So be forewarned that obtaining a waiver will probably be time-consuming and require you to do a lot of paperwork. You may want to wait to discuss the option of requesting a waiver with your teenager, since school officials may not want or know how to arrange for a waiver. In addition, your teenager may be tempted to give up too soon on a subject that she is capable of mastering.

4. POOR NOTE TAKING

Students with attention deficits may have trouble taking notes in class because of poor listening comprehension, difficulty picking out main points, inattention, poor fine motor coordination, or slow processing speed (slow listening comprehension and writing). Because note taking requires such intense concentration for them, they may avoid it. Dr. Steven Evans and his colleagues found that students who were taught improved note taking skills increased their comprehension, made better grades on daily assignments, and were less disruptive.

Obtain a Copy of a Classmate's or Teacher's Lecture Notes. Your teen might be able to obtain copies of lecture notes from another student, or perhaps the teacher may be willing to provide a copy of her notes. Or the teacher may provide guided lecture notes that summarize the critical information, including key words and concepts being presented. This way, your teen can concentrate on what the teacher is saying, and not have to take notes, listen, and keep up with the lecture. According to one study on ADHD, students' comprehension improves when they are given the notes, even though they don't actually take the notes themselves.

Use NCR Paper. Non carbon replica (NCR) paper, a chemically treated paper like that used in some checkbooks, can also be used to make a duplicate copy of notes. One student might take notes on this lined paper and then tear off the bottom copy for your teen.

Cue Student When Important Points Are Made. Sometimes it is very helpful for teachers to state the obvious: "This is important." "Write this down. This will be on the test." Or the teacher could ask students, "Of all the things we've discussed this morning, tell me the three most important things you've learned. What do you think will be on the test?" Ultimately the teacher is helping students learn how to identify key points in her lectures.

Poor Reading Skills or Reading Comprehension*

Up to 39 percent of students with ADHD have difficulty with reading. Some have problems with slow reading, and others, difficulty comprehending and remembering what they have read. Although not all teenagers have difficulty with vocabulary words, Dr. Zentall explains that they may have trouble comprehending long passages. In large measure their limited working memory, a key component of executive function, again emerges as one of the primary reasons for problems remembering the key points of what they have read or heard. This may explain why students sometimes complain that they can't remember what they have read, and then have to reread the whole page.

Other researchers have found that when youngsters with ADHD read silently, they are more likely to make errors and have poorer comprehension since

they tend to skip words, phrases, or lines. Several factors combine to make reading comprehension difficult for these teenagers, including inattention, distractibility, working memory problems, impulsivity, and losing their place on the page.

1. SLOW READING FLUENCY AND COMPREHENSION

Use a Bookmark. Your teen can slide a ruler or bookmark down the page as she reads so that she doesn't lose her place.

Use Published Book Summaries. Commercially available book summaries such as *Cliff Notes* provide a brief synopsis of the plot, description of characters, and chapter summaries. These may be a helpful supplementary aid for students who have reading comprehension problems.

Use Books on Tape or CD. "Talking Books," books recorded on audiotape cassettes or compact disks, can be a wonderful study aid for some students, both at home and school. The student reads a book while the same material is played on a tape recorder or CD player. Two national organizations, "Talking Books" and "Recording for the Blind and Dyslexic," record many books, including textbooks. Most schools have access to this resource. Parents also may obtain this free service independent of

the school system. In addition, many classic books that are required reading for high school students are available on tape or CDs from school or public libraries.

> *"Since my high school age son has started reading books on tape, he has completed a book a week for the last three months. These books were required reading for graduation from his private school."*

Several special services are provided free by "Talking Books" including a special cassette or CD player, books from classics to bestsellers, mailing and return costs. Teenagers whose ADD or ADHD adversely affects their ability to learn are eligible to use these services. An application must be completed by a physician or other professional to certify the presence of a specific learning disability or an attention deficit. Applications are available from most local libraries or directly from these organizations. For more information on this free service, please contact your local library or:

> National Library Service for the Blind and
>   Physically Handicapped (NLS)
> Library of Congress
> Washington, DC 20542
> 1-800-424-8567
> E-mail: nls@loc.gov
> www.loc.gov/nls
>
> Recording for the Blind and Dyslexic (RFB&D)
> (a one-time membership fee of $25-$35)
> 20 Roszel Road
> Princeton, NJ 08540
> 1-800-221-4792
> E-mail: custserv.rfbd.org
> www.rfbd.org

Recordings for the Blind is the only organization to provide *textbooks* on tape.

Weak Spoken Language Skills (Oral Expression*)

Some teenagers with attention deficit disorders are extremely verbal and love making speeches in public, but others absolutely dread it. In fact, about one-third to one-half of these teenagers have problems with expressive language. This is about two or three times the rate for teenagers without attention deficits. Interestingly enough, Dr. Barkley and Dr. Zentall have both observed that teenagers with ADHD are *more* likely than their peers to talk during spontaneous conversations, but *less* likely to talk when asked to respond to a specific request. Responding to a question or statement requires more organization and careful thought. Again, slow processing speed and limited working memory capacity may contribute to this problem.

> *"When my daughter tells me about something that has happened, the story comes out all jumbled up. She can't organize her thoughts to tell the story in logical order."*

1. DIFFICULTY ARTICULATING CLEAR ANSWERS

Teenagers with attention deficits may have trouble organizing their thoughts and expressing them in a logical, sequential order. This can show up in two ways. First, some youngsters talk nonstop and have trouble giving brief, concise answers. Second, youngsters who process information slowly need more time to think before responding to questions. This problem increases if the student is nervous, self-conscious, or anxious about her answer.

> *"My son has difficulty sorting out what's important, so he says it all. Rather than give the main idea, he painstakingly repeats every detail."*

Be Positive and Supportive. Many of these teenagers need more help and understanding than other students. By being supportive, the teacher creates a positive learning environment in which students are not afraid to ask questions or make mistakes. Teachers can help by praising correct answers or efforts to answer a question, giving students time to think of their answer, and avoiding criticism or put-downs.

Teach Mechanics of Outlining and Sequencing. With time and practice, these students can often learn to express themselves more clearly. They can practice telling about events in a story in sequential order. What happened first? Next, and so on? If your teenager has to make an oral presentation, help her outline the speech.

2. AVOIDS RESPONDING IN CLASS

Students who have problems with verbal expression may be less likely to volunteer to answer questions in class. They may avoid making presentations to the class. Sometimes they are afraid to ask for help or to ask a teacher to repeat information.

"I don't like to raise my hand in class and ask questions. I am afraid that my mind was drifting off and I may look dumb. I'm afraid to ask a teacher a question if it isn't clear. I feel like I shouldn't ask questions about things she has already said. It would be redundant."

"My son was frightened to death of having to make a presentation in class. Once he took an F on his report rather than speak in front of his classmates."

Cue Student Prior to Being Called Upon. Teachers may cue the teenager prior to calling on her. The teacher may also assign specific problems (questions) to each student and say, "In a few minutes, I want each of you to tell me how to do your problem."

Provide Less Threatening Opportunities to Speak Publicly. You and your teen's teachers can devise less threatening opportunities for her to practice public speaking—through school clubs, debate team, theater groups, boy scouts or girl scouts, church or synagogue, or at family events or holiday programs.

Don't Penalize for Limited Class Participation. Sometimes a portion of the grade is based upon class participation. Perhaps the teacher will agree not to penalize her grade for lack of class participation.

3. SLOW RECALL OF FACTS

Even when students with attention deficits are able to memorize material such as multiplication tables or history facts, their recall of information may be slower. Youngsters who have ADD inattentive usually have the most difficulty with slow retrieval of stored information. Some medications, such as Lithium at higher doses, may also slow the ability to recall facts quickly.

Give More Time to Respond. Teachers may need to give your teenager more time to think when asking her to respond orally to questions in class. They might also call on another student and then come back to her.

"I'm not stupid. I knew the answer but the teacher didn't give me enough time to think about my answer."

Weak Written Language Skills (Written Expression*)

Our teens may have trouble:
1. writing their own ideas down on paper, and
2. reading and comprehending what someone else has written.

Reasons may include: slow processing speed, poor organizational skills, limited working memory, inattention, slow recall of information, poor fine motor coordination, and avoidance of unpleasant tasks.

As reported earlier, about 65 percent of children with ADHD in one study also have serious problems with written expression. On a positive note, Dr. Zentall notes that some teenagers with attention deficits write more creative stories. At school, difficulty with written language can lead to serious problems.

"Steven had great difficulty writing as early as fifth grade, but, because he could read three grade levels above his grade, we never thought that he had a learning disorder. It was not until the tenth grade that we figured out he had ADHD. After we got him on the correct medication, everything except writing improved. His junior year, it became clear it would be impossible for him to pass the state exit exam in writing. In hopes of getting an exemption on the state required test, we had him tested and his writing disorder was diagnosed. It's sad that it took over six years to figure this out. I don't quote Hillary very often, but it does take a village to help parents raise an ADHD child."

1. WRITES SLOWLY ON ASSIGNMENTS

Because of the problems described in the preceding paragraphs, these teenagers may work very slowly on their homework, schoolwork, and tests. Some students may take twice as long to complete written assignments.

Use a Computer. Hopefully, one day, all students will have their own computer to use at school. Until then, if your teenager has illegible handwriting and writes slowly or laboriously, ask the teacher if a computer, perhaps a smaller, cheaper AlphaSmart, is available for her to use when writing compositions at school.

Reduce Amount of Writing. Talk to the teachers about ways of avoiding unnecessary writing. If your

teenager writes very slowly, she could photocopy pages of textbooks in subjects such as history, science, or government. She could then highlight important facts, or highlight answers to questions. She could also just fill in the blanks with answers to questions. There is no need to ask her to write the whole question plus the answer.

2. PRODUCES LESS WRITTEN WORK

Slow processing may mean that a student produces less written work and reads less material. Obviously, these students require more time for completing written and reading assignments.

Shorten Assignments. For example, in math, teachers may assign every other or every third problem.

Use Alternatives to Writing. If your teenager finds writing more difficult than public speaking, it may be helpful if she is allowed to: a) make oral presentations, or b) record homework on a tape recorder for assignments other than written English compositions, or c) use voice recognition software that then prints out what the student dictated. However, reviews on the effectiveness of voice recognition software are mixed, with some saying the written product isn't always accurate. Plus, it takes time to "train" the program to recognize your voice, and colds or voice changes can confuse the software. *Dragon Naturally Speaking 8* is often suggested as one of the better voice recognition software programs. This program costs roughly $250. Talk with school personnel about the practicality of using these programs.

3. HAS DIFFICULTY WRITING ESSAYS AND REPORTS

These teenagers may have difficulty organizing and expressing their thoughts in a clear, orderly manner as required for writing essays or reports.

Teach Strategies for Essay Writing. Sometimes their organizational skills improve if students with attention deficits learn the standard format for writing a five-paragraph essay: an introductory and closing paragraph plus three body paragraphs. Ideally, your teen will be given a copy of the essay writing guidelines, possibly in the form of a graphic organizer to take home so you can work with her on these skills.

Use Note Cards or Post-It Notes for Main Ideas. Another strategy that can help with written language problems is to have the teenager write main ideas on 3 x 5 cards or Post-It Notes. She can then rearrange the cards/notes in groups for each paragraph, next she can arrange them in proper sequence before writing the report. She can refer to the cards/notes as she writes her paper, or, if appropriate, use them later to study for an exam.

4. DIFFICULTY TAKING TESTS

Teach Test Taking Skills. Dr. Don Deshler reported that students who were taught test taking skills scored ten points higher on tests. For example, students may use "brain dumping" to jot down key information they might forget as soon as they walk in and sit down. Or skim ahead to find out which questions are worth more points and spend more time on those.

Give Extended Time or Shorten Tests. If students have slow processing speed, reading comprehension problems, or slow retrieval of information, they will require more time or a shorter test.

Provide a Reader for Tests. If your teenager has great difficulty reading or responding in writing on tests, the teacher or a student could read the test questions aloud and let her respond orally. Or the test could be recorded on a tape recorder so that the student can listen to it again as needed.

"I would go over the test with Cassie and find that she knew much of the material. She would say, 'I didn't even see that question on the test—no wonder I didn't answer it.' Sometimes she gave ridiculous answers to questions. When we looked over the questions, we would look at each other in disbelief. Then she would give the correct answer aloud. Finally, I asked for someone to read the test to her since she seemed to do far better when asked questions verbally.

"It was constantly a struggle to have teachers remember to line up a reader for each test. Frequently we ran into regular education teachers who were adamantly opposed to 'babying' kids with SLD. One teacher said there is nothing wrong with this kid that a little bit of hard work won't cure. I think he was just a 'hard liner' who felt these children didn't have any problems."

General Strategies for Strengthening Key Deficits

This section offers suggestions that can help with any of the language deficits discussed in the section above, including problems with speaking, reading, writing, and math.

Learning Styles

Talk with a teacher or school psychologist to identify your teenager's *learning style.* In other words, through what senses does your teen learn best? Some people are visual learners and learn better when they can see printed materials. Others are stronger auditory learners and learn more effectively when they hear academic material. In earlier times, before the advent of computers and video games, most students were auditory learners. Today that trend is shifting so that more students, especially those with attention deficits, are visual learners. Students should be taught in a manner that builds on the strength of their learning style.

Information about your teenager's learning style is vital for planning academic interventions. Sometimes, because of inattention, memory problems, and listening comprehension difficulties, our teenagers have trouble with auditory learning. That is, they may have great difficulty learning from a teacher's lecture or verbal directions. Adding a visual component—with written handouts or written directions—may help. Experiential "hands-on" activities and or interactive computer software also help students learn more easily.

Poor Memorization Skills

Many teenagers with attention deficits have difficulty memorizing information and then quickly retrieving it. In addition, they may have trouble with their limited working memory capacity—in other words, holding information in mind, manipulating it, and then coming up with an answer. Their problems with working memory, a key executive skill, may be caused by a combination of factors: poor strategies for memorizing, poor complex problem-solving strategies, limited working memory capacity, difficulty focusing attention, and poor organizational skills. The good news, however, is that teenagers with ADD or ADHD *can* memorize information if they are taught specific techniques.

"Initially I thought my son couldn't learn to memorize. Then when I tried some of the memory strategies in Teaching Teens, I realized he could memorize information if I used the right strategies."

Dr. Zentall reports that students with ADHD make fewer auditory memory errors when teachers use visual cues in addition to verbal instruction. For example, they are more likely to remember information (spelling words) the teacher *says* when they also *see* it (flashcards).

Teenagers with attention deficits who have serious memory problems are at significant disadvantage in school. Students who are good at memorizing usually make better grades. It is therefore critically important to make accommodations for memory problems.

"Shawn had trouble memorizing, but we thought it was because he didn't care. If he didn't like the teacher, or if he couldn't see an immediate useful application for the information, he wouldn't even try to memorize. If he really liked the teacher, then he would make a real effort to learn something—but his memory was very short-lived."

Subjects that require rote memorization of isolated facts such as math, algebra, spelling, history, and foreign languages can be especially difficult. This section covers suggestions for dealing with problems with rote memorization. Math in particular presents one of the biggest challenges and is addressed later in this chapter.

1. DIFFICULTY MEMORIZING INFORMATION

Effective strategies for memorizing include acronyms, acrostics, visual posting, and use of graphic organizers.

Use Mnemonics. Using mnemonics, or memory tricks, a student figures out a way of thinking about facts or concepts that will help him remember them more easily. For instance, students are often taught the acronym "HOMES" to help remember the names of the great lakes (Huron, Ontario, Michigan, Erie, and Superior). This technique can be especially helpful when memorizing information in subjects such as history, geography, biology, or chemistry.

Use Flashcards. If your teen is *required* to memorize facts, work on one set of facts at a time until she has mastered them. Hold up the flashcards. If she answers correctly, she gets to keep the card. Otherwise you keep the cards she doesn't know. Next, review the cards she missed the first time through. The review continues until she has collected all the cards. This is an especially good technique when she sees the facts, says them aloud, hears you state the correct answer, and is then handed a card.

Forgetfulness

Forgetfulness is one of the more exasperating characteristics of teens with attention deficits. Many have a terrible time remembering:

1. class- and homework assignments,
2. to bring home the correct book,
3. to complete homework,
4. to take it back to school, and
5. to turn it in.

Sometimes their homework makes it to their school locker but never makes it to the classroom. If they miss a test, they forget to request a make-up exam, even though their grade may be lowered significantly. They forget to complete major class projects. Poor organizational skills and listening comprehension, in addition to memory problems, contribute to their apparent forgetfulness.

"If my son needs help, I am going to help him without feeling guilty. If he is able to learn the material but forgets his book, or the page number, or can't organize a semester's worth of information to study for a final exam, are we supposed to let him fail? What are we grading: the subject or organizational skills? I'll take an F in organization and a C in Math any day!"

"A 12-year-old girl with ADD inattentive called our office in a rage. A teacher had given her a zero on a test because she had forgotten to put her name on her paper. The child's actual test score was 91. A call to the teacher revealed that she did not give her a zero but gave her credit for the 91. The poor exasperated teacher had hoped to scare her into putting her name on future papers."

Forgetfulness is one of the major diagnostic criteria for attention deficit disorders, and as such should be carefully addressed at school. Effective strategies include using an assignment book, emailing assignments home, appointing "row captains" to check that peers have written down assignments, using Palm Pilots, and keeping two sets of books at home.

1. FORGETTING HOMEWORK AND OTHER ASSIGNMENTS

Forgetting homework and long-term projects are often major problems for these students.

Check to See If Assignments Are Written. The teacher or another student may check the teen's assignment sheet each day to see if she has remembered to write down the assignments. When she gets in the habit of keeping up with her work, teachers will no longer need to provide this much supervision. Some students find it helpful to use their computer, a Zire, or Palm Pilot to write down assignments.

Ensure Assignments Are Known. Several options are available: post homework on the web, ask the teachers to email it home, call another student or return to school and check the chalk board for assignments. Some parents must be notified of due dates for long-term projects as part of an IEP or Section 504 Plan (see Chapter 14). Other helpful tips include using daily or weekly reports and monitoring make-up work to ensure that no assignments are overlooked.

Weak Math Skills

Many teenagers with attention deficits have serious weaknesses in their math skills. Two major problems are relevant here: *memorization difficulties* and *slow math calculation* (processing speed).* Some may even have a Nonverbal Learning Disability (NVLD), a deficit in visual spatial skills and visual spatial processing which is often associated with math disabilities. Children with NVLD will often score markedly higher on verbal subtests of the WISC than on nonverbal ones.

One general recommendation to help with math homework is to shorten assignments. If your teenager can't complete math assignments in an hour or less, consider asking her teacher to shorten the class or homework assignment. This ensures that she knows the math concepts but doesn't burden her with lengthy homework assignments. The teacher can discuss this reduced assignment privately with your teenager so other students are not aware it is occurring. Most likely your teen will experience problems if he or she processes slowly or has problems holding all the required information in working memory.

1. CAN'T MEMORIZE MULTIPLICATION TABLES

Memorizing basic math facts and recalling them quickly is a critical skill. Memorization of multiplication facts enables a student to complete complex math problems more quickly. Teachers in elementary school drill children to increase their speed working these basic math problems. Yet, some teenagers are unable to memorize and recall basic math facts even with intensive practice sessions—they are unable to "automatize" math facts quickly.

Students with attention deficits often have a *slower speed of calculating math problems* than other children with comparable intelligence. Poor memorization skills, slow computation, and inattention may make it extremely difficult for teenagers to develop a solid foundation of basic math facts upon which to build more complex math concepts.

When students enter middle school without having mastered the multiplication tables, they may be penalized unfairly. They may know the math concepts but work so slowly that they cannot finish assignments in class. Furthermore, if teachers insist that they continue trying to memorize multiplication tables, valuable time will be taken away from the major class objective: learning more advanced math functions.

"*Our son has great difficulty memorizing anything even though he is extremely bright. Although he passed high school algebra and geometry, he still has not memorized his multiplication tables.*

"*He and I spent hours drilling multiplication facts, which he promptly seemed to forget the next day. This process continued for weeks. I battled my own ambivalent feelings about my son's ability to remember and memorize things. Was he not trying? Did he not care? Was he just being lazy? Finally, I realized he was doing his best. He could not memorize things very easily.*

"*Because the ability to memorize had been one of my greatest strengths in school, it was even more difficult to accept my son's disability in this area. I didn't fully appreciate that the ability to memorize was a God-given gift.*"

If your teenager cannot memorize multiplication tables, it is not the end of the world. Most adults use a calculator when they need to multiply. In fact, a good question to ask about material that must be memorized is, "Do adults in the real world use this information frequently?" In real life, most adults use calculators to balance their checkbooks, and spell- and grammar-check functions on their word processor to correct letters they are writing.

Use a Calculator or Multiplication Chart. Perhaps when your teenager reaches middle school, teachers will allow her to use a calculator or multiplication chart while working math problems. Consequently, she can work on mastering each new math concept as it is presented without being slowed down by not knowing multiplication tables. And she may actually learn some of the tables from punching the numbers into the calculator.

Even organizations such as The College Entrance Examination Board recognize the practical use of calculators and now allow students to use calculators when taking the SAT. As discussed in Chapter 14, the use of a calculator may need to be specified in your teen's IEP or 504 plan for him to be allowed to use it on tests.

"*Cassie's math disability is described in her IEP as 'the inability to retain math facts over time.' She wonders why no teachers ever said, 'That's not a problem. She knows the process. She can get an answer with a calculator. Let's just go on from there.'*"

"*Thank goodness teachers are willing to shorten math assignments. Otherwise, my son would have been up half the night working on math that others could finish in an hour.*"

Other effective strategies include using manipulatives, rap tapes, rhyming and chanting, math software, math shortcuts, and programs like *Times Tables the Fun Way*.

2. DIFFICULTY MASTERING ALGEBRA

The transition from grade school math and its concrete facts to the more abstract concepts of algebra is incredibly challenging for most of our teens. Remember, too, these students have significant deficits in working memory that may interfere with their ability to do well in algebra. These students have difficulty holding all the necessary information in mind while doing an algebra or math problem. For example, they must remember the problem, remember the proper steps in order, quickly retrieve necessary math facts and formulas, remember how to do the problem, and then hold information in mind while solving the problem. Furthermore, slow processing speed also means that they will take significantly longer than their classmates to do their homework.

Use Concrete Teaching Strategies to Teach Abstract Algebra Concepts. Obviously, making these abstract concepts concrete is very difficult for teachers.

Unfortunately, only a few programs have been developed to show teachers how to do this.

One program that impresses me was developed by Brad Witzel, Ph.D., Winthrop University. The program starts with concrete, hands-on activities to demonstrate the abstract concepts; next moves on to representational drawings for the concrete steps; and finishes with the transition to traditional algebra. Research on this program has been impressive with participating students outperforming students in traditional algebra classes two to one. For more information on the *Multisensory Algebra Guide*, visit www.msalgebra.com (803-389-8501).

Use Paired Learning. Paired learning or class-wide peer tutoring is a very effective interactive learning strategy. After the teacher demonstrates the problem, students pair off, make up their own problem example, swap problems with their partner, compare answers, and if answers aren't the same, determine why not. Ed Thomas, Ph.D., has developed strategies like paired learning for both middle and high school teachers, *Styles and Strategies for Teaching Mathematics* (www.thoughtfuled.com).

Reduce Demands on Memory. By reducing the memory demands on these students, their limited capacity is freed up to focus on solving the problem. Here are a few suggestions from *Teaching Teens*:

1. Leave an example of the solved problem on the board during class;
2. Use a calculator for math computation;
3. Use graphic organizers;
4. Use mnemonics.

3. DIFFICULTY WITH MULTI-STEP MATH

Many teenagers with attention deficits have problems with the multi-step math that is involved in algebra and other advanced math classes. Typically, they want to take shortcuts. For example, they like to do much of the work in their heads, skip steps, and never write everything down on paper. Sometimes they write their numbers and problems very small, all on one line. As a result, they make "careless" errors. It is often difficult to follow what they have done because their writing is so poor and so small. If they write slowly, they may skip steps because they are afraid they will not have enough time to finish the assignment. Poor working memory, short attention span, slow processing speed, and organizational skills also contribute to problems in this area.

"Stephen can do long division in his head but fouls up on paper because he can't line the numbers up correctly. His teacher agreed to let him give the answer without showing all his work as long as he continues to get the answers correct."

Write Problems Correctly. You or the teacher can demonstrate how to write the problem, spacing it correctly on the paper. It may be helpful for you to "talk through" the problem, step by step. Have your teen write on one line for each step of the math problem. Since this is a basic concept, take care to do it tactfully, in private, and not embarrass her by making her appear stupid in front of other students or friends.

Shorten Assignments. With shorter assignments, these students may also be more inclined to write down all the steps required for completing each problem. Specific strategies for mastering math and algebra also include group response and use of graph paper and graphic organizers.

Poor Fine Motor Coordination

Fine motor coordination problems are also common and may result in poor handwriting, avoidance of writing, a preference for printing (instead of writing cursive), and low output of written work (homework or classwork).

1. POOR HANDWRITING

Teachers may complain that your teenager's writing is hardly legible. Like many of these teenagers, she may prefer to *print* rather than write in cursive. It seems these children often have good reasons for the things they do, even if they aren't apparent to adults; Dr. Mel Levine explains that printing requires less memory than writing cursive.

"Both of our sons had very poor handwriting. One son wrote extremely small letters and numbers and he also wrote very slowly. Homework took forever to complete. Both boys preferred printing their schoolwork rather than writing in cursive even in middle and high school.

"Alex's writing was not very good, plus he wrote very slowly. His first grade teacher made him write his whole name, Alexander. By the time he laboriously finished writing his name, the rest of the class had almost finished the assignment. Finally, I was able to convince the teacher that it was okay for him to write 'Alex' and not the sixteen letters which comprised his first and last names."

Accept Poor Handwriting and Printing. Urge teachers to allow your teenager to print his schoolwork as long as it is legible. Ask them to accept her writing as is without badgering or subtracting points from her overall grade.

Use a Computer. Encourage your teen to do her school work on a computer.

Do Not Ask to Write Sentences as Punishment. Writing 500 sentences such as "I will not talk back to my teacher" for punishment is inappropriate for youngsters who have fine motor coordination problems.

"My son had to write 500 sentences in high school because he didn't do his homework. He forgot to do the sentences and the teacher added another 100 sentences for each day he was late. He writes so slowly. This was a terrible punishment. He truly didn't think he would ever finish writing. I finally helped him finish his sentences."

2. DIFFICULTY COMPLETING BOARD WORK

Some of these students have difficulty quickly copying work from the board. They may have difficulty looking back and forth from the chalkboard to their paper, keeping their place, and completing the assignment. Limited working memory capacity, poor fine motor coordination, and slow processing skills may contribute to this problem.

Minimize Board Work. Reducing the amount of work students are expected to copy from the board should help. Ask the teacher to give your teenager a written copy of the material on the board.

Poor Motor Coordination

Some teenagers with ADD or ADHD have trouble participating successfully in physical education classes. In fact, approximately half of these youngsters have poor motor coordination. Poor concentration and distractibility may also be problems in P.E. classes and organized sports. Teenagers may have trouble staying with the group and paying attention when the teacher is talking. In addition, they can have difficulty with the transitions and rule changes that are so often a part of sports. For example, at the beginning of P.E. class, they might be allowed to be talkative and active, but then suddenly they have to change (transition) to quietly listening to the teacher. In addition, some of these teenagers, especially those with ADHD, may not have

the social skills required for cooperative interactions in P.E. classes and sports.

1. DIFFICULTY PARTICIPATING IN SPORTS

Participate in Sports Where Success Is More Likely. Hand-eye coordination is often a major problem for those who struggle with sports. Since their gross motor skills may be stronger, they may do well in sports such as swimming, soccer, karate, or wrestling. They may not do as well playing baseball, basketball, tennis, or racquetball.

Work with the School to Schedule P.E. Classes. To help make P.E. class a more positive experience, check with the guidance counselor to see which sports are taught when. Perhaps, your teenager can then sign up for P.E. when sports like soccer or wrestling are taught.

Give the Student a Job Helping the Teacher. Sometimes the teacher may tap a student's high energy by giving her a job during class. For example, handing out towels or giving out or taking in equipment may be jobs she would be willing to do. Having a job may help her feel successful in P.E. class, even if she is not athletic.

Other Factors Affecting Completion of Schoolwork

Although these issues were discussed in earlier chapters, a brief discussion about their impact on school performance, plus some suggestions for you to give teachers, are provided in this section. Remember, too, that some teenagers with ADD or ADHD also meet criteria for learning disabilities, depression, anxiety disorder, oppositional defiant disorder, or conduct disorder.

1. HYPERACTIVITY, TALKING, AND DISRUPTION OF CLASS

Most teenagers are restless, rather than hyperactive, in the classroom. Teenagers who still have hyperactive tendencies may talk loudly, interrupt others, or monopolize conversations. They may act out to draw attention to themselves or enjoy being the center of attention. When not on medicine, the "class clown" may wait for the exact moment to deliver a classic line that sends the whole class into peals of laughter.

Provide Opportunities to Be the Center of Attention. Be proactive. Encourage your teenager to participate in activities such as theater or debate team that allow her to act or speak and be the center of attention.

Find Activities to Allow Movement. Some of these youngsters need to move when they are studying or at least take a break from sitting. As long as they can finish their work and don't disrupt the rest of the class, let them sit, stand, or move as needed. Some students can do two things at one time. If restlessness or hyperactivity is severe, ask them to carry messages to the principal's office or assist the teacher with other chores.

Assign Two Work Stations. If teens are still very restless, particularly in long classes such as in block scheduling, the teacher may assign two seats or work stations so that they can move from their seat to a nearby table to work for a while.

2. MEDICATION

Major problems can arise at school when the student forgets to take her medication or it wears off. The teenager can't concentrate on academics and is more likely to make impulsive decisions that get her into trouble. Thankfully, the longer-acting medicines now available can last throughout the school day. However, if problems suddenly flair up at school after a period where the student has been successful, a good review and fine-tuning of medication, dosages, and timing of administration is critical.

Discreetly Ask If Medication Was Taken. If the teenagers only rarely appears inattentive, suggest that someone discreetly check to see if she forgot her medication that morning. Consider leaving some medication at school so your teen can go to the office and take the medicine if needed.

If Taking Short-acting Medication, Monitor School Performance. If a student is taking a shorter-acting medication like Ritalin or Dexedrine, it may wear off during the school day. Even medications like Adderall (not XR) and Metadate ER may last only six or so hours. If the student took medication as early as 6:00 a.m., it may wear off by lunchtime.

Schedule Key Academics at Times When Medication Is Working. Schedule important academic classes or classes in which your teenager has the most trouble paying attention for times when medication has its maximum effect. Mornings are generally better for most of our students.

If Problems Arise, Ask When They Occur. If your teenager is not doing well academically or misbehaves only during one or two classes, discuss this with teachers. Identify the time of day the problems are occurring. If it is either late in the morning or afternoon, the medication may have worn off. Long-acting medications that peak in the afternoon may result in early morning academic problems. Don't forget to calculate how long your teen's medicine should last.

Adjust Medication Schedule or Dose. Your teenager may be able to take medications at a different time, or you may consider switching to longer-acting medication. These long-acting medications last eight to twelve hours, so the need for a midday dose will be eliminated.

3. OTHER SYMPTOM-RELATED PROBLEMS

Issues that may cause problems at school—uneven academic performance, low energy or lethargy, sleep disturbances, coexisting conditions such as depression, self doubts, emotionality, and oppositional behavior—are discussed in Chapters 7 and 12. It is important to make certain that whenever any of these problems crop up, the teacher knows that they are all part of having the disorder—typically, your teen is not just deliberately misbehaving.

Exceptions to the Rule

Not all teenagers with ADD or ADHD do poorly in school. Some are outstanding students even without medication. For example, nearly half of the major speakers at a recent national CHADD conference identified themselves as having ADD or ADHD. These speakers included professionals with Ph.D.'s and M.D.'s. Most likely, these adults were extremely bright, learned to compensate for their inattentiveness, had milder cases of attention deficit disorder, and were able to do well in academic settings in spite of their disability. As mentioned previously, children and teenagers with attention deficits *can* learn to compensate and find ways to succeed.

"As a child, I was chronically in trouble. I received straight A's in all my classes and U's in conduct. I lived in the corner when I was in the second grade. I smuggled books in under my clothes so I would have something to read. When I got in trouble, I gave my teacher 'drop dead looks.' In the third and fourth grades

I would lose my temper and get paddled at school. I was chronically on restrictions at home. My ADHD wasn't diagnosed until I was studying for my Ph.D. in psychology, when academic demands became so much greater."

Conclusion

Since success in school is so critical, I have identified numerous effective intervention strategies in all three of my books. Obviously, you are not expected to use all of these strategies. Use as few interventions as are needed to help your teenager succeed.

If you try to use too many strategies, you and your teenager may get caught up in a colossal power struggle. Your teen may resent being forced to use so many accommodations, especially if he or she is viewed as being significantly different from other friends. You both will be worn out and your teenager will be well on his or her way to hating school and you. As a parent, I personally avoided implementing any major strategies unless my son was in danger of failing classes or his self-esteem was being damaged because of his poor grades. Of course, if your teenager expresses a desire to make better grades, you should work with him or her to make any accommodations that might help.

Use common sense in deciding when and how to use accommodations. For example, younger children need to practice multiplication tables with their peers when they are first introduced in elementary school. In later grades, if it becomes obvious that your teenager cannot memorize multiplication tables, then advocate for accommodations such as using a calculator or a sheet with the multiplication tables listed on them.

Ask your teenager for input about accommodations. Remember, she may feel uncomfortable or embarrassed when accommodations are made in class. Be sure to handle accommodations as discreetly as possible. Ideally, only your teenager and the teacher should know about the change.

Periodically reassess the accommodations being used to see if any can be eliminated. Bear in mind, however, that some accommodations may be needed throughout your teenager's high school and college career. The underlying goal is to teach your teenager increased self-reliance, self-advocacy, independence, and strategies for compensating for the challenging symptoms of ADD or ADHD. As your teenager assumes more responsibility for her schoolwork and other activities of daily living, you will want to continually reduce your involvement in her life.

Table 13-1 Identifying Common Learning Problems and Providing Accommodations in the Classroom

Common learning problems, the behavior observed, and possible classroom accommodations are presented below. Your teenager may be experiencing some but not all of these learning problems. The accommodations listed in the last column may be used for more than one behavior listed below. If your teenager doesn't know how to study or is disorganized, someone must act as an "academic coach."

You may identify which learning problems your teenager may be experiencing and possible accommodations. Then discuss this information with a teacher or treatment professional whom you trust to see if he or she agrees with your initial assessment.

Learning Problems	Behavior Observed	Accommodations *[Accommodations listed in this column may be used for more than one deficit]*
Inattention		
Poor concentration	▪ Difficulty completing work (Changes from one task to another) ▪ Forgets assignments or books (See section on Memory below)	▪ Give frequent positive feedback ▪ Provide more supervision ▪ Ensure assignments are known ▪ Monitor homework ▪ Use weekly report ▪ Provide reward for completing work ▪ Take medication when doing schoolwork ▪ Study with a friend
	▪ Tuning out and daydreaming (Difficulty paying attention in class; Easily distracted; Doesn't seem to listen)	▪ Use high interest material ▪ Use hands-on interactive learning ▪ Use a multisensory teaching approach ▪ Make eye contact ▪ Seat away from distractions ▪ Cue/use private signal system ▪ Cue prior to important announcements ▪ Ask for a reminder ▪ Keep instructions brief and simple ▪ Divide work into smaller segments ▪ Schedule short work period ▪ Find activity to allow movement
	▪ Lack of attention to detail (Make "careless errors"; Don't notice changes in math signs so may add all problems regardless of sign; Have trouble finding errors in grammar, punctuation, capitalization, and spelling)	▪ Use color as aid to learning ▪ Encourage to double-check answers ▪ Highlight signs in color until student becomes aware and no longer needs cue ▪ Highlight potential errors in color ▪ Have student read material aloud ▪ Modify grading system ▪ If never double-check answers (too tired or too much homework), parent highlights errors and teen corrects
	▪ Lack of awareness of grades (Don't know when failing)	▪ Monitor school work ▪ Obtain information about grades ▪ Graph or average grades
Impulsivity		
	▪ Getting into trouble at school (Noncompliance, forgetfulness, talks back to teachers, walks out of class, defiance, skips school, smokes at school, fights, carries a weapon to school, speaks and acts without thinking)	▪ Help succeed academically ▪ Keep rules simple; state clearly ▪ Remind of consequences of breaking rules ▪ Notify school of potential problems ▪ Consider medication ▪ Request a classroom aide ▪ Ask about a FBA or BIP ▪ Shorten the school day

Learning Problems	Behavior Observed	Accommodations
	■ Impulsive learning style (Starts without reading directions, rushes)	■ Review instructions with teen ■ Highlight instructions ■ Mark out wrong answers on multiple choice ■ At home, double check answers with teen
Executive Function Deficits		
	■ Disorganized (Appears lazy, difficulty getting started and finishing school work, doesn't understand directions, forgets assignments, to turn in papers; see Memory below)	■ Find a tutor or academic coach ■ Seek a structured classroom ■ Establish routine ■ Keep an assignment notebook or Palm Pilot ■ Develop an organizational notebook ■ Make lists/use Post-it notes
	■ Lost possessions; e.g., homework, books, clothes	■ Make teacher aware of problem ■ Put homework in same place each night ■ Put names on possessions ■ Check lost and found at school
	■ Difficulty being prepared to do school work	■ Request flexibility from teachers ■ Place homework in notebook night before ■ Turn in work before leaving school
	■ Difficulty getting started (starts and stops work)	■ Monitor getting started; "jump start" ■ Prompt to start working ■ Use cue to get attention
	■ Procrastination	■ Prompt on assignments and due dates
	■ Messy desk, notebooks & lockers (can't find homework, books)	■ Help organize locker ■ Clean out locker and notebook periodically ■ Look for lost papers in locker & notebook ■ Don't throw away completed papers
	■ Difficulty managing and being aware of time (impaired sense of time; forget and are late for appointments)	■ Make teacher aware of problem ■ Set wrist watch alarm or beeper ■ Remind of key times ■ Teach awareness of time; time management ■ Practice time estimation
	■ Difficultly remembering and organizing long-term projects	■ Give accommodations for long-term projects ■ Use graphic organizer for long-term projects ■ Require notification of long-term projects in IEP/504 plan
Language Deficits (Slow Processing Speed for some; impacts listening, speaking, reading, or writing)		
	■ Difficulty understanding instructions (Lose main point in instructions) (Confused with verbal directions)	■ Keep instructions brief and simple ■ State directions clearly: "Number 1. Do all the odd problems. Number 2. Do all five problems on the next page." ■ Use cue to get attention
	■ Difficulty following verbal instructions (Don't always "hear" instructions)	■ Ask student to repeat instructions ■ Write instructions on Post-it notes
	■ Difficulty learning foreign language	■ Use tips on memorization ■ Ask for accommodations ■ Consider seeking waiver to exempt
	■ Difficulty taking good notes (Takes notes very slowly)	■ Get copy of notes from student or teacher ■ Use NCR paper or carbon paper ■ Ask for a notetaker in IEP/504 Plan ■ Get guided lecture notes from teacher ■ Record lecture on tape ■ Cue for important points; Teacher may say: "This is a major point."

Learning Problems	Behavior Observed	Accommodations
Reading Comprehension	■ Poor reading comprehension (slow reading, loses place, skips words) ■ Can't remember what she reads (Difficult reading; stops and starts over; slow reading; loses place, skips words)	■ Slide a paper or ruler down page ■ Use published book summaries ■ Use Talking Books at home & school ■ Check audio or video tapes from library ■ Use Kurzweil Personal Reader
Written Language (written expression)	■ Writes slowly, takes longer to complete ■ Produces less written work ■ Difficulty writing essays, reports & tests (Difficulty organizing thoughts and ideas for writing) ■ Difficulty taking good notes ■ Difficulty taking written tests; may take twice as long; may have trouble understanding questions and expressing and organizing answers	■ Use computer; laptop at school ■ Use computer-aide instruction ■ Reduce amount of written work ■ Shorten written assignments ■ Teach strategies for composition writing ■ Use alternative to writing; e.g., tape record report ■ Use note cards for main ideas ■ Modify the test/administer untimed ■ Provide a reader for tests ■ Use voice recognition software to dictate essays ■ Teach test taking strategies
Spoken Language (oral expression)	■ Difficulty articulating clear answers (Trouble giving brief, clear answers) (Slow cognitive processing speed) ■ Avoids responding in class ■ Slow recall of facts (Reluctant to raise hand or answer questions; problems with memorization & retrieval)	■ Be positive & supportive ■ Make teacher aware of problems ■ Teach outlining & sequencing ■ Give notice prior to being called on ■ Provide less threatening situations to speak publicly ■ Don't penalize for limited class participation ■ Give more time to respond
General Tips for Strengthening Language Deficits		■ Seat away from distractions ■ Keep instructions brief and simple ■ Ask teacher to make accommodations or shorten assignments ■ Allow to receive peer tutoring ■ Allow more time for doing work and tests ■ Identify learning style/teach to strengths
Memory		
	■ Difficulty memorizing ■ Difficulty with rote memorization (Difficulty with subjects requiring memorization: spelling, history, algebra & foreign languages)	■ Teach strategies for memorizing ■ Use flashcards or tapes ■ Use color to highlight error ■ Use word associations ■ Use mnemonics ■ Use choral response ■ Use spell check or dictionary ■ Don't count off grade for spelling ■ Seek a waiver for foreign language
Weak Math Skills	■ Can't memorize multiplication tables (Poor basic math skills; slow recall of basic addition, subtraction, multiplication, division facts) ■ Difficulty with multi-step math (Take short cuts, do math in head, skip steps, don't write work down, write small, make "careless errors") ■ Difficulty mastering algebra	■ Give chart with multiplication tables ■ Allow use of calculator ■ Ask teacher to shorten assignments ■ Reward accuracy/reduce work ■ Use flashcards ■ Use choral response to memorize ■ Write problems correctly ■ Use graph paper ■ Use math short cuts ■ Modify assignments, reduce amount of work ■ Teach concrete strategies (www.msalgebra.com) ■ Use paired learning ■ Reduce demands on memory

Learning Problems	Behavior Observed	Accommodations
Forgetfulness	■ Forgets to bring home assignments, worksheets, books, etc. (Forgets homework assignments) ■ Forgets or can't find books, pencils, paper, folders, report covers ■ Forgets to do homework & make-up work ■ Forgets to bring work to school; forgets to turn in ■ Forgets to put name on paper	■ Work with teacher ■ Keep assignment book ■ Check that assignments are written down ■ Ensure homework is known ■ Have another student prompt about homework ■ Ask teacher for written weekly assignments ■ Call friend to confirm homework when teen can't remember ■ Ask about homework assignment routine ■ If parent picks up at school, check assignments and books ■ Keep extra supplies at home ■ Get two sets of books; keep one at home and one at school ■ Parent prompts ■ Monitor make-up work ■ Put school work in same place each night ■ Allow flexibility in turning work in late ■ Buy a name stamp

Motor Skills

Learning Problems	Behavior Observed	Accommodations
Fine Motor Skills and Written Language	■ Poor handwriting, illegible (Avoids writing, writes slowly, produces less written work, prints instead of writing cursive) ■ Difficulty doing board work	■ Accept poor handwriting & printing ■ Allow to use a computer ■ Modify assignments; shorten ■ Give untimed tests ■ Do not write sentences as punishment ■ Minimize board work; give written copy
Motor Coordination	■ Poor coordination ■ Difficulty participating in sports	■ Select PE classes where can succeed; e.g., swimming, soccer, wrestling ■ Work with counselor to schedule PE ■ Help with transitions to and from PE ■ Give job to help teacher

Other Factors Affecting Completion of Schoolwork

Learning Problems	Behavior Observed	Accommodations
	■ Talking and class disruption	■ Allow to be center of attention ■ Find activity to allow movement ■ Assign two work stations
	■ Forgotten or ineffective medication	■ Check to see if medication taken ■ Monitor grades ■ Complete teacher med rating form ■ Schedule key academics when meds working best ■ Find out time of day problems occur; compare with med effectiveness ■ Adjust meds ■ Refer to Chapter 6
	■ Sleep	■ Refer to Chapter 9
	■ Coexisting conditions such as depression	■ Refer to Chapter 7

14

Legal Leverage for Pursuing Academic Success

To ensure school success for students with attention deficits, parents must become educated advocates. First and foremost, they must learn about three federal laws:

1. The Individuals with Disabilities Education Act (IDEA),
2. Section 504 of the Rehabilitation Act of 1973, and
3. the Americans with Disabilities Act (ADA).

These laws provide guidance for the education of all students with disabilities. Students with ADD or ADHD often qualify for services under IDEA or Section 504 because of their major academic challenges. In addition, the ADA provides important protections for students with attention deficit disorders during extra curricular activities and postsecondary education.

Do Students with Attention Deficits Need Special Education?

Roughly 90 percent of students with attention deficits will face serious struggles at school at some time during their academic career. It is therefore reasonable to assume that the majority of students would benefit from extra supports or accommodations in the classroom. The term "special education" in this section is used broadly to include necessary educational services for children under either IDEA or Section 504. In a more narrow legal sense, "special education" is a term found in IDEA legislation.

Let's first define some terms, though, so you can understand exactly what is and is not meant by "special education."

Special Education: Under federal law, students who are legally entitled receive *"special education and related services and supplementary aids and services,"* which are specially designed to meet the unique learning needs of students with disabilities. These services may or may not be provided in the regular classroom. A "statement of the program modifications" must also be provided. Note that accommodations can be provided informally by teachers whether or not a student has been found eligible for special education. However, if teachers refuse to provide accommodations without "proof" that a student needs them, parents must seek a formal evaluation under IDEA or Section 504 to determine if their teenager is eligible for special education under the law.

In other words, special education services are provided along a continuum. Many students receive accommodations within the regular classroom without other students even being aware that they are receiving special education. Other students, with more intense needs, may need to leave the regular classroom to receive specialized instruction for one or more classes.

According to one researcher, Robert Reid, Ph.D., a Professor of Special Education at the University of Nebraska, approximately 30 to 50 percent of students with attention deficits will qualify for special education services under IDEA *by the time they reach adolescence.* That is, they will be found legally entitled to special education under IDEA, the main special education law in the U.S. However, Dr. Reid also explains that these students don't necessarily require placement in a special education classroom, but rather can be successful in regular classroom settings with appropriate accommodations.

Accommodations: An accommodation is a change that is made in schoolwork to enable a student with a disability to learn but without affecting the content of what he is learning. Examples include being given a copy of notes taken by a fellow classmate (a notetaker) rather than having to take your own notes or being given extended time on a test. The student takes the same test as his classmates, but has more time to finish it. Additionally a student may be allowed to use a calculator for school work and tests.

Modifications: A modification is a change that is made to the *content* of what a student is learning because a disability interferes with his ability to learn at the same pace as peers without disabilities. Examples include being required to learn only some of the material that is covered in math class, or using textbooks that are written at a lower reading level than other students are using. Most students with attention deficits receive accommodations rather than modifications, however.

Related Services and Aids and Supplemental Supports: These terms may refer to a range of services from counseling and speech therapy to skills training. For example a student with an attention deficit may benefit from study and organizational skills classes, anger management and time management training,

test taking skills, problem solving strategies, notetaking skills, ADHD education, or counseling or parents may benefit from parent training. *Assistive technology* should also be provided. For instance, these teens might benefit from use of a calculator, a computer, or special software programs like *Inspiration* to assist with a written expression deficit.

If your teenager has academic or behavior problems that make it difficult for him to succeed in the classroom, it is important for you to learn how the various federal laws may help him. Other important laws, policy statements, and court rulings are discussed later in this chapter.

The Challenges of Interpreting the Law

Keep in mind that it is extremely difficult to provide up-to-date, accurate information about federal laws because explanation of any law requires interpretation. If you ask two lawyers, you may get two different interpretations, just as you would if you asked a school official and a parent, or two different judges. In addition, the interpretation of the law may change overnight on the basis of important court rulings that become known as *case law.* Furthermore, states may pass laws and regulations that may provide more detail or protections than the federal law does. For example, states may specify the number of days during which an evaluation and special education placement must occur, or add to the list of objects qualifying as weapons. And local school districts will have their own individual policies and procedures. So the information given in this section is stated in general terms and is not intended as legal advice.

Attention Deficit Disorders and Special Education Law

For several decades, federal laws have guaranteed special educational services for students with a variety of disabilities. Until the last few years, however, it has been extremely difficult to use these laws for the benefit of students with attention deficit disorders. One reason was that attention deficit disorder wasn't listed as an eligible condition for special education services in IDEA, the federal special education law, until 1997. Even with legal eligibility now spelled out in the law, however, some parents are still struggling to get needed services for their children with ADD and ADHD. Across the country, access to services has been uneven. Some communities do an excellent job of following the law. Unfortunately, others do not. Even though the law has made it clear that children with ADD and ADHD may be eligible for services, I still receive emails from desperate parents who cannot get the help they need from their local school system.

The bottom line is that parents must educate themselves about these important federal laws, if their children are to receive the services they deserve. But let's be very clear, students with ADD or ADHD are not automatically eligible for services; they must meet specific criteria that will be described in this chapter.

Key elements of this chapter include information on program eligibility under federal laws and official interpretations of the laws that are relevant to students with attention deficits. Common roadblocks to services are also addressed. In addition, this chapter contains specific suggestions for working with the school system to ensure your teen's academic success. Additional detail on these laws and specific academic and behavioral intervention strategies are provided in our companion guide, *Teaching Teens with ADD and ADHD,* Summaries 39-50.

Begin with the Right Attitude

Although this chapter talks about laws and legal rights, the underlying message is one of cooperative planning and respect between educators and parents to help students be successful in school. As you work with school officials, it is important to assume good intentions. Keep in mind, it will take the combined wisdom and experience of both teachers and parents to implement a successful educational plan.

Of course, in an ideal world, school officials would provide whatever resources a student needed to be successful, and laws like IDEA and Section 504 would be unnecessary. Unfortunately, that's not the case. So this chapter is designed to give you guidance in situations where your school is not meeting your child's needs in compliance with the law. Keep in mind, however, your strategies for dealing with the school system should be based upon their level of professionalism, knowledge, competence, and understanding of attention deficit disorder. Hopefully you will be one of the fortunate families whose school system is topnotch. If not, this chapter's for you.

Common Roadblocks to Services

You may be thinking that you don't need to read this chapter because you've been told by school officials that your child isn't eligible for special education services under IDEA. So, before we get to the facts on the law, let's talk about the obstacles and misinformation that may have already been thrown in your path. Here are my "Cliff Notes" comments regarding eligibility so you can make an informed decision about whether or not you should read any further.

"They say my son isn't eligible for services...."

Some school systems act responsibly, gather the facts, and readily acknowledge when a student with an attention deficit qualifies for services. But other school systems may be resistant. Occasionally parents are told their teen is not eligible for services under IDEA, when in fact he is. Sometimes school officials may simply be misinformed. Or they may not have conducted a proper evaluation or considered all the options for services. So, you must educate yourself and ask questions. On the other hand, school officials may be correct, and your teenager may not be eligible for services.

If school officials tell you your teen isn't eligible for services, ask them to explain their reasons for this decision in writing. In particular, ask them which disabilities they were evaluating your child for. As discussed later, many teens qualify under the category of "other health impairment" (OHI), but some might qualify under the category of specific learning disability (SLD) and a few, Emotional and Behavior Disorder (ED). Make sure the school has evaluated your child for all of the disabilities you believe he might have. In addition, if your teen was evaluated for SLD before 2004, be aware that criteria for diagnosing SLD have changed. See page 299 to see if these changes might affect your child's eligibility.

"What if my child isn't failing any classes? Can he still get services?"

> *"A school counselor said that because my daughter wasn't failing, that she would not qualify for IDEA."*

Federal law makes it clear that a student does *not* have to be failing to be eligible for services under IDEA. According to an April 5, 1995 policy statement from the Office of Special Education (OSEP), U.S. Department of Education:

"The evaluation should consider information about outside or extra learning support provided to the child when determining whether a child who received satisfactory grades is nevertheless not achieving at age level. The child's current educational achievement may reflect the service augmentation not what the child's achievement would be without such help." The federal regulations also indicated that the student 'could be passing from grade to grade.'"

In other words, students with attention deficits may be passing their classes primarily because of taking medication or the extraordinary efforts of parents or tutors. If these supports are withdrawn, the impact on the teenager's academic performance may be significant. Furthermore, it is not unusual to find that some teenagers with attention deficits are successful in school because of the Herculean efforts of both parents and the teen. In any of these cases, the school cannot rule that the student is ineligible for special education solely on the grounds that he is not failing his classes. Of course, if the student *is* failing, the need for intervention is obvious.

"What about my daughter who is on grade level but is bright and not achieving up to her potential?"

These children may be eligible for services in certain situations. The 1995 OSEP memo also noted that: a student may be eligible for services "if the team determines that the child does not achieve commensurate with his or her age and ability levels…."

One simple way of interpreting this statement is that "age level" refers to being on grade level and "ability level" refers to children who are intellectually capable of functioning at a higher level of academic achievement.

"Could my son with a high I.Q. be eligible for services?"

Yes, the 1995 OSEP memo continues by stating that "there is no categorical exclusion for children with high IQs…therefore, if a student with a high I.Q. is not achieving at this expected performance standard,"… and also meets eligibility criteria, the student can be eligible for services. The student could have dual classification as Gifted-OHI or Gifted-LD. "Each child who is evaluated for a suspected learning disability must be measured against his own expected performance, and not against some arbitrary general standard."

These statements indicate that a gifted child who may be achieving on grade level could still be eligible for services. Furthermore, some students with attention deficits may score high on most achievement test categories, but have really low scores on math computation or written expression sufficient to meet eligibility criteria.

Making These Laws Work for You

Access to services should follow a pretty predictable path. First, when it becomes clear your teen is struggling, the teacher might give him a few extra supports or accommodations, known as *pre-referral intervention strategies*; next, the teacher may refer the student to an educational team for help; and finally the student may be evaluated to determine eligibility under either Section 504 or IDEA. At this point, the question parents must answer is which law—IDEA or Section 504—will offer the supports your child needs to be successful in school. First let's take a look at both laws. Hopefully this information will help you make an informed decision.

Individuals with Disabilities Education Act (IDEA)

The Individuals with Disabilities Education Act (IDEA) mandates that students with disabilities receive a free, appropriate public education. Under this law, the federal government provides funding to the states so they can develop and maintain quality special education programs. To qualify for these funds, states must guarantee students with special needs a variety of services and rights. IDEA has been revised several times since it was first passed in 1975 as the Education for All Handicapped Children Act (Public Law 94-142). Important revisions made in 2004 will be highlighted throughout this chapter.

Key Provisions of IDEA

Key provisions and new requirements of IDEA are listed below along with a more detailed discussion of each service in subsequent sections. Revisions effective with the 2004 law are noted because your school system may be making decisions based upon old guidelines and not know about these changes. New requirements or changes will be <u>underlined</u> and any commentary will be in [brackets]. Typically, any other specific questions you may have about IDEA may be answered at websites like www.ideapractices.org, which was developed by the Council for Exceptional Children (CEC). Key provisions of IDEA include:

1. A Free Appropriate Public Education (FAPE)
2. Involvement of Parents in Educational Decisions
3. Nondiscriminatory Evaluations and Assessments
4. An Individualized Education Program (IEP)
5. An Education in the Least Restrictive Environment (LRE)
6. A Right to Remedy or Due Process

1. A Free Appropriate Public Education

Under IDEA, children with disabilities are guaranteed a "free appropriate public education" (FAPE), designed to meet their individual needs. "Free" means that the education must be provided at no cost to the parents and child. "Public" mean that the education will ordinarily be provided in a public school, but if the school system is unable to provide an appropriate education for your child, then they may have to pay for his education, even if it must be provided in a private school or residential school. What constitutes an "appropriate" program will be determined by you, your child, and a group of educators. Although each state has different names for this group of educators who work with parents, a few common terms include IEP Team or ISP Team. Pertinent information about your child's education will be written down in an *Individualized Education Program* (IEP), as explained below.

2. Involvement of Parents in Educational Decisions

Parents should be *equal partners* in the process of developing an educational plan for a student. At first, you may feel intimidated by this process, especially since you may be heavily outnumbered, so to speak; the only noneducator working with a team of educators. But just remember, you bring invaluable information to this process. *Parents often know their child best and have learned over the years which intervention strategies are most effective!*

Dixie Jordan, a child advocate and an authority on IDEA, has wisely observed that parents may "not always know what will work with their adolescent, but they certainly know what has *not* worked." Jordan is the author of *Honorable Intentions*, a book to help parents navigate the special education system. The book is especially helpful for parent of students who have serious emotional problems. Much of her expertise comes from being a parent of a young adult with ADHD and also a veteran of numerous IEP meetings that she has attended with parents.

You can educate yourself by reading books and talking with other parents or teachers so that you feel confident enough to be an active participant—don't be afraid to speak up. Some parents take advocacy a step further and bring their own draft "IEP" to the meeting, or, more realistically, a list of issues that must be addressed in the IEP, plus strategies that they think might work. In addition, you might consider hiring an educational consultant or psychologist to accompany you and speak as an informed advocate on your child's behalf.

3. Nondiscriminatory Evaluations and Assessments

Only students with certain disabilities and levels of impairment are eligible for services under IDEA. Before a student can begin receiving special services or accommodations, he must be formally evaluated by the school system to determine whether he qualifies. When evaluating a child, schools must ensure that:

- Parents receive a written notice before their child is tested;
- Parents give written consent prior to testing, for a first-time assessment;
- Parents have the opportunity to refuse assessment, in writing, if they believe it is not needed;
- Parents give their consent before the child is placed in special education;
- Student records are kept confidential;
- Parents are allowed access to all student records;
- Evaluations are conducted by multidisciplinary teams—that is, by a group of people who each have expertise in different areas, including someone knowledgeable about attention deficit disorders;
- Evaluations are nondiscriminatory or culture (bias) free;
- If any of the above rights have been violated, parents have a right to an impartial

"mediation" or "due process" hearing by a person who is objective and who is not directly involved in the case; and

■ Parents may request an independent evaluation, at no cost, if they disagree with school evaluation results.

Ultimately, the school system has the right to determine what constitutes their evaluation. They decide how extensive the assessment should be and which, if any, tests should be given. Often the school system will implement "pre-referral strategies" in the student's classroom first before conducting a more formal evaluation. In other words, they make simple changes in the curriculum or environment to see if that will solve the student's problems. If these strategies don't work, then a more formal evaluation will be conducted to determine if the student is eligible for services.

They may do the evaluation in phases. When attention deficit disorder is suspected, the first phase may consist only of:

1. a classroom observation by a school psychologist,
2. a review of current school records plus samples of class work,
3. a teacher conference, and
4. an interview with the parents.

The evaluation might not include any formal testing.

If school staff suspect an eligible disability, a permission form will be mailed home for the parents to sign authorizing an evaluation. After the evaluation is completed, parents will be invited to a meeting to discuss the results. If the student is determined to be eligible for special education, an IEP will be developed jointly by the parents and school.

According to federal law, a reevaluation must be conducted every three years (unless the parents and school agree reevaluation is unnecessary) or earlier if educational or related services needs warrant it, or upon a parent or teacher's request.

ELIGIBILITY CATEGORIES

In conducting an evaluation, the school tries to determine whether a student has one of the thirteen disabilities listed in IDEA as qualifying a student for special education (provided that that disability has an impact on the student's ability to learn). The two major disability categories that teenagers with ADD and ADHD are mostly likely to qualify under are "other health impairment (OHI) and "specific learning disability" (SLD).

"What is OHI and why do I need to know about it?"

OHI is critically important to know about because the law specifically lists ADD and ADHD as eligible conditions under the OHI category. According to federal policies, students with attention deficits should now be considered for eligibility under this category first instead of Specific Learning Disability (SLD) or Emotional or Behavior Disorder (ED). This definition of other health impairment (OHI) is quoted from federal law.

> OHI "means having limited strength, vitality or alertness, including a heightened alertness to environmental stimuli, that results in limited alertness with respect to the educational environment, that…
> a. is due to chronic or acute health problems such as asthma, attention deficit disorder, or attention deficit hyperactivity disorders, diabetes, epilepsy, a heart condition, hemophilia, lead poisoning, leukemia, nephritis, rheumatic fever, and sickle cell anemia; and
> b. adversely affects a child's educational performance."

Please note that this law uses the term *educational* performance not *academic* performance. This means that additional factors other than just test score discrepancies should be considered in determining eligibility for services. For example, "relevant functional, developmental, and academic information" may include factors such as grades, homework completion, independent work habits, alertness, sleeping in class, class participation and attendance, ability to complete tests within class time frames, relationships with peers, and compliance with rules.

The "limited alertness" or inattention exhibited by our teens is an important diagnostic criteria for OHI. Many states require a medical report as part of their assessment process. Your teen's physician will need to fill out and sign a medical evaluation form. Depending on your relationship with your teenager's doctor, you might photocopy the medical report form in Appendix 4 of this book and fill out a draft copy for him or her to use as a reference. In addition, a sample OHI School Eligibility Report is provided in Appendix 6. OHI is discussed in greater detail in *Teaching Teens*, Summary 42.

If your teen is really struggling but doesn't meet OHI or SLD criteria (below), then the next step is to ask that he or she be considered under Section 504 criteria.

What is SLD and what do I need to know about It?

For years the major category for evaluating students with attention deficit disorders for special education has been Specific Learning Disability (SLD), so without thinking some schools still automatically use these criteria. Evaluations for OHI may be done so seldom that schools may mistakenly use SLD eligibility criteria instead of the appropriate ones from OHI.

Until late 2004, eligibility criteria for SLD required that the student have a significant discrepancy between academic achievement and intellectual ability. For example, scores on reading and math grade level tests would be compared with scores on an IQ test to see whether the student was not achieving in school at a level commensurate with his intellectual ability. Thanks to 2004 IDEA revisions, states now are allowed to waive the requirement for a "severe discrepancy" between achievement and intellectual ability. Schools are required to consider many components of a student's life in determining eligibility under SLD, such as those factors described in the previous paragraph, rather than solely focusing on test scores. Schools must consider "relevant academic, developmental, and functional performance." In addition, the focus is clearly on providing positive interventions when students are struggling academically or behaviorally.

Key IDEA Revisions Related to Evaluations

Evaluations to be comprehensive. The child's present levels of "academic achievement and the related developmental needs" of the child must be evaluated. [The child's developmental delay due to ADHD or ADD should be considered.]

Discrepancies in test scores no longer required for eligibility. Schools are no longer required to use a severe discrepancy between achievement and intellectual ability to determine eligibility for specific learning disabilities.

Some children in private schools to receive services. Some children with disabilities in private schools are eligible for services from the public school system. In fact, IDEA's "Child Find" provision mandates that they "find" and serve these children in private schools and that a "proportionate amount of federal funds" must be spent on them.

Unfortunately, information about changes in federal requirements may trickle down slowly to some local schools. So, it may be awhile before families receive the full benefit of these changes in the law.

CONFLICTS OVER EVALUATION

Two key areas of potential conflict exist between parents and school personnel regarding evaluations:

1. timing (how soon can it be done), and
2. adequacy of the evaluation.

When the issue of an evaluation surfaces, it is often in the midst of a crisis—your child is not doing well at school. You want the evaluation done *yesterday*. But school officials may have a backlog of children awaiting evaluation. Ask how long your child must wait for an evaluation in your state. Federal law requires schools to complete the evaluation within 60 days from the day parents sign a permission slip for testing.

Consider a Private Evaluation. There are at least two situations in which parents may elect to seek a private evaluation.

1. If you disagree with the results of the school's evaluation—perhaps because you believe it is inadequate since no IQ or academic achievement tests were given—you may request that a new evaluation be done privately. For example, if the school system is not familiar with the concept of executive function deficits, an evaluator may overlook this problem that could be one of the major underlying causes of the student's academic failure.

If you request another evaluation, the school district is responsible for arranging and paying for it—unless they believe it is unnecessary or prove that their evaluation is correct. If the school disagrees, they must request a due process hearing to deny your request. Since a due process hearing generally costs much more than a complete evaluation, most schools are unlikely to take this route. If you want an independent evaluation paid for at public expense, make the request in writing to the school system. The school may have an approved list of qualified professionals from which parents may choose.

2. If the school can't comply with the 60-day timeline, you may decide to seek testing at your own expense. Tell them you are seeking private testing and ask them for a list of approved evaluators in your community. If results from independent testing help in determining school services needed, the school system *may* have to reimburse you for testing. But don't count on this, since the legal process of securing payment for the testing may be expensive and time consuming, plus it may be difficult to meet the school's evaluation criteria. For example, private evaluations may not include the same tests required by the school system.

Assessment Doesn't Mean Just Testing. Keep in mind, testing won't provide a magic answer. Sometimes a good teacher or parent interview will give the school more helpful information than a test. Some of the more subtle challenges that our children face such as deficits in executive skills don't easily show up on formal tests. If the school psychologist can identify the problem without formal testing, that's wonderful. The most important action is to implement effective intervention strategies.

4. An Individualized Education Program (IEP)

At the heart of each student's educational program is a document called the Individualized Education Program (IEP). The IEP is developed at a meeting between parents and school personnel, where they *jointly* decide "what the child's needs are, what services will be provided to meet those needs, and what the anticipated outcomes may be." Four key issues should be considered in this process:

1. the strengths of the child,
2. the concerns of the parents,
3. the results of the evaluation, and
4. the academic, developmental, and functional needs of the child.

As indicated earlier, each state has timelines for evaluating the student and scheduling an IEP meeting. For example, Minnesota allows thirty school days while other states may allow up to six weeks.

Unfortunately, after the IEP meeting, some schools are very slow implementing services. Federal law states only that the IEP must be "implemented as soon as possible following the meeting." So ask when services will begin. It is reasonable to expect that they will start within five school days after the IEP meeting. For students who change schools, please note that as of 2004, when a child with a disability transfers to a new school district, the receiving school must provide the student services currently listed in his IEP until an IEP meeting has been scheduled and a new IEP created. [Parents should take a copy of the old IEP to the new school.]

COMPONENTS OF AN IEP

Several federally mandated components of an IEP are listed below and discussed in more detail in subsequent sections. Parents should look for statements in the IEP that address each of the following topics:

1. "The child's present levels of educational performance." The statement must address "the child's present levels of academic achievement and <u>functional performance</u>." All areas of performance and development, including academic, social, and behavioral issues, as well as difficulties with executive skills such as organization and slow processing speed, should be considered.

Frequently the primary focus of IEPs for students with attention deficits is on misbehavior. Recent research findings, however, are guiding us toward a different approach—*focus on academics first*. According to Dr. George DuPaul, a noted Lehigh University researcher on the education of those with ADHD, students who receive academic instruction such as tutoring, show improvements in both academic performance and behavior; however, the converse is not true. Behavioral interventions alone do not bring about academic improvements.

2. "Measurable annual goals for both academic and <u>functional</u>" issues." (The 2004 amendments to IDEA eliminated the requirement for short-term objectives for the majority of students.)

A goal is simply a statement of what special education is supposed to help your child achieve during the course of the school year. For example, one goal for a student with an attention deficit might be to complete and submit homework in a timely manner. One way to make this measurable would be to add "at least 85% of the time." Another goal may be to reduce emotional or angry outbursts.

3. "Special education and related services and <u>supplementary aids and services</u>" (accommodations and supports) that will be provided for the child and the name of the person responsible for arranging the service.

Special education refers to any specialized instruction your teen might need (such as tutoring in math or resource room assistance in reading). "Related services" refers to therapy or other services your teen might need in order to help him achieve the goals on his IEP. For example, a related service for a student with a goal to reduce angry outbursts might be anger management training.

Intervention Strategies. Simply stating student goals in isolation is of no value. The key here is that *the intervention plan must clearly state what the teachers and parents are going to do to provide the support necessary for the student to achieve this goal*. In other words, the IEP must include a list of the accommodations and supports needed for school success. For instance a "row captain" or class buddy will check to see that assignments are written down daily and turned in when they are due. Parents must monitor homework completion at home. An aide or buddy may meet the student at his locker to see that the right books are taken home.

4. How much time the student will spend in a "special education" setting outside of a regular classroom.

5. When the services will start, *how often* they'll be provided, *where*, and for *how long.*

6. Modifications or accommodations on district or state assessment tests.

For example, some students with ADD or ADHD get extra time to complete the tests; others are allowed to write their answers in the answer booklet rather than filling in "bubbles" on an answer sheet.

7. How progress will be measured and how and when parents will be informed of progress.

8. A transition plan including transition services, <u>courses of study, measurable postsecondary goals, and transition assessments</u> for <u>students age 16</u> and older to prepare them for life after high school.

5. An Education in the Least Restrictive Environment (LRE)

IDEA guarantees a free appropriate education in the least restrictive environment (LRE). The LRE is de-

fined as the educational setting that allows the student with special needs to be educated, "to the maximum extent appropriate," with children who don't have disabilities. In other words, qualifying for special education under IDEA does not automatically mean placement in a special education classroom. *If a student can make good progress in the regular classroom with some modifications, accommodations, or supports, that is where he should be served.* Or, if he only needs to leave the regular classroom for special instruction in one or

two subjects, then he should still spend the majority of his time with classmates who don't have disabilities.

A full continuum of options ranging from classroom accommodations to placement in a self-contained special education classroom must be available. Students should be provided services in the least restrictive environment in which they can succeed academically.

6. A Right to Remedy or Due Process

If you and the school system disagree about your child's educational plan (IEP), you can follow formal and informal avenues of complaint. On an informal basis, you may be able to iron things out with your teenager's teacher, principal, or director of special education simply by notifying them that you disagree with your child's plan and are requesting a meeting to talk things over.

MEDIATION

School districts must offer a procedure called "mediation" that allows the parents and school to informally resolve complaints fairly quickly and with a minimum of antagonism. Federal law requires that mediation services be offered free for children eligible for services under IDEA. If you are dissatisfied with the results of the mediation, you still have the right to file for a due process hearing.

A mediator meets with you and school officials to:
1. discuss the points of disagreement,
2. listen to possible alternatives suggested by you and the school,
3. suggest other alternatives, and
4. help you and the school system agree upon a compromise.

Frequently, mediation is preferable to filing for a due process hearing. You may be more likely to get services you want through mediation than through a due process hearing. Realistically, your chances of winning a due process hearing vary greatly from state to state. But even if you don't want mediation, it is mandatory for parents to attend a meeting to listen to the benefits of mediation. As a result, many parents have accepted mediation and the number of due process hearings have actually dropped over the last few years.

DUE PROCESS HEARINGS

If local mediation fails, or you choose not to try it, you can request a *due process hearing* by notifying the superintendent of schools in writing. Based upon your state timelines, a hearing must then be scheduled and a decision rendered within a certain number of calendar days, perhaps 45 or so from the date your request is received. You can request a due process hearing when you have a dispute about almost any aspect of your child's educational program, including identification, evaluation, placement, and provision of educational services.

A due process hearing has all the major elements of most legal court procedures. Parents and school officials each have an opportunity to argue their case before a hearing officer, often an attorney or administrative law judge who is not a state employee. This hearing officer must be impartial—he or she must not have a stake in one or the other side's winning. In some states, parents may select a hearing officer from a list supplied by the school system.

Parents may:

1. access all school records,
2. present testimony and evidence,
3. bring witnesses to testify,
4. subpoena or compel witnesses to appear,
5. cross examine witnesses,
6. present results of an independent evaluation, and
7. hire an attorney at their own expense.

Ask your state department of education for a copy of state hearing procedures. Then check them to determine your state timelines regarding several key issues. For example, you should know that evidence that has not been disclosed at least five days prior to the hearing most likely will be prohibited. Also check the number of days the hearing officer has before he must present his findings. If you disagree with the results, you also may have only 30 days to appeal this ruling.

The student will remain in his current education placement until completion of the due process hearing with two exceptions:

1. the parents agree to removal from the class, or
2. the student's offense involved weapons or drugs, or the student inflicted "serious bodily injury" to another person. "Serious bodily injury" is defined as "injury that involves a substantial risk of death, extreme physical pain, protracted and obvious disfigurement, or protracted loss or impairment of a bodily member, organ, or mental faculty."

If parents win the lawsuit, the school system *may* be required to reimburse their attorney's fees.

Work positively to resolve conflicts; avoid antagonism. Whenever possible, parents should try to resolve conflicts with the school quickly and with as little antagonism as possible. If parents use a "sledge hammer"

to obtain services, the relationship between the family and school may be damaged forever. Unfortunately, if the school system is refusing to provide services that the student is eligible for, the family is probably dealing with a pretty damaged and entrenched school system. Other students who come along after a due process hearing may benefit—although the student initiating a due process hearing may suffer. Of course, retaliation against a student or parent is expressly prohibited, but in reality, subtle discrimination is very difficult to prove. Regrettably, systems change is often glacially slow.

Section 504 of the Rehabilitation Act of 1973

Section 504 of the Rehabilitation Act (P.L. 93-112) is a *civil rights law that prohibits discrimination* against people with disabilities by any program or activity that receives funding from the federal government. (Title II of the Americans with Disabilities Act (ADA) expands the prohibition of discrimination to other settings, including in private, non-parochial schools and in the workplace.)

Since most schools in the United States receive at least some federal funding, this law can be used to obtain many important educational rights and benefits for students with disabilities. This law provides a broader definition of disability and has fewer regulations than IDEA, so it may be easier to qualify for and receive services under Section 504 than IDEA. At the same time, Section 504 offers fewer protections if the child breaks school rules, as will be explained subsequently. The Office for Civil Rights (OCR) develops regulations for and monitors administration of Section 504.

Section 504 states: *"No otherwise qualified individual with a disability in the United States…shall, solely by reason of her or his disability, be excluded from the participation in, be denied the benefits of, or be subjected to discrimination under any program or activity receiving Federal financial assistance."*

29 USC s 794(a), 34 CFR s104(a)

"An individual with a disability is a person who:
- has a physical or mental impairment that substantially limits one or more major life activity;
- has a record of such an impairment; or
- is regarded as having such impairment."

34 CFR s104.3(j)(1)

In a 2003 *Attention* magazine article, Mary Durheim, a certified mediator and hearing officer for Section 504, explains that some terms such as *"substantially limits"* are not defined in federal regulations. Durheim explains that each local school district will make a determination of "substantially limits" based upon the nature and severity of the person's disabling condition. "Major life activities" may include caring for oneself, performing manual tasks, walking, seeing, hearing, speaking, *learning, concentrating,* or working. With these clarifications, it's easy to see why students with ADD or ADHD frequently qualify for eligibility under Section 504.

Services and Rights Under Section 504

Many of the rights and safeguards mandated by IDEA are also available under Section 504. For example, Subpart D - Preschool, Elementary, and Secondary Education guarantees "a free appropriate public education to each qualified person with a disability…regardless of the nature or severity of the person's disability."

In practice, access to services for students with attention deficits via Section 504 varies across the country based upon regional interpretations. In some areas, most students struggling with ADHD or ADD and related learning problems are considered eligible for a 504 Plan. In other areas, where the law has been interpreted conservatively, fewer students with attention deficits meet 504 eligibility criteria, unless they also meet the more stringent IDEA eligibility criteria.

For a 504 evaluation, Durheim explains that the 504 Committee must consider several sources, not just a doctor's report: for example, "grades over the past several years, teacher reports, information from parents or other agencies, state assessment scores or other school administered tests, observations, discipline reports, attendance records, health records and adaptive behavior information."

A letter from your physician documenting the attention deficit is often required. However, the medical diagnosis alone is not sufficient documentation for meeting eligibility requirements.

Provisions of Section 504. Section 504 or subsequent court rulings require:
- Free appropriate public education (FAPE);
- Placement in the least restrictive environment (LRE);
- Nondiscrimination in assessment and evaluation;

- Periodic reevaluations of students receiving related special education services; every 3 years or for "any significant change in placement";
- Revision of an accommodation plan at any time, if needed;
- Opportunities to take part in extracurricular and non-academic activities;
- Provision of non-academic services; such as counseling, transportation, physical education, or health services;
- Consideration of the child's disability in determining disciplinary action. A procedure similar to a "Manifestation Determination Review" discussed below may be conducted, even if the school doesn't call it that.

Under Section 504, parents have the right to:
- Receive notice prior to evaluation or placement;
- Review pertinent school records for the student;
- Request an impartial hearing regarding school actions, if needed;
- File a complaint with the school district section 504 coordinator;
- File a complaint with the regional Office for Civil Rights.

Violations of IDEA are often violations of Section 504 also; most due process appeals may be filed under one or both laws.

Differences between IDEA and Section 504. Unlike IDEA, Section 504 does *not* mandate:
1. A written plan (although a written plan is usually developed anyway);
2. Parental involvement in decision-making; (although parents are usually included);
3. Formalized testing;
4. Reimbursement of an outside independent evaluation if parents disagree with the school's evaluation.
5. *The eligibility criteria for Section 504 are broader* than those for IDEA. Often, struggling teenagers with an attention deficit who are unable to qualify for services under IDEA will qualify under Section 504. But teenagers who qualify under IDEA are always eligible under Section 504.

6. The effectiveness of services delivered under IDEA is held to a higher standard than under Section 504. Educational services offered under IDEA must be sufficient to allow the student to "*benefit*" from his schooling. Under Section 504, educational services must be "*comparable*" to those received by non-handicapped students, with no requirement that the student benefit from the services.

7. *IDEA only covers students through high school*, whereas Section 504 covers students in technical school, colleges, and universities as well.

8. Students usually receive accommodations under Section 504. However, they may be *less likely to receive more costly related services* such as speech therapy since school systems are not reimbursed for providing these services as they are under IDEA.

SECTION 504 PLANS

Even though development of a written "Section 504 Plan" is *not* required in federal law, many states have elected to require one anyway. Development of written plans is often viewed as a "best practice" policy that can also be helpful to school systems by documenting their educational efforts. Most likely, you will have a planning meeting to discuss your teenager's academic needs with his teachers and other school personnel. So development of a written plan, based upon that meeting, would be a logical action.

Ultimately, an IEP or "504 Plan" is often a primary source of *documentation* for taking an untimed SAT or ACT. If you make the school aware that documentation may be needed for accommodations in technical school or college, most likely they will develop a written plan for you.

In many ways, a Section 504 Plan is like a stripped-down version of an IEP. So the materials related to writing IEPs both in this book and in *Teaching Teens,* Summaries 41, 44-46, should be a tremendous help as you formulate your ideas regarding your teen's needs. Since OCR has given no formal guidance about 504 Plans, the document may be whatever your local school system wants it to be. Many county policies governing Section 504 Plans follow the basic format of an IEP. Typically a plan will identify the teen's strengths, learning or behavior problems, goals and objectives, classroom accommodations, and possibly transition issues.

Placement. Most eligible students are taught in regular classrooms, but if the student's disability is so disruptive that others cannot learn, then the child may be placed elsewhere. In this situation, most likely, the school will seek eligibility under IDEA since they will be reimbursed for services rendered.

Discipline. Before taking any disciplinary action against one of these students, just like under IDEA, the school must consider the relationship between the disability and the misbehavior. However, according to Matthew Cohen, a special education attorney and former CHADD president, the consequences for inappropriate behavior will be regulated only if:

1. there is a plan/statement for doing so in the 504 Plan, and

2. if the student is excluded for more than ten days.

You can read more about these two issues in the subsequent section on IDEA's *Manifestation Determination Review*, and the subsequent section on school suspensions and in *Teaching Teens,* Summary 40, #7. Guidelines for disciplinary procedures unique to your community will be contained in your local school's Section 504 Policies.

GETTING MORE INFORMATION ABOUT SECTION 504

Every education agency is required to have a local 504 coordinator on staff to respond to questions and concerns from families. Local school systems have varied in their compliance with this requirement. Some systems have taken this very seriously and have hired a Section 504 coordinator whose primary responsibility is to manage the 504 system, while others have identified an existing staff member to take on the extra responsibilities.

If you have questions about Section 504, talk with staff at your local school first. If they are unable to answer your questions satisfactorily, call your local 504 coordinator about rights and possible resolution of problems. If you are not satisfied with the coordinator's response, you may contact the regional Office for Civil Rights (a federal agency) for additional information:

Office for Civil Rights
U.S. Department of Education
Washington, DC 20202-1100
1-800-421-3481; email: ocr@ed.gov
www.ed.gov/about/offices/list/ocr/index.html
(or enter Office for Civil Rights on your Internet search engine)

The Educational Dilemma Facing Parents

Now that you have an overview of the laws, which, if any, federal program should you consider? Does it matter whether it's IDEA or Section 504? Both IDEA and Section 504 offer similar important advantages. IDEA, however, offers more protections if your child is more likely to get into trouble at school and it establishes higher academic standards—the child must receive "educational benefit" from the services in the IEP. Similar advantages shared by IDEA and 504 include:

Service in a Regular Classroom. Eligible students may participate in *regular classes* and still receive services under IDEA or Section 504. The adolescent does not have to be placed in a separate, "self-contained" classroom.

An Educational Plan. IEPs or Section 504 Plans must be developed which document all needed services and accommodations to the teenager's academic program. If the planning team agrees, certain protections may be written in the IEP, particularly with regard to any potential disciplinary issues.

Alternative Disciplinary Actions. Each school system has a student code of conduct that may also state consequences for specific misbehavior. However, if the student's inappropriate behavior is caused by his disability, with certain exceptions—"inflicted serious bodily injury, drugs, alcohol or weapons"—he may be exempt from standard disciplinary actions. Unique consequences may be imposed instead. IDEA or 504 eligibility may give the parents the legal reason they need to request that these students be disciplined differently (for example, switching classes or teachers, or being given in-school suspension instead of at-home suspension).

Easier School Transfers. In some school systems, students protected by IDEA or 504 may transfer to another school more easily without requiring school board approval. Some teenagers have burned so many bridges within a school that transferring to a new school for a fresh start may be appropriate.

Which Program Should You Pursue First?

There is no clear cut answer to this question. From a practical standpoint, however, you may find some advantages to seeking Section 504 eligibility first. For starters, these services are:

1. *Easier to access.* Because Section 504 eligibility criteria are very broad, it may be easier for students with ADD or ADHD to qualify for services under 504 than under IDEA.

2. *Implemented rapidly.* Accommodations may be implemented in the regular classroom more rapidly under Section 504. Whereas the evaluation and eligibility procedure under IDEA may take two to three months, Section 504 requires no lengthy evaluation.

SEEK ELIGIBILITY UNDER IDEA IF...

1. *Serious misbehavior may occur.* Dixie Jordan never recommends Section 504 and argues that parents should make an all-out effort to obtain IDEA eligibility. Seeking IDEA eligibility is especially important if the student has ADHD, serious emotional problems, or is likely to act impulsively without thinking of the consequences. Under these conditions, our teens may impulsively misbehave and be suspended or expelled. See "Addressing Problem Behaviors," below, for more information.

2. *More services may be needed.* Technically, more services can be provided to students under IDEA, but in reality the typical services that benefit our children most are also available under Section 504. However, since schools are not reimbursed for services delivered under 504 but are under IDEA, they may prefer to provide more expensive services through IDEA. This may be an important consideration if your child has SLD in addition to an attention deficit disorder and may need special-

ized instruction in reading, tutoring, or services during the summer.

If your child is declared ineligible under IDEA, then definitely pursue services under Section 504. Note: *If you think your child may need accommodations or services in college or technical school, it is essential to obtain IDEA or 504 eligibility no later than high school.* IEPs and 504 Plans are often important documentation required for college eligibility.

Making Certain the IEP or Section 504 Process Works

Regardless of the program parents pursue, neither will automatically guarantee that your child will receive the services he needs. That will come about only if the parent is educated and closely monitors the process. When the IEP or 504 plan is not working, parents must act immediately and request a meeting to determine what should be done to correct any problems. First let's talk about the IEP meetings. Section 504 meetings are often held in a similar manner, although they may not be as formal since there are not as many rules and regulations nor protections.

What You Should Know about IEP Meetings

Several facts related to IEP meetings are important to parents.

Participants. At a minimum, three or four participants should be invited to develop the IEP: you, the special education teacher, a regular education teacher (if your child is included in regular classes for any part of the day), and someone who is authorized to commit district resources. Ideally, others will be invited at the discretion of you or the school: for example, the school psychologist, a former teacher, the guidance counselor, or a vocational expert. If it is the first IEP, someone who is knowledgeable about the evaluation *must* attend. Minor changes can be made to the IEP with the parent's concurrence, without requiring a full-blown IEP meeting.

Parents have a right to invite their teenager, a friend, an advocate, or other person, such as private therapist or school personnel, to attend and participate in development of the IEP. If your child is struggling and your school is not being cooperative, I strongly encourage you to bring someone with you to supply professional expertise or simply moral support. If possible, include your teen in this meeting, unless you anticipate that the meeting will be a negative experience for him. Some high school teens actually take charge of their IEP meetings.

You should receive advance notice of attendees for the IEP meeting. If you anticipate disagreements over the content of the IEP, a representative from the district office is essential since he or she has authority to resolve disagreements between parents and the school. If an important member is missing, ask that the meeting be rescheduled. Participants should plan to stay for the whole meeting.

*B*oth Erik and Katie attend their IEP meetings and take a very active role, telling the committee what is most helpful to them and which accommodations they would like to have. Erik typically chairs his meeting and once asked that study skills class be discontinued because he no longer needed it. He credits his study skills class as being one of the most helpful service he received in high school.

Transition Plan. By age 16, your child's IEP team will develop a transition plan to discuss goals and services that will enable him to make a successful transition to post secondary education or a career. When the transition plan is developed, it would be a good idea to invite someone who is knowledgeable about vocational issues, possibly a representative from the vocational school or the state Vocational Rehabilitation Services. Revisions to IDEA clearly state that transition services must be "designed within a result-oriented process," including measurable postsecondary goals, assessments, and guidance on specific courses required for the student's hoped-for career.

Scheduling. Meetings to develop an IEP must be scheduled at times that are convenient for *both* parents and school officials. If the time scheduled is not convenient for you (for instance, it may cause you to lose a half day's pay or work), ask to reschedule. Everyone who has a contribution to make should be present and have a chance to give input.

Being Prepared. It is critically important for parents to be prepared when they attend the IEP meeting. As explained in the Parent IEP Checklist, Table 14-3, there are several important things you can do. Ideally, you will actually develop a draft IEP, or at a minimum, summarize your child's learning challenges, identify your main concerns (for example, passing algebra), and list possible supports and accommodations that might be helpful. If this task seems overwhelming, consider asking an outside professional to help you complete the checklist in Table 14-3.

"My advice to parents going to a school meeting is to always be armed with information. I put together a three-ring binder with everything in it—medical diagnosis, psychological reports, medications, etc. When the assistant principal told me my son didn't qualify for special education under learning disabilities, I was ready. Normally I am an easy-going person, but I told her to stop right there—my son did meet criteria for Other Health Impaired. I told her that unless she was ready to dispute the neurologist's diagnosis of Tourette syndrome, she had no other choice but to give my son services. She was shocked, and stammered that she didn't know about OHI."

Developing the IEP or 504 Plan. A completed IEP or 504 plan should *not* be presented for your approval before there has been a full discussion of your child's needs and the services to be provided. You may find that in practice, a *draft IEP or 504* has been developed to serve as a springboard for discussion at the meeting. You are encouraged to begin developing your own version of an IEP or 504 plan for your child before the meeting. Using information in this book and *Teaching Teens*, plus your child's old reports cards, previous evaluations, and standardized tests, you can identify potential learning problems and needed accommodations. Do not hesitate to ask that the IEP be changed to better meet your teenager's needs. See the next section for more information.

Monitor Development of the IEP or 504 Plan. You must make certain the system is working in your teen's best interests. All accommodations that your child is to receive—even those he will receive in the regular classroom—must be included in the IEP, in writing. Hopefully, the 504 Plan will be put in writing.

When you get your copy of the IEP or 504 plan, check to see that all services are written down. Ask questions and don't be afraid to request services you think your teenager needs. See the parent checklist in Table 14-3 for actions that may help ensure development of an effective educational plan.

Although federal Section 504 legislation does not include the following three requirements, check your local school system's Section 504 Implementation Guidelines if you have questions.

Signing Permission Forms for the IEP. After the IEP is finalized, you will be asked to sign it.

Technically, parents are *not* required by federal law to sign the IEP. But here are situations in which your signature is needed.

1. If it is your child's first IEP, the school *must* obtain your written permission before they can *place* your teenager in special education.
   a. If, however, the plan is an updated version of a previous plan, the school *can* implement the IEP without your written permission.
2. In this case, if you disagree with the IEP that has been developed, you should state this in writing.
3. Or sign the IEP but with a written note that you do not agree with it.

Unless you object in writing, the school may, after 10 days, implement the IEP without your permission. Therefore, it is critical that you state any objections to the IEP *in writing* and request a meeting to resolve points of disagreement.

Implementing the IEP. Under federal law, the IEP must be implemented immediately.

Annual Updating of the IEP. Each student who is receiving services under IDEA must have a valid IEP in effect at the beginning of each school year. If, however, you or school personnel feel that your teenager's educational needs have changed or that he is not progressing satisfactorily, you may request a meeting to review and revise the IEP at any time. Under IDEA, students *must* be provided special education services until:

1. the student has met the goals and objectives stated in the IEP and parents and school agree the services are no longer needed,
2. the student graduates, or
3. the student turns 22.

Tips for Talking with IEP or Section 504 Team Members. If the teen is still struggling, most parents come to the IEP or 504 meeting feeling frustrated, irritated, and perhaps frightened. After all, these educators are supposed to be the experts and if they don't know what to do, how can you possibly figure out the answers?

Even if you are experiencing these upsetting emotions, try to avoid blaming, criticizing, or inadvertently implying the school isn't doing its job—even though that may be true. If you put educators on the defensive, they may be less likely to help you. It's been my experience that most teachers want to help, but don't always know what to do. Unfortunately, if that occurs, that means that you, the parent, often must educate school officials. Of course, you may reach a point where you have to be forceful and direct, but try a positive approach first. Here are a couple of suggestions:

Try using "I" language to express how you are feeling (worried, helpless, frustrated), rather than blaming the school ("you haven't..."). You may also *make a statement describing the problem* or give a suggestion for solving it. You may find it helpful to reread the section in Chapter 8 on "maintaining good communication" through use of "I" messages. These same strategies are effective with teachers.

> **Say:** "We need to figure out why my son is on the verge of failing four classes. Is it because he is making low test grades or low homework grades?"
> Or if you don't know what to do, just say "Our present strategy isn't working. What should we try now?"

> **Avoid saying:** "You haven't been following the IEP or 504 plan." Or, "You aren't doing anything to help my child."

In reality, we parents are very much like our children; we can't learn everything we need to know all at once—the educational law, plus effective communication skills. You may be struggling simply to master basic facts about the law. So deal with that first and then work on your communication skills. This is another good reason to take a professional with you to the IEP or 504 meeting. Since he is not emotionally involved, he may be able to keep a cool head and stay focused on what needs to be done.

Developing and Implementing Effective IEPs and 504 Plans

While I was rewriting this chapter, I received an email from a mother whose 13-year-old son was failing several classes even though he has an IEP. Unfortunately, this is not an uncommon occurrence. Let's call the student Thomas. His IEP is included in Appendix 5, along with specific suggestions for improving it and general comments for developing an effective IEP. To help parents create an effective IEP, three helpful tools are offered.

1. Table 14-1 contains a list of common ADHD behaviors that may be appropriate to include in your educational plan.
2. A checklist of actions parents should take before, during, and after an IEP meeting is also available in Table 14-3.
3. The federally mandated components of an IEP that are of importance to parents are discussed in more detail in the sample IEP in Appendix 5. Although the discussion in this section focuses on IEP development, the principles are the same for Section 504 Plans.

The school identified Thomas's primary problem as not completing or turning in homework, which is one of the most common problems among students with attention deficits. His IEP was actually a pretty good one, but the implementation plan had a few shortcomings:

- All teachers did not follow the IEP.
- Interventions to improve homework completion were *not* made at the "point of performance"—the moment Thomas had to decide which books to take home (see discussion in Chapter 8).
- Even though he was eligible, no arrangements were made for extended time on tests.
- Changes were made to the IEP without parental input (for example, the extra set of books was no longer provided for home use).

"My Son Has an IEP But He's Still Failing..."

A complaint I hear from parents from time to time is that even though their child has an IEP or Section 504 Plan, he is still failing. Again, parents are encouraged to look at the common behaviors in Table 14-1 and the sample IEP in Appendix 5. You should also be aware that an IEP or 504 Plan may be ineffective for a variety of reasons, for example:

1. All learning problems have not yet been identified;
2. Deficits in executive skills have not been addressed;
3. Effective accommodations or modifications have not been put in place;.
4. Appropriate accommodations are not yet being provided; and perhaps most importantly,
5. Teachers are not following the requirements of the IEP or 504 Plan.

Table 14-1 Common Characteristics of ADHD to Address in the IEP or 504 Plan

Several characteristics and skill deficits related to attention deficits may affect learning. Consider including specific strategies to address these characteristics in an educational plan.

1. **Forgetfulness** [*This is not simply a matter of choice or laziness; it is one of the diagnostic criteria for attention deficits.*]

   Consequently: Students cannot always remember to write down and turn in their assignments.

   Strategy: Prompts at the "point of performance" from the teacher or another student will probably be necessary. For example:
   - A row captain" will check each student's notebook to ensure that all assignments are written down.
   - Another student will write down and give the list of assignments to the student.
   - The teacher will email assignments home or send home a written list of all assignments.
   - Parents must monitor homework completion.

2. **Impulsivity** [*Impulsivity is also a diagnostic characteristic of ADHD.*]

   Consequently: Students may use poor judgment and act impulsively, such as talking back to a teacher or skipping school.

   Strategy:
   - Have the student write a letter of apology.
   - Provide training in anger management; teach conflict resolution skills.
   - Offer an acceptable alternative to blowing up. Allow the student to visit the guidance counselor when he feels he is about to lose control.
   - Consult with the teen's physician about this problem behavior.

3. **Poor organizational skills** [*This is a key executive skill.*]

   Consequently: Students may not be sufficiently organized, nor remember, to gather all the correct assignments, books, and materials to complete homework.

   Strategy: Provide interventions at the "point of performance."
   - A teacher aide or another student may have to meet the student at his locker after school to help him gather the correct books and assignments.
   - Attend a study skills class.

4. **Slow processing speed and/or slow retrieval of information.** [*This problem is more common among students with ADD inattentive.*]

   Consequently: Students can't complete school work or tests as quickly as their peers and may avoid answering questions in class.

   Strategy:
   - Shorten assignments.
   - Give extended time.
   - Give some lead time before answering questions in class.

5. **Limited working memory capacity** [*This is another key executive skill.*]

   Consequently: Students may have difficulty:
   - Remembering what is read
   - Comprehending what they read (weak reading comprehension)
   - Writing essays and reports
   - Working complex math or algebra problems

   Strategy: Reduce demands on working memory.
   - Use graphic organizers, calculators, lists of formulas, or word lists.
   - Teach memory strategies.

(Table 14-1 continued on next page.)

(Table 14-1 continued)

6. Written expression deficits [*Requires strong executive skills including working memory and reconstitution (problem solving)*]

Consequently: Students may have wonderful ideas that they are unable to capture, organize, and write down on paper.

Strategy:

- Teach writing skills and give memory prompts.
- Allow the student to dictate his thoughts. Parents may act as a recorder or scribe.
- Provide graphic organizers for essay writing as in Teaching Teens, Appendix A-3.

7. Homework not submitted. [*Homework assignments may be too long because teachers underestimate how long it will take students with learning problems to complete work.*]

Consequently: Students may avoid doing homework or fail to turn it in.

Strategy:

- Reduce the amount of written work so that all homework can be completed in no more than two hours per night.
- Shorten assignments.

8. Up to a 30 percent developmental delay and related deficits in executive skills. [*Students with either ADD or ADHD may seem less mature because of this developmental delay.*]

Consequently: Teenagers may be delayed up to 4 to 6 years in their self-control and many of their executive skills (for example, the ability to be organized, to get started on work, remember things, control emotions, use self-talk to direct behavior, and complete the complex problem-solving required to write essays and compute math or algebra problems).

Strategy: Provide "developmentally appropriate supervision," which means more supervision, more often, than for other students.

9. Ineffective medication levels. [*MTA researchers found that many students with ADHD were on lower than optimal doses of medicine.*]

Consequently: Students may not have reached peak medication levels that allow them to achieve maximum academic performance. Or perhaps medication has worn off later in the school day or during the homework hours.

Strategy: Ask teachers to complete the medication rating scale in Appendix 1. If the results show that your teen is still having difficulty paying attention, then talk with your doctor about medication.

10. Sleep disturbance and impaired sense of time. [*Over half of all students with attention deficits have sleep problems and many also lack the ability to accurately judge the passage of time.*]

Consequently: These students may have trouble waking up and getting to school and class on time. Plus, they often have trouble estimating how long projects will take.

Strategy:

- Develop a plan to address sleep problems; ask your doctor for help.
- Teach time management and how to schedule backward.
- Provide a watch with an alarm.

List behaviors of concern in "Present Levels of Performance." Of course, any of the problems listed in this table or elsewhere in this book must be identified in the Present Level of Performance section of the IEP or 504 Plan. Only issues identified in the "Present Levels" section must be addressed with accommodations. After problems are identified, then the strategies from this book or *Teaching Teens* can be included in the third section of the IEP, "special education, related services, and supplementary aids and services." Identifying potentially problematic ADD or ADHD behaviors in the IEP is one way of documenting evidence that the disability is linked to inappropriate behavior.

Regardless of the reasons for the ineffective IEP or 504 Plan, the bottom line is this—if your teen has an educational plan and is still struggling or perhaps even failing, something is terribly wrong! ***Changes must be made to the IEP or 504 Plan to enable the student to be successful in school!*** If your teen continues to be unsuccessful in school, you have the right to request a meeting at *any* time to revise the IEP. The Student Support Team (SST) and parents must reconvene and make appropriate changes. This may also be a good time to ask if a functional behavior assessment (FBA) could be conducted to aid in development of a behavioral plan. These plans may be referred to as a Behavior Intervention Plan (BIP) or Behavior Management Plan (BMP). See the subsequent discussion on FBA and BIP.

Here's what Dixie Jordan has to say about students who have an IEP, yet are failing in school:

"We should never have a child with an IEP who is failing. That is a clear signal that something is terribly wrong with the IEP. Perhaps, expectations were too high, interventions were not intensive enough, or the duration of the intervention was not long enough. School failure is a signal for scheduling an IEP meeting immediately and revising the goals or adding needed services."

Addressing Problem Behaviors

Ordinarily behavior problems are addressed by the regular school discipline policies. For students with attention deficits, sometimes the imposed consequences are overly harsh when you take into consideration that their misbehavior is often impulsive, not malicious and is linked to their disability. By planning ahead and including a statement in the IEP or Section 504 Plan, parents may be able to ensure that *reasonable* disciplinary actions are utilized instead.

State Alternative Disciplinary Procedures. According to Dixie Jordan, it is important to state alternative disciplinary procedures in the IEP or 504 Plan in the section regarding accommodations. For example, the statement might read something like this:

"When (name) exhibits behavior problems that are a manifestation of his ADHD such as (impulsivity, forgetfulness, impaired sense of time, or other ADHD related behaviors), the IEP team or its designee is authorized to institute an alternative disciplinary consequence."

To prevent behaviors that may result in suspensions, Jordan also advocates that IEP or Section 504 goals and related intervention strategies be written to specifically instruct the student in acquiring the necessary behavior or skills. The purpose of these strategies is not to take advantage of or browbeat the school system—but to ensure the teen is treated fairly through:

1. the use of direct instruction to correct the problem behaviors, or
2. the use of reasonable consequences.

If the school is reluctant to do this, then remind them that IDEA and Case Law on Section 504 mandate that misbehavior linked to the disability be taken into consideration during disciplinary actions. Surely they won't object to a simple restatement of the law. Jordan says that punishing a student with ADD or ADHD for a lack of social behavior skills is *"akin to punishing a child with a visual impairment for not being able to read."*

Prevent Reoccurrence of Misbehavior. School personnel should also implement a strategy to prevent misbehavior from occurring again in the future. For example, if a teenager talks back to a teacher:

- The student may be required to apologize to the teacher or attend an anger management class.
- School personnel may establish a crisis plan for the student to go to the counselor if he is losing control.
- Teachers may be trained in strategies to "defuse" angry situations so students are less likely to talk back.
- Perhaps parents will talk with the doctor about adjusting medication so impulsive talking back to teachers is reduced.

An FBA and BIP may also be developed to identify and address problem behaviors. Some schools do a better job of this than others.

A 12-year-old middle school student (ADHD) with a Section 504 Plan had major disciplinary problems at school. Just two months into the school year, he had received six disciplinary notices for several "ADHD behaviors" like disrupting class, by talking; being disrespectful by mumbling under his breath, rolling his eyes, and throwing a book; being tardy, acting silly, and marking in his pencil tray. He had also received two after-school detentions and two suspensions from school. The boy was not on medication. The school did not convene an SST meeting to discuss these issues until after the father requested it. Then they developed a plan that simply stated actions the student must take—be on time to class, complete and submit work on time, and control his emotions—without any statement of supportive accommodations he should receive. When the father requested an FBA, he was advised by the uninformed school psychologist that his son was not eligible for that service.

Examples of Alternative Disciplinary Strategies. If more serious misbehavior occurs, modifications in traditional consequences might be requested. In all these cases, the IEP Team or their designee, such as a guidance counselor or vice principal, could determine reasonable consequences for the offenses. These alternative strategies might be suggested to the IEP Team or principal to prevent future fighting.

- Provide in-school suspension instead of "out-of school" suspension.
- Allow the student to make-up any work without a grade penalty while he is suspended (critically important if the student is on the verge of failing a class).
- Teach anger management or conflict resolution strategies.

Here is an example of alternative disciplinary action that was instituted because of parental advocacy. Hopefully, this plan has also taught the teen a valuable lesson about the seriousness of his actions.

"A student with ADHD and anxiety gave one of his antidepressants to a friend who probably had undiagnosed ADHD, was extremely anxious, and was really struggling in school. Meanwhile, another student gave him one of his Adderall to help him concentrate. The medication combination caused the student to pass out in class. When questioned, the story about the exchange of medications came to light. Under regular school discipline policies, all three children could have been expelled for exchanging drugs at school. Of course, this behavior is terribly inappropriate and must be addressed, but expulsion and suspension could be considered discriminatory. In-school suspension would have been a reasonable alternative.

"Fortunately, one of the parents was an expert on the law. When the father met with school officials, a young school psychologist said, "You agree, don't you, that this behavior was not linked to ADHD (impulsivity) because they planned the day before to bring medicine?" If the parents agreed, then the students would have been punished according to regular school discipline policy. The father disagreed explaining that even though the action was planned ahead by one day, it was still undertaken impulsively without any thought of

the full implications of their actions. The two boys just wanted to help their friend.

The principal has the authority to suspend any student up to ten days for any reason, but he elected not to do that. These parents were very fortunate. The consequences could have been devastating to these students. Typically an IEP meeting would then be scheduled to decide a proper consequence. Ultimately, this student's consequences included attending Saturday school, attending a drug education class, and talking with a police resource office."

Using Positive Behavior Supports

Recent changes in IDEA require more frequent use of positive behavior supports to prevent behavior problems. The reason for this change is simple; punishment alone is ineffective. The Office of Special Education has established a technical assistance center, known as PBIS or Positive Behavior Interventions and Supports, to disseminate information on effective strategies for changing behavior. Instead of a punishment- or coercion-based model of changing behavior, PBIS encourages defining, teaching, and supporting appropriate student behavior. This system is based upon the belief that there is a reason for most misbehavior and adults should work with the student in compassionate ways to correct the behavior. PBIS may be implemented for individual students or school wide.

Develop a Positive Behavior Plan. When students have broken the rules, the bottom line goal is to teach them the correct behavior, not just punish them for lack of skills. Legally, as stated earlier, the school cannot just punish IDEA eligible students but must develop a strategy to prevent future problems. One way to handle that is to develop a positive plan that might be called a behavior intervention plan (BIP) or a behavior management plan (BMP). Typically the BIP is based upon information obtained from a functional behavior assessment or FBA. These tools are discussed in more detail in this section.

1. The BIP should include strategies for *teaching desired behaviors;* for example, constructive ways to handle anger or strategies for remembering homework assignments.
2. A positive BIP should help prevent potential problems in the future.
3. Furthermore, a positive BIP is mandatory for any IDEA eligible student who is removed from class because of behavior problems.

School-wide PBIS programs have shown impressive changes in student behavior: higher student grades, higher test scores, increased school attendance, decreased referrals to special education for evaluation, decreased disciplinary referrals, and decreased suspensions and expulsions. This compelling research has convinced the state of Illinois to implement PBIS statewide. Visit www.pbis.org for more detailed information on PBIS, school-wide programs, functional behavior assessments, and behavior intervention plans. You might share this information with your school officials. Perhaps they will consider implementing a school-wide PBIS program.

Using FBA to Develop a BIP

When a student has had several disruptive incidents at school, especially if they place the student at risk of a school suspension, the IEP Team should meet to discuss strategies to prevent reoccurrence. As you may recall, the functional behavior assessment (FBA) provides a mechanism for gathering needed data about who, why, when, and where of the inappropriate behavior, and the BIP lays out the implementation strategy. A formal FBA is typically done by a school psychologist, but in reality teachers and parents do this informally every day as they assess a student's progress. Both teachers and parents can improve the quality of their FBA by following the guidelines below and in *Teaching Teens*, Summary 63 and Appendix B5.

An FBA might help explain why the student is not completing assignments. It may also help identify learning problems underlying the student's failure to complete his work. In addition, an FBA can be extremely helpful by identifying the event that triggers problem behaviors and in developing an effective behavior intervention plan. If teachers don't suggest using these strategies, then parents should ask school officials to consider using them. A good FBA for students with attention deficits should address several key issues:

- *Behavior:* What is the behavior of concern?
- *Context:* Where and when did the problem occur? Who was involved?
- *Antecedent or "trigger":* What happened just prior to the problem that may have triggered it?
- *Contributing factors:* What is going on in the student's world that may affect his behavior? (For example, does the behavior occur when the student forgets to take his medicine or the medication has worn off?)

- *Function of Behavior:* What seems to be the purpose or reason for the behavior? Inappropriate behavior usually serves one of two functions for students:
    1. to obtain something, or
    2. to escape something. The psychologist or teacher may interview the teacher who observed the misbehavior and perhaps the student also to glean information. The student may also be observed. The team may then discuss the results of the FBA and attempt to determine the reasons for the misbehavior and potential effective intervention strategies.

    Note: With students who have ADD or ADHD, *the neurological problems linked to ADHD are often responsible for the "function and why" of behavior!* It's not always a matter of thoughtful choice. If a teen with an attention deficit does something inappropriate, it may be as simple as he thought it, so he impulsively did it. There may be no conscious motive to "get something or to escape something."

- *Teacher response and student reaction:* What did the teacher do? What did the student do after the teacher responded? (The teacher's response often serves as a consequence that may either escalate or deescalate the situation.)
- *Continuation of behavior:* Why is the behavior continuing to be a problem? What is maintaining it?
- *Rewards:* What does the student view as a reward or positive reinforcements?
- *Previous interventions:* What interventions were tried previously? What worked best? Both parents and teachers should be asked these questions.

Georgia Sugai, PH.D., PBIS Director, tells one of my favorite stories related to the value of FBAs. After one student, let's call him Perry, had misbehaved on several occasions, one of the only consistent findings was that it occurred only on those mornings when it rained. The teachers were at a loss to determine the relevance of the rain. When they checked further, they found that Perry rode with his father on rainy days. The father criticized and nagged him for the duration of the morning ride. So by the time the boy arrived at school, he was about to explode. The BIP included meeting Perry at the door on rainy days and taking him aside to "soothe ruffled feathers," giving him a snack, and calming him down. This intervention solved the problem. One of the lessons learned from this child is *that typically there is a reason for the misbehavior but it may not be obvious at first.*

Behavioral Intervention Plan (BIP)

Once the IEP team or teacher has analyzed the information gathered from the FBA, they must develop a theory of why the misbehavior occurred. Next they will use this theory and information to develop an effective BIP. As explained in Perry's example, once the teachers realized that the car ride with his father was the trigger for the misbehavior, they developed an effective intervention plan. Typically the plan will be discussed at a team meeting, recorded in writing, and all teachers who are involved with this child will be made aware of the intervention strategies and receive copies of the plan. (A sample FBA and BIP, plus blank forms, are provided in *Teaching Teens*.) The information collected through this process will provide invaluable assistance as the IEP is written.

Unfortunately, behavioral strategies aren't always effective with teens with ADHD. Typically, interventions may work for a couple of weeks and then are no longer effective. Remember, one key is to intervene at the *point of performance*—in other words, the time and place when the teen needs to use a specific skill. See Chapter 8 for details.

Participation in Extracurricular Activities

Taking part in extracurricular and non-academic activities, such as sports, band, debate team, cheerleading, or clubs, is very important to most adolescents. Unfortunately, some teenagers with attention deficits are denied the opportunity to participate in activities because of poor grades. "No pass, no play" standards typically *do* apply to these students. To be eligible to participate in school activities, the student must meet the same grading criteria as other students—for example, earn a required number of credits, maintain a C average, and not fail more than one class. However, if your teen is in danger of losing eligibility for sports or other activities, there is one hope—*intervene early*—

prevent school failure by seeking IDEA or Section 504 eligibility, identifying learning problems, and implementing accommodations.

Now that earlier diagnosis and treatment are occurring, hopefully examples like the following one will be avoided. Educators are more aware of ADD, ADHD, and related learning problems, and are more likely to provide supports.

"A high school junior with ADHD did not participate in the state championship wrestling tournament. He failed chemistry because he forgot to turn in a chemistry project that was due after Christmas. Subsequently, he started taking Concerta his senior year and passed all his classes. He won the state tournament in his weight class his senior year. No special accommodations had been made in the regular classroom."

Getting help after the fact... One possible gray area may exist for getting assistance after your teen is on the verge of failing or has failed a class—try to find a new issue that was not considered in earlier discussions with the school. For example, if the disability was not diagnosed until recently, you might argue that:

1. you have only recently recognized (if true) that your teenager has an attention deficit,
2. medication levels have been inadequate (if true) and are being adjusted, or
3. deficits in executive function or learning disabilities have just been identified.

Seek your physician's or counselor's help, since the school may be more likely to listen to a "professional" opinion. They can lay out the rationale for reconsideration of your child's grade and ask if your child could submit late make-up assignments or retake the final exam on medication. If your teen completes the required schoolwork, his grade could be revised, making him eligible to continue participating in the sport. Obviously, the failure to identify ADHD or learning problems is not an issue of bad faith on either side, because you both have overlooked the diagnosis of the attention deficit.

Here are a couple of rationales for making this request:

1. Section 504 states that a student is eligible for services if he "*has a record of such an impairment*" or "*is regarded as having such impairment.*" In these situations, clearly school officials were aware there were problems—written documentation of failing grades and repeated failure to submit

homework were recorded in progress reports and cumulative student records.

2. The second argument is that the existing IEP or Section 504 Plan was not working if the child still failed. The implication is that the school has also failed to do its job.

The decision on a request of this type is a judgment call and will be based upon the goodwill of school officials. It's one option that may be worth trying, but there are no guarantees that it will work. Once you get the student back on track, hopefully ongoing support from the IEP or 504 Plan will be sufficient to prevent future failure and the threat of losing eligibility.

IEP and Section 504 Strategies to Prevent Suspensions

For students in danger of suspension, the IEP or 504 Team must develop an adequate "individualized behavior management plan" to prevent reoccurrence of the problem behaviors resulting in suspension from school. For example, having a substitute teacher or guest speaker often triggered problems for one student with ADHD. School officials were aware of this problem, but no intervention strategies were developed to reduce the likelihood of it happening again.

Positive strategies that could be incorporated into the IEP or 504 plan include:

1. Substitute teachers will be notified of potential problems and told how to best work with this student.
2. A classroom aide or other school official may provide extra supervision in the classes the teen has with a substitute.
3. The teen will be allowed to return to a former teacher's classroom for the periods a substitute is present.
4. The teen will be taught the procedures to follow when:
   a. substitute is present or
   b. the teen feels he may blow up—for example, going to the guidance counselor's office until the period is over.

The best strategy is to be proactive. As explained earlier, request that a disciplinary plan or statement be added to the IEP or 504 Plan. If your teen is having problems with behavior or deficits in executive skills, it is critical to include a statement in the accommodations section stating the process to be followed when the student has violated the regular school policies. Examples of common ADD/ADHD behaviors to consider addressing in the plan were listed in Table 14-1. In addition, intervene early with appropriate accommodations to greatly reduce the likelihood of school failure and disciplinary problems.

Suspensions and Expulsions

Teenagers with attention deficits who are impulsive, argumentative, easily frustrated, and struggling academically are likely to have conflicts with school officials. The potential for conflict grows when school administrators don't understand attention deficit disorders and incorrectly perceive the teenager's noncompliance, anger, and defiance as willful, malicious misbehavior. As discussed earlier, 46 percent of the students with more complex cases of ADHD had been *suspended* from school, according to a study by Dr. Russell Barkley. Eleven percent had been *expelled* from school. The rate of suspensions and expulsions in the general population is much lower—for example, 23 and 5-6 percent respectively. However, don't forget that the percentage of suspensions and expulsions in the general ADHD population is about half what it is in clinical studies.

Some teenagers with attention deficits have been suspended or expelled inappropriately for long periods of time for non-dangerous misbehavior that is linked directly to their disability. Parents should keep in mind that *depriving a student of an education because of misbehavior related to his disability*, particularly if no attempt has been made to teach the student the proper behavior, *is out of compliance with IDEA and is discriminatory under civil rights law (Section 504)*. Some of the examples given below fall in this category, but occurred prior to the more recent revisions to IDEA which require positive behavior supports.

As clarified by a Supreme Court ruling, children who are covered by IDEA *cannot be suspended for more than ten days for an infraction related to their disability* (with a couple of exceptions involving drugs, weapons, or danger to self or others). School systems must also abide by a variety of other safeguards in determining how to discipline a student with special needs. Plus, if parents disagree with the decision to expel, they may request a due process hearing.

"A middle school student was expelled the remainder of the school year for a collection of less serious, defiant behaviors. He refused to take a bandanna off his head as he was waiting for a bus after school."

"A high school student was expelled for the remainder of the school year for a collection of noncompliant behaviors. The last straw occurred when he got off the bus, left school property, and crossed the street to a convenience store. He was offered the option of attending an alternative night school. He was having tremendous academic problems but no accommodations had been made to the regular classroom."

Before a student is readmitted after a suspension or expulsion, a meeting should be held to address the behavior that resulted in the suspension. Objectives in the IEP or 504 plan should be rewritten to prevent misbehavior that may cause another suspension. Conducting an FBA and then developing a BIP should prove helpful.

Manifestation Determination Review

Before a school can suspend, expel, or place a child in an alternative setting for more than 10 days, a Manifestation Determination Review *must* be conducted for students who are served under IDEA to determine whether the misbehavior is attributable to the student's disability. If the behavior is related to the student's disability, then the IEP Team must take this information into consideration as they determine appropriate services, placement, and disciplinary consequences. This policy gives schools flexibility to discipline this student differently than stated school policy. Hopefully, you have already anticipated this possibility by having a statement included in the IEP or 504 about disciplinary actions. Behavior *not* linked to a disability can be dealt with through the standard school district policy. The district must, however, continue to educate the student. Refer to IDEA revisions, below.

"One student who was eligible for services under Section 504 had been suspended and was in danger of being expelled because he forgot and accidentally brought a can of smokeless tobacco to school. After finding the tobacco, school officials searched his locker and car and found a pocket knife. This young man had never been in trouble before. Since he was suspended for more than 10 days, a manifestation determination review should have been conducted. However, the school did not mention this procedure to the parents and may not have been aware that it was required."

Documenting the Disability/Behavior Link. Unfortunately, some schools will say that obvious "ADD/

ADHD behaviors," including impulsively speaking or acting before the student thinks of the consequences, are not related to the disability. Hopefully, by listing impulsivity as an issue under "present level of performance" in the IEP or 504 plan, it may be easier to show that the misbehavior was linked to a student's disability. After all, impulsivity—a primary diagnostic characteristic of attention deficits—is often the underlying cause of misbehavior. Even when taking medication, or if it was forgotten or has worn off, our children may still act impulsively. Federal intent regarding this topic seems pretty clear based upon these comments in federal law. Misbehaviors and disabilities are linked if:

1. The child's disability impairs "the ability of the child to understand the impact and consequences of the behavior subject to disciplinary action"; and
2. the child's disability impairs "the child's ability to control the behavior subject to disciplinary action."

Appealing a Decision. If the school rules that the behavior is not related to the disability, then parents can appeal it by asking for mediation or a due process hearing.

One mother reported that her son was given a drink that "tasted funny" while at school. He took a sip and got rid of it by passing it on to someone else. Later he learned it had alcohol in it. The school wanted to suspend him for having alcohol on the premises. At the Manifestation Determination Review, they ruled that this behavior was unrelated to his disability. The mother is appealing.

Unfortunately, the mood of the courts and OCR varies over time and by region of the country. For example, depending upon the prevailing political winds, OCR may not appear as sympathetic to parental concerns and may not be very strict in their interpretation of their own policies. So using your powers of persuasion rather than relying on legal clout becomes critically important.

"Stay Put" Provisions. Pursuant to IDEA, a student must "stay put" in his current placement pending an official decision regarding disciplinary action to be taken by the school. The student cannot be removed arbitrarily except in certain situations related to dangerousness, drugs or weapons, or with the parents' consent.

Interim Alternative Educational Settings. If a student poses an immediate and substantial risk of injury or harm to self or others, the school can make a unilateral decision to immediately place the student in an Interim Alternative Educational Setting (IAES) for up to 45 days without going through a Manifestation Determination Review. IAES placements are discussed in greater detail in *Teaching Teens*, Summary 40, but can include special education schools for students with behavior problems.

Appropriate "Discipline." Some school systems struggle to provide appropriate "discipline" for adolescents with attention deficits. Obviously, these teenagers should not be allowed to misbehave any more than other students should. On the other hand, neither should they be made to feel that they are criminals. *Reasonable consequences, which are instructive, not just punitive, should be used.* For example, don't just suspend or send the teenager to detention because he misbehaved when a substitute was present. As discussed earlier, teach him how to handle this problem in the future or give him a safety release valve—going to the guidance counselor's office. Because many teenagers with ADD or ADHD are struggling academically, suspending them greatly increases the risk of school failure and dropping out of school.

Dealing with the issue of misbehavior of students with attention deficits is especially difficult now because of the horrific school violence at Columbine and other schools. School officials are justifiably afraid and may be more likely to overreact to misbehavior from our students. The fine line the school must walk is to hold your child accountable for his behavior but not discriminate against him because of his ADD or ADHD. Your job as an advocate is made harder when you try to explain that your teenager's ADD or ADHD is the major cause of his misbehavior. Clearly, if the aggression is potentially life threatening, school officials must act. Unfortunately, it is sometimes difficult to know if a crisis situation is life threatening when you are in the middle of it. See "Relevant Policy and Court Rulings" below.

What If You're at Your Wit's End?

Most families are able to work successfully with the public schools. If, however, your teenager is eligible for services under IDEA or 504, yet his school experiences are extremely negative for a whole grading period or longer, and you feel the school is unable or unwilling to meet his needs, it is time to take action. Here is a summary of the options discussed in this chapter. You may want to take a few minutes and re-read the earlier section on "My teen has an IEP but is still failing...."

1. Request a school meeting to discuss problems and *develop* or *revise the IEP* or the *504 Plan*.

2. Complete the *medication rating scales* in Appendix 1 and *talk to your doctor* again to be certain that medication levels are correct.

3. If the school (IEP/504 Team) still does not meet your teenager's needs as required by IDEA or Section 504, talk with the principal. If that doesn't resolve the issue satisfactorily, *contact the director of special education, the local 504 coordinator, the superintendent, or school board member for advice.* At this point, it is very important to make concerns and requests in writing.

4. Consider *mediation* to resolve your differences with the school system.

5. As a last resort, if you and the school cannot agree on your child's needs, or if you believe that the proposed program will not meet his needs, consider requesting a *due process hearing* under IDEA or Section 504.

6. If you decide to take legal action, contact your superintendent of schools, state director of special education, or regional Office for Civil Rights to find out how to file a formal complaint.

7. If you want your child to remain in the public school but want to avoid a confrontation with school officials, consider *other options*: hiring a tutor, hiring an educational consultant or psychologist to go to school and work with the teacher and/or your child in the classroom, or requesting a change in teachers.

8. If the school agrees that they cannot meet your child's needs, *seek placement* in an alternative public school or a private school.

However, an outside placement will be very expensive and most schools are unlikely to be willing to cover these expenses.

Relevant Policy and Court Rulings

In addition to the three key federal laws, several policies and court rulings have had a significant bearing on the provision of educational services to students with learning handicaps.

The 1991 U.S. DOE /OCR Memo

Before attention deficits were listed as examples of qualifying conditions under Other Health Impairment in IDEA regulations, a joint memo of the U.S. Department of Education and the Office of Civil Rights clarified the legal rights of students with ADD and ADHD to special education. This joint memo remains one of the *most important documents* ever issued regarding the education of children and adolescents with attention deficit disorder. This landmark policy stated that youngsters with attention deficits who ex-

Key IDEA Revisions to Disciplinary Guidelines

Greater discretion given to schools.

Schools may consider "any unique circumstance on a case-by-case basis" when deciding whether to remove a child who has violated school rules from his current placement. [This change could be good or bad. Principals may deal more harshly with our children or they may take into consideration "ADHD behaviors" when deciding upon disciplinary measures.]

Positive behavioral interventions required for students with behavior problems.

When a child's behavior impedes the child's learning or that of others, the IEP team must consider the use of positive behavioral interventions, supports, and other strategies to address the behavior.

Causing bodily injury to others warrants removal from school.

"Inflicted serious bodily injury upon another person" was added to "weapons and drugs" as reasons for removal from school.

Manifestation Review required to determine when misbehavior is linked to disability.

Any child may be suspended with cause for up to 10 days. However, for longer than that, a *manifestation determination hearing* must be held to determine if inappropriate behavior by a child is linked to his disability. All relevant information in the student's file including the IEP, teacher observations, and input from parents will be used to determine if the misconduct was:

  a. caused by, or had a direct and substantial relationship to, the child's disability; or
  b. the direct result of the school's failure to implement the IEP.

If behavior and disability linked, FBA and BIP required.

If the school, parents, and members of the IEP team decide the conduct was a manifestation of the child's disability, the team will "conduct a functional behavioral assessment and implement a behavior intervention plan." If a BIP is already in place, it should be reviewed and modified as needed to address the behavior. The child must be returned to his original placement, unless he is dangerous or unless the parent agrees to an alternative placement.

Children facing disciplinary action, but not currently served by IDEA possibly eligible in certain circumstances.

The school is "deemed to have knowledge" that a child has a disability if, before this misbehavior,

  a. the parent expressed concern in writing to anyone at the school that his child needed special education services,
  b. the parent requested an evaluation, or
  c. the teacher or other school personnel expressed specific concerns about behaviors directly to the director of special education or other supervisors; unless the parent has refused an evaluation.

Documentation of previous problem behaviors in the child's cumulative folder at school may also be relevant in this situation.

REVISIONS RELATED TO MEDICATION
No forced medicating of children.

Schools cannot force parents to give their children medication as a condition of attending school. However, the law also states that teachers are *not* prohibited from sharing observations and information about students with parents.

perience *"limited alertness, which adversely affects their educational performance"* should be eligible for extra supports and accommodations under the IDEA category of *"other health impairment."* Key elements of this memo were incorporated into the 1997/1999 IDEA regulations. The memo further states that if students are not eligible for services under IDEA, they may be eligible under Section 504. Thus, depending on the severity of their condition, children with ADD or ADHD *may* fit within that definition.

The memo goes on to list specific classroom *accommodations* that might be appropriate. A summary of these recommendations plus other possible classroom accommodations are included in Table 14-2.

The memo also clarifies parents' rights to request an evaluation of their child: "Under Section 504, if parents believe that their child is handicapped by their attention deficit the local education authority (LEA) must evaluate the child to determine whether he or she is handicapped as defined by Section 504." Parents may also request an evaluation under IDEA. A school system may, on rare occasions, however, refuse to do an evaluation if they are positive that the ADD or ADHD is not affecting a child's school performance—for example, she is making straight A's and is working above grade level without significant supports from parents. Most likely, they will "evaluate" the student regardless. Of course, the school is not mandated to "test" a child. Ultimately, the school determines what constitutes the evaluation. As a result of this memo, many local school systems have been more responsive to teenagers with attention deficits. Other schools have circumvented this requirement by doing a very limited evaluation.

Table 14-2 Summary of U.S. DOE Memo
Classroom Accommodations for Students with ADD or ADHD

Several examples of accommodations that may be used in regular classrooms are listed below. The accommodations listed in the left column were recommended in the US DOE 1991 memo. Some of the classroom accommodations discussed earlier are listed in the column on the right. You may need to read Chapter 13 for a more detailed explanation of possible accommodations. Obviously, accommodations are selected based upon each student's individual needs, learning problems, and symptoms of their attention deficit.

US DOE /OCR Suggestions:
- structured learning environment
- repeat and simplify instructions
- provide visual aids
- use behavior management
- adjust class schedules
- modify test delivery
- use tape recorder
- computer aided instruction
- audio-visual equipment
- modified textbooks or workbooks
- tailor homework assignments
- consultation
- reduce class size
- one-on-one tutors
- special resources
- classroom aides
- notetaker
- services coordinator
- modify nonacademic times (lunchroom, recess, PE)

Other Accommodations:
- seat near teacher
- seat positive role models nearby
- reduce distractions
- pair students to check work
- pair with student who checks to see if assignment is written down
- give untimed tests
- use calculator
- give guided lecture notes
- provide chapter outlines
- simplify directions
- don't reduce grade for handwriting
- consider multiple-choice tests
- use Books on Tape
- use extra set of books at home
- use weekly progress reports
- consider oral tests
- teach study skills
- put assignments in writing for month
- use color to highlight info. to be memorized, or common errors
- use flash cards

A U.S. Supreme Court Ruling Regarding Suspensions and Expulsions

As the result of a 1988 Supreme Court decision (Honig vs. DOE), the Office for Civil Rights (OCR) issued a memo clarifying how suspensions and expulsions for special education students should be handled. A student with an attention deficit who qualifies for services under IDEA or Section 504 now has several safeguards regarding suspensions and expulsions. Much of the Court's ruling has been incorporated into IDEA. However, here are a few key points.

- Protected students may not be suspended or expelled, for more than 10 days, without a reevaluation, and without affording the required due process procedure.
- A suspension/expulsion for more than 10 days constitutes a "significant change in placement," which is prohibited by federal law.
- Students may be suspended for 10 days or less with no need to determine if misconduct is caused by their disability. Schools cannot impose a series of suspensions that are each of 10 days or fewer in duration.
- Reassessment must involve review of current information to determine if "misconduct is caused by the child's handicapping conditions."

Case Law Related to Section 504 Protections

Mary Durheim, a certified mediator, has identified several relevant court rulings related to removal of students from school. Here are brief descriptions:

- *Behavior management plans (BMP).* The repeated removal of a student from the classroom and the failure to formalize a plan for addressing the student's misconduct can deny the student an equal opportunity to participate in and benefit from the school district's educational programming in violation of Section 504 (New Hampshire; OCR 1992).
- *Misbehavior; BMP.* When a student who is disabled within the meaning of Section 504 manifests repeated or serious misconduct such that modifying the child's negative behavior becomes a significant component of what actually takes place

in the child's education program, an individual BMP may be required. The plan should ensure that the disabled child is able to successfully maintain the placement that is determined to appropriately meet his educational needs." (Elk Grove (CA) Unified School District; OCR 1996).

- *Discontinuation of medication.* OCR concluded that a school district failed to promptly hold a Section 504 meeting to address the behavior of a student with ADHD. The student had been taken off his medication and as a result his behavior changed. Thereafter, he was suspended on two occasions for misbehavior. According to OCR, once the district was aware of these changes, it was required to develop an individual BMP for the student (Westside Union (CA) School District; OCR 1995).

Working in Good Faith with School Officials

Now that all the legal issues are out on the table, let's talk about the *common struggles parents and school staff share* as they deal with ADD or ADHD and the importance of parents and teachers *treating each other with mutual respect*. Together you must learn to manage this challenging condition, to understand the emotional aspects of coping with an attention deficit, and implement federal mandates.

Because an attention deficit disorder can be a difficult and frustrating disability for the teenager, parents, and school, the potential exists for hostile confrontations. When nerves are frayed, tempers may flare on either side, especially during crises. Clearly, the parents of most students with attention deficits have the legal backing of IDEA and Section 504 and are negotiating from a position of strength with their local school system. For example in Utah, if a school system is found guilty of discrimination under IDEA or Section 504, the state-issued insurance will not cover the system's legal expenses.

Most of the time, parents can get what they need from the school by educating themselves and using a positive but firm approach. Mutual respect and courtesy are appropriate in these negotiations, until or unless school officials refuse to cooperate. Always assume good intentions of others until proven wrong. Many caring and well-intentioned educators are eager to help students with attention deficits. You should first try to work in good faith with local school officials to develop an appropriate educational plan for your teenager.

The comments from a county director of special education below convey a willingness to work with parents that is shared by many educators. You must find a "voice of reason" within your school system.

"I really appreciate parents who come to me, without hostility, and are willing to work together toward a positive solution for the student. If parents feel the school is not responding properly, I encourage them to find a higher level official (director of special education, school superintendent, or school board member) and give school people the opportunity to do the right thing."

Now you know your rights and what the school should be doing to help your teen. However, if your child's needs continue to be unmet, this chapter has provided you with the knowledge you need to pursue necessary legal action.

Table 14-3   Parent IEP Checklists

BEFORE the IEP Meeting

Before the IEP meeting, hopefully parents will take the time to do some homework in preparation for the meeting. If completing the tasks below seems overwhelming, consider asking an outside professional to help complete the following checklist.

_____ 1. Contact the school to schedule a meeting.
_____   Ask which school staff will attend.

_____ 2. Consider inviting someone to attend the IEP meeting with you. *(For example, spouse, another parent, advocate, counselor, or psychologist)*
_____   Notify the school in advance who will attend with you.

_____ 3. Review old report cards, IEPs, and psychological evaluations.
_____   Make copies for the IEP meeting of any relevant non-school evaluations.

_____ 4. Identify key problem areas: academic, behavioral, executive function deficits. *(For example, writing essays, working Algebra problems, remembering homework assignments, completing long-term projects, and organization.)*
_____   Consider asking a professional (educational consultant or psychologist) to review this material and attend the meeting with you.

_____ 5. Identify accommodations or supports that you think will be helpful. *(For example, extended time, shortened assignments, tutoring, prior notification of long-term projects, or an organizational coach.)*

_____ 6. List strategies that have worked in the past.

_____ 7. List classes in which your child is struggling.

_____ 8. Identify the reasons you think he or she is failing. *(For example, failure to complete homework, poor test grades, or forgetting to make up tests.)*

DURING the IEP Meeting

IDEA states that parents are *"equal participants"* on the IEP Committee in making educational decisions regarding their child. During the meeting, parents should feel free to suggest the special supports or accommodations their child needs to be successful in school. During the discussion of current education performance, parents have an opportunity to educate teachers and administrators about the specific impact two key factors may have on their teen's school performance:

1. the 30 percent developmental delay (4-6 years) experienced by teenagers with ADHD
    a. thus the need for more support and supervision than their peers; in other words "developmentally appropriate supervision"
2. executive function deficits such as disorganization, limited working memory capacity, impaired sense of time, or weak complex problem-solving skills.
    a. thus the need for extra supports such as "point of performance" prompting regarding homework assignments, compensatory tools such as graphic organizers, study guides, and calculators, and direct instruction of strategies for writing essays and computing math or algebra problems.

Here is a checklist of issues that should be addressed during the IEP Meeting. As needed, refer to the model IEP in Appendix 5 to determine which details to include in the document.

Current Status

_____ 1. Statement of progress toward current objectives

_____ 2. Present level of performance

_____ 3. How the disability affects child's school performance

_____ Identify Problematic ADHD diagnostic criteria: forgetful, impulsive, disorganized, not finishing work, lack of attention to detail. Don't forget executive skill challenges: _limited working memory, slow completion of work_ (slow processing speed and retrieval of information), _difficulty getting started_ (activation), _late to school & poor time estimation_ (inability to accurately judge passage of time), and _difficulty writing essays and completing math problems_ (analysis, synthesis, & reconstitution)

Goals

_____ 4. Measurable annual goals

_____ 5. Method for measuring progress toward goals

_____ How and when will it be reported to you

Services

_____ 6. Special education services to be provided (specialized instruction)

_____ 7. Accommodations to be provided (adjustments to environment, written work, testing, etc.)

_____ 8. Related service to be provided (occupational therapy, speech therapy, etc.)

_____ 9. Supplementary aids or services (use of calculator, word processor, etc.)

_____ 10. Modifications of the curriculum

_____ 11. Accommodations on district or state assessment tests, if appropriate

_____ 12. Transition services (beginning at age 16)

_____ 13. Extended School Year services if needed

_____ 14. Supports needed for teachers such as consultation from the school psychologist or a behavioral aide a few hours a day.

Behavioral Interventions

_____ 15. Positive behavior strategies

_____ 16. Behavior Intervention Plan (BIP) if needed

_____ 17. A statement about how discipline will be handled

_____ 18. Statement of exceptions to district student discipline policies, plus reasons for same

Plan Implementation

_____ 19. Date to begin

_____ 20. Length and frequency of services

_____ 21. Location, specification of time spent outside a regular classroom

_____ 22. Person (by job title) providing service

_____ 23. Signatures of committee members and parents

Hopefully, you will agree with school officials regarding the IEP, but if not, don't be afraid to say so. If they insist that you sign the document, then write a statement that you do not agree with the plan. Most likely the local school will work with you to address your concerns. If not, you'll have to decide if you want to go to mediation or file for a due process hearing.

AFTER the IEP Meeting

Parents must monitor implementation of the IEP to ensure that it is effective. Otherwise parents may drift along, assuming everything is fine, then suddenly learn that their teen is failing at the end of the grading period.

_____ 1. Be an active member of the IEP Team.

     _____ Review the IEP regularly.

     _____ Review progress toward goals.

     _____ Give feedback about the effectiveness of the IEP to teachers.

     _____ When it's working, don't forget the positives; express thanks.

     _____ Tell teachers which strategies are working best.

     _____ If the teen is still struggling and isn't making progress, **request another IEP meeting.**

     _____ Raise issues of concern at teacher conferences.

     _____ Know who is responsible for giving copies of the IEP to your child's teachers who may not have attended the meeting.

     _____ Discuss components of the IEP with key teachers.

     _____ Participate in the annual IEP review.

     _____ Save your child's IEP and progress reports each year.

_____ 2. Get involved at school.

     _____ Volunteer, attend school functions, or join the PTA.

_____ 3. Communicate regularly with teachers.

     _____ E.g., phone calls, email, notes, or teacher conferences.

_____ 4. Share educational information about ADD/ADHD in small doses with school officials.

_____ 5. Attend relevant training the school may offer.

Adapted from checklists developed by Mary Durheim, Educational Consultant, Section 504 hearing officer, CHADD President; Dixie Jordan, author, consultant, PACER Center; and Chris A. Zeigler Dendy.

After High School… What Next?

Many teenagers with attention deficits feel anxious about what they will do after high school graduation. Those who have had a terrible struggle in school may dread thinking about additional education, especially college or even classes at a technical school. Although most of them are aware that additional education will help them get a better paying job, they may doubt their ability to do the required school work.

"At the end of Cassie's junior year in high school she started worrying, 'What will I do after high school? I'm too dumb to go to college. It's not possible. I don't know what I want to be or I don't know what I want to do.' We talked a lot about how everyone feels that way and that's an okay feeling. As long as your parents are willing to support you in college, you might as well give that a try. You can figure out what you want to do and we'll help you get there. Cassie said that college wasn't a bad place to spend time while you were trying to figure out what you wanted to do with your life."

In addition to earning a higher income, additional schooling may enable your teenager to select a more satisfying career than simply doing unskilled labor. Another advantage is that she has more time to mature while in a somewhat protected school or college environment. At age 18, she may not be ready for the routine and monotony of a traditional 40-hour work week. By the time she reaches 21, she may be acting more like a typical 15- or 16-year-old. So, between the

ages of 18 and 21, she will become more mature and perhaps be ready to tackle technical school or college. Or she may make a more successful transition to the adult work world. But be patient. You may end up on a "six- or eight-year" college plan.

According to Dr. Barkley's long-term study of youths with more complex cases of ADHD, only 5 percent graduated from college compared with expected rates of 35-40 percent for non-ADHD students. If your teen is to be successful, given her developmental delays, you must arrange for additional supports and accommodations that are appropriate for a younger teen.

Educational Opportunities after High School

Several opportunities are available for post high school training and education:

1. on-the-job training,
2. the military,
3. Job Corps,
4. technical institutes,
5. two-year community colleges, and
6. four-year colleges and universities.

Although college is not appropriate for every student with an attention deficit, the majority would benefit from some specialized training after high school. You and your teenager should consider which educational option is most appropriate for your family. Your teenager should not be afraid to consider college as an option if she has average intelligence or above; has adequate reading, writing, and math skills; adequate SAT/ACT scores; and is willing to attempt college-level work.

Many students with attention deficits are very smart and have mastered academic skills despite poor grades in high school. Some teenagers thrive in technical institutes or college and actually make better grades than they did in high school. They especially like the increased freedom higher education offers, such as flexibility in scheduling classes and fewer hours spent in class each day, plus being treated with greater respect by college faculty than by their high school teachers.

Many families are not aware that under Section 504, special supports and accommodations are available for students with ADD or ADHD in all these programs, except, of course, the military.

Bear in mind that timetables for starting and graduating from a technical institute or college may vary among these teens. Some students may prefer to take a year off and work first. Others may attend a technical institute or college for a year, work for a while, and then return to school. Attending school on a co-op program—taking classes while also getting credit for working in a related field—is also an option. Some start and go straight through to graduation, even though it may take longer to graduate. Remember, however: taking a couple extra years is not much time when compared with the rest of one's life.

Should Your Teen Consider the Military?

Joining the military could be a good choice for some teens who have attention deficits, but it could be a disaster for others. Teens who are successful in the military typically loved ROTC in high school and, at least by high school age, knew they wanted to go into the armed services. Most teens with attention deficits, however, would hate the discipline of the military and some would have difficulty keeping their mouths shut and staying out of trouble.

Some teens with ADD or ADHD who have had their hearts set on getting into the military may be disappointed. Generally speaking, the military doesn't want recruits whose successful functioning is dependent on a daily medication, whether it is for diabetes, asthma, or ADHD. Ironically, rates of untreated ADHD among military personnel are quite high—two times greater than in the general population. You will find a very helpful fact sheet on "ADHD and the Military" at the National Resource Center on ADHD (www.help4ahdh.org). This fact sheet explains that eligibility criteria are divided into two categories:

1. skill and aptitude for military services, and
2. physical standards for military service.

Aptitude. Potential recruits must take a written test called the *Armed Services Vocational Aptitude Battery* (*ASVAB*). It addresses eight key areas: general science, arithmetic reasoning, word knowledge, paragraph comprehension, auto and shop information, mathematics knowledge, mechanical comprehension, and electronics information.

Physical Standards. A physician will take a complete *medical/psychiatric history* and conduct a *physical examination*. By wordy regulation, rejection by the military is linked to "a history of impulsiveness, immatu-

rity, instability, that will interfere with military performance as evidenced by the inability to maintain a reasonable adjustment in school." So, if your teen has been reasonably successful in school or work for a period of time without medication, probably for at least a year, she may be eligible for a waiver. This is a fairly new option, and I have not heard of anyone who has applied for the waiver, either successfully or unsuccessfully.

A couple of things about serving in the military make it easier for teenagers with attention deficits to be successful, even without medication. They provide a lot structure; someone always tells recruits what to do and when to do it. Recruits get lots of exercise, which also helps their brain work better. Typically, the teen really wants to be there and wants to do well, so he or she is highly motivated.

Unfortunately, a few recruiters under pressure to meet quotas have encouraged teens not to disclose their ADHD. Some of these "don't ask, don't tell" recruits have made it through basic training and done really well, while others were "separated" from the military. But of course as you will read in the following paragraphs, it is risky. You could be dishonorably discharged or perhaps even prosecuted for providing false information.

"My 24-year-old son was so happy when he entered the military. His recruiter was anxious to meet his quota and encouraged him not to disclose his ADHD. Unfortunately, during basic training, he injured his knee. While discussing his medical history with the base doctor, he listed Ritalin as one of his past medications. My son explained that he had ADHD, but hadn't taken any medicine since high school graduation six years earlier and had successfully held down jobs in a local factory. The doctor explained that didn't matter; he had to disclose the ADHD even though he hadn't been on medicine for a long time. The question on his original application was asked in such a way that I don't think he even realized it included ADHD: 'Have you ever been treated for a psychiatric disorder? Taken a psychiatric medication? Or seen a psychiatrist?'

"He was immediately sent to see the base psychiatrist and legal staff. Subsequently, he was placed in a separation unit along with many other recruits who were being 'separated' from the military for 'failure to disclose.' Thankfully he did not receive a dishonorable discharge. They even said he could reapply to the military in three years. The good news is that he has a job that he loves and is doing well now."

"My son had been off medication for a year and the recruiter advised him not to tell anyone about his ADHD. Basically the military had a 'don't ask; don't tell' policy. After the second day of basic training, the boys were exhausted, physically and emotionally. Military personnel took advantage of this vulnerability to ask them one last time if they had anything they needed to disclose—after all, the military 'knows everything.' My son told them about a suicide gesture, but did not tell about his ADHD. He was referred to a psychiatrist for an evaluation. My son explained to the doctor that it was just an impulsive act by a stupid kid and that he was fine now. He said all the right things that the doctor needed to hear and there were no other problems. Today, he is a successful and proud Marine."

What If Your Teenager Didn't Finish High School?

Teenagers may be surprised to learn that they can go to the Job Corps, a technical institute, or college even if they didn't graduate from high school. An important first step will be to take a test that documents that she has an education that is the equivalent of a high school degree. Once she has passed a high school equivalency test, she may be able to get a better job or apply to a technical institute or college.

Nationally, a high school equivalency test, the *GED (General Education Development),* is available for students who didn't graduate from high school. The same GED test is administered in each state. Students must make a score of 2250 to pass it. The good news is that 97 percent of colleges accept the results of this test for admissions. The GED test includes five sections:

1. writing,
2. social studies,

3. science,
4. literature and the arts, and
5. mathematics.

Students must obtain passing scores on each section, although the cut-off score may vary from state to state. If a student passes some sections of the test, she is only required to retake the sections she failed. Accommodations, such as untimed tests or oral administration, may be made for students who have learning problems and are eligible for services under Section 504. Remember, if your child qualifies for an IEP, she also qualifies for coverage under Section 504.

Although most teens would prefer to have a high school diploma, getting a GED is an impressive accomplishment. Some pretty famous people, including Bill Cosby, actor Christian Slater, a state governor, and a U.S senator got their starts with a GED. According to the GED national office, students who pass the GED outperform 40 percent of high school graduates. In fact, researchers tell us that they do just as well in college and other training programs as traditional high school graduates. Passing the GED makes a pretty strong statement: even though your teen may not have made good grades, she still learned a lot.

If your teenager is interested in getting a GED, there are a variety of ways to go. She can just sign up to take the test and see how she does. Or she can take a pre-test and then attend study sessions at a community school, community technical institute, or community college to master areas of deficiency. A few training programs are offered online to help students prepare for the GED. Check with your local vocational institute to determine the specific guidelines, testing dates, and fees in your state. Some states have incentive programs for completing a GED. When a student completes her GED in Georgia, for instance, she is given a voucher to use toward continuing her education. Visit www.acenet.edu for more information on the GED.

Is Technical Training the Way to Go?

At least a couple of options are available for acquiring technical training: Job Corps and technical colleges.

Job Corps

Job Corps, a service of the U.S. Department of Labor, provides a no-cost education and vocational training program for youth ages 16-24 and could be an excellent option for some of our students. Two hundred of these programs with an average enrollment of 200-300 students are available throughout the country.

Students can enroll to learn a trade, earn a high school diploma or GED, and get help finding a good job. Job Corps students are paid a monthly allowance, plus may receive support from the program for up to 12 months after they graduate. The majority of students live on-site at the program. You may obtain more information on the program serving your local area by calling 1-800-733-jobs (1-800-733-5627) or visiting their website: www.jobcorps.org.

Eligibility. Eligibility requirements include:
1. ages 16 to 24,
2. a U.S. citizen or legal resident,
3. meet income requirements, and
4. be ready, willing, and able to participate fully in an educational environment

To determine financial eligibility, the program considers several factors including the number of people in the family, household family income, and the presence of a disability. Although this program is not just for families who are living in poverty, adults who are eligible for Food Stamps or other public assistance program should be eligible for Job Corps. By age 18, young adults may be considered a "single head of household," so their eligibility is determined on the basis of their financial income alone.

Programs. Typically, vocational training may be offered in the following areas:
1. Brick masonry,
2. Carpentry,
3. Culinary arts,
4. Health occupations technology,
5. Heating and air-conditioning,
6. Information technology,
7. Office administration,
8. Cosmetology,
9. Auto mechanics,
10. Licensed practical nurse,
11. Computer engineering,
12. Legal secretary,
13. Drafting,
14. Medical records technician, and
15. Welding.

Each program is unique and may offer different opportunities. For example, the program in Gadsden, Alabama, happens to be on site at the local community college so they also offer college courses.

"The Job Corps program in Dennison, Iowa is an excellent one. When we refer someone to the program, we don't worry about financial eligibility. After all, most of our referrals are young single people who are not making very much money anyway. In addition to the programs listed above, our program offers training as a certified nurse assistant (CNA) and an unarmed security guard. Our 'solo mom' program is another unique component we offer. A single mother between the ages of 16 and 24 can take up to three children with her to the program. The program provides housing, day care, and Headstart on site. This program really gives these young moms a wonderful chance to learn the skills necessary to become self-supporting, contributing members of the community. It's an impressive program!"

— Nancy Sayres, Parent Coordinator, Southern Prairie AEA

Technical Institutes and Two-Year Community Colleges

Because of the burgeoning employment opportunities in technical fields, the role of technical institutes is becoming increasingly important. Technical institutes provide training for a wide variety of careers in business and industry (see Table 15-1.) Students can obtain several levels of training, although the names of these levels may vary from state to state. For example, a certificate, a diploma, or associate degree may be awarded. Associate degrees that may be awarded by a technical institute include an associate of applied technology (AAT) or an associate of applied sciences (AAS), which require no further training. Community

---

Table 15-1   Programs of Study at Northwestern Technical College (GA)

Associate degrees, diplomas, or certificates are offered in a variety of programs.

Associate Degrees or Diplomas are offered in these areas:

- Accounting
- Administrative office technology
- Computer programming
- Internet specialist
- Management & supervisory development
- Microcomputer specialist
- Networking specialist
- Cardiovascular technology

- Criminal justice
- Early childhood care & education
- Medical assistant
- Occupational therapy assistant
- Pharmacy technology
- Surgical technology
- Drafting
- Electronics

Certificate Programs:

- Bookkeeping specialist
- Customer service specialist
- CISCO specialist
- Data management
- Document design & production
- Employee relations
- Help desk support specialist
- Java programmer
- Medical receptionist
- Medical transcriptionist
- Microsoft officer user specialist
- Microsoft Windows
- Network security
- Office support assistant
- Organizational leadership
- Technical communications
- Telecommunications management
- Web designer

- Word processing specialist
- Child development associate
- Criminal justice records
- Emergency medical technician
- Medical coding
- Nail technician
- Patient care
- Pharmacy assistant
- Phlebotomy
- Machinist
- Mechanical drafting
- CAD operation
- Commercial truck driving
- Drafting
- Electrical controls systems
- Engine lathe operator
- Milling machine operator
- Welding & joining

colleges offer degrees such as Associate of Arts (AA) or Associate of Science (AS) that can be used as a stepping stone toward a bachelor's degree at a four-year college or university.

These training programs certify that graduates have specialized skills in any one of several areas:

1. business technology,
2. health technology,
3. industrial technologies, and
4. personal and public service technologies.

Graduation Requirements. Most *diploma* programs may be completed in a year (four quarters) to a year and a half (six quarters). Completing classes for a *degree* may require six to eight quarters. The AAT or AAS degree requires basic academic classes such as English composition, math, algebra, and psychology, in addition to basic technical classes. Many four-year colleges and universities accept credits from the associate degree programs toward their own graduation requirements.

Admission Requirements. Admission requirements vary, but typically may include: a high school diploma or equivalent (GED), minimum age of 16 (some programs such as emergency medical technician may require 18), and scores from a state placement exam. For students seeking a degree rather than a diploma or certificate, SAT or ACT scores may also be required. Entry into some programs of study may be open at the beginning of each quarter. Other programs may have limited admission only during the fall quarter.

Advantages of Technical Schools. Many teenagers with attention deficits do well in technical institutes. *First,* they are taking courses they really want to take. *Second,* instructors may treat them more like adults and be more flexible. *Third,* most classes involve more action and hands-on learning and less reading and writing than high school classes. *Fourth,* less time may be spent in class when compared with a six-hour high school day. *Fifth,* the time required for completion of a certificate or diploma is shorter than for a four-year college degree. Some students may have taken some vocational classes in high school, but this is not necessary for admission to a technical institute.

The Parent's Role. Parents will probably need to help their teenager plan ahead, identify key deadlines, submit an application, and link them with staff at school who can help them make choices about classes and a program of study. If your teenager is interested, *you may*

have to take the initiative to get the ball rolling. You can request a catalog which explains admission requirements and programs offered. You may even have to help him fill out the application and mail it in. Special supports provided under Section 504 are usually described in their catalog under sections related to "Student Services."

Financial Aid and Job Placement. Two other services that are also available through most technical institutes and colleges are financial aid, such as low interest loans and scholarships, plus job placement services.

Can My Teen Really Go to College?

Are Low Grades an Obstacle to Admission?

Some teenagers with attention deficits do not get very high grades in high school. Fortunately, most colleges consider both grade point averages and scores on the SAT (Scholastic Assessment Test) or ACT (American College Testing). Although making good scores on the SAT or ACT is important, students who make low scores on these tests should not be discouraged. They can still be accepted into certain colleges.

Admission Criteria. Visit a few college websites or order college catalogs to review their admission criteria. Students who are in danger of making low scores on the SAT or ACT tests have other options that may enhance the likelihood that they may be accepted by a college. *First,* students who have documented learning disabilities or an attention deficit which adversely affects their ability to learn may be given *accommodations* such as extra time on the SAT and ACT. *Second,* students may be *admitted on the basis of high school grades alone,* assuming their grades are pretty good, but test scores are low. *Finally,* if both the test scores and grades are low, the student may be admitted on a conditional status.

College Admissions Tests

Teens must take a test of general knowledge like the SAT or ACT for admission to most, but not all, colleges. These tests generally measure overall language and math skills. In 2005, the SAT added an essay section. The ACT also has a section that includes science. Additionally, optional testing in other subjects is available. Both tests now offer an optional Writing Test that may or may not be required by your college. The SAT also offers tests in higher math, history, biology, chemistry, physics, and foreign languages. Individual college admission requirements vary, so you must find out if any optional tests are mandatory.

After recent changes to the SAT and errors in scoring nearly 5,000 tests, more colleges have been making the SAT/ACT optional for admission. This decision followed on the heels of a 20-year study by Bates College that showed no difference in the grades and graduation rates of students who did and did not take the SAT. This trend in optional testing seems to be growing. Colleges that do not require SATs or ACTs are listed on www.fairtest.org.

Required Eligibility Documentation. Meeting eligibility criteria for disability-related accommodations for both the SAT and ACT has gotten increasingly more difficult since 1995. Officials from the College Board and Educational Testing Services (ETS) who develop and administer the tests were afraid that students were taking unfair advantage of test accommodations by falsely claiming that they had ADHD. Both SAT (ETS) and ACT have endorsed a policy statement developed by a respected group of experts known as the ADHD Consortium to determine eligibility criteria for accommodations on tests. According to this policy, an IEP or Section 504 Plan alone is not sufficient documentation for testing accommodations.

Talk with your local counselor for more details regarding SAT or ACT requirements for accommodations. Also refer to these ADHD guidelines on either the SAT or ACT website. If an additional evaluation is needed, the professional who assesses your teen will need a copy of these guidelines so she can address all key issues in her final report. Here is an overview of the policy requirements.

- A licensed professional must complete the evaluation (psychologist, physician)
- Evaluation must be no older than three years
- Documentation must be comprehensive
    - ❑ Evidence of early impairment
    - ❑ Evidence of current impairment
    - ❑ Alternative diagnoses ruled out
    - ❑ Relevant testing
    - ❑ Identification of DSM-IV criteria
    - ❑ A specific diagnosis (use direct language; avoid use of broad terms such as, "suggests ADHD", or "is indicative of")
    - ❑ An interpretative summary
- Each accommodation requested must include a rationale. Information from an IEP or Section 504 Plan should be helpful.

Accommodations. The two or three accommodations that may be most helpful to our students include untimed tests, use of a computer for the writing test, and testing in a separate room or at least with fewer students. According to SAT and ACT guidelines, the student *must currently be receiving the same accommodations* for tests in school that she is requesting for the test. Therefore, it is critical that these accommodations are incorporated into their IEP or Section 504 Plan. Keep in mind that accommodations offered by the SAT may differ slightly from the ACT. For example, as explained in the following paragraphs, the ACT offers one option which allows more time for the test.

Untimed SAT or ACT. Students with ADD or ADHD might consider taking the timed, regularly administered SAT or ACT first, perhaps in the spring of their junior year. Then, if needed, untimed testing may be scheduled. If the teenager does well on the regularly administered SAT or ACT, she may not even need extended time. Otherwise, the difference between the two scores may give a better indication of the student's academic potential when accommodations are made for the learning problem. So it could be helpful for the college to compare scores for both the timed and untimed tests.

"According to SAT data, the average student who retakes the test shows an increase of 15 to 20 points on each of the verbal and math sections. My son who has ADD inattentive with slow processing speed took the SAT untimed and scored an increase of 270 total points over the timed testing session."

Until 2003, SAT and ACT scores earned by students who had extended time were flagged. Colleges that received copies of your teen's scores found the term "Nonstandard administration" on the SAT report and "Special" on the ACT. Advocates worried that this practice could negatively influence a college's decision to admit a student. As the result of a 1999 lawsuit against the College Board (SAT), the SAT (ETS) and ACT no longer flag test results.

Review the SAT and ACT Testing Guidelines. Be certain to look over the test booklets for both the ACT and SAT to see if you should make any suggestions to your teenager. For example, it may be okay to guess on the ACT since a student's score is not penalized for incorrect responses. However, wrong answers are penalized on the SAT. Policies may change with time so ask your counselor about the advisability of making educated guesses. Additional test taking tips plus sample questions are available at each website. Computer programs and books are available for your teenager to work on as a practice exam for both the SAT and ACT.

ACCOMMODATIONS ON THE SAT

Students must qualify for accommodations on the SAT through the College Board, Services for Students with Disabilities (SSD). Each student must complete the *SSD Student Eligibility Form* that is available from local school counselors. Once your application has been submitted and approved by the College Board, you can register online to take the SAT. The application to take the SAT with accommodations must be submitted at least six to eight weeks before the test date. The approval process takes a while, so submit the application as early as possible. To determine current fees, testing dates, and sample questions, visit their website, www. collegeboard.com.

Some experts argue that students with ADHD (not ADD inattentive) should not be given extended time on tests. This could be true if a student rushes through her work, finishes ahead of her peers, and then has to sit there for the "extended" test time. On the other hand, students with inattentive ADD, especially if they read, write, or process information slowly, should request untimed testing.

In truth, the SAT offers *extended time,* not unlimited time. Typically, that might be roughly one and a half times the regular testing time, or four and a half hours. Students can spend the extra time on any portion of the SAT they wish. A team from your local school will decide exactly how much time your teen will be allowed.

ACCOMMODATIONS ON THE ACT

Students with an attention deficit can also apply for testing accommodations by the American College Testing program (ACT). The ACT is a multiple-choice test that covers four skill areas: English, mathematics, reading, and science. Roughly three hours is allowed to complete the test. The Writing Test, which became available in 2005, measures skill in planning and writing a short essay. Six testing dates are available each year, but not all dates will include the Writing Test. Approval of the application will take 35–40 days, so check submission dates. Current fees, testing dates, and sample questions are displayed at their website. Visit www.act.org for more details.

The ACT has two time options available to students with disabilities. *Extended Time National Testing,* up to five hours, is offered at a national testing site on a regularly scheduled test date, which will be on a Saturday. Under the *Special Testing* option, the student and test supervisor jointly determine a test date and time. An application for extended time is available online or from your school counselor. If needed, the test may be administered over several days. Each student is responsible for finding someone at her school or a local college or technical school, perhaps a guidance counselor, who will agree to be her supervisor and administer the test. Then the supervisor must submit a request for special testing to ACT approximately four to six weeks before the regular ACT application deadline.

Conditional Admissions

Some community colleges and smaller four-year colleges may accept students with low SAT and ACT scores. Basically, this is a conditional acceptance. Some colleges and universities also have lower SAT admission scores for students who have documented learning disabilities. Students accepted into college on a conditional status first must take remedial courses in areas where they have deficits. If a student is required to take only one remedial class such as algebra, then she may also take another regular college course. Prior to their enrollment, students may have to take a placement exam covering basic math and English concepts. Students who score well on placement exams may not have to take remedial classes.

Remedial Classes. In these situations, students may be placed in remedial classes, or *developmental studies,* for no credit during the first quarter. Remedial classes are usually required for two or three basic academic areas—for example, English composition and algebra. In addition, students may be required to take a reading or basic study skills course.

Taking a developmental studies course can be advantageous for students with attention deficits because it gives them an opportunity to adjust to college life while taking noncredit courses. The student continues taking the class until skill mastery is achieved. At the end of the quarter, if mastery is not achieved, the grade report indicates "course in progress." If skills are mastered, a "satisfactory" (S) grade is given and the student moves into the next remedial class or regular college classes. Students may take the same remedial class for three or four quarters until they master the course content. If a student can't master the content in that time, the college may place her on probation and ask her to stay out of school for a year.

Making Up High School Deficiencies. Students who do not take all the necessary college preparation classes in high school can still go to college. The student may be given a conditional admission and allowed to make up any deficiencies during her first year in school. For example, if she did not take a foreign language, she might take one college-level course to make up for the deficiency or might even qualify for a waiver. Developmental studies classes in math may help a student who did not take all the proper algebra courses. If your teenager is not required to make up difficult deficiencies during her first year at school, she may want to put it off as long as possible to give herself time to adjust to school and develop confidence that she can handle college-level work.

Choosing a School

Technical School or Community College vs. a Four-Year College

The key elements that help students with attention deficits achieve academic success after high school are: *classroom accommodations, staff guidance in course and faculty selection, and monitoring and support* especially during the first year in college. These elements can be found in many technical institutes, community colleges, and larger four-year universities. Some universities have highly specialized and intensive programs for students with documented learning problems. You and your teenager will need to do your homework and decide which program meets your family's needs.

Living at Home vs. on Campus. Perhaps the biggest issue to consider in deciding between a community college and four-year college is whether your teenager is ready to live away from home. Students who attend a nearby community college or technical school often live at home, while those who attend four-year colleges often live on campus.

Living at home may be a good choice for students:
1. who need and are willing to accept additional academic supports from their family;
2. who have limited financial resources; or
3. whose families are reluctant to pay tuition and related expenses when they are not certain that their teenager can cope successfully with the demands of college.

Some parents feel more comfortable with the teenager living at home for the first few quarters un-til she demonstrates she can handle college class work. Sometimes the curriculum at a community college may be geared to meet the needs of students with weaker academic backgrounds. In addition, faculty at community colleges may teach smaller classes and offer more individualized attention.

You may want to encourage your teenager to go away to college if you feel she can handle college classes, especially with Section 504 supports in place. There are some advantages to letting students with an attention deficit begin taking on the responsibilities of living on their own in a somewhat sheltered college environment. In addition to learning academics, college students develop important life skills, such as getting their own meals, managing money, keeping their room clean (maybe, maybe not), and paying bills on time.

Forgive me for saying this, but conflict in the family may also be reduced when the teenager is no longer living at home. Parents don't have to deal with the little things that drive them to distraction: leaving clothes all over the floor, coming in late, being late for meals, not completing chores, and arguing over school work.

"When my son was getting ready to leave for college, he said in a somewhat embarrassed tone, 'Mom, I'm sorry to say this, but I can't wait to get away from home.' My laughing response was, 'I hate to tell you this too, but I can't wait for you to leave.'"

Typical problems these teenagers face living on campus and suggestions for handling them are discussed later in the chapter.

Selecting a College

When selecting a college, students with ADD or ADHD should consider many of the same factors that other students do:
1. geographical location;
2. cost;
3. co-ed vs. single sex; and
4. college majors offered.

Other critical considerations for students with an attention deficit include the college's responsiveness to students with special needs such as ADD or ADHD, and the level of support it provides. Your high school guidance counselor may provide more insights to which college might be the best match for your teen.

Ideally, during the junior year of high school, you and your teenager will identify a few schools or colleges, visit their campuses, and talk with student services staff. Granted, it is sometimes difficult to do things in an ideal sequence with these teenagers. So if you start later, during the senior year or after high school graduation, don't panic. It is never too late.

Special Programs. In recent years, more colleges are trying harder to meet the needs of young people with learning problems including ADD and ADHD. Of course, they are mandated by law to do so, but some are going above and beyond the legal requirements. *Some colleges actually specialize in educating young people with learning disabilities.* These colleges offer special assistance and accommodations such as untimed tests, use of calculators, computer labs, tutoring, and individual student monitoring. Universities that specialize and offer a comprehensive program, typically offer more intensive support for an additional fee.

Some of the better-known universities include Landmark College, West Virginia Wesleyan, University of Denver, and the University of Arizona. Other smaller, less well-known universities also have been very helpful to students. At the University of Denver, students with attention deficits are assigned a specific counselor who works with them one on one to learn needed organizational and time management skills. Like many universities, they offer a tutoring program. Uniquely, they have also hired an organizational specialist who provides individualized consultation. Students may also receive instruction in the use of *Outlook*, a Microsoft program, to enhance their time management and organizational skills.

Most major universities have full-fledged programs for students with learning disabilities. Typically, projected annual costs for a freshman are higher, with costs decreasing each year as less supervision is needed.

Landmark College, a two-year program in Vermont, is well known because it exclusively serves students with dyslexia, learning disabilities, and attention deficits. The intensive Landmark program provides a one-to-five faculty-to-student ratio to ensure that students master skills. Tuition and housing are costly, but if the Landmark program interests you, you may want to find out whether tuition and fees may be deductible as a medical expense for federal income tax purposes. (School tuition may be tax deductible if your child is attending the school for remediation of learning disabilities.) Bear in mind that Landmark is a two-year college, so you would need to make sure that credits earned there would be accepted by the four-year college your child would attend afterwards.

Many colleges, even those that don't specialize in serving LD students, let students with learning disabilities take extra time for completing tests or let them take smaller class loads and still be considered full-time students. Special academic advisors may be available to advise them and consult with their professors. Other colleges provide limited supports as required by Section 504, but do not offer a full range of services.

Several guides for colleges with programs for learning disabilities or attention deficit disorders are available, including *Peterson's, Bear's,* and *K.W.'s.* These guides list universities and colleges plus the services they provide for students with learning problems, expenses, housing, majors, graduation requirements, and a profile of their students. You may find it interesting to review the information they provide on specific topics. For example, Peterson's offers guides on distance learning programs and Bear's has a guide to the best computer degrees by distance learning. These guides are available at most local libraries and larger bookstores.

Smaller Colleges May Be Better. Generally speaking, if your teenager does not select a college with a specialized program for students with learning disabilities, *a smaller college may be a wise choice,* at least for the first two years. Typically, classes are smaller and faculty may be more willing to provide individualized support. At some smaller colleges, such as Reinhardt College in Georgia, parents pay double the regular tuition to receive intensive supervision and supports. West Georgia College is an example of a small public college (7,000 students) that has provided excellent supports to students with learning disabilities even though they do not have a comprehensive program. One family found the College of Charleston, South Carolina, responsive to working with students with ADD or ADHD.

Cooperative Education (Co-op) Programs. Some colleges offer a combination of degree-related work experience interspersed with college classes. Co-op programs and internships offer several advantages for students with attention deficits: 1) Students make business contacts with potential employers. 2) Learning is more meaningful because it is done in a real world setting, not just an abstract educational setting. And 3) the students get a temporary break from boring yet demanding academic requirements. Some students with attention deficits need variety and tire of the monotony of classes, quarter after quarter.

Your teenager can apply for a co-op program through her college, which will help her find an employer. Or you may know a business that would be a good match for her career interests and arrange the placement yourself.

Selecting a Major Field of Study. Once your teenager has an idea of what she wants to major in, you can help her start searching for a suitable college program. Obviously, selecting a major that offers a more active, hands-on program could be an advantage—for example Georgia Southern's printing management program or Troy State's land surveyor program. Sometimes talking with people who currently work in her field of interest can help a teen identify colleges that offer a suitable program. Some teenagers may start college and have no idea what their major will be. Usually, this is not a problem.

"Our son was interested in a major in printing management because he wanted to work in the paperboard packaging industry. We found out that Georgia Southern University and Clemson (SC) offer printing management degrees. Our son earned his degree from Georgia Southern and is now working as the general manager for a paperboard packaging company."

Quarter vs. Semester System. At one time, schools that operated on a quarter system might have been a slightly better choice for students with ADD or ADHD. However, some colleges have modified their systems so that a quarter and semester system are more similar. Under a quarter system, classes typically meet more frequently (daily), for shorter periods of time (one hour), and end sooner (after ten weeks). Final exams are completed before Winter Break and students can relax and enjoy the holidays without worrying about returning to finals.

Under a semester system, classes meet two or three times a week for one hour and the semester lasts fourteen weeks. Classes may begin earlier in the fall so they are finished by the holidays. One advantage the semester system offers is the novelty of not having to go to the same class, five days a week. On the other hand, if classes vary each day, students may have difficulty remembering which classes to attend on which days. If these may be issues for your teen, then review the class schedules that are available at the colleges of your choice.

"Recently, my son's college shifted to a modified quarter system. I guess faculty preferred having more than the allotted 50-minute class period for teaching. One of my son's major classes (Spanish) meets for one and a half hours three days a week and the other (Computer programming) meets two hours twice a week. Of course, the first week after the change, he forgot to go to his computer class. He took awhile to get used to the schedule change and having to attend classes only three days a week."

Visit the College. You may want to review Peterson's or Bear's guide and decide which colleges in your home state look interesting. Then contact a few and ask what services they offer for students with learning disabilities including attention deficits. If possible, visit the colleges and meet with the Section 504 coordinator or staff in the student services office. Ask what services and accommodations can be provided for your teenager.

Paying for School

Expenses will vary depending upon where the student attends school. Classes at a technical institute should be the cheapest. One technical institute estimated that the total cost of tuition, books, and tools for a four-quarter program would be approximately $2,000 a quarter. Expenses are somewhat higher at a community college. Since the student generally lives at home, however, she does not incur any extra expenses for housing or food.

Expenses at public universities are significantly less than those at private universities. Tuition and fees at a moderately priced public college may be $2,000 to $4,000 per semester. If you live on campus, other expenses include dormitory rent, food, books, recreation, and general living expenses.

Seek Financial Aid. Your teen may be eligible for low interest loans, grants, or scholarships. Grants and scholarships do not have to be repaid. If your child's grades are not good enough to get a scholarship her first year in college, she may consider applying the next year if her grades improve. Loans are available from a variety of sources and most must be repaid after graduation. Low interest loans are available to most students when starting college and may be continued as long as they are maintaining passing grades.

To find out what financial aid your teen may qualify for, contact the director of financial aid at your teen's college. The director should know if special scholarships or other sources of financial aid are available for students with disabilities. The high school guidance counselor may also know about sources of financial aid, particularly at state and local colleges. You can also consult a book such as *College Costs and Financial Aid Handbook,* published by the College Board. This book lists grants, scholarships, and loans available, includes a worksheet to determine financial need, and gives step-by-step directions on how to apply. Some states have created programs whereby a student who maintains a certain grade point average may receive funds to pay toward their college expenses.

Scheduling Classes

Take Fewer Classes. When scheduling classes the first year, you may want to advise your teenager to *take a lighter course load*. Usually, 12 credit hours is considered a full academic load on a semester system. That may mean two 5-hour courses and 2 hours of P.E. on a quarter system or four 3-hour courses on a semester system. At some colleges, students with learning disabilities may be considered full-time students with fewer hours.

For students who struggled in high school, taking a lighter academic load will reduce stress, increase the likelihood of success, and help build self-esteem. However, full-time status may be important if your teenager's car insurance rates are lower as a full-time student and if you want to continue to cover her under your health insurance policy. Although your teenager may take longer to graduate, you are buying time for her to mature, develop better study habits, and take increasing responsibility for her school performance and career selection.

Balance Degree of Class Difficulty. Your teenager may need to balance her academic load with difficult and easier courses, especially during her first year in college. She should schedule at least one class she enjoys, plus consider taking a P.E. class. If possible, she should avoid taking several demanding academic courses such as English 101 and college algebra during the same quarter. Your teen should be aware that some faculty advisors may push her to follow a standard class schedule so as to keep her on track for graduation in four years. This might require her to take English 101 and algebra the same quarter. You and your child should hold firm in asking for a schedule that is best suited to her needs. If needed, seek support for your decision from the college Section 504 coordinator. It may help to explain that graduating is more important than the length of time required.

"My son took a computer class, developmental studies algebra, and a PE class his first quarter in college. He loved computers so it only made sense to get him into those classes as soon as possible. My son lacked confidence in his ability to make it in college. He needed to have a successful first quarter under his belt to get hooked on believing he could actually pass college classes and eventually graduate."

Schedule Personal Growth or Career Planning Courses. You and your teenager may want to review a list of potential courses before she meets with her advisor to schedule classes. A brief description of the content of each class is offered in the college catalog. She may want to consider taking career studies or psychology courses designed to introduce career options, give students personal insight into their own behavior, or teach study skills. These courses have valuable practical application to everyday life. Plus, the class may be less demanding academically and may be paired with more demanding academic courses such as college algebra.

To Work or Not to Work? Something else to consider in helping your teenager schedule her time is whether or not she should also have a part-time job. Some students with ADD or ADHD can manage jobs while attending school. Often, teenagers who were formerly hyperactive have enough extra energy to also juggle a job. You may, however, want to encourage your teen to wait until her second or third semester in college until she is certain she can master the academics.

Exempting College Classes. Although many students with attention deficits struggle in college, others do not. In fact, some may earn college credits while in high school or exempt some basic courses. College credits may be earned by taking Advanced Placement Courses (AP) and the accompanying test of skill mastery. Or you could take the CLEP, College-Level Examination Program which is one way of earning credit for what you already know. Both tests were developed by the College Board. Check out both tests at www.collegeboard.com. Although AP testing may be better known, the CLEP is also accepted by most colleges.

"My son took the CLEP in hopes of exempting two college biology courses. He made 49 on the test but had to make 50 to pass. He was so close, but the rules are inflexible. He had to take both courses, and I'm proud to say he made A's in both."

Making the Grade

Most colleges require students to maintain a certain cumulative grade point average (GPA) to stay in school, participate in extracurricular activities such as sports or fraternities, and also to graduate. If the GPA drops too low, the student is given an academic warning. If grades are low for two consecutive quarters or semesters—below a C average—she may be placed on probation and ultimately asked to leave school for a quarter or longer. Since no grades are given for developmental studies classes, the cumulative GPA is not brought down before the teenager has a chance to adjust and succeed in a college environment.

How the GPA is figured may vary from college to college. On a four-point system, the GPA is calculated by first multiplying the *credit hours* for each course by the *grade points* earned. Next divide the total *grade points* by the number of *credit hours*, which gives the GPA. The grade points for letter grades are usually: A - 4; B - 3; C - 2, D - 1; F - 0. For example, a student who was taking 11 hours of classes and received a B and a C in the 5 hour courses and a D in a 1 hour course would have a 2.36 GPA.

$$
\begin{aligned}
&\text{B (5 hrs)} \times 3 = 15 \\
&\text{C (5 hrs)} \times 2 = 10 \\
&\underline{\text{D (1 hrs)} \times 1 = 1} \\
&\phantom{\text{D (1 hrs)} \times 1 = } 26 \div 11 = 2.36
\end{aligned}
$$

To be "in good academic standing," students must usually maintain a 2.0 (C) average.

Seek Help from Student Services. Most colleges and universities have a student services department that offers *counseling* and other supportive services such as *tutoring, class and teacher advisement, and early registration*. Each college must have a Section 504 coordinator, who may also be located in the student services department. Typically there will be one person who is the major contact person and advisor for each student with a learning disability. This person can familiarize you and your teenager with various procedures at the college. Encourage your teenager to work closely with her advisor in the student services office.

Assuming you have your teenager's permission, you should feel free to call the advisor and ask questions occasionally as needed. Since most teenagers in college are 18 and legally adults, however, faculty members cannot disclose information about their academic performance without their permission. Grades are mailed to the student, not the parents.

Transferring to Another School. For a variety of reasons, our students may decide to transfer to a different college. Transferring to a college within the same state should not present problems. However, colleges in different states may require different core courses thus increasing the total number of courses taken. For example, one state may require two semesters of U.S. history and another one will accept one semester each of U.S. and world history. So finishing all core courses at the first college before transferring out of state could be important.

Section 504

Section 504 of the Rehabilitation Act requires that all technical institutes and colleges receiving any federal funds must provide special supports for students with learning problems. A detailed description of this law is provided in Chapter 14. Schools that receive federal funds usually have a statement in the front of their school catalog indicating that they are in compliance with Section 504 or other appropriate federal laws. If an attention deficit adversely affects a student's ability to learn, these institutions must make accommodations in her environment similar to those listed in Chapter 14, Table 14-2.

Applying for Section 504 Supports. Ideally, your teenager should contact the college early, six months to a year prior to entry, to apply for admissions, and, once accepted, request special supports and accommodations under Section 504. If your teenager hasn't planned ahead, this process can be completed at some colleges within three to six months. You will need to provide documentation of the adverse effects of ADD or ADHD on her ability to learn. Check in the college catalog for details regarding the procedure for applying for support under Section 504.

Reluctance to Accept Help. Some teens may be reluctant to accept supports in college. When teens transition from one school level to another, pride and a normal desire to do things without medication may influence their thinking. They may want to try college classes without any supports. Just to be safe, however, you should suggest that the teen go ahead and complete the application for eligibility under Section 504. Then once she gets to school, she can decide whether or not she needs accommodations. It may be halfway through the semester before she can determine if she needs extra help. But if she does need help, the accommodation can be implemented immediately.

Qualifying for Section 504 Supports. Requirements for documentation vary from state to state. Ask faculty in the student services office what information is required. The following information may be required:

1. A *letter from a physician* stating that your teenager has ADD or ADHD and perhaps a little history of when it was first diagnosed, her response to medication, and performance at school.
2. A *psychological evaluation that is less than three years old*, including
   a. an intelligence test such as the WISC, and
   b. an academic assessment such as the Woodcock Johnson.

   Since SAT and ACT evaluation standards have become more stringent, this may also carry over into requirements for college admission. So, ask in advance what information is required for the psychological evaluation. Some universities conduct their own evaluations and will not accept evaluations from other sources.
3. A copy of your teen's high school *IEP or Section 504 Plan*.

Accessing Services. If teens qualify for services, staff in the student services office will work with students to develop a list of accommodations and then write a letter stating the student's learning problems and needed accommodations. Your teenager will be responsible for taking this letter to her professors at the beginning of each quarter. See the sample letter in Table 15-2. Reminders to take these letters to their professors will probably be necessary.

Some teens, eager to assert their newfound independence, may want to try class work on their own without asking professors for special help. You may have to be patient with this, but if your teen begins struggling, tactfully suggest, "Now may be a good time to consider taking the letter to your professor." If you think she will not be receptive to this suggestion from you, make a confidential call to the Section 504 Coordinator and make her aware of your teen's struggles. Your teen may be willing to listen to this same advice when it comes from the Coordinator.

You and your teenager should not be embarrassed to ask for support under Section 504. Faculty can discreetly provide assistance so that no one realizes your teen is receiving accommodations. She will participate in regular college classes with all other students.

"College athletes are provided a very intense level of supervision and support to help them complete school work. After all, they must pass classes to retain their eligibility to play. This level of involvement is comparable to that provided by parents of students with attention deficits, but no one seems to think very much about this. No one ever says to coaches, 'You're too involved. These students should be able to do this on their own. Let them fail, then they'll learn the lesson.' Coaches understand the obvious—some students need more support if they are to succeed in college."

Section 504: Aids and Accommodations

Institutions vary in the sophistication and intensity of services and accommodations offered. Any of the accommodations listed below are pretty basic, however, and should be available if your child qualifies for services under Section 504 or received services under IDEA while she was in high school. College guides like Peterson's and Bear's list accommodations offered by each college.

Request Extended Test Time; Use of Calculator. If your child needed these accommodations in high school, there's a good chance she will need them in college. Talk with your teenager and ask her what supports she thinks she may need. If she doesn't want any accommodations, she doesn't have to give the letter from student services to any of her professors. But if she realizes three weeks into a class that she is in trouble, she can turn them in then.

"My son has problems with his working-memory, couldn't memorize his multiplication tables, and reads and writes slowly. The college agreed to give extended time for tests, use of a calculator, and accommodations in requirements for English 101 regarding compositions that must be written in class. He had problems organizing his thoughts and getting them down on paper. The professor taught him specific skills plus provided him a written outline for preparing his essays. By the final exam, he was complying with the same requirements as all other students. The professor was flexible and supportive. She taught him the skills he lacked. This enabled him to overcome his deficits in this area."

Use a Laptop Computer for Composition. Many colleges require that the majority of essays for English 101 be written in class. This ensures that the composition is actually written by the student and not someone else.

Table 15-2   Sample Student Disability Report

Report date: October 19, 2006

Joanna Jordan, Coordinator
Disabled Student Services

STUDENT DISABILITY REPORT

Student's Name: <u>Katelyn</u>   **SS#:** _____

Major: _____   **Minor:** _____   **Advisor:** _____

Kind of Disability: <u>Attention Deficit Disorder, Learning Disability</u>

General Description of Student's Disability:
Katelyn is easily sidetracked. Her processing of the written word, both in reading and writing, takes longer than usual.

How the Disability Affects Student in Class:
1. She takes a long time to read a test, write answers, and proof what she has written.
2. She has a hard time keeping her attention on the class content.
3. She has problems with organization and self-starting.
4. She takes a very long time to organize thoughts and get them on paper.
5. She is unable to calculate math quickly, and has been unable to memorize multiplication tables despite years of effort and high intelligence.
6. She has test anxiety as a major consequence of contending with ADD and LD during her school years.

Strengths and Additional Resources:
1. She will have her textbooks on tape.
2. Electronics and computer science are strengths.
3. She has a personal computer for word processing.
4. The <u>untimed</u> SAT was 270 points higher than the timed SAT.

Classroom Accommodations That Can Aid the Student in Reaching Standards and Requirements of Her Courses:
1. Extended time on all tests.
2. Extended time for all in-class compositions.
3. Extra time on the Regents' Exam, (a state-mandated writing test).
4. The use of a calculator on math tests.

Special test situations can be arranged with Mrs. Frances Martin, Office of Testing and Developmental Studies, ext. 555.

**If you have questions or wish further information, please call Joanna Jordan,
Student Development Center, ext. 554.**

If a student has an attention deficit and slow processing speed, she will have a hard time finishing a composition in a one-hour class period. Having a laptop computer would be an excellent resource for students with this problem. Some colleges provide laptops for students that are ultimately paid for through the student's tuition.

Use Technology. Obviously, having a computer to use in her dorm room would be wonderful. Access to encyclopedia software programs and the Internet would be very helpful. This could be a real asset to a student who occasionally forgets or puts off going to the library to research a report. If your teenager will accept help from you, she could send English essays to you for editing via email or fax. The big questions are how much extra academic help your teenager will accept…and how much you are capable of providing.

Seek Computer-Aided Instruction. Students with ADD or ADHD may do better in classes in which lessons and exercises can be completed on a computer.

Ask for a Notetaker. Students may request a notetaker. Non carbon replica (NCR) paper can be used so that the student immediately has access to a copy of the class notes each day (Chapter 13). Colleges will usually make arrangements for a notetaker for the student. Often, the notetaker won't even know your teenager's identity. Some professors may be willing to give the student a copy of their class notes.

Ask for Tutoring. Most colleges and universities offer free tutoring. Your teenager can ask her professor or the counselor for details about obtaining assistance. Encourage her to take as much responsibility for getting help as possible. Remember, however, that even if she is willing to accept this responsibility, she may continually forget to ask for help. Sometimes teenagers with attention deficits have trouble getting started on new initiatives on their own. You may need to make the initial call to find out details about tutoring and then give your teen the phone number to make a follow-up call to schedule an appointment. You may have to remind her to follow through.

Participate in Early Registration, Class, and Professor Selection. Students who qualify for Section 504 supports are often eligible for early registration, which gives them first choice of class times and professors. If your teen has a sleep disturbance or trouble getting organized in the morning, being able to choose classes with a later starting time can be a real boon. She can also ask her advisor or Section 504 Coordinator to help select professors who work well with and are supportive of students with learning disabilities. If faculty members are unknown, or if the college is too small to provide this service, either you or your teenager could call the chairman of a department and ask which faculty members work best with learning disabled students.

Make Schedule Adjustments. If your teenager discovers a scheduling problem, her advisor may, with permission from the professor, "force" her into a class that is full and closed to other students. This may be helpful if your teenager forgets to go to early registration or has to drop and add a class at the beginning of a quarter and the class she needs is already filled.

Dropping and Adding Courses. Most colleges have a cut-off date after which a student may no longer "drop" a class without receiving an F. It is important for parents to be aware of this date, especially if your teen is forgetful and has enrolled in a difficult class. If she tells you she needs to drop a class, ask when the cut-off

date is or look up the date yourself in the college catalog. And of course, remind her to complete the proper paperwork—a drop/add form signed by the instructor and taken to the registrar's office.

If the professor is willing, exceptions may be made for students who have learning problems. They may be permitted to withdraw after the cut-off date without having their grade point average penalized with an F. You shouldn't count on this option as a routine way of dropping a class, but it may be used occasionally in unusual circumstances. Your child should talk with her advisor in the student services office if she needs this help.

It may be advantageous at times to allow your teenager to drop a course she is failing. Receiving an F significantly lowers a student's grade point average. As a result, a student with ADD or ADHD may find that she is unable to graduate because her grade point average is too low. The student may need to take unnecessary courses with the added pressure of having to make A's or B's to pull up her average.

Consider Requesting a Waiver. Some colleges will allow a teenager with serious learning problems to apply for a waiver and exempt a subject related to their learning deficit. Typically, the college may require a course substitution such as Spanish Art Appreciation for a foreign language. Or you might check to see if a "computer language" course counts as a foreign language. The decision is typically made on a case-by-case basis after considering a student's specific learning problems and her major. Obviously, it would be difficult to exempt math if you were planning to be an engineer. Obtaining a waiver for a student with an attention deficit may not be easy and may require a good bit of time to work out the details with the disability services office staff.

Potential Academic Pitfalls in College

The symptoms of ADD or ADHD continue to affect many teenagers in college and their chosen careers. The same characteristics of the attention deficit that made high school difficult may continue to pose problems in college. As a parent, you need to be knowledgeable and anticipate the challenges the disorder will bring in this setting.

Many of these teens recognize their strengths and "challenge areas." For example, they probably know that they are forgetful and are sidetracked easily. It is important to show respect for this awareness and involve your teen in the problem-solving process. For example, you might say something like: "Sometimes you have difficulty remembering things. Would you like me to remind you when your psychology report is due, or when the deadline is for paying your parking ticket?" Or you may give her a copy of *A Bird's-Eye View* to use as a reference book. Hopefully you have previously discussed these issues during teachable moments so that she may actually try some of the advice.

How Much Should You Help? If your teenager made passing grades in high school, you may let her tackle the first quarter or semester on her own before you offer to help her. You may subtly ask questions to see how her grades are coming along during the first few weeks. If you sense she is struggling, talk with her to see how much help she needs and is willing to accept. Perhaps you may help her make arrangements for classroom accommodations and special supports.

Don't be surprised if your teenager doesn't want any help. She may be hesitant or embarrassed to ask for assistance because she doesn't want to be different from other students. Sometimes this reluctance or refusal to ask for help is difficult for parents to accept. Understandably, you may become very frustrated or angry. You might try reasoning with your teenager and then wait for her to seek you out. Be aware that she may be more likely to ask if she knows she is in control and the final decision to request help is hers. If she reaches a point where she is in danger of failing a class, she will probably agree to accept assistance.

"When my son went away to college, I told him I would help him as much or as little as he wanted. He was an adult now and I would trust his judgment. We made arrangements for accommodations such as untimed testing, use of calculator, and teacher and class selection assistance. Then as the quarter progressed, I asked a few questions. 'How did you do on your first algebra test?'

As long as he was passing, I didn't have much to say. When he started struggling in college algebra, I asked him if he thought he needed help from a tutor. At first he said no, but eventually he agreed. When he was ready, I made the first call to the tutor, found out the details, called my son, and gave him the number. He followed up and made the appointment. Sometimes, my son is shy about taking the first step. I didn't push him. The decision was his but I helped him follow up on the details."

Hopefully, most parents won't need the suggestions given in the following sections. But if your teenager has a more complex case of ADD or ADHD and is really struggling, these suggestions may be helpful.

Being Disorganized

Your teenager's ability to get organized and stay on top of her schoolwork will probably need monitoring, especially during her freshman year. Try to spot problems early so appropriate help can be provided. Although it will be more difficult for you to provide support or prompt your teenager about due dates on assignments, it can be done even if she is living away at school. Ideally, however, you should try to find someone at college who can help provide needed supervision.

Teach Self-Monitoring. Allow your teenager to monitor her own progress, unless she requests your assistance. This is especially important if she is passing her courses. You may need to remind her of events occasionally.

Consider an Electronic Device. Many students have improved their organizational skills by purchasing a *Palm Pilot, iPAQ,* or simply using the calendar feature on their laptop PC. They can list assignments, meetings, due dates, or medication. The device will beep to remind students when school work is due or when it's time to take medication. Teens often like electronic gadgets, so may be more willing to use them. Cheaper versions available include a *Zire* and Sharp *Wizard.*

Keep "A Month at a Glance" Calendar. Your teenager might write all her major assignments and test dates on a monthly calendar. The calendar could be hung on the wall so that she sees it on a daily basis or could be a small one she carries in her book bag or notebook. This calendar will enable her to see assignments and tests plus due dates at a glance during the next 30 days. With a weekly calendar, she may fail to see a test that is scheduled on Monday of next week until too little time is left for studying. If needed, you may also make note of key dates and remind your teenager of them.

Use Time Management. You may help your teen learn to fill out her month-at-a-glance calendar, especially in planning backwards from an assignment due date to allow enough time to complete a report or project. But remember, time management is one of their greatest deficits so *external* prompts such as reminders from their Palm Pilot, "WatchMinder" or from you will be needed.

Seek Help from the College. Universities with comprehensive or specialized programs for students with learning disabilities may offer extra help to these students. For example, students may schedule regular meetings with their advisor in student services to review their weekly calendar, assess progress and identify problem areas, monitor homework assignments, help schedule time for studying, or develop timelines for completion of major class projects. Some colleges arrange for a student volunteer to call or meet with a student with learning problems at least once a week to discuss their school progress.

Consider a Coach. Coaches can assist with either academics or activities of everyday living. Having a coach may be preferable to having a more traditional tutor. After all, the organizational issues are often more challenging than specific academic courses. Even though tutoring may be free, your teen may not take advantage of this service for a variety of reasons. For example, tutoring in specific subjects is usually offered at set times and set locations. Sometimes, your teenager may have trouble getting organized to go to the location where tutoring is offered. She may be embarrassed and find excuses not to go.

An academic coach can help your teenager organize assignments, monitor completion of homework, provide some tutoring or editing, and offer encouragement and moral support. If your child is willing to work with a coach, talk with someone in the student services department, the college tutoring service, or the psychology or social work departments to see if any graduate students may be interested in the job. You may pay $15 to $25 an hour for this service. Once you find a coach, you and your teenager will have to explain what you want him or her to do and provide information on attention deficits. Or in many situations, parents will still be serving somewhat reluctantly as a coach for their teen.

Inattention and Forgetfulness

Inattention can cause significant problems, especially during the early college years. Students with ADD or ADHD are forgetful, don't plan ahead, and seldom complete assignments ahead of due dates. They are more likely to remember routine assignments such as writing an essay every week. However, they may forget one-time special assignments.

Notify the Professor of ADD or ADHD. Your teenager must remember to take the letter from student services regarding needed accommodations to her professor at the beginning of every quarter. Don't be surprised if she forgets the letter. You will probably need to remind her to give it to her instructors.

Obtain a Copy of the Class Syllabus. Many faculty members provide each student with a class syllabus. This should make it easier to know what assignments are due and when. If she agrees to accept some prompting about her school work, ask her to give you a copy of the syllabus. You can then remind her, with her permission, *before* major assignments are due. At the beginning of the quarter, you can also discuss all assignments for the class with your teenager, pointing out those that look like they will take extra time. As your teenager gets used to the college routine and takes on more responsibility, you can phase out this assistance.

Ask for a List of All Assignments. If the professor doesn't give a syllabus, your teenager could ask for a written list of all class assignments at the beginning of the quarter. If needed, this request could be included in her 504 letter to the faculty as an accommodation.

Record All Test and Project Due Dates. Your teen should record all test dates, special projects, and reports and their due dates in her electronic device, computer, and possibly her month-at-a-glance book. You may want to review this with her by phone or on a weekend visit early in the quarter. With her permission, photocopy her schedule and help her monitor test and due dates. It is not unusual for a student with an attention deficit to walk into class totally unaware that the test is today rather than tomorrow.

Call and Wish Good Luck on Tests. The evening before a test, call and wish your teen good luck. Of course, what you are actually doing is reminding her that she has a test tomorrow.

Monitor Key Events. With your teenager's consent, you or the coach may help monitor key activities. For example, "When is your meeting with your advisor for early registration?" "What classes do you want to take next quarter?" "When is your deposit due to guarantee your dormitory room?" Or, most importantly, "When is the deadline to apply for graduation?" Of course, you won't get much cooperation if you bombard her with all these questions at once. So be selective in your questioning.

Be Aware of Graduation Requirements. It is especially important to make sure your teenager fulfills all the requirements needed for graduation. Your teenager and her advisor must check to see that she has taken all the core curriculum courses such as English, math, history, and science. Depending on your teen's maturity, you may have to go so far as to compare her college transcripts with the graduation requirements listed in the college handbook. If your child enters college with a deficiency in high school graduation requirements, she will have to take those make-up courses early in her college career.

Plan for Exit Exams. In some states or universities, students must pass tests demonstrating that they have mastered basic skills, or they cannot graduate. In Georgia, for example, students must remember to sign up for the Regents Exam in writing after completion of English 102. They must write a standard five-paragraph essay in an hour. The essay is graded by faculty from other colleges in the state. If a student forgets to take the exam before she has earned a certain number of hours, she may not be allowed to take additional courses or may have to take unnecessary remedial courses.

Use Audio Tapes or Compact Disks with Texts. If your teenager has trouble concentrating when she reads, audio tapes or compact disks may be helpful. "Books on Tape" may help her read and comprehend material in college texts, particularly in subjects such as literature and history that require more reading and memorization. Information on Recording for the Blind and Dyslexic is available in Chapter 13. They have a large collection of college textbooks recorded and can mail them within 24 hours. Books that aren't currently on tape or CD may require three to four months advance notice to be recorded. Although this is a wonderful service, some students may not want to use it. As long as they are passing the class, *they* should make the decision about whether or not to use the service.

Can't Get Started on Homework

Many college students with attention deficits report difficulty getting started on homework. Of course, now we know that this problem is linked to their deficits in executive skills. They may not always complete their homework but continue their high school habits of trying to pass tests on the basis of what they learn in class. Although they may still be able to do this in some college classes, it will be increasingly difficult. They will encounter more challenging classes that require more studying and completion of homework.

Prompt Getting Started. If your teenager is struggling, an academic coach can prompt her to get started on homework. With your teenager's permission, the coach will call and remind her to start homework, perhaps at the same time each day. Setting aside a couple of hours to study each day, for instance 2 to 4 pm, should be helpful. If a coach isn't available, you may have to prompt your teen during her freshman year to ensure she gets off on the right foot.

"Sometimes I remind my son to start his homework, get up, or take his medication by leaving a message on his answering machine or cell phone."

Jump Start Homework. Physical activity may help prime your teen's mental activity. Some suggestions you can share with your teen:
1. Walk around for a few minutes as you start reading;
2. begin drawing a mind map as you brainstorm your essay; and
3. set a timer as to when you should begin your homework.

Forgetting to Take Medication

Remembering to take medication may be a major problem for college students with attention deficits. Taking medication, however, may mean the difference between passing and failing classes. If your teenager continually forgets her medication, first ask *her* how she would suggest solving the problem. She may find it helpful to read "What do I need to know about my medicine?" in our survival guide for teens, *A Bird's-Eye View*.

"One teenager took his medication during the first two quarters of his freshman year. He passed his classes. The third quarter his prescription ran out and he kept forgetting to ask his dad to get it refilled. He failed a couple of classes. It never even occurred to his mom or dad that they might fill the prescriptions for him. "

Remind to Take Medication. Ideally, your teenager will remember on her own. Suggest that she put her medicine in a weekly pill box with compartments for each day. Then put the box in the same place each day. Have her put the medicine where she is most likely to see and remember to take it—by the bathroom sink, kitchen table, or bed. You may have to remind her to fill the containers each weekend. If she comes home every weekend, if necessary, fill the weekly container for her then. You may have to call her for a while to remind her to take the medication, especially her freshman year, until she gets into a routine of taking it regularly. Perhaps she can find someone at school such as her coach, girlfriend, or roommate who will be willing to remind her to take her medicine.

Provide Medical Supervision. It may be best if your teenager continues with her present family doctor if she goes away to school. Her physician knows her and her needs best, since they have worked together for a number of years. You and your teenager can monitor the effectiveness of medication and talk with your doctor about any needed adjustments. Typically, by this age, your child doesn't visit her pediatrician or psychiatrist very often, perhaps a couple of times a year for her annual physical and monitoring of her stimulant medication.

On the other hand, you may decide that your teenager should have a physician at school, particularly if she is going to school out of state and seldom comes home. Or if she is interested and wants counseling on a regular basis, you may ask the student services advisor for names of a good psychiatrist, counselor, or physician. You will need to find a doctor who specializes in treating attention deficits, make an appointment, and sign a release to have copies of your records sent from your family doctor.

Getting Prescriptions Filled. If your child is away at school for weeks at a time, you could have her prescription mailed to her at college and let her get it refilled there. Of course, she may have trouble remembering to get the prescription filled and then to put meds in her weekly container.

Monitor Medication Needs. Your teen's medication needs may change over time. Some teens will continue the same medication throughout their high school and college careers. Others may develop a tolerance that makes the medication seem less effective and need to change to a different medicine. Others may not need any medication, especially as a junior or senior, if they are taking high-interest, active courses in their major field. As time goes on, your child may feel she can study and pay attention in class without medication. Or she may need to take meds less often, perhaps only on days she has challenging subjects. Your child may be the best judge of her need for medicine. Obviously, if she stops taking her medicine and begins failing her classes, you would discuss this with her. State the obvious: "It seems like your grades started going downhill when you stopped taking your medicine. What do you think is the problem? Do you think it would help to start taking it again?"

Experiencing an Emotional Crisis

If your teenager fails a test or breaks up with her boyfriend, she may experience an emotional crisis while she is miles away from home. Hopefully, you have helped her understand that the characteristics of the attention deficit—impulsivity, forgetfulness, difficulty getting started, and low frustration tolerance—may cause problems that eventually snowball into a major crisis. With luck, your teachings will have helped her develop good coping skills over the years.

Call Home and Develop a Plan. Many times calling home and talking with you may help your teen cope with her crisis. Remember that you can try several techniques discussed in Chapters 8 and 9:

- *Listen* while she tells you her feelings about the pain, self-doubt, embarrassment, and fears about failure. This may take awhile—maybe even an hour.
- *Use active listening*, then develop a plan to cope with the problem so she doesn't feel powerless and depressed. For example, a crisis may be triggered because she forgot she was having a test, didn't study, and failed an exam.
- Next, when you think she's ready, begin *problem solving*. Ask her what she can do to correct the problem or what would make her feel better?
  - She could take the "504 letter" about accommodations to the professor if she forgot to turn it in earlier in the quarter.
  - She could start taking her medication again if she has not been taking it regularly.
  - She can schedule a conference with her professor, explain what happened, and ask if she can do work for extra credit.
  - She may schedule an appointment with her student services advisor to ask for advice.

- ❑ Or do something physical—swim, play tennis, or lift weights.
- ❑ Or spend time with a friend or boyfriend.

Handling a Crisis. If your teenager is experiencing a major crisis and you are concerned, encourage her to talk with her student services advisor. With her permission, you may call her advisor to get his or her opinion on how serious the problem is. Or you may decide to drive to school and see her yourself to determine how serious the crisis is. Teenagers with attention deficits may be reluctant to open up and discuss painful problems with someone they don't know—"Sometimes the last person you want to see during a crisis is some stranger." If she needs to see a doctor, the advisor may send her to a local doctor, emergency room, or to the college infirmary, if staff are properly trained.

Career Choices

Teenagers with ADD or ADHD have a wide range of intellectual abilities and interests, and may therefore pursue a wide variety of vocations. There are adults with attention deficits in traditional careers such as

medicine or law, as well as those with jobs that tap their creative and physical abilities, such as art, modeling, electronics, music, computers, or working on cars. Others find that college is not for them and that learning a trade such as carpenter, chef, plumber, hair stylist, car mechanic, or heating and air conditioner repairman has greater appeal. Finding a job that can hold their interest and commitment for a long time is critically important. Many prefer jobs that are active, include changes in routine, and involve a variety of different issues or people throughout the work week.

"When Steven graduated from high school, he didn't know what he wanted to do. In some ways he was afraid to try college but he decided to go for one year. At the end of that first, he dropped out. He knew he liked 'detailing' cars, which involves thorough hand washing, waxing, and buffing. He went to work at a shop that specialized in detailing cars and worked

there for three months. He pursued his dream, grew tired of it, and realized he did not want to do that for the rest of his life. Next, he got a job with a manufacturing company that made dies for printing companies.

"Subsequently, his ADHD was diagnosed when he was 20. He went back to college on Ritalin and graduated with a degree in printing management. This job is ideal for him. It requires a lot of activity, both interpersonal and physical. He must interact with many people, plus he has the opportunity to move around a lot. It is not a traditional paper-pushing desk job. Once he graduated from college, he no longer needed to take medicine. Today he is the general manager of a manufacturing plant."

Selecting the right career is crucial and will require more planning for students who have attention deficits. The career your teenager selects should maximize her strengths and minimize deficits such as poor organizational skills or lack of attention to detail.

"One day when Cassie came home and saw a stack of papers I had to read for work she said, 'If I had to read a six-inch stack of papers to make a living, I'd kill myself.'"

"At 16, Alex seems to feel trapped in his career choices. He told me that all my husband and I do is sit and work at a desk and how boring that was to him. Yet he feels the only way he can make money is to get a job that requires sitting behind a desk. We discussed other career options which don't just require people to sit behind desks."

"After high school graduation, my daughter who has ADHD took a job working for a company that provides temporary office help. It is a perfect job for her. She is enthusiastic about going to work each Monday and doesn't get tired of the job because she meets a new group of people and assignments every two weeks or so. They love the work she does. She is very bright and is a quick study in a new office."

Please keep in mind that some extremely bright teenagers with attention deficits excel academically in both high school and college. They may be skilled at many things and have trouble narrowing their job options. And then again, they may have trouble staying focused long enough to make a career decision.

"I thought it was interesting that the only two high school Merit Scholars I know both diagnosed themselves as having ADHD. Both were struggling to select a

career path. One had difficulty selecting a college and the other struggled with the decision about what he wanted to do after graduation."

Identify Skills and Interests

Identifying your teenager's skills and interests should be helpful in finding a good career match for her. You and your teenager can begin talking informally about these issues in high school.

- What does she enjoy doing?
- What special skills does she have?
- What vocations match her strengths and interests?
- What does she do with her spare time?
- Is she outgoing and does she enjoy talking a lot? Work in sales might be a perfect choice.

"My sister with ADHD has a job that is perfect for her. She is a chiropractor. She is very outgoing, sees lots of different patients each day, is active and moving around all day long, and enjoys the diversity of her patients' problems. She is always upbeat and witty. Her patients love her entertaining personality. The down side is that she avoids paperwork like the plague. Ironically, our mother is her office manager and after 40 years she is still stuck with the job of trying to get my sister to do her 'homework.'"

Listed below are several steps you and your teenager can take to help find the most appropriate career.

Vocational Testing. Vocational interest testing can be conducted in high school, a technical institute, or college to help identify a student's strengths and career interests. In college or technical school, the student services section can help schedule the testing; in high school, the guidance counselor can. This testing is usually free.

The *Strong Interest Inventory* is one vocational test that some colleges use. Students answer questions about things they like or dislike. The scores give them a pattern of interests and show how their interests compare with those of successful people in different occupations. Scores are obtained for six general occupational themes:

1. Realistic;
2. Investigative;
3. Artistic;
4. Social;
5. Enterprising; and
6. Conventional.

Approximately 115 possible occupations are listed within these themes.

"My son's best scores were found in the Realistic and Investigative Occupational Themes. He scored very high on the Basic Interest Scales for Adventure and average on Nature, Agriculture, Military Activities, Mechanical Activities, Medical Science, and Medical Service. Vocations in which he scored similarly to successful people currently working in the field included emergency medical technician, radiological technologist, veterinarian, electrician, computer programmer, farmer, police officer, enlisted military personnel, geologist, optometrist, bus driver, and photographer.

"He received a very low score on the Conventional Occupational theme of the Office Practices scale. Specific occupations in which he received lower scores and probably would not be well suited were accountant, business education teacher, public administrator, foreign languages teacher, minister, social worker, elected public official, and not surprisingly, school administrator.

"This test turned out to be a pretty helpful guide regarding his special talents and interests. Six years later he graduated with a forensics degree and a minor in computers. He was also a licensed private investigator."

Computerized Career Programs. Interactive computer programs are available that explain details regarding various careers. For example, Educational Testing Services has developed SIGI PLUS, which describes detailed aspects of numerous occupations: work activities, settings, educational requirements, average income, top earning potential, average work week, and employment outlook. This computer software or similar programs are available on most college campuses. Talk with staff in the counseling and career planning office at your college or visit www.sigiets.org for more information.

Personality Testing. Another test that may be helpful is the *Myers-Briggs Personality Inventory*. The teenager answers approximately 100 questions about herself and the way she conducts her daily life. Based upon her scores, one of sixteen personality styles that describes her will be identified. This test provides labels for differences in personality that we observe in work colleagues and family on a day-to-day basis.

This is an interesting exercise that may help these teens gain insight into their personality, how they think, make decisions, and live. The more she understands about herself and how she relates to others, the more she may learn to get along better with people and be more productive at work. One teenager with ADHD who took the test was astounded that the test described her so well. Many young adults are curious about who they are and what makes them tick. This test takes advantage of their natural curiosity.

Opposite extremes of four basic categories are identified on the Myers-Briggs:

1. Energy preferences: *Extrovert–Introvert;*
2. Perceptual preferences: *Sensing (realistic)–Intuitive;*
3. Decision-making preferences: *Thinking (Objective)–Feeling;*
4. Lifestyle preference: *Judging (goal directed)–Perceiving (flexible/spontaneous).*

Some teenagers with ADHD may be described as an Extrovert, Intuitive, Feeling, and Perceiving (spontaneous). Certain personality types are better suited to particular careers. For example, as noted in the Strong Inventory, the teenager who had an attention deficit probably would not make a good accountant because she would have to pay attention to details, be objective, deal with routine, and finish up quickly. This information may also explain why people with different personality types have problems in relationships. Obviously, conflicts may result between a teenager and her parents if they have the opposite characteristics of Introverted, Sensing (realistic), Thinking (objective), and Judging (goal directed).

"My son's personality type is Introvert, Intuitive, Thinking, and Perceiving. I am an Introvert, Sensing, Feeling, and Judging. Sometimes we drive each other crazy because I want to make a list, start work immediately, finish, and mark things off my list. Being organized is very important to me."

According to Kathleen Nadeau, Ph.D., author of several books on ADHD, those of our teens who are described as "perceiving" tend to be mood driven with regard to their work. They do their best work when they are in the mood to work. So sometimes you have to be flexible and let them work on their own timetable, even though it may not match yours. For example, she may not divide a project up into nice equal segments. She may skip two nights and then work until midnight finishing up an assignment.

Special Courses. Teenagers can continue to explore job options in college through career study and personal development classes. Students don't have to declare a major upon entering college. During the first two years, most students take basic academic requirements anyway, such as algebra, English, and history. Some college courses offer an opportunity to explore career options and to make decisions about a college major. The curriculum may include vocational testing, career discussions, filling out job applications, strategies for job interviews, and writing resumes and letters for job interviews.

Some colleges also offer psychology courses related to interpersonal relationships and personal growth and development. A course of this nature should be helpful to a teenager with an attention deficit. Typically, the classes are more interactive and require less written homework. Class participation is the key variable in the student's grade. If the student attends class every day and actively participates, she should receive a good grade. An A or B added to her grade point average would be a nice bonus.

Summer Jobs. Summer jobs offer an important opportunity to explore career options and master basic work ethic skills. Seemingly simple job skills, such as getting up, being on time to work, and remembering and following directions, are important skills for *any* teenager to learn, especially if she has ADD or ADHD. Administrative and organizational skills may also be learned on the job. In addition, working during the summers can help students obtain first-hand knowledge about various careers.

Exploring vocational interests is an extremely important benefit of a summer job. For example, some teenagers, especially boys, may be drawn to jobs that don't require a postsecondary education. Once a teenager actually does the work eight hours a day, some of the appeal may wear off. She may realize that she doesn't want to spend the rest of her life doing that kind of work.

It is important for your teenager to select a job that she enjoys so that she will want to go to work. You may need to help teach her responsible work habits. Make certain she has her own alarm clock. Wake her up if she oversleeps. If sleeping late becomes a major problem, discuss it with her and develop a plan to solve the problem. See Chapter 9 in this book and "Night Owls & Morning Zombies" in *A Bird's-Eye View* for more information on handling sleep problems.

Dr. Barkley has found that teenagers with ADHD do as well with summer jobs as teenagers who don't have ADHD. Perhaps the short duration of the job, the nature of the job (usually relatively active, unskilled work), having a job they like, and novelty make it easier for them to hold summer jobs successfully.

"Steven worked as a lifeguard during the summers. Even with his ADHD, he did an excellent job. He loves being the boss and was really good at his job. He had to open and close the pool on his own, watch all the children, monitor the chemicals, schedule the other lifeguards, and relate to the homeowner association president and members. He passed difficult lifeguarding, first aid, and CPR classes. His ego was boosted by this experience. This was great management training for him."

Meeting Professionals in the Field. Another way to find out more about various careers is to talk with professionals currently working in the field. If your teenager expresses interest in such a meeting, you might line up informal interviews through your personal and professional contacts.

"My son struggled finding a career after high school. After talking with a friend of mine who is a nurse, he thought that sounded really interesting. He recently started training as a nurse and loves it."

Life's Other Important Lessons

Teenagers with attention deficits experience tremendous changes when they go away to college. Just living on their own for the first time is a major adjustment. Getting up and going to class is a demanding endeavor for many. Writing checks, balancing checkbooks, washing clothes, and keeping up with homework assignments are a lot for these teenagers to juggle, especially with the organizational problems so many of them face. Again, be reminded that teaching your teen the basic concepts underlying these skills is important, but does not guaranteed that they will use these skills when they are needed. After all, they lack the necessary executive skills required for many of these tasks.

"Our daughter received numerous parking tickets that she never paid. One day the campus police impounded her car and towed it away. She called home all upset, asking if she could borrow $500 to pay parking fines and charges to get the car back."

Do Checkbooks Balance?

The answer to this question is an emphatic "No" if it is directed to a college freshman with ADD or ADHD. How much money is in her bank account is a complete mystery. Even remembering to record basic information about checks, such as to whom they were written and the amount, may be difficult. Some students may use check cards or bank automatic teller machine (ATM) cards almost exclusively. If the teller machine indicates that money is in the account, they withdraw it. They may forget they wrote a check the day before that has not cleared yet. "Bounced" checks due to insufficient funds may cost an additional twenty to thirty dollars. A student may write a six-dollar check that ends up costing much more.

Obviously, this behavior can be very irritating to parents. Fortunately, the ability to manage money tends to improve with age. By the time your child is a senior, she should be able to manage her money more effectively, but don't be surprised if problems continue. In the interim, however, you must come up with a plan to teach her how to handle her finances.

Parents must decide how to deal with money matters. Some parents are so worried about their teenager succeeding academically, they cut the student some slack with finances, especially during the first couple of years. If she has problems managing money, ask her to help solve the problem. Just punishing her will not help her learn to manage money better.

"Because our son's confidence in his ability to do college work was so tenuous, academics were our greatest concern. We made certain our son was on solid ground academically before we began pressing him for greater financial responsibility. When he was a junior, we gave him a set allowance and told him he had to live within that amount. Although he was somewhat resentful at that time, he later thanked us."

Teach Money Management. Spend some time with your teenager before she goes away to college and teach her how to handle a checkbook—filling out a check, listing the check and number in the checkbook, subtracting the check, and keeping a running balance. Explain how checking accounts, check cards, and ATM cards work. But again, teaching skills is not magic. Because of their disorder, there is a high probability they will still have problems with money management and impulsive spending.

Limit Access to the Checking Account. You may decide to give your child a limited number of checks and to pay major bills such as tuition, dorm room, and a college meal plan yourself. She can pay for her books or other designated expenses. Then you can allow her to withdraw a set amount of money each week from the ATM for an allowance. You could try transferring the money in a week at a time. She can withdraw her weekly allowance on Saturday and pay her miscellaneous expenses in cash. Or you could send her an allowance in a weekly check. As long as she has a meal plan, she won't starve if she runs out of cash. Sometimes a boyfriend may be the lifesaver who helps her balance her checkbook and be aware of how much money she has in the bank.

Consider a Check Card. Check or debit cards look like a credit card but the money is subtracted from your account immediately. One advantage of the check card is that it is declined or approved when you try to pay for a purchase. If you don't have enough money in your account, your check card will be declined. You avoid bounced-check charges from the bank, returned-check charges to the merchant, and the hassle of having to make the check good.

One disadvantage of check cards is that you don't have the option of filing a disputed payment claim and withholding payment like you can with your credit card company. Thus you have little leverage to force the seller to replace or repair any damaged or faulty merchandise. One way to avoid this problem is to use a credit card instead. If your check card is stolen, your account could be emptied overnight. Some cards cover this theft and others do not. Our teens are also less likely to keep a running account of their balance and may be clueless about how much money they have left. Study the pros and cons of this option to decide what is best for your teen.

Deposit Extra Money. You or your teen might deposit a little extra money in her account. One teenager told me she put $50 extra in her account as a safety cushion. If she makes a mistake on the account balance, she won't bounce any checks. To use this method, your teen must be organized enough to keep a running account of her finances. Otherwise, she will just spend the $50 cushion.

Use Overdraft Protection. Another option is to obtain overdraft protection or a personal line of credit. With this protection, a check will not bounce. The only cost will be interest, usually only a few dollars or cents, for money the bank advanced to the account to cover the check, instead of a $20 or $30 service charge for a bounced check. However, if your teenager knows about this service, she may take advantage of it and write checks for more money than she has available. Some banks will call you if your teen has had to dip into overdraft protection.

Managing Personal Earnings or Scholarship Funds. Your teenager may have a job or receive a check from a school loan or scholarship. Regardless of where the funds come from, she will need help managing her money. Sit down with her and explain how to develop a budget. Show her how to write down the exact amount of each monthly expense such as the phone, cable TV or satellite, rent, or quarterly expenses such as books and class registration fees. Then when she subtracts expenses from her income, she knows how much money she will typically have left to spend after bills are paid. If she is earning her own money, she will probably be more cautious about spending it. But she may still have problems managing it very well.

To Charge or Not To Charge?

College students often receive applications for credit cards and are notorious for piling up significant debt. In spite of this debt risk, some parents may still *want* their teenager to have a card, perhaps for safety reasons and convenience. They may not want their teenager to drive home from college without a credit card in the event she needs gas or has car trouble. If you allow your teen to have credit cards, you will need to closely monitor their use since most of these teenagers may spend money impulsively and will have trouble using a credit card wisely. This could be an opportunity to teach your teen the importance of paying off her card each month and avoiding credit card debt.

Set Guidelines for Credit Card Usage. Talk with your teenager about proper use of a credit card. You may teach the importance of keeping charges at a minimum and paying them off in full each month. You may also explain that many teenagers with attention deficits are prone to impulsive spending and may run up credit card bills. Express your hope that she will avoid that pitfall. Explain how much you pay for interest when you don't pay the card off each month.

Limit and Monitor Card Use. Let your teenager know what she should and shouldn't use her credit cards for. For example, you may want to designate their use only for emergencies or for expenditures you authorize in advance. You may also explain that you intend to monitor monthly statements and then review charge card expenditures with her. If bills are sent to a school address and you are paying the bill, you should review them with her each month. This may prevent her running up a huge credit card bill without your knowledge. If she is paying the bill but has a high balance, you could talk with her about ways to reduce her debt, such as paying more than the minimum required each month.

Will She Remember to Pay Fees and Bills?

No, she probably won't remember to pay her bills without being reminded. She may forget to pay her school fees, tuition, and other bills. And if she lives off campus in an apartment, she may also forget that rent, utilities, cable TV or satellite, and telephone bills must be paid. To keep your teenager from running up late payment fees or having services disconnected, you may have to step in and help, especially the first year or two.

Remind about Bill Payment. You may need to remind her of due dates, such as rent due the first day of the month. You may need to ask for registration forms and bills for tuition and pay them yourself. Students don't always realize that bouncing too many checks and failing to pay bills may result in a bad credit rating for both themselves and their parents, if they have co-signed.

Set Up a Bill Paying Reminder System. Here is one low-tech strategy that may be effective since it uses visual cues. Several stores carry a rectangular box that contains 31 slots, one for each day of the month. This box can be placed near the entry way so that as bills are opened they can be slotted on the proper due dates and you have a nice visual reminder to pay your bills. Or she may program reminders into her Palm Pilot, iPAQ, or computer.

Bill Parents Directly. If your teenager often forgets to pay bills, you may want to have some bills sent directly to you and gradually phase in her full responsibility for payment by her senior year.

Can She Get Along with a Roommate?

Sometimes relationships between a teenager with an attention deficit and her roommate can be strained. These teens are not known for their neatness. Clothes and possessions can pile up quickly when two people share a room measuring ten by twelve. Thoughtfulness or an awareness of how they affect others is not usually one of their strong suits. Loud music or talking while

their roommate is trying to study is not going to go over real well. The teen-aged "night owl" may also create problems for her roommate. Or if she can't wake up of a morning, her roommates may be irritated by loud alarms that ring forever while the ADDer obliviously continues sleeping. Sometimes both roommates may have an attention deficit, which creates another set of problems. If you are lucky, your teenager's college will send out surveys before school begins in an effort to match roommates who have similar living and study habits. Still, there is no guarantee that your teenager and her roommate will hit it off.

Talk with Your Teenager. Before your teen leaves home, you may want to talk to her about the need to respect the rights of her roommate and discuss potential areas of conflict.

Talk with the Resident Assistant (R.A.). Most colleges have resident assistants (R.A.'s) who live on each floor of a dorm. These upper-class students receive a free room in exchange for providing support, supervision, and mediation for students who live on their hall. If your teen runs into problems with her roommate, suggest that she talk to her R.A. and ask for assistance in resolving their problems.

Change Roommates. If serious problems arise, your teen may be able to change roommates immediately. She may feel, however, that she can wait for a new quarter or school year. She can begin looking for someone more compatible who shares common interests.

Request a Private Room. Sometimes when a teen with an attention deficit finally gets around to studying, her roommate may be watching a movie or talking on the phone. It doesn't take much to distract these teens. The first thing you know, good intentions for studying are down the tube and your daughter is watching the movie with her roommate. If available, your teenager may be better off in a private room.

Get an Apartment or Live at a Fraternity House. Parents may face a dilemma about where the student should live. Some parents insist that their freshman teen live in a dorm the first year of college. If they do well, the parents may allow them to live off campus in an apartment or at a fraternity during their sophomore year. This final symbolic step of living out from under any adult supervision may be difficult for you to accept. You will have to make a judgment call as to whether or not your teenager is ready for this level of independent living. Questions to ask yourself include:

- *First,* has she been responsible about studying during her freshman year and passed the majority of her classes? If so, chances are that she will manage living in an apartment successfully. You might tell her: "As long as you study and pass your classes, I'll support your living in an apartment."
- *Second,* are family finances sufficient to pay for an apartment or will she get a job?
- *Third,* do you think your teen can be responsible about paying bills? Remember: if needed, you can handle this by direct billing and paying the rent, phone, power, or cable TV bills yourself.

When students live in their first apartment, their sense of pride in living on their own may mean they keep their place fairly clean. Then again, your teen's room may still be a pigsty, but if she can live in it and get her studies done, so be it.

Should She Drive a Car to School?

As Chapter 9 discusses, driving can land many of these teenagers in difficulties ranging from minor parking violations to serious accidents. In deciding whether your teenager should have access to a car at college, think carefully about her ability to handle this privilege responsibly. In particular, ask yourself how likely she is to drive when her medication has worn off, and how likely she is to have an accident.

Allow Limited Driving. If you have serious reservations about your teenager driving a car to school, you might let her take a car her second quarter at school and see how well she handles it. After the quarter is over, does she have passing grades? Did she get any tickets or have any accidents? Has she received a ticket for DUI? A logical consequence for any problems in these areas may be reduced driving privileges or taking the car away from her for a while.

Establish a Gas Allowance. Some students get jobs so that they can earn money to help pay for their gas. Other parents prefer to have their children focus all their energies on schoolwork and give them an allowance for gas each month. Any charges over that amount must be paid for by the student. If you want to encourage your teen to come home more often, you could offer to pay for the gas required for the trip home.

Encourage Her to Ride with Others. If she has received an occasional ticket or had an accident, encourage her to ride with others at night (that is, if these problems occur at night). She may be willing to ride with her boyfriend or roommate. Or encourage her to take her medication at 5:00 p.m. or so when she is driving after dark.

Talk about Drinking and Driving. As discussed in Chapter 9, tell her that drinking and driving is a nonnegotiable area. Drinking impairs drivers with ADHD even more than those who don't have this condition. Explain that you love her too much to allow her to risk her life while drinking and driving. If she is with someone who is drinking, tell her to get out of the car and call a taxi or friend to come get her.

Should Your Teenager Join a Fraternity or Sorority?

Some teenagers will want to join a fraternity or sorority. Parents must weigh the advantages and disadvantages, plus consider costs, to make a final decision.

Weigh the Pros and Cons. One advantage to joining a fraternity or sorority is that students must maintain passing grades to be eligible to join and participate in fraternity activities. In addition, teenagers make a lot of new friends who can provide important social and business contacts in the future. They are also encouraged to participate in intra-fraternity sports.

Although parents may worry about drug and alcohol abuse, fraternities are under strong pressure from college officials to prohibit use of illicit substances. Sanctions are stiff for violations, especially use of drugs. Fraternities and sororities may be placed on probation or banned from campus for a year or more.

On the minus side, a fraternity or sorority may demand so much time or put such an emphasis on partying that members may fail some of their classes. Your teenager is going to be drawn to people she enjoys and with whom she feels comfortable. You will probably not have much influence over the sorority she selects. The good news is that students can't remain active in a fraternity or sorority if they fail classes. Remember also that most of these groups are okay or else they will have been disbanded.

"At first I worried about my son joining a fraternity. When he decided he wanted to join, I agreed but with some reservations. However, it has been a great experience for him. He actually worries about his grade point average so that he can be active in the fraternity. He tends to be introverted and it has helped him become more outgoing. The fraternity has given him certain responsibilities. He had to clean the fraternity house and participate in a pledge class project to improve the house. He has helped wire stereo systems and outside lights. He participates in inter-fraternity sports. He acts as photographer for the fraternity. He has been able to use so many of his talents. It has been a great confidence builder."

Consider the Costs. Before your teen joins a fraternity or sorority, be sure she knows the costs involved. Costs vary from college to college. Some groups have a one-time initiation fee plus monthly dues. Being a member of a fraternity or sorority is important enough to some teenagers that they are willing to work a part-time job so they can belong to one.

Parental Involvement: When to Let Go?

Because some teenagers with attention deficits have struggled so much in high school, both parents and teenagers may face college with a great deal of anxiety. Some parents may think that their teenager should be independent, now that she is 18 and legally an adult. Yet, they also recognize that she is more like a younger teen in many ways and is not ready for total independence.

"As a mental health professional, I have felt very guilty about my involvement in my son's academic life. All through high school, I kept trying to find someone else to be his 'academic coach' but never found anyone to replace me. Although my son was bright, high school was such a struggle for him. If I had totally stopped monitoring his performance, I'm not certain he would have graduated.

"A few months ago I talked to a mental health professional in another state who also has a son with ADHD. We discovered we have both struggled with and felt a lot of guilt about this same dilemma. When do we let go? She

told me how her son had called her from college, really upset about his first big test in history, a subject that was very difficult for him and required a lot of memorization. They talked by phone and she decided to go down to the college and help him study. After they made the decision, they both cried. She decided then, that you stop helping them when they no longer need help. He is making every effort to make it academically on his own. There is no reason to feel guilty for helping him.

"From a practical perspective, parents are paying thousands of dollars a year for their child's education. What would be gained by letting him fail classes?"

Faculty at West Virginia Wesleyan have found that students with learning disabilities usually need the most assistance their first year in college. As students learn how to study and gain confidence, they need fewer supports each subsequent year. As a result, special fees for extra supervision decline each year. *Getting over the hurdle of her first year in college may well be the most critical challenge your teenager faces.* After a successful semester or two, she should build confidence in her ability to make it on her own.

"Although I still feel guilty at times that I am so involved in my son's life, the good news is that each year he needs less help from me. He has assumed increasing responsibility for his schoolwork, payment of rent, and self-care. Now that he knows how to seek help from student services, he is helping his girlfriend, who is a freshman, do all her paperwork for special accommodations for her ADD inattentive."

Some Closing Thoughts

You must be careful about how involved you get in your teenager's college career. If you are too controlling or demanding, your teenager may rebel. Power struggles may undermine and detract from her academic efforts. On the other hand, if you are paying for your teen's education, you certainly have a right to expect a certain level of effort from her. But if she is doing her best and still fails a class because of learning problems, the best course is usually to be as supportive as possible and make sure that appropriate accommodations are provided. Knowing about Dr. Russell Barkley's research that your 18-year-old may be more like a 12- or 14-year-old in some respects gives you the necessary permission to provide the extra supports that your teen needs to be successful in college and life.

16

Parents Have Permission to Take Charge

"Parents are probably the greatest single factor in determining whether or not a teenager with an attention deficit disorder receives needed services."

Some teenagers with ADD or ADHD need little outside help to succeed at school and at home. Perhaps parents may only have to monitor progress reports and periodic report cards and oversee their medication, but otherwise teens can manage on their own. Other teenagers with more complex attention deficit disorders, however, must struggle to cope, even with a variety of interventions at home and at school.

If your teenager is struggling, give yourself permission to become more involved and to take charge of coordinating services, if need be. You're probably the best person to take charge, anyway.

First, you know your teenager best and have a tremendous emotional investment in his success! *Second,* because of the parent-child bond, you'll stick with your teen long after others have given up and are no longer involved. As a parent you have an intense emotional investment that enables you to be creative and tenacious, just as this book strongly advises.

Remember, do whatever it takes to help your teenager succeed! After reading this book, you should feel comfortable developing a plan to help your teenager adjust successfully at home, school, and in the community. And you should understand and appreciate your own critical role in this process.

"I decided after five psychologists, four pediatricians, one neurologist, and many others that I was my daughter's best case manager. It was up to us to decide what to do. We know our daughter best. Professionals leave—parents stay!"

Put Together a Winning Team

If your teenager is struggling at home or school, you need to work *together* with the teacher, counselor, and physician to develop an *individualized, comprehensive treatment plan*. As discussed throughout the book, the family/school/physician partnership is the *cornerstone* of successful home and school experiences for teenagers with attention deficits. This partnership must truly include the parents and teenager as respected members of the treatment team. The critical role the family plays in treatment must not be underestimated.

"Parents and teenagers have great inner strength and ability that frequently are overlooked in the traditional therapeutic process."

Identify a Case Manager. If your teenager is receiving specialized services from a variety of professionals, *someone must coordinate the services they provide.* Typically, each professional is a specialist in his own field and may not be knowledgeable or feel comfortable monitoring your teenager's progress in other areas. For example, the doctor may not know if your teenager has learning problems or whether classroom accommodations are needed. The teacher may not know that your teenager is on medication, whether it is effective, when medication changes are made, the time of day medication may wear off, or whether your teenager has sleep disturbances that affect his schoolwork.

Ideally, the doctor and school personnel should communicate with each other periodically. For example, exchanging information about the effectiveness of medication at school is very important. With this information, adjustments can be made to the medicine, dosage amounts, and the time administered to maximize medication benefits. Unfortunately, this communication seldom occurs. Consequently, someone must look at the whole child, monitor his functioning in every setting, and provide feedback to all professionals involved. You, as a parent, are often the best person to take on this responsibility. In Kansas, thanks to a federal grant, some parents are being trained to act as case managers for their children who have serious emotional problems. They have been extremely effective in coordinating services.

The School's Role. School personnel are extremely valuable allies who can ensure a successful academic experience for your teenager. Approaching them with a positive attitude, expecting them to cooperate fully, is very important. Chapters 11 through 13 offer guidance on working with school personnel to make sure that your teenager's learning problems are identified and that appropriate accommodations are provided in the classroom. The federal laws discussed in Chapter 14 should provide legal leverage, if needed, to obtain appropriate services at school.

The Physician's Task. Building a strong partnership with the physician is also crucial. As Chapters 5 and 6 explain, this partnership is the key to finding the right medication regimen. Your family must work with the doctor to determine which medications and dosages seem to work best. If maximum benefits are not obtained from medication, your family may need to talk with your physician about making adjustments. If these changes are still not successful, you can request a consultation with a psychiatrist in hopes of finding a more effective medication regimen.

The Parents' Job. You may want to attend a parenting class, an ADHD education class, or get counseling for yourself to help you be a more effective parent and advocate. Learning new parenting strategies, tips for promoting resilience and self-confidence, and ways of diffusing potentially volatile situations are essential skills for parents to master. In fact, these strategies may result in greater long-term dividends than sending your teenager to someone to be "fixed." You will be better prepared to handle crises if you have developed effective communication and parenting skills. Researchers like Dr. Barkley remind us that counseling is not that effective for our children nor for adults. Barkley explains that ADHD is not a knowledge deficit; it is a performance deficit. Dr. Sam Goldstein often tells audiences, children with ADHD know what to do, but don't always do what they know. *Education about ADHD is one of the very best tools to help you and your teen cope successfully with this challenging disorder!*

Developing an Individualized Treatment Plan

This chapter will help you develop an individualized treatment plan for your teenager. By filling out the blank forms in this chapter, you can address each of five potential problem areas:

1. your teenager's self-esteem and coping skills;
2. family life;
3. medication;
4. school performance; and
5. community activities.

It may help to refer to completed sample forms contained in earlier chapters. If need be, remember to ask for help from your teenager's physician, teacher, school counselor, social worker, or psychologist to complete the treatment plan. Other parents may also be able to help you develop a plan. You can meet parents through programs at CHADD, ADDA-SR, ADDA, Federation of Families, Mental Health Association,

NAMI-CAN, or other support meetings. Addresses for these organizations are listed in the Resource Guide.

As you develop your treatment plan, remember that you should seek services in the most normal manner possible. It is important that services not be stigmatizing, traumatizing, intrusive, or overly restrictive. Try first to obtain services for your teenager in her natural environment—through supportive services offered at home and in a regular classroom at school, rather than through residential treatment.

Do not feel as if you have to complete all the forms or try all the strategies recommended in this book. If your teen's problems are simple, you may decide to fill out only a few forms. You may even be able to develop an informal plan in your head. Use this material in whatever way is helpful to you. Again, do not feel guilty if you cannot complete this process alone. Complete as much as you can and then ask someone else for help.

"At first I thought there was no way I could develop an individualized treatment plan for my son. But when I realized how useful it would be for him, I felt compelled to get it done. I sat down and worked and worked with it. My advice to other parents is to find an experienced parent who can hold your hand while you go through this process.

"The individualized treatment plan worked perfectly for my son. Of course, we had periods of adjustment and it took awhile to get the details worked out. When I showed the school people all these forms I'd completed for the individualized treatment plan, they were really impressed and treated me with more respect. Once we all agreed on a plan, things worked much better at school. They were more in tune with what was going on because we worked hard to put the plan into action. We had really begun to work as a team. When a crisis came up, we handled it together."

You may find it helpful to complete the action steps listed below:

Identify Strengths and Build Self-Esteem

Develop a Unique Profile (Form 1). Each teenager with an attention deficit is unique. Some have serious learning problems; others do not. Some have major deficits in executive skills; others do not. The many factors listed on this form can all affect a teenager's self-esteem, performance in school, and outcome in life. Some problem behaviors, such as academic failure or friends who are a bad influence, can be changed;

others cannot. Identify the things you can control and make an effort to change them. Completing this form will increase your awareness of your teenager's unique characteristics. (See Table 1-2, Chapter 1.)

Identify Strengths (Form 2). Teenagers with ADD or ADHD can be extremely charming and creative. Take the time to identify *your* teenager's strengths by completing Form 2. It is also important to make your teenager more aware of her strengths. Many teenagers with ADD inattentive may only see their failures and shortcomings. Parents, too, may tend to focus on problem behaviors. Reading about the concept of reframing negative characteristics, as discussed in Chapter 4, should help you and your teenager redirect your thinking in a more positive way. (See Table 4-1.)

Follow the Guiding Principles for Interactions. Guiding principles for parent/teenager interactions are discussed in Chapter 8: give unconditional positive regard, treat as an equal partner, maintain good communication, provide structure and supervision, look for the good, be positive, help build self-esteem, avoid negatives, weather each crisis as it occurs, and nurture yourself. Obviously, it is important to encourage your teenager to move toward independence, accepting increased responsibility over time. In addition, treat him with respect by involving him in decisions affecting his life. (See Table 8-4.)

Build Self-Esteem (Form 3). Develop a plan to build self-esteem, as discussed in Chapter 7. Encourage your teenager to pursue his interests. Give him opportunities to participate in activities that make him feel special. Identify interests or talents such as sports, art, and music in which he can develop skills. Let him select the activities he likes best. Completing this form will help guide your efforts. (See Table 8-2, Chapter 8.)

Provide Appropriate Medication

Assess the Effectiveness of Medication (Form 4). Monitoring your teenager's response to medication is critical and is discussed in detail in Chapter 6. Finding the right medication(s) requires fine tuning; seldom will a family luck out and find the right medication and dosage on the first try. Informal reports from parents, teachers, and the teenager are needed to determine whether academics and behavior have improved. Completing this form can help you judge whether medication is working to improve behavior and school performance. Your physician may also monitor possible effects and effectiveness of medication through use of formal measures such as behavior rating scales. Most behavior rating scales, however, can pick up a reduction in inappropriate behavior, but may not capture increases in attention and improvement in school work. Parents, teachers, and teens should complete this form. If improvement is not significant, go back to the drawing board and fine tune medications or make classroom accommodations. (See Table 6-7, Chapter 6.)

Chart Peak Medication Time (Form 5). Sometimes it helps to chart the period of time when medication should be effective, based upon the information provided in Chapter 6. Charting can help you understand just how long medicine should last. Once stimulant medications are absorbed, they reach a peak time of effectiveness and then their effectiveness gradually decreases until the medicine is out of the body. For example if Adderall XR or Concerta is taken at 7:00 a.m., don't expect it to last past 4 or 5 o'clock. Typically the teen may need a small dose of a short-acting medicine for homework. During the years when primarily short-acting medications were prescribed, it was critical to chart medication coverage to ensure all day coverage

at school. Fortunately, charting medication is not as essential as it once was.

Charting is still critical for any medications that last less than six or so hours. For example, the effect of some intermediate time release medications such as Metadate ER, Ritalin SR, regular Adderall, and Dexedrine SR last from 6 to 8 hours. Depending on when your teen takes his medicine—for example, at 6:00 am—it could wear off by lunch or two o'clock. If your teenager is having problems at school, check to see if his problems are related to times when his medication has worn off or he has totally forgotten to take it.

Note the time he takes medication, how long it takes to become effective, when it wears off, and time of each class. Then compare this with which classes he may be failing or where behavior problems occur. For example, you may discover that he is passing English at 10:00, but is failing and talking back to teachers in algebra at 2:00, when medication has worn off. You may need to consider changing medications, take more medicine or take it later in the morning, or reschedule classes. (See Table 6-6, Chapter 6.)

Discuss Medication Change with Your Physician. If anger, irritability, frustration, or aggression continue to cause problems at home and school, changes in medication may be needed. "Rebound" or academic frustration may be causing the problem, or the right medication or correct dosage may not yet have been found. Talk with your physician about the possibility of adjusting current medication. Don't be afraid to tactfully suggest changes: "A speaker at CHADD mentioned that Adderall XR, Concerta, and Strattera last several hours, eliminating the need for a noon dose. Could we try one of them?"

When a teenager says, 'Concerta didn't work' or 'I don't like the way it makes me feel,' parents should ask questions and get more details. This doesn't necessarily mean that the medication isn't working. The frequency, dosage, or medication strength may be wrong. Ask your teen to work with you and the doctor. 'We should be able to make adjustments in the medication to address your concerns.'

As discussed in Chapter 6, the doctor may explore a variety of options:

1. increase the dosage;
2. change to a long-acting medication;
3. give a smaller dose for short-acting medication later in the day; or
4. prescribe stimulants plus an antidepressant.

For those who may respond best to short-acting medications:

1. give stimulants more frequently during the day (3 or 4 doses); or
2. combine regular and sustained release (SR) stimulants such as Ritalin.

For years traditional wisdom dictated that other interventions such as a positive behavior modification program should be tried first, then medication should be prescribed to correct the remaining problem behaviors. As explained in Chapters 1, 5, and 6, research has proven that wisdom wrong! So if an attention deficit has been diagnosed after a careful evaluation and the teen is struggling at home and school, then medication should be given immediately. Behavioral strategies may be implemented simultaneously.

Consider a Psychiatric Consultation. If you and your family physician are unable to resolve the problems with anger, aggression, impulsivity, irritability, or sleep disturbances, you might consider a psychiatric consultation. As discussed in Chapters 5 and 6, psychiatrists are sometimes more knowledgeable about a broader range of medications that may be used to treat coexisting problems. When Adderall, Concerta, or Strattera is not enough, medications such as Zoloft, Celexa, or Lexapro may be beneficial. Third tier medications such as Clonidine or Depakote may also help. Sometimes combinations of these medications may be prescribed.

Seek Additional Treatment Resources as Needed. If your teenager continues to struggle with some of the more serious problems discussed in Chapter 10 (suicidal thoughts or drug abuse), you may need to consider other treatment options that are discussed in Chapter 5. Options include special education classes, a classroom companion, an academic coach, respite, intensive in-home services, a day treatment program, after school programs, summer programs, and as a last resort, residential treatment. Again, remember to first consider services that will enable your teenager to remain in his home and local school.

Identify Challenging Behaviors

Identify Challenging Behaviors at Home and School (Form 6). You and your teenager should identify the behaviors that are most challenging at home. Teachers should help identify the behaviors that are most challenging at school. Completing this form should help you identify these behaviors and possible intervention strategies. If there are several problems, pick one or two behaviors of greatest concern to start working on and develop a plan for intervention.

Parents should also keep in mind the value of Functional Behavior Assessments (FBA) in determining the "trigger" contributing to misbehavior and helping identify key target areas for intervention. FBAs are discussed in Chapter 14 and more detailed guidelines and blank forms are available in *Teaching Teens*.

Select Appropriate Interventions. Chapter 8 discusses general principles helpful in raising a teenager with an attention deficit. In addition, intervention strategies for dealing with common behaviors are included in Chapter 9 (Table 9-1) and more serious problem behaviors in Chapter 10 (Table 10-4). Remember, if you can't change your child, change the environment. Work with the school to anticipate problem situations and develop a plan to cope with them.

Eliminate Academic Agony

Make School More Positive (Form 7). Chapter 11 discusses steps to help make school a more positive place for your teenager. (You can also refer to *Teaching Teens with ADD and ADHD*, the companion guide for this book, for more suggestions.) Decide which action steps you should take on Form 7, below, and check them off when you have finished them.

Identify Learning Problems and Make Accommodations (Form 8). Although you *could* leave your teenager's education up to his teachers, he will be much more likely to succeed in school if you get involved. Along with teachers, you should identify your teenager's academic strengths, learning problems, deficits in executive skills, and possible classroom accommodations. Form 8 can help you to do so. To complete Form 8, you will need: old report cards (teacher comments and grades); standardized test scores; IQ test scores, such as the WISC, indices and subtest scale scores if available; academic achievement tests, such as the IOWA; and Table 13-1, "Identifying Common Learning Problems" in Chapter 13. (See Table 12-2, Chapter 12; Tables 14-1 & 14-2, Chapter 14.)

It may take several attempts, with input from trusted teachers, doctors, and other professionals, to fine tune the information. Once the form is completed, however, it will be invaluable during future school years.

You can use it to discuss the best teaching strategies with new teachers at the beginning of each school year.

Make accommodations to the regular classroom as soon as possible. Then monitor your child's progress to determine if accommodations are effective. Does his academic performance improve? If not, adjustments to the original treatment plan may be needed. Remember to ask your teenager which interventions and accommodations he needs and is willing to accept.

Work on the Home Front to Avoid Academic Hassles. Chapter 12 suggests strategies for ensuring that your teenager completes his homework assignments and improves his performance at school. If needed, you can identify which strategies to use by checking off needed interventions on Table 12-2 in Chapter 12, plus Summaries 24-27, *Teaching Teens.*

Use Federal Laws to Obtain Educational Services. Many teenagers with attention deficits have serious learning problems including deficits in executive skills that interfere with their ability to learn. Remember that the federal laws discussed in Chapter 14 guarantee that students with disabilities, including ADD or ADHD, have a right to a free appropriate public education. This includes providing accommodations in the regular classroom.

Treat Teachers as Respected Allies. How you approach school personnel about potential learning problems and accommodations is extremely important! Treating the teacher as an ally and partner is more likely to be successful. Most people do not respond favorably to an adversarial approach. You may want to try saying something like this:

"My son has some serious learning problems that are causing him problems at school. I have tried to identify his learning problems and some potential accommodations that may help him do better academically. The information contained in this chart [Form 8] reflects information you have provided me, plus input from other sources: previous teacher conferences, standardized tests, past homework efforts, report cards, past academic and intellectual assessments, and my own observations. I need your help to fine tune this document and make it more accurate and helpful. You may have some ideas I haven't even thought of."

(If the form is completed near the end of the school year): *"Identifying learning problems and accommodations now should help him next year when we start off the new school year. We'll have this information to help the next teacher."*

Determine Who Will Monitor and Provide Support to Improve School Performance. Some parents avoid involvement in school-related work because it becomes such a hostile battlefield. Instead, they hire a neighbor, friend, relative, private tutor, or staff at an after school program to take on these responsibilities. Other parents are actively involved, even in high school and college. These parents are able to monitor and tutor their teenager without major battles.

Plan for the Future

When the time is right, begin planning for your teenager's future after high school. According to federal law, planning for the transition from high school must begin early for eligible students, at least by age 16. As explained earlier, the transition plan must be results oriented. Information in Chapter 15 will help you schedule an untimed SAT or ACT if needed, explore career options, and learn about technical school or college. Don't forget that protections under Section 504, including classroom accommodations such as untimed tests, continue through technical school and college. Apply early and provide documentation to support your request for accommodations.

Nurture Yourself

Parents can burn out from the demands of raising a teenager with an attention deficit. As discussed in Chapters 3 and 8, if you don't nurture yourself, you won't have any emotional energy left to give to your child. This makes taking good care of yourself a crucial element of the treatment program for your child. Sometimes what you may need most is for someone to listen with a sympathetic ear while you vent your emotions. If you have emotional support, plus information learned from other parents, a teacher, counselor, or your doctor, then you can be more patient and understanding, and can take crisis situations in stride more easily.

Participate in Parent Groups. You may benefit from participating in local parent education and support groups such as those offered by CHADD, ADDA-SR, Federation of Families, LDA, MHA, or NAMI-CAN. These groups are a wonderful source of information and support for families. Other suggestions for nurturing yourself are offered in Chapter 8.

Learn New Parenting Skills. Becoming a more effective parent will give you greater confidence as you face the challenge of raising a teenager with an attention deficit. Suggestions for improving your parenting skills are given throughout this book.

Educate Yourself and Your Teen about ADHD. Experts tell us that one of the most effective ways to cope with attention deficits is to fully educate yourself about the condition. This strategy is even more effective than counseling. Education may be obtained from a variety of sources: reading books from my reading list, attending conferences or parent training, viewing videos, reading CHADD or ADDitude newsletters, and attending local parent support groups.

Some Final Thoughts for Parents

Sometimes it is difficult for parents to know when their teenager has reached his maximum potential. When have the best medications at the right dosages been prescribed? When have all learning problems been identified and proper accommodations made? When should parents stop pushing the system to help their teenager?

*Keep pushing the system
until your teenager succeeds!*

"As a parent of a teenager with ADD, I didn't know how long to keep pushing for answers to my son's problems. I wondered, 'Maybe this is as good as we can make it for him.' Things had improved at home and medication helped him concentrate better at school. But his grades were still terrible and he was just barely getting by in school. I stopped pushing for answers because I thought he had reached his optimum level of functioning.

"In retrospect, I realize he had serious learning problems and deficits in executive skills that were never identified or treated. His big academic breakthrough came in college when he received accommodations such as extended test time and use of a calculator. After barely graduating from high school, he has just finished a successful freshman year in college. My son was unable to articulate his learning problems and their negative impact until he was a college freshman. He is so much happier and self-confident now.

*"My advice to parents is: **If your teenager isn't doing well at home and school, something is still wrong. Keep searching for answers, such as adjustments in medication or classroom accommodations, until your teenager succeeds in both environments!**"*

In trying to help your teenager successfully cope with his or her attention deficit, you may need to play the role of a detective who is trying to solve a mystery. You will have to continue to ask questions and seek answers as you unravel the mysteries of ADD or ADHD and your teenager's unique problems and needs. For some parents, answers won't come easy. You may have to be tenacious in seeking solutions to your child's problems. The good news, however, is that parents of teenagers with attention deficits are no longer alone. Thanks to many parents who have traveled this lonely road and discovered strategies for coping successfully, more information than ever is now available about these teenagers. Hopefully, the information learned from other parents and professionals which is shared in this book will make your search less lonely and overwhelming.

Form 1 Understanding Teenagers with Attention Deficit Disorders

Name: _____ Age: _____ Date: _____

By completing this form, parents should gain a better understanding of their teenager's unique characteristics, personality, strengths, difficulties, and how he or she is different from other teenagers with an attention deficit. In addition to the list of symptoms, all the factors listed below also influence the teenager's behavior, self-esteem, and ability to cope successfully with ADD or ADHD. The severity of the behavior will also vary. Please circle words that best describe your teenager.

DIAGNOSIS: Symptoms of ADD or ADHD may range from mild to severe.

ADHD	mild	moderate	severe
ADD Inattentive	mild	moderate	severe

Coexisting Diagnoses: ADD and ADHD frequently coexist with other disorders

Anxiety	mild	moderate	severe
Depression	mild	moderate	severe
Executive Skill Deficit	mild	moderate	severe
Learning Disability	mild	moderate	severe
Learning Problems	mild	moderate	severe
Sleep Disturbance	mild	moderate	severe
Oppositional Defiant	mild	moderate	severe
Conduct Disorder	mild	moderate	severe
Substance Abuse	mild	moderate	severe

FACTORS INFLUENCING ADD OR ADHD: Other factors influence a teenager's personality and ability to cope successfully with attention deficit disorder. These factors may also vary in intensity: mild/moderate/severe. Teenagers with ADHD and ADD Inattentive may be almost exact opposites in some behaviors. Circle the words that describe your teenager's behavior most of the time.

TEMPERAMENT	GENERAL ISSUES	FAMILY STRESS FACTORS
calm / fidgets	Self-esteem: fair / good	Family understand ADD/ADHD: yes / no
easy going / aggressive	Response to meds: fair / good	
low energy / high energy	Intelligence: average / high	Reasonable discipline: yes / no (not too harsh or lenient)
depressed / happy	Inattentive: yes / no	
irritable / pleasant	Impulsive: yes / no	Open communication: yes / no
sullen / charming	Disorganized: yes / no	Few hostile interactions between teen and parents: yes / no
shy / class clown	Loses things: yes / no	
anxious / relaxed	Forgets things: yes / no	Relatives understand ADD/ADHD (supportive): yes / no
cautious / daring	Complies with requests: yes / no	
gives up / tenacious	Will do chores: yes / no	Family stresses (money, illness, divorce, remarriage): yes / no
compliant / defiant	Truthful: yes / no	
copes well / frustrated	Difficulty falling asleep: yes / no	Moved to new community: yes / no
calm / angry outbursts	Difficulty waking up: yes / no	Attending new school: yes / no
quiet / talks a lot	Restless: yes / no	Two parent family: yes / no
	Self-centered: yes / no	Step parents: yes / no
	Accident prone: yes / no	
	Interrupts: yes / no	
	Few friends: yes / no	

AREAS OF SUCCESS	**POTENTIAL PROBLEM AREAS**	**MORE SERIOUS PROBLEMS**
sports: yes / no	Argues: yes / no	Lies or cons others: yes / no
computers: yes / no	Loses temper: yes / no	Starts fights: yes / no
Game Boy: yes / no	Blames others: yes / no	Bullies or threatens others: yes / no
music/art: yes / no	Annoys others: yes / no	Physically cruel to others: yes / no
drama: yes / no	Easily annoyed: yes / no	Physically cruel to animals: yes / no
debate: yes / no	Spiteful/vindictive: yes / no	Steals without confronting: yes / no
cheerleading: yes / no	Defies/disobeys: yes / no	(shoplifting, credit card fraud)
religious activities: yes / no	Skips school: yes / no	Robs someone: yes / no
hunting/fishing: yes / no	School suspension: yes / no	Breaks into houses, cars: yes / no
academics: yes / no	School expulsion: yes / no	Destroys other's property: yes / no
add others:	Drops out of school: yes / no	Sets fires: yes / no
	Speeding tickets: yes / no	Uses weapons to harm: yes / no
	Substance abuse: yes / no	Forces others to have sex: yes / no
	Sexually active: yes / no	Substance abuse: yes / no
	Access to weapons: yes / no	Runs away from home: yes / no
		Pregnancy: yes / no
		Suicide risk: yes / no
		Car accidents: yes / no
		Before age 13:
		Stays out all night: yes / no
		Truant from school: yes / no

SCHOOL PERFORMANCE	**LEARNING PROBLEMS**	**SPECIFIC LEARNING DISABILITY**
Good handwriting: yes / no	Poor concentration: yes / no	Verbal expression: yes / no
Good reading skills: yes / no	Poor organizational skills: yes / no	Listening comprehension: yes / no
Good writing skills: yes / no	Poor memory: yes / no	Written expression: yes / no
Good vocabulary: yes / no	Lacks attention to detail: yes / no	Reading comprehension: yes / no
Good spelling skills: yes / no	Slow reading: yes / no	Mathematics calculation: yes / no
Good math skills: yes / no	Poor reading comprehension: yes / no	Mathematical reasoning: yes / no
Good organization: yes / no	Slow writing: yes / no	Basic reading skills: yes / no
Good at times tables: yes / no	Slow math calculation: yes / no	
Good at history: yes / no	Poor handwriting: yes / no	
Good at foreign languages: yes / no		
Dislikes school: yes / no	**SCHOOL ENVIRONMENT**	
Forgets assignments: yes / no		
Forgets make-up work: yes / no	School personnel:	
Forgets special projects: yes / no	Positive: yes / no	
Forgets instructions: yes / no	Flexible: yes / no	
Difficulty getting started: yes / no	Accommodations: yes / no	
Test anxiety: yes / no	Reasonable discipline: yes / no	
Failed a class: yes / no	Section 504 elligible: yes / no	
Failed a grade: yes / no	IDEA eligible: yes / no	

Form 2   Discovering Your Teenager's Strengths

Individualized Treatment Planning: "Do Whatever It Takes"

Name: _____ Age:_____ Grade: _____ Date: _____

List your teenager's strengths that you observe at home, at school, and in the community. Remember to reframe negative behaviors more positively as described in Chapters 4 and 8.

STRENGTHS

Home/Community   **School**

_____   _____

_____   _____

_____   _____

_____   _____

_____   _____

_____   _____

_____   _____

_____   _____

_____   _____

_____   _____

_____   _____

EXAMPLES OF REFRAMING NEGATIVE BEHAVIOR:

Examples of reframing negative behaviors may help parents develop a list of their teenager's strengths. Remember, the desirability of behaviors changes over time. Characteristics that are not valued in children in school may be valued in the adult business world. Discuss the teenager's strengths with him. Ask him to add to the list.

bossiness	"leadership" (albeit carried too far)
hyperactivity	"energetic," "high energy," "does ten projects at one time," "works long hours"
strong willed	"tenacious"
day dreamers	"creative," "innovative," "imaginative"
daring	"risk taker," "willing to try new things"
laziness	"laid-back," "Type B personalities live longer"
instigator	"initiator," "innovative"
manipulative	"delegates," "gets others to do the job"
aggressive	"assertive," "doesn't let people take advantage of him"
questions authority	"independent," "free thinker," "makes own decisions"
argumentative	"persuasive," "may be attorney material"
poor handwriting	"maybe they'll be a doctor one day"

Form 3   Building Self-esteem

Individualized Treatment Planning: "Do Whatever It Takes"

Name: _____ **Age:** _____ **Grade:** _____ **Date:** _____

IDENTIFY INTERESTS: Encourage your teenager to pursue his interests Give him the opportunity to participate in activities that make him feel special. Build on strengths listed in Form 2. List interests or talents such as sports, art, music, or debate that could be developed further through special training.

_____   _____

_____   _____

_____   _____

_____   _____

_____   _____

_____   _____

_____   _____

_____   _____

PARTICIPATE IN ACTIVITIES TO BUILD SELF-ESTEEM: Parents may arrange for their teenager to participate in a variety of activities: computer classes, art classes, scuba diving class, modeling, Boy or Girl Scouts, acting in school plays, hunting, fishing, motorcycle racing, water or snow skiing, canoeing, baseball/football/wrestling teams, tennis or golf lessons, summer sports camps, gymnastics, karate, or cheerleading camp. Religious activities should also be considered if appropriate: summer camps, Bible school, singing in a choir, public speaking on programs, or activity retreats (snow skiing, camping). Let the teenager select those activities he likes best. If he has no special interests, parents may sign him up for a variety of activities and see which skills emerge as strengths.

_____   _____

_____   _____

_____   _____

_____   _____

_____   _____

_____   _____

Form 4   Assess Medication Effectiveness

Individualized Treatment Planning: "Do Whatever It Takes"

Name: _____   Grade: _____   Date & class: _____

Completed by: _____   Time of day observed: _____

Medication: _____   Dosage: _____

To assess the impact of medications on a student's school work, each parent and teacher should answer several key questions. When medication is working properly and learning problems have been identified, the student should be doing much better in school. Please circle the number that best describes the student's behavior.

Academic Performance:

	Strongly Agree	Agree	Neutral	Disagree	Strongly Disagree
When the student is in my class, s/he					
1. Pays attention	1	2	3	4	5
2. Completes class & homework	1	2	3	4	5
3. Does work correctly	1	2	3	4	5
4. Complies with requests	1	2	3	4	5
5. Makes passing grades	1	2	3	4	5

ADD/ADHD-Related Behaviors, including Executive Function Deficits

If the student is on medication and is not doing well in school, what else could be causing continuing problems? Are there any ADD/ADHD-related behaviors that are interfering with the student's ability to succeed in school?

ADD/ADHD-related Behaviors:

The student:

6. is organized (finds and turns in work)	1	2	3	4	5
7. remembers things (assignments, tests, etc.)	1	2	3	4	5
8. manages time well/ plans ahead	1	2	3	4	5
9. is on time to class	1	2	3	4	5
10. is on time to school	1	2	3	4	5
11. thinks before acting or speaking	1	2	3	4	5
12. is awake and alert in class	1	2	3	4	5
13. gets along with friends	1	2	3	4	5
14. gets angry easily & blows up	1	2	3	4	5

Are you aware of any sleep problems? The student

15. falls asleep easily	1	2	3	4	5
16. wakes up easily	1	2	3	4	5

Comments: _____

_____

_____

_____

Form 5 Chart Peak Medication Time

Individualized Treatment Planning: "Do Whatever It Takes"

Name: _____ Age: _____ Grade: _____ Date: _____

Medication: _____ Dosage: _____

Chart the period of time each day when medication is effective. Compare this with when misbehavior or class failure is a problem. Medication wearing off may be a major contributing factor. Classes or times for taking medication may need to be changed. Please note the time when: (1) Meds are taken; (2) Meds start to work; (3) Meds have worn off; and (4) Each class is scheduled. Give the same information if a second dose is given at school. Refer to Table 6-6 in Chapter 6.

Time	Medication/dose	Class/activity	Medication Effectiveness
7:00 A.M.			
7:30			
8:00			
8:30			
9:00			
9:30			
10:00			
10:30			
11:00			
11:30			
12:00 P.M.			
12:30			
1:00			
1:30			
2:00			
2:30			
3:00			
3:30			
4:00			
4:30			
5:00			
5:30			
6:00			
6:30			
7:00			
7:30			
8:00			
8:30			
9:00 +			

Form 6   Identifying Challenging Behaviors

Individualized Treatment Planning: "Do Whatever It Takes"

Name: _____ Age:_____ Grade: _____ Date: _____

Identify two or three challenging behaviors both at home and school and select intervention strategies. Information in Chapters 9-12 should be helpful in completion of this form.

CHALLENGING BEHAVIORS

At Home/School	Intervention/Comments

Form 7   Make School More Positive

Individualized Treatment Planning: "Do Whatever It Takes"

Determine which of these action steps will increase academic successes and help make school a more positive place for your teen. Then check each step off as it is completed.

Chapter 5

_____ Ensure peak medication effectiveness is reached during school hours

Chapter 6

_____ Identify and treat coexisting conditions

Chapter 11

_____ Educate school personnel about ADD and ADHD
_____ Educate yourself about school philosophy
_____ Request a teacher assignment
_____ Schedule a conference
_____ Notify school officials that your teenager has ADD or ADHD
_____ Treat teachers with respect
_____ Build rapport with school before a crisis
_____ Find the "Voice of Reason"
_____ Work through the guidance counselor
_____ Phase out interventions over time, if appropriate
_____ Be knowledgeable: sound knowledgeable!!!
_____ Express appreciation

Chapter 12

_____ Monitor and provide assistance with homework

Chapter 13

_____ Identify learning problems, including deficits in executive skills
_____ Identify accommodations needed for academic and executive skill deficits
_____ Request services in a regular classroom
_____ Obtain assistance with or without IDEA eligibility
_____ Request a teacher change, if needed
_____ Develop a contingency plan for crisis

Chapter 14

_____ Know key provisions of IDEA and Section 504
_____ Request an evaluation for services under IDEA or Section 504
_____ Participate in development of the IEP or Section 504 Plan

Form 8   Identifying Learning Problems and School Accommodations

Individualized Treatment Planning: "Do Whatever It Takes"

Name: _____ Age: _____ Grade: _____ Date: _____

Identify potential learning problems and possible classroom accommodations. Material in Chapter 13 should be helpful in completion of this form. After you have done the first draft, discuss it with a trusted former teacher, a counselor, guidance counselor, school psychologist, a child study team at school, or your teenager's physician to confirm and, if needed, correct your assessment.

Learning Problem	Behavior Observed	Classroom Accommodations

17

Words of Wisdom from the Kids

My intense interest in attention deficit disorders first began in the late 1980s when our sons, Alex and Steven, were diagnosed with ADD inattentive and ADHD, respectively. As teenagers, they shared many of the typical characteristics of the condition. However, they were also different in many ways. One has high energy and loves to talk; the other is quieter and more laid back. One has coexisting problems with executive skills such as organization, memory, and time management; the other does not.

Actually, Alex and Steven "inherited" each other as brothers by virtue of my marriage in 1986. Alex's ADD inattentive was diagnosed in 1987, when he was 12 years old. Steven was diagnosed as having ADHD in 1989, when he was 20. Imagine our surprise several years later when our 35-year-old daughter, Audrey, was also diagnosed. As with many parents, her ADHD was discovered after her son was diagnosed. Although the disorder appears to have skipped both my husband and me, we each have other relatives who also seem to have attention deficits.

Over a period of several years, we observed that several of our sons' friends appeared to have similar symptoms. At first we thought it was our imagination—projection possibly—but referral to a physician confirmed a diagnosis of ADD or ADHD for six or seven of their friends. As explained earlier, young people with attention deficits may feel more comfortable with teenagers who think and act like them and tend to gravitate toward each other as friends.

My circle of friends and professional colleagues who have children with ADD or ADHD has broadened considerably over the past twenty years. Through this communication network, I have had the opportunity to interview several teenagers with attention deficits from across the country. Each teenager's story and experiences are similar yet different in some ways. Some of the young men and women have co-occurring learning disabilities, anxiety, depression, or oppositional defiant disorder, and others do not.

A Unique Perspective. This 2006 edition includes interviews with some of our original teen contributors at age 16 and then again as young adults. It is my hope that parents will be inspired by the successes these young people achieved despite their attention deficits. The chapter also includes interviews with some new teens on the block. These interviews highlight the uniqueness of each teenager. The contrasts in their experiences may help parents understand the differences between the types of attention deficit disorder, the complications that arise when attention deficit disorder is accompanied by learning disabilities or deficits in executive skills, and the frustrations of dealing with the disorder.

The young people who contributed to this chapter range in age from 14 to 30. The feelings they describe—their pain, confusion, anxiety, fears, and joys—as well as their academic difficulties despite good intentions, touch the heart. Their stories of living with an attention deficit are sensitive and insightful, and reflect their courageous spirits. Having ADD or ADHD isn't easy, but these teenagers have developed a better understanding of their disorder and have learned to cope successfully. You may want to share these inspiring stories with your teenager.

ADD and ADHD: 15 Years Later...

As parents of teenagers with attention deficits, my husband and I were often frightened about what the future held for our children, especially during the disastrous middle and high school years. If you have that same concern, this next section will be of special interest to you. Three of the teens from the original 1995 edition of this book were interviewed fifteen years later to see how they were faring. Although there were no Rhodes Scholar in the bunch, these young people have done exceptionally well, considering their challenges. My husband and I are extremely proud of them. For the most part, they are good, hard working, honest, young adults. Among the group of eight teens who were part of our local "ADHD family," two are college graduates, two became Marines, three work in management positions, and one former class clown now gets paid for doing special promotions for a rock radio station. Most of them have been married and have children and a few are divorced. Consistent with national statistics, a couple have had serious drug problems. One has had serious brushes with the law.

Audrey and Steven Today

Obviously we are very proud of our children. Audrey, a former assistant vice president of a bank, made the difficult but necessary choice to be a stay-at-home mom. Steven is now the general manager of a successful manufacturing plant. Both are also active in their communities: Audrey as a PTA president, Sunday school superintendent, and church deacon; Steven as a Sunday school teacher, baseball and soccer coach, and chairman of the school's annual mother-son fishing tournament.

Both are also parents of children with ADHD. Audrey's son, Nathan, who is 14, is featured in our survival guide for teens, *A Bird's-Eye View of Life with ADD and ADHD*. Steven's 11-year-old son, Hunter, enjoys baseball and fishing. Both were diagnosed early, by first grade or so, and have done extremely well on medication. We are very blessed that our grandsons both began treatment early, are doing well in school,

and have thus far avoided the academic struggles their parents faced. For pictures and more information about our family, visit www.chrisdendy.com.

Our Son Alex, Then and Now

Profile: *Alex has ADD inattentive (without hyperactivity) and has learning problems that include slow cognitive processing speed and deficits in executive skills, including poor working memory. He is 30 now and a college graduate. He is a jack-of-all-trades at a company that sells guns and specializes in hand-loading ammunition. He was diagnosed at age 12.*

Alex at Age 16

When you have a disability like ADD, you don't know what "normal" attention and concentration are. You just assume that everyone concentrates the same way you do. It's like having a vision problem. You don't know what the real world looks like or that you have a vision problem until you are tested and get glasses. In the same way, you don't know you have ADD and problems with attention and concentration until you take Ritalin and find out what is it like to be able to concentrate.

Second grade is where the trouble started. This is where I discovered writing, and that I didn't like it. One day when I was frustrated, I stopped writing. When the teacher asked me to do the work, I told her to do it herself.

Third grade I didn't get along with my teacher at all. She couldn't understand why I was so slow, so I spent a lot of time with the principal. This teacher was so bad that even my mom didn't like this woman. I wasn't doing so well in school and they referred me to be tested. I scored pretty high and they said I was eligible for the gifted program.

Fourth grade I was moved to a new school. This school was much more fun and easier than my old school. I liked my teacher that year. She was nice to me.

Fifth grade I was lucky enough to get the same teacher again. This class helped me with my work habits. The thing I liked best about this class was its pets, especially the snakes. I liked taming wild snakes, and I was bitten almost every day.

I was not prepared for sixth grade. It was exactly like high school. I had six classes, six teachers, and six homework assignments every day. This was a very big change for me, but I hung in there.

Seventh grade I moved to Georgia from Tallahassee, Florida. The schools became a little bit less like high school since I had three teachers instead of six. I again got myself into trouble by cursing at a teacher. This incident helped me in a way, because I became good friends with the principal.

Eighth grade I was transferred to another school. Mr. Ford, the principal, also transferred to this new school. That year one of my teachers was not a friendly teacher, but I controlled my temper this time.

Ninth grade wasn't as bad as I had thought it would be. Some of the work was harder for me, which caused me to slack off a little bit. The Ritalin helped me a lot when trying to stay on task.

My sophomore year seemed to be a little bit easier, but I still slacked off some. I would usually have low grades that I would pull up near the end of the semester. My grades were pretty much borderline, but I had a few high grades.

So far my junior year has been the same with borderline grades.

Sometimes I was a troublemaker at school. I didn't like to do the work. Sometimes I made fun of the teacher. Teachers said I didn't assert myself very much. Mom said that teachers told her that I was never a discipline problem. I guess the things I did to make them mad were pretty subtle. I didn't do anything real bad.

I like for my teachers to treat me with respect. If a teacher is nice to me, then I usually do better in that class. If I don't like them and I think they're mean, sometimes I will fail the class.

When I'm not on Ritalin, I tend to be more impulsive and more aggressive. I go on instinct. When I am on my medicine, I actually think about my decisions more clearly and what will happen if I do something. I can do my work. I can really concentrate a lot better. I can sit for two or three hours and work on my homework.

I am not constantly on Ritalin so I can't constantly think about what will happen. I forget why I was grounded and feel like my parents are just being mean to me. It doesn't connect in my mind that I really did something wrong. Punishment doesn't work a lot of times because it doesn't connect in my mind.

I've been stopped for speeding lots of times. I hate to tell you but I was stopped for speeding seven times in the first seven months I was driving. I have slowed down a lot. Tickets and speeding are starting to connect in my mind a little more now. I have to go to court and pay money. They take my license away. But once you get your license back and are out driving, you forget. You don't realize that they can take it away again. I always say I won't do this again after I get a ticket. Getting a ticket really upsets me and I feel really stressed out. My Toyota 4-runner is the love of my life. I live to drive.

If you asked me to describe myself, I'd say I try to be generous to other people a lot. I get along well with a lot of people. I have a lot of friends. My friends say I'm a take-charge kind of guy. I am adventuresome. I like to come up with ideas. I try to make things fun.

Alex at Age 30

AFTER HIGH SCHOOL

After I graduated from high school, I moved away to attend college. I guess I did okay grade-wise, but it was tough at times. Some of my classes were hard, plus getting up on time was really difficult. I also had a lot of other things I wanted to do. I was really active in my fraternity; and my fraternity brothers elected me to our executive committee. I was the D.J. for a lot of our parties.

After awhile I got really tired of school, so I stayed out of college for a year. During that time I took a course and became a licensed private investigator. For a couple of years I worked as a P.I., even after I returned to college.

I had trouble deciding on a major: at first I thought computers, then maybe communications. Finally I settled on forensics. My last few years in college I was a much better student. I graduated from college with a 3.22 grade point average with a major in forensics and a minor in computers. One thing that really helped was finally getting my medication right. My major professor and I got along really well and I became very involved in activities in the criminal justice department. My classmates elected me vice president and later president of the criminal justice fraternity.

While I was in college my mother and I wrote a book for teenagers with attention deficits—*A Bird's-Eye View of Life with ADD and ADHD*. I like to do a lot of different things, so I was able to contribute on several levels. Since I have lived with ADD all my life, as the coauthor, I had lots of firsthand experiences to write about. In addition, I also brainstormed with mom about specific content ideas for the book. My other contributions included the design of the book cover, internal layout of the text, using professional publishing software, cropping and inserting pictures, creating the scientific drawings, and the final rendering of the cartoons. Since the publication of our book, I've been invited to participate on numerous panel discussions about attention deficit disorders around the country and in England.

My strong computer skills enabled me to create and serve as webmaster for the website for our family business, Cherish the Children—www.chrisdendy.com. Whenever there's a computer crisis, I'm the "go-to-guy." In addition to my love for computers, I've always enjoyed a wide variety of activities including scuba diving and photography.

MY WORK NOW

Today I work for an ammunition company that produces specialized rounds for military and law enforcement applications. Our equipment and ammunition are in great demand because of their high quality and are often the preferred choice of gun manufacturers and government agencies alike. As the director of research and development, I have been in charge of designing several special purpose rounds. I also double as the advertising director: I designed their business logo and have created several unique magazine ads. Right now I'm working on the company website. My life is never dull at work: we have a testing facility behind our shop where I frequently test fire the rounds I'm designing in machine guns and large caliber rifles.

In addition, I have also enjoyed working occasionally for a major national beverage company. I have helped with sales promotions at bars, concerts, and NASCAR races.

MY CHALLENGES AT WORK

The company where I work has had great advantages for me. The work pace is not as hectic and my boss is pretty flexible. In addition, I especially like the fact that my work responsibilities vary greatly. I've done everything from advertising, installing and wiring our new computer network and phone system, and computer repair, to selling guns and ammunition, loading ammunition, assembling machine guns, and my favorite—research and development.

At this point in my life, I've become more organized: my computer and PDA/phone have helped a great deal with that. I use the PDA calendar function so that I am reminded of birthdays, appointments and deadlines. In some ways time management is still difficult, but I've gotten better. I've learned to allow more time when traveling or completing job assignments. I still take medication and that makes a huge difference.

MY LIFE AT HOME

I'm still single, but I've found an extraordinary girlfriend. She's smart, beautiful, and best of all, she likes me as much as I like her. We complement each other in many ways. She has high energy and enjoys adventure. For Valentine's Day, she treated me to a weekend trip where we both went hang-gliding. Thank goodness she's pretty patient and can accept me for who I am. We have great communication skills. Although we still have disagreements, I'm proud of the fact that we can talk through any issues of concern. My sleep problems that were so bad in college are pretty much under control now. When my alarm goes off, I get up with few if any problems.

MY ADVICE

At times having ADD was really tough for me. So when I think back about how I coped with my attention deficit, I think about the helpful things my parents did. Amazingly my parents didn't seem to get discouraged or think I was a lost cause. Perhaps most importantly, my parents wouldn't give up on me, even when I was in my rebellious teenage stage. Thankfully, they never said I've had enough (at least not that I know of and not out loud) and never called the state to come to pick me up. I guess what helped me the most was having a good life coach during my teenage years and into adulthood. My parents were always there for me. They helped me stay on top of things, especially my school work, and kept me from getting discouraged.

I think disciplining teenagers with attention deficits takes a certain balance between not spoiling and not beating a kid when they've made a mistake. Obviously, you don't want to be too lenient—you don't want to give in to every whim of your child. On the other hand, you want to set certain limits without disciplining them too harshly either. If you find the right balance, it works out great. I was lucky to have that balance with my parents.

Being educated about my ADD was also incredibly helpful. Because my parents were motivated to learn all they could about attention deficits, I was educated all along from age 12, when I was first diagnosed, until today. That helped me understand what was going on with my own thought processes. I knew what to look for when I was fading or when I was struggling with a problem. My bottom line advice is this: believe in your child and yourself and don't ever give up!

Alex's Friends Lewis and Shawn

Most of Alex's friends also had ADHD and hung out at our house. Eventually, as a matter of self-defense, we referred all of them in for diagnosis and treatment. The first picture of Alex and his friends was taken when they were high school juniors and the second taken at an informal ten-year reunion the boys arranged. Standing in the same order from left to right in both pictures: Shawn, Lewis, Robert, Alex and Chad. We are incredibly proud of each of these young men and their unique accomplishments. Each has struggled but found a special niche in life—a radio special promotions guy, a salesman, and an electrician. This section contains two interviews with Lewis and Shawn—one at age 16 or 17 and then again as young adults.

Alex and his friends: Then…

Lewis

Profile: *Lewis has ADHD and learning disabilities. His learning disabilities were diagnosed in second grade, but ADHD wasn't diagnosed until he was a junior in high school. Today he is 30 and is working for a leading new rock radio station in Atlanta doing special promotions. He is hugely popular when he does live onstage performances. He has recently received a promotion and is also the on-air back-up traffic reporter.*

Lewis at Age 17

My mom tells me I was born two months premature. I weighed 2 pounds 11 ounces. I had to stay at the hospital for six weeks before I could go home.

I was always getting into stuff. I was always curious about things and had to explore or check out everything. My mom must have thought I was a terror. Once I vacuumed all the water out of the toilet. One time I got a can of mace and accidentally sprayed it in my face.

I stuck rings in light sockets and knives in the toaster . . . I got shocked. I did it at least four more times even though I got shocked. Once I played in a big bed of fire ants. I was covered with bites. I ran in the house and jumped in the bathtub.

I used to talk a lot when I was little. Kids in school called me "motor mouth." If I thought of something, I just said it. I wouldn't think twice. It would just come out.

When I was growing up, people say I was in constant motion. I guess some people thought I was "hy-

and now.

per." Some people thought I was downright "crazy." I couldn't sit down for a long time. I had trouble sitting down even when I wanted to. I couldn't sit still for school, reading, or even watching TV.

I have always loved entertaining people and making them laugh. When I was in elementary school, I got on top of a car and started dancing just to make people laugh. Unfortunately, my mom and dad weren't laughing when the principal had them come to school to talk about my antics. I have always had a lot of friends.

Teachers have told me that they can see I'll be famous someday. I had long talks with my teachers while I was standing in the hall. Since I was in the hall almost every day, I had my own special spot in the hall. I would peek in the room and make faces. The other students would laugh a lot. I would wander off and peek in the bathroom. I'd run in, flush all the toilets, put soap in all the sinks and on the mirrors, and run back to my spot in the hall.

Usually, teachers seated me up front near their desk or back in the cubbyhole. Sometimes I had to sit in the corner. I'd get mad. It didn't work. I'd still turn around and get someone's attention. I had to sit in a cubicle with high sides in third through seventh grades. They put me there so I wouldn't disturb the other students.

In the second grade they found out I had a learning disability. I thought I was in "dumb classes." People started making fun of me. They thought I was abnormal. That's why I guess I kept being funny: to let them know I was just like them . . . maybe even better.

I'm still in a resource room. In one way I am glad I am getting extra help. On the other hand, I don't like getting put down by other students asking "Why are you in that class? Are you dumb? Are you abnormal?" I don't want people to know I'm in a resource room except my close friends. But I am coping better with being in the resource room.

Once I asked my teacher a question about a math problem. In front of the whole class, she asked my why I needed so much extra help. She said, "If you need extra help, then you need to go to the resource room." I was embarrassed and very angry with my teacher for being so insensitive.

I never made very good grades in school when I was little. Now that my ADHD has been diagnosed, I have made better grades. I made my first A in a class …biology. Ritalin lets me concentrate better and focus on what I am doing. I don't shout out in class. I raise my hand. I think my temper is going down. I take time to do my work right rather than doing it half way. When I'm on time-release Ritalin, I can actually feel it kick in. In class one day I was making chicken noises. About three minutes later I felt it kick in and I started doing my work. Teachers ask me if I have taken my medicine. They know when I have and when I haven't. In fact, if I hadn't taken my medicine, I wouldn't be able to sit here long enough to write this story about my life.

When I started taking Ritalin, I took it only when I went to school. My mom had never been around me when I was on Ritalin. Then one day I started a new job and took my medicine before I went to work. So when I came home, the medicine was still working. My mom said that I could actually stand still long enough to have a conversation with her.

Although my family knew I had a learning disability when I was real young, no one ever even mentioned that I might have ADHD. When I was 16, I met Alex in driver's ed class and spent the night the first night I met him. His mom, Ms. Dendy, got to know me and asked if I had ever been checked for ADHD. I found out that Alex and a lot of my friends also had attention deficit disorders. It made me feel more confident in myself when I knew that it wasn't me alone in the dark. Other friends were in the same boat with me.

Lewis at age 30

AFTER HIGH SCHOOL

Right after graduating from high school, I ended up moving to Pennsylvania to live with my father's family. I didn't take any medication. Although I went to work every day as a mason tender—laying concrete blocks—I didn't have any structure. I was so daring that I scared the veteran workers because I would be up five stories high, jumping from one scaffold to another. After all those years in school, I was just having fun. But those times were so hard for me. I knew I really needed medicine. After two years, I moved back to Georgia and tried to get back on my feet. I started taking medicine again.

In some ways it was hard to come back to Georgia because I didn't have any family there anymore. I lived with some friends until we had to move because we couldn't pay the rent. Then I moved in with Alex and his parents for about a year until I could save up some money and could get a good job.

Chris suggested I meet with Vocational Rehabilitation. That got me a job landscaping yards and businesses. After about a year of installing sod, plants, and trees, my boss asked me to learn about irrigation systems. I studied hard and took books and videotapes home so I could learn the trade. Eventually they asked me to be their full-time irrigation man. I was really pretty good at it. You can even ask Chris. I put a sprinkler system in her yard and it still works great! Of course I made certain I took my medication while I was installing it or I would forget what I was doing.

Next I started my own business and ran that for about a year. I thought it would be a cake walk because I knew irrigation so well. I guess I was 21 or 22 and the sky was the limit for me. When I first started I had pretty good referrals from friends and people who knew my work. I thought business would come to me, but I couldn't get enough reliable work. Of course, then I didn't have any insurance and couldn't afford to see my doctor or buy my medicine. I had to work 24-7. I'd start working as soon as my eyes opened and worked at night until they closed. I discovered that I was not organized enough. Looking back on it, I realize I was not ready to be in business on my own, age-wise and experience-wise. I knew I needed medicine but I couldn't afford to get it.

All this time, I didn't give up on my lifetime dream of doing comedy. I did standup in comedy clubs in downtown Atlanta. I also did some comedy in Tennessee and Alabama, plus my dad's company flew me up to entertain at their company Christmas party. I also attended classes to practice my stand-up "improv" comedy.

In 1999 I was selected as the best comic in Atlanta in one contest. Then in 2000 I won the late night laugh-off on WB 36 TV in Atlanta. One of the prizes was a trip to Las Vegas. While we were on that trip, I asked Jill to marry me. Winning the laugh-off opened the door to a great marriage and my job at the radio station.

MY WORK NOW... TRAFFIC BACKUP

Today I have my dream job, but it wasn't easy getting here. I work at the best new rock radio station in Atlanta. When I first started working there part-time, I had to work two other jobs to pay my bills. I worked full time in a medical warehouse cleaning up after sick patients and that was pretty bad.

The favorite part of my job at the station is standing up in front of live audiences and doing my comedy. Technically, my job titles are Street Team Coordinator, Remote Tech, Promotions Assistant, and Back-up Traffic Reporter. I've been there five years and I continue to get promotions plus more opportunities to be on stage entertaining. As a supervisor, I have to hire and manage 27 interns who help us handle our promotions. Here are two examples of our promotions: a local benefit for groups like CARE for tsunami relief and some high school gigs for the great American Smoke Out.

In my job as remote tech, I go to our promotion two hours early, talk with the client, and set up the tent and equipment. Then the disk jockey arrives just in time to do the actual show. My favorite event is the Atlanta Midtown Music festival when I get to perform live on stage. One year I built a PVC catapult and shot Jell-O, grapes, and fish heads into the crowd. We had the largest crowd of any stage.

One afternoon in a crisis, my boss came in and said, get ready, you're going on the air live in a couple of hours to do the traffic report. I was shocked . . . and scared because of my learning disability in reading. But I did just fine. In fact, my bosses say I'm a superstar. As backup traffic reporter, I pull news off "traffic pulse" and listen to other stations that have traffic helicopters. I give five reports an hour on major accidents all around Atlanta. My boss let me know she is a big fan of mine. She says nobody on the face of the earth can do what I do for the radio station. I boost morale.

In some ways it's really funny; everyone at work knows I take medicine. Sometimes they even ask me, "Did you remember to take your medicine?" But they also want to make sure it wears off before I go on stage for a live promotion—because I'm funnier off my medicine. I see no shame in having ADHD. I tell everyone, even the crowds at promotions. If I blurt out something, I might say, "Sorry I gotta focus now, I got ADHD." They always laugh. I've learned to use it to my advantage. When I first came to work, one of my supervisors was talking to me. I had to laugh because he had ADHD too and was taking Adderall. We compared notes on our medications.

I'm proud I've been able to help others who have it too. Once a salesman came up to me. He said he thought he might have ADHD and had been wanting to try medicine. He got diagnosed. He thanked me several times for opening up and telling him about it. Having ADHD is like being in a brotherhood. All of us who have it feel a certain bond.

MY CHALLENGES AT WORK

My greatest challenge now is managing the 27 staff who report to me. I have to keep their lives organized too. Each intern or "roadie" has at least 2 gigs a month, but can do more. I have appointed 6 captains. I also set up a system so that each day I put up a list of new gigs on our website. The roadies can sign up for the gigs they want. I update the website everyday. There is a lot of paperwork to keep up with. I have to tell them where to meet and what time. In addition I make certain they are not overworked. I try to teach them to be energetic and smile. I try to utilize everyone's strengths and be aware of their weaknesses. They seem like kids—they're just 18 to 24 years old.

At work I have learned to get organized. In my job there are 50 million things going on at the same time. I have to write things down and highlight things. On my ride in to work, I take my 5 mg of regular Dexedrine. It keeps me so focused. As soon as I get in I've learned to focus on the most important things first—I send emails and organize schedules. I get most of the important things done before 2 or 3 o'clock. Toward the end of the day when my medicine wears off, sometimes I'll take another one if I need it. I don't see myself ever being able to stop taking medicine.

MY LIFE AT HOME

I work all day long and then drive 2 hours to get home. Even though my work schedule is really crazy, I try to leave it all at work once I get home. It's all about family; I'm a dad and husband first and foremost. Jill, my wife, is my best friend. I'm so comfortable around her and I can tell her anything. We have a truly loving family. She is very organized and pays all our bills. My check gets direct deposited into our account. We have bought our own home.

Our 2-year-old son, Ryley, is the joy of my life. We ride bikes and skateboards together. Jill takes care of Ryley and keeps house. She has always been in my corner and wanted me to do what I needed to do to be happy. When I wanted to go to work at the radio station, she told me to go for it. She always said and made me believe that good things happen to good people.

MY ADVICE

I know that nothing in life is ever easy. But once I was diagnosed and had the right medicine, my life was so much better. I really feel like ADHD is nothing to be ashamed of. Having ADHD—if anything—means you have a little advantage over everyone else because you think outside the box. You're not narrow-minded. Now if we could just break down the wall of fear and misinformation that medicine is bad and all you need is discipline. That's just not the truth. Medicine can't fix everything, but it helps you cope with the ADHD. Once you learn to cope with your ADHD, life is so much easier. I AM myself on medicine and not just a zombie. Medicine just helps me be more focused. I grasp a lot more and retain a lot more. It helps me think clearly.

Shawn

Profile: *Shawn has ADD Inattentive, which was diagnosed when he was 15. Once his ADD was diagnosed, he made mostly straight As in high school. After graduation, he attended college on an academic scholarship for a while, but decided that he wanted to become a Marine instead. Today he is a top salesman for a billion-dollar company.*

Shawn at Age 16

My ADD without hyperactivity was diagnosed when I was 15, and I started taking medication then. Up until that time I had never done very well in school and it seemed like I was always in trouble with my parents.

I guess I thought I was lazy and stupid. I couldn't concentrate. Like, when I was reading, I would be thinking about something else. After I read something, I would realize I couldn't remember what it was about. My handwriting was never very good. My parents had me checked for learning disabilities when I was in the sixth grade but they couldn't find any.

I used to think, "I can get one zero in class and it won't hurt." One zero turned into more and more. Then it got to where I didn't really care. I would get too far behind and couldn't catch up.

During class I tended to be real tired and sleep a lot. I tended to sleep in classes like English that have a lot of book work. If teachers talked too much, it seemed like it just went right through my brain. If I missed a little, I couldn't catch back up.

When I came home from school each day, I was in a real bad mood. I would start yelling over the least little thing. My grades got worse in school as time went by. I got C's in elementary school, some D's and F's in middle school, and then mostly D's and F's my freshman year in high school, except in wood shop. I've always been good working with my hands, so I made good grades in shop.

I always had trouble getting started on my homework. I would write down my assignments and bring them home. Then I would forget to bring my book home. Sometimes I remembered my homework at bedtime or in the morning just before I went to school. In elementary school, I had to go to after-school detention for not doing my homework at least once a week. My teachers said I was never a discipline problem, though.

I used to start a lot of projects but never seemed to get them finished. I would start out with lots of good ideas and good intentions. Then I would slack off and do a crappy job. It was the same with sports. I'd go out for soccer, baseball, and football, do real well for a little while, then get bored with it and want to do something else.

I wanted to do better in school, but somehow I never could. I would start out okay the first two weeks. Then I slacked off.

We moved around a lot and I thought that was why I had so many problems at school. I know I have developed bad work and study habits. I missed out on a lot of basic skills in math and English.

I forgot my chores a lot. If Dad asked me to bring my dirty clothes down within the next hour, I forgot to do it. I forgot to bring in the newspaper. I forgot to clean my room. I never seemed to think about the consequences.

I felt like my parents didn't trust me. Sometimes I didn't always tell them the truth because I knew they didn't trust me anyway. Sometimes I'd tell them I was spending the night with one friend, but really stay with another. I knew they wouldn't let me stay with that friend. I got in so much trouble that at one point it felt like I had been grounded my whole life. I guess my parents just thought I was lazy. They were worried about what I would do in life when I grew up. At times they may have been ashamed of me. Thank goodness, things are a lot happier now. Since I've been taking Ritalin, I have not been grounded.

When I turned 15, my parents wouldn't let me get my learner's permit to drive. I had to wait until I was 16. They were worried about the way I drove. When I'm not on my medicine, I drive real bad. I forget to stop at red lights and sometimes I stop at green lights.

Besides making me a better driver, medicine has made a big difference in my grades. My grades went from D's and F's my freshman year to mostly A's and B's my sophomore year when I started taking Ritalin.

Now I go to school early. I always look at my books to make certain I haven't forgotten something. If I have forgotten something, I can do the work then before I go to class.

I really like my grades now. I have more free time. I can get most of my work done in class. My parents let me do more things. They trust me more and are real proud of me. They are very happy about my grades.

If I had to describe myself, I would say that I am quiet and easygoing. Most of the time I go with the flow. I don't argue a lot. I'm not hyperactive. People seem to like me a lot. I get along with most everyone. My friends say that they have never seen me angry. My friends can count on me. I like to try exciting things. If someone tries something new I want to try it too.

I have had a job for several months now and I love it. They really like my work and trust me and put me in charge sometimes if they are gone for a while. I don't like to have a lot of free time and just sit around home. I am saving up my money for a car.

Shawn at age 30

AFTER HIGH SCHOOL

After high school I stopped taking medication and went to college on scholarship for a while. I was sitting in class one day when I realized I hadn't heard a word the instructor had said. I decided that not everyone needed to go to college. I could go into the service and get paid while I received training. I got up and walked out of class and decided to join the Marine Corps.

I really enjoyed the Marines. My Dad served in the military, and after Desert Storm, I really wanted to go. It was an excellent decision for me; I'd do it again. I've always liked structure and discipline. For me, boot camp was easy. The camaraderie was wonderful; I made some of the best friends in my life. The Marines have a long history; our motto, semper fidelis, means always faithful. I'm very proud that I was a Marine; not everyone can say that.

MY WORK TODAY

Today I am one of the top salesmen in the country for a company that sells special batteries. We charge, test, and rebuild batteries for forklifts. For a while, I was a branch service supervisor and supervised a total of 20 guys in 2 shops. Lots of guys who worked for me probably had undiagnosed ADHD. My bosses always said that I did such a great job, they couldn't run the shop without me. About 2 years ago, I got promoted and now I have customers all across the state of Georgia.

MY CHALLENGES AT WORK

I still have the same problems as before, like remembering everything and staying organized. But they're just not as bad as they used to be. I'm older and I've learned to deal with them better. I've got lots of responsibilities and I know I have to get them done. When you're younger you're carefree; when you're older you have more worries.

My memory is the worst thing. When I worked as a supervisor, I was always juggling lots of things at the same time. I would have five things to do and forget one of them, within just a 20-minute span. An hour later, I'd finally remember it. But there haven't been any problems with my boss because I get things done. My handwriting is still terrible, so now I use a computer a lot more. Sometimes I'd get a little aggressive with my temper when people didn't do their work; I'd set them straight.

I'm proud that I have learned to compensate. I write stuff down; I use a lot of yellow stickies [Post-it notes].

Over the years, my organization has gotten a lot better, especially in the last few years. When I was a supervisor, I developed a system that works for me. We had a lot of truck batteries in and out every day and I had to keep up with a lot of details. So I created a new computerized filing system using Excel software for keeping track of customer batteries, the loan or rent—status sheet, and a spread sheet—log out. When my bosses went out of town, they left me in charge. They knew everything would be okay. They said I'll go far.

I get along well with both bosses. I'm overworked—50 or 60 hours a week—and my bosses know it. I really enjoy our company perks; I get a vehicle, a retirement package (401K), and an expense account. I found out about the job through my Dad, who worked for the same company. My bosses say that they have never had a harder or more dedicated worker than I am.

MY LIFE AT HOME

I'm single now and have to travel all the time. Recently I bought a two-bedroom condo. When I was married, my wife got angry because of my attention span. She said I didn't listen to her. In the middle of conversations, sometimes I'd walk away and watch TV. Sometimes I forgot to take out the garbage, but I always remembered to mow my yard. I married too young, so I'm not in a rush to settle down again any time soon. Sometimes I think it probably wouldn't hurt to take medication again. But for now, I've learned to cope with my ADD. I know I'll keep getting better and better.

MY ADVICE

My advice to teenagers is "Don't give up!" Don't let anyone make you think you're stupid; once you say that and give in to it, nothing is going to get better for you. It's just going to get worse. If you feel like you're stupid, you may just give up. But once you realize that isn't true, you'll feel a lot better. When you have no hope, at some point—you give up.

For me the hardest time of my life was from fourth until tenth grade when my ADD was finally diagnosed. I reached a point in high school when I just didn't care anymore. But once I started taking medicine and could pay attention, things got easier. I wanted to do better in school. I wanted to go to college. Remember, though, you can't use ADD or ADHD as an excuse. You can't just take medication alone and expect things to be perfect. You still have to try to make yourself better.

The New Teens on the Block

Comments from a few new teens who have attention deficit disorders have been added to this section. Their insightful comments are impressive and may be of help to you.

Emily, Age 17

Profile: *Emily, who has ADD inattentive, was not diagnosed until her freshman year in high school. Initially*

school officials thought her problems at school were due to laziness and/or depression. She did not receive any accommodations until her sophomore year. Once she began taking medication, her grades improved significantly. She hopes to be a fashion designer in New York someday.

When I was younger I did my homework and got really good grades. I could do my work even in distracting settings because I can multitask and the work was simple. My problems first started in sixth grade, when memorization became a necessary part of the curriculum. I have the worst time memorizing things. Then in seventh grade when I had to start writing essays, I got my first C. Before that I'd always made straight As.

I always knew I was different; that I learned differently. When I was asked to sit and write essays or do journal entries in English class, I just couldn't do it and none of my peers were having difficulty. I knew something was wrong. I should have been able to do that, but why couldn't I? I just had so much trouble concentrating and I was curious to find out why.

"IT'S ADD; NOT JUST DEPRESSION!"…
THE STRUGGLE TO GET DIAGNOSED

Mom thought I might have ADD but no one would listen to her, except Chris Dendy. Everyone else just kept saying, "Emily's depressed. She needs to see a therapist." I guess I was depressed, but only because I kept trying so hard in school but not making the grades that reflected my level of knowledge. The school just believed that I wasn't trying hard enough. They tried to put me in modified classes for less intelligent students. They gave me relatively easy tests which were untimed and I got really good scores but it took me three times as long as it should have. Even the guidance counselor didn't understand—and *she* had a diploma in special education. The school personnel on the whole were entirely useless. Finally, I was diagnosed the middle of my freshman year. Although I already knew I had it, I was relieved that I was finally going to get the help and hopefully the understanding I needed. I was reading a lot about ADD and thinking—that's definitely me. Wow! That makes a lot of sense. *A Bird's-Eye View of Life with ADD and ADHD* has helped a lot.

It was a nightmare getting diagnosed. It took forever before the school finally accepted my diagnosis and did something to help me. I didn't get any accommodations until my sophomore year, and I started the impossible fight for diagnosis the beginning of ninth grade. First, someone at school told Mom that she had to have a neuropsychologist diagnose me. Then, after

Emily

she did that, they retracted their previous statement and the school psychologist said we needed a diagnosis from a "real" doctor (medical doctor).

MEDICATION AND MY SCHOOL WORK

I started taking Adderall XR during the middle of my freshman year. When I first started taking it, I was amazed. I wrote a history assignment that ended up being two pages, front and back. Ordinarily, I'd be stunned if I wrote just half a page. In biology, I had been making D's because the class was all memorization. Not to mention, the class was the last period of the day after my gym class and I was always so tired and eager to get home. My teacher had a terrible monotone voice and was the most boring man I have ever met. I spent most of my time in class doodling and drawing. But I've always gotten into trouble for doodling in class. After I started the Adderall XR, my grades got a lot better. I made a C the next marking period. The final marking period, I made a B.

Now I'm making pretty much straight A's. My mind is hyperactive, but my body is not. Before I started taking Adderall XR, I needed to be doing at least four things at once to keep my mind occupied or else I got really bored. I am pretty impatient, especially on the computer. When I took regular Adderall and Ritalin, it wore off after lunch. I felt so frustrated I was ready to hit someone and had less patience than usual. Then I switched to Adderall XR and that worked much better.

Adderall doesn't make me finish things, but it helps me clear my train of thought. If I sat down and tried to write without my medicine, my brain would be like a big cloud of information. By the time I finished thinking of a whole sentence, I'd already forgotten what the first part of the sentence was. When I first started writing essays, I was a perfectionist. And couldn't move on to the next sentence until the one I was writing was perfect. That led to countless hours of frustration and, inevitably, procrastination. Now I've learned to get all my ideas on paper first or at least take it paragraph to paragraph and edit things once an idea is complete. But being on Adderall helped me learn some methods around my disability, so even without it I can manage a paper with less frustration. Albeit it's much easier to write when I have taken medicine.

MY IEP

My IEP really helps me. I'm allowed to hand in assignments late and am given extra time on tests. I'm just looking for understanding that I'm not a bad kid. I'm not being obstinate or making excuses when I say "I forgot." I really do forget.

I really need extra time in English because I write a lot slower. Capturing my ideas in words and getting them down on paper is very hard. My English teacher and I have a really good understanding between us. She is lenient with me about handing in assignments. Now I have extra time on essays. I'll sit down and do half the essay right away. One paragraph can take a couple of hours. I usually finish it over the course of a week. I get nine-tenths done, but the hardest time is finishing what I started. But when I do get it written, the quality is really good.

Even now, school is still really hard but I have help and it's not as hard as it used to be. At times I hate it, but most kids do.

Actually, I don't look at my ADD as a disability. If you were to reverse the classroom situation so that students have to be creative and not simply memorize and repeat like parrots, I'd excel and other students would be the ones with disabilities.

MY STRENGTHS AND TALENTS

I love the fact that I can excel creatively. I use a different part of my brain; I learn differently. Since you asked me my strengths, I'd have to say that I'm good at drawing, painting, sewing, and working on computers. But moreover, I enjoy doing those things and that's what counts. I especially love to draw people. At times when I'm doodling in class, a doodle will turn into an entire page of artwork and that's when I realize that I haven't been listening to a word the teacher said. I make a lot of my own clothes too. I wear long skirts, corsets, Victorian jewelry, and lace-up boots just because it pleases me. I'm also good at fixing computers and figuring out how they work. I think I do this because I get so angry when they're running slow.

MY DREAMS FOR THE FUTURE

When I think about the future, it's a little scary. I really want to go into illustration or perhaps fashion design. But it's really hard to get into fashion design. One day I may start my own business or sell my clothes in a boutique. I've already taken classes at the Fashion Institute of Technology in New York City and hopefully will be accepted there for college.

Spencer, Age 17

Profile: *Spencer is a junior who was diagnosed with ADD inattentive when he was 14. In 2005, he was a speaker on a teen panel at the CHADD Conference in Dallas. At school, he earned a spot on his high school's varsity lacrosse team. Currently he takes Strattera and Provigil to help him stay alert and concentrate at school.*

EXERCISE

When I spoke on the teen panel in Dallas, I learned that exercise helps us concentrate better in school. This year I have weight training first period and I can tell a big difference. I am less drowsy and better able to function in early classes. I also have la-

Spencer

crosse practice for four hours each day after school. Algebra is one of my earliest and toughest classes. Now I can think more clearly in algebra, I get started

more easily, and focus more on the task at hand, instead of what's going on around me.

MEDICINE

Right now I'm doing pretty well on my medicine. We made some changes recently and now I take half my Strattera in the morning and half at night. That way it doesn't affect my stomach as much. Before, it made me nauseous and I felt really hot and sweaty. Now I can eat breakfast and not feel sick. Medicine helps me focus. If I don't take it, it's pretty bad—it makes a huge difference. Otherwise I'm fidgety and can't focus on anything. If I don't take my medicine, I'm really sleepy and just want to put my head down and sleep. Even when I try to read something, my head is in other places.

HAVING ADHD

I found out I had ADD in the eighth grade and I really didn't know what to think of it. I didn't know what it meant. Although school is tough, I have also found almost a Zen mindset advantage in creativity. Ideas just come to me. I don't really have to think about them. Ideas just pop into my head and it just seems right. Sometimes I'm pretty good writing persuasive papers as far as the content goes; but I overlook and don't always think about the grammar and other stuff that much.

ADVICE TO OTHERS WITH ADHD

Once you find what works for you, stick with it. Perhaps it's the right medicine, routines, process for doing things, homework routine, or whatever. I use a small card to keep up with my homework. I usually get an agenda book but I always lose it. So I just put a note card in my pocket each morning before I leave home, then pull it out and write down the assignments for each class. My dad lays the cards out every morning by my medicine. The card has columns, classes, rows, and space to write assignments. Then in the afternoon when I go to my locker, I check my card to see what I have left to do. I also came up with the idea to carry only one binder and I put everything in it. Before I had one for every class and I'd always lose them.

Alyssa, Age 16

Profile: *Alyssa is a sophomore who was diagnosed with ADHD when she was in the third grade. In 2005, she was a speaker on a teen panel at the CHADD Conference in Dallas. At school, she makes really good grades and takes honors classes. She loves to write and three of her articles have been published. In addition, she participates in a* *leadership group with the Girl Scouts known as S.A.I.L., Strong And Independent Leaders. Currently she takes Concerta and Welbutrin.*

HAVING ADHD

When I was in the third grade and the doctor told me I had ADHD, I didn't really mind. Actually my mom and I diagnosed the ADHD and the doctor confirmed it. At first I didn't have a full concept of it; I found that out later on. The doctor explained why I acted the way I did and that was kind of nice. Finally I knew why I was different from all the other kids and that helped me understand why it was hard for me to make friends. I was relieved.

LEARNING ABOUT ADHD

I first started to understand ADHD when I went to one of Mrs. Dendy's conferences. I remember the one where Lewis from 99 X rock radio spoke; he was so funny. I also read *A Bird's-Eye View of Life with ADD and ADHD*. I learned even more when I was on the teen panel at the CHADD conference in Dallas. Now I know that I should exercise more. Then I'll have more dopamine and I wouldn't need to take as much medicine.

MY INTERESTS AND SPECIAL TALENTS

I think my ADHD gives me a great imagination that helps me be a better writer. I have had some of my articles published already. My first article on bullying was published in a Girl Scout magazine. The last one was an article I wrote about my friend Christina, who is blind.

I also found some other good things about having ADHD listed in an article called "25 positive things about ADHD." For example, I am always ready to talk and I can talk a lot. If the teacher asks a question in class, I can usually answer it. I've been told that I have a great personality and am very articulate, especially for someone my age. I also need less sleep and can get more done. And I get along really well with adults and enjoy hanging around younger children. Unfortunately, I can't baby-sit yet, because my attention span is not long enough. In fact, after watching my little sister for a couple of hours, my mom said that I didn't need to baby-sit someone else's kids. I definitely have to agree with that. I love animals too.

THE GREATEST CHALLENGE

Although I like being different, at times it can be the hardest thing about having ADHD. Some people, especially from my same race, don't accept me the way others do. The girls especially don't seem to like me. They don't like it when I can answer so many questions in class.

Alyssa

MY WORK AT SCHOOL

Mostly I make really good grades and am also in some honors classes. However, I don't like math too much. There are just too many numbers to remember. Because I have algebra and science, it's almost like I have two math classes. I have too many formulas to memorize. The worst grade I received last semester was an 89 in algebra 1, Part II. Right now I actually have a 96 in world geography. Last semester I was in honors literature and this semester I'm talking honors British literature. I also love playing my viola in the orchestra.

I love reading and writing. That makes me the happiest. I love to read fantasy stories. My favorite author is Amelia Atwater-Rhodes. Everything she writes is so vivid. She gives so many details when she writes; it really feels as though I can see the characters. Her characters act so human. I now have all seven of her books. She wrote her first book when she was only 13.

When I was younger, I did really, really badly on my multiplication tables. I remember I studied all night for the multiplication quiz. I knew just about everything on it because my mom was testing me. Mom watched me study. The next day when I took the quiz, it was all gone—bye-bye. I failed that test and I was so sad. My grandmother was a math teacher and we would study all day together. By the next day, everything I learned was all gone. She even said something was wrong. Now I do know most of the multiplication tables. I've picked up some tricks. I find the nearest fact I know, and then add to it. For instance, for 8x6, I multiply 8 x 5 to get 40 then add 8.

MY DREAMS FOR THE FUTURE

I want to be a lawyer when I get older. First I may publish books so I'll have enough money for college. Then I can study to be a lawyer.

Appendices

Appendix 1: Medication Rating Scale 384

Appendix 2: Sample Contract 385

Appendix 3: The ABC's of ADD and ADHD: Impact on School Performance 387

Appendix 4: Sample Medical Report 390

Appendix 5: Developing and Implementing Effective IEPs 391

Appendix 6: OHI School Eligibility Report 394

APPENDIX 1   Medication Rating Scale

Name: _____   Grade: _____   Date & class: _____

Completed by: _____   Time of day observed: _____

To assess the impact of medications on a student's school work, each teacher should answer several key questions. When medication is working properly and learning problems have been identified, the student should be doing much better in school. Please circle the number that best describes the student's behavior.

Academic Performance:

	Strongly Agree	Agree	Neutral	Disagree	Strongly Disagree
When the student is in my class, s/he					
1. Pays attention	1	2	3	4	5
2. Completes class & homework	1	2	3	4	5
3. Does work correctly	1	2	3	4	5
4. Complies with requests	1	2	3	4	5
5. Makes passing grades	1	2	3	4	5

ADD/ADHD-Related Behaviors, including Executive Function Deficits

If the student is on medication and is not doing well in school, what else could be causing continuing problems? Are there any ADD/ADHD-related behaviors that are interfering with the student's ability to succeed in school?

ADD/ADHD-related Behaviors:

The student:

6. is organized (finds and turns in work)	1	2	3	4	5
7. remembers things (assignments, tests, etc.)	1	2	3	4	5
8. manages time well/ plans ahead	1	2	3	4	5
9. is on time to class	1	2	3	4	5
10. is on time to school	1	2	3	4	5
11. thinks before acting or speaking	1	2	3	4	5
12. is awake and alert in class	1	2	3	4	5
13. gets along with friends	1	2	3	4	5
14. gets angry easily & blows up	1	2	3	4	5

Are you aware of any sleep problems? According to parents, the student

15. falls asleep easily	1	2	3	4	5
16. wakes up easily	1	2	3	4	5

Comments: _____

_____

_____

_____

_____

_____

APPENDIX 2   Sample Contract

This contract between _____ (teenager) and _____ (parents) is hereby entered into this _____ day of _____, 2_____.

Whereas, _____ is a mature and responsible teenager;

Whereas, _____ is at least 16 years of age, has a driver's license, and wishes to drive a car;

Whereas, _____ likes to go to the mall, movie theater and participate in other activities with his friends;

Whereas, _____ likes to spend time with friends, invite them on outings and to our home;

Whereas, _____ likes to watch TV in his room, talk on the telephone, play video games, and watch movies on the VCR; and

Whereas, _____ likes to party, have a good time, buy cassette tapes, water ski, hunt, fish, swim, and ride a dirt bike.

Therefore, be it agreed that _____ and parents have developed the following statements to help ensure that s/he continues to enjoy the above listed activities and that the parents are able to enjoy being parents. Both parties agree to do their best to comply with the following statements:

With regard to school issues, _____ agrees to:

1. complete school assignments and turn them in on time.
2. complete and turn in all homework.
3. start his/her homework after dinner. No TV or talking on the telephone until homework is completed except if s/he deems a break is necessary.
4. be responsible for finding out about and completing any make-up work or make-up tests.
5. make every effort to pass all subjects.
6. bring home a weekly report in any subject that s/he may be in danger of failing.
7. show parents completed homework assignments each evening.

In return, the parents agree:

1. not to nag him/her about school work.
2. to provide assistance if requested.
3. to ask to see completed homework daily (or once a week).
4. if necessary, to give one reminder after dinner that homework must be started.
5. if necessary, to check the weekly school report to see if all school work has been completed.
6. to allow him/her (on a school night) to use the telephone and watch TV in his/her room, drive with a parent, go to the mall, and spend time with friends, once all school assignments are completed.

If in the unlikely event _____ should fail a subject, allow him/her to drive and spend time with friends each week that he brings home a passing weekly progress report.

With regard to driving privileges, _____ agrees to:

1. wear a seat belt.
2. drive the speed limit or less.
3. take medication when driving.
4. be home by 10:30 on school nights or 12:30 on weekends.
5. pay for any gasoline used above gas allowance.
6. never drink and drive.
7. pay fines for any speeding tickets.
8. call parents for advice and/or transportation at any hour, from any place, if he/she is ever in a situation where he/she has been drinking or a friend or date who is driving him/her has been drinking.

In return, parents agree to:

1. provide a car to drive (or let teen drive the family car or help teen pay).
2. pay for car insurance (or pay half the car insurance or teen pays all).
3. provide a gasoline allowance (one tank every two weeks or teen pays all).
4. come and get teen at any hour, any place, no questions asked and no arguments at that time, or parents will pay for a taxi to bring teen home safely. I expect we would discuss this issue at a later time.

In the unlikely event _____ receives a speeding ticket, s/he will pay any fines plus lose driving privileges for a week (a weekend, more or fewer days).

All parties signing this contract are doing so in good faith and with the belief that the terms of the agreement will be implemented in a fair manner. Exceptions to these rules shall be mutually agreed upon with the parents. If a dispute should arise, he/she can negotiate with parents to make changes to the contract.

Let all men know by the signing of this document that these statements are agreed to by all parties.

_____
(Parents)

_____
(Teenager)

_____
(Date)

Parents are encouraged to modify this contract to meet your family's needs. This contract can be helpful by stating guidelines for your teenager regarding school issues and driving privileges. Although the sample contract identifies important issues, you can design it specifically for your child. For example, curfews may be earlier or he may have more limits on his driving because he is only fifteen. Just having a contract will not magically make your teenager comply with these guidelines but will clearly state his privileges, limits, and responsibilities. You will need to remind him of responsibilities such as wearing a seatbelt. The contract may also be modified if sections of it are not applicable or no longer effective. For example, in a large town, a tank of gas may only last a week. If your teenager has had numerous speeding tickets, you may need to talk to the doctor about giving him medication at night when he is driving, send him to another driver training course, or take driving privileges away for a longer period of time.

APPENDIX 3 The ABC's of ADD and ADHD: Impact on School Performance
Chris A. Zeigler Dendy, M.S.

ADD and ADHD are neurobiological disorders which affect approximately 5 to 12 percent of all children. Researchers believe that neurotransmitters, the chemical messengers of the brain, do not work properly, causing symptoms of ADD or ADHD. Inattention and impulsivity, the two major characteristics of attention deficits, can make complying with parental requests and succeeding in school more difficult for these children. Symptoms of ADD and ADHD vary from mild to severe. Some children with attention deficits do extremely well in school. However, for many others, underachievement in school is a hallmark characteristic of the condition.

Three major types of attention deficit disorder have been identified:

- ADHD (predominately hyperactive-impulsive);
- ADHD inattentive (predominately inattentive without hyperactivity—schools call this ADD); plus
- ADHD, combined type (a combination of both hyperactivity and inattention).

Children who have ADHD tend to be very energetic, talkative, and outgoing. In contrast, children with ADD inattentive, previously called ADD without hyperactivity, tend to have less energy, are less likely to talk in class, and are more introverted. Although many children are diagnosed and treated in elementary school, some (especially those with ADD inattentive or mild cases of ADHD) are not diagnosed until high school or college.

A Developmental Delay. Although they may be bright intellectually, many **children with ADD or ADHD lag behind their peers developmentally by as much as 30 percent** in certain areas, according to research by Dr. Russell Barkley. This translates into a *delay of 4-6 years* for teenagers. As a result, they may seem immature or irresponsible. They are less likely to remember their chores or assignments and complete their work independently, are more likely to say things or act impulsively before thinking, and the quality and amount of their work will fluctuate from day to day. Consequently, parents and teachers may need to provide more positive feedback, supervise school work more closely, give reminders of homework, and communicate more frequently with each other to help the child cope with this disability.

Deficits in Executive Function. Sometimes very bright students with attention deficits do poorly in school. Recently, Dr. Russell Barkley's research has focused on the role **weak executive functioning** plays in school failure (deficits in working memory, control of emotions and behavior, internalizing language, problem-solving, and organization of materials and action plans). Deficits in executive skills make writing essays and computing more complex math very difficult. For more details, refer to Chapters 1 and 3 and read the related article on my website, www.chrisdendy.com.

Treatment. Research has shown that **medication can help most children** with ADD and ADHD improve their performance at home and school. Medications commonly used to treat attention deficits such as Adderall, Concerta, Strattera, Ritalin, or Dexedrine help the neurotransmitters norepinephrine and dopamine work properly. When medication is effective, attention and concentration improve, more chores and school work are completed, compliance with adult requests increases, hyperactivity and impulsivity decrease, and negative behaviors decrease.

Frequently, **ADD or ADHD may coexist with other major problems**—learning disabilities (25-70%), sleep disturbances (56%), anxiety (27-44%), depression (29-45%), bipolar disorder (6-12%), oppositional behavior (45-84%), substance abuse (10-40%), or conduct disorder (25-50%)—which further complicates a student's treatment and school work.

The majority of children with ADD or ADHD experience difficulty in school (90%). Common learning problems and their practical implications for home and school performance are described below. However, keep in mind that each child with an attention deficit is unique and may have some, but not all of these problems.

1. **Inattention and Poor Concentration:** difficulty listening in class; daydreams; spaces out and misses lecture content or homework assignments; lack of attention to detail, makes careless mistakes in work, doesn't notice errors

in grammar, punctuation, capitalization, spelling, or changes in signs (+,-) in math; difficulty staying on task and finishing school work; distractible, moves from one uncompleted task to another; lack of awareness of time and grades, may not know if passing or failing class.

2. **Impulsivity:** rushes through work; doesn't double-check work; doesn't read directions; takes shortcuts in written work, especially math (does it in his head); difficulty delaying gratification, hates waiting.

3. **Language Deficits:** slow processing of information; reads, writes, and responds slowly; recalls facts slowly; more likely to occur in children with ADD inattentive. Three language-processing problems may be common among children with ADD or ADHD.

   a. **Listening and Reading Comprehension**: becomes confused with lengthy verbal directions; loses main point, difficulty taking notes; difficulty following directions; may not "hear" or pick out homework assignments from a teacher's lecture; poor reading comprehension, can't remember what is read, must reread material.

   b. **Spoken Language** (oral expression): talks a lot spontaneously (ADHD); talks less in response to questions where they must think and give organized, concise answer; avoids responding in class or gives rambling answers.

   c. **Written Language:** slow reading and writing, takes longer to complete work, produces less written work; difficulty organizing essays; difficulty getting ideas out of head and on paper; written test answers or essays may be brief; responses to discussion questions may be brief.

4. **Poor Organizational Skills:** disorganized; loses homework; difficulty getting started on tasks; difficulty knowing what steps should be taken first; difficulty organizing thoughts, sequencing ideas, writing essays, and planning ahead.

5. **Impaired Sense of Time:** loses track of time, is often late; doesn't manage time well, doesn't anticipate how long task will take; doesn't plan ahead for future.

6. **Poor Memory:** difficulty memorizing material such as multiplication tables, math facts, or formulas, spelling words, foreign languages, and/or history dates.

7. **Math Computation:** difficulty automatizing basic math facts such as multiplication tables; cannot rapidly recall basic math facts.

8. **Forgetful:** forgets chores or homework assignments, forgets to take books home; forgets to turn in completed assignments to teacher; forgets special assignments or make-up work.

9. **Poor Fine Motor Coordination:** handwriting is poor, small, difficult to read; writes slowly; avoids writing and homework because it is difficult; prefers to print rather than write cursive; produces less written work.

Difficulties in school may be caused by a combination of several learning problems: a student may not take good notes in class because he can't pay attention, can't pick out main points, and/or his fine-motor coordination is poor. A student may not do well on a test because he reads, thinks, and writes slowly, has difficulty organizing his thoughts, and/ or has difficulty memorizing and recalling the information. Identification of learning problems plus implementation of appropriate accommodations in the regular classroom are critical.

Under IDEA and/or Section 504, children with ADD or ADHD whose ***ability to learn is adversely affected*** by the disorder are eligible for accommodations.

Common classroom accommodations that are extremely helpful to children with attention deficits include:

- untimed tests;
- use of calculator or computer;
- modification of assignments (e.g., fewer math problems);
- elimination of unnecessary writing (e.g., write answers only, not questions);
- reduced demands on limited working memory capacity;
- written homework assignments given by teachers;
- notetakers or guided lecture notes.

Accommodations should be individualized and made to accommodate each child's specific learning problems.

Other factors related to ADD or ADHD may also influence the child's school work:

1. **Restlessness** or hyperactivity in younger children: Can't sit still in seat long enough to complete work.
2. **Sleep Disturbances:** Children may come to school feeling tired; may sleep in class. Many children with attention deficits (56%) have difficulty falling asleep at night and waking up each morning. Approximately half of them wake up tired even after a full night's sleep. Good sleep is important because memory is often consolidated during sleep. Children may have battles with their parents before arriving at school. This suggests that there are problems with the neurotransmitter serotonin.
3. **Medication Wears Off:** With the advent of long-acting medications like Adderall XR, Concerta, and Strattera, problems with medication wearing off at school are less common. However, the effects of short-acting medications such as Ritalin or Dexedrine (regular tablets) wear off within three to four hours and children may begin having trouble paying attention around ten or eleven o'clock in the morning. Even the intermediate range medications (6-8 hours) like Adderall, Metadate ER, Ritalin SR, or Dexedrine SR may wear off by early afternoon. Class failure, irritability, or misbehavior may be linked to times when medication has worn off.
4. **Low Frustration Tolerance:** Children with attention deficits may become frustrated more easily and "blow-up" or impulsively say things they don't mean, especially as their medication is wearing off. They may blurt out answers in class. Or they may be argumentative or impulsively talk back to a teacher. Transitions or changes in routine, such as when substitute teachers are present, are also difficult for them.

Since most children with ADD or ADHD are not as easily motivated by consequences (rewards and punishment) as other children, they may be more difficult to discipline and may repeat misbehavior. Although they would like very much to make good grades on a test or at the end of the semester, these rewards (grades) may not occur quickly enough nor be strong enough to greatly influence their behavior. Frequently, they start out the school year with the best intentions, but cannot sustain their efforts. Positive feedback or rewards are effective but must be given immediately, must be important to the child, and must occur more frequently than for other children. Consequently, sending home daily or **weekly reports** regarding school work should help improve grades.

Giving children choices regarding chores or homework—for example, at home, selecting their chore, or determining which homework subject is first and establishing a starting time—will increase compliance, productivity, and reduce aggression (at school, selecting topics for essays or reports).

Typically their misbehavior is not malicious but rather the result of their inattention, impulsivity, or failure to anticipate the consequences of their actions. As my friend and colleague Sheryl Pruitt explains in *Teaching the Tiger*, "Ready. Fire! And then, Aim...oops!!" may more accurately describe the behavior of children with attention deficits. They may not think before they act or speak. They also have trouble controlling their emotions. If they think it, they often say or do it. If they feel it, they show it. Belatedly, and with remorse, they realize they should not have said or done certain things.

Youngsters with ADD or ADHD have many positive qualities and talents (high energy, outgoing charm, creativity, and figuring out new ways of doing things). These traits are often valued in the adult work world, but may cause difficulties for these students and their parents and teachers. Their high energy, if properly channeled, can be very productive. Although sometimes exasperating, they can also be extremely charming in their self-appointed role as class clown. Typically, children with ADD inattentive tend to be quieter and present few, if any, discipline problems. When they become adults, children with attention deficits can be very successful. Having parents and teachers who believe in a child is essential for success!

APPENDIX 4 Sample Medical Report *[Comments in brackets are the author's and are not part of the report.]*

Gwinnett County (GA) Schools Medical Report

Name: _____ Age: _____ Date: _____

1. **Diagnosis and medical history:** ADD inattentive diagnosed at age 12, have treated child since 2003; anxiety; sleep disturbance; Mathematics Disorder.

   [A diagnosis of the attention deficit should be listed, plus coexisting conditions and any learning problems. The doctor can give a diagnosis of any "Learning Disorders" he has detected from his evaluation such as "Mathematics Disorder" (DSM IV). See Chapter 12 for more details.]

2. **Current medication/list side effects:** Adderall XR 30 mg once daily; Dexedrine 5 mg p.m. for homework, as needed; Lexapro 10 mg near bedtime. If he forgets his medication, he may be inattentive and impulsive at school.

   [Medications should be listed, and related problems mentioned: for example rebound, irritability in the afternoon as shorter-acting medication is wearing off; loss of appetite.

   With the availability of long-acting medications like Adderall and Concerta, many problems from earlier years are now avoided, for example, no midday doses can be forgotten nor are they required now.]

3. **Describe any condition that may interfere with regular attendance or functioning in school:** Although the student may act indifferent, he is actually quite anxious and wants to do well in school. He still struggles with certain executive function skills, particularly organization and time management, even when taking his medication. The teenager has learning problems that interfere with his ability to do well academically, for example;
   - slow cognitive processing (reads and writes slowly, slow calculation of math problems, which means the student will produce less written work);
   - poor memory (difficulty memorizing multiplication tables, spelling, and foreign languages);
   - inattentive and forgetful;
   - impulsivity and low frustration tolerance (says or does things without thinking, is more likely to blow up when upset);
   - a sleep disturbance (sometimes can't fall asleep at night and has trouble waking up the next morning, may be late to school or sleep in class or be irritable at school the next day, or may be late.)
   - forgetting medication; or short acting medication that may wear off earlier in the school day.

   A copy of our psychological and academic assessment is attached.

   [Lack of all day medication coverage may cause problems at school. For example, a few students may still take short-acting medications that don't last the entire school day. Students who take these meds may be inattentive or act or speak impulsively when it is wearing off. If the student is having problems only during certain times of the day, you may want to double-check to see if medication has worn off. If this is a problem, the doctor will work with you to correct the problem by changing the medication, dose, or time it is administered.

   Some doctors can explain how your teenager's learning problems will adversely affect his performance at school. They may obtain information from an in-depth evaluation, including intellectual (IQ) or academic functioning as assessed by their staff. Some physicians also review school evaluations and test data (old school psychological evaluations, IOWA scores, report cards) and point out areas of academic deficits, or share information from Table 12-2 about common learning problems and accommodations.]

4. **Medical Prognosis:** Good, if the teenager continues to take medication and the school provides appropriate classroom accommodations.

5. **Recommendations and Comments:** Based upon our evaluation, this child will need some accommodations to succeed in school. Other patients with similar problems have found the following accommodations extremely helpful: untimed tests, use of a calculator, written homework assignments, and someone to meet him at the locker to review homework assignments and help him select the right books to take home. I have prescribed medication that should help reduce problems with his inattention, anxiety, and sleep disturbances.

   It would be helpful if his most important academic classes are scheduled earlier in the day when his physical and intellectual energy levels are higher and his medication may be at maximum effectiveness. Placing him with teachers who are positive but flexible and understand attention deficit disorders is also important.

APPENDIX 5 Developing and Implementing Effective IEPs
[Comments in brackets are the author's and are not part of the report.]

As discussed in Chapter 14, sometimes students with ADD or ADHD have IEPs but are still failing. Obviously the IEP is not working. This appendix includes the IEP for Thomas, the failing student introduced in Chapter 14, as well as specific suggestions for improving his IEP and general comments for developing an effective IEP for any student with ADD or ADHD. To help parents create an effective IEP, a checklist of actions they should take before, during, and after an IEP meeting is also available in Table 14-3.

Strategies for Improving Thomas's IEP. If we are to identify the best methods for helping Thomas, we need to play detective and determine why he is failing. If possible, we need to figure out *why* he is not completing or turning in his work. Typically, it is best to identify a few core problems first and work to resolve those issues. A variety of factors, including deficits in executive skills, may contribute to his failure to submit completed homework. When these factors are taken into consideration, the strategies used and teacher attitudes may change.

Not every student with an attention deficit will need the supports identified below for Thomas. Even then, the goal is to provide the supports for a while, and then teach skills or compensatory strategies so that, if possible, these accommodations are no longer needed.

INDIVIDUALIZED EDUCATION PROGRAM: Actual IEP with Comments

Name: _____ Age: _____ Date: _____
School:_____ Grade: _____

1. **Present level of educational performance.** "Include specific descriptions of strengths and needs that apply to current academic performance, behaviors, social/emotional development, other relevant information and how the student's disability affects his/her involvement and progress in the general curriculum."
   [General Comments: Here are quotes regarding Thomas's present performance from two separate IEP meetings during the past two years. In the Spring of 7th grade, he was failing most of his classes.]

   A. Present Performance:
   Winter of 7th grade: "When given a task, Thomas is determined to do it right. He participates in class and seeks assistance when needed. He does not always take materials home or turn in completed homework."

   Spring of 6th grade: "Thomas has made improvements in completing assignments and turning them in on time but continues to have difficulty with this. He has a set of textbooks to keep at home so he does not have to remember to bring them home every night. However, he is still responsible for bringing home the added materials that he may need. This is also a challenge for him. He is capable of writing assignments down in his planner on a regular basis but often needs an incentive or reminder to do this. Even after a reminder is given, it is beneficial for the teacher to initial his planner each period to verify that the assignments are written down completely and correctly."

   B. Strengths: *"Thomas is polite and well-mannered. He has a good speaking voice. He reads with expression."*

   C. Parent Concerns, if any, for enhancing the student's education: "Bring up his low grades, completing assignments."

   [General Comments: In the present performance section, parents and teachers must identify all behaviors and academic skills, including executive function deficits, that should be addressed in the IEP. Goals and objectives will be developed to address only those concerns that are identified in this section, so it is critically important for you to raise key issues here. Be aware that some school officials may list problem behaviors only and fail to identify underlying learning issues that may be contributing to the academic problems.]

   [Specific Comments on Thomas's IEP
   The school identified one major issue of concern: completing and turning homework. If, however, we are to identify the best methods for helping this particular student, we need to know more. If possible, we must determine why the student is not completing his work. A variety of factors, including executive function deficits, may contribute to his failure to

submit completed homework. For a more detailed discussion of potential factors affecting Thomas's academic performance plus suggestions for implementing a more effective IEP, please read Table 14-1.

Based upon an interview with Thomas's mother, there are several important issues that she identified in addition to the organizational and homework issues listed in the IEP; for example, difficulty taking tests, slow processing speed, getting no credit for assignments submitted late, and difficulties memorizing vocabulary meanings, remembering his block schedule, and speaking in class. These issues should be identified in this first section of the plan.]

2. Goals and Objectives

A. Annual goal: "Thomas will improve organizational skills and turn in homework assignments."

[General Comments: Goals must be written for the student to accomplish by the end of the school year. Although generally speaking goals are broadly stated, the new laws indicate they must also be measurable.

Your teen's annual goals should address the major stumbling blocks that are preventing him or her from being successful in school. Beautiful, measurable goals can be written but if they don't address the major issues that are preventing your teen's school success, they are worthless.]

[Specific Comments on Thomas's IEP

These are certainly worthy and appropriate goals, but in spite of the IEP, Thomas was still failing most of his classes. To be effective, the IEP must include effective intervention strategies, an active monitoring plan, plus constant fine-tuning. In addition to academic issues, executive function deficits must be addressed. For example, specific intervention strategies are needed to teach improved organizational skills or compensatory strategies.]

3. Educational Services to Be Provided: Appropriate supplementary aides, services, and accommodations for instruction and testing, and/or supports for school personnel.

A. Recommended Special Education Program(s): "Other Health Impairment (OHI), consultation in a regular classroom setting."

[General Comments: "Educational services" includes both special education and related services. "Special education" is instruction individually tailored to meet a student's unique learning needs. It is usually provided by teachers with special training and expertise in meeting the needs of students with learning difficulties. It may be provided inside or outside of the regular classroom. Special education teachers may also provide consultation to a teen's classroom teachers.

Before you attend your child's IEP meeting, you should decide on your own what services might benefit your child and why. For example, you could say, "My son could benefit from another student reminding him to write down and then turn in homework assignments…or to provide training on test taking skills. Could the guidance counselor or someone work with him to help him develop those skills?" A list of other possible accommodations that students might receive are found in Table 14-2.]

B. Recommended Related Services: "none"

[General Comments—Related Services: The IEP must list any "related services" which are necessary for the student to succeed in school, for example: 1) counseling, 2) parent counseling and training, 3) psychological services, 4) social work services, 5) audiology, 6) speech therapy, 7) physical therapy, 8) occupational therapy, and 9) assistive technology.

Most students with ADHD have organizational and time management issues which might benefit from some skills training in these areas. **Keep in mind earlier research that shows that the benefits of skills training are limited. At a minimum, these students need basic skills knowledge but may not remember to apply the knowledge when it is needed. To be effective, supervision and prompts must be provided at the "point of performance" where the skill is needed.]**

C. Accommodations: This school system uses a general checklist to indicate the specific accommodations to be provided. Thomas will receive four accommodations.

"Thomas qualifies for services due to Other Health Impaired. He is in all regular education classes except Study Skills. He rarely did homework in Study Skills, stating he did not have any. He was not using his agenda on a regular basis. At the semester, Thomas was failing Social Studies, Language Arts, and Math. He is receiving accommodations and modifications in all classrooms. He is given graphic organizers, extended time, preferential seating, and study guides. The committee decided to put Thomas on consultative services due to the stigma he associated with Study Skills. He will receive all classes in regular class. He will not be removed any part of the day. The special education teacher will consult with mainstream teachers.

[Specific Comments on Thomas's IEP

The decision to keep Thomas in a regular classroom with supports is a reasonable choice. Dropping the study skills class (a related service), however, is questionable, unless it is replaced with supervision at the "point of performance."

Study skills class would be a great place to teach organization skills, identify the reasons for the failure of the IEP, and change the implementation plan so that the IEP is effective. Teachers could also monitor his agenda to make certain that homework assignments are completed and up-to-date.

A study skills class that is run like an old fashioned study hall will not be effective with most of these students. In truth, study skills classes must offer careful monitoring and supervision for each student, not just babysitting. The current system of simply asking Thomas if he has homework is not working. Supervising teachers must know with certainty what the assignments are.

One way to correct some of the past problems with the study skills class would be to improve the communication between classroom teachers and the person in charge of study skills class. Until Thomas gets in the habit of doing his homework, the study skills teacher should have a copy of all homework assignments and check to see that they are completed. If he does not complete all his homework in study skills class, then someone must ensure he takes home his assignments and the right books. Direct supervision at the point of performance is critical, for example, meeting Thomas at the locker with a list of homework assignments to select books needed to take home. Just telling him at 8:30 in the morning to remember to take his books home for his math homework is ineffective.]

D. Anticipated Frequency and Location: Services will begin in the fall and continue for the school year; special education consultation will be provided once a week for 30 minutes in a regular classroom; he was not deemed eligible for extended school year services.

[General Comments: The IEP must state the beginning date, duration, and location for each special education and related service your child is to receive, as well as how long he is expected to receive the service. The amount of time not spent in a regular classroom setting must also be indicated. The person who will be responsible for implementing each objective should also be identified.

Some students may need a summer program to build academic skills that are closer to grade level, to keep from falling behind academically or to improve their behavior at school. This may be an opportunity to discuss the need for "year-round programming." For some students with attention deficits, however, the last thing they need is to attend summer school.]

E. Modifications in Statewide or District Wide Assessments: "extended time"

[General Comments: If the student doesn't take the same assessment tests as all other students, the school must list any assessment not being done, the reasons why, and the alternative assessment that will be given.]

4. How Progress toward the Annual Goal Will Be Measured. "For all objectives: daily agenda/planner check, work samples, teacher grade book."

[General Comments: This section of the IEP lists what specific tests or other measures are to be used to determine if the IEP goal and objectives are being met.]

5. An Individualized Transition Plan: "Upon completion of high school, Thomas plans to attend college and major in P.E. He enjoys golf."

[General Comments: A transition plan must be developed when a student turns 16. This plan must help the student make the transition from high school to: "post secondary education, vocational training, integrated employment (including supported employment), continuing and adult education, adult services, independent living or community participation." Activities should be based upon "the individual student's needs taking into account the student's preferences and interests, and shall include instruction, community experiences, the development of employment and other post-school adult living objectives, and when appropriate, acquisition of daily living skills, and functional vocational evaluation."]

[Specific Comments on Thomas's IEP

Hopefully when Thomas turns16, the school will begin developing a more detailed transition plan complete with some specific objectives that will help him achieve his career goals. For suggestions on effective transition planning, see Summary 48 in Teaching Teens.]

APPENDIX 6   OHI School Eligibility Report

After the school has your doctor's medical report, they will gather relevant school data, and complete an eligibility report. Georgia's eligibility report includes the following issues that are relevant to ADD and ADHD:

OTHER HEALTH IMPAIRMENT (OHI)
SCHOOL ELIGIBILITY REPORT (GA)

I. Educational and Assessment Data
- A. Medical evaluation (less than one year old. This section will be a summary of the information from your doctor's medical report.)
  - ■ Date of evaluation:
  - ■ Diagnosis/prognosis of health impairment:
  - ■ Information regarding limitations to alertness.
  - ■ Information regarding surgeries, medications, special health care procedures, diet or activity restrictions.

- B. Educational evaluation:
  - ■ Dates, instruments [tests], results
  - ■ Informal assessment of education performance; date & results

- C. Psychological evaluation:
  - ■ Dates, instruments, results

- D. Based upon the above information, education deficits are noted in the following areas:

_____ academic functioning	_____ adaptive behavior
_____ gross/fine-motor development	_____ communication skills
_____ social/emotional development	_____ other areas; specify

II. Conclusion:
  Summarize the documentation that educational deficits have resulted from the health impairment.

  _____ The student <u>does</u> <u>(does not)</u> meet OHI eligibility criteria.

Resource Guide

All Neurobiological Disorders

The common link between all these disorders is that their cause is thought to be related to neurotransmitters that are not working properly.

National Institute of Mental Health (NIMH)
Public Info. and Communications Branch
6001 Executive Blvd., Room 8184, MSC 9663
Bethesda, MD 20892-9663
866-615-6464
www.nimh.nih.gov
Fact sheets, booklets, and other publications on all mental disorders, including a detailed booklet on depression, dysthymia, and bipolar disorder.

Koplewicz, Howard. *It's Nobody's Fault: New Hope and Help for Difficult Children and Their Parents.* New York: Three Rivers Press, 1997.

Kutscher, Martin. *Kids in the Syndrome Mix of ADHD, LD, Asperger's, Tourette's, Bipolar, and More.* Philadelphia: Jessica Kingsley, 2005.

Wilens, Timothy. *Straight Talk about Psychiatric Medications for Kids.* New York: Guilford Press, 2004.

ADD and ADHD

Children and Adults with Attention Deficit/
    Hyperactivity Disorder (CHADD)
8181 Professional Place – Suite 150
Landover, MD 20785
301-306-7070
www.chadd.org
www.help4adhd.org
*The leading organization in the U.S. providing information and resources for **children** with attention deficits, their families, and the professionals who serve them. They also provide websites, conferences, a newsletter, on-line chats, advocacy, and 250 local parent support groups.*

ADDA: Attention Deficit Disorders Association
P.O. Box 543
Pottstown, PA 19464
484-945-2101
www.add.org
*The leading organization in the U.S. providing information, networking, and resources for **adults** with attention deficits and the professionals who serve them. They also provide a website, a conference, and a newsletter.*

ADD Resources
223 Tacoma Avenue South
Tacoma, WA 98402
253-759-5085
www.addresources.org

An organization providing information and resources for those with AD/HD concerns. They have a website with over 100 free articles, a free monthly eNews, teleclasses, and webcasts. They host two conferences annually and run five local support groups in Washington state.

Attention Deficit Disorder Association—
    Southern Region (ADDA-SR)
12345 Jones Rd. Suite 287-7
Houston, TX 77070
281-897-0982

A strong regional organization providing ADHD information and resources in Texas and surrounding states. They also provide websites, conferences, a newsletter, advocacy, and 18 local parent support groups.

Anxiety

Anxiety Disorders Association of America (ADAA)
8730 Georgia Ave., Ste. 600
Silver Spring, MD 20910
240-485-1001
www.adaa.org

Information about five anxiety disorders: Panic Disorder, Obsessive-Compulsive Disorder, Post Traumatic Stress Disorder, Generalized Anxiety Disorder, and Phobias. Fact sheets, a medication update, and an online newsletter.

Manassis, Katharina. *Keys to Parenting Your Anxious Child.* New York: Barron's, 1996.

Asperger's Syndrome

Autism Network International (ANI)
P.O. Box 35448
Syracuse, NY 13235-5448
www.ani.ac

Autism Society of America (ASA)
7910 Woodmont Ave., Suite 300
Bethesda, MD 20814
800-3AUTISM
www.autism-society.org

O.A.S.I.S (Online Asperger Syndrome Information and Support)
www.aspergersyndrome.org

Atwood, Tony. *Asperger's Syndrome.* London: Jessica Kingsley, 1998. (Also see the author's website: www.tonyattwood.com)

Bruey, Carolyn. *Demystifying Autism Spectrum Disorders.* Bethesda, MD: Woodbine House, 2004.

Bipolar Disorder

Child and Adolescent Bipolar Foundation (CABF)
1000 Skokie Blvd., Ste. 425
Wilmette, IL 60091
847-920-9498
www.bpkids.org

Fact sheets, a chat room, experts to answer questions on-line, bookstore, and science-based research.

Depression and Bipolar Support Alliance
730 N. Franklin St., Ste. 501
Chicago, IL 60601
800-826-3632
www.dbsalliance.org

Information on research, new publications, plus a bookstore related to depression and bipolar.

Madison Institute of Medicine:
    Lithium Information Center (MIM)
7617 Mineral Point Rd., Ste. 300
Madison, WI 53717
608-827-2470
www.miminc.org

Facts on treatment of bipolar, depression, OCD, and anxiety.

Papolos, Demitri and Janice. *The Bipolar Child.* New York: Broadway, 2002. (Also see the authors' website: www.bipolarchild.com)

Sommers, Michael. *Everything You Need to Know about Bipolar Disorder and Manic Depressive Illness.* New York: Rosen, 2002.

Waltz, Mitzi. *Bipolar Disorders: A Guide to Helping Children and Adolescents.* Sebastopol, CA: Patient-Centered Guides, 2000.

Depression

Depression and Bipolar Support Alliance
(*See under* Bipolar Disorder)

National Mental Health Association (NMHA)
(*See under* Conduct Disorder)

Cobain, Bev. *When Nothing Matters Anymore: A Survival Guide for Depressed Teens.* Minneapolis: Free Spirit, 1998.

Garland, E. Jane. *Depression Is the Pits, but I'm Getting Better: A Guide for Adolescents.* Washington, DC: Magination Press, 1998.

Manassis, Katharina and Annemarie Levac. *Helping Your Teenager Beat Depression: A Problem-Solving Approach for Families.* Bethesda, MD: Woodbine House, 2004.

Emotional Disorders (Including Conduct Disorder)

The national organizations below also have state and/or local chapters that can provide information and support.

The Federation of Families for Children's Mental Health (FFCMH)
9605 Medical Center Dr., Ste. 280
Rockville, MD 20850
240-403-1901
www.ffcmh.org

The National Alliance for the Mentally Ill (NAMI)
2107 Wilson Blvd., Ste. 300
Arlington, VA 22201
800-950-6264
www.nami.org

The National Mental Health Association (NMHA)
200 N. Beauregard St., 6th Floor
Alexandria, VA 22311
800-969-NMHA
www.nmha.org

Learning Disabilities and Academic Challenges

All Kinds of Minds
1450 Raleigh Road, Suite 200
Chapel Hill, NC 27517
888-956-4637
www.allkindsofminds.org

All Kinds of Minds is a nonprofit institute that helps students who struggle measurably improve their success in school and life by providing programs that integrate educational, scientific, and clinical expertise. Their website provides resources to help parents, educators, and clinicians understand why a child is struggling in school and how to help each child become a more successful learner. The website includes a free monthly newsletter, articles by Dr. Mel Levine and others, discussion groups, and a LearningBase and Parent Toolkit with practical strategies for supporting learning differences.

Learning Disabilities Association of America
4156 Library Rd.
Pittsburgh, PA 15234
412-341-1515
www.ldanatl.org

A national nonprofit organization with state and local affiliates, the LDA provides information and support for parents and teachers, advocates for laws and policies that will help people with LD, publishes a journal, position papers, etc.

LD Online website
www.ldonline.com

Online articles, resources, and forums to help parents, teachers, and self-advocates understand many different types of learning disabilities and learn strategies and information to help individuals with LD be more successful at home, school, and on the job.

Schwab Learning website
www.greatschools.net

A website established by Charles and Helen Schwab, whose family members have struggled with dyslexia and learning differences. The site provides parents much needed information and resources for helping their children with learning difficulties succeed in school.

Substance Abuse

Al-anon/Alateen
1600 Corporate Landing Pkwy.
Virginia Beach, VA 23454
757-563-1600
www.al-anon.alateen.org
Support for families of adults or teens with alcohol problems.

Alcoholics Anonymous World Services
P.O. Box 459
New York, NY 10163
212-870-3400
www.alcoholics-anonymous.org
Offers help to young people and families who are struggling with substance abuse issues. Finding an AA or NA group that is appropriate for teens will require careful search. A listing of local chapters may be found in your telephone directory under "Alcoholics Anonymous" or via the AA website.

Narcotics Anonymous
P.O. 9999
Van Nuys, CA 91409
818-773-9999
www.na.org

National Clearinghouse for Alcohol and Drug Information
800-729-6686
www.ncadi.samhsa.gov

National Crime Prevention Council
1000 Connecticut Ave., NW
Washington, DC 20036
202-466-NCPC (6272)
www.ncpc.org

National Institute on Drug Abuse (NIDA)
6001 Executive Blvd.
Bethesda, MD 20892
301-443-1124
www.nida.nih.gov
www.teens.drugabuse.gov (NIDA for Teens)

Growing Up Drug Free: A Parent's Guide to Prevention
(available by calling 800-624-0100; also available online on a variety of sites such as www.drugfree.org/Files/Parents_Guide)

Tourette Syndrome

Tourette Syndrome Association (TSA)
42-40 Bell Blvd.
Bayside, NY 11361
718-224-2999
www.tsa-usa.org
Fact sheets, information on treatment and research, plus a list of famous people who may have this condition.

Tourette Syndrome "Plus" website
www.tourettesyndrome.net
A comprehensive source of resources and information on Tourette syndrome, OCD, Asperger syndrome, ADHD, and other neurobiological disorders.

Comings, David E. *Tourette Syndrome and Human Behavior.* Duarte, CA: Hope Press, 1990.

Dornbursh, Marilyn and Sheryl Pruitt. *Teaching the Tiger: A Handbook for Individuals Involved in the Education of Students with Attention Deficit Disorders, Tourette Syndrome, or Obsessive Compulsive Disorder.* Duarte, CA: Hope Press, 1995.

Marsh, Tracy. *Children with Tourette Syndrome: A Parent's Guide.* Bethesda, MD: Woodbine House, 1992, 2006.

Bibliography

Academic/School Issues

Crutsinger, C. *Thinking Smarter: Skills for Academic Success*. Carrollton, TX: Brainworks, 1992.

Davis, L., Sirotowitz, S. & Parker, H. *Study Strategies Made Easy*. Plantation, FL: Specialty Press,1996.

Dendy, C., editor. *CHADD Educator's Manual*. Landover, MD: CHADD, 2006.

Dendy, C. *Teaching Teens with ADD and ADHD: A Quick Reference Guide for Teachers and Parents*. Bethesda, MD: Woodbine House, 2000.

Deshler, D., Ellis, E.S. & B.K. Lenz, *Teaching Adolescents with Learning Disabilities: Strategies and Methods*. 2nd edition. Denver, CO: Love Publishing,1996.

Dornbush, M.P. & Pruitt, S.K. *Teaching the Tiger: A Handbook for Individuals Involved in the Education of Students with Attention Deficit Disorders, Tourette Syndrome, or Obsessive Compulsive Disorder*. 2nd edition. Hope Press. Duarte, CA, forthcoming.

DuPaul, G.M. & Stoner, G. *ADHD in the Schools*. 2nd edition. New York: Guilford Press, 2004.

Ellis, E. *Using Graphic Organizers to Make Sense of the Curriculum and Strategic Graphic Organizer Instruction*. Masterminds, 1998.

Frender, G. *Learning to Learn: Strengthening Study Skills and Brain Power*. Nashville, TN: Incentive Publications, 2004.

Jones, C. *Practical Suggestions for ADHD*. Moline, IL: LinguiSystems, 2003.

Koplewicz, H.S. *It's Nobody's Fault: New Hope and Help for Difficult Children*. New York: Random House, 1996.

Levine, M. *Educational Care*. 2nd edition: Cambridge, MA: Educators Publishing Service, 2002.

Parker, H. *Problem Solver Guide for Students with ADHD*. Plantation, FL: Specialty Press, 2002.

Parker, H. *The ADD Handbook for Schools*. Plantation, FL: Specialty Warehouse, 2005.

Pfiffner, L.J. *All About ADHD: The Complete Practical Guide for Classroom Teachers*. New York: Scholastic, 1996.

Rief, S. *The ADHD Book of Lists*. San Francisco: Jossey-Bass, 2003.

Rief, S. *How to Reach & Teach Children with ADD/ADHD*. 2nd edition. San Francisco: Jossey-Bass, 2005.

Teeter, P.A. *Interventions for ADHD: Treatment in Developmental Context*. New York: Guilford Press, 1998.

University of South Florida. *A School-Based Guide for Youth Suicide Prevention.* (http://fmhi.usf.edu; search Publications for "suicide.")

Medication

Wilens, T. *Straight Talk about Psychiatric Medications for Kids.* Revised edition. New York: The Guilford Press, 2004. *(Most books in this section also give information on medication, but Dr. Wilens's is more detailed.)*

Parent Education

Brookes, R. & Goldstein, S. *Raising Resilient Children: Fostering Strength, Hope, and Optimism in Your Child.* Lincolnwood, IL: Contemporary Books, 2001.

CHADD Parent to Parent Training: http://www.chadd. org; 800-233-4050.

Copeland, E. & Love, V. *Attention, Please! A Comprehensive Guide for Successfully Parenting Children with Attention Deficit Disorders and Hyperactivity.* Plantation, FL: Specialty Press, 1995.

Fowler, M. *Maybe You Know My Teen.* New York: Broadway Books, 2001.

Hagar, K., Goldstein, S. & Brooks, R. *Seven Steps to Improve Your Child's Social Skills.* Plantation, FL: Specialty Press, 2006.

Jensen, P. *Making the System Work for Your Child with AD/HD.* New York, Guilford, 2004.

Quinn, P.O., Nadeau, K. & Littman, E. *Understanding Girls with ADHD.* Silver Spring, MD: Advantage Books, 2000.

"What We Know" (WWK) fact sheets from CHADD. www.help4adhd.org/en/about/wwk.
   Fact sheets can be downloaded on a variety of topics, including: *Managing Medication for Children and Adolescents with ADHD* (WWK #3); *Educational Rights for Children with ADHD* (WWK # 4); *AD/HD and Coexisting Disorders* (WWK #5); *Complementary and Alternative Treatments* (WWK #6): *Psychosocial Treatment for Children and Adolescents with AD/HD*

(WWK #7); *Time Management* (WWK #11); *Succeeding in College* (WWK #13).

Parenting Challenges/Discipline/Defiance

Barkley, R.A., Edwards, G.H. & Robin, A.L. *Defiant Teens: A Clinician's Manual for Assessment and Family Intervention.* New York: NY: Guilford Press, 1998.

Barkley, R.A. *Taking Charge of ADHD: The Complete Authoritative Guide for Parents.* Revised edition. New York: Guilford Press, 2000.

Goldstein, S. & Brooks, R. *Understanding and Managing Children's Classroom Behavior.* 2nd edition. New York: John Wiley & Sons, 2006.

Goldstein, S., Brooks, R. & Weiss, S. *Angry Children, Worried Parents: Seven Steps to Help Families Manage Anger.* Plantation, FL: Specialty Press, 2004.

Greene, R.W. *The Explosive Child: A New Approach for Understanding and Parenting Easily Frustrated, Chronically Inflexible Children.* New York: Harper Collins, 2001.

Heininger J.E. & Weiss, S.K. *From Chaos to Calm: Effective Parenting of Challenging Children with ADHD & Other Behavioral Problems.* New York: Perigee Books, 2001.

Illes, T. *Positive Parenting Practices for Attention Deficit Disorder.* Jordan School District, Utah, 2002.

Snyder, M. *ADHD and Driving: A Guide for Parents of Teens with ADHD.* Whitefish, MT: Whitefish Consultants, 2001.

Social Issues

Begun, R.W., editor. *Ready-to-Use Social Skills Lessons & Activities for Grades 7-12.* San Francisco, CA: Jossey-Bass, 1996.

Cohen, C. *How to Raise Your Child's Social IQ: Stepping Stones to People Skills for Kids.* Washington, DC: Advantage Books, 2000.

Goldstein, A.P. & McGinnis, E. *Skills Streaming the Adolescent: New Strategies and Perspectives for Teaching Prosocial Skills.* Champaign, IL: Research Press, 1997.

Hagar, K., Goldstein, S. & Brooks, R. *Seven Steps to Improve Your Child's Social Skills.* Plantation, FL: Specialty Press, 2006.

Lavoie, R. *It's So Much Work to Be Your Friend.* New York. Touchstone (Simon and Schuster), 2005.

McDougall, N. & Roper, J. Creative Coaching: A Support Group for Children with AD/HD (for elementary and middle school age students). Chapin, SC: Youthlight, 1998. (www.youthlight.com)

Novotni, M. *What Does Everybody Else Know That I Don't Know?* Plantation, FL: Specialty Press, 1999.

Sheridan, S. *Why Don't They Like Me? Helping Your Child Make and Keep Friends.* Longmont, CO: Sopris West, 1998.

Social Skills in Adults (What We Know Series #15). www.help4adhd.org/en/about/wwk.

Bullying Prevention

Olweus Bullying Prevention Program. Clemson University. Contact Marlene Snyder, Ph.D. at nobully@clemson.edu; www.clemson.edu./olweus/; www.modelprograms.samhsa.gov.

Materials for Children and Teens

Crist, J. *ADHD: A Teenager's Guide.* Plainview, NY: Childsword/Childsplay, 1997.

Dendy, C. & Zeigler, A. *A Bird's-Eye View of Life with ADD and ADHD: Advice from Young Survivors.* Cedar Bluff, AL: Cherish the Children, 2003.

Dendy, C. *Teen to Teen: The ADD Experience.* Cedar Bluff, AL: Cherish the Children, 2003. (Video available in English and Spanish.)

Hallowell, E.M. *A Walk in the Rain with a Brain.* New York: Regan Books, 2004. (A rhyming picture book for younger children.)

Hallowell, E.M. & Corman, C.A. *Positively ADD.* New York: Walker Books for Young Readers, 2005.

Nadeau, K. *Help 4 ADD @ High School.* Silver Spring, MD: Advantage Books, 1998.

Packer, A. *Bringing Up Parents,* Minneapolis: Minneapolis: Free Spirit Publishing, 1993.

Quinn, P.O. & Stern, H.J. *Putting on the Brakes: Young People's Guide to Understanding ADHD.* Washington, DC: Magination Press, 2001. (For grades 3-8.)

Walker, B. *The Girl's Guide to AD/HD: Don't Lose This Book.* Bethesda, MD: Woodbine House, 2005.

"What We Know" (WWK) fact sheets from CHADD. *What about Medicines for ADHD?*; *What Is ADHD Anyway? Questions from Teens.* www.help4adhd.org/en/about/wwk.

Professional Books

These books are recommended for parents who want more in-depth information:

Barkley, R.A. *Attention-Deficit Hyperactivity Disorder: A Handbook for Diagnosis and Treatment.* 3rd ed. New York: Guilford Press, 2006.

Barkley, R.A., Edwards, G.H. & Robin, A.L. *Defiant Teens: A Clinician's Manual for Assessment and Family Intervention.* New York: The Guilford Press, 1998.

Brown, T. *Attention Deficit Disorder: The Unfocused Mind in Children and Adults.* New Haven: Yale University Press, 2005.

Goldstein, S. & Goldstein, M. *Managing Attention Deficit Hyperactivity Disorder in Children: A Guide for Practitioners.* New York: John Wiley and Sons,1998.

Jensen, P.S. & Cooper, J.R. *Attention Deficit Hyperactivity Disorder: State of the Science – Best Practices.* Kingston, NJ: Civic Research Institute, 2002.

Robin, A.L. *Adolescents with ADHD: Diagnosis and Treatment.* New York: The Guilford Press, 1998.

Teeter, P.A. *Interventions for ADHD: Treatment in Developmental Context.* New York: Guilford Press, 2000.

Index

1-2-3 Magic, 165
Abbreviations, for types of ADHD, 2
Abilify, 135
Abney, Billy Shaw, 226, 229
Academic problems. *See* School problems
Accidents, 15, 187, 214-15
Accommodations, school
   definition of, 294
   examples of, 84-85, 319, 388
   for college admissions tests, 331, 332
   for common learning problems, 288-91
   involving teen in choosing, 287
   planning form for, 368
Achenbach Child Behavior Checklist, 46
ACID Test, 42-43
ACT, 330-32
Activation, 3
Activities. *See also* Sports
   dangerous, 187-89
   extracurricular, 314-15
   family, 146, 183-84, 185
   high interest, 269
   teen, 155-56, 185, 193
ADD (inattentive type). *See also* Attention deficit
   disorders; Behavior
   as categorized in DSM, 10, 11
   as separate disorder, not ADHD subtype, 15, 49
   attention problems and, 30
   characteristics of in adolescence, 49-50
   childhood characteristics of, 15

   coexisting disorders and, 129
   compared to ADHD, 51, 191-97
   friends and, 16, 50
   lack of research on, 128
   medical conditions confused with, 48
   medications helpful for, 101, 115, 117, 118, 194
   prevalence of, 11
   scores on IQ tests and, 44
ADDA, 89
ADDA-SR, 89
Adderall, 101, 102, 105, 108, 109, 110, 111, 113-14, 116
Addiction, 102, 115, 136. *See also* Substance abuse
ADHD (hyperactive and/or combined type). *See also*
   Attention deficit disorders; Behavior
   characteristics of in adolescence, 48-49, 50
   childhood characteristics of, 14
   compared to ADD, 51, 191-97
   disorders associated with, 28
   new theories about, 29
   prevalence of, 11
   scores on IQ tests and, 44
AD/HD and Driving, 216
AD/HD and the Nature of Self-Control, 30
ADHD/NOS, 50
AD/HD Reports, 30
Adolescents and ADD, 82
Adoption, 10
Adults with ADD/ADHD
   behavior of, 70
   diagnosis of, 12

medication and, 103, 126
percentage who have symptoms after adolescence, 11, 96
research on, 26
success of, 96
who are parents, 66, 126, 162
Advice on ADHD from the Real Experts, 82
African Americans, 76
After school care, 94
Aggression. *See also* Conduct disorder; Oppositional defiant disorder
causes of, 206
fighting and, 204
in bipolar disorder, 134
in conduct disorder, 140
increased, in one-parent families, 62
medication for, 141, 182
related to depression, 117, 133
Aide, classroom, 243, 272
AIDS, 219, 221-22
Al-Anon/Alateen, 211
Alarm clocks, 191
Algebra, 283-84
Alcohol use. *See also* Substance abuse
driving and, 211, 222
facts about, 209
maternal, 11, 28, 209
of teens with ADD/ADHD, 137
with antidepressants, 118, 210
with stimulants, 210
Alcoholics Anonymous, 213
Allergies, 15, 194, 261
American Coaching Association, 92
American Psychiatric Association, 8, 222
Americans with Disabilities Act (ADA), 302
Amphetamine, 105
Anafranil, 118, 130
Anemia, 194
Anger. *See also* Tantrums
coping with, 149, 157-58
difficulties handling, 56-57
directed at parents, 181
parents', 60, 167-68, 170
related to homework, 256-57
suicide and, 224
Antecedents, 162
Antidepressants, 117-19, 133, 182, 224
Antihistamines, 114, 190
Antipsychotics, 119
Antisocial personality disorder, 140
Anxiety, 35, 50, 84, 117, 119, 128, 129-30, 191

Appetite, effects of medication on, 112
Arguments, 182
Aricept, 116
Arousal, 3
Arrests. *See* Law, brushes with
Assignment books, 273
Asthma, 15
Asperger's syndrome, 138-39
Atomoxetine. *See* Strattera
Attention, difficulties with. *See* Inattention
Attention deficit disorders. *See also* ADD; ADHD; Coexisting conditions; Executive function; Girls with ADD/ADHD; Treatment
ABCs of, for teachers, 387-89
age at diagnosis, 8, 37
and relative numbers of ADD vs. ADHD diagnosis, 11
causes of, 23-30
core characteristics of, 1-2, 4-5, 51
diagnostic criteria for, 8-10
diagnosis of, 31-52
environmental trauma as cause of, 11
famous people with, 72
former names for, 49, 52
health problems and, 15
iceberg image and, 12, 13
keys to good outcome and, 20-21
learning problems associated with, 269-80
myths about 16, 32-33
names for, 2, 10
"outgrowing," 10-11
"over-diagnosis" of, 11-12, 32-33
prevalence of, 10-11
protective factors for, 79
reframing perceptions of, 69-70, 73-74, 89, 146
reasons for delay in diagnosis of, 32-37
ruling out other conditions and, 48
shortcomings of research about, 11
treatment overview for, 21
types of, 2
uniqueness of teens with, 16-17, 33
variability in, 1-2
Attention-deficit/hyperactivity disorder, 50. *See also* Attention deficit disorders
Attorneys, 219
Atwood, Tony, 139
Autism, 138
Barkley, Russell, 3, 4, 8, 15, 29, 30, 49, 54, 57, 83, 101, 103, 131, 137, 140, 159, 178, 215, 219, 230, 235, 265, 268, 325
Bauermeister, José, 36, 76
Bedtime routine, 189-90

Bed wetting, 15, 117

Behavior, challenging. *See also* Conduct disorder; Discipline; Impulsivity; Oppositional defiant disorder; Rules
attention-getting, 195
avoiding confronting teen about, 55
behavior intervention plans for, 162, 312-13, 318
depression and, 204
FBAs and, 162, 247, 272, 313-14
form for charting, 366
function of, 313
in adulthood, 70
influences on, 150-51
learning from other teens, 84
medication for, 119
noncompliance, 54
not overreacting to, 73
overview of, in teens with ADD/ADHD, 4-6, 171, 198-201, 203, 230-32
parents' different perspectives on, 57-58
relationship to ADD/ADHD, 145, 180, 316
relative incidence of in ADD vs. ADHD, 11, 50
risk taking and, 187-89
strategies for handling, 158-67, 357

Behavior intervention plans (BIP), 162, 312-13, 318

Behavior management programs, 89-90

Behavior Rating Inventory of Executive Function, 45

Behavior rating scales, 46, 122, 356

Behavioral and Emotional Rating Scale (BERS), 46

Behavioral Assessment System for Children (BASC), 46

Behavioral charts, 159-60

Behavioral specialists/aides, 93

Benadryl, 114, 190

Biederman, Joseph, 8, 34, 130, 139, 206

Bilbow, Andrea, 138

Bipolar disorder, 114, 119, 128, 133-35, 137, 182

Bird's Eye View of Life with ADD and ADHD, 2, 82, 172, 371

Bladder control, 15

Blood pressure, 113, 119

Books on tape, 278, 343

Boredom, 185

Brain. *See also* Neurotransmitters
areas involved in ADD/ADHD, 25
diagram of, 25
differences in, 26-27
injuries to, 28
PET scan of, 26

Brain chemicals. *See* Neurotransmitters

Breakfast, taking medications at, 114

Brooks, Robert, 20, 67, 72, 154, 175, 180

Brothers and sisters. *See* Siblings

Brown, Thomas E., 3, 49, 117, 263

Brown Attention-Deficit Disorder Scales, 46, 47

Bullying, 206-207

Buspar, 130

Buzogany, Bill, 28

Calculators, 283

Calendars, 179, 252, 341

Calhoun, Susan, 236

Camps, summer, 93-94

Capsules, difficulty swallowing, 109, 111

Cars. *See* Driving

Career choices, 92, 345-48

Carter, Dale, 161

Case law, 320

Case managers, 354

Catapres. *See* Clonidine

CDC National Clearinghouse and Resource Center of ADHD, 88-89

CDC Youth Risk Behavior Survey, 204, 205

Celexa, 117, 119, 130, 194

Cell phones, 179

Central auditory processing disorder, 275

Cerebral palsy, 141

CHADD, 30, 33, 87, 88, 95, 105, 245

Cherish the Children, 372

Child Behavior Checklist, 122

Choices, 147, 240

Chores, 152, 158, 176

Cigarettes. *See* Smoking

Class clown, 49, 194-95

CLEP tests, 336

Clinical sample, 127, 222, 237

Clonidine, 101, 114, 119, 131, 132, 141, 190, 206

Clyburn, Mary Kay, 252

Coaches, 84, 92-93, 98, 133, 153, 238, 273, 342

Cocaine, 208, 212

Coexisting conditions. *See also* Anxiety; Bipolar Disorder; Depression
medications for, 117-19
prevalence of, 79, 127
residential treatment for, 95
support groups for, 89
types of, 128

Cognitive processing speed. *See* Processing speed

Cognitive tempo, sluggish, 15, 49, 193

Colic, 15

College
admission to, 330-32
community, 329-30, 333
difficulties at, related to ADD/ADHD, 340-45

driving at, 351
emotional crises at, 344-45
fraternities and sororities, 351-52
grades at, 336-37
graduation rate, 234, 326
money management at, 348-50
paying for, 335-36
remedial classes and, 332-33
roommates and,350-51
scheduling classes at, 336
Section 504 supports at, 337-40
selecting, 333-35
taking medication at, 343-44
Color highlighting, 271, 272
Comings, David, 131
Communication. *See also* Language deficits; Nagging;
   Speaking
   arguments and, 182
   difficulties between parent and child, 55
   positive, 160-61, 239-40
   strategies for effective, 86, 87-88, 148-50, 157
   with school, 255-56, 307-308
Computers, 252, 279, 280, 338-39
Concerta, 101, 102, 105, 108, 109, 110
Conduct disorder, 128, 130, 136, 137, 140-41, 204,
   206, 226
Connors' Behavior Rating Scale, 46
Connors' CPT, 47
Consequences, logical, 165-66, 261. *See also*
   Incentives; Punishment
Continuous performance tests, 47
Contract, behavior, 152, 216, 385
Correspondence courses, 260
Costly, Virgil, 227
Counseling. *See also* Guidance counselor
   for parents, 90-91, 170
   for teens, 83-84, 261
Court, 218, 226-29
Credit cards, 349-50
Crises, 55, 94, 95, 167-68, 246-47, 344-45
Criticism, sensitivity to, 181
Curfews, 211
Cylert, 105
Cymbalta, 119
Dating. *See also* Sexual behavior
   single parents and, 63-64
   teens with ADD/ADHD and, 197
Daydreaming, 49, 194, 270. *See also* Inattention
Daytrana, 109, 110
Deaths, medication-related, 113
Decongestants, 114

Defiance, 5, 54, 204-206, 265, 269. *See also* Power
   Struggles; Rules
Denckla, Martha, 3
Dendy, Steven, x, 369
Dennis, Karl, 80
Depakote, 119, 135, 141
Depersonalizing problems, 148
Depression. *See also* Bipolar disorder
   family history of, 132
   in girls, 132
   in parents, 46, 54, 56, 168, 170
   in teens with ADD, 50, 84
   incidence of, 128, 132
   medications for, 117-19
   signs of, 132-33, 204
   sleep problems and, 132, 191
   suicide and, 223, 224
Deshler, Don, 280
Desipramine, 131
Desks, messy, 274
Developmental delays, related to ADD/ADHD, 3, 4,
   34, 93, 147, 235, 322, 387
Dexedrine, 110, 111, 112, 216
Dextroamphetamine, 106, 107, 108
DextroStat, 110
Diagnosis, differential, 48
Diagnostic and Statistical Manual of Mental Disorders.
   See DSM
Digit span, 43
Discipline. *See also* Punishment
   at school, 305, 311-12, 316-317
   disagreements about, 57
   ineffective, 144, 179-80
   revised IDEA guidelines regarding, 318
   stepparents and, 65
   unwanted advice about, 59, 62
Discontinuation syndrome, 118
Disorganization. *See* Organization
Distractibility, 29, 253
Divorce
   dating after, 63-64
   statistics, 54, 62
   stress related to, 62-63
Doctors. *See* Physicians
Dopamine. *See* Neurotransmitters
Douglas, Virginia, 52
Drinking. *See* Alcohol use
Driven to Distraction, 84
DriveRight, 217
Driving
   at college, 351

accidents and, 214-15
contract for, 216
drinking and, 211, 222
linking to behavior, 152, 193
medications and, 215-16
speeding tickets and, 166-67, 214, 216-18
training for, 215
unauthorized, 174, 214
Drug abuse, 102, 103, 208-209. *See also* Substance
    abuse
Drug interactions, 114
Drug testing, 212
Drugs, illegal, 102, 207, 208. *See also* Substance abuse
DSM, 8, 9, 10, 48, 49, 52
Due process hearings, 301-302
DuPaul, George, 93, 300
Durheim, Mary, 303, 320
Dyslexia, 275
Dysthymia, 133
Ear infections, 15
Ecstasy (drug), 209
Effexor, 119, 130, 194
Effort, persistence of, 29
Eligibility categories, special education, 298-99
Emotional and Behavioral Disorder (ED), 141, 236, 298
Emotions. *See also* Anger; Depression; Frustration
    difficulty controlling, 139, 180-81, 273
    executive function and, 3
    intense, 54-55
    parents', 53-54, 58-62, 168, 170, 204, 307
    talking about, 149, 150
Energy, low, 49, 193, 194, 263
Epson, David, 71
Epstein, Michael, 46
Errors, careless, 271
Evaluations, ADD/ADHD
    AAP guidelines for, 38
    by school, 37
    components of, 38-48
    conflicts over, 299
    differential diagnosis and, 48
    for special education, 297-300
    private, 37-38, 299-300
    reasons to consider, 36-37
    receiving results of, 48
Evans, Steven, 28, 100, 126, 276
Executive function
    assessment of, 44-45
    components of, 3
    delayed maturation of, 3
    demands on, at school, 6, 236, 322

distractibility and, 29
    effects of stimulants on, 100
    problems related to deficits in, 7, 214, 273-75, 387
Exelon, 116
Exercise, 131, 133, 170, 184, 190, 263
Expectations, 146, 147, 174, 235
Explosive Child, The, 74, 163, 206
Expulsion. *See* School problems
Extended time, 44, 194
Extracurricular activities, 314-15
Faber, Adele, 88
FairTest, 331
Family activities, 146, 183-84
Fathers, teens' behavior with, 57-58. *See also* Parents
FBA. *See* Functional behavior assessment
FDA warnings, 113-14, 116, 118
Federation of Families for Children's Mental Health, 89
Fetal alcohol syndrome, 28, 141
Fighting, 204. *See also* Arguing; Aggression
Focalin, 108, 110, 111, 112, 216
Foods, taking medication with, 114
Foreign languages, 44, 276, 340
Forgetfulness
    at college, 342-43
    at school, 282
    handling at home, 176
    taking advantage of, 164
Forgiveness, 170
Fragile X syndrome, 141
Fraternities and sororities, 351-52
Free Appropriate Public Education (FAPE), 297
Friends
    criticizing, 164
    desirable vs. undesirable, 211-12
    difficulties making, 16, 51, 195-97
    importance of, 196
    with ADD/ADHD, 192-93
Frustration
    handling, 168, 181-82
    increased academic demands and, 7
    tolerance, 5, 54, 158, 265
Functional behavior assessment (FBA), 162, 247, 272,
    311, 313-14
GED, 327-28
Gelperin, Kate, 113
Gender Issues and ADHD, 24
Generalized anxiety disorder, 129
Genes
    involved in ADHD, 26, 27
    role of in risky behavior, 5, 26
Gifted students, 296

Gioia, Gerald, 45
Girls' Guide to AD/HD, 82
Girls with ADD/ADHD
    academic problems of, 35
    behavioral disorders in, 35
    brain inactivity in, 26
    difficulties in diagnosing, 8, 11-12, 34-35
    effects of adolescence on, 12, 35
    emotionality of, 54, 117, 181, 182
    expectations for, 146
    friendships and, 196
    medication and, 117
    menstruation and, 54, 118, 181
    numbers of, 10
    paucity of research on, 12
Gittleman-Klein, Rachel, 137
Goals
    IEP, 300, 392
    teen's vs. parent's, 72
Goldstein, Sam, 20, 58, 67, 131, 354
Gordon, Gale, 56, 113, 115, 120
Gordon Diagnostic System, 47
Grabowski, Audrey Dendy, 370
Grades. See also Homework; Reports, weekly
    at college, 336-37
    effects of zeroes on, 257-58
    keeping in perspective, 72
    lack of awareness of, 271
    pressure about, 264
    required for college admission, 330
Grandiosity, 134
Grandma's Rule, 161
Gratification, delayed, 5, 6, 158, 271
Greed. See Materialism
Green, Ross, 74, 145, 163, 206
Growth rate, 113
Guidance counselor, 242, 246-47
Guns, 222, 224-25
Haldol, 119
Hallowell, Edward, 84, 96
Hallucinations, 134
Handwriting, 284-85. See also Motor skills
Hartsough, Carolyn, 261
Healing stories, 71-72, 146
Heart problems, 113, 114
Helbing, Joan, 152, 246
Henggeler, Scott, 94, 226
Heroin, 208
High school
    diagnosis of ADD/ADHD in, 34
    failing to graduate from, 327-28

transition from, 301, 358
transition to, 7
Hinshaw, Stephen, 113
Hispanics, 36, 76
History facts, 44
Holidays, 186
Homework
    amount of time to spend on, 254
    conflicts over, 249, 250, 266
    difficulties with, in college, 343
    emotional blow ups over, 256-57
    finding out assignments, 252, 282
    keeping track of, 254-55, 273, 274
    math, 282-84
    modifying, 244, 253-54, 280
    strategies for completion of, 252-55
    study routine and, 251, 262
    taking medication during, 251
    turning in on time, 274
Homosexuality, 222
Hormones, 12, 35, 54, 120, 181
Hospitalization, 94, 95
How to Talk So Kids Will Listen and Listen So Kids Will
    Talk, 56, 87
Howard, Marion, 221
Humor, keeping sense of, 73
Hyperactivity. See also ADHD
    as old diagnostic name, 52
    extreme, 14
    handling at school, 285-86
    in adolescence, 262
    myths about, 16, 32
Hyperfocusing, 29, 175
Hyperkinetic Syndrome, 10, 52
ICD-9-CM, 10
IDEA. See also IEPs
    compared to Section 504, 303-304, 305
    coverage of, related to ADD/ADHD, 294-95
    key provisions of, 297-302
    revisions to disciplinary guidelines of, 318
IEPs, 300-301, 306, 308-11, 315-17, 391-93
IEP meetings, 306-308, 322-24
Immaturity, 3, 174, 223. See also Developmental
    delays; Independence; Responsibility
Impulsivity
    as cause of behavior problems, 5, 158, 316
    at school, 271-72
    handling at home, 174
    medication for, 197
Inattention. See also Daydreaming
    at college, 342-43

at home, 175
at school, 269-71
boring tasks and, 4, 29
reasons for, 29
Incentives, 153, 158, 159, 216. *See also* Contracts,
behavior
Inderal, 119
Independence, 90, 172-73
Individualized Education Programs. *See* IEPs
Individuals with Disabilities Education Act. *See* IDEA
Inhalants, 208, 209
Instructions, difficulty following, 276. *See also*
Listening; Rules
Insurance, automobile, 218
Intensive in-home services, 94
Interim Alternative Placement Setting (IAES), 317
International Coach Federation, 92
Interrupting, 195
IQ tests, 40-44
Irritability, 134, 182. *See also* Anger; Frustration
Islands of Competence, 154
It's Nobody's Fault, 206
Jensen, Peter, 2, 33, 77, 78, 85, 230
Job Corps, 328-29
Jobs, summer, 347-48. *See also* Career Choices
Jordan, Dixie, 297, 305, 311
Juvenile justice systems, 226
Kaplanek, Beth, 85
Katz, Mark, 20, 67, 68, 71
Kaufman Test of Educational Achievement, 40
Klein, Rachel, 226
Koplewicz, Harold, 206
Kurlman, Roger, 131
Lahey, Ben, 96, 140
Lambert, Nadine M., 237, 261
Landmark College, 334
Language
expressive, 49
internalizing, 3
Language deficits
incidence of, 275
poor listening comprehension, 275-77
Larsen, William, 118, 132
Law, brushes with, 5, 55, 140, 219, 225-29
Laws. *See* IDEA; Section 504
Lawyers. *See* Attorneys
Laziness, 4, 7, 59, 172, 269
Learning disabilities
attention deficits and, 7, 41
colleges for students with, 334
common, 7, 235, 269, 275

criteria for diagnosis of, 234-35
IDEA and, 299
incidence of, 128, 235
Learning style, 281
Least restrictive environment (LRE), 301
Lethargy. *See* Energy, low
Levine, Melvin D., 186
Lexapro, 117, 119, 130, 194
Listening
active, 149
comprehension, 51, 275-77, 388
strategies for helping with, 175-76
Lithium, 135, 141
Liver problems, 116
Lockers, 274-75
Losing things, 177, 273-74
LSD, 209, 212
Luvox, 119
Lying, 140, 183
Mandelkorn, Theodore, 96, 107, 120
Mania, 134
Manic depression. *See* Bipolar disorder
Manifestation Determination Review, 316-17, 318
Mannuzza, Salvatore, 226
Marijuana, 208-209, 212
Marks. *See* Grades
Marriages. *See also* Parents
second, 64-66
stress on, 168, 170
Materialism, 186
Math, difficulties with, 40, 43-44, 282-84
Math disability, 275
Mattox, Gail, 76
Maturation, delayed, xi, 325. *See also* Developmental
delays
Mayes, Susan, 236
Mazlish, 88
Mediation, 301
Medical conditions, ruling out, 48
Medical report, sample, 390
Medication holidays, 114-15
Medications. *See also* Medications, stimulant
alcohol and, 118, 201
antidepressant, 117-19, 182
changed response to in adolescence, 120
combining, 117
common concerns about, 103-104
determining right one to use, 120
educating teen about, 122, 124
effectiveness of, 77, 79, 85, 101, 364
effects of not taking, 102-103

for aggression, 141
for coexisting conditions, 117-19
for impulsiveness, 174
for problem behaviors, 119
for school problems, 245, 251
for sleep problems, 190
forced, at school, 318
interactions of, 114
irritability and, 182
need for, in adulthood, 99
non-stimulant, 115-17, 120
overdoses of, 224
parents' attitudes toward, 99
percentage of children with ADD/ADHD
   prescribed, 33
rating scale for, 384
refusing to take, 124-25
remembering to take, 124
taking at college, 343-44
taking at school, 125-26, 245, 286
tolerance of, 108
Medications, stimulant. *See also* under specific
   brand names
abuse of, 104, 112, 115, 209
as controlled substances, 105
build-up of, 108
combining several types of, 108
compared to illegal drugs, 102
dosage of, maximum, 107-108
dosage of, determining optimal, 109-10, 120-21, 122
dosage of, typical, 106-107
dosage of, too low, 79, 107
effect of, on behavior, 100
effect of, on brain, 24, 101-102
effect of, on sleep, 190
effectiveness of, 29, 105-106, 120, 356, 364
first choice of, for younger children, 112
generic, 106
"holidays" from, 114-15
ingredients of, 105
length of effectiveness, 107, 110, 121
list of, 105
most prescribed, 111
number of children taking, 33
poor response to, 135
rebound effect and, 113, 182
safety of, 113-14
side effects of, 112-14
research on, 100, 112
special considerations in taking, 114
time of day to take, 192

time of day when effective, 121-22, 365
time release options of, 107-11
Memory
   sleep problems and, 389
   slow retrieval of facts from, 279
   strategies to assist, 281-82
   working, 3, 43-44, 277
Mental retardation, 4, 141
Messy room. *See* Room, messy
Metadate, 110, 111
Methamphetamine, 209
Methylin, 110
Methylphenidate. *See also* Medications, stimulant
   brand names of, 105
   effect of, on brain chemicals, 102
   generic, 106
   strength of, 107
   tics and, 131
Middle school
   bullying in, 206-207
   diagnosis of ADD/ADHD in, 34
   transition to, 7
Milich, Richard, 15, 49
Military, 326-37
Minorities, 10, 35-36
Mistakes, careless, 271
Modafinal, 116
Modifications, 294
Money, as reward, 186. *See also* Incentives
Money management, 348-50
Mononucleosis, 194
Mood disorders, 128, 132-35. *See also* Bipolar
   disorder; Depression
Mood stabilizers, 119, 135
Morning battles, 191-93
Mothers. *See also* Emotions; Parents
   depression in, 56
   teens' behavior with, 57, 58
Motivation, apparent lack of, 49. *See also* Laziness
Motor skills, 16, 184, 284-85, 388
MRI, 47
Multiplication tables, 282-83
Multisensory Algebra Guide, 284
Multisystemic therapy, 94
MyADHD.com, 244
Myers-Briggs Personality Inventory, 346-47
Nadeau, Kathleen, 12, 24, 146, 347
Nagging, 61, 85, 124, 147, 163-64
Narcolepsy, 263
Narcotics Anonymous, 213
National Alliance for the Mentally Ill (NAMI), 89

National Center for Gender Issues and ADHD, 12

National Clearinghouse for Alcohol and Drug Information, 211

National Institute on Druge Abuse (NIDA), 211

National Library Service for the Blind and Physically Handicapped, 278

National Mental Health Association (NMHA), 89

National Resource Center on ADHD, 326

Neuroleptics, 119

Neurotransmitters

    differences in, in ADD/ADHD, 23-24

    dopamine, 24, 26, 101, 102, 178, 194

    effects of medication on, 100-102

    effects of on behavior, 101

    norepinephrine, 24, 101, 102, 115, 194

    role of, 23

    reuptake of, 23

    serotonin, 24, 101, 117, 189, 194, 206

Nicotine, 116, 137, 208

NIMH/MTA study, 78-79, 90, 107, 120, 127, 130

"No," saying, 163, 164

Noncompliance. *See* Rules, following; Power struggles; Stubbornness

Non-stimulant medications. *See* Strattera

Nonverbal learning disability, 275

Norepinephrine. *See* Neurotransmitters

Norpramin, 118, 131, 224

Note taking, 276-77, 339-40

Obsessive-compulsive disorder (OCD), 117, 118, 128, 130

Office for Civil Rights, 304

Office of Special Education (OSEP) policy memo, 295, 296

OHI. *See* Other health impairment

Olanzapine, 119

Olweus Bullying Prevention Program, 207

Oppositional defiant disorder (ODD), 128, 139-41, 204, 206

Oral expression. *See* Speaking difficulties

Organization

    problems with, at college, 341-42

    problems with, at home, 177-78

    problems with, at school, 273-75

Other health impairment (OHI), 298, 394

Overdoses, 224

Panic attacks, 130

Parents and Adolescents Living Together, 148

Parents of teens with attention deficits. *See also* Supervision

    as cause of ADD/ADHD, 2, 23

    as partners with professionals, 50, 52, 77-78, 242-43, 320-21, 353-54

    attitudes of, 71, 78

    behavior checklists and, 46

    communication problems of, 55-56

    concerns of, about future, 20, 61-62

    conflicts between, 57

    counseling for, 90-91

    denial and, 36

    depression and, 46, 54, 56

    differing perspectives of, 57-58

    emotions experienced by, 53-54, 58-62, 168, 170, 204

    involvement of, with college, 341, 352

    involvement of, with school, 237-38, 297

    isolation of, 62

    maintaining relationship of, 58

    mentioning possible diagnosis to, 192

    "over-involved," 4, 93, 237

    power struggles and, 5

    prevalence of ADD/ADHD in, 10, 27

    respite for, 93

    second marriages and, 64-66

    single, 62-64

    strategies for, 67-74, 85-92, 97, 143-70

    support groups for, 88-89

    supportiveness of, 20-21

    training for, 85, 87

    with ADD/ADHD, 66, 126, 162, 238

Parties, unauthorized, 173

Patch, methylphenidate, 109

Patterson, Gerald, 148

Paxil, 117, 118, 119, 130

Pelham, William, 94, 100, 107, 111, 126

Personality testing, 346-47

PET scan, 25, 47

Petitions, court, 228

Phelan, Thomas, 74, 145, 147, 163, 165

Phones, cellular. *See* Cell phones

Physical examination, 48, 113, 194, 263

Physician's Desk Reference (PDR), 107

Physicians, 37, 48, 76

Pills, difficulty swallowing, 109, 111

Playing a Poor Hand Well, 68

Pliszka, Steven, 130

PMS, 181

Poetry, 69

"Point of performance," 159, 322

Police, 217

Poly-pharmacy, 117

Popper, Charles, 133

Positive behavior supports, 312-13. *See also* Behavior intervention plan

Poverty, 11

Power struggles, 162, 165, 182, 287. *See also* Behavior, challenging; Stubbornness
Pragmatic language disorder, 138
Praise, 160-61
Pregnancy, 219, 221
Prematurity, 28
Premenstrual syndrome, 181
Prince, Jeff, 109, 118
Problem solving, 157
Processing speed, 44, 49, 129, 194, 227, 279. *See also* Cognitive tempo
Procrastination, 179, 274
Profanity. *See* Swearing
Propanolol, 119
Protective factors, 79
Provigil, 116
Prozac, 117, 118, 119, 130
Pruitt, Sheryl, 131, 174
Psychiatrists, 117, 224, 357
Psychologists, 224
Psychotic episode, 133
Punishment. *See also* Discipline
   and teens with conduct disorder, 206
   as last resort, 164-67
   incentives as alternative to, 153
   ineffective, 144
Quetiapine, 119
Quinn, Patricia, 12, 24, 82, 96, 101, 117, 129, 134
Raising Resilient Children, 67
Ratey, John, 84, 96
Reading difficulties, 40, 194, 277-79
Rebound effect, 113, 182
Reconstitution, 3, 236
Recording for the Blind and Dyslexic, 278
Recreation, family, 146
Reid, Robert, 294
Related services, 294, 300, 304
Religion, 156
Remeron, 119
Reminyl, 116
Reports, weekly, 255-56, 270
Resilience, 20, 67, 142
Respite care, 93
Responsibility, increasing, 153-54, 161, 245
Restlessness, 185, 262
Retention, school, 236
Rewards. *See* Incentives
Risk-taking behavior. *See also* Driving
   among all adolescents, 204, 205
   brushes with law and, 5
   examples of, 187-88

gene for, 5, 26
   handling, 188
Risperdal (risperdone), 119, 135
Ritalin, 105, 108, 110, 111, 112, 216
Robin, Arthur, 133
Rohypnol, 209
Room, messy, 166, 177-78
Roommates, 350-51
Rouse, Gerald, 228
Routine, need for,151, 189-90, 251
Rules
   breaking, 167
   difficulty following, 4, 173, 180
   family, 151
Running away, 229
Russell, Ari, 137
SAT, 330-32
Sayes, Barbara, 117
Schedules. *See* Time management
School. *See also* High school; Homework; Middle school; Special education; Teachers; Tests
   avoidance of, 39, 260-62
   boarding, 94
   communicating with, 255-56
   discipline at, 305
   limiting failure at, 165
   making more positive, 241-47, 261, 367
   making up credits at, 259-60
   negative feelings about, 263-65
   need for stimulation at, 29
   notifying about ADD/ADHD, 243
   summer, 166
   taking medication at, 125-26
School problems. *See also* Discipline; Grades; Learning disabilities; Special education
   accommodations for, 84-85, 288-91
   addressing on IEP or 504 plan, 309-10
   alternative disciplinary procedures and, 311-12
   characteristics of ADD/ADHD related to, 7, 387-89
   difficulties speaking in class, 279
   expulsion, 237, 272, 315, 320
   failing a grade or class, 236, 258-60, 267, 308, 311
   general strategies for resolving, 238-41
   importance of resolving, 237
   in higher grades, 7
   learning problems, 269-80
   medication and, 125-26, 245, 286
   prevalence of, 6
   related to type of attention deficit, 11
   skipping or dropping out, 229, 234, 236
   sleep disturbances and, 262

specific ADD/ADHD symptoms and, 262-64

statistics on, 237

strategies for resolving, 317-18, 357-58

summary of, 51, 236-37

suspension, 237, 272, 312, 315, 320

teenager's role in resolving, 147

troubleshooting, 91-92

truancy, 237

tutoring for, 93

underachievement, 1, 6, 32

uneven performance, 6, 29, 262

School work, monitoring, 244, 270. *See also* Homework

Section 504 of the Rehabilitation Act, 302-304, 305, 314, 315-16, 320, 326, 337-40

Selective serotonin reuptake inhibitors. *See* SSRIs

Self-blame, 71

Self-centered attitude, 186-87

Self-esteem, 7, 20, 154-56, 222, 355, 363

Self-Esteem Teacher, The, 72, 154

Self-talk, 3

Seroquel, 119, 135

Serotonin. *See* Neurotransmitters

Serzone, 119, 130

Severe Emotional Disturbance (SED), 141

Sexual awareness, 134

Sexual behavior, 219-22. *See also* Dating

Sexually transmitted diseases, 221

Shaping behavior, 161

Shaywitz, Bennett and Sally, 34

Siblings

    conflicts with, 164, 195

    emotions of, 56-57

    incidence of ADD/ADHD in, 10, 27, 57

Single parents. *See* Parents of teens with ADD/ADHD

Sleep disturbances

    bipolar disorder and, 134

    causes of, 191

    effects of, on school performance, 262, 389

    medication and, 108, 112-13

    prevalence of, 5, 128, 131

    strategies for handling, 189-91

    types of, 16, 131-32

    treatment of, 132, 190

Sluggish cognitive tempo. *See* Cognitive tempo

Smoking. *See also* Nicotine

    among teens with ADD/ADHD, 208

    maternal, 11, 28

Snyder, Marlene, 216

SOAR, 93

Social skills, 196. *See also* Friends

Social skills training, 196

Software, voice recognition, 280

Speaking difficulties, 51, 227, 278-79

Special education. *See also* Accommodations; Evaluations; IDEA; School; Section 504

    definition of, 293-94

    eligibility for, 295-96, 298-99

    percentage of students with ADD/ADHD who need, 294

    related services and, 294

Specific learning disability (SLD), 234, 298, 299. *See also* Learning Disabilities

SPECT scan, 47

"Speed," 209

Speed governor, 217

Speeding. *See* Driving

Spelling, 44

Spencer, Tom, 115, 130

Sports, 156, 184-85, 193, 285

SSRIs, 117-19, 130

"Stay put," 317

Stealing, 140

Stimulant medications. *See* Medications, stimulant

Straight Talk about Psychiatric Medications for Kids, 105, 129

Strattera, 101, 105, 106, 115-16, 216

"Streetwise," 215

Strengths, focusing on, 68-70

Stepparents, 64-66

Strong Interest Inventory, 346

Stubbornness, 5, 54, 162, 265. *See also* Power struggles

Study buddy, 251

Substance abuse 136-38. *See also* Alcohol use; Drug abuse

    as self-medication, 207

    dealing with, 212-14

    prevention of, 209-12

    research on, 136-37

    risk of, among teens with ADD/ADHD, 128, 207

    signs of, 136

    treatment of, 137-38

Sugai, Georgia, 313

Sugar, 28

Suicide risk, 104, 116, 118, 119, 222-24

Summer camps, 93-94

Summer jobs, 347-48. *See also* Career choices

Supervision, 153-54, 189, 211, 240-41

Support groups, parent, 88-89, 354-55, 359

Surviving Your Adolescents, 74, 147, 164

Suspension. *See* School problems

Swanson, James, 26, 100, 111

Swearing, 182

Talking back. *See* Arguments
Tantrums, 134, 163, 265. *See also* Aggression; Anger
Teachers. *See also* School
  ABCs of ADD/ADHD for, 387-89
  ability of, to share observations about child, 318
  and behavior checklists, 46
  and need to provide more supervisions, 52
  as partners with parents, 242-43, 253-54
  asking for help from, 240
  educating about ADD/ADHD, 245
  effective teaching and classroom management
    strategies for, 268
  medication rating scale for, 384
  monitoring medication effectiveness and, 120
  requesting, 246
  substitute, 162
Teaching Teens with ADD and ADHD, 2, 156, 230, 267
Teaching the Tiger, 131
Technical institutes, 329-30, 333
Teen to Teen, 82
Teenagers with ADD/ADHD
  books for, 82
  coaches for, 84, 92-93, 98
  counseling for, 83-84, 261
  difficulties in diagnosing, 48-49
  diminished hyperactivity in, 32
  educating about attention deficits, 80, 82, 172
  educating about medication, 122, 124
  healing stories for, 71
  role of in own treatment plan, 77-78, 85, 86, 147
  skills training for, 82-83, 86, 156-57
  strengths of, 68-70, 355, 362
  uniqueness of, 16-17, 33, 355, 360-61
  videos for, 82
Television, 28
Temple, Robert, 113
Tenex, 119, 131, 141
Test of Variables of Attention (TOVA), 47
Test of Written Language (TOWL), 41, 45
Tests. *See also* Evaluations; Extended time
  academic achievement, 40
  Advanced Placement, 336
  CLEP, 336
  college admission, 330-32
  continuous performance, 47
  discussing results of, 48
  erratic performance on, 40
  extended time on, 44, 194
  GED, 327-28
  IQ, 40-44
  personality, 346-47

  stimulants and, 100
  taking, 280
  untimed, 304, 331
  used in ADD/ADHD research, 47
  vocational, 345
Therapy, multisystemic, 94
Thorazine, 119
Thrill seeking, 175
Tics, 114, 117, 119, 128, 131
Time. *See also* Extended time
  awareness of, 178, 275
  management, 157, 179, 275, 341-42
  procrastination and, 179, 274
Timers, 178, 251
Tired of Yelling, 115
Tofranil, 118, 130, 132, 224
Tolerance, medication, 108
Thyroid problems, 28
Tofranil, 190, 194, 206
Topomax, 135
Tourette syndrome, 114, 119, 131
Tranquilizers, 119
Transition plans, 306
Traumatic brain injury, 141
Trazadone, 190
Treatment for ADD/ADHD. *See also* Medication
  accommodations at school, 84-85
  AD/HD education, 80, 82, 89, 172
  challenges of, in adolescence, 76
  coaching, 84, 92-93, 98
  combined, 79, 96
  coordinating, 354
  counseling, 83-84
  effective, 29, 77, 79, 96
  factors influencing successful, 98
  individualizing, 354-59
  key principles guiding, 77, 97
  need for multimodal, 28, 75
  parents' role in, 77-78
  research into, 78-79
  residential, 94-95
  skills training, 82-83, 86, 156-57
  teenager's role in, 77-78, 85, 86, 147
  unproven, 95
  wraparound, 80-81
Tricyclic antidepressants, 118, 130-31
Tutoring, 93, 243, 340
Twins, 27
Unconditional positive regard, 146-47
Underachievement. *See* School problems
U.S. DOE memo, 318-19

VanDenBerg, John, 80
Video games, 29, 47, 175
Visteryl, 130
Vitamins, 263
Vocational testing, 346
Volkmar, Fred, 139
Volkow, Nora, 102
Waking up, 191. *See also* Sleep disturbances
Walker, Beth, 82
Walter, Warren, 45
Waugh, Lyndon, 115
Weapons, 222, 224-25
Wechsler Individual Achievement Test (WIAT), 40, 41
Wechsler Intelligence Scale for Children (WISC), 40-44, 45
Weekends, medication on, 108
Weight loss, 112
Weiner, Jerry M., 102
Weiss, Gabrielle, 20, 142, 143, 234
Wellbutrin, 119, 133
Wender, Paul, 24
Werner, Emmy, 68
White, Michael, 71
Wiesner, Lisa, 139
Wilens, Timothy E., 103, 113, 119,129, 137, 207
Williams syndrome, 141
Witzel, Brad, 284
Wolraich, Mark, 11
Woodcock-Johnson, 40
Working. *See* Career choices
Wristwatch, 178
Writing. *See also* Handwriting; Motor skills
    dictation as alternative to, 253
    difficulties with, 41, 44, 51, 194, 236, 279-80
    healing stories, 71-72, 146
    note taking and, 276-77, 339-40
Zametkin, Alan, 25, 26
Zeigler, Alex, x, xi, 83, 369, 370-72
Zentall, Sydney, 29, 57, 69, 96, 172, 269
Zoloft, 117, 118, 119, 130, 133, 194, 206
Zyprexa, 119, 135

About the Author

 **Chris Abney Zeigler Dendy** has over forty years combined experience in a variety of professional roles. Those roles include teacher, school psychologist, mental health counselor, administrator, lobbyist, advocate, author, and publisher. More importantly, she is the mother of three grown children and grandmother of three, all with attention deficit disorders. She has served on the CHADD National Board of Directions, Executive Committee, and President's Council. Because of her outstanding contributions to the field of ADHD, she was inducted into the prestigious CHADD Hall of Fame in 2006. She was one of the co-founders and clinical advisor for CHADD Gwinnett (GA). Her books draw upon her extensive professional experience plus personal experience of raising children with the condition. A popular speaker, Chris and her husband, Tommy, have traveled the country providing training in over 40 states and in England.